Enterprise Java™ Programming with IBM® WebSphere®

IBM Press

Enterprise Java™ Programming with IBM® WebSphere®

WebSphere

Kyle Brown • Gary Craig • Greg Hester
Russell Stinehour • W. David Pitt • Mark Weitzel
Jim Amsden • Peter M. Jakab • Daniel Berg

♦Addison-Wesley
Pearson Education

Boston • San Francisco • New York • Toronto • Montreal
London • Munich • Paris • Madrid • Capetown
Sydney • Tokyo • Singapore • Mexico City

The publisher offers discounts on this book when ordered in quantity for bulk purchases and special sales. For more information, please contact:

U.S. Corporate and Government Sales
(800) 382-3419
corpsales@pearsontechgroup.com

For sales outside of the U.S., please contact:

International Sales
(317) 581-3793
international@pearsontechgroup.com

Visit Addison-Wesley on the Web: www.awprofessional.com

A CIP catalog record for this book can be obtained from the Library of Congress

For information on obtaining permission for use of material from this work, please submit a written request to:

Pearson Education, Inc.
Rights and Contracts Department
75 Arlington Street, Suite 300
Boston, MA 02116
Fax: (617) 848-7047

ISBN: 0-321-18579-X
Text printed on recycled paper
First printing

Dedications

Kyle Brown—As with all my books, this is for Ann and Nathaniel, who cheerfully supported me during its making. This one is also for Vera Whiteside and Stan Blank, who first gave me the inspiration to dare to dream such a thing was possible.

Gary Craig—To my wife Judy, and my three terrific children, Andrew, Megan, and Taylor, for their support and the sacrifice they endured over the course of this project.

Greg Hester—I would like to thank my wife, Sherry, and my four children for their patience while I worked on this book. Without their love and support, this book would not have been possible. I'd also like to thank God for the many blessings and opportunities.

Russell Stinehour—I would like to thank my wife, Lee Ann, and my children for their patience while I missed family functions to work on this book. Lee Ann is a patient saint and a real asset in editing my work. I would also like to thank Greg Hester and David Pitt for their support to me personally. It's nice to be able to work with your friends on a daily basis. I thank God for blessing me to be able to work on this book and for CrossLogic.

W. David Pitt—To my daughter Lauren for her enthusiasm in pointing out our first edition in retail bookshelves.

Mark Weitzel—This book is dedicated to Marialana, for her support, encouragement, and Love— and for Big Sky. And to Montana and Reece, for their patience and understanding when this work had to come first. I also owe special thanks to Kyle Brown and Steve Graham for their advice and friendship.

Jim Amsden—I'd like to thank my wife Marjorie, and son Carl for their support in this endeavor, and for their continued patience during the next one. I'd also like to thank Kyle for the wonderful opportunity to participate with such a great team of co-authors.

Peter M. Jakab—To my wife Mabel, my daughter Jessie and my son Justin. Without their support and encouragement this book would not have been written. And lastly, to Shadow, our black lab, who always kept me company during the long days and nights writing this book.

Daniel Berg—I would like to dedicate this book to my lovely wife Michelle. She has selflessly supported me in this endeavor. For this I have to say thank you and I love you. I would also like to dedicate this book to my fellow J2EE team members. Their hard work, dedication, and talent made it possible to create an amazing J2EE development tool in WebSphere Studio.

Table of Contents

Foreword

I don't often find books like this one terribly interesting. Books on a specific technology, such as WebSphere, are often handy if you're using that technology—but they don't contain any great insights. I look to these books to tell me exactly which animal I need to sacrifice with which incense in order to get a job done. And this book does tell you that for these tools.

What makes this book stand out is that it doesn't stop at that. As the old adage says, a fool with a tool is still a fool. If you're developing enterprise applications with a technology like J2EE, it's easy to be a fool. There are lots of ways you can mess things up, and all the wizards and cute graphical interfaces in the world can't save you!

So this book also tells you how to reduce your foolishness by passing on design advice. The authors have been building these kinds of applications since before Java was invented. Kyle Brown, in particular, has more than once steered me around a nasty distributed rock. So here, you don't just find chapters on how to build a servlet, and what the transaction attributes are for Enterprise JavaBeans—they actually give you some advice on how to design these things. Rather than just give a simple solution, suitable for a hands-on tutorial, they talk about the trade-offs you'll need to make in putting an Enterprise Java application together. As a result, you may find some of this book hard work, but by putting the effort in to understanding it you'll avoid many of the pitfalls that regularly send these kinds of projects to the great cubicle farm in the sky.

In particular, the authors put a strong emphasis on layering—centering their design around a five-layer architecture. While carefully separating layers are an odd complexity for simple examples, they are a key life vest for serious enterprise applications. Time and time again, I've seen teams begin by reluctantly following layers, shrinking from the fact that simple logic gets separated into several different classes. Then slowly, they appreciate that the layers allow changes to be made more easily, that layers make a system easier to test and easier to root out bugs. If there is any advice in this book that I must echo, it is to follow the layering architecture, even if it seems awkward to you. You future self will thank you for it.

When the first edition came out, it was easy to find books on J2EE technology but impossible to find any books giving good design advice. Indeed this was the first book that contained substantial design advice on J2EE and as such influenced many writers of enterprise design books—it certainly was very useful for me.

The second edition builds on this by building its design advice on the work that has appeared since the first edition was published. It spends a lot of time showing you how to take some of the common enterprise application patterns and implement them in J2EE. As such it both integrates and extends the work of authors like myself, and lays out more foundations for our future work.

So if you're a WebSphere developer, buy this book for its tutorial on WebSphere, but treasure it for its design advice. If you don't develop in WebSphere, or even J2EE, get this book for its design advice anyway.

—Martin Fowler
Chief Scientist, Thoughtworks

Preface

Here We Go Again

The first edition of *Enterprise Java Programming with IBM WebSphere* was the first book that addressed J2EE development within the context of an application server and Integrated Development Environment. The feedback about the first edition was very positive, and led us to conclude that we had made the right choice—that developers usually learn J2EE technologies and the details of an application server together and that a single book that teaches both is valuable.

Since we published the first edition, a lot has changed. When we wrote the first edition, we couldn't use J2EE in the title because IBM was not yet a licensee of the newly developed J2EE brand, even though WebSphere Application Server implemented all of the technologies in the nascent J2EE 1.0 specification. Also, when we wrote the first edition, IBM's premier development environment for WebSphere was VisualAge for Java; that environment has since been superseded by WebSphere Studio Application Developer.

In this edition we will build on the firm foundation laid in the first edition, and expand the coverage of topics to include all of the major parts of WebSphere Application Server 5.02 and WebSphere Studio Application Developer 5.0. Those who have read the first edition will find a lot that is new; new readers can be assured that we've built on a strong foundation of describing the more mature parts of J2EE, while also describing new technologies like Web services and the EJB 2.0 specification.

About Us

Despite everything that has changed about the subject matter of our book, one thing has not changed—the experiences and intent of the author team. In one respect, we're probably a lot like most of you—we came to Java, J2EE, and WebSphere after gaining experience in other OO languages and programming environments. While the details of the systems that we have worked on have differed, they all shared some common features. What we hope to do is to introduce J2EE, WebSphere, and WebSphere Studio by referring you to the things you already know, while showing you some best practices that we've learned in building client/server and enterprise systems both before the age of Java and in the J2EE universe.

The Goals We Have Set

We set forward to achieve several goals in the writing of this book. They are to:

- Introduce developers to the primary J2EE technologies.
- Teach developers how to apply these technologies within the right architectural framework.
- Demonstrate how WebSphere Application Server implements the J2EE standard, and what advantages it gives to developers as a J2EE application server.
- Demonstrate the advantages WebSphere Studio Application Developer conveys as a platform for developing J2EE programs for deployment on WebSphere Application Server.

Of these four goals, the most important one is listed second: to teach developers how to apply J2EE technologies within the right architectural context. It has been our experience that teaching someone a new technology without teaching how to apply it is a terrible mistake. A lot of our time as consultants is spent getting customers out of problems that have been created either by trying to make a technology do something it was not intended to do or by viewing one particular technology as a hammer and all problems as nails.

While we can convey some of this architectural context by teaching you the dos and don'ts of the technologies, most of you are like us—you learn best by doing. To help you gain a feel for the J2EE technologies we will cover, you will want to walk with us through the example system that we are building and find out for yourselves how the pieces fit together. It is only by seeing the entire system end-to-end, and by working through the example on your own, that you will start to understand how the different APIs interrelate and how WebSphere implements the abstract specifications.

So, we want to welcome you on an adventure. It's been a long, hard road for us in mastering these technologies, tools, and techniques. We hope we can make the way easier for you who are following us. It will take a lot of preparation and effort for you to really learn how and why to apply these technologies, and how best to take advantage of the features of WebSphere, but we feel that the effort is worthwhile.

J2EE is a terrific architecture for building scalable, manageable server-side systems, and IBM has developed a wonderful set of tools that make those technologies real. We hope that by the time you reach the end of this book, you will understand and agree with why we think so highly of these tools. We also hope that this book will enable you to start designing and building these large-scale, enterprise systems that J2EE, WebSphere, and WebSphere Studio Application

Developer make possible. Thanks for coming along with us on this journey, and good luck in reaching your destination.

Acknowledgements and Thanks

Building a book like this is a team effort. We would like to acknowledge all of those team members who contributed to this book but whose names are not mentioned on the cover. Without the important contributions from these people, this book would not have been possible. These include Keys Botzum, Jaime Niswonger, Rachel Reinitz, Scott Rich, and Geoff Hambrick. We would also like to thank the remarkable group of people who have participated as reviewers of this project and provided very insightful feedback and help. That dedicated group consisted of Keys Botzum, John Smith, Dan Kehn, Roland Barcia, Paul Ilechko, Johannes DeJong, and Bobby Woolf. You have our gratitude and our thanks.

August 2003
Raleigh, NC
Asheville, NC
Kansas City, MO
Toronto, ON

Introduction

Welcome to *Enterprise Java Programming with IBM WebSphere, 2nd Edition*. This book was designed to help you understand how to design, build, and deploy applications based on the Java 2 Enterprise Edition (J2EE) using the IBM WebSphere family of tools and runtime. This book was written for technical managers seeking guidance in understanding J2EE and WebSphere; architects who wish to design scalable, secure enterprise applications; and for the day-to-day developer who wishes to create more robust, consistent code.

You'll find our approach to be a bit different than other books. Rather than simply focusing on the bits and bytes of each technology component that makes up WebSphere, we take a slightly broader view. We will show you how J2EE and WebSphere combine to form an architecture and runtime suitable for large, mission-critical applications.

If you have already invested in the award-winning WebSphere Studio family of tools, or you are considering doing so, this book will ensure that you get the maximum productivity benefits WebSphere has to offer. Through hands-on examples, we will illustrate how the IBM WebSphere Studio family of tools helps you master enterprise application development. These examples will also demonstrate some of the J2EE best practices which are intended to make your development tasks easier, your code more maintainable, and your enterprise projects successful. Along the way, we will also provide rationale for our approaches to building enterprise applications. We will start by discussing the importance of enterprise development, explaining the development process, and presenting the topology of properly layered enterprise applications.

1.1 Why Software Development Must Consider the Whole Enterprise

The explosive growth of the Internet has created a truly global marketplace. Because this marketplace is accessible by any customer, anywhere in the world, even small companies have the potential to compete against multinational conglomerates. However, the irrational exuberance for Web-based business-to-business (B2B) and business-to-consumer (B2C) opportunities of the late 1990s is being tempered by the reality that enterprise applications require a sound architecture in order to provide reliability, scalability, performance, and security. To ensure viability in this network economy, companies are using technology to fundamentally change the way they do business. For example, technology is being used to:

- **Enhance communications** through a distributed, connectionless network; providing access to information anywhere, anytime. Mobile computing solutions expand the reach of information by providing wireless solutions that utilize the same technologies and network.

- **Leverage existing technologies**, making existing resources more productive and useful to an increased number of users. It is expensive to produce information—consider the time and effort involved in building a stock transfer or insurance processing system—yet providing an access wrapper into these proven systems is, relative to their total cost, fairly inexpensive. Thus reusing information in new contexts, rather than reimplementing, is a sound business decision. In fact, the wrapping of existing technology is proving to be a significant driver for the success of Web services.

- **Improve the visibility of information and data,** opening new and existing sources of information to a larger population of customers, vendors, employees, and others. Static information can be quickly and easily updated while dynamic solutions can be delivered with minimal effort and programming resources.

- **Fulfill the promises of distributed computing** with flexible, and easy-to-implement programming languages, tools, components, and interfaces. The complexity of building distributed systems, combined with compatibility issues between distributed models such as CORBA and DCOM, created high barriers to entry. Previous attempts at distributed computing tended to break down in heterogeneous environments. To address these issues, the industry has adopted Web services and, in the larger sense, a service-oriented architecture as the base distributed computing model. Combined with the power of the J2EE architecture, this distributed computing technology can be utilized to deliver flexible, high-performance, and standard solutions that can be easily changed to reflect new requirements and design needs.

- **Streamline and reengineer business processes** to do business in ways never before imagined. Self-service applications have moved information closer to the end user and reduced administrative personnel. Electronic-commerce (e-commerce) transaction-based applications have increased marketplace competition and changed the way many companies present and sell goods and services. Internet technologies have lowered the barrier of entry for many start-up ventures and entrepreneurs; allowing them to compete with larger companies. The Web has equalized the playing field for businesses, making many small ones appear larger and many larger companies move like smaller businesses.

In this chapter, we will begin by looking at the motivations for enterprise application architectures and we will end by summarizing the focus of each chapter in this book. We will look at information technology (IT) issues, focusing on the process requirements of building enterprise solutions and look at what is needed overall to respond to competition, business pressures, and new requirements.

1.2 How Iterative Development Addresses Key IT Management Issues

To effectively build, deploy, and maintain an enterprise application, the project team should follow a proven process that supports an iterative development lifecycle, such as the Rational Unified Process (RUP).

Regardless of whether the development team follows a widely recognized process or creates its own, it should:

- **Focus on feasibility issues early in the development cycle**—the project can be built incrementally by providing tangible value at each iteration in the cycle (Figure 1.1). The most difficult feasibility issues are addressed early in the process.

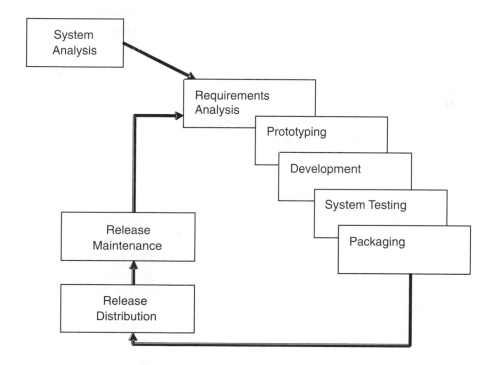

Figure 1.1 Iterative development process.

- **Build on early success**—breaking the project up into smaller "chunks" allows the development team to deliver iterations early in the development cycle instead of waiting for the "big bang" delivery of the project as in the more traditional waterfall development process.
- **Ensure early participation and commitment by end users**—while facilitating early discovery of requirements.
- **Reduce risk to the overall project**—while increasing concrete deliverables risk can be reduced with each iteration

1.3 Today's Enterprise Applications Have New Requirements

With increased competition, lower projected e-commerce profit margins, increased legal issues, and new IT management requirements, three things are expected in today's enterprise applications:

- **Solution value**—solutions that rely on a layered architecture that leverages reuse and dynamic, scalable solutions that can be easily changed to meet new business needs.
- **Speed to market**—a focus on the business domain and not the application infrastructure can help meet the ever-growing strategic application backlog. By using a repeatable standard development process that reuses legacy information and systems, a development team can begin to bring solutions to the marketplace sooner.
- **Secure solutions**—by protecting assets, legally and technically, an IT organization can not only produce flexible solutions, it can also give the enterprise a strategic advantage in the marketplace.

1.4 What Is the Starting Point?

So how do you achieve solution value, and how do you begin to organize your thoughts on where to start in application development? If we had to identify the single architectural principle that is the foundation of J2EE and at the heart of the WebSphere product family, we would have to choose *layering*. Commonly, application development is accomplished in a vertical fashion. At a minimum the division and estimation of work is determined by defining the application's primary user interfaces.

Business rules, behavior, and data are obtained and manipulated based upon activity conveyed via the user interface. It is the responsibility of the architecture to provide a blueprint that guides developers on when and how objects are defined during the development process. The importance of establishing this blueprint is realized in support of the iterative development process, where vertical slices of application functionality are delivered in iterations made up of *planning*, *development*, and *assessment* activities. The architecture must support vertical and horizontal dimensions of an application. Horizontal development activities consist of applying *logging*, *exception handling*, and *start up/shutdown* mechanisms. Basically, this is behavior that must be provided by all applications. Vertical activities involve implementing slices of application functionality from presentation to data source access. Having the infrastructure in place to allow development to occur in these two dimensions is the responsibility of the architecture.

Most experienced IT professionals will agree that developing and adhering to a standard architecture is key to the success of large-scale software development. Computer science pioneer Edsger Dijkstra validated this notion when he developed *THE* operating system in 1968. Since then, layered architectures have proven their viability in technological domains such as hardware and networking.

Layering has proven itself in the operating system domain; however, the same benefits are available when applied to e-commerce or thin-client oriented applications. Layered architectures have become essential in supporting the iterative development process by promoting reusability, scalability, and maintainability. Next we will define and justify a layered architecture for J2EE and WebSphere that is the foundation for the remainder of this book.

1.5 What Is a Layered Architecture?

What is a layered architecture, and what does *layering* mean? Application layering is the separation of architectural concerns whose boundaries are supported by interface contracts. Typically, these layers are stacked vertically so that each layer interacts only with the layer directly underneath it (Figure 1.2).

Because an interface contract exists between each layer, changes can be affected on Layer 3 with minimal side effects on Layer 1. Moreover, Layer 3 can be totally replaced, as long as it meets Layer 2's contract, without affecting Layer 1. This property is known as strict layering.

As mentioned earlier, the principle of layering is core to J2EE and WebSphere. From the J2EE perspective, this concept has been the driving force behind much of the standards work that defines the platform. This can be seen in how presentation and data access are designed. The WebSphere Application Server fully leverages this architecture by allowing individual layers to be scaled and distributed independently.

Critics of strictly layered architectures argue that performance, and sometimes extensibility, are sacrificed since more activity is required to propagate down through the layers. Extensibility can suffer if contracts defined between the layers are not robust enough to handle future requirements. However, being able to strategically distribute the application layers, use the domain layer across multiple applications, and easily configure different data sources and user interfaces overcomes such criticism.

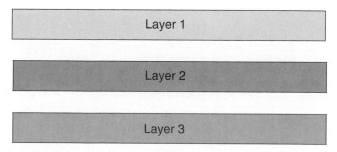

Figure 1.2 Layers.

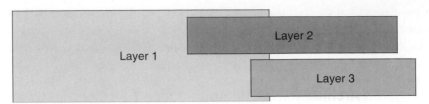

Figure 1.3 Nonstrict layering.

Nonstrict layering (Figure 1.3) allows higher layers to access any layer defined below it and answers the critics' arguments against performance and extendibility; however, it nullifies the benefits of strict layering.

1.5.1 Common layering schemes

Traditional two-tier client/server-based applications can be partitioned into two layers—presentation and data access. A two-tier Graphical User Interface (GUI) application would simply query a data source, compute, and display the information to the user. A consequence of this simple architecture is that knowledge about the business domain is both scattered throughout the user interface, and is forced into complex database schemas.

Object technology encourages not only the abstraction and reuse of presentation logic, but also business processes and data. Therefore, decoupling application logic from application presentation results in scalable three-tier distributed systems that allows objects defined to model business data and processes to be used across application boundaries. With the explosion of the Internet and related technologies, enterprise application requirements have made the existence of layered application architecture imperative.

The most common layers of an application can be partitioned into presentation, domain, and data source sections (Figure 1.4). The most important layer is the domain. This is where business process and state are captured. Presentation layer objects either consume or exercise domain objects. Data source objects defined in the data source layer access specific data sources on behalf of domain objects requesting or saving state.

It is not enough to merely stipulate the layers in a graphic and expect developers to properly partition application elements into a layered architecture. Developers must implement functionality within each layer in a consistent fashion. Moreover, message interaction between layers must be formalized.

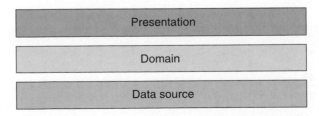

Figure 1.4 Client/server layers.

Formalizing layer interaction should involve a decoupled design that includes appropriate indirection in support of layer substitution. Additionally, behaviors prescribed across all applications, namely exception handling, logging, start up, and shutdown operations, should be formalized and consistently applied.

1.5.2 Layered Architecture Definition

The primary motivation for layering is to create and preserve a reusable domain model that spans application boundaries. Other advantages to this architecture are that it helps organize the project and allows construction and validation of each layer to vary independently. Of course this can be accomplished with three layers; however, introducing two additional layers between presentation and data source layers further decouples the domain from application presentation and data source requirements (Figure 1.5). An example of layer substitution would be enabling the domain layer for pervasive devices or a voice response unit. In Figure 1.5, this would imply creating only the new presentation layer constructs and the necessary mediators to interact with the existing domain model.

Let's take a closer look at each of the roles and responsibilities of the layers in this five-layer architecture.

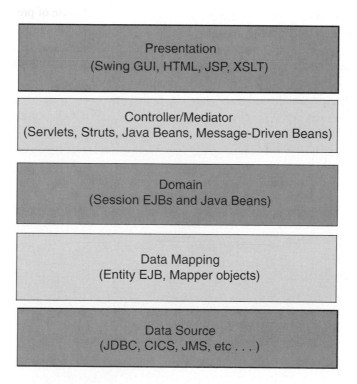

Figure 1.5 Five-layer architecture.

1.5.2.1   Presentation

The presentation layer consists of objects defined to accept user input and display application outputs. The most common presentation technologies that can be used with J2EE are:

- HTML/JSP (with servlets acting as *controllers* as we see in the next section)
- XML and XSLT (again with servlets acting as controllers)
- Applets (using AWT or Swing)
- Applications (using AWT or Swing)

We will discuss the relative merits and proper uses of these technologies in Chapter 5 and revisit them with regard to deployment issues in Chapter 22. Chapters 5–15 describe the technologies used in developing presentation and control layers in J2EE.

1.5.2.2   Controllers and Mediators

Because a primary goal of layered applications is to enable domain logic to be reused in different presentations, how the user interacts with the business model needs to be isolated. This is the role of the controller. Whatever the presentation technology happens to be, requests for domain state and behavior will be done via a controller object defined for the particular presentation requirements; e.g., HTML, Swing, or pervasive devices. This controller object implements the mediator design pattern from [Gamma]. An important design requisite involves making sure that domain-specific logic is not defined in presentation object methods, but rather, is obtained from a mediator referenced domain object. Additionally, application navigation topology is defined within this layer.

Application presentation objects interact with a domain model in generalized ways, regardless of the presentation technology. For instance, a GUI will present a list of choices which are composed of a collection of domain model objects; the same collection can be used to populate an HTML list. For that matter, the same collection could be used to provide a list of choices in a voice response unit interface (Figure 1.6).

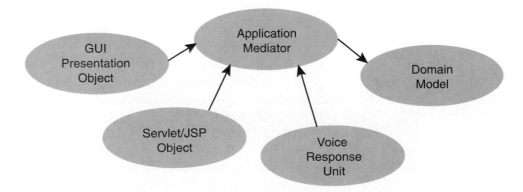

Figure 1.6 Mediators used by multiple presentation technologies.

Mediators capture and decouple application-specific functionality from presentation technology by performing domain model requests for presentation or controller objects that drive a specific application use case. Mediator classes are defined to satisfy a specific application user interface function or use case; therefore, they are less granular than controllers. For example, a single mediator can be used to implement a user registration function with a wizard-like interface. Mediators implement behavior that would usually end up in presentation classes as methods/scripts. Moreover, consistently applying mediator objects offers more than loose coupling between a domain model and presentation technologies. Mediators provide a convenient and consistent way to transfer application state between user interfaces, eliminating the typical highly parameterized approach. Additionally, transaction behavior finds an appropriate location in mediator objects since navigation and units of work constraints are tied to application-specific functionality.

The key to mediators' presentation independence is the enforcement of strict layering, meaning that mediators should not contain any references to presentation objects. However, they are free to reference domain-object public state and behavior. Care must also be taken not to define domain-logic in mediators. This pitfall can be avoided by applying a simple experiment. Ask yourself, "Can I still perform or obtain the requested domain operation using only existing domain objects?" If the answer is "No, I need a mediator object," then the mediator is implementing behavior that belongs in the domain.

1.5.2.3 Domain

The domain layer is the hardest part of a layered system to understand, and the most challenging to implement. To understand what a domain object is, you have to go back to the basic roots of object-oriented (OO) programming. When we learn Java programming or OO, design the first examples seen are usually in terms of concrete objects. This might be an example of a control system like in [Booch] where the objects modeled are physical like TemperatureSensors and AirConditioners, or it might be through a simple game where objects like playing cards are modeled.

Unfortunately, when many programmers start looking at their own day-to-day problems they instead see more abstract things like windows and database tables, not the nice, concrete things seen in the books and tutorials. This is unfortunate, since modeling the aspects of a business in software can be one of the most powerful tools that a programmer can bring to bear on solving the hardest problems in software development. Capturing business abstractions in objects can make a system much more powerful by making it more flexible and can create a critical distinction between the parts of a system that represent the business problem being solved (its essence) and the accidents of implementation resulting from choices in technology that might be transitory.

Domain objects are usually implemented as standard Java classes or plain old Java objects (POJOs). J2EE provides another option for implementing domain objects that we will examine more closely in later chapters. A programmer can choose to implement his domain objects as Enterprise JavaBeans (EJBs), which conveys some benefits in terms of distribution, transaction capabilities, and persistence. Even when EJBs are used, a mix of standard Java classes and EJBs should be employed, as we will examine in greater detail in Chapters 19 and 30.

1.5.2.4 Mapping

A consequence of building a domain layer, as we have described, is that it should not be concerned with purely implementation-specific details. For instance, one of the most common questions in enterprise programming is how to extract data from or update data in a database. Rather than making this behavior part of the domain object, a second set of objects is required to perform this function. Separating the behavior in this way conveys a number of benefits, including making it possible to change implementation details like database vendor or database schema without changing the domain implementation.

A design like this requires a separate layer, often called *mapping* or *persistence*, that can move data from domain objects to back-end data sources and vice versa. There are several open source and commercial products, like Apache Castor, CrossLogic's Universe, and Oracle's TopLink that can add this behavior. However, for a programmer using J2EE, the common way that this behavior will be used is through the APIs provided by the EJB container. As we will describe in Chapters 19 and 23, the EJB container in WebSphere provides a simple and consistent interface for data persistence using entity beans. However, we may still need to implement some mapping functions even in designs using EJBs when we need to move data between Java-Beans and EJBs. We will cover this topic in-depth in a later chapter.

1.5.3 Data Source Access

At some point in your application, you have to retrieve and store data, or communicate with external systems. Undoubtedly relational databases (DB2, Oracle, Informix, etc.) are the most common way IT organizations store and query enterprise data. Recognizing this profound market share, Sun delivered the JDBC (Java Database Connectivity) API. JDBC allows the production and execution of vendor-neutral Structured Query Language (SQL).[1] Developers can use standard ANSI SQL against any JDBC-compliant driver. The specific API and types of available JDBC drivers are beyond the scope of this discussion; refer to the JDBC specification, available on Sun's Java Web site (*http://www.java.com*), for more information.

However, there are other common data access mechanisms in J2EE as well. Enterprise information systems (EIS) such as CICS, SIEBEL, SAP, or J.D. Edward's OneWorld are a common part of today's enterprise landscape.

J2EE offers two ways to connect to EIS: Java Message Service (JMS) and the Java2 Connector Architecture (J2C). JMS provides asynchronous access to corporate data, while J2C provides synchronous access to these EIS systems.

Finally, you may access external systems through Web Services, which is the newest mechanism for providing open access to enterprise services. We'll examine JMS in Chapter 27 and we'll cover Web Services in Chapters 32 to 34. We will not cover J2C in-depth in this book.

---

1.   The JDBC specification also applies to nonrelational data sources.

However, vertical layers are not enough to build and deliver complex enterprise applications. Application layers must be complemented with application services and test facilities.

1.5.4 Application Services

There are application responsibilities that developers must apply to all application development efforts. Implementing these activities consistently using a design that is extendable will facilitate reuse and minimize side effects when requirements change. Moreover, standardizing these services across all applications can yield efficiencies in determining and communicating new development and in maintenance activities.

Obvious application responsibilities include error handling, status tracing, application start up and shutdown, accessing externalized properties, and applying preferences. A design must be put in place that not only allows developers to consistently apply error handling across all applications, but also supports the ability to install and change these behaviors on an application basis. For example, application status is sometimes reported to a console. What happens if the application is server-based and a console does not exist? A design should allow error logging and tracing to be routed to a flat file, perhaps in addition to the console.

1.5.5 The Virtues of Test Scripts

The primary design intent of a layered architecture is decoupling a problem space domain model from presentation and data source requirements. Reuse of the domain, at least across application boundaries, can be achieved if isolation is accomplished.

Creating test scripts that exercise domain model behavior helps to verify domain isolation and provides other significant benefits. In fact, test scripts should be developed for all the different layers of your application. We will cover this in Chapter 17.

Figure 1.7 provides the high-level picture of an enterprise application topology where vertical layers are supported by application services and test frameworks.

1.6 Layered Architecture Benefits

With increased competition, lower projected e-commerce profit margins, increased legal issues, and new IT management requirements, what is needed is an architecture that provides:

- **Solution value**—reliance on a layered architecture that leverages reuse produces dynamic, scalable, solutions that can be easily changed to meet new business needs.
- **Speed to market**—a focus on the business domain and not the application infrastructure can help meet the ever-growing strategic application backlog. By using a repeatable standard development process that reuses legacy information and systems, a development team can begin to bring solutions to the marketplace faster.
- **Secure solutions**—by protecting assets, legally and technically, an IT organization can not only produce flexible solutions, it can also give the enterprise a strategic advantage in the marketplace.

That architecture framework is the J2EE platform.

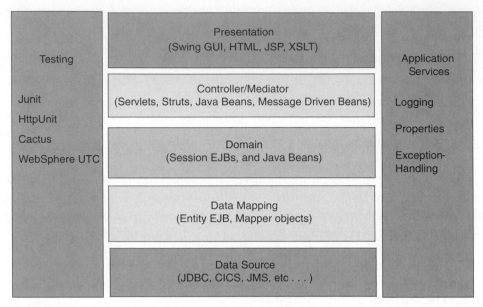

Figure 1.7 Mediators used by multiple presentation technologies.

1.7 Summary

Now that the architectural design and business rationale for the J2EE framework have been presented, we can discuss the organization for the rest of this book. Loosely speaking, it will follow the J2EE architecture, where Web constructs are presented first, followed by business model development, then EJBs, followed by Web Services. The list which follows is a high-level breakdown and is intended for those readers who prefer to tackle sections in their own preferred order. Chapters 1 through 4 present an overview of J2EE, WebSphere Application Server Version 5.0, and the case study used throughout the book. These chapters present the foundation for the book and are highly recommended.

- Chapters 5 through 15 focus on building Web-based applications, and present in-depth information on topics such as using the Struts framework for proper Model-View-Controller (MVC) partitioning, servlets and JavaServer Pages (JSPs), and session management.
- Chapters 16 and 17 emphasize techniques for building and testing the business model. A particularly useful section on leveraging JUnit is contained in this portion of the book.
- Chapters 18 through 31 provide extensive coverage of the EJB architecture. These chapters cover everything from basic usage of session beans to advanced object relational mapping. They also cover EJB transactions and the J2EE security model.
- Chapters 32 to 34 are about Web Services. These chapters describe the latest support provided by WebSphere Application Server for this exciting technology. Several examples are presented on how to create and deploy business objects as Web Services.

This section concludes with a collection of best practices around the usage of this technology.

- Chapter 35 summarizes the lessons learned in this book.

If this seems like a great deal of information, that's because it is! Building secure, well-performing, transaction-aware, distributed applications remains a complex and difficult task. It's quite easy to get lost in the specifications and overwhelmed by technology. The good news is that J2EE's layered architecture, along with a powerful set of tools, like those built by IBM, and a good reference guide packed with a healthy dose of common sense, like this book, will help you manage this complexity and deliver robust, scalable, enterprise solutions.

CHAPTER 2

Introduction to the
Case Study

Learning a new technology is often complicated by the fact that most sources of information tend to throw a lot of acronyms and new terms at you without providing any context. It's just as important to understand where and why to use a new technology as it is to understand how to use it. In this book we'll present most of the examples of how you use each technology in the context of a case study about a company developing a simple J2EE application for tracking hours spent on projects.

This sort of time tracking—for instance, consultants and legal firms track time spent on projects so that they can bill their hours—is common in many companies. Many other companies have in-house service groups (such as IT organizations) that must track time for internal billing purposes. What's more important, though, is that the example is complicated enough, both from a UI and a domain object perspective, to provide a backdrop complex enough to show you how to apply J2EE technologies in a real-world environment.

2.1   Case Study Analysis and Design Artifacts

While a book of this nature is not an appropriate place to discuss all of the ramifications of performing a detailed analysis and design of a Web-based application, we hope to convey a sense of the kind of process that is followed, and some of the artifacts that can be produced. In designing our application, we took a simple use-case driven approach, similar to that described in [Fowler]. We will show the analysis and design artifacts using UML[1] notation, again as described in [Fowler].

---

1.   Unified Modeling Language as defined by the Object Management Group standard.

WHAT TYPE OF A&D PROCESS IS APPROPRIATE FOR WEB APPLICATIONS?

A question we are commonly asked in our consulting practice is what advice we can give about setting up a development process for Web applications. Simple question. Difficult answer. The problem is that Enterprise Java applications can be approached from two sides—Web-up and enterprise-down.

The Web-up approach is where a Web site built using ad-hoc, seat-of-the-pants development methods must suddenly be rearchitected to scale up to thousands—or millions—of users to meet new demands. In this case, we see that there is often no development process in place, as it has not been necessary in the small-team environment that most Web shops employ. The enterprise-down approach is where a traditional IT organization finds it must reinvent itself to address the needs of customers and partners on the global Internet. In this case, there is often a set of development practices in place, but they do not necessarily apply to the development tools, techniques, and timescales that Web development necessitates.

We have found a happy medium where most groups doing Enterprise Java development can reside. We often recommend that our clients begin by looking at two books—*Extreme Programming Explained* by Kent Beck [Beck] and *UML Distilled* 3rd Ed. by Martin Fowler [Fowler].

Extreme programming (XP), the subject of Beck's book, is a radical revisiting of old theories about software development. It proposes a very rapid, highly productive development cycle that is characterized by constant testing, minimal up-front design, and tight control of software iterations. We have seen several cases where small teams (in the range of 3 to 10 programmers, which is about the limit of what XP can handle) can produce very high-quality software in a very short time using this process. On the other hand, there is often a need for some slight formalism in analysis and design artifacts, specifically where developers are learning new technologies, and need to be able to see, at a glance, where the new technologies fit into an overall picture of a software system. For this purpose we often recommend that an XP-like process be combined with some (but not all) elements of UML. Since many Web programmers (coming from both sides) are very visual people, we have seen that they may prefer a more diagrammatic approach to rapid design than the text-based CRC-card approach suggested by [Beck]. We often take this XP-plus-UML approach ourselves, and it is what we recommend for most small teams beginning to learn Enterprise Java technologies.

However, there may be a need for a more large-scale approach. If a team is large (over 15 people) or it must produce specific requirements and design documentation to fit an existing corporate or governmental process, then a more elaborate technique like RUP (described in [Jacobson]) may apply. While RUP is a well-understood and complete process, we feel that it may be overkill in many cases, as it does not accommodate itself well to either Web timescales or team sizes. However, there are those cases for which it must be chosen.

Another approach that is just emerging, and is particularly well-suited for developing enterprise applications, is model-driven development (MDD). MDD separates concerns by developing a platform-independent model (PIM) of the business application. This model focuses on the business domain, simplifying the domain discovery process by separating the complexities introduced by architecture and implementation domains.

The PIM is then translated by automated tools to a platform-specific model (PSM), using translation patterns that are developed for a particular deployment architecture and implementation language, like J2EE. These transformation patterns can be developed by platform experts and provide an excellent way of formalizing and codifying the architectural rules and best practices. See *http://www.omg.org* for further details.

You must consider carefully your timescales and the size of your team before you select a development process. The same process may not be appropriate for different projects.

2.1.1 Problem Statement

All analysis and design must start with some statement of the problem to be solved. This can be as simple as the user stories defined in [Beck] or as complex as a traditional functional specification. Ours is simple, and is closer to a user story than a functional specification. It is described here:

A SIMPLE PROBLEM STATEMENT

Corporate personnel perform various activities throughout a given business day. These activities are most often dictated by assigned projects. As such, time spent on project-specific activities are tracked and reported on a specified basis. Summary information can then be compiled and applied against project and budgetary plans.

Ensuring that time is appropriately entered for projects is accomplished through a time-sheet approval process. Authorized employees will have the ability to preview pending time sheets and mark them as being approved. Additionally, employee time sheets can be automatically approved.

The system will be used frequently for short periods of time on a daily basis from a variety of locations. Therefore, quick and convenient access to the time entry portion of the system is required.

Another part of design is to specify the tasks that a user must perform in order to use the system. These can be in the form of user stories as described earlier. [Beck] describes how to enter these on task cards that can be used to partition development and prioritize the order in which functions will be developed and delivered. [Fowler] describes these tasks as scenarios that can be used to build use cases. Our system tasks are specified next.

2.1.2 System Tasks

1. Employees can enter half-hour time increments against any available project.

2. Employees can enter time-sheet information on a weekly basis.

3. Managers can ask for summary reports including the details of actual hours charged against any given project.

4. Managers can ask for summary reports including the details of actual hours charged for any given employee.

5. Both employees and managers should be able to access the system from any corporate standard Web browser with intranet access.

6. Employees can modify entered time sheets before they are approved.

7. Authorized personnel can view and approve time sheets on a department or project basis.

8. Authorized personnel can define projects, employees, and departments.

2.1.3 Use Case List

Use cases can provide a more formal process than the XP described in [Beck]. They can be used to specify user interactions with a system, or system-to-system interactions (which can be useful in specifying B2B applications). In the following section we will list the use cases that we have derived from our user tasks, then show their write-ups and UML diagrams. Here are the use cases we derived:

1. Employee enters daily time entries against project(s)

2. Employee creates a new time sheet for a week-ending date

3. Employee updates a time sheet that is not yet approved

4. Manager approves employee time sheets

5. Manager unapproves employee time sheet

6. Manager requests a report of pending time sheets

7. Manager requests a report of approved time sheets

2.1.4 Use Case Diagrams

By examining our list of use cases, we have discovered two actors that participate in our use cases. They are:

- Employee—Enters daily time associated with projects
- Manager—Authorizes employee time sheets.

We show the use cases and relationships with our defined actors in the use case diagram (Figure 2.1).

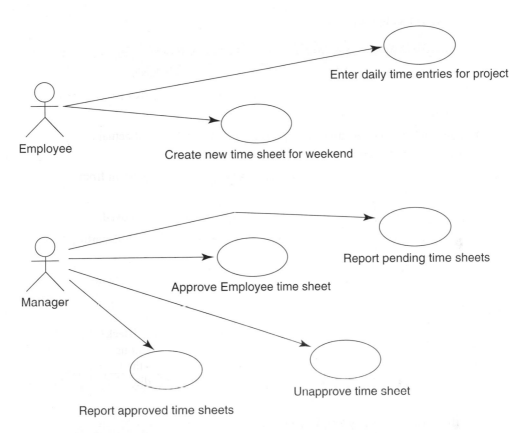

Figure 2.1 Use case diagram.

2.2 Use Case Definitions

Table 2.1 shows the use cases that we have defined for the case study. We are using the simplified use case format described in [Fowler].

2.3 Designing the Case Study Domain Model

Now that you understand the requirements, how will we implement them? As you read in the previous chapter, a key design point in the development of any system is understanding the domain model, or the business classes that make up the system. In our simple problem domain, there are only four basic concepts that we need to consider: Employee, TimeSheet, TimeSheetEntry, and Project.

The most basic object in our time sheet system is an Employee. We have to identify an Employee in order to create a time sheet for him, so this is an obvious part of our model. However, this is an interesting small subsystem. In addition to simple attributes like a name, an Employee may have a home address. Likewise, Employees may belong to Departments. We use

Table 2.1 Use cases for the case study.

USE CASE: Employee enters daily time entries for a project(s)
Primary Course

1. Employee requests time sheet for a week-ending date and Employee name
2. System checks for existence of time sheet.
   2a. If it exists, present to Employee
   2b. If does not exist, see Create employee time sheet use case and present to Employee
3. Employee sets day of week
4. Employee selects project and enters hours worked on project
5. Employee requests system to save changes and system confirms

Alternative Course
Line 5: Employee aborts time sheet entry

USE CASE: Approve employee time sheets
Primary Course
1. Manager selects Employee from Employee list 2. System finds and displays pending time sheets for selected employee 3. Manager selects and marks displayed time sheets and requests system to mark as authorized

USE CASE: Create employee time sheets
Precondition: Employee and week-ending date is known
Primary Course
1. System creates time sheet and associates Employee and week ending date 2. System puts new time sheet in pending state and commits

USE CASE: Unapprove employee time sheet
Primary Course
1. Manager selects time sheet for employee and week-ending date 2. System searches for and displays pending time sheet 3. Employee toggles time sheet state to pending
Alternative Course
Line 2: If not found display available time sheets

Table 2.1 Use cases for the case study. (Continued)

USE CASE: Approve employee time sheet
Primary Course
1. Authorized Employee selects time sheet for Employee and week-ending date 2. System searches for and displays pending time sheet 3. Employee toggles time sheet state to approved
Alternative Course
Line 2: If not found display available time sheets

USE CASE: Display pending time sheet
Primary Course
1. System displays list of pending employee, weekend, and totals for pending time sheets

USE CASE: Display approved time sheets
Precondition: Approved time sheet for Employee exists
Primary Course
1. System displays list of approved time sheets by employee, weekend, and summarizes total hours

creating and managing Employees to show you some of the different choices you can make in designing applications with the WebSphere product family.

TimeSheets are the next most critical part of our model. TimeSheets have a date associated with them that indicates the ending date for this time sheet. Likewise, they have two different Employees associated with them; the Employee who submits the time sheet, and the Employee who approves it (the Employee's manager). However, it's not enough to simply have a TimeSheet object—we also have to track how time is entered by project for each particular date against that TimeSheet. We've chosen to model that with a collection of TimeSheetEntries, each of which stands for a particular combination of date, project, and hours.

A simple UML diagram showing the different relationships in our model is shown in Figure 2.2.

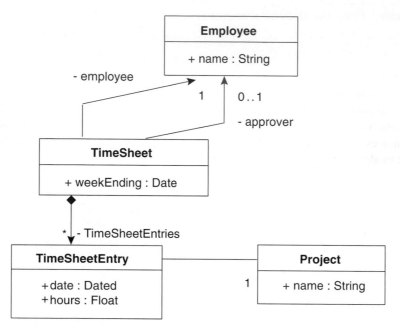

Figure 2.2 TimeSheet design.

2.4   Using the Case Study in Our Book

As we discussed at the beginning of this chapter, this simple case study is complex enough that we can demonstrate the choices you can make when using it to design J2EE applications. It's not a one-object toy application, but it's not overly complicated. We'll use it in several ways as we proceed through the chapters.

Employee management (creating, removing, and updating Employees in a relational database) is a topic that we'll revisit several times so that you can learn how to understand the trade-offs that the various parts of WebSphere and J2EE give you. We'll examine a simple Employee Management System in Chapter 7, and discuss different design aspects of implementing the database access and user interface portions in Chapters 12, 13, 14, and 21. We'll also examine how to secure that part of the application in Chapter 29.

The TimeSheet entry and display portion of the case study is another rich area that we'll explore repeatedly. In Chapters 11 and 15, we'll talk about two different choices for implementing part of the Web-based user interface of the application. In Chapters 23, 24, and 25, we'll introduce how to implement database persistence in that part of the application using some of WebSphere's built-in persistence capabilities. In Chapters 30 and 31, we'll examine how to put all of the technologies together into a single whole that uses all the different pieces you've examined in the previous chapters. Other chapters will also often refer to smaller portions of the case study presented in previous chapters to illustrate the differences in alternative technologies where you have a choice between two or more options.

Later on, as you learn more about building user interfaces with J2EE and the WebSphere product family, we will show you what the user interface of our case study system will look like.

2.5 Summary

In this basic overview of our case study, you've gained an understanding of the basic problem that our examples will solve, and of the business object design that we will use to solve it. In the chapters that follow, you'll learn how to use WebSphere and J2EE to implement this business model and the choices for providing a user interface for manipulating this business model and for persisting the model objects to a relational database.

CHAPTER 3

J2EE Overview

Over the years, the Java technology platform has grown out of its original applet client/server origins into a robust server-side development platform. Initial platform packages introduced built-in threading support and provided abstractions to I/O and networking protocols; newer versions of the Java Software Development Kit (SDK) continued to enhance these abstractions and introduce newer framework offerings.

The momentum of producing technology frameworks supporting enterprise server-based development has continued, and has been formalized into the J2EE platform offering. The motivation of this offering is to provide developers with a set of technologies that support the delivery of robust enterprise-scale software systems. IT professionals are presented with an ever-changing business and technology landscape. Technology professionals must balance the demands for new automation requirements against the existence of existing line of business applications; simply using the technology du jour perpetuates the problem of integrating existing legacy systems. The goal of the J2EE platform is to offer a consistent and reliable way in which these demands can be met with applications that possess the following characteristics:

- **High Availability**—Support and exist in a 24/7 global business environment.
- **Secure**—Ensure user privacy and confidence in business function and transactions.
- **Reliable and Scalable**—Support high volumes of business transactions accurately and in a timely manner.

This chapter offers an overview of the J2EE architecture, a brief discussion of the specification's component design and the solutions they provide, and describes which J2EE technologies this book will focus on.

First, some background.

All J2EE technologies are built upon the Java 2 Standard Edition (J2SE). It includes basic platform classes, such as the Collections framework, along with more specific packages such as JDBC and other technologies that support client/server-oriented applications that users interact with through a GUI interface (e.g., drag-and-drop and assistive technologies). Note that platform technologies are not limited to framework implementations. They also include development and runtime support tools such as the Java Platform Debugger Architecture (JPDA).

Technologies specific to developing robust, scalable, multitiered server-based enterprise applications are provided within the J2EE platform offering. While still supporting client/server-based architectures, J2EE platform technologies provide support for distributed computing, message-oriented middleware, and dynamic Web page development. This chapter and most of this book will deal specifically with some of these technologies. In particular, WebSphere 5.0 (the focus of this book) implements the J2EE 1.3 platform specification. A list of the technologies from J2EE 1.3 (along with the supported levels) is shown in Table 3.1.

Table 3.1 J2EE technologies.

Supported Technology	Level required by J2EE 1.3
Java IDL (Interface Definition Language) API	(Provided by J2SE 1.3)
JDBC Core API	2.0 (Provided by J2SE 1.3)
RMI-IIOP API	(Provided by J2SE 1.3)
JNDI API	(Provided by J2SE 1.3)
JDBC Extensions	2.0
EJB (Enterprise Java Beans)	2.0
Servlet API	2.3
JSP (JavaServer Pages)	1.3
JMS (Java Message Service)	1.0
JTA (Java Transaction API)	1.0
JavaMail	1.3
Java Activation Framework (JAF)	1.0
JAXP (Java API for XML Parsing)	1.1
Java 2 Connector Architecture (J2C)	1.0
JAAS (Java Authentication and Authorization Service)	1.0

Table 3.2 J2EE 1.4 technologies implemented
by WebSphere 5.0.

J2EE 1.4 Technology
JAX-RPC (Java API for XML-based RPC)
SAAJ (SOAP with Attachments API for Java)
JMX (Java Management Extensions)

In addition to the required technologies for J2EE 1.3, WebSphere Application Server 5.0 implements a number of J2EE-compatible technologies in advance of support of J2EE 1.4. In particular, WebSphere also supports technologies which will be required in J2EE 1.4 (Table 3.2).

3.0.1 J2EE Component Design

One of the most appealing features of object technology is its ability to combine function and data into a single element, also referred to as an object. Arguably, a single object implementation could be classified as a component, but components offer more functionality than providing access to data and performing functions against this data. Flexibility is achieved with designs that can consist of multiple classes related through composition and inheritance. The word component implies that they are a part of something whole, indicating that components require some kind of reference problem space where they can be applied. The J2EE specification provides this frame of reference for components that can be used, extended and combined by developers to deliver robust enterprise applications.

J2EE components defined for the platforms exploit the OO nature of Java by applying design patterns that provide both white and black box extensibility and configuration options. The platform components use inheritance and composition throughout their design, providing a way for custom configuration by developers. Also, defining components in an abstract way can allow systems built using those components to work regardless of how each vendor implements each concrete component implementation.

Studying these design techniques employed in the platform implementations can help make your own designs more elegant. These object design techniques are nothing new and have been applied throughout the years in other OO languages. Two design themes that take different approaches in supporting component configuration are discussed in the following sections.

3.0.2 Configurable Implementations

A specific design technique often used in the J2EE platform is the notion of describing completely abstract designs (through the use of interfaces) that allow the entire implementation to be configurable. This means that developers are aware of, and have visibility to, a set of interface types without regard to how they are implemented; implementation is the vendor's responsibility. This allows developers to choose the best available solutions. Figure 3.1 shows the dual relationship interfaces create between developers and vendors.

Figure 3.1 Relationship between developers and vendors.

3.0.3 Configurable Algorithms

Not all technology implementations are exclusively interfaces. Most have a combination of generalized class definitions that interact with interface types. Consider the servlet package; it provides a `javax.servlet.GenericServlet` implementation that is defined abstractly along with providing a servlet interface type. While this may seem redundant, designers of the servlet API have provided a way for developers to take advantage of an abstract configurable algorithm, and have provided an abstract configurable implementation that can serve as the basis of a concrete implementation. (For more on this dual nature, see the discussion comparing abstract classes and interfaces.)

> ### *ABSTRACT CLASSES OR INTERFACES?*
>
> Inheritance is a feature of the OO paradigm that captures the imagination of developers when they first encounter this technology. The ability to define and classify hierarchies of data structures and create state and behavior that is extended for specific functionalities provides an excellent way to deliver solutions that can be extended in a white box manner.
>
> White box-based designs utilize inheritance by implementing a base class that is extended by developers, and the appropriate elements are overridden with the desired functionality. Java provides language constructs that help communicate what can and cannot be overridden at construction time. Methods and class definitions can be defined as abstract, requiring developers to supply concrete implementations. Access modifiers such as final and private can be utilized to prohibit methods from being overridden. Combining these elements effectively can yield what is referred to as a configurable algorithm. The base class implements generalized methods that perform a set of algorithmic steps. Within this scope of base methods calls, abstract methods appear that are overridden, fulfilling a given method's implementation.
>
> Using inheritance exclusively can result in deep hierarchies that may lead to coupled implementations, usually the result of an abstract design that requires a large number of abstract methods to be implemented. Java interfaces provide an alternative abstract mechanism that allows for a more independent implementation without regard to an existing hierarchy.
>
> Inheritance is useful for designs that have algorithms or behavior that can be generalized and utilized by extending classes. Designs that require most or all of its implementation to be defined by extending classes can be

communicated using interface definitions. Implementers are given complete freedom in how the interface methods carry out their operations. However, interfaces enforce a more rigid contract, and changing an interface design can make a larger impact on existing implementations. Therefore, an effective way to evolve a design, in lieu of booking a lot of initial design time, is to initially utilize inheritances and let an abstract design evolve. Once the required signatures have been discovered, and it turns out that a configurable implementation is necessary, interface(s) can be produced.

Configurable implementations utilizing interfaces are the underpinnings of providing vendor-independent J2EE technology designs.

Interfaces and effective abstractions are the means by which J2EE components achieve vendor neutrality. The J2EE specifications simply define the APIs, types, life cycles, and interactions of objects within the technology frameworks. Vendors can then apply their efforts toward the agreed-upon contracts and specifications. Developers write to these specifications. You may ask: "Won't that create a dependency on these contracts, and if they change,won't my code be affected?" The short answer is yes, you are dependent upon versions of these contracts, but engaging them in a consistent way and knowing that they are community supported should help minimize this concern.

In addition to describing WebSphere Application Servers as a J2EE implementation product, this book will provide patterns and approaches for neutralizing this dependency.

3.0.4 Who Defines These Specifications?
Another key advantage of Java and the J2EE standard is the way in which component solutions are identified and defined. Early on, Sun promoted the openness of the Java language, initially by giving it away.

Advancement of Java technology and the formulation of the J2EE specification have been carried out by the JCP (Java Community Process). Community is the operative word; any interested individual or organization can participate. For individuals participation is free; organizations pay nominal dues. Delegates from the membership propose, review, and accept technology specification proposals. While not an open source initiative, but under a community license that still allows Sun to be steward of the language, the JCP encourages community participation.

Ideas are proposed through the creation of a Java Specification Request (JSR). Members evaluate and vote on the JSR for merit. Once accepted the JSR becomes an official technology component and goes through the design and development process by a committee made up JCP members—usually a cross section of well-known vendor members.

The advantage of community participation is the proliferation of new frameworks/components that are derived and designed from a wide point of view, arguably larger than proprietary-based technology that may be more influenced by market pressures. These market pressures still exist in the JCP environment, but the checks and balances of the membership can make them have less influence over the manner in which the problem is solved.

Of course, there is a down side to this approach. Whereas a company can be very nimble in getting a solution out the door by using a custom-built design, standardized solutions must receive approval and validation from the community which can take time.

3.1 Why J2EE?

Reuse is an adjective that can beckon the attention of developers, managers, and bean counters. It promises savings in the form of shorter development efforts and higher quality. Unfortunately, reuse has been oversimplified, and overhyped, resulting in a minimized impact. For instance, some reuse (of the base class libraries) occurs just through using Java as a programming environment. If you add J2EE components, more reuse occurs. Of course, this is not the business domain type of reusability that would allow us to snap together applications as in the proverbial IC chip analogy made by Brad Cox. Nevertheless, Java's OO nature and the standards of J2EE are a progression toward achieving high degrees of reuse.

J2EE-based technologies provide what can be classified as horizontal technology reuse (Figure 3.2). Contracts, primarily in the form of Java interfaces, allow developers to use vendor-supplied technology solutions with a high degree of transparency. Imagine if the JDBC specification did not exist and developers had to write directly to vendor-supplied APIs; of course, then-

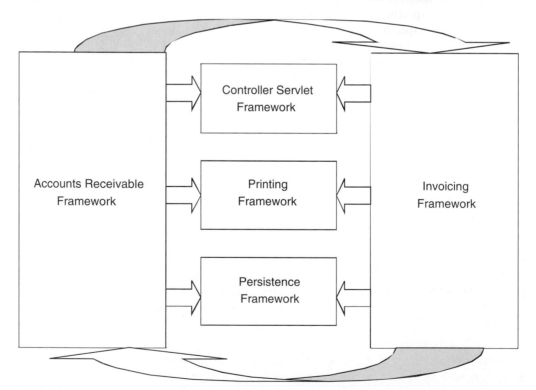

Figure 3.2 Horizontal technologies.

good OO developers would build designs that would decouple and wrapper vendor-specific APIs with a neutralized access API. Even though SQL is also a standard, each new target SQL-based data source would require a modification to this neutral API.

Fortunately, the JDBC specification allows the burden of access APIs to be moved to vendors. Developers simply acknowledge the specified contracts and generalized implementations and use them in applications to execute SQL against any vendor honoring the JDBC specification, which most, if not all, do.

Other horizontal technologies are vendor neutralized in a similar approach, allowing developers to concentrate on application-specific logic by using standards-compliant solutions. This frees developers from worrying about having to produce or refactor a horizontal implementation. Instead, the best vendor-supplied solutions can be engaged, resulting in shorter delivery times of applications that are robust and scalable.

3.2 J2EE Architecture

Planes, trains, and automobiles are all assembled using well-accepted blueprints and parts supplied by countless vendors. One way that this is carried out is through industry-accepted blueprints that define specifications for construction and how they are to be used. Under this same premise, the J2EE specification defines these interfaces, their life cycles, and interactions they must carry out. The specification also describes roles that can be held by resources involved in the development and deployment of server-based applications.

The J2EE specification introduces an architectural concept of a container. Containers are defined to house J2EE components within a layer boundary. Containers manage component relationships within tiers and resolve dependencies of components between these tiers. Figure 3.3 illustrates the J2EE containers and their associated component dependencies.

To understand where these components exist within the topology of an application, consider that a given application can be partitioned as follows:

- **Client Container**—User interface implementation resident on a client workstation.
- **Web Container**—Server-based user-interface implementation accessed via HTTP.
- **EJB Container**—Captures and defines enterprise business data and function; provides a mechanism for distribution of business objects and for transactional support of complex business interactions.
- **Information Systems Back End**—A database, messaging system, or EIS that provides data and functions to the system.

Applications may utilize all or, at a minimum, the client and Web tiers; within each tier J2EE technologies will be engaged to perform application functions. Some will occupy an obvious tier, as is the case with the JSP/Servlet technologies. Obviously, these belong in the Web tier. Other technologies play a supporting role and may appear in any or all tiers. For instance, it's easy to see the requirement of interprocess messaging (JMS) appearing in all of the client, Web, and EJB tiers.

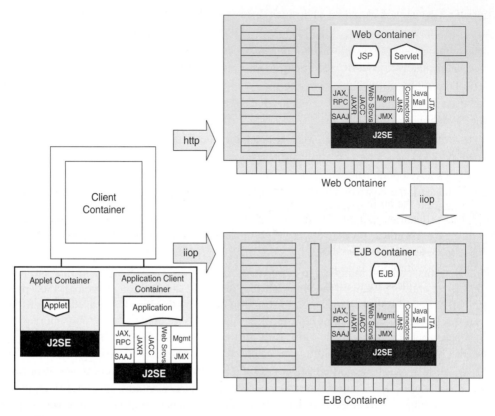

Figure 3.3 Container diagram.

Notice the presence of J2SE in every container definition diagrammed in Figure 3.3. This reflects the foundation for all containers. Other technologies shown may or may not appear within a container definition because they are determined by application requirements. The following sections describe components defined within container boundaries.

3.2.1 JDBC

Potentially the catalyst technology for Java, JDBC allows developers to interact with vendor-enforced JDBC data sources using generic interfaces. Statement execution, connection resolution, and result set processing can be carried out using the specification interfaces. Although in most cases the data source is relational-based, the specification interfaces does not require this.[1] This allows developers to execute SQL in a vendor neutral fashion.

---

1.   The JDBC design is slanted toward row-based result sets, therefore the majority of JDBC support comes from relational database vendors.

3.2.2 Servlet/JSP

Servlet technology is the mechanism used to create dynamic Web pages, in the same spirit that early Common Gateway Interface (CGI) technology was used to provide a personalized interaction with a Web site. Servlet technology allows browser resident clients to interact with application logic residing on the middle tier using request and response mechanisms of the HTTP protocol.

JSP technology is built upon servlet technology. Its purpose is to help blend HTML-based page definition and dynamic-based Java expressions into a single HTML-like document resource.

3.2.3 EJB

EJBs support the ability to create distributed components that can exist across Java application process boundaries and server topologies. More than simply providing access to distributed objects, the specification supports transactions with two-phase commit support, security, and data source access.

EJB technology is utilized to help support scalable application architecture by making enterprise business logic and data available and accessible to Web container function. EJBs' ability to support transactions across server boundaries in a distributed fashion is key to supporting large-scale, transaction-based applications.

3.2.4 Connector

EJB technology provides a distributed transaction-based environment for external resources. In many, but not all, cases these sources are relational based. The connector specification provides a mechanism for EJB technology to interact with other, non-relational resources in an implementation-independent manner.

3.2.5 JMS

JMS provides vendor-neutral point-to-point and publish/subscribe messaging solutions. The JMS service provider will provide an implementation based upon the JMS APIs. JMS is the primary mechanism in J2EE for allowing asynchronous communication between components. It can be used to provide asynchronous update of components running in networked client containers, or it can be used to allow asynchronous communication with back-end EISs.

3.2.6 Java Mail

This technology is a framework that implements an interface to an e-mail system. The framework is provided with J2EE in binary form. Also included is a set of APIs that support POP3 and SMTP mail protocols. While we will cover the other core J2EE APIs in this book, we will not cover Java Mail in any depth because, in truth, this API is rarely used.

3.2.7 JTA

Transaction support is abstracted using Java Transaction API (JTA). This API provides a generic API that allows applications, applications servers, and resource managers to participate in defining and executing heterogeneous transaction boundaries.

3.2.8 JAX-RPC

Java API for XML-based RPC (JAX-RPC) allows Java developers to create client and end-point Simple Object Access Protocol (SOAP)-based Web service functions. Developers can utilize Java-based classes to define Web services and clients that exercise Web-services, effectively shielding the developer from the complexity of interacting with the SOAP protocol. As with SAAJ and JMX, JAX-RPC is a required part of the J2EE 1.4 platform.

3.2.9 SAAJ

This technology (SOAP with Attachments API for Java) provides a Java API that allows the formatting of XML messages in conformance with the SOAP specifications. This should not be confused with JAX-RPC, which also supports SOAP, but provides Web services support for message composition and support for SAAJ, which allows the attachment of MIME-encoded binary documents to SOAP messages. SAAJ is a required part of the JAX-RPC API, so we will discuss it only within the context of JAX-RPC.

3.2.10 JMX

Java Management Extension (JMX) allows a generalized way that distributed and Web-based applications can provide monitoring and instrumentation services, independent of the vendor application server. We won't discuss programming to this API in WebSphere, but we will discuss how it is used in WebSphere administration.

3.3 J2EE Platform Roles

Besides defining a standard blueprint for vendor neutral enterprise computing components, the J2EE specification identifies roles that participate in producing, creating, and supporting information systems built upon the J2EE platform. These roles as defined in the J2EE 1.3 specification are described in the sections which follow.

3.3.1 J2EE Product Provider

The role is responsible for providing the J2EE containers that house the specification components. In addition, they are required to provide deployment and management tools used to manage J2EE applications deployed to the product. IBM plays the role of a product provider with its WebSphere application server product.

3.3.2 Application Component Provider

This role identifies the provider of components such as enterprise bean developers, and HTML document designers, and programmers that create components used to produce J2EE applications. This book exists primarily to educate developers who will fill this role.

3.3.3 Application Assembler

The act of using J2EE components to construct an application is the role defined by the specification—an application developer. Assembly implies that components are created and defined within an Enterprise Archive (EAR) file for deployment to containers. We will discuss integrating J2EE components and packaging them as EAR files for deployment.

3.3.4 Deployer

The deployer is responsible for deploying enterprise Java components into an operating environment that has a J2EE server supplied by a product provider. Deployment is typically made up of three steps: (1) installation, which involves moving the application (.ear) to the server environment; (2) configuration of any external dependencies required by the resource; (3) Execution of the installed application.

 While our primary focus is application development, and not deployment, we will discuss areas where the two roles meet.

3.3.5 System Administrator

This role is not new to the J2EE landscape. Administrators are responsible for configuring and monitoring the operating environments where J2EE servers exist, tasks are accomplished by using the appropriate tools from the J2EE product provider. We will not examine this role in our book. For more information on performing system administration with the WebSphere family of products, see [Francis] or the WebSphere Application Server InfoCenter.

3.3.6 Tool Provider

Tool providers furnish tools that help with the construction, deployment, and management of J2EE components. Tools can be targeted to all platform roles defined by the specification. This book describes WebSphere Application Developer, used to develop components, making IBM a tool provider.

 Currently, the specification does not require or provide a mechanism by which these tools are standardized. However, the specification has referenced a possibility of this being so in the future.

3.4 J2EE Versions and Evolution

Java's momentum has moved it from a niche programming language into a mainstream language that is robust enough for a spectrum of applications from scientific to business. Java's object-based environment allows the fundamental language to remain relatively stable with extensions coming in platform technologies, such as those defined in J2EE. Developers and vendors fulfilling these technology specifications with best-of-breed implementations have arguably formed a so-called critical mass. There is no reason why this momentum should not continue; new versions of current technologies along with new technologies will continue to augment the J2EE technology platform. Already, a single J2EE version increment from 1.3 to 1.4 has introduced Web services technology and XML support.

What does this mean to the Java developer? One point of view is that change in designs and APIs leads to a maintenance nightmare. Another, more optimistic view, is that smaller development cycles will result in more stable and robust software. Developers can protect themselves from API creep through consistency, generalization, and the application of design patterns. This book will not only describe how these technologies are used, specifically with IBM WebSphere, but will provide patterns that can be used to implement these technologies in a malleable way.

3.5 A J2EE Perspective

It is not enough to download the J2EE platform components and start writing enterprise applications with just any tool. Choosing the right development environment and application server determines whether complexity will be shielded and managed, or be an ever-present struggle during the development process. Realizing the full potential of J2EE technologies requires more than just a tool—it requires a pattern-based approach that engages tool-produced artifacts.

Many choices are available to the developer who wants to use J2EE technology. Some are free, others are vendor-supported. Obviously if you are reading this you are interested in the IBM WebSphere suite of products. The remaining chapters capture and describe the complete cycle from development to deployment utilizing the WebSphere Studio Application Developer product and its integrated tooling support. Besides providing a complete tutorial on how to utilize these tools and the application server, we will describe design approaches and patterns that can help make your development and deployment process, as well as the resulting software, flexible to better meet changing business needs.

As we discussed in Chapter 1, we see the idea of layered application architecture as being critical to J2EE, and to understanding the architecture of the WebSphere product family. Figure 3.4 illustrates how the different technologies we've just covered fit into that layered architecture.

At the top of our architecture is the presentation layer. We'll discuss providing presentation layers based on HTML using Java servlets, JSP, and eXtensible Stylesheet Language Transformations (XSLT). XSLT, not a J2EE technology, is a mechanism for transforming XML documents into HTML (commonly used along with servlets and JSP). We will also consider Web services in this layer, even though they are considered to be a program-to-program communication mechanism. We'll also examine how to test servlet-based applications using the open-source HTTPUnit tool.

Next comes the controller/mediator layer, which captures the notion of application flow and adapts the domain model layer to the presentation layer. We'll examine several ways of implementing controller logic, including implementing it with servlets, using the Struts open-source application framework, and even using message-driven beans (which are EJBs called through JMS) as application controllers for asynchronous logic flows.

In the domain layer, we'll examine how to implement domain logic using Java Beans (or, more correctly, Plain Old Java Classes) and EJBs. We'll also show you how to test your domain logic using the open-source JUnit toolkit. To support the persistence of objects in the domain

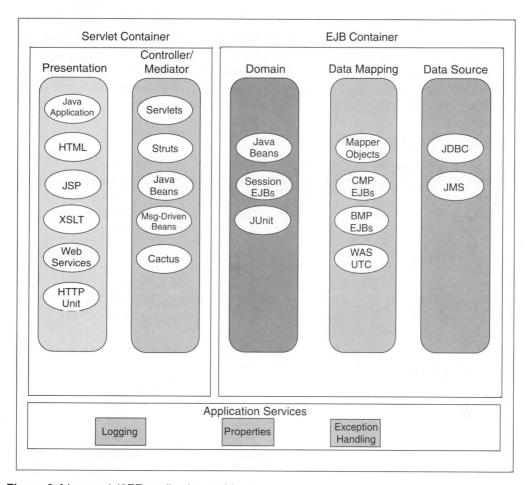

Figure 3.4 Layered J2EE application architecture.

layer, we'll examine the mapping layer in depth, discovering how to use mapper objects, bean-managed persistence (BMP) and container-managed persistence (CMP) entity EJBs.

In addition to showing you how to test with JUnit, we'll show you how to use the Web-Sphere Studio Universal Test Client. Finally, we'll examine the two most common sources of data for J2EE programs, JMS and JDBC.

While the book will proceed roughly in the order we've outlined, it won't cover the layers in strict order because not every system uses every technology we've described. Instead, you can rely on the application architecture graphic (Figure 3.4), which will appear at the beginning of every chapter starting in Chapter 5, to help you understand where the technologies fit into the overall J2EE architecture.

3.6 Summary

This chapter described Java's evolution from an initial way of delivering client/server type applications via the Web, to a robust OO platform that can support large-scale multiuser enterprise applications. With the addition of J2EE-based technologies, which are supported by the Java community at large, Java technology is a viable choice for developing applications of varying deployment topologies, platforms requirements, and business requirements.

What Is WebSphere?

One of the more confusing things about starting to use IBM's implementation of the J2EE technology is understanding what people mean by WebSphere. Developers often refer to WebSphere when they are, in fact, speaking about WebSphere Portal Server, or WebSphere Commerce Server, or even WebSphere MQ!

Why? There is no short answer, so first we will establish what WebSphere means, then understand how everything named WebSphere fits into the picture.

WebSphere is not a product. From its inception, WebSphere has been an IBM brand. One of the first products[1] introduced under the brand was the IBM WebSphere Application Server (WAS), which is what most people simply call WebSphere. However, the use is so common that you may even find references to WebSphere (meaning the application server) in this book.

After the introduction of WAS, several more products were added to the product family. By the time WAS 5.0 was released, the WebSphere product line had settled into a consistent set of offerings divided into three categories: Foundation and Tools, Business Portals, and Business Integration (Figure 4.1).

- **Foundation and Tools** represents the heart of the WebSphere product line; the WAS, the WebSphere Studio product line, and the WebSphere tools for host integration. In this book we will focus on the first two elements.
- **Business Portals** include WebSphere Portal Server (products for building internal and customer-facing portals), WebSphere Commerce Solutions (including WebSphere Commerce Portal, an extensive set of tools and frameworks for building large-scale

---

1.   The very first shipped product under the WebSphere product family name was WebSphere Performance Pack, now part of WebSphere Application Server, Network Deployment Edition.

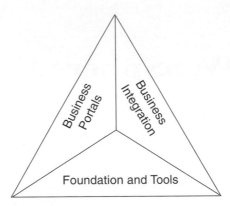

Figure 4.1 WebSphere family of products.

Internet commerce Web sites), and the WebSphere Everyplace family (including tools and frameworks for communicating with cell phones, PDAs, and pervasive computing devices).

- **Business Integration** includes the WebSphere MQ family of products for enterprise messaging, workflow, systems integration, as well as the WebSphere Business Integrator family of products for application integration.

IBM also offers other strategic product families that work with the WebSphere product line:

- The Tivoli family of products for systems management and security provide additional capabilities for WebSphere. For example, Tivoli Access Manager can provide integrated security management for products like Web servers and CRM applications that lie outside of the bounds of the WAS. Likewise you can use products like IBM SecureWay Firewall to secure your network resources, and IBM Directory Server to provide a Lightweight Directory Access Protocol (LDAP) repository for maintaining the identities of the users on your network.
- The Rational family of products for application development like Rational Rose and Rational XDE allow you to integrate the J2EE development you perform in WebSphere Studio into the Rational Unified Development Process.
- The DB2 family of Information Management products like DB2 Universal Database provides superior performance and scalability for your database needs.

We will not touch on the capabilities provided by these tools, with the exception of IBM DB2 Universal Database, which we will use in our examples. Of course, at the heart of the WebSphere product strategy is the interoperability that adhering to J2EE standards provides you. While you can achieve easy interoperability and excellent results by using tools like DB2 and IBM Directory Server, WebSphere works well with other relational database providers like Oracle and Sybase, or with other LDAP tools like Microsoft Active Directory or Sun ONE Directory Server.

4.1 WebSphere Foundation and Tools

WebSphere Foundation and Tools is made up of the products needed to quickly build and deploy J2EE-compliant applications on the most scalable, fastest J2EE application server on the market. There are two primary product groups within this family: WebSphere Studio (development tools) and WAS (deployment platforms).

4.1.1 WebSphere Studio

WebSphere Studio is a unique family of development tools based on the open-source Eclipse architecture. The Eclipse architecture is a plug-in based approach to IDE development that allows users and third parties to freely extend the base IDE with their own plug-ins. Eclipse provides the common code base in all of the WebSphere Studio family products for the basic Java IDE capabilities (Java code editing, incremental compilation, debugging, and source code control). Each product in the WebSphere Studio Family extends these capabilities with additional functions and features. The primary members of the WebSphere Studio family are:

- **WebSphere Studio Site Developer**—An environment that allows developers to build and test dynamic Web sites using JSPs and Java servlets. It includes the HTML and DHTML authoring and editing capabilities of the WebSphere Studio Homepage Builder product, combined with additional wizards and features for developing JSP and servlet applications and Web services. The applications we build in chapters 1–16 can be developed using these features.
- **WebSphere Studio Application Developer**—This product extends WebSphere Studio Site Developer with additional capabilities for developing applications using EJBs. WebSphere Studio Application Developer also contains features for working with relational database schemas and for performance profiling applications. Beginning in Chapter 17 we will examine applications that can be built using these features.
- **WebSphere Studio Application Developer Integration Edition**—WSAD IE provides features that extend WebSphere Studio Application Developer with the ability to develop for many of the special features of WebSphere Application Server Enterprise Edition (such as process choreography). In addition, WSAD IE provides support for developing applications that use the J2C specification for access to EISs such as CICS. The tools provided in WSAD IE support technology that is complimentary to the core J2EE platform such as workflow management and business rules, and will not be covered in detail by this book.
- **WebSphere Studio Enterprise Developer**—WSED is designed to integrate traditional transaction-based systems with the WebSphere e-business platform and supports traditional z/OS development with COBOL and PL/1. The test and debugging support allows developers to interactively debug Web, CICS, and IMS transaction environments.

4.1.2 WebSphere Application Server Family

Once you have developed and tested an application using WebSphere Studio you are ready for the next step, deployment. There are three members in the WAS family. They provide different capabilities for scalability and manageability, and provide other programming model possibilities through extensions to the J2EE programming model.

- **WAS** is the cornerstone of the WebSphere product family. WAS 5.0 is a J2EE 1.3-compliant application server that provides complete support for all aspects of the J2EE programming model. WAS (the base edition, sometimes called the core server) is targeted for small, departmental applications that do not require deployment on more than one machine.[2]
- **WebSphere Application Server, Network Deployment Edition (WAS ND)** provides the ability to deploy applications that support failover and load balancing across multiple machines. WAS ND combines the cloning features that were previously part of WAS 4.0, Advanced Edition, together with features from what was previously marketed as Tivoli's WebSphere Edge Server. We will discuss some of the key features of WAS ND in this book, especially as they apply to writing scalable, reliable applications using the J2EE programming model.
- **WebSphere Application Server, Enterprise Edition (WAS EE)** provides programming model extensions that go above and beyond the J2EE specification. Some of the capabilities address common problems faced by enterprise-scale application developers that have not yet been incorporated into the J2EE specification, while others are truly unique to IBM's vision of enterprise development. WAS EE includes enhancements to the basic CMP EJB model, features that are in anticipation of later versions of the J2EE specification (like Async Beans), and features that support development of very-large scale applications like WebSphere Business Choreographer. We will occasionally point out some features of WAS EE in the context of the problems that they solve (in Chapter 28, we will discuss how some WAS EE features address shortcomings in the current EJB specification) but this book will not cover all of the features of WSAD EE in detail.

Two other members of the WebSphere product family should be mentioned, even though they fall outside of the continuum of products just discussed. They are:

- **WebSphere Application Server, Express Edition**—WebSphere Application Server, Express is a combination of WebSphere Studio Site Developer and a version of WAS that only supports a J2EE Web container. This would be appropriate for developers of small-scale applications that do not need to use the power of EJBs.

2.   In the previous version, these capabilities were part of what was known as WebSphere Application Server, Advanced Single-Server Edition (AEs).

• **WebSphere Application Server for zOS**—This product is a version of WAS specifically targeted at the zOS (OS/390) platform. It is fully compliant with the J2EE 1.3 specification, and code written for WAS will deploy and run without change on this platform. Likewise, it shares the same Web-based administrative console feature as WAS. However, some of the advanced capabilities of the zOS platform allow the product to take advantage of that platform's unique scalability in ways that differ from the scalability mechanisms used in WAS ND.

In the next section, we will look at each of the three major products in the WAS family in more detail and discuss the major features and capabilities of each.

4.1.3 WebSphere Application Server (WAS)

The WAS family of products is scalable. It provides a fully compliant platform for J2EE and key Web services open standards, making WAS production-ready for the deployment of enterprise Web services solutions. Product packaging is based on the core product, IBM WAS 5.0, which provides the base administrative console; an updated Application Assembly Tool for creating, editing, and viewing J2EE applications; the Application Client Resource Configuration Tool (ACRCT); and the Tivoli Performance Viewer on a single node configuration.

WAS 5.0 includes:

• Support for J2EE 1.3 (including built-in JMS and full J2C support)
• New Web services integration (including support for JAX-RPC and JSR109[3])
• An XML-based administrative repository (no database required as in previous versions)
• A Web-browser based administrative console
• Support for JMX

At runtime, WAS consists of a *server* process (which is a single JVM instance) that can run several J2EE *applications* (each packaged and deployed as separate enterprise archive [EAR] files). One of the applications running on each stand-alone WAS instance is the administrative application, which allows you to manage and configure the server from a Web-based administrative console.

4.1.4 WAS Network Deployment (ND)

WSAD ND is unique in that it does not require you to install additional software on most server machines; all you need on most machines in your network is the base WAS. The WAS ND installation is simple because you are required only to install the additional software that makes up ND on a machine in the network to create a *deployment manager* node. A *node* is the term in WAS ND for a collection of managed processes (usually corresponding to one physical system with a single IP address, although this can get complicated if you consider SMP configuration).

---

3.   Introduced as a technology preview in WAS 5.0 and fully supported in WAS 5.02.

Nodes are grouped into a higher level grouping called a *cell*. The servers and applications in a cell are administered using the management tools located on the network deployment manager node. A *cluster* in WSAD ND is a collection of server processes all running the same enterprise application(s).

HTTP and RMI-IIOP traffic is load balanced across the different servers in the cluster according to the settings configured in the administrative console. You can create as many clusters within a cell as you choose, depending upon the scalability and failover needs of your applications. Just like servers and applications, clusters are created using the tools available on the network deployment manager as well.

4.1.5 WAS Enterprise Edition (WAS EE)

WAS EE includes both WAS and WSAD ND. Enterprise extensions expand the J2EE programming model through custom APIs. These extensions work on both a single server with WAS, or in a multiserver environment with both WAS and WSAD ND.

Each enterprise extension stands alone as a component feature. You probably would not need to use all of the extensions on any one system. In a large network of heterogeneous networks and applications, WAS EE provides extensions for legacy systems to improve throughput, resource utilization, and systems management.

Enterprise extensions provide a greatly enhanced programming model. These extensions support features such as process automation services and dynamic business policy management. WAS EE also has EJB CMP extensions, container-managed messaging, Business Rule Beans, last-participant transaction support, and dynamic EJB-QL queries (the last two are covered in later chapters).

4.2 The WAS Core Architecture

At last it's time to look deeper into the process architecture of WAS. We will first examine the components of a base WAS installation, and then examine how an installation of WSAD ND differs from an installation of base WAS.

Let's begin by talking about how the J2EE specification describes a standard for packaging applications. An enterprise application contains the hierarchy of resources for your J2EE application to function. It can contain any combination of the following:

- **Web modules (Web archive [WAR] files)**—These files contain servlets and JSP components as well as other classes and resources (like property files and static web content) used by those components.
- **EJB modules (packaged into EJB Java archive [JAR] files)**—These files contain EJBs and their associated classes.
- **Application client modules**—These files contain the code for application clients that use EJBs and other J2EE services. This code runs on the client, not on the server. We will cover this in detail in Chapter 22.

- **J2C connector modules (resource archive [RAR] files)**—These files contain J2C connectors and their definitions. If, for instance, you needed to connect to a mainframe CICS transaction, you would need to include an appropriate J2C connector enabling this inside your EAR file.
- **Utility JAR files**—If you have Java code that is used by more than one module within your EAR, it is a best practice to separate it into its own JAR file and package that file in the EAR file as well.

Each of the J2EE module files has a similar structure. They are all packaged as JAR files, which combine Java .class files for a logical set of packages and any necessary configuration property files together with a JAR manifest. In addition to Java .class files, a J2EE module will also contain deployment descriptors (which are specific to each module type) and IBM extension and binding documents (again, specific to each module type).

Enterprise applications are packaged together as EAR files. A typical example of how an EAR file is laid out is shown in Figure 4.2.

WebSphere is different from some other application servers in that it adheres strictly to the J2EE specification and does not allow deployment of applications in any way other than through the standard EAR format (e.g., there is no special directory in WebSphere in which you can place JSP or servlet .class files in order to make them run).

We will revisit EAR files (and their constituent parts) in later chapters. For now, you need to have a basic understanding of EAR files to understand how applications are deployed into WAS, and how this fits with the WAS process model. Figure 4.3 shows the parts of a base WAS installation.

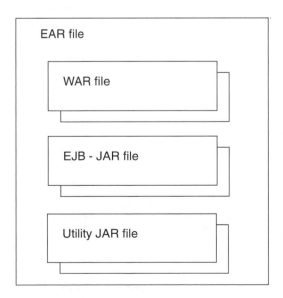

Figure 4.2 Typical EAR file structure.

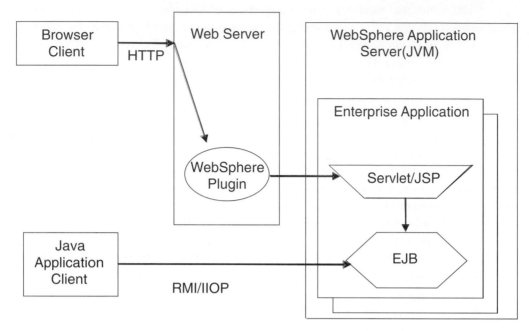

Figure 4.3 WAS process architecture.

By far the two most common means for a user to access a WebSphere application is by requesting HTML (Web) pages from a servlet or a JSP, or by using a desktop application client written in Java that connects to services provided by EJBs running inside a WebSphere server.

Let's first consider the servlet or JSP path. The URL that the user connects to will not, in fact, be hosted by a WebSphere application server instance itself, but will instead refer to a Web server. This may be an open-source Web server like Apache, or a commercial one like Microsoft IIS, or the IBM HTTP Server (powered by Apache) which ships as part of the WebSphere base installation. This Web server must have installed within it a piece of extension code provided as part of WAS, and which is installed as part of the WebSphere installation process.

This piece of code is called the WebSphere plug-in, and it is responsible for identifying those URLs that represent services (servlets, JSPs, and other files) provided by a WebSphere application server and passing the requests on to an appropriate WAS instance.

WebSphere requires this level of indirection for a couple of reasons.

First, in most real-life situations, you would want to combine an application written in WebSphere with other Web content. This could be static HTML, JPEG or GIF files, animations written using Macromedia Flash, or even entire applications written in technologies like Perl or Microsoft ASP.NET. WAS's plug-in approach allows you to accomplish this with a minimum of additional setup. The WebSphere plug-in uses a simple XML configuration file that identifies the URLs (and virtual hosts) that correspond to WebSphere applications, and identifies the server name to which it should route requests for those URL-host combinations. The Web server and whatever other plug-ins it may host handle all other content not identified in this file.

The second reason WebSphere uses a Web server plug-in is that in WAS ND the plug-in can also spread work among several different WebSphere application server instances. We will discuss more about this behavior of the plug-in in the next section.

Once the plug-in identifies the correct final endpoint for an HTTP request, it forwards it to a WAS instance. An application server instance is a JVM that can host any number of enterprise applications, each representing different logical applications. Once the server identifies the URI for the request it can then find the appropriate enterprise application that contains that URI and invoke the Web component (servlet or JSP) that will handle the request. That component may make requests of other J2EE components (other servlets or JSPs, EJBs, etc.) or it may obtain information from an external data source like a relational database. In the end, though, it returns an HTTP response back to the browser, usually in the form of a Web page.

The other path is much simpler, but less common. In it, an application written in Java makes a request of an EJB running in a WAS using the RMI/IIOP protocol. We'll cover that architecture in detail in Chapter 22.

There are other ways to make requests of components running inside WebSphere, such as through Web services or CORBA, which we will cover in later chapters. What we covered here are the two basic approaches; other mechanisms are variations of them.

Now that you understand how a request is handled by a WebSphere installation, you're ready to understand how enterprise applications are placed into a WAS instance and what other administration steps can be done to make the application server instance ready to run the enterprise application.

4.3 Administering a local WAS Server

In WebSphere (both base and ND) you use a web-based WebSphere Administrative Console[4] to administer applications. The WebSphere Administrative Console is a WebSphere application much the same as any other WebSphere application. If you haven't enabled security, you will only be prompted for a username for change control. Otherwise, you will need to login with a valid user ID and password, which has been granted administrative access.

Once you login, you are able to:

- Manage enterprise applications (including installing, starting, stopping, updating, and uninstalling)
- Manage users, groups, and other security configuration information
- Manage your WebSphere Environment (managing virtual hosts, updating the plug-in configuration, set up shared libraries)

---

4.   For those who can't wait to try this out, the URL to access the console is *http://localhost:9080/admin* (for stand-alone) and *http://localhost:9090/admin* (for Network Deployment).

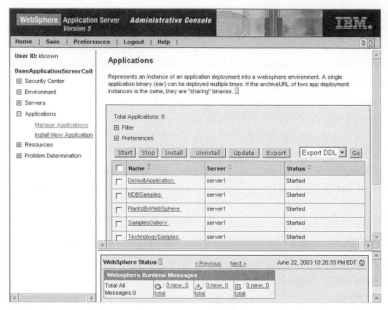

Figure 4.4 WebSphere Administrative Console.

- Manage servers (create servers)
- Manage resources (JMS, JDBC, JCA, URL, and JavaMail)
- Perform problem determination (view logs, turn tracing on or off)

An example of a page from the WebSphere Administrative Console is shown in Figure 4.4, where we show the Administrative Console open to the page used for administering enterprise applications.

Upon reflection, it may seem there is a chicken-and-egg problem here. If the administration application is a WebSphere application, and (as you've just seen) you need to use the administration application to create, start, and stop Web applications, then where did the administrative application come from? In fact, the base WebSphere solves this bootstrapping problem by configuring a default server with a preinstalled administration application that allows you to perform these tasks. To perform administration you have to start the default server (which you can do by using the startServer script, or by using the Start Server Windows Start menu option available within the WebSphere program group).

In order to deploy an enterprise application you would use the WAS Administrative Console to:

1. Create virtual host aliases for the enterprise application so clients can access the enterprise application.

2. (Optional) Create an application server.

3. Create an enterprise application and associate it with application servers.

We will cover some of the facilities of the administration console in later chapters. It is beyond the scope of this book to describe all the features of server administration in WAS. For that, refer to the WebSphere InfoCenter[5].

Now you know a little bit about how you configure WAS, and how you install enterprise applications into WebSphere Application Server, but we still haven't explained what happens when you perform these actions in the administrative console. The answer to that is simple: When you install a server, the console is simply expanding the EAR file into a specific installation directory known to the WAS instance and updating a set of XML configuration files. Any other configuration changes also update the XML configuration files as well.

The fact that every configuration can be represented by values in these XML files is what makes it possible to replicate configurations across multiple machines in a network in WAS ND, as you will see next.

4.4 Leveraging the Scalability of WAS ND

We should note that describing how to administer and configure WS ND is beyond the scope of this book. For detailed information on configuring ND, refer to the InfoCenter or [Francis]. However, understanding the terminology used in WAS ND will help you understand how things are organized in the base WAS, and also will help you understand some of the programming features that take advantage of scalability that we will cover in later chapters.

IBM WAS ND 5.0 provides centralized administration of multiple nodes. As we discussed earlier, in all versions of WAS, a node is a logical grouping of managed processes that usually corresponds to a physical system with an IP address. Node names usually are identical to the host name for the system. IBM WAS 5.0 (Base) resides on a single node. In the base product each installation is unaware of other installations.

In WAS ND, a WebSphere *node agent* manages all WebSphere processes on a node. The node agent represents the node in the WebSphere management cell.

The network deployment manager node contains a WAS ND manager that communicates with the independent node agents running in each node in the cell. Nodes synchronize configuration files and installed application files. Most resources in a WebSphere cell reside on one node. Some resource types, such as virtual hosts and enterprise applications, are not associated with a specific node. For a node to be managed by the deployment manager, it must contain IBM WAS. It is not necessary for the deployment manager node to contain IBM WAS.

Nodes in a cell can run while the network deployment manager node is not running. When the network deployment manager node is online, it coordinates synchronization with each node agent. You can attach the administrative console to a node, cluster, or cell to monitor nodes.

A cell is where you can find configuration information for objects in your distributed WebSphere set of nodes. A cell is comparable to a WAS 4.0 administrative domain. A cell contains

---

5.   The WebSphere InfoCenter is the WebSphere Application Server product documentation. It is available at *http://www.ibm.com/software/webservers/appserv/infocenter.html*.

clusters, each of which is a set of servers under workload management. An EAR file is deployed onto all of the servers within a cluster (the cluster members). Since they all run the same software the cluster members are all equivalent, which is what allows WAS to perform workload balancing across a cluster. In addition to cluster configuration, a cell contains configurations pertaining to:

- Physical hosts where an application server is installed
- Application servers
- Enterprise applications installed on application servers
- Resources providing support to applications, such as JAR files and data sources for data access

WAS 5.0 node configuration data is stored in XML files. You can use either the admin console or the wsadmin scripting facility in interactive or batch mode to update the configuration XML files. The wsadmin scripting utility is a tool that supports many scripting languages, including JavaScript, JPython, and Jacl (derived from Tcl). You can use it to access JMX-managed beans (MBeans) that control WAS servers.

A deployment manager retains master configuration files for each server in each node. Each node and server likewise has its own local copy of the configuration files. When you make a change to the master files in the deployment manager, the changes are synchronized to the appropriate copies of those files on the affected nodes. Synchronization between local and cell configuration files occurs at events such as server startup, or on a timed basis. Figure 4.5 shows a diagram of this architecture.

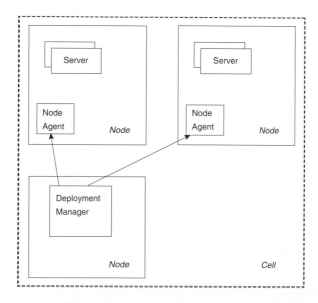

Figure 4.5 Cell architecture in WAS ND.

Clusters are the equivalent of WAS 4.0 server groups. A cell can have zero or more clusters. Vertical clusters have servers on the same node under workload management. Horizontal clusters have servers on multiple nodes under workload management. An example of this kind of arrangement is shown in Figure 4.6.

Normally, traffic is balanced among the members of a cluster using a simple algorithm like round-robin or random routing. WAS ND's workload management can also route both HTTP and IIOP traffic based on server weighting, to provide better control. Also, you can define a backup cluster to mirror and provide failover for a production cluster.

A sample topology for an application deployed in a WAS ND cluster is shown in Figure 4.7. In Figure 4.7 we also show how the pieces of WAS ND interact to provide scalability and protection from failure. Here, the Network Dispatcher component of the WebSphere Edge Server (which is part of WAS ND) receives incoming HTTP traffic that represents requests for either servlets or JSPs residing in WAS, or for static content residing in the IBM HTTP Server (IHS). This traffic is split (load balanced) among two or more installations of the IHS. Static content is served directly from the IHS.

Requests for dynamic content (meaning URLs corresponding to servlets or JSPs) are passed on to the WAS instances behind the IHS instances by the IHS plug-in. The IHS plug-in provides a second layer of load balancing to the different members of the WAS ND cluster.

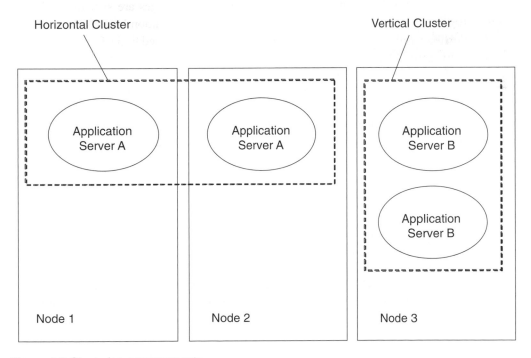

Figure 4.6 Clustering arrangements.

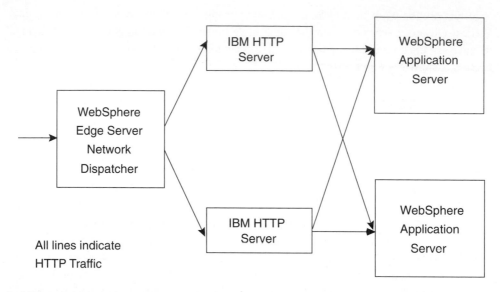

Figure 4.7 WSAD ND HTTP load balancing.

So, in this topology you are protected from any single point of failure (presuming, of course, that a backup network dispatcher is in place). If an IHS server fails, the other server will continue to handle requests, and the network dispatcher will notice the failure and stop routing requests to the server that is offline. Similarly, if an application server in the cluster fails, the plug-ins in the IHS instances will notice the failure and stop forwarding requests to that instance as well.

You should care about this configuration because there are programming model ramifications of this deployment model. For instance, in Chapter 9 you will learn about how HTTPSessions are shared across members of a cluster and what impact that has on the design of your servlets.

4.5 Summary

IBM WAS 5.0 contains many new features and enhancements that simplify Web application deployment and management. An enhanced admin console, configuration management, and cluster and node management allow IBM WAS 5.0, the application server, to manage complex J2EE applications.

In the chapters that follow we will discuss the technologies needed to implement enterprise applications. We will also demonstrate the application development tools and deployment through our case study.

Presentation Layer Patterns

The user interface of an application provides the basis in which the end user, in many cases your paying customer, judges its value. If you doubt this, reflect on the experiences and emotions you have whenever you are exposed to a new development tool interface. More than likely your initial impression comes from cosmetic appearances like color schemes, widget layout, etc. A bad initial impression can influence your perception of the actual effectiveness of the tool. Next, users place weight on the intuitiveness of the application's features. In short, can the user do what he wants to do without instruction or documentation?

From a developer's perspective, constructing an effective and intuitive interface is an endeavor that can satisfy the hidden artist in all of us, but the underappreciated value of a given application is in the elegance of the design applied to its construction. Developers value applications that have been consistently constructed and are therefore easily maintained and enhanced. A balance between providing a user with an elegant user interface experience and allowing developers to modify and even replace implementations is the rationale behind the application layers discussed in earlier chapters.

Consistently separating business logic from the user interface allows the modification of the user interface to occur with minimal effect on the business or domain implementation. Decoupling the user interface from the domain also means that GUI technologies can change without affecting the rest of the application. This may not have been a reality in the early client/server days where client-side GUIs were the norm, but interface technologies delivered via the Internet make it likely—if not probable—that user interface technologies will continue to evolve. This evolution is even more reason to decouple the user interface from business function and data.

Decoupling is a key feature of the layered application architecture presented in the previous chapters. This chapter introduces the user interface technologies and frameworks that will be discussed in upcoming chapters and occupy the presentation controller/mediator layers of the

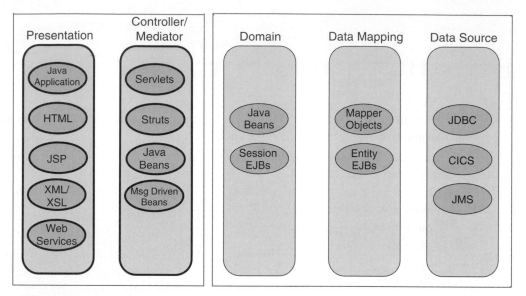

Figure 5.1 Presentation layer elements of the road map.

application architecture. The road map diagram for the book is shown in Figure 5.1 and high-lights the relevant layers

In addition, we'll cover why and how capturing application logic in a separate layer bene-fits decoupling. Finally, we'll discuss how the well-known Model View Controller (MVC) design pattern fits into the decoupling equation.

5.1 Java User Interface Technologies

Java's original intent was to allow an application to be deployed to a client from a Web server. User interfaces were constructed with graphical widgets in the same way that window-based user interfaces were. The novelty was that the application could be accessed with a Web browser; applets would provide the same functionality that a standard client/server-based user interface would. Browsers only required the presence of a Java virtual machine (JVM) . Initially, these VM implementations were built into the browser executable.

The problem arose when the JVM specification changed, adding new features, thus mak-ing older browser software unable to execute new Java applets. Making the VM a plug-in solved this problem, but created another. The original user interface framework in Java (AWT, or the Abstract Windowing Toolkit) relied upon a *peer*-based design. User interface widgets were actu-ally rendered as platform-specific user interface widgets. The design utilized a toolkit pattern that associated Java class widgets with the appropriate platform user interface widget. Each VM knows what type of platform it has been deployed on, so it can access the appropriate operation systems resources.

While the toolkit may seem clever, it limited the family of available widgets to the operating system with the smallest number of widgets. This caused many initial Java applications to rely upon third-party user interface frameworks that violated the platform independence and standardization of Java. This problem was ultimately solved with the introduction of Java Swing that rendered user interfaces entirely in Java, eliminating the reliance on available operating system widgets.

However, by then, Servlet/JSP technology had appeared and provided an easy way to deliver thin dynamic Web-based applications with plain old HTML.

At this point, development momentum quickly shifted to this new cost-effective way to deliver applications, commonly referred to as server-side Java development; implying that all of the Java-based application is resident on the server side. Even though this allowed easy deployment and ubiquitous access for the user, HTML-based user interfaces did not provide the rich navigability features that were common in client-side GUIs.

Even interface technologies such as JavaScript cannot satisfy all user interface requirements. Designing an application in a decoupled way minimizes the reliance on a specific user interface technology. Upcoming sections will discuss how this decoupling takes place.

First, we'll discuss some popular user interface technologies. Upcoming chapters will describe each of these technologies in detail, along with how they are engaged within the WSAD toolset.

5.1.1 Servlet/JSP

Using servlet and JSP J2EE components, developers can generate HTML in response to individual user requests. This offers the thinnest of client workstation profiles. All that is required is a browser and connectivity using the HTTP protocol. HTML interfaces provide a colorful and visually aesthetic user interface with its ability to lay out and integrate graphics and text.

Servlets and JSPs are essentially synonymous, at least when speaking of the mechanics of how Java models the HTTP protocol. Both allow server-side Java logic to be exercised and HTML tags returned for rendering by the browser at runtime. In fact, JSPs are translated into Servlets (see Chapter 10) by the Web Container. This implies that defining a JSP is really a programming endeavor; however, through the use of tag libraries and well-placed scriptlet tags, it's conceivable that JSP construction can be performed by more graphically inclined personnel who are conditioned to ignore Java-based tags and scriplets.

JSPs are documents like HTML, and are constructed much like HTML documents, often using the same HTML editor. The door is open for tool support and the robust knowledge of putting together HTML-based interfaces.

The down side of the technology is attempting to implement interfaces that require robust viewing and editing capabilities against large amounts of data. Users accustomed to robust user interface controls, such as fully editable tables and menu options activated using keystroke combinations, can find JSP/Servlet interfaces limiting. A user will appreciate a highly-customized, quickly interactive application when it must be used for long periods of time or when it requires the viewing and editing of large amounts of data. HTML-based user interfaces don't naturally support this type of intensive user interaction.

5.1.2 XML/XSLT

An alternative way to generate dynamic HTML is through XSL, a technology which allows the transformation of XML documents into other XML documents. HTML is XML-based, so it provides a convenient way to transform presentation-neutral XML into dynamic HTML documents that can then be presented to the user. Chapter 15 provides a detailed discussion of how XSLT can be used to generate dynamic HTML within a Java application, so this discussion will only contrast this user interface approach against the JSP/Servlet way of HTML generation.

The primary benefit of representing user interfaces in XML is the ability to use XML technology and tools to separate business data from user interface rendering in order to repurpose or process the XML into any format for various devices. Rendering a user interface in a pervasive device, kiosk, or Web browser is only a matter of processing the XML with different XSL templates.

From the Java standpoint, the application has to worry only about the logical elements that appear in the XML document tree. An XML-based interface not only decouples the presentation from underlying business and application logic, it decouples the user interface from platform and interface technologies.

Another advantage is the ease of change or rebranding efforts. XSLT is a powerful scripting language that is applied at runtime and does not have to be compiled and deployed in the same manner as JSP/Servlet elements. These features allow programs written using XSLT to be more easily customized than those using JSP. Also, when an interface is written using XSLT, the only logic contained in the XSLT stylesheet is that which is responsible for transforming XML into HTML tags; this ensures that proper layering is preserved.

While one could say JSPs provide the same level of modification, JSP implementations combine HTML tags and Java expressions. Developers are free to import and define complex and lengthy Java expressions intertwined within HTML tags, and often delivery timelines can influence developers to overload JSP implementation with Java logic, even if a formal design approach exists.

XSL-based interfaces are fed XML generated with Java, which keeps long ugly methods that produce the XML separate from the presentation logic. The redeployment and compilation of modified JSPs require special access visibility and may have side effects.

Performance is the most obvious trade-off when comparing JSP/Servlet-based interfaces against pure XML-based user interfaces. The parsing and styling of XML produced for the interface is often done dynamically, and parsing can consume many machine cycles. In addition, XSLT is not a language that is universally understood, presenting a moderate learning curve. Likewise, tools support for XSLT is limited. However, by using XSL caching and XSLT compilation technology many performance issues can be easily overcome.

Also, as we will see in Chapter 15, WSAD contains numerous tools and development aids in its XML perspective for XML and XSL Web interface development.

5.1.3 Swing-Based GUI

It would be naive to think that client/server-based applications have been completely superseded by Web-delivered applications. Applet technology and/or distributed technology support still accommodate the traditional client-based GUI in a J2EE-based application.

Java Swing technology provides a way for workstation resident and operating system-independent GUIs to be constructed. This requires the presence of a JVM for the platform to be resident. These user interfaces are constructed using Java Swing technology that provides a robust set of interface widgets that can be constructed in an infinite number of ways. Standard features include things such as menus, tables, and robust list elements that support integrated graphics allowing the delivery of elaborate and responsive user interfaces.

Responsiveness is probably the most common reason users demand a client-side user interface. Applications that carry out frequent lookup and modification of data can benefit from the navigation control and robust set of interface widgets available with the Swing-based user interfaces.

Swing-based applications can, and should, utilize server-based J2EE technologies. EJB, JMS, and SOAP technologies can be exploited to diminish the impact on the client resident user interface. Likewise, the layered architecture approach proposed by this book supports the ability to engage both Web- and client-based user interfaces using the same business domain implementation. Essentially, Web-based clients access the system via the Web container, while Java-based clients access the system via the EJB layer. Since the Web container uses the EJB container to gain access to business logic, this provides consistency and reuse.

5.2 Decoupling the User Interface

The early JSP specifications (prior to JSP 1.0) identified two types of architectural models. Model 1-type architectures don't formalize how the presentation-based elements interacted with the rest of the application, which can include everything from business logic defined in Java objects and database calls. In a sense they rolled everything together into a single element. Model 2-based architectures do formalize the way in which the presentation interacts with the underlying objects that carry and define business function and data.

This separation of concerns, which the Model 2 approach dictates, supports the ability to change the user interface with minimal impact on the business layer implementation. In addition, Model 2 offers greater opportunity to scale predictably, which is necessary for maintenance, and change requirements typical during the lifetime of an application's user interface. Figure 5.2 illustrates the separation of elements in the Model 2 architecture.

5.2.1 MVC Pattern

The Model 2 approach is really an implementation of an older design pattern originally developed for Smalltalk user interfaces called the MVC pattern.

MVC, like other design patterns, provides a blueprint for reoccurring design problems. In other words, design patterns are abstract designs that help identify the structure and elements involved in a specific design solution. From this, a concrete implementation can be produced.

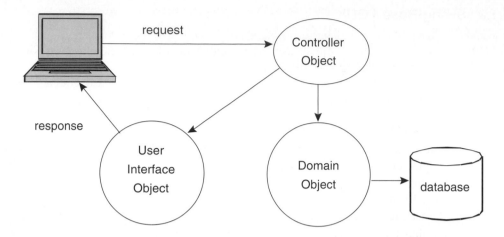

Figure 5.2 Model 2 architecture.

Originally, the MVC pattern was applied to GUI-based user interfaces. In this implementation, view elements were identified as GUI components or widgets and controllers were elements that joined these elements, along with the underlying data structures or objects that supplied the data of a specific user interface. Today, the pattern is commonly related to the Web-based Java world by referring to JSPs as the view element, Servlets are controllers, and Java objects constitute the model. Figure 5.3 shows the MVC pattern applied to both GUI and Servlet/JSPs.

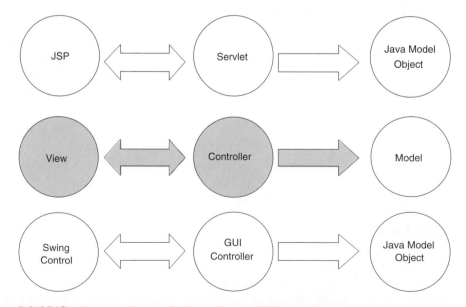

Figure 5.3 MVC pattern applied to GUI and Servlet/JSP technologies.

All too often lip service is paid to an MVC-based implementation. Just because a JSP submits to a servlet that than interacts with a Java class, does not mean you will gain the benefits proposed by the MVC pattern. Formality and consistency are the keys to applying the MVC pattern successfully, so that the benefits of maintainability and scalability can be achieved. Successful architectures utilize the MVC design, but go a step further and generalize and prescribe the way the MVC sequence is applied in developer code.

5.2.2 Single Servlet vs. Multiple Servlet

Two models are commonly encountered when applying the MVC pattern to the JSP/Servlet model. The single servlet approach utilizes a single gate-keeping servlet that funnels all JSP (view) requests and then engages and/or creates another controller instance.

In contrast, the multiple servlet models each controller implementation as a separate servlet. Which approach to take is debatable; however, the single servlet model ensures a common entry point and thus may provide more opportunities to generalize. However, the single servlet model also requires some sort of dispatching mechanism, either elegantly through Java reflection, or (more commonly) through something as inelegant as a switch statement. Chapter 12 provides an in-depth discussion of servlet-based design considerations. Figure 5.4 provides a simple example comparing these two approaches.

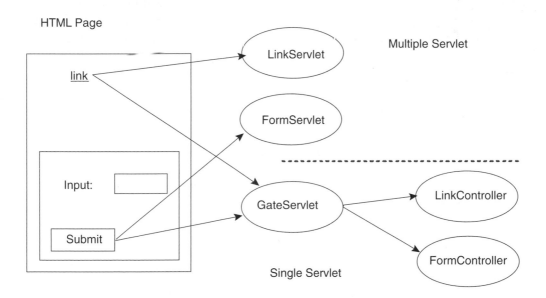

Figure 5.4 Single versus multiple servlet designs.

5.2.3 The Struts Framework

Struts is a robust MVC-based implementation that follows the single servlet approach. Entire books have been devoted to the Struts framework, and that alone indicates the robustness of the framework. WebSphere Studio has integrated tools supporting the framework. An introduction to Struts and how it is used within WebSphere Studio can be found in Chapter 14.

While the MVC pattern effectively separates view logic from business logic, it does not decouple an application from a specific user interface technology. This notion might not be obvious; the next section will discuss how another architectural layer can help decouple user interfaces even further.

5.2.4 Logical View Logic

MVC architectures assume that an applications business function and data is captured and defined as JavaBeans. JavaBeans have become somewhat passé, and the "bean" terminology can actually confuse developers into thinking they are a part of EJBs. Many developers are not familiar with JavaBean technology. Those that are consider it GUI-based, and therefore have a hard time seeing why a design would use them to define business logic.

In fact, JavaBeans can exist in nonvisual implementations. And any Java class that implements the `java.io.Serializable` interface, has getter/setters methods, and a zero-argument constructor can be considered a JavaBean. This confusion can be alleviated by not using the JavaBean reference and simply referring to them as POJOs.

Another opportunity for decoupling can be had if another layer of objects is placed between the presentation objects (view/controller) and the POJOs defined for the application domain logic. This new layer captures view-specific behavior in a logical way, logical in the sense of behavior specific to a particular user interface's demands on the business object POJOs. Figure 5.5 depicts this relationship.

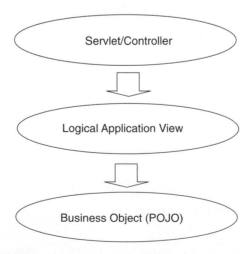

Figure 5.5 Logical view layer.

The layered application described by this book defines this layer of objects as the mediator layer. It is responsible for defining and referencing state that services a specific application view, but, interestingly, it is not coupled to a specific user interface technology. Thus, the logical presentation or mediator layer can be utilized by Web, client, XSL, or any user interface technology. The next sections clarify their existence.

5.3 Mediating Logical View Logic

Capturing and extracting logical view logic might initially seem like an extra hurdle to perform at the cost of providing more indirection and bolstering the OO critic's accusation of lasagna type coding[1] designs. Lasagna coding comes with OOP; it is managed through generic implementations that promote a consistent implementation by all developers.

As earlier sections indicated, decoupling the user interface from the underlying domain implementation is accomplished by applying the MVC pattern; however, formalizing how controllers and view implementations interact with the domain provides further decoupling and supports the ability to interchange user interface technologies, along with some other benefits.

The formalization of view and controller interactions is accomplished through capturing requests and behavior made to domain objects in a separate layer. This layer provides a barrier between the presentation layer and the domain. Within the mediator layer, mediator objects are created for each specific application view. Mediator implementations define state and function used by view and controller implementations for a specific user interface. Figure 5.6 illustrates the mediator and its place in the layered application architecture.

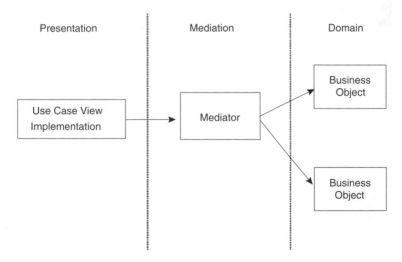

Figure 5.6 Mediator layer.

---

1. Lasagna coding is a metaphor referring to the nature of OO designs that include many coupled methods and layers of object message execution sequences.

Mediators capture what can be considered interaction logic that is gleaned from user interface functionality. To help capture the spirit of mediator design, the following sections describe some examples of mediator-bound behavior.

5.3.1 List Support

All user interface technologies support some kind of mechanism to display lists of data. Table definitions and form lists are utilized to display dynamic HTML with JSP/Servlet technology. List and table controls are available in all operating systems as widget controls. List behavior is even used to support menu selections in a voice response unit.

Mediators define methods that reference and retrieve lists of domain objects. Mediators can also define convenience methods that extract and format properties of domain instances into collections that are accessed by the user interface. Figure 5.7 illustrates this type of support.

5.3.2 Selected Object

User interfaces are, in most cases, providing a user the ability to display or modify a domain instance. Mediators can define references to specific objects that have been navigated to through some kind of finding method or from a selection from a list of domain objects.

5.3.3 Communicating Validation Messages

Mediators also provide a convenient way to capture and format validation messages generated from the domain layer object. View resident logic, such as JavaScript, can validate formatting of data types and simple checks for the presence or absence of required fields. This is collectively referred to as syntactic validation. However, other, more complex types of validation rules, such as range value checks, are best defined in domain layer code.This placement allows these checks to be reused across application boundaries. Mediators can exercise these validation rules and

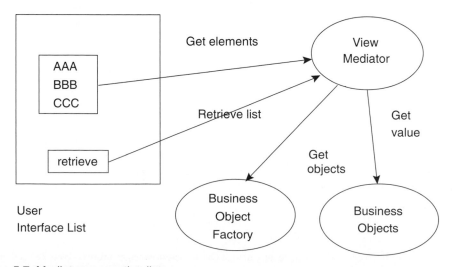

Figure 5.7 Mediator supporting lists.

capture their results, formatting them into ready to consume structures that view layer implementations can access consistently.

5.3.4 View Transition Support

Navigation between user interfaces often requires transferring values. Mediators provide a convenient and common object to carry out this transition. JSP/Servlet-based user interfaces can place object references in either session or request attribute objects that are available between interface transitions. Instead of allowing developers to put arbitrary objects in the session or requests, a generalized mechanism can be provided that supports mediator types. GUI-based interface transitions can apply a similar generalized mechanism that passes mediator references among panels, frames, etc.

This type of consistency eases maintenance by allowing developers to rely upon this pattern and structure. It also provides a place were other types of generalizations can be applied.

5.3.5 Collapsing Object Graphs

Java developers, when developing a user interface, often take Java object graphs and pull selected properties into some kind of user interface form for editing or viewing. In many cases, especially HTML-based interfaces, this means that Java data types are converted into strings for display. The same process is performed in reverse when values input into the user interface must be reconstructed into an object graph.

This type of logic is not necessarily coupled to a specific user interface technology; therefore, defining this logic within a mediator allows it to be reused across disparate interface technologies. Mediators essentially provide a façade interface between a user interface form and a domain object graph. Logic in the mediator can provide methods that perform the previously described pulling and pushing mechanism. Figure 5.8 (on the next page) illustrates the role the mediator plays in collapsing an object graph for a user interface form.

Mediators can act as a façade on business object graphs that are deep and require a lot of transformation prior to display. Defining this type of logic at the mediator layer allows other technologies to gain access to object graphs in an easier to use, linear structure.

5.4 Summary

Decoupling the user interface technology is an obvious goal of the MVC architecture. Upcoming chapters of this book, specifically Chapters 7, 8, 13, and 14, will describe how tools integrated within WSAD can be engaged to create dynamic HTML-based user interfaces with JSP/Servlet and the Struts framework. The result is a rapid application development environment that produces implementations compliant with the MVC approach.

This chapter also introduced the mediator layer that captures logical application user interface state. Not only does this additional layer provide further decoupling, but is supports the ability to replace user interface technologies and provides a consistent mechanism to capture technology neutral requests of domain objects with a consistent implementation.

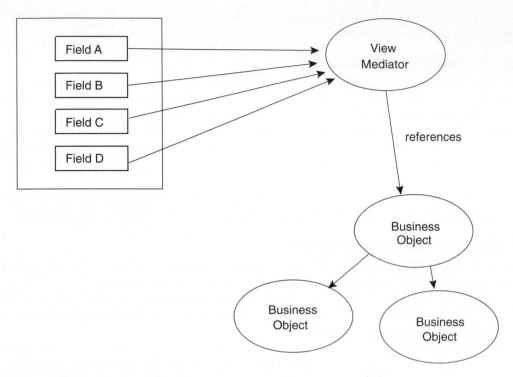

Figure 5.8 Collapsing a user interface.

Servlets

Now that we've examined some of the architectural issues surrounding the use of server-side programming and J2EE, we can look in-depth at the first of the APIs that make up the programming model. In this chapter, we will introduce you to the concept of a servlet and discuss what servlet programming entails. We will discuss the following:

- HyperText Transfer Protocol (HTTP) basics
- Servlet concepts
- Servlet life cycle
- Example servlet
- web.xml deployment descriptor file
- Filters
- Servlet API
- Arguments for using servlets

This chapter, which fundamental concepts about the servlet API, will focus entirely on the servlet container as shown in Figure 6.1. In the next chapter, we will examine how to take the examples and principles that we will review in this chapter and apply them within the WebSphere Studio environment.

6.1 HTTP Technology Primer

HTTP is the basis for Web browsing. HTTP is built upon TCP/IP and is considered an application-level protocol for distributed, collaborative, hypermedia information systems. It is a request/response-oriented protocol where an HTTP client makes a request, and an HTTP server services that request and subsequently responds.

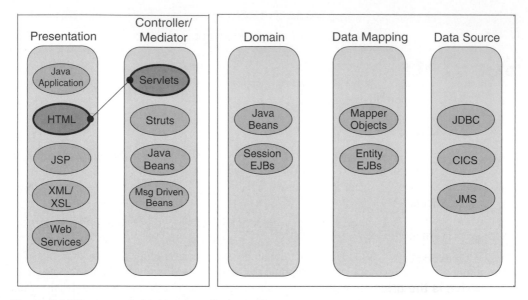

Figure 6.1 Where servlet technology fits in road map.

When looking at HTTP from an application-programming point of view, the first thing to understand is that HTTP is connectionless and stateless. HTTP is based upon a Web server (sometimes referred to as HTTPD [HTTP daemon]) receiving a request and then formulating a response to a client. It is connectionless because neither the client nor the server retains any state information regarding the application data. It is up to the application programmer to maintain any state information necessary to the application[1].

In most cases, the client is a Web browser but could be an application, a Java applet, or another Web server. While this request/response protocol is not as sophisticated as the newer connection-oriented protocols such as Internet Inter-ORB (Object Request Broker) Protocol (IIOP), it has proved very flexible in allowing a wide variety of vendors to create Web servers, Web browsers, and other HTTP-based systems.

6.1.1 Uniform Resource Identifiers

URIs have been called many different names: Universal Resource Identifiers, Universal Resource Locators, WWW addresses, Uniform Resource Locators (URL) and Uniform Resource Names (URN). URLs and URNs are kinds of URIs. URL is specific to the HTTP scheme while URN is not. As far as HTTP is concerned, URIs are simply formatted strings that identify—via name, location, or any other characteristic—a resource. URIs in HTTP can be represented in absolute form or relative to some known base, depending upon the context of their

---

1.   We will see later that the servlet API provides ways of maintaining application state information, but this is not
      part of HTTP.

use. The two forms are different in that an absolute URI always begins with a protocol name followed by a colon.

HTTP does not place any limits on the length of a URI. Therefore, HTTP servers should support this requirement. However, programmers formulating a URI ought to be cautious about depending on URI lengths above 255 bytes, because some older client or proxy implementations might not properly support these lengths.

6.1.1.1 HTTP URL

Each Web resource (an HTML page, a JSP page, a servlet, etc.) that can be requested from a Web server must have a unique name associated with it. That unique name is called a URL. For discussion purposes, let's consider a URL as a way to uniquely identify a Web page, which exists on a particular Web server. For example, to access the index.html page on the *www.abc.com* Web server, the absolute and explicit URL would be *http://www.abc.com/ index.html*. The format of a URL is as follows:

```
protocol://hostname<:port>/identifiers
```

6.1.1.2 What is the difference between a URI and URL?

According to the specification [RFC 2396] all URLs are URIs. However, URIs allow Web services to be defined in a way that they are not bound to a specific server. This has many advantages.

1. A URL explicitly locates a service to a specific Web server and port. If it becomes necessary to create services and pages that can be hosted on various Web servers, there arises a need to have a way to identify those pages without locating them. The URI provides the unique name for a service, hosted on any Web server.

2. In addition to being able to relocate a service or set of pages to another Web server, many times it is desirable to replicate these services or pages to several servers to avoid the single-point-of-failure problem. If one of these servers terminates, then other mechanisms such as a network dispatcher can safely send requests to another Web server, which has replicas of those services or pages. The use of a nonlocated URI helps the developer to avoid making code changes to the service or page when deploying to different machines.

> ### AN EXAMPLE OF URLS AND URIS
>
> A fully specified URL is always of the form:
>
> *http://www.mycompany.com/mydirectory/mypage.html*
>
> However, a URI may be fragmentary like:
>
> */mydirectory/mypage.html*
>
> This difference will become important when we get to the point of specifying URIs that refer to HTML and JSP pages. By only referring to a

partial address (e.g., URI) , you keep your HTML tags (and JSP and servlet code) from being tied to a single machine name.

6.1.2 Requests, Responses, and Headers

HTTP is a simple protocol based on a client sending a request to a Web server and then getting a response. When the client sends a request, the request contains all of the information that the Web server needs to process the request. Both the request and the response contain a start-line, zero or more header fields (also known as "headers"), an empty line (i.e., a line with nothing preceding the CRLF) indicating the end of the header fields, and possibly a message-body.

6.1.2.1 Headers

The headers section of a message contains a general-header section (headers that are applicable to both the request and the response and specific headers), an entity-header section, and either a request-header section or response-header section, depending upon the type of message. The general-header section contains items such as Cache-Control, Date, and Transfer-Encoding. The Transfer-Encoding header can impact the message length as the encoding type may increase the size of the body of the message.

The request-header section contains headers such as Host, Accept-Charset, and Referer. The Referer header specifies the URL of the page from which the request came from while the Host header contains the name of the target host specified in the request (the host which is processing the request).

The response-header section contains headers such as Age, Location, and Server. The Server header specifies the name of the server that generated the response.

Entity headers define metainformation about the entity-body or, if no body is present, about the resource identified by the request. Some entity-headers include Allow, Content-Encoding and Last-Modified.

6.1.2.2 Requests

In the case of a request message, the start-line is the request itself. An HTTP request is characterized by a method token, followed by a Request-URI and a protocol version, ending with a CRLF. The method token is one of GET, POST, OPTIONS, HEAD, PUT, DELETE, TRACE, CONNECT, or some extension method as defined by the implementation.

When using HTTP methods to create a request, the application programmer should understand that the writers of the HTTP protocol consider some methods as safe and others as unsafe. This definition of a safe method was noted in the HTTP specification so that user agents can be written to make a user aware of the fact that a possibly unsafe action is being requested. It is thought that the safe methods will not generate side effects as a result of calling them. The protocol does not enforce this idea of safe methods nor can it, as implementers are free to create servers that handle these requests in any way that they see fit. Two key HTTP request methods are particularly important to the programmer (GET and POST). GET is a safe method while POST is unsafe since it is expected that POST will cause side effects by posting some new data:

- **GET**—An HTTP GET request is what happens when you type in a URL at a browser. It literally means, "GET a file and return its contents." In the context of a servlet, this means return some dynamic content to the user as HTML.

- **POST**—An HTTP POST request is what happens (usually) when you type information into an HTML form and press SUBMIT. It is called post because it was originally intended to represent POSTing a message to an Internet newsgroup.

6.1.2.3 Responses

After receiving and interpreting a request, the server must respond. The response message contains a start-line—the status of the request. This status-line contains the HTTP protocol version followed by a numeric status code and its associated textual phrase, with each element separated by spaces. The status code is a 3-digit integer result code of the attempt to understand and satisfy the request. The textual phrase is for debugging purposes.

The first digit in the 3-digit code defines the class of the response. The last two digits do not have any categorization role but instead help to uniquely identify the response. There are 5 values for the first digit:

- **1xx**: Informational—Request received, continuing process
- **2xx**: Success—The action was successfully received, understood, and accepted
- **3xx**: Redirection—Further action must be taken in order to complete the request
- **4xx**: Client Error—The request contains bad syntax or cannot be fulfilled
- **5xx**: Server Error—The server failed to fulfill an apparently valid request

As with any HTTP message, after the start-line (status-line in the response case), the message headers are given, followed by the message-body. The message-body contains the actual data, which will be displayed in the Web browser.

6.1.3 Pulling It All Together

When using HTTP, there are numerous scenarios. In an effort to pull together the ideas presented here about URIs and messages over HTTP, we need to take a look at the GET and POST requests and how the interaction between the client and server occurs.

We show a GET request round-trip in Figure 6.2. The request is for the URL of *http://web-server/index.html*. Note that when using a Web browser and HTML to make HTTP requests, a GET request could be made in several ways. Here are the well-known ways:

1. By typing the URL into the URL line of the Web browser and pressing ENTER.

2. By clicking on a link, which appears inside an HTML page. The link is coded using the `<A HREF="url...">` tag.

3. By clicking a button on a form, which appears inside of an HTML page. The FORM tag would need to specify a method of GET as in the tag `<FORM method="GET" action="url...">`.

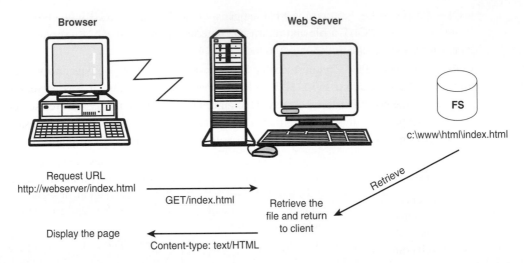

Figure 6.2 HTTP GET request in action.

The Web server, upon receiving this request, maps the request to a file located on the Web server file system (e.g., C:\www\html\index.html) and then responds with the contents of that file to the browser. The entire transaction involves one connection to the Web server and an almost immediate response.

In Figure 6.3, we show a POST request round-trip. This request is for the URL *http://webserver/servlet/Register*. Note that when using a Web browser and HTML to make HTTP

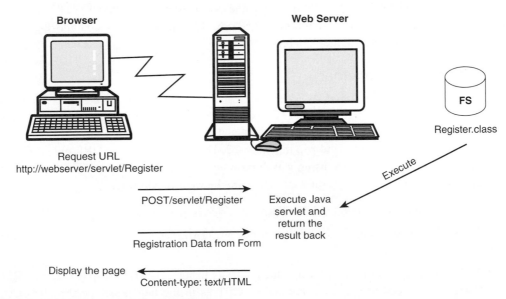

Figure 6.3 HTTP POST request in action.

requests, a POST request can only be made by clicking a button on a FORM which appears inside of an HTML page. The FORM would need to specify a method of POST as in the tag `<FORM method="POST" action= "url...">`.

The Web server, upon receiving this request, transfers it to the servlet engine, which loads the requested servlet by searching the classpath and then runs the servlet. Next, the Web server (or Web container) reads the posted data and performs the requested operation. Lastly, the Web server (or servlet engine) responds with a message that is displayed in the browser. The entire transaction involves at least one connection to the Web server with an almost immediate response.

6.2 Servlet Concepts

A servlet is a Java class that runs within a JVM associated with a Web container. While Java is well suited for client use, it is equally well-suited for server use.

A servlet, as a standard server-side Java program, extends the functionality of a Web server. When a Web container receives a request for a servlet (through a URL), it loads the servlet into the JVM associated with the Web server (if not already loaded) and executes the servlet. When the servlet completes its task, it sends any generated output (the response) back to the Web browser. You can write servlets for administrative purposes, such as managing Web server log files or for sending alert E-mails to administrators. However, what is more interesting and more pervasive is the use of servlets in IT applications that run on the Web.

We have already seen how the MVC design pattern can help break a system down into layers. In this scenario, the servlets will cooperate with a set of POJOs or EJBs to perform the real work of an application. When following this principle, servlets act as a part of the controller layer for applications that run on the Web. Servlets become glue between ordinary HTML (the view) and the POJOs or EJBs (the model). Servlets can then add functionality to the overall Web application by providing session management, user authentication, and user authorization.

6.2.1 Support for Servlets

Sun Microsystems provides the Java 2 SDK Enterprise Edition (J2SDKEE), which contains classes in support of servlets, JSP, and a basic Web server for testing servlets, HTML, and JSP.

J2SDKEE also contains basic tools for testing EJBs and other J2EE APIs, which will be discussed later. You can download the J2SDKEE from *http://java.sun.com/j2ee/1.4/download.html#sdk.* At the writing of this book, IBM WAS 5.0.1 implements the Servlet 2.3 specification, which is also implemented in J2SDKEE 1.3. As a result, all references to the servlet API in this book are for the Servlet 2.3 specification.

Since WebSphere Studio has an open design, you could use the J2SDKEE Web server from within WebSphere Studio to develop and test your servlets. However, WebSphere Studio contains the built-in WebSphere Test Environment (WTE), a servlet development and test environment that is based on IBM WAS. The integrated WTE can be used in WebSphere Studio instead of J2SDKEE to develop and test servlets more effectively.

6.2.1.1 Servlet Engines

There are three basics types of servlet engines—stand-alone, add-on, and embedded. Each has its advantages and disadvantages.

Stand-alone Servlet Engines   A stand-alone engine includes the normal HTTP server functions and has built-in support for servlets. This is desirable because the installation and configuration concerns are greatly minimized in the beginning as the Web server and servlet engine are integrated in a single installation. This is the approach taken, for instance, by the Apache Tomcat Web container. It can be a drawback, because stand-alone servlet engines cannot take full advantage of advanced Web server features like caching or the ability to coexist with other languages like Perl. Also, stand-alone engines are usually not as well integrated with other parts of the J2EE specification like EJBs or JMS as more comprehensive solutions may be.

Add-on Servlet Engines   Add-on servlet engines function as a plug-in to an existing Web server. As the name suggests, add-on servlet engines add servlet support to a server that was not originally designed with servlets in mind. This solution is desirable in that it solves the problem mentioned in the stand-alone solution of allowing the user to keep up with the latest servlet APIs apart from the Web server.

There is a trade-off: The initial configuration may be difficult, as integration problems may have to be solved by the user instead of the vendor. IBM WAS falls into this category. IBM WebSphere provides a small plug-in, which installs into an HTTP server. The HTTP server will then detect which URLs refer to applications deployed in WebSphere and forward the servlet requests to a stand-alone application server through HTTP.

Embeddable Servlet Engines   An embeddable engine is generally a lightweight servlet deployment platform that can be embedded in another application. That application becomes the true server. An example of this is Sun's JavaServer Engine, which can be embedded into other servlet engines where the other engines compliment or add on to the basic functionality of the embedded servlet engine. IBM WTE, included within WebSphere Studio, is such a servlet engine; actually, it's the complete WAS packaged slightly differently. Since the WTE uses the same code as used by the production product, you can be sure that applications developed in the WTE will work as-is in the deployed environment.

The overall architecture of a servlet appears in Figure 6.4.

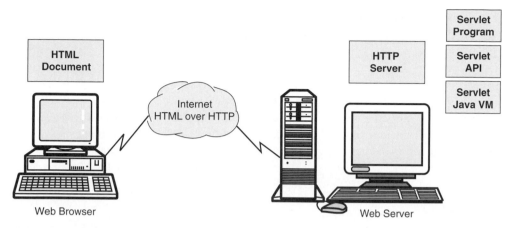

Figure 6.4 Servlet architecture.

6.3 Servlet Life Cycle

The servlet life cycle defines the process used to load the servlet into memory, execute the servlet, and then unload the servlet from memory. A Web browser requests a servlet through a URL.
The URL can be on the location line of the Web browser or it can be a link embedded in the
HTML document being viewed. A typical servlet URL appears as *http://localhost/**helloctx**/Hel-
loServlet*. The word *helloctx* in the URI path represents the context root for the Web module and
lets the Web server know that the request is for more than just an HTML page. *HelloServlet*, in
the URL, is the name (as defined in web.xml—more on this later) of the desired servlet. Figure
6.5 shows the servlet life cycle.

   To create a servlet, you must first create a subclass of the GenericServlet class or one of its
subclasses. Typically, you will subclass the class `javax.servlet.http.HttpServlet`, which
means that your servlet will be invoked through HTTP. You are not required to add any code to
your servlet at this point. However, if you issue an HTTP request to your new servlet in this
state, it will respond with the default error that says that a GET or POST request is not supported. Thus, from a compile-time perspective, there are no required methods. However, as you
will see, you will want to code at the very least a `doGet()` or `doPost()` method to make your
servlet useful.

   When your servlet is first requested, the Web server requests that the servlet engine load the
appropriate servlet class and all of its required classes into memory on the servlet engine node.

   Control then passes to the `init()` method in the servlet. `GenericServlet` provides an
empty `init()` method. If you wish to perform initialization tasks, such as reading external cus-
tomization files, you need to provide an `init()` method in your subclass. The `init()` method
receives only one call, and that is immediately after your servlet is loaded into memory. It is a
good idea to always call the super class's `init()` method if you provide your own `init()`
method. This ensures that any setup required by the servlet engine or other super classes is done.

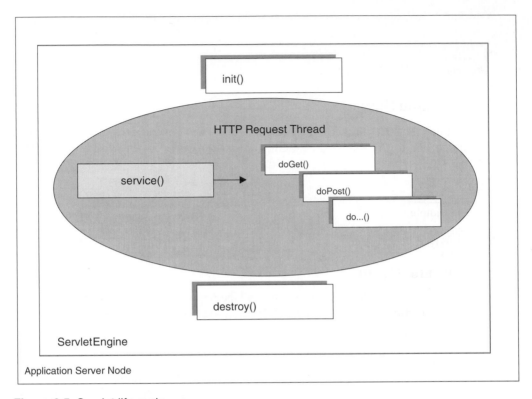

Figure 6.5 Servlet life cycle.

The init() method is the perfect place to perform operations that are done only once for the life of a servlet such as reading a properties file that contains configuration information for the application. Other items that can be accomplished in the init() method include caching reference data for quick access, clearing log files, or notifying other services that this service is now available.

Each time the servlet is requested (including the first time after the init() method is called) the service() method is dispatched on a separate thread for each request. Generic-Servlet provides an empty service() method. You must override this method if you want to do any real work. Since the service() method is called in its own thread, the servlet engine is free to take additional requests for the same servlet or another servlet that it executes in another thread.

The service() method is where the work of the servlet is accomplished. Note that in the HttpServlet the service() method has been specialized into the doGet(), doPost(), doDe-lete(), etc. methods. Since the service() method is always executed inside a new thread, you must be careful to ensure that everything done in the service() method is thread-safe (reentrant).

When the Web container deems it necessary, the destroy() method of the servlet is called and the servlet is unloaded from the server's memory. If you provide a destroy() method in your servlet, it is called. Common tasks performed by the destroy() method include closing all files and other administrative items.

6.4 An Example Servlet

Now let's examine the code for a complete servlet. As we mentioned, a single URL presents a servlet to the outside world, exactly as a CGI script is represented to the Web browser. However, unlike a CGI script, information about the request made of the servlet is not passed as environment variables that must be parsed. It is instead given to the servlet as a set of well-defined Java objects. To illustrate this point, let's examine the simplest possible servlet, the Hello World example.

```
/**
 * This class is a simple sample servlet
 */
import java.io.*;
import javax.servlet.*;
import javax.servlet.http.*;

public class HelloServlet extends HttpServlet {
/**
 * This method handles an HTTP GET request and outputs
 * HTML to print "Hello IBM WebSphere World" to a browser.
 */
public void doGet (HttpServletRequest req, HttpServletResponse res)
res)
throws ServletException, IOException{
    PrintWriter out = null;
   res.setContentType ("text/html");
   out = res.getWriter ();
   out.println ("<html>");
   out.println ("<head><title>Sample</title></head>");
   out.println ("<body>");
   out.println ("Hello IBM WebSphere World!");
   out.println ("</body>");
   out.println ("</html>");
}
```

}To run this servlet, assuming the host *localhost* is defined, the Web and application server are appropriately configured to have a context root of *helloctx*, and that the HelloServlet.class file is placed in the appropriate location. You would enter the URL *http://localhost/helloctx/HelloServlet* on the URL line of a Web browser. The words *Hello IBM WebSphere World* would then be shown in your Web browser.

Our simple servlet class extends the class `javax.servlet.http.HttpServlet`. Think about `HttpServlet` and its descendents as being servlets that speak HTTP as their native language. The key thing to understand about `HttpServlet` is that they typically handle GET and POST requests. `HttpServlet` subclasses handle one or both of these methods by overriding either `doGet()` or `doPost()` respectively. In our case we're overriding `doGet()`, so the information sent back will be displayed on a client's browser if she types in the URL corresponding to our servlet (e.g., send a GET request).

WHICH SERVLET METHODS DO I OVERRIDE?

The `HttpServlet` class defines a special do [Request Type] method (or a service handler) for each of the HTTP Request types that were previously discussed. These methods are simply defined as protected void methods—they are not declared abstract. The `service()` method defined in `HttpServlet` is written to automatically call the appropriate service handler based on the type of request that is received. In your servlets, you will generally choose to override only a small subset of these methods—generally `doGet()` or `doPost()`.

Sometimes, the same servlet will need to handle both GET and POST requests. If the code in each of these methods is different (e.g., you want to do something different for each request type) you should override both `doGet()` and `doPost()`. On the other hand, if you need to implement the same logic for both request types, then you should probably override `service()` instead.

Now, exactly how is the reply Hello IBM WebSphere World sent back to the browser? As you can see from the example, the route we use is an object that implements the interface HttpServletResponse. HttpServletResponse allows you to do several things:

- Set the MIME type (or content-type) of the HTTP response header. This can be any valid MIME type (like image/jpeg or audio/wav. Most of the time the response type will be text/html, which means you are sending back HTML to be interpreted and displayed by the browser. The method `setContentType(String)` sets the content type.
- Set the HTTP header values with `setHeader(String, String)`. This is useful if you want to disable browser and server page caching for a response page. Note that all headers must be sent before any output is written to the servlet output stream. This is because HTTP specifies that headers appear before the message body in the response. The headers are implicitly written to the servlet output stream the first time the servlet explicitly writes to the stream.

- Obtain a PrintWriter for output with `getWriter()`. When you are sending HTML as your content type, you want to make it human-readable. `PrintWriter` facilitates this by adding CR/LF on the end of your text lines with the `println()` method . Additionally, other writers allow for National Language support and translation of Unicode characters to UTF. In all other respects, `PrintWriter` acts like an output stream. You can also obtain an `OutputStream` with `getOutputStream()`.
- Redirect the browser to a different page with `sendRedirect(String)`

In our example we're simply setting the content type of the response, opening a `Print-Writer` for output, and sending several lines of HTML text back to the browser. This is what most servlets end up doing for output. They may obtain part of the information they display from an outside source (say, from a socket to another server, or a JDBC query). However, the mechanics of sending HTML to the client is the same regardless of the source.

Those of you with keen attention to detail will have noticed that `doGet()` also takes a second parameter, `HTTPServletRequest`, which we did not use. Servlets that need to process input from the browser use this interface. The code in a `doGet()` or `doPost()` method typically use the `HttpServletRequest` methods `getParameterNames()` `getParameter()` and `getParameter-Values()` to read in the HTTP parameters sent as part of a POST request or of a query string.

The servlet then makes decisions based on those parameters, or records them to persistent storage. If we make a small modification to the HelloServlet servlet, we can send a message parameter to the servlet and have it display that message instead of the common "Hello IBM WebSphere World!" message. Examine the new code and note the lines in bold type.

```
/**
 * This class is a simple sample servlet, which takes a message
parameter
 */
import java.io.*;
import javax.servlet.*;
import javax.servlet.http.*;

public class HelloServlet extends HttpServlet {
/**
 * This method handles an HTTP GET request and outputs
 * HTML to print "Hello IBM WebSphere World" to a browser.
 */
public void doGet (HttpServletRequest req, HttpServletResponse res)

throws ServletException, IOException{
PrintWriter out = null;
res.setContentType("text/html");
out = res.getWriter ();

// Changed Code
String theMessage = req.getParameter("mymessage");
```

```
if (theMessage == null) {
theMessage = "Hello IBM WebSphere World!";
}
    out.println("<html>");
    out.println("<head><title>Sample</title></head>");
    out.println("<body>");
    out.println(theMessage);
    out.println("</body>");
    out.println("</html>");
}
}
```

To run this servlet you would use the same URL as before with an additional Query-String. An example URL of this type might be: *http://localhost/servlet/HelloServlet?mymessage=Hello+Parameter*. The words *Hello Parameter* would then be shown in your Web browser. Without the + sign in the URL the space and Parameter portion of the URL would be lost. The + can be used for spaces to ensure that the full message will survive the network send. You could use %20 to represent the space as well.

If you examine the code changes, you can see that the difference is the use of the **req.get-Parameter("mymessage")** to obtain the data passed on the URL. The `getParameter()` method takes one argument which must be a String and is the case-sensitive identifier of the parameter in the request. The name of this parameter key must match exactly the name used on the Query-String. If it does not match, `getParameter()` will return a null. If null is returned, then the method will set the variable `theMessage` to "**Hello WebSphere World!**" The last thing done to the code was to change the `out.println()` to use the newly created variable, `theMessage`.

SOME COMMENTS ABOUT HELLOSERVLET

One of the things that makes it difficult to explain the servlet API is that the simplest examples, like the one we have shown here, are not truly representative of the way in which servlets are used in practice. In particular, you should avoid hard-coding HTML into your servlets. Remember from our overview discussion of the J2EE APIs and the MVC design pattern that servlets will act as mediators that will tie together domain logic and display logic in the form of JSPs. In general, you should avoid placing HTML in your servlet code; if you place HTML in your servlets, it becomes more difficult to change the look of your Web sites since you must change your Java code even if all that changes is the HTML that is returned.

6.5 Web Deployment Descriptors

Deployment descriptors are text-based XML files that describe how a J2EE component is deployed into an application server. Deployment descriptors allow additional attributes such as security settings and initialization properties, which are not represented in Java code, to be associated with the component. J2EE defines several deployment descriptors; however, there are three major ones:

- J2EE enterprise application deployment descriptor—application.xml
- EJB module deployment descriptor—ejb-jar.xml
- Web module deployment descriptor—web.xml

In this chapter, we have focused solely on servlets and as such the only descriptor we will describe at this point is web.xml. Later we will discuss the application.xml and ejb-jar.xml files.

The web.xml deployment descriptor is included in the Web WAR file and describes to the Web container how the items in the file are to be deployed and used in the Web container. A simple web.xml, which sets up a servlet mapping for the HelloServlet created previously, follows:

```xml
<?xml version="1.0" encoding="UTF-8"?>
<!DOCTYPE web-app PUBLIC "-//Sun Microsystems, Inc.//DTD Web
Application 2.3//EN" "http://java.sun.com/dtd/web-app_2_3.dtd">
<web-app>
<display-name>Hello Web Module</display-name>
<servlet>
<servlet-name>SimpleHello</servlet-name>
<display-name>SimpleHello</display-name>
<servlet-class>HelloServlet</servlet-class>
</servlet>
<servlet-mapping>
<servlet-name>SimpleHello</servlet-name>
<url-pattern>sayHello</url-pattern>
</servlet-mapping>
<welcome-file-list>
<welcome-file>index.html</welcome-file>
</welcome-file-list>
</web-app>
```

Notice that there are essentially three key elements in the web.xml file: (1) The servlet element associates a name with a Java class name for the servlet. (2) The servlet-mapping element associates a URL pattern with the named servlet. (3) The welcome-file-list element gives a list of files that can be used as the home page for the WAR file that contains this web.xml file. By convention, the welcome files are returned by default if no specific file is requested.

Once a servlet is named in a web.xml file, initialization parameters can be specified and the servlet can be marked for initial startup. Additionally, other elements, which deal with EJB references, security, and environment variables can be specified in the web.xml file.

6.6 Filters

A filter is an object that can transform a request or alter a response. It can be created and configured to intercept requests before a servlet is called, and it can intercept responses before con-

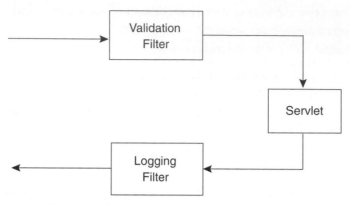

Figure 6.6 Filters applied to servlets.

tinuing. The filter interface is the base interface for the filter features and was included in the servlet API 2.3.

One of the more powerful features of a filter is that it can be applied at deployment time. Once a filter has been coded, it can be applied to any servlet by adding filter elements to the web.xml file. Filters can also be chained so that several are applied to a single servlet. (Note: At no time is it necessary to alter the servlet code.) Filters can also be used to preempt the execution of a servlet. For instance, you may want to perform some sort of input validation before a servlet is invoked (and reject the request if validation fails) and perform logging on all responses as they are returned. An example of the type of design approach you may take with filters can be seen in Figure 6.6.

A filter has an API similar to that for a servlet. A filter has an init() method which is executed the first time the filter is accessed. A destroy() method is provided so that the filter writer can gain control before the Web container unloads the filter. The doFilter() method is where the actual work of the filter is accomplished.

An example filter that can be applied to the HelloServlet is one that will add the current date and time to the response. This DateTimeFilter will contain only the doFilter() method. The doFilter() method accepts a parameter of type FilterChain which provides the filter with the means to request that processing continue down the chain. In doFilter(), the chain.doFilter() method is called which will cause the servlet and all other filters downstream to be called. After the call to chain.doFilter(), HttpServletResponse is used to obtain the PrintWriter object. Then the date and time are added to the response by using PrintWriter. Here is the code for the filter:

```
import java.io.IOException;
import java.io.PrintWriter;
import java.util.Date;

import javax.servlet.Filter;
import javax.servlet.FilterChain;
```

```
import javax.servlet.FilterConfig;
import javax.servlet.ServletException;
import javax.servlet.ServletRequest;
import javax.servlet.ServletResponse;
public class DateTimeFilter implements Filter {
public void destroy() { }
public void init(FilterConfig config) throws ServletException { }
public void doFilter(
    ServletRequest req,
    ServletResponse resp,
    FilterChain chain)
    throws ServletException, IOException {

    chain.doFilter(req, resp);

    // Get the output writer from the response
    PrintWriter out = resp.getWriter();
    // Add the Date/Time String to the response
    out.println("<B>" + new Date() + "</B>");
    }
}
```

In order to use the filter, the web.xml file must be updated so the filter is applied to the HelloServlet. Or, instead of specifying a particular servlet, it is possible to apply the filter to all servlets. By adding the elements which to the web.xml file as subelements of the web-app element, the filter will be called each time any servlet in this Web application is called.

```
<filter>
<filter-name>DateTimeFilter</filter-name>
<display-name>DateTimeFilter</display-name>
<filter-class>DateTimeFilter</filter-class>
</filter>
<filter-mapping>
<filter-name>DateTimeFilter</filter-name>
<url-pattern>/*</url-pattern>
</filter-mapping>
```

Now, when the HelloServlet is called, the output will resemble the following:

Hello IBM WebSphere World! **Sat Nov 5 22:50:24 EDT 2003**

Filters are very powerful. If you wanted to create one which skips calling the servlet and other filters in the chain, your filter simply omits the invocation of `chain.doFilter()` in its `doFilter()` method.

In this section we have only touched on filters and how they can be used. There are many other uses that you can explore on your own.

6.7   Servlet API Classes and Interfaces

The J2SDKEE 1.3 API contains a rich set of classes and methods that enable the servlet developer to code complex Web applications in a well-implemented manner. The API is contained in three packages:

- javax.servlet
- javax.servlet.http
- javax.servlet.jsp

Each package contains several interfaces and classes that define the API. In this section we will only briefly cover the `javax.servlet` and `javax.servlet.http` packages. The classes in the `javax.servlet.jsp` package will be discussed later. As we look at the interfaces defined in these packages, you should understand that the servlet engine provider would supply implementations for these interfaces. However, you will want to write code which only uses the API as it appears in an interface where supplied and not any vendor-specific class.

6.7.1   javax.servlet package

The `javax.servlet` package contains the basic API for servlets but is not tied to a particular scheme or protocol for how servlets may be used. See Table 6.1 for a list of the classes and interfaces in the `javax.servlet` package.

Table 6.1 javax.servlet package interfaces/classes.

Interfaces
Filter
FilterChain
FilterConfig
Request Dispatcher
Servlet
ServletConfig
ServletContext
ServletContextAttributeListener
ServletContextListener
ServletRequest
ServletResponse
SingleThreadModel

Table 6.1 javax.servlet package interfaces/classes. (Continued)

Classes
Generic Servlet
ServletContextAttributeEvent
ServletContextEvent
ServletInputStream
ServletOutputStream
ServletRequestWrapper
ServletResponseWrapper
Exceptions
ServletException
UnavailailableException

6.7.2 javax.servlet.http package

The javax.servlet.http package contains the API for servlets that will be used as HTTP servlets. See Table 6.2 for a list of the classes and interfaces in the javax.servlet.http package.

Table 6.2 javax.servlet.http package interfaces/classes.

Interfaces
HttpServletRequest
HttpServletResponse
HttpSession
HttpSessionActivationListener
HttpSessionAttributeListener
HttpSessionBindingListener
HttpSessionContext
HttpSessionListener
Classes
Cookie

Table 6.2 javax.servlet.http package interfaces/classes. (Continued)

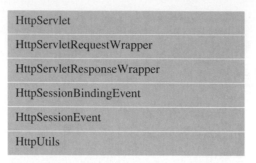

HttpServlet
HttpServletRequestWrapper
HttpServletResponseWrapper
HttpSessionBindingEvent
HttpSessionEvent
HttpUtils

For a more details on the servlet API refer to the servlet API Javadocs available from the Help menu in WebSphere Studio, and also for download from *http://java.sun.com.*

6.8 Summary

In this chapter we have covered the basics of HTTP, servlet concepts, and the basics of servlet programming. Anytime you begin to code in a client/server or distributed environment, the complexity of the task is going to increase. However, with the robust HTTP protocol as an underlying mechanism for servlets and the highly usable JSDK 2.1 servlet API, a programmer of moderate skill can be very productive with servlets in a very short amount of time.

Developing Servlets Using IBM WebSphere Studio Application Developer

In the previous chapter, we learned the basics of HTTP and servlets. Now it's time to put these concepts to work. Java servlets are one of the simplest ways to extend the capabilities of a Web server with business-specific behavior. To build, deploy, and test servlets, it helps to understand how to use the available tools effectively, in particular, WebSphere Studio Application Developer (WSAD) and other products in the WebSphere Studio product family as described in Chapter 2.

WSAD is a collection of tools to provide a workbench tailored to the development of Web, J2EE, and Web services-based applications. In this chapter, you will learn how to develop servlets using WSAD. We'll start with a brief introduction to WebSphere Studio Workbench and the WSAD-integrated set of tools contained in the Workbench. Then we'll take a use-case approach to explore the steps required to develop a typical servlet-based example. In Chapter 8, we'll examine how to deploy, test, and debug the servlet-based application developed here.

We will develop a simple example that allows us to view and update employees in a database. Figure 7.1 shows the architectural roadmap used to implement the example. We'll cover creating a simple model based on POJOs, persisting instances of the model in a database accessed through JDBC, developing static HTML, processing input forms, and handling servlet requests and generating HTML responses. This architecture is certainly not the most sophisticated, and it has many drawbacks, as we'll discuss. However, it has all the pieces of the layered architecture:

- **Presentation**—HTML, some of which is created by servlets.
- **Controller/Mediator**—In this case, the servlet engine in the application server itself supports the controller/mediator layer through servlets.
- **Domain Model**—There's only one domain model object, Employee, but it's still a domain model.

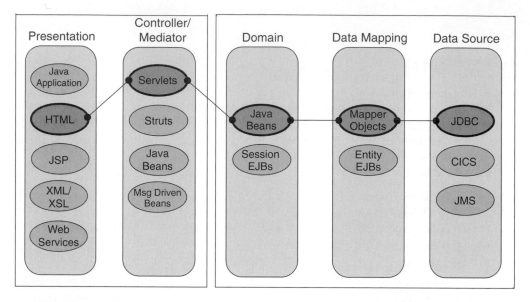

Figure 7.1 Architectural Roadmap.

• **Data Mapping**—We use the Active Record pattern to map the Employee to its data source.
• **Data Source**—The actual data is in an EMPLOYEE table in a relational database accessed through JDBC.

Throughout the development steps, we'll look closely at the features of WSAD. There are a lot, and we won't try to cover all of them here. Instead, we'll highlight those used to build our end-to-end example in the context in which they are used. In Chapter 13, we'll look at this same example to see how it can be simplified using JSPs and more sophisticated persistence implementation mechanisms.

7.1 The IBM WebSphere Studio Family of Tools

J2EE specifies a number of roles played by participants in the development process. WSAD in turn provides an integrated development environment (IDE) for developing J2EE applications that organizes the tools in a manner appropriate for each role. Tools are available for authoring Web content using HTML, CSS, XML, XSL, XML Schema, Java programs, EJB components and deployment descriptors, Web services, as well as tools for integration with relational databases, application profiling, and debugging. Like any craft, your knowledge and efficient use of available tools will go a long way toward improving the result (your applications), as well as reducing the level of frustration that would otherwise accompany the construction process. The WSAD Help system introduces the tool components that make up the platform. For details select *Help>Help Contents*, and follow the links to *Application developer information>Product overview>Application development tools*.

7.1.1 WebSphere Studio Workbench Overview

Aside from viewing Help, a brief introduction of WebSphere Studio Workbench (WSWB, or just Workbench) will be helpful in getting you started on the tasks you'll be performing in the rest of the chapter. The Workbench is IBM's branded version of the Eclipse tool integration platform. WSWB is functionally equivalent to Eclipse, the basic difference being that IBM provides fee-based defect and problem support of WSWB, while Eclipse is supported via the open source community process (mailing lists, newsgroups, bugzilla, and so on).

WSAD extends WSWB with a set of plug-in extensions that provide the J2EE and Web services authoring, deploying, and testing tools. If you are familiar with the Eclipse development environment, you already know a lot about using WSAD. We'll provide additional details throughout the development of the example where they can be better understood in the context in which they are used. As always, additional detailed information is available from WSAD Help. From the Help contents, follow *Application developer information> Getting Started>Workbench fundamentals*. For more information on the Eclipse tool integration platform, see *http://www.eclipse.org*.

Install WSAD on Windows platforms using the typical Install Shield tools, or on Linux or other UNIX platforms using the install tools typically used for those platforms. Installation is very straightforward and requires very little input. Once installed, you can start WSAD using the installed menu item, or by invoking `wsappdev.exe` in the installation folder.

Before starting WSAD though, we should think about how to organize our work. Eclipse and WSWB use the notion of *workspaces* to partition the development of related applications. Each workspace has an associated directory that contains metadata about the configuration of the workspace, information about the projects in the workspace, the state of the workspace when it was last shut down, user interface layout, etc. For example, you could use different workspaces for managing collections of closely related projects.

You could use one workspace for all projects but this could get cumbersome as the number of projects increases. The biggest advantage of multiple workspaces is that they each remember their own Workbench configuration and state. You can also import preferences from another workspace to save reentering. When you first start WSAD, a dialog displays the default workspace and gives you an opportunity to change it to a location of your choice, and optionally to permanently change the default (Figure 7.2).

You can accept the default, but if you'd like to have multiple workspaces or put the workspace somewhere else on your computer, you can browse to or enter a new workspace path. A workspace is simply a folder in your local file system. We recommend using a number of different workspaces for managing collections of related projects. You can do this by creating shortcuts (or links) to *<WSAD Installation Folder>\wsappdev.exe* in the desktop start menu. After creating the shortcut, edit its properties and add a *–data <workspacePath>* parameter. Then WSAD will use different workspaces for each shortcut used to start it.

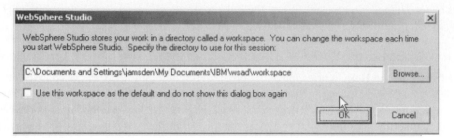

Figure 7.2 Selecting a workspace.

A workspace contains any number of projects. Projects contain the development resources that taken together produce an application or some reusable application component. Each project has one or more natures, which define the semantics of the project. The resources in the project, what happens when the resources change, how resources are edited, and what actions are available define a project's semantics. For example, when a Java source file in a Java project changes, the corresponding Java class file is recreated, and all of the Java files that depend on that file (i.e., import it) are also recompiled. Similarly, when a servlet source changes in a Web project, not only is the file recompiled, it is also redeployed to the Test Environment so the changes are visible the next time the servlet is invoked (more on this later).

Inside a project are resources organized in folders. Workbench provides a Navigator view for navigating the projects in a workspace, and the resources in the projects. Figure 7.3 shows the Servlet Example project in the navigator view.

The resources displayed in the resource navigator have pop-up menus that offer choices specific to the selected resource(s). Tools installed into Workbench contribute these choices. Each resource has a type, generally distinguished by its file extension. For example, .java files are Java resources while .html files are HTML files. Each file can be associated with one or more editors, one of which is the default editor invoked when you double-click it.

The editors that are configured for the resource types can be seen by right-clicking the file and selecting *Open With* (the default is first and indicated by a check in front of the menu item), or by examining the workbench preferences. To see the workbench and other tool preferences, select *Window>Preferences* from the menu bar, and expand *Workbench> File Associations*. You can use this preferences page to add new resource types and associate them with either Workbench (internal) editors, or external editors that run in the underlying operating system. For example, you might associate *.jar with your favorite ZIP utility so you can simply double-click to examine its contents.

Each editor provides a way of viewing and manipulating the specific resource type. Editors may have other associated views that provide alternate ways of looking at or modifying a resource. For example, most editors also contribute to the outline view to provide a quick way of navigating the contents of a resource or to provide context-sensitive menu items on selected items in the resource. Many views and some editors also contribute to the properties view to

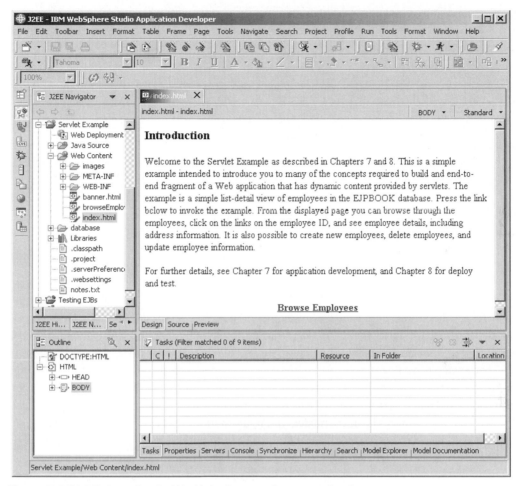

Figure 7.3 WebSphere Studio Workbench on workspace-wsbook.

show the detailed properties of a selected item in the editor. Figure 7.3 also shows the HTML page editor opened to index.html with the outline view showing the HTML tags in the file.

When you save a resource, Workbench optionally performs an incremental build of the project, updating any item that depends on the saved resource. The project nature determines what builders run, and how they react to changes in the project's resources. The tasks view displays any information, warnings, or errors resulting from a build. Double-click entries in the task view to open the resource editor and navigate to the cause of the error.

Not only does Workbench provide projects as a way of organizing resources, it also provides perspectives as a way of organizing the Workbench user interface. This, along with specialized project types and wizards, is how Workbench organizes itself to support roles-appropriate tools. Each plug-in extension to the Workbench can contribute any number of perspectives. A perspective groups together the most common views, editors, and actions that support a set of tasks associated with a user's role. The Workbench has a number of predefined perspectives that other tools can enhance with their own views, editors, or actions. Some products, such as WSAD, define new perspectives that group their own editors and views with some of those that come with the base Workbench to support a specific solution. Independent of how a perspective was defined, an Eclipse user is free to modify it or define entirely new ones, since, after all, a perspective is just a designer's idea of how users performing a particular set of tasks might best organize their workbench. You can:

- Position views at the left, right, or bottom of the workbench window by dragging the view title bar
- Resize views by dragging their borders
- Open additional views from the *Window>Show View* menu item
- Stack views in tabbed panes
- Choose which sets of perspective menu items are available with *Window>Customize Perspective…*
- Create and save custom perspectives

To see the available perspectives, select menu item *Window>Open Perspective*. The cascaded menu lists the most common and recently opened perspectives. Select *Others…* to see them all. It is often useful to switch perspectives as you change roles in developing an application. For example, you might be developing the HTML client resources for a Web application, and then have to edit the Java servlets that generate HTML responses. The Web perspective provides views and navigators for both activities, but if you're doing a lot of Java development, perhaps for your application's business model, you might want to switch to the Java perspective.

Alternatively, if you're developing EJBs, you'll probably want to switch to the J2EE perspective. Figure 7.3 shows the default, or *Resource,* perspective with a few additional views opened in the bottom pane. You can quickly switch between other perspectives that are also open by pressing the shortcut buttons along the left side of the Workbench window.

A word of caution: Not all perspectives behave the same. Menu items that look the same between perspectives may actually do different things. For example, selecting a file in the navigator and invoking the *Rename…* pop-up menu item renames the file in the file system as expected. However, if you select a .java file from the Java perspective and invoke *Rename…*, the Java tools perform a refactor operation that updates all the references to the class corresponding to the .java file.

Similarly, renaming an HTML file in the Web perspective will update all the links to that file. Therefore, it's always a good idea to do things in the most resource-specific perspective. Each perspective generally names and/or organizes the menu items differently to help avoid confusion.

Workbench also provides support for working in a team and for version and configuration management. Rather than requiring a specific repository, Workbench supports integration with many different repository management systems. Typical Workbench configurations include support for the Open Source CVS, Rational ClearCase, or Merant PVCS. Depending on your installation, you may have any or all of these.

Workbench also supports development with no repository manager at all, or simple resource sharing through a nonversioning WebDAV-enabled repository.

Workbench uses an optimistic resource-sharing policy. The resources in your workspace are in your own private space on your local hard drive. Of course, you could share your drive with others, but a workspace usually provides a private scope in which you can do your work independently of other developers who may be working on the same or related resources. When you are ready to integrate your work with others, you can synchronize your workspace with the shared repository.

Synchronization detects changes you've made compared to the versions in the shared repository and gives you a chance to merge your work with the work of others into your workspace. When you are satisfied that the changes are properly integrated, you can commit your work, saving it to the shared repository where it will then be available to other team members for further development and integration.

Finally, each tool can contribute its own help to the Help system. Help is available both through the *Help>Help Contents* menu item and by pressing F1 to get context-sensitive help based on the current cursor location. We'll be referring to specific sections of the Help system throughout the book. Take a minute to become familiar with the available help so that you'll have a better idea where to look when you need it.

Each Workbench configuration will be slightly different depending on what plug-ins have been included, so it's hard to predict what might be available in any given Workbench instance. We recommend [Shavor] for more in-depth coverage of the basic features that Workbench offers, such as team development support.

7.2   Building an Example Servlet with WSAD

Now that you know what WSAD is capable of, it's time to get started building the servlet example. Instead of implementing a simple Hello, World servlet, we believe you'll get a lot more out of an example that is closer to something you might actually build yourself. Figure 7.4 shows what the finished example looks like when run.

Selecting the Browse Employees link invokes the application and provides a simple list-detail display of the employees in the WASBOOK database. Figure 7.5 shows the list with Jane Doe's details. You can display a particular employee's details by clicking the link on their ID. The HTML isn't that pretty, but we want to keep it as simple as possible in order to focus on the semantics.

In this chapter, we'll develop enough of the example to create employees, and display and update their details.

Now that you're familiar with the example, let's see what's involved to build it using Java servlets. Follow these steps in implementing the servlet example using WSAD:

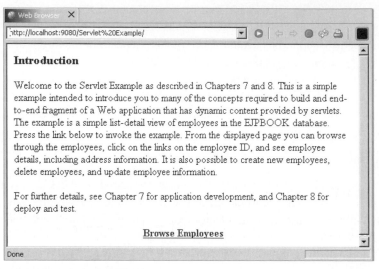

Figure 7.4 Servlet example index.html.

Figure 7.5 The Servlet example List-Detail pages.

1. Create a Web project

2. Build a business model with Java Objects

3. Persist the model using JDBC

4. Create and edit HTML for the list-detail user interface

5. Create the servlet for accessing and updating the model

The following sections cover each step in detail. These steps are typical of what you need to do to create any dynamic Web application using servlets.

7.2.1   Create a Web project

A WSAD Web project extends the Java project with perspectives, wizards, editors, views, and builders for developing static and dynamic Web applications. To create a Web project, start up WSAD on your workspace and open the Web perspective by selecting *Window>Open Perspective>Other...* from the menu bar. Select *Web* from the list of available perspectives (Figure 7.6).

Next, create a Web project by selecting *File>New>Web Project*. This will bring up the *Create a Web Project* wizard as shown in Figure 7.7.

First, you must enter the *Project Name*. By default, all projects and project resources are stored in folders under your workspace folder with the project folder name the same as the project name. However, you can choose to create a folder for your project anywhere in the file system with any name you want.

If you use an existing folder, the resources in that folder are automatically included in the project. For this example, we'll leave *Use default* selected and let the wizard assign the *New project location*. Next, specify that this project is a *J2EE Web Project* so you can add dynamic

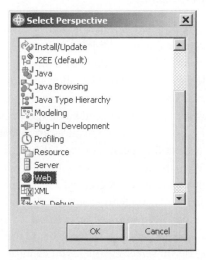

Figure 7.6 Select Perspective.

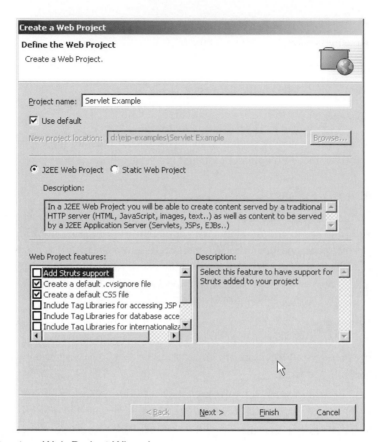

Figure 7.7 Create a Web Project Wizard.

content in the form of servlets. A static web project contains resources accessible through a traditional HTTP Web server that contains no additional business logic (servlets, JSPs, or EJBs). Therefore, you can deploy static Web applications to a simple HTTP server without a J2EE deployment descriptor. The *Web Project features* list allows you to select things the wizard will automatically add to your Web project.

For our simple servlet example, we don't need anything special and want to create most of the resources ourselves anyway. So make sure no features are selected and press *Next*.

The next page (Figure 7.8) is for specifying the J2EE settings for a J2EE Web project. These settings configure the Web application server with information required to run our Web project. As we discussed in Chapter 4, an EAR collects J2EE client, Web, and EJB modules for deployment on a J2EE application. An EAR file contains all the information needed to deploy and run the complete application. An *enterprise application project* is one that contains an EAR. In Chapter 8, you'll see how to deploy EAR projects to the server. You can use an existing EAR project or create one. If you select *Existing*, you can use the *Browse...* button to select

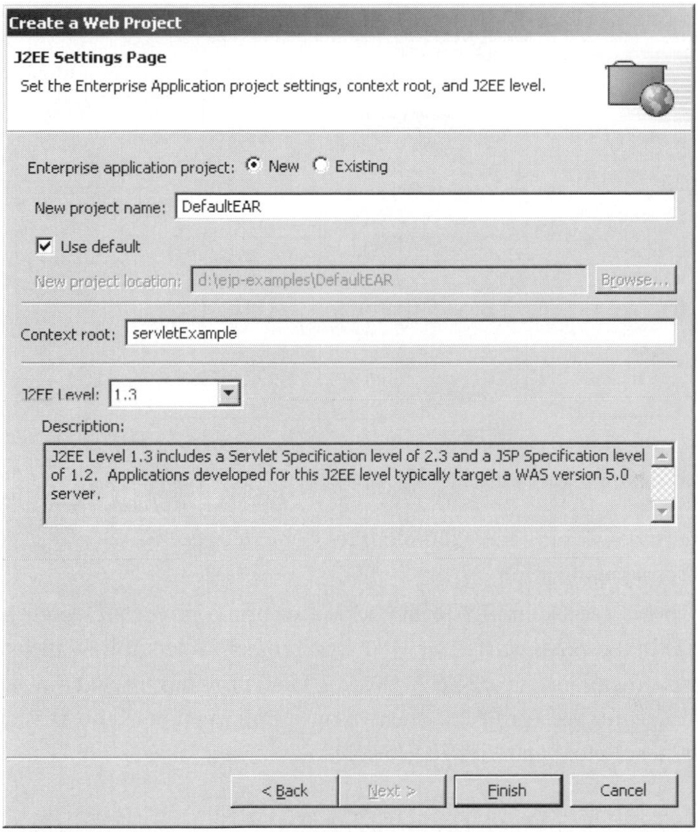

Figure 7.8 J2EE Settings page.

an EAR project from your workspace. Select *New* to create an EAR project, enter DefaultEAR as the project name, and select *Use default* (the same as you did for your Web project). The *Context Root* is the URL prefix used to access resources in your Web project. Select a context root that easily identifies your Web application, but is not too difficult to type. It's also a good idea to avoid spaces in the context root, as they have to be escaped in URLs. For example, if you use servletExample as your *Context Root*, you would use *http://localhost:9080/servletEx-ample/index.html* to access the project's home page. Next, select *J2EE Level* 1.3 to specify that you want to use its associated level of the Java servlet specification, namely Level 2.3[1]. WebSphere Application Server 5 and the WebSphere Test Environment that is part of WSAD support J2EE Level 1.3, and that's the level we'll be covering in the book. So, that's the level

---

1.   In other words, the J2EE 1.3 specification includes the Servlet 2.3 specification, as we discussed in an earlier chapter.

Figure 7.9 Servlet example project.

you'll want to use in developing the example. Press *Finish* to create your Web Application and DefaultEAR enterprise application project.

Figure 7.9 shows the DefaultEAR and servlet example projects created by the *Create a Web Project* wizard in the *J2EE Navigator View*. The project folders follow the structure defined by the J2EE 1.3 specification. The *J2EE Navigator View* provides a few conveniences over the simple *Navigator View* for Web projects. The two most important conveniences are quick access to the deployment descriptors and viewing Java resources in packages rather than folders in the file system.

In the servlet example, the *Web Deployment Descriptor* corresponds to the `web.xml`, `ibm-web-ext.xmi`, and `ibm-web-bnd.xmi` files that are in the Web content/WEB-INF folder. These files correspond to the J2EE Web archive (WAR) deployment descriptor, the IBM Web application extensions, and the IBM WebSphere bindings respectively. You can edit these files indi-vidally, but it is much easier to double-click *Web Deployment Descriptor* and edit them as a group using WSAD's Web deployment descriptor editor. The WSAD Web deployment descrip-tor editor is more than just a text editor on a number of integrated XML files. It presents a higher level view of the semantics of a Web deployment descriptor rather than the details of its persis-tence format. Similarly, the EAR deployment descriptor in the DefaultEAR project corresponds to the J2EE deployment descriptor `application.xml` in the META-INF folder.u

If you would like to avoid a lot of typing, you can import the rest of the files for the sample servlet from the CD-ROM. See Appendix A for instructions on loading the workspace contain-ing the examples and the case study.

7.2.2   Building a business model with Java objects

Chapter 5 introduced different presentation patterns including MVC, the central pattern used throughout the book. The initial focus of MVC is the application business model, which is what

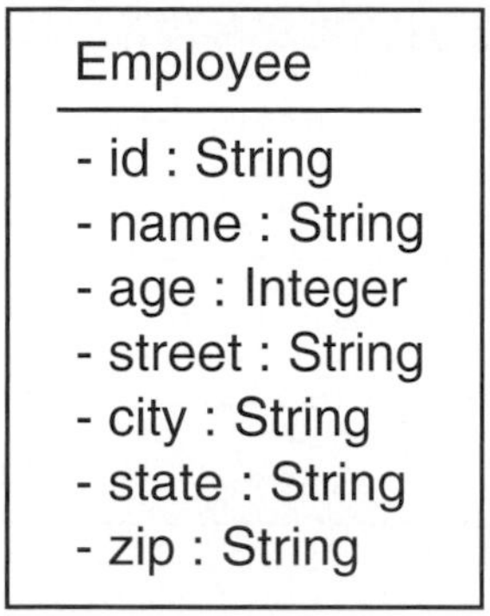

```
┌─────────────────────────┐
│  Employee               │
│  ─────────────────────  │
│  - id : String          │
│  - name : String        │
│  - age : Integer        │
│  - street : String      │
│  - city : String        │
│  - state : String       │
│  - zip : String         │
└─────────────────────────┘
```

Figure 7.10 Servlet example model.

you will be building in this section. The model for our servlet application is intentionally simple in order to cover the end-to-end details of application development in the smallest space possible. It consists of an employee with properties for name, age, and address information (Figure 7.10).

To build the model, you first have to create a Java package to contain the model classes. Select the *Java Source* folder in the *Servlet Example* project, right-click and select *New>Package*, enter com.wsbook.servletexample.domain for the package name, and press *Finish*. Next, create the model class. Select the package you just created, right-click, and invoke *New>Class*. Figure 7.11 shows the dialog used to create a class called Employee.

This dialog is self-explanatory, but there are a couple of things that are of interest. First, you can specify an *Enclosing type* to create an inner class. You can enter a superclass name, or browse existing classes that are visible to your project by selecting *Superclass*, and you can specify any additional interfaces the class should implement. Finally, the wizard can generate some commonly required methods for you, including stub implementations for inherited abstract methods. Fill in Employee for the class *Name* and press *Finish*. The next section covers the code for the Employee JavaBean, along with its persistence implementation using JDBC.

The Java editor has many nice features, far too many to describe here. Here are a few useful ones that might not be obvious for first-time users:

- Invoke content assist by pressing CTRL+SPACE, use the up and down arrow keys to scroll through the selections, press return to accept a selection. You can use content assist to fill in variable and method names, discover method parameters, add structured blocks of code, or just reduce typing.
- Quick fix is available for some errors in the Java source. Click the light bulb in the left margin, or select the *Quick Fix* menu item from an item in the tasks view.
- Position the cursor over almost any text to get a Help description, or click any identifier and press F3 to go to that definition. This is particularly useful for quickly navigating to other classes.

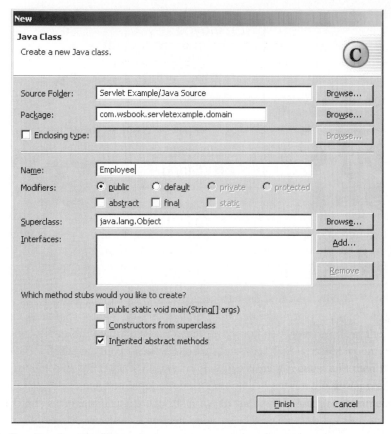

Figure 7.11 Creating the Employee class.

- Select an undefined class name referenced in a Java source file and press CONTROL+SHIFT+M to add the required import statement automatically at the beginning of the file. Alternatively, press CONTROL+SHIFT+O to organize your import statements, removing any that are unnecessary, adding any that are missing, and sorting them in the ordered specified in the Java preferences.
- Add a try/catch block around selected code by selecting *Source>Surround with try/ catch block*. The editor will automatically add catch statements for each exception raised in the selected code.
- Use *Source>Generate getter and setter…* to generate accessor methods for a field.
- Use *Source>Override methods…* to generate stub implementations of superclass methods, or unimplemented abstract methods.
- Use *Refactor* to change your Java source, updating all references in the current workspace.

For further details, see *Help>Help Contents>Java Development*, especially, *Tips & Tricks*.

7.2.3 Persist the Model using JDBC and the Active Record Pattern

Now we're ready to look at persisting objects in the business domain model. There are a number of patterns and tools for persisting an object model in a relational database. Since persistence is such an important topic and we want the example to be typical of what you might need to do, we'll cover one of the simple patterns in this section. Later in the book, you'll see other patterns and how to use local entity EJBs to persist business domain objects and map them to existing relational databases.

In this chapter, we'll use JDBC directly so you can contrast the approaches. We'll do this by implementing a simple object-to-persistence store mapping technique based on the Active Record pattern [Fowler]. This pattern puts the responsibility for implementing persistence in the business object itself. Active Record is useful when the domain object is simple, does not participate in an inheritance hierarchy, or has few associations with other domain objects. So, it's a good fit for our example, which only has one domain object. First, we have to create the database and populate it with test data.

> **ACTIVE RECORD IS USUALLY NOT THE BEST CHOICE**
>
> The Active Record pattern is a very convenient way to add persistence to a domain model, especially in a situation where you have a small number of domain objects and limited associations between them. However, in most cases, you will want to separate the persistence code from the domain code by introducing a data mapping layer based on the Broker pattern or Data Mapper pattern [Fowler]. These patterns will then store and load domain objects to/from the database. Chapter 16 covers the Data Mapper pattern.

Space does not permit covering all the details for creating a database, creating a schema for the example, setting authentication, and populating the tables with sample data, especially given the variability in popular database management systems. Instead, we'll give an overview using IBM DB2 to show what the example needs from a typical database management system. See the documentation for your system for specific details. Listing 7.1 is a DB2 command line processor script file that creates a database for our example.

Listing 7.1 Create sample database script initializeDatabase.clp.

```
drop database EJPBOOK;
create database EJPBOOK;
connect to EJPBOOK;
grant connect on database to user "GUEST";
create schema acme;
create table acme.employee (
    id       varchar(10) not null primary key,
    name     varchar(60),
    age      integer,
    street   varchar(60),
    city     varchar(60),
```

```
    state       varchar(60),
    zip         varchar(30)
);
grant all on table acme.employee to user "GUEST ";
commit work;
connect reset;
terminate;
```

This script creates a database called EJPBOOK, connects to the database, creates the employee table, and grants privileges necessary for user GUEST to connect to the database and access the employee table. You can execute the script by entering *db2cmd db2 –t –f initializeDatabase.clp* from an OS command prompt. The -t command argument tells the command processor to use a semicolon to separate commands, something that is useful for long commands like the create table statement. You can also create an external tool in Workbench for executing any selected DB2 script. Select *Run>Configure…*to invoke the *External Tools Configuration* dialog. Click *New…* and enter the information as shown in Figure 7.12. The Workbench provides a

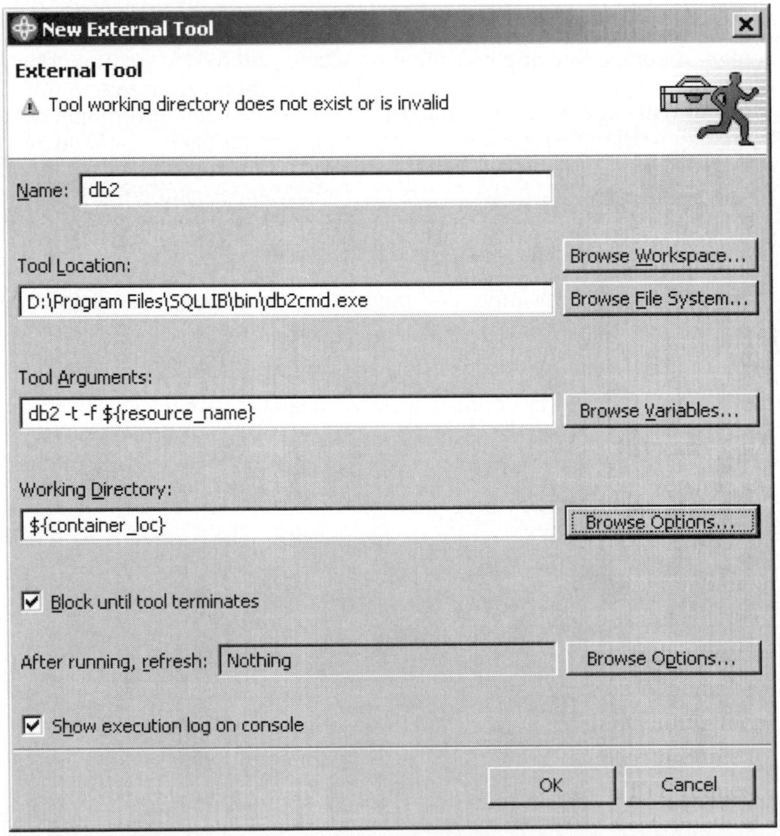

Figure 7.12 Configuring an external tool.

number of convenience variables for accessing information from the workspace. You specify these variables using the format ${variable-name}. For example, ${resource_name} would evaluate to the name of the selected resource. Press the *Browse Variables...* button to see what variables are available, and to insert them into the field.

Execute a DB2 script file by selecting the file and invoke *Run>External Tools>*db2. Other database systems can use a similar technique and script.

Now let's look at the code for the Employee class as given in Listing 7.2. Note that in Listing 7.2 and most later listings we have omitted comments for brevity. Browse the code on the CD for the complete listing.

Listing 7.2 Employee.java.

```java
package com.wsbook.servletexample.domain;

import java.sql.Connection;
import java.sql.PreparedStatement;
import java.sql.ResultSet;
import java.sql.SQLException;
import java.util.ArrayList;
import java.util.Collection;

import javax.naming.InitialContext;
import javax.sql.DataSource;

import com.wsbook.servletexample.ApplicationProperties;
import com.wsbook.servletexample.exception.DuplicateKeyException;
import com.wsbook.servletexample.exception.MappingException;
import com.wsbook.servletexample.exception.NoSuchObjectException;

public class Employee {
        private String id = "";
        private String name = "";
        private int age = 0;
        private String street = "";
        private String city = "";
        private String state = "";
        private String zip = "";

        public Employee() {
                super();
        }
        public Employee(String id) {
                this.id = id;
        }

        public boolean equals(Object anObject) {
                if (anObject == null) {
                        return false;
                }
                if (!(anObject instanceof Employee)) {
                        return false;
                }
                Employee anEmployee = (Employee) anObject;
```

```java
            return anEmployee.getId().equals(getId());
}

public String getId() {
      return id;
}

public String getName() {
      return name;
}

public int getAge() {
      return age;
}

public void setName(String value) {
      name = value;
}

public void setAge(int value) {
      age = value;
}

static final String authId =
ApplicationProperties.getDatasourceSchemaName();

protected static final String _createString =
      "INSERT INTO "+authId+".EMPLOYEE "+
      "(ID, NAME, AGE, STREET, CITY, STATE, ZIP)"+
      "VALUES (?, ?, ?, ?, ?, ?, ?)";

protected static final String _readString =
      "SELECT * FROM "+ authId+ ".EMPLOYEE " +
      "WHERE ID = ?";

protected static final String _findAllString =
      "SELECT * FROM "+authId+".EMPLOYEE ";

protected static final String _updateString =
      "UPDATE "+ authId+".EMPLOYEE "+
      "SET NAME=?, AGE=?, STREET=?, CITY=?, STATE=?, ZIP=? "+
      "WHERE ID = ?";

protected static final String _deleteString =
      "DELETE FROM "+authId+".EMPLOYEE  WHERE ID = ?";


public void create() throws SQLException, DuplicateKeyException {
      Connection connection = null;
      try {
            connection = getConnection();
            PreparedStatement ps =
            connection.prepareStatement(_createString);
            ps.setString(1, getId());
            ps.setString(2, getName());
            ps.setInt(3, getAge());
            ps.setString(4, getStreet());
            ps.setString(5, getCity());
```

```
                        ps.setString(6, getState());
                        ps.setString(7, getZip());
                        int rows = ps.executeUpdate();
                        if (rows != 1) {
                                throw new DuplicateKeyException(
        "Duplicate employee "+id);
                        }
                } finally {
                        close(connection);
                }
        }

        public static Employee findByPrimaryKey(String id) throws
SQLException, NoSuchObjectException {
                Connection connection = null;
                try {
                        connection = getConnection();
                        PreparedStatement ps =
        connection.prepareStatement(_readString);
                        ps.setString(1, id);
                        ResultSet rs = ps.executeQuery();
                        rs.next();
                        return load(rs);
                } finally {
                        close(connection);
                }
        }


        public static Collection findAll() throws SQLException {
                ArrayList list = new ArrayList();
                Employee emp = null;
                Connection connection = null;
                try {
                        connection = getConnection();
                        PreparedStatement ps =
        connection.prepareStatement(_findAllString);
                        ResultSet rs = ps.executeQuery();
                        while (rs.next()) {
                                emp = load(rs);
                                list.add(emp);
                        }
                        return list;
                } finally {
                        close(connection);
                }
        }

        private static Employee load(ResultSet rs) throws SQLException {
                Employee emp = new Employee();
                emp.id = rs.getString(1);
                emp.setName(rs.getString(2));
                emp.setAge(rs.getInt(3));
                emp.setStreet(rs.getString(4));
                emp.setCity(rs.getString(5));
                emp.setState(rs.getString(6));
                emp.setZip(rs.getString(7));
                return emp;
```

```java
    }

    public void update() throws SQLException, MappingException {
        Connection connection = null;
        try {
            connection = getConnection();
            PreparedStatement ps =
connection.prepareStatement(_updateString);
            // can't update the id
            ps.setString(1, getName());
            ps.setInt(2, getAge());
            ps.setString(3, getStreet());
            ps.setString(4, getCity());
            ps.setString(5, getState());
            ps.setString(6, getZip());
            ps.setString(7, getId());
            int rows = ps.executeUpdate();
            if (rows != 1) {
                throw new MappingException(
"Unable to update employee "+id);
            }
        } finally {
            close(connection);
        }
    }

    public void delete() throws SQLException, MappingException {
        Connection connection = null;
        try {
            connection = getConnection();
            PreparedStatement ps =
connection.prepareStatement(_deleteString);
            ps.setString(1, getId());
            int rows = ps.executeUpdate();
            if (rows != 1) {
                throw new MappingException(
"Unable to delete employee "+id);
            }
        } finally {
            close(connection);
        }
    }

    public static Connection getConnection() throws SQLException {
        // get a connection
        DataSource ds = getDataSource();
        return ds.getConnection(
ApplicationProperties.getDatasourceUserId(),

ApplicationProperties.getDatasourcePassword());
    }

    public static DataSource getDataSource() {
        DataSource ds = null;
        try {
            InitialContext context = new InitialContext();
            ds = (DataSource) context.lookup(
ApplicationProperties.getDatasourceJndiName());
```

```
        } catch (javax.naming.NamingException ne) {
                MappingException e = new
    MappingException(
    "NamingException: cannot find DataSource in initialContext");
                ne.printStackTrace();
        }
        return ds;
    }


    protected static void close(Connection conn) {
        try {
                if (conn != null) conn.close();
        } catch (SQLException e) {
        }
    }
}
```

The Employee class has accessor methods to get and set its attributes. Only some of the accessors are in the listing (see the example code for the complete implementation, including JavaDoc comments). The id attribute is read-only, so it does not have a set accessor. The Active Record pattern includes SQL statements and methods for typical CRUD (Create, Read, Update, and Delete) operations. Each of these operations is implemented by getting a connection to the database, preparing the corresponding SQL statement, filling in query or update parameters, executing the statement, and processing the results, raising any necessary exceptions. Notice the use of class ApplicationProperties that has static methods to get the database URL, schema name, and password. ApplicationProperties uses a Java ResourceBundle to get configuration properties from a Java .properties file. Listing 7.3 is an example application.properties file.

Listing 7.3 Listing 7.3 Sample Application Properties.

```
com.wsbook.servletexample.mapping.datasource.name=java:comp/env/
jdbc/EJPBOOK
com.wsbook.servletexample.mapping.datasource.schemaname=jamsden
com.wsbook.servletexample.mapping.datasource.userid=guest
com.wsbook.servletexample.mapping.datasource.password=guest
```

7.2.4 Create and Edit HTML for the List-Detail User Interface

Now that the model is complete and able to be persisted in a database, we're ready to start looking at the user interface. For maximum flexibility, availability, and ease of installation, we'll host the user interface in a Web browser, and implement it using HTML. Our example is typical of what many Web applications have to do: Display a list of model items, let users select from the list, and display and update details of the selected item. HTML is a language for describing user interfaces. HTML doesn't know anything about the model or how is it used by the application. That's where servlets come in. By using mediators and domain objects, servlets provide dynamic content for the pages and logic for updating the model using the information returned from an HTML form.

Take another look at Figure 7.5, which shows the employees list and the details for employee Jane Doe. The HTML page consists of three frames to hold the banner, the employee list, and the details for the selected employee. The employee list is a table with columns displaying some subset of the employee data to help users in choosing a selection. An HTML form displays the employee details. Another table is used to organize and lay out the labels, fields, and buttons on the form.

In this section, we'll cover the development of the static HTML used to access the employee list and organize its contents. In the next section, we'll look at the servlets that actually provide and update the dynamic data. WSAD provides a number of excellent tools for developing HTML and XML documents. These tools are best used from the Web perspective, so if you don't have that perspective selected, select it now by either clicking the *Web* perspective button in the shortcut bar on the left side of the Workbench window (its icon looks like a globe) or select *Window>Open Perspective>Web*.

Web applications generally have a welcome page, often the home page, or first page introducing the application. Its role is to orient the user and provide organized links to the rest of the application. Index.html, index.jsp, welcome.html are typical names for welcome pages. Specifying a URL for a folder without specifying a file in that folder access the welcome page by default. For example, *http://localhost:9080/servletExample/index.html* and *http://localhost:9080/servletExample/* would access the same page. You can specify the welcome pages in the Web deployment descriptor, but we'll look at that in Chapter 8.

Next select the *Web Content* folder, right-click, and select *New>HTML/XHTML File*. Fill in index.html for the file name, and take the defaults for the rest of the fields. To get descriptions of other fields available from the *New HTML/XHTML File* wizard, press F1. Press *Finish* to create the file and open Page Designer on the contents. Notice that the wizard generated initial contents based on the selected generation model and markup language.

Figure 7.3 shows the Web perspective with Page Designer opened in the index.html file. Before getting into the details of using Page Designer, let's look at the views that are in the Web perspective. Remember you can add or remove any views you want or reposition the views to suit your taste. The layout in Figure 7.3 is the default layout for the Web perspective. If you have made changes to the perspective, you can reset the perspective to the default layout by selecting *Window>Reset Perspective*. Recall that the Web perspective uses the *J2EE Navigator* by default instead of the resource *Navigator* in order to provide easier access to the *Web Deployment Descriptor* and to display Java source in packages instead of file folders to make it easier to navigate.

Use the *Server Configuration* tab to configure different application servers for deploying and testing your applications (Chapter 8 covers this topic). The bottom left pane provides views for navigating and modifying HTML. The *Gallery* provides a number of page layouts and styles, images, wallpapers, Web art, MIDI sounds, and style sheets from which to choose. The *Thumbnail* view shows small graphic summary views of the files in your project, or in the *Gallery*. You can select elements from the thumbnail view and add them to your Web page.

The *Library* view provides a list of active elements that you can add to your HTML pages including JavaScript and JSP elements. This makes it very easy to add rich content and actions to your page without having to know all the JavaScript details. We'll be using the JSP elements in Chapter 13.

The *Outline* view shows an outline of the HTML source and provides an easy way to navigate the document. In particular, use the outline view to navigate to the location of specific HTML elements in the Page Designer design view since the actual elements aren't directly visible in that view. The *Attribute* view shows all the Page Designer attributes of the selected item in the design view. Contrast with the *Properties* view, which shows all the HTML attributes of the selected HTML element and their current values. This is a great way to see what attributes are available on an HTML element.

The properties view isn't open by default in the Web perspective, but you'll find it helpful if you like to do a lot of HTML source editing. To add the view, select *Window>Show View>Others...* and then select *Basic>Properties*. Then position the view where you want it by dragging its title bar. You may want to arrange the view at the bottom left because you don't generally look at attributes and properties at the same time. The *Links* view lets you look at the links to and from a file selected in the *J2EE Navigator* view. This is a great view for finding and fixing broken links.

Finally, there's the Page Designer editor itself. Page Designer is a multipage editor that provides three presentations of the edited file: design, source, and preview. The design view is a WYSIWYG editor that is best for doing general editing because you can see what the page will look like as you edit. Use the gallery and library views to add layout, static content, and dynamic content to your page. Use the attributes view to edit the details of the selected element.

Note that when viewing the attributes of a link, the attributes of the text are shown when the cursor is positioned in the text inside the anchor element. To display and edit the link's URL reference, make sure the cursor is positioned at either the beginning or the end of the anchor text. The Source pane is for directly editing the HTML source. Use the properties view as a convenient way to edit the attributes of the selected HTML element. Nondefault values of properties are automatically added to the HTML element. Full content assist is available by pressing CONTROL+SPACE anywhere. Use content assist to see what HTML elements or attributes are valid at the current cursor location or to select a value for an attribute. In addition, allowing the cursor to pause over an element displays Help on that element.

You can also open the source directly by selecting an HTML file from the navigator and selecting *Open With>Source Editor*. This might be necessary when editing pages with multiple frames, some of which cannot be displayed, perhaps because they reference servlets instead of HTML pages. The preview view lets you see what your page will look like when viewed in a Web browser. This view also shows how existing Windows applications built with ActiveX are integrated into Workbench. On Windows systems, the HTML viewer used in the preview view is actually Internet Explorer.

Page Designer has lots more features, enough for its own book. This introduction should be sufficient to get you started and we'll cover more details throughout the book. As always, additional detail is available from the product's online Help.

Now back to the example. Add some content to your index.html welcome page that introduces users to your Web application and provides initial access to its functionality. Use headings, paragraphs, alignment, style sheets, etc. to make the page look the way you want. We'll keep the HTML intentionally simple in our example in order to focus on the overall application flow. Add a link to your page to a file called browseEmployees.html, which will contain the frames to lay out the employee list and details.

Select the *Web Content* folder again, and create another HTML file called browseEmploy-ees.html and enter the code shown in Listing 7.4. The page contains three frames: One for the banner at the top, a resizable frame for the employee list, and one, on the bottom, for the employee details. The *src* attribute of the banner frame references banner.html, so create that file and add some interesting looking banner from *Gallery>Image->Banner* or create your own using *File->New>Other...>Web>ImageFile* to create an image file and edit it with WebArt Designer.

The *src* attribute for the list frame is BrowseEmployees, the URL used to access the servlet that provides the employee list from the database. We'll develop this servlet in the next section. Notice the information marker next to the line that references the BrowseEmployees servlet. This marker indicates there is a broken link in the file. You can also see the broken link from the links view when you select browseEmployees.html from the J2EE Navigator view and in an error in the tasks view. The error will go away when you create the servlet and add it to the Web application deployment descriptor.

The detail frame doesn't have an *src* attribute. A link provides the content generated by the BrowseEmployees servlet, which uses the detail frame as its target. This frame will be empty the first time you access the browseEmployees.html file.

Listing 7.4 browseEmployees.html.

```
<!DOCTYPE HTML PUBLIC "-//W3C//DTD HTML 4.01 Transitional//EN">
<html>
<head>
<meta http-equiv="Content-Type" content="text/html; charset=iso-
8859-1">
<title>Servlet Example</title>
</head>
<frameset rows="50,*, 240">
<frame name="banner" scrolling="no" noresize src="banner.html"
    marginwidth="0" marginheight="0" frameborder="0"/>
<frame name="list" scrolling="auto" src="BrowseEmployees"
    marginwidth="50" marginheight="20"frameborder="1"/>
<frame name="detail" marginwidth="0" marginheight="20"
        frameborder="0"/>
<noframes>
```

```
<body>
<p>This page uses frames, but your browser doesn't support them.
</p>
</body>
</noframes>
</frameset>
</html>
```

7.2.5   Create the servlets for accessing and updating the model

Now we're finally ready to create our first servlet. The `browseEmployees.html` file had a link in the list frame to `BrowseEmployees`. This URL references the servlet that accesses the database to get a list of employees and presents the result as an HTML page displayed in the frame. Select package `com.wsbook.servletexample` in the Java Source folder, right-click, and select *New>Servlet*. Fill in *com.wsbook.servletexample* for the *Java package*, and *BrowseEmployees* for the servlet *class name*, and press Next.

Figure 7.13 shows the second page of the new servlet wizard. Use this page to select which servlet methods you wish to implement. These methods correspond to the HTTP methods

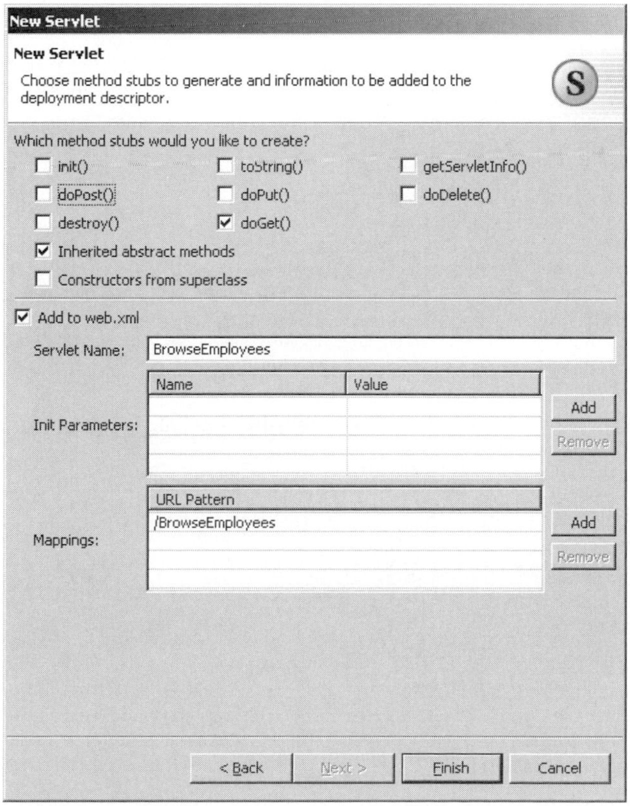

Figure 7.13 New servlet wizard.

that can be used to access and update Web content. The employees list is read-only, and requires no parameters, so we'll implement `doGet()` which, you'll remember, is used to return a page.

Make sure you select the *Add to web.xml* option. This adds the servlet to the Web application deployment descriptor so it can be accessed through a specific URL. We'll look at the details in the next chapter when we prepare to execute the application.

Note the *Mappings:* section. By default, WSAD added URL mapping */BrowseEmployees* to the mappings, which in turn adds it to the Web deployment descriptor. This means that this URI can be used by an HTTP client application to cause the Web application server to invoke the `doGet()` method of the `BrowseEmployees` servlet. The URL mapping will also fix the broken link we had in our `browseEmployees.html` file. You can have many mappings to the servlet in order to provide access through different URLs. We only need the default, so press *Finish* to create the initial servlet code. When you do, you'll see that the broken link warning is removed from the tasks view.

Next, update the code of BrowseEmployees.java to match Listing 7.5.

Listing 7.5 BrowseEmployees.java.

```
package com.wsbook.servletexample;

import java.io.IOException;
import java.io.PrintWriter;
import java.sql.SQLException;
import java.util.Iterator;

import javax.servlet.ServletException;
import javax.servlet.http.HttpServlet;
import javax.servlet.http.HttpServletRequest;
import javax.servlet.http.HttpServletResponse;

import com.wsbook.servletexample.domain.Employee;

public class BrowseEmployees extends HttpServlet {

        public void doGet(HttpServletRequest req,
        HttpServletResponse resp)
                throws ServletException, IOException {

                PrintWriter out = resp.getWriter();
                out.println("<HTML>");
                out.println("<BODY>");
                out.println("<h3 align=\"center\">All Employees</h3>");
                out.println(
                        "<TABLE align=\"center\" BORDER=\"yes\"
CELLSPACING=2 CELLPADDING=0 WIDTH=\"70%\">");
                out.println("<TR>");
                out.println("<TD><center><b>Id</b></center></TD>");
                out.println("<TD><center><b>Name</b></center></TD>");
                out.println("<TD width=\"40\"><center><b>Age</b></
center></TD>");
                out.println("</TR>");
                try {
```

```
                Iterator employees = Employee.findAll().iterator();
                while (employees.hasNext()) {
                        Employee employee = (Employee)
                                        employees.next();
                        out.println("<TR>");
                        out.println(
                                "<TD><A HREF=\"EmployeeDetails?id="
                                        + employee.getId()
                                        + "\" target=\"detail\">"
                                        + employee.getId()
                                        + "</A></TD>");
                        out.println("<TD>" + employee.getName() +
                                        "</TD>");
                        out.println("<TD width=\"40\">" +
                                employee.getAge() + "</TD>");
                        out.println("</TR>");
                }
        } catch (SQLException e) {
        }
        out.println("<TR>");
        out.println(
                "<TD colspan=\"3\"><A href=\"EmployeeDetails\"
target=\"detail\">Create Employee...</A></TD>");
        out.println("</TR>");
        out.println("</TABLE>");
        out.println("</BODY>");
        out.println("</HTML>");
    }

}
```

This code is typical of a servlet that provides dynamic content. It first accesses the output `PrintWriter` from the `HttpServletResponse` in order to write output back to the Web browser, which displays it in the list frame of the `browseEmployees.html` page. Most of the rest of the code outputs the HTML for the output page. It uses a table to display the employee ID, name, and department. This is sufficient information to help users identify which employee they would like to update. The code uses the Employee `findAll` static method to access the database and then obtains an Iterator over the set of employees. It then iterates over the set of employees to display each employee in an HTML table row.

Notice that the employee ID is placed inside an HTML anchor element that specifies a link to `EmployeeDetails` with an ID argument containing the employee ID. This link is used to invoke the `EmployeeDetails` servlet, which displays the employee details in the detail frame of `browseEmployees.html`. There is also a special row added to the bottom of the table that contains a link to `EmployeeDetails` with no argument so users can create an employee.

Create another servlet in the same package called `EmployeeDetails` that also implements the `doGet()` method. The code is given is Listing 7.6.

Listing 7.6 EmployeeDetails.java.

```java
package com.wsbook.servletexample;

import java.io.IOException;
import java.io.PrintWriter;
import java.sql.SQLException;

import javax.servlet.ServletException;
import javax.servlet.http.HttpServlet;
import javax.servlet.http.HttpServletRequest;
import javax.servlet.http.HttpServletResponse;

import com.wsbook.servletexample.domain.Employee;
import com.wsbook.servletexample.exception.NoSuchObjectException;

public class EmployeeDetails extends HttpServlet {

    public void doGet(HttpServletRequest req,
    HttpServletResponse resp)
        throws ServletException, IOException {

        String employeeId = req.getParameter("id");
        Employee employee = new Employee();
        if (employeeId != null) {
            try {
                employee =
                Employee.findByPrimaryKey(employeeId);
            } catch (NoSuchObjectException e) {
                e.printStackTrace();
            } catch (SQLException e) {
                e.printStackTrace();
            }
        }
        PrintWriter out = resp.getWriter();

        out.println(
            "<!DOCTYPE HTML PUBLIC \"-//W3C//DTD HTML 4.01
Transitional//EN\">");
        out.println("<html>");
        out.println("<head>");
        out.println("<title>Employee Details</title>");
        out.println(
            "<meta http-equiv=\"Content-Type\" content=\"text/
html; charset=iso-8859-1\">");
        out.println("</head>");
        out.println("<body bgcolor=\"#FFFFFF\"
text=\"#000000\">");
        out.println("<h3 align=\"center\">Employee Details</
h3>");
        out.println("<div align=\"center\">");
        String action = "UpdateEmployee";
        if (employeeId == null) action = "CreateEmployee";
        out.println(
            "<form name=\"updateEmployee\" target=\"_top\"
method=\"post\" action=\""+action+"\">");
        if (employeeId != null)
```

```
                    out.println(
                        "    <input type=\"hidden\" name=\"id\"
value=\""
                            + employee.getId()
                            + "\"/>");
                out.println(
                    "    <table align=\"center\" border=\"1\"
cellpadding=\"0\" cellspacing=\"0\" width=\"70%\">");
                if (employeeId == null) {
                    out.println("      <tr>");
                    out.println("        <td width=\"60\">");
                    out.println("          <div align=\"right\">Id:</
div>");
                    out.println("        </td>");
                    out.println("        <td>");
                    out.println(
                        "          <input type=\"text\" name=\"id\"
size=\"70\" value=\""
                            + employee.getId()
                            + "\"/>");
                    out.println("        </td>");
                    out.println("      </tr>");
                }
                out.println("      <tr>");
                out.println("        <td width=\"60\">");
                out.println("          <div align=\"right\">Name:</div>");
                out.println("        </td>");
                out.println("        <td>");
                out.println(
                    "          <input type=\"text\" name=\"name\"
size=\"70\" value=\""
                        + employee.getName()
                        + "\"/>");
                out.println("        </td>");
                out.println("      </tr>");
                out.println("      <tr>");
                out.println("        <td width=\"60\">");
                out.println("          <div align=\"right\">Age:</div>");
                out.println("        </td>");
                out.println("        <td>");
                out.println(
                    "          <input type=\"text\" name=\"age\"
size=\"70\" value=\""
                        + employee.getAge()
                        + "\"/>");
                    out.println("        </td>");
                    out.println("      </tr>");
                    out.println("      <tr>");
                    out.println("        <td width=\"60\">");
                    out.println("          <div align=\"right\">Street:</div>");
                    out.println("        </td>");
                    out.println("        <td>");
                out.println(
                    "          <input type=\"text\" name=\"street\"
size=\"70\" value=\""
                        + employee.getStreet()
                        + "\"/>");
                    out.println("        </td>");
```

```
            out.println("      </tr>");
            out.println("     <tr>");
            out.println("       <td colspan=\"2\">");
            out.println(
                "             <table border=\"0\" cellpadding=\"0\"
cellspacing=\"0\">");
            out.println("           <tr>");
            out.println("             <td width=\"60\">");
            out.println("               <div align=\"right\">City:</
div>");
            out.println("             </td>");
            out.println("             <td>");
            out.println(
                "               <input type=\"text\" name=\"city\"
size=\"27\" value=\""
                + employee.getCity()
                + "\">");
            out.println("             </td>");
            out.println("             <td width=\"30\">");
            out.println("               <div align=\"right\">State:</
div>");
            out.println("             </td>");
            out.println("             <td>");
            out.println(
                "               <input type=\"text\" name=\"state\"
size=\"6\" value=\""
                + employee.getState()
                + "\">");
            out.println("             </td>");
            out.println("             <td width=\"30\">");
            out.println("               <div align=\"right\">Zip:</
div>");
            out.println("             </td>");
            out.println("             <td>");
            out.println(
                "               <input type=\"text\" name=\"zip\"
size=\"10\" value=\""
                + employee.getZip()
                + "\">");
            out.println("             </td>");
            out.println("           </tr>");
            out.println("         </table>");
            out.println("       </td>");
            out.println("     </tr>");
            out.println("     <td colspan=\"2\">");
            out.println("       <div align=\"center\">");
            out.println(
                "         <input type=\"submit\" name=\"submit\"
value=\"Submit\" align=\"center\">");
            if (employeeId != null) {
                out.println(
                "         <input type=\"submit\" name=\"submit\"
value=\"Delete\" align=\"center\">");
            }
            out.println("       </div>");
            out.println("     </td>");
            out.println("   </tr>");
            out.println(" </table>");
```

```
                    out.println("</form>");
                    out.println("</div>");
                    out.println("</body>");
                    out.println("</html>");
        }
}
```

This code is similar to the previous servlet. It again uses the Employee class to access the database, but this time using the findByPrimaryKey method for a specific employee identified by the id HttpServletRequest parameter. Recall that the BrowseEmployees servlet provided this parameter in the link that invokes the EmployeeDetails servlet. An HTML form contains the employee information using input fields so users can update the employee data. At the bottom of the form, there are a couple of submit input elements for updating and deleting the employee. The form action is UpdateEmployee, and it uses the POST method instead of GET.

Recall that an HTML form puts all the input fields into HttpServletRequest parameters. HTTP can communicate parameters using headers or in a request entity body. In both cases, the parameters are in the form "?name=value" and are parsed so getParameter can be used to access the parameter by name.

However, most Web application servers limit the size of HTTP headers, limiting the number of parameters that can be passed in an HTTP GET method. Therefore, it is generally best practice to use the POST method for passing data in HTML forms.

The HTML form generated by the EmployeeDetails servlet passes each of the form input fields as a parameter using the input field name as the parameter name.

Next, we'll create another servlet that will use this information to update the employee in the database. Create a servlet called UpdateEmployee, but have this servlet implement the doPost() method instead of doGet(). This is because the form's action tag invoked the UpdateEmployee servlet using the post method. Listing 7.7 contains the code for the UpdateEmployee servlet.

Listing 7.7 UpdateEmployee.java.

```
package com.wsbook.servletexample;

import java.io.IOException;
import java.sql.SQLException;

import javax.servlet.ServletException;
import javax.servlet.http.HttpServlet;
import javax.servlet.http.HttpServletRequest;
import javax.servlet.http.HttpServletResponse;

import com.wsbook.servletexample.domain.Employee;
import com.wsbook.servletexample.exception.MappingException;
import com.wsbook.servletexample.exception.NoSuchObjectException;

public class UpdateEmployee extends HttpServlet {
```

```java
public void doPost(HttpServletRequest req,
HttpServletResponse resp)
    throws ServletException, IOException {

    // Retrieve the Employee information
    String employeeId = req.getParameter("id");
    Employee employee = null;
    try {
        employee = (Employee)
            Employee.findByPrimaryKey(employeeId);
    } catch (NoSuchObjectException e) {
        System.out.println(
          "***Error, employee doesn't exist");
    } catch (SQLException e) {
        e.printStackTrace();
    }

    // see what button the user pressed
    String action = req.getParameter("submit");
    if (action.equals("Delete")) {
        try {
            employee.delete();
        } catch (SQLException e) {
            e.printStackTrace();
        } catch (MappingException e) {
        }
    } else {
        employee.setName(req.getParameter("name"));
        try {
    employee.setAge(
            Integer.parseInt(req.getParameter("age")));
        } catch (NumberFormatException exc) {
            System.out.println(
              "***Error, employee id must be a number");
        }
        employee.setStreet(req.getParameter("street"));
        employee.setCity(req.getParameter("city"));
        employee.setState(req.getParameter("state"));
        employee.setZip(req.getParameter("zip"));
        try {
            employee.update();
        } catch (MappingException e) {
            System.out.println(
              "***Error, couldn't save employee or address");
        } catch (SQLException e) {
            e.printStackTrace();
        }
    }
    // refresh the employee's list so it shows the updates
    resp.sendRedirect("browseEmployees.html");
}

}
```

UpdateEmployee is an example of a controller servlet that handles user input and invokes operations on the business model in order to implement some business use case; in this case, updating the business data. This servlet again uses the Employee class to get a particular employee by ID, and then uses parameters from the HttpServletRequest that were provided by the HTML form to update the employee information. Notice that the code does little data validation, and errors are handled by simply raising exceptions, which will result in the servlet displaying a standard error page that you typically wouldn't present to your users in a real application.

Servlets generally catch these errors and send output that is more suitable in a generated error HTML page. However, we'll ignore this for now in order to keep the code simple. Notice the last line in the UpdateEmployee servlet. This code redirects the request to the browseEmploy-ees.html page in order to refresh the employee list with the updated employee information.

7.3 Some Problems with This Example

Our servlet example was simple, but covered many of the steps required for Web applications using dynamic data and shared business logic. This simple example might make you wonder what else you need. We'll soon discover that as we scale up the functionality, complexity, persistence, transaction, and security needs of our applications, this simple pattern won't be nearly enough.

As a final look at what we've learned in this chapter, let's look at what was tedious or inflexible and in doing so, briefly introduce some the additional features of J2EE and WSAD that we will explore in the coming chapters.

- Editing HTML inside Java source was difficult to develop and error prone. There was no way to use the WSAD HTML editor for WYSIWYG editing, formatting, preview, content assist, attributes, etc. This resulted from the unintegrated mixture of two languages. Later we'll see how JSP addresses this issue.
- All the data parameters passed into the servlets used to update the database were passed as strings with no data validation. The Struts framework provides additional facilities and validation that will help you simplify and standardize your forms data processing.
- The EmployeeDetails servlet mixed display and control logic for accessing employees in the same component making control logic more difficult to reuse in other user interfaces. Using JSP and the Struts framework to separate reusable business logic from reusable user interface modules addresses this issue.
- Developing the database mapping code using the Active Record pattern was reasonably simple, but somewhat tedious. In addition, it was only one business object with no associations, no inheritance, and no data transformations between the data in the object model and tables in the relational database. This simple solution will not scale up well to more complex models and database schemas. J2EE local container-managed entity beans solve this problem by automatically generating all database assess code and providing a tool for interactively mapping object and relational models for those cases where the defaults are enough.

- Mixing persistence into the model classes couples them to a particular database implementation. We need an approach that provides a common interface for persistence, but allows for variability of both the objects being persisted, and the persistence mechanisms used.
- A lot of database code in the Employee class is generic and unnecessarily repeated in each domain object. Other object-to-relational mapping patterns factor out the common code so you need to implement only the things that are specific to the object. We'll look at another approach for developing the domain model in Chapter 16.
- Our sample application didn't use transactions except at the database access level, or security beyond what could be set on individual Web resources and the database itself. J2EE EJBs address this functionality by supporting a rich, role-based security model and method-level access control.

7.4 Summary

Web-based application development involves myriad different file and resource types. If not efficiently managed, the process of moving from development to test, and ultimately a production environment, can result in what might feel like an endless cycle of regressions due to these files being out of synch.

Having a good, well-integrated, well-understood tool set that knows the relationships between the artifacts of an application and how to manage change will go a long way to improving and shortening the development process and increasing the quality of the resultant applications.

WSAD is more than just another HTML authoring tool; it provides a complete, IDE for J2EE applications and Web services. In this chapter, we covered an overview of WSAD and WebSphere Studio Workbench that provides the Eclipse-based tool integration environment. We then looked at the steps required to create and edit a simple, but complete, Web application based on J2EE servlets using WebSphere Studio Application Developer. Along the way, we took a more detailed look at just a few of the tool components that make up WSAD.

In the next chapter, we'll look at how to deploy and test this simple application within WSAD. Later chapters will address alternative J2EE design choices using this application as an example.

Testing Servlets Using WSAD

In Chapter 7, you learned how to develop a simple servlet-based Web application. In this chapter, we'll finish the example by deploying it to an application server, running the application, and doing simple debugging. Specifically we'll:

1. Edit the Web deployment descriptor

2. Deploy to an enterprise application

3. Configure the WSAD test environment and publish the application

4. Start the WSAD test environment

5. Run the application on the test server

6. Edit HMTL and servlet code and retest

7. Debug a servlet

The following sections cover each step in detail. Refer to Chapter 7 for a description of the sample application, the architecture used, and the implementation code.

8.1   Edit the Web Deployment Descriptor

The Web application in Chapter 7 contains a business model, a list-detail view of the model, and a controller servlet that updates the model. In order to execute this Web application, we must first describe it to the application server so it knows what's in the application, what resources it uses, and how to invoke it. That's the role of the J2EE Web application deployment descriptor. The Web application deployment descriptor is an XML file called `web.xml` in the WEB-INF folder of a Web application. To open the Web deployment descriptor editor as shown in Figure 8.1, either double-click the `web.xml` file directly or double-click Web Deployment Descriptor (which appears right under the Web project name) from the J2EE navigator view.

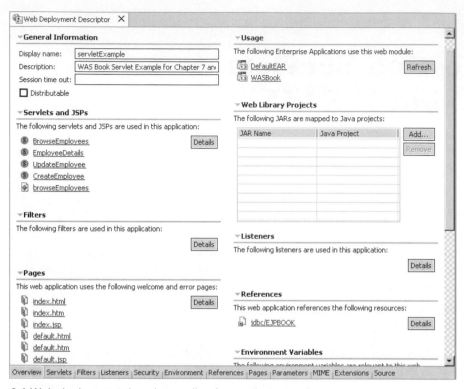

Figure 8.1 Web deployment descriptor editor for servlet example.

This editor displays information in the `web.xml` file combined with information in the WebSphere bindings file (`ibm-web-bnd.xmi`) and WebSphere extensions file (`ibm-web-ext.xmi`). These XML files contain extensions to the deployment descriptor that are supported by IBM WAS 5.0. You can edit all three files as a single logical unit with the deployment descriptor editor, which organizes the information in the deployment descriptor into a number of tabbed pages. The following paragraphs provide an overview of the editor tabs, including further information on settings required for the sample application. For a complete description of the editor, see the WSAD Help.

The Overview tab provides the most commonly updated information, giving at a glance the Web application name, description, the servlets contained in the application, the welcome and error pages, etc. It also shows the enterprise applications that use this Web application. See the next section for details on how to add a Web application to an enterprise application so a J2EE Web application server can execute it.

The Servlets tab provides additional details about the servlets in the Web application. Figure 8.2 shows the servlets page with the BrowseEmployees servlet selected. Notice that the details shown for the servlet are the same information that we entered in the new servlet wizard. You can edit that information here if needed. Note that you can expand and contract the subsec-

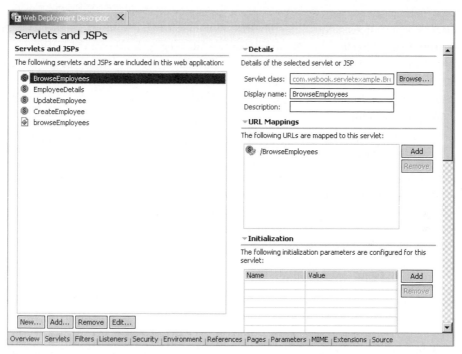

Figure 8.2 Web deployment descriptor editor.

tions of the form to display or hide information as needed. Use this feature to hide deployment information that you don't need to change. The editor remembers the expansion state of each section so they are displayed the same way the next time the editor is opened.

The Filters tab attaches filters to a servlet. You'll remember from Chapter 6 that you can attach filters to servlets in order to provide further processing on their input or output.

The Listeners tab is for adding servlet context or HTTP session listeners that are notified when the servlet context or HTTP session is initialized, changed, or destroyed. You can use listeners to handle change events in the servlet context or HTTP session instead of having to distribute or duplicate change-event management code in many different servlets.

The Security tab is for managing access control to Web application resources. Use the Security Roles subtab to define roles played by users of your application, then switch to the Security Constraints subtab to create specific access control or security constraints. Each security constraint can have a number of Web resource collections that specify the permitted HTTP methods and URL patterns for identifying the resources in the collection. The security constraint also specifies which security roles are able to access the resources identified by the Web resource collection. We will examine this more in a later chapter.

The Environment tab defines variables available to all servlets in the Web application. Use this tab to define constants used in your servlets, but that may need to be customized by users or administrators instead of being fixed in the code itself.

The References tab specifies other resources referenced by this Web application including EJBs, JDBC data sources, and JSP tag libraries. We'll be looking at the References tab in more detail in subsequent chapters, but in this chapter, we do need to configure the JDBC data source that is used to access the employees database. Figure 8.3 shows the Resource subtab. Create a resource reference by pressing *Add* at the bottom of the resource references list. Name the new reference as shown in Figure 8.3, or use the name you specified for the data source name in the application.properties file:

```
com.wsbook.servletexample.mapping.datasource.name=java:comp/env/
jdbc/EJPBOOK
```

Resources specified in this way are placed in the `java:comp/env/` namespace. That is, they are looked up in the application using names like `java:comp/env/jdbc/EJPBOOK` instead of their specific, global Java Naming and Directory Interface (JNDI) names. The global JNDI name is specified under the WebSphere Bindings in the JNDI Name field on the References page.

For our database access, specify the name used by the Web application server to look up the data source. Figure 8.3 uses `jdbc/EJPBOOK` as the nonlocal JNDI name to indicate the resource is a JDBC data source, and the rest of the name corresponds to the sample employee database. You can use any JNDI name you want as long as it doesn't conflict with some other reference name for the servlet; however, it is useful to use names that easily identify the accessed resource.

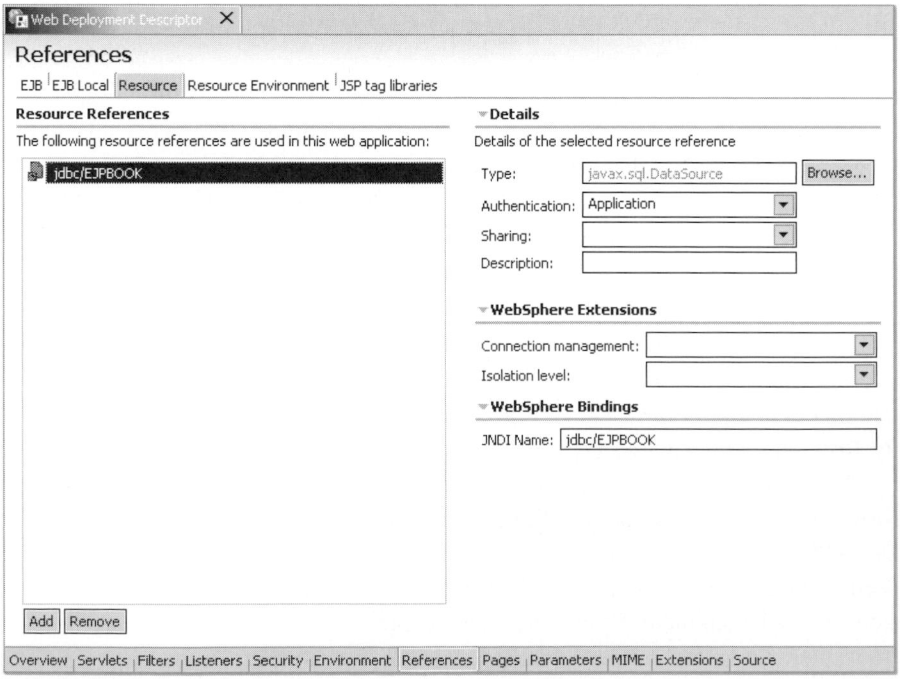

Figure 8.3 Configuring the JDBC resource.

You can use the nonlocal JNDI name directly in the application, eliminating the need to specify a resource reference in the Web application deployment descriptor. However, this can create problems when the same application is deployed on more than one Web application server. It may be necessary for the application to access its resources from a different JNDI server with a different name. By defining resource references in the Web deployment descriptor, the resource `java:comp/env/` reference can be mapped to a different JDBC URI without having to change the servlet source code. In addition, by creating a local resource reference, the application is informing the application server that it uses this resource. The application server will alter the classpath, as well as take other steps to support this usage.

Welcome and error pages fall under the Pages tab. Welcome pages specify the default pages used when a URL refers to a folder containing a collection of resources. The default is based on the order given in the list, with the resources at the top selected first, if more than one welcome page exists in the folder. Use error pages to specify a URL for a page that is to be displayed instead of a default page when a particular HTTP error occurs. For example, specify pageNotFound.html for error code 404 to provide an HTML page to display when a resource does not exist.

Use the Parameters tab to add default parameter values into the Web application context. These parameters are available through the application context. Use the MIME tab to specify custom MIME types for file extensions. These MIME types will be automatically included in HTTP headers when the Web application server accesses a resource with the custom extension. Browsers typically use the MIME type header information to know how to display the resource.

The Extensions tab specifies Web application extensions supported by WAS. One useful extension is the default error page. Use this parameter to enter or select the default error page displayed on any HTTP error other than those overridden in the Pages tab.

The MIME filters group is an alternative to servlet filters. MIME filters either transform the contents of an HTTP request or response or modify HTTP headers. MIME filters forward HTTP responses with a specified MIME type to one or more servlets where the response can be translated to some other MIME type. Other extensions are covered throughout the book as needed.

You can edit the deployment descriptor XML source directly using the source page. Note that the source page only displays the contents of the web.xml file, which contains the J2EE 1.3 standard deployment description information. To see or edit the source for the WebSphere bindings and extensions, open the ibm-web-bnd.xmi or ibm-web-ext.xmi in the WEB-INF folder using the XML or default text editor. Changes to the source page are immediately reflected in the other design pages and vice versa.

8.1.1 Deploying to an Enterprise Application

Now that the Web application is described in its deployment descriptor, we are ready to send it to an application server and start testing. As we described in Chapter 4, J2EE 1.3 application servers run enterprise applications described by enterprise application deployment descriptors. In order to deploy a J2EE 1.3 Web application, it must first be added to an enterprise application, which is then deployed to an application server. The same Web application can be deployed in more than one enterprise application, and on more than one application server.

The easiest way to deploy a Web application using WSAD is to simply run it on a server; it will be automatically deployed, if necessary. To do so, select the Sample Servlet project, right-click, and select *Run on Server…*. The first time you run the project, the server selection dialog is displayed. Click the *Advanced* button and the server selection wizard shown in Figure 8.4 is displayed to create a server to use.

Select the Create a new server radio button, then the WTE server. This server is built into WSAD and simplifies development by running the Web application inside WSAD and directly from the files located in the Workbench's projects. Check the toggle *Set this server as project default* (do not prompt) to set this server as the preferred one for the Sample Servlet project (you can create as many servers as you want) and select the preferred server in the server preference properties of the Web project. To see the Web project properties, select the project, right-click, and select properties. The properties you set when you created the Web project are available in the properties dialog and can be updated as needed. In particular, see the Server Preference, and Web properties pages.

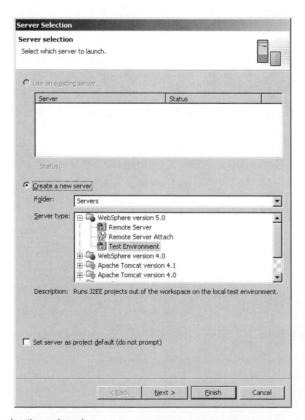

Figure 8.4 Server selection wizard.

Click *Next* on the Server selection wizard and answer *yes t*o the prompt for creating a server project. Server projects contain server configurations that you can use to deploy and test your J2EE applications. On the next page, you can set an HTTP port number for the server. If you have created many servers, make sure each one is listening on a different HTTP port if you intend to run them at the same time. Otherwise, the server won't be able to start up if its port is already in use. Click Finish to create and start up the server. You'll see a Web browser open up in WSAD as shown in Figure 7.4. Click the Browse Employees link and see what happens.

Don't be alarmed about all those errors that appeared in the console window from the Web server! One of the challenges of Web application development is that errors that occur in components of your application are often reported through the application server rather than directly by your application, or they appear as errors returned to the client Web browser, long after the error occurred. However, it's generally easier to find the error than it may appear. Usually the first error is the one you want to resolve. The others are just cascading errors caused by the first one. So let's look at the console output and see what caused the problem—

```
[10/28/02 9:57:06:123 EST] 726cdc0b Helpers      W NMSV0605E: A Reference
object looked up from the context "java:" with the name "comp/env/jdbc/
EJPBOOK" was sent to the JNDI Naming Manager and an exception resulted.
Reference data follows:
ReferenceFactoryClassName:com.ibm.ws.util.ResRefJndiLookupObjectFactory
Reference Factory Class Location URLs: <null>
Reference Class Name: java.lang.Object
Type: ResRefJndiLookupInfo
Content com.ibm.ws.util.ResRefJndiLookupInfo@9851c1 ResRefJndiLookupInfo:
Look up Name="jdbc/EJPBOOK";JndiLookupInfo: jndiName="jdbc/EJPBOOK";
providerURL=""; initialContextFactory=""

Exception data follows:
javax.naming.NameNotFoundException: jdbc/EJPBOOK
      at
com.ibm.ws.naming.jndicos.CNContextImpl.doLookup(CNContextImpl.java:1502)
      at
com.ibm.ws.naming.jndicos.CNContextImpl.doLookup(CNContextImpl.java:1456)
...
```

From the console output we can see that a `javax.naming.NameNotFoundException` was raised when the Employee `getDataSource` method attempted to lookup the data source named `java:comp/env/jdbc/EJPBOOK`. That's because we haven't yet created a data source for the server configuration to tell it where the data source is and how to access it.

Recall that we created a reference in the Web deployment descriptor to a `javax.sql.Data-Source` resource called `jdbc/EJPBOOK` that also used `jdbc/EJPBOOK` as the JNDI name. However, we never created the resource in the JNDI server. The next two sections cover the remaining configuration operations.

8.1.2 Configure the Enterprise Application to Deploy the Web Application

Now that the Web application has been deployed, let's look at what has happened. First, refer-ring to Figure 7.8, recall that when you created the Servlet Example Web application, you had to specify an enterprise application to deploy the Web application to a J2EE Web application. Second, when you ran the Web application on a server, the servlet selection wizard (Figure 8.4) was displayed because there were no defined servers, and, therefore, the Web application has no preference.

Selecting the Web application and invoking *Run on Server* uses the enterprise application specified when the Web application was created and invokes the server selection wizard to create a server instance, or reuse one, and publish the enterprise application to that server. Each of these activities can be done manually, enabling more configuration control.

To edit the enterprise application, expand the project corresponding to the enterprise appli-cation you entered when creating the Web application as shown in Figure 7.8. If you took the default, the enterprise application would be DefaultEAR. Double-click the EAR Deployment Descriptor in the DefaultEAR project (right under the project name), or edit the `applica-tion.xml` file in the META-INF folder. This invokes the Application Deployment Descriptor editor shown in Figure 8.5.

The Overview tab provides an overview of the enterprise application giving its name, description, a list of Web and EJB archive modules that are included in the application, and other details as specified in the J2EE 1.3 specification.

Use the Modules tab to add or remove Web or EJB modules to/from the enterprise applica-tion. An enterprise application can host any number of WAR files, JAR files, and other project

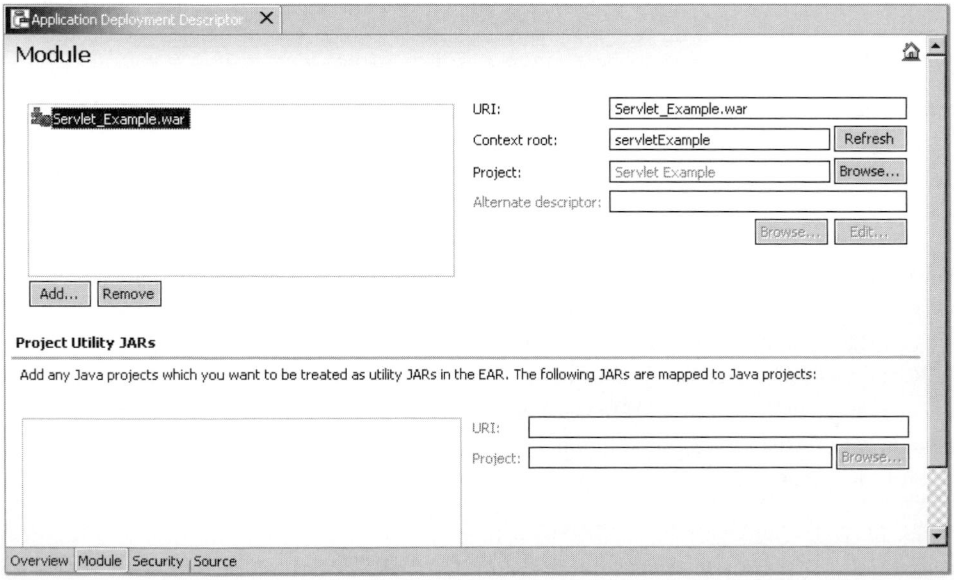

Figure 8.5 Application deployment descriptor, module page.

utility JARs that contain Java classes used by other modules in the enterprise application. Notice that the create Web application wizard shown in Figure 7.8 added the sample servlet application to the DefaultEAR file since we selected that option. You can also add and remove modules from the enterprise application using the buttons at the bottom of the module list.

Each module has a URI to the WAR or JAR file that provide the module implementation, and the context root that specifies the URL prefix used to access resources in that module. The context root must match the value given in the Web properties of the Web application project. The Security tab allows you to define security roles for the enterprise application, and assign particular users or groups to those roles.

The Source tab allows you to edit the contents of the XML `application.xml` document directly, again with full content assist.

8.1.2.1   Configure the WSAD Test Environment and publish the application

Returning to the runtime error we saw when we tried to display the employee list, recall that the problem was that the data source for accessing the database using the `jdbc/EJPBOOK` URL was not defined in the server. We're now ready to fix this problem. First, select the Server Configuration tab to display the Server Configuration view. You can also open the server perspective, but the Web perspective provides everything you need. Server Configuration lists all the configured servers in the servers project. You can create as many server projects as you want, and each server project can contain any number of application servers and server configurations. You can use different application servers to test your application in various ways including WebSphere 4.0 and 5.0 servers running on the localhost machine, a remote server, the TE server built into WSAD, or the Apache Tomcat server. We'll be using the TE because it is the easiest to use during Web application development and testing since the Web application is published in-place. The test environment server accesses the Web application components directly from the project resources instead of having to publish them to a server every time a resource changes.

You can also create a number of server configurations for different testing scenarios, and associate a server configuration with a server before starting it up. To change the server configuration, select the server in the list, right-click, and expand the Switch Configuration submenu to select from the server configurations that are compatible with the selected server.

You can edit the server configuration by double-clicking its entry, or you can edit the server and its current configuration at the same time by double-clicking the server. The only difference is the addition of the Server tab when editing the server. Referring to Figure 8.6, the Server tab shows the server name and a toggle for enabling JavaScript debugging. The rest of the pages are for the current server configuration.

The Configuration tab specifies overall configuration information such as the configuration name, whether the server uses single or multiple class loading policy, and if the administration console and universal test client (UTC) applications are enabled in this configuration. We'll be seeing more about UTC when we test EJBs in see Chapter 20.

The Paths tab specifies the classpath for the server. You shouldn't generally need to add any classpath entries when deploying Web applications as WAR files in an enterprise application

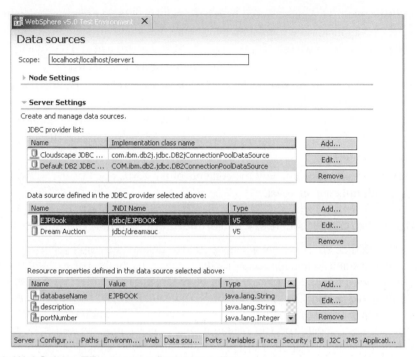

Figure 8.6 WebSphere TE server configuration editor.

since the J2EE deployment descriptors provide the information required by the application server to load classes.

The Environment tab specifies any additional JVM arguments and environment variables required by the Web application server. The Web tab allows you to edit the MIME type to file extension mapping. Put any custom MIME types used by your application here. You can enable URL rewriting and cookies for the Web application server on this page.

The Data source tab is where you configure data sources referenced by your Web application. There are two sets of entries—Node Settings and Server Settings. Node settings apply to all servers running on a particular computer. Server settings are for a particular server running on a node. Note that the TE will only support a single server, so configure the data source in the server settings. The JDBC Provider list shows the JDBC data sources available on the node. These are generally filled in automatically, but you can add, remove, or edit entries in the provider list.

Select the *Default DB2 JDBC Provider* and click *Add* next to the Data source defined in the JDBC provider selected above: list. The Modify Data Source wizard shown in Figure 8.7 is displayed.

Enter a name for the data source, something that distinguishes it from other data sources provided by the same JDBC provider. Be certain to enter the same JNDI name that you used for the `javax.sql.DataSource` resource reference in the Web application. The defaults are proba-

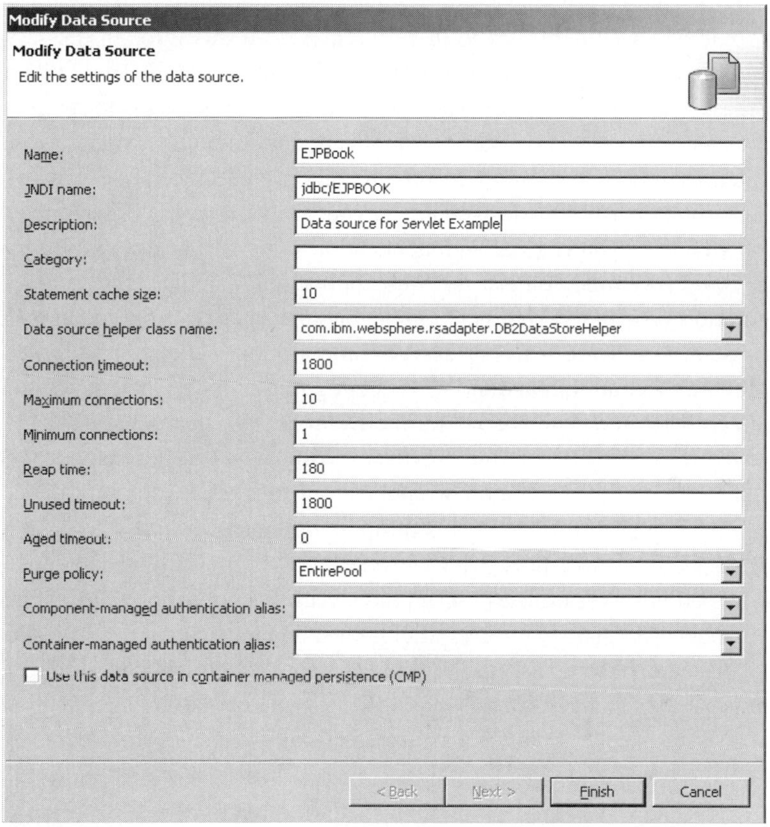

Figure 8.7 Modify data source.

bly fine for the rest of the settings. The values shown in Figure 8.7 are specific to DB2. Other servers require similar information, but the dialog may look different.

Click *Finish* to update the settings for the data source. Now the data source is defined in the server configuration, and when the server starts up, there will be an entry in the JNDI server called jdbc/EJPBOOK that will provide access to the data source resource required by our sample application.

Remember that a server configuration can be used to configure more than one application server. So the configuration information you have provided to configure the TE can be reused to configure the production server.

8.1.3 Start the WTE

Now we're ready to try running the application again. You could just select the Servlet Example Web project or index.html and invoke *Run on Server…*, but let's start the server manually this time to see what's going on.

Before starting the server, make sure the enterprise application that contains your Web application module has been deployed to that server. We did this through the server selection wizard shown in Figure 8.4 when we attempted to run the index.html file from a Web application that was not yet associated with a server. There are a couple of other ways to set the server for an application. You can see what server your Web application is configured to run on by opening the Web application project properties and selecting the server preference page. This will allow you to select a server from the list of those available in your workspace, or allow you to prompt for a server selection whenever you run the Web application. This will bring up the server selection wizard (Figure 8.4) every time you run the Web application. Another approach is to select the Server Configuration view in the Web perspective, or server perspective, and expand the Server Configurations item. You'll see a list of server configurations, one of which we created and edited in the previous section. Expand the server configuration to see the enterprise applications that have been deployed in it. You should see the DefaultEAR enterprise application in the list since we deployed it to this server in the previous section. You can select the server configuration, right-click, and add or delete enterprise applications to/from the configuration.

Next, start the application server that is hosting your enterprise/Web application. From the Web or server perspective, select the Servers view. You'll see a list of the servers available in your workspace as defined in server projects. Select the server that is hosting your application, right-click, and select *Start*. This starts the server after publishing any enterprise applications deployed to that server that need to be republished. Publishing an application will copy necessary files from the application project folders to locations required by the particular Web application server. The WTE copies very little since the application runs directly from the project folders.

You will see a number of messages in the Console view. This view shows the content of the application server log, standard output, and standard error for the application server. You'll be making more use of the console output when debugging your Web applications. There should be a number of lines similar to those which follow, indicating that the DefaultEAR application and servlet example Web module started successfully. You should also see the last line indicating the server is open for e-business. This indicates the server started successfully and is ready to process requests.

```
[10/30/02 20:24:08:078 EST] 170ab85d ApplicationMg A WSVR0200I: Starting
application: DefaultEAR
[10/30/02 20:24:08:218 EST] 170ab85d WebContainer A SRVE0169I: Loading Web
Module: servletExample.
[10/30/02 20:24:08:448 EST] 170ab85d WebGroup      I SRVE0180I:
[servletExample] [/servletExample] [Servlet.LOG]: JSP 1.2 Processor: init
[10/30/02 20:24:08:949 EST] 170ab85d WebGroup      I SRVE0180I:
[servletExample] [/servletExample] [Servlet.LOG]: SimpleFileServlet: init
[10/30/02 20:24:09:099 EST] 170ab85d WebGroup      I SRVE0180I:
[servletExample] [/servletExample] [Servlet.LOG]: InvokerServlet: init
[10/30/02 20:24:09:149 EST] 170ab85d ApplicationMg A WSVR0221I: Application
started: DefaultEAR
[10/30/02 20:24:13:045 EST] 170ab85d HttpTransport A SRVE0171I: Transport
http is listening on port 9,080.
```

```
[10/30/02 20:24:15:609 EST] 170ab85d HttpTransport A SRVE0171I: Transport
https is listening on port 9,443.
[10/30/02 20:24:15:859 EST] 170ab85d JMXSoapAdapte A ADMC0013I: SOAP
connector available at port 8880
[10/30/02 20:24:16:139 EST] 170ab85d RMIConnectorC A ADMC0026I: RMI Connector
available at port 2809
[10/30/02 20:24:16:279 EST] 170ab85d WsServer    A WSVR0001I: Server server1
open for e-business
```

If necessary, go back to the Web perspective, select index.html in the Web Content folder of the Servlet Example, right-click, and select Run on Server…, or open your favorite Web browser and enter and browse *http://localhost:9080/servletExample/index.html*. The port specified in the URL is the one for the application server on the Ports page of the server configuration editor as shown in Figure 8.6. Click the Browse Employees link and you should see an empty list of employees. Test the application by creating, displaying, and updating some employees.

8.1.4   Edit HMTL and Servlet Code and Retest

This is where WSAD really shines. You can change almost anything in your project, including servlet code, go back to the Web browser, refresh, and immediately see the effect of your changes. Well, it's almost that easy. More accurately, what you have to do to effect a change depends on what kind of resource you change, and the Web application server used to run the application.

We'll look at the more common scenarios used during development here. If you encounter a different server configuration, consult the server documentation for details. When in doubt, you can always restart the server. Here are the general rules for using the WTE:

1. If you change *any* resource in the Web application you can see the changes by simply refreshing the view in the browser.

2. If you change *any* resource in the enterprise application project hosting your Web application, you must restart the EAR project. Select the EAR project in the J2EE Navigator view, right-click, and select Restart Project.

3. If you change *anything* in the server configuration, you must restart the server.

For further details, including special cases for using Tomcat to test Web applications, see the WSAD Help at *Web developer information > Application testing and publishing > Concepts > When the test server requires restarting*.

8.1.5   Debug a Servlet

Debugging distributed applications was once difficult because the application code ran inside a Web application server in a different operating system process, and often on a different machine. Inserting print statements and examining server logs was often the best you could do. WSAD and the WTE make Web application debugging a breeze. You can set a breakpoint anywhere in your servlet code or Java code used by your servlets, and debug the server-side of your application as easily as a simple Java main program. In this section, we'll provide an overview of the WSAD debugger and show you how to debug the Sample Servlet Web application.

To debug a Web application first start the application server in debug mode. If the server isn't running, select the index.html file in the Web Contents folder of the Servlet Example, right-click, and select *Debug on server…*. This will start the Web application server in debug mode and launch a Web browser on the selected resource. If the server is running, stop and restart it in debug mode. From the Web, J2EE, or server perspective, select the server's view; select the server in the list that is hosting your Web application, right-click, and select *Stop*. After the server stops, right-click again and select *Debug*, which starts the server in debug mode, which means the JVM is listening for debug commands.

It also opens the Debug perspective. Now switch back to the Web perspective, select the index.html file in the Web Content folder of the servlet example, and select *Run on Server* or *Debug on Server*. Both do the same thing once the server is running in debug mode.

The index.html file comes up as usual. It isn't a dynamic page, so there's nothing to debug. Now click the Browse Employees link. Initially, the application server is in step-by-step mode, meaning you'll see the dialog in Figure 8.8 displayed every time a servlet is invoked. This dialog indicates which servlet and servlet method are being invoked, and on what server. You can choose to step into the servlet method, skip debugging this servlet, or disable step-by-step mode.

You can use step-by-step mode for debugging servlet code, but if your application has a lot of servlets, and most of them work properly, this can be tedious. You might instead prefer to disable step-by-step mode and set a breakpoint in the specific servlet you're trying to debug. Note that if you disable step-by-step mode, the servlet remains suspended at the first line of code in the servlet, and the debug perspective won't be displayed when you press *OK* in the Step-by-Step Debug dialog shown in Figure 8.8. To proceed, switch to the debug perspective and press *Resume*.

So let's try setting a specific breakpoint.

Open the BrowseEmployees servlet (com.wsbook.servletexample/BrowseEmployees.java in the Java Source folder), and double-click in the vertical ruler (left margin) at the left of the line of code where an iterator is accessed over all the employees in the database. This puts a break-

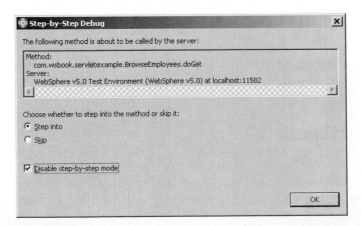

Figure 8.8 Step-by-step debug.

point marker at that point in the code as shown by the blue dot in the vertical ruler of Figure 8.9. You've already seen such markers indicating errors in Java code or broken links in the HTML code. Other kinds of markers can appear in this margin, each with its own icon. Markers can show the location of information, warnings, or errors in the Tasks view, breakpoints as shown here, or arbitrary bookmarks you might create for your own purposes. For example, right-click in the left margin to set a bookmark. Use the Bookmarks view to navigate to your bookmarks.

Now go back and run the index.html file on the server again, and click its Browse Employees link. This time the Workbench switches to the debugger perspectives shown in Figure 8.10 and pauses execution at the line containing the breakpoint. In the figure, we've pressed single step a couple of times so there's an interesting variable to look at.

Now let's take a closer look at the views in the debug perspective. The Debug view shows a list of the concurrent threads in the WTE server application with the thread suspended at the breakpoint expanded to show the stack trace. Click on any entry in the stack trace to display the application source code at that point, and to display the variables that are available at that point in the program. If the source is not available, you'll see the Class File Editor which shows the public interfaces available in the class, and any other information available in the Java .class file, but you won't be able to see any local variables if the class file was not compiled with debug attributes. There are a number of things you can do while the thread is suspended such as setting or clearing breakpoints, examining variables, or evaluating expressions. We'll look at each of these as we examine the other views in the debug perspective. First, let's explore how to step through the code in order to get to the point where we'd like to explore the state of the code in more detail.

```java
public void doGet(HttpServletRequest req, HttpServletResponse resp)
    throws ServletException, IOException {

    PrintWriter out = resp.getWriter();
    out.println("<HTML>");
    out.println("<BODY>");
    out.println("<h3 align=\"center\">All Employees</h3>");
    out.println(
        "<TABLE align=\"center\" BORDER=\"yes\" CELLSPACING=2 CELLPAD
    out.println("<TR>");
    out.println("<TD><center><b>Id</b></center></TD>");
    out.println("<TD><center><b>Name</b></center></TD>");
    out.println("<TD width=\"40\"><center><b>Age</b></center></TD>");
    out.println("</TR>");
    try {
        Iterator employees = Employee.findAll().iterator();
        while (employees.hasNext()) {
            Employee employee = (Employee) employees.next();
            out.println("<TR>");
            out.println(
                "<TD><A HREF=\"EmployeeDetails?id="
                + employee.getId()
                + "\" target=\"detail\">"
                + employee.getId()
                + "</A></TD>");
            out.println("<TD>" + employee.getName() + "</TD>");
            out.println("<TD width=\"40\">" + employee.getAge() + "</
            out.println("</TR>");
```

Figure 8.9 Setting a breakpoint.

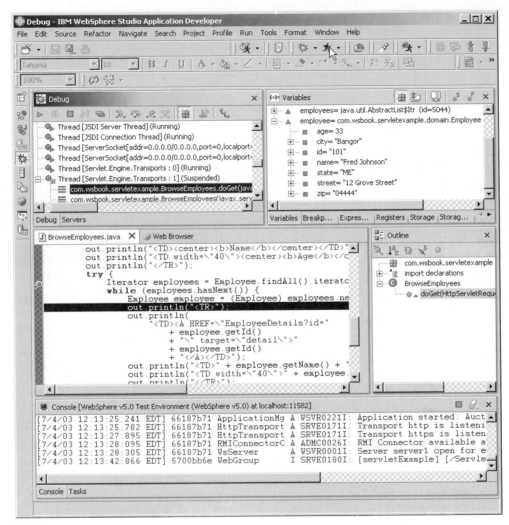

Figure 8.10 Debug perspective.

There are a number of ways you can control execution of a program being debugged:

- Step into a function and pause at the first line of code in the function (F5)
- Single step over a line at a time (F6)
- Run to return, or the first return statement encountered in the current function (F7)
- Resume execution (F8)
- Run to the line containing the cursor (assuming it's after the current line)

To invoke these operations you can use the buttons in the Debug view title bar, invoke menu items in the *Run* menu, or use the function keys as shown in the previous list. The function keys

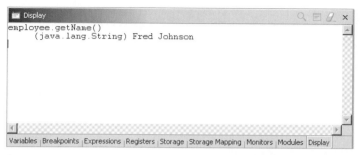

Figure 8.11 Debug views.

are generally the easiest once you get used to using them. Try pressing F6 a couple of times until you're suspended at the first `println` statement as shown in Figure 8.10. You're now at a point where you can explore some of the other views in the debug perspective as shown in Figure 8.11.

One of the most useful debug views is the Variables view shown in Figure 8.11. It shows the variables visible at the point where the program is suspended. You can see the values of fields of the object upon which the method is invoked by expanding the *this* entry. Other variables in the list are the method parameters and local variables. Expand any tree entry to see the names and values of its member variables. When variables change from one single step to another, their color changes to red so you can easily see what changed.

You can simplify the variable names in the list by toggling the *Show Qualified Names* button in the Variables view title bar. This toggles displaying fully qualified names for Java classes. Turning this off shortens the names, but doesn't tell you what package the classes are in, and may show ambiguous names if different classes have the same name in different packages. You can also control the display of type names for field names by pressing *Show Type Names*.

You can toggle displaying details of the selected field by toggling Select Detail Pane. Turning on the detail pane shows the result of invoking the `toString` method on the selected variable in the bottom pane of the variables page.

The Breakpoints page lists the breakpoints set in the running application. You can select a breakpoint and disable or remove it from the list. Disabling a breakpoint leaves it in the list, but the application will not suspend when reaching it. Disable breakpoints that you want to skip for the moment, but may want to reuse later in the debug session.

You can also set a count to specify that a breakpoint must be reached a certain number of times before suspending execution. This is useful when attempting to suspend the application in a loop after a certain number of iterations.

It is also possible to set breakpoints when any Java exception is thrown.

Often when debugging an application, stepping over a statement will result in an exception being raised in some nested function call. You can set a breakpoint on the exception to suspend where the exception occurred rather than in handlers at other locations in the application. Figure 8.12 shows additional properties on a breakpoint that you can set.

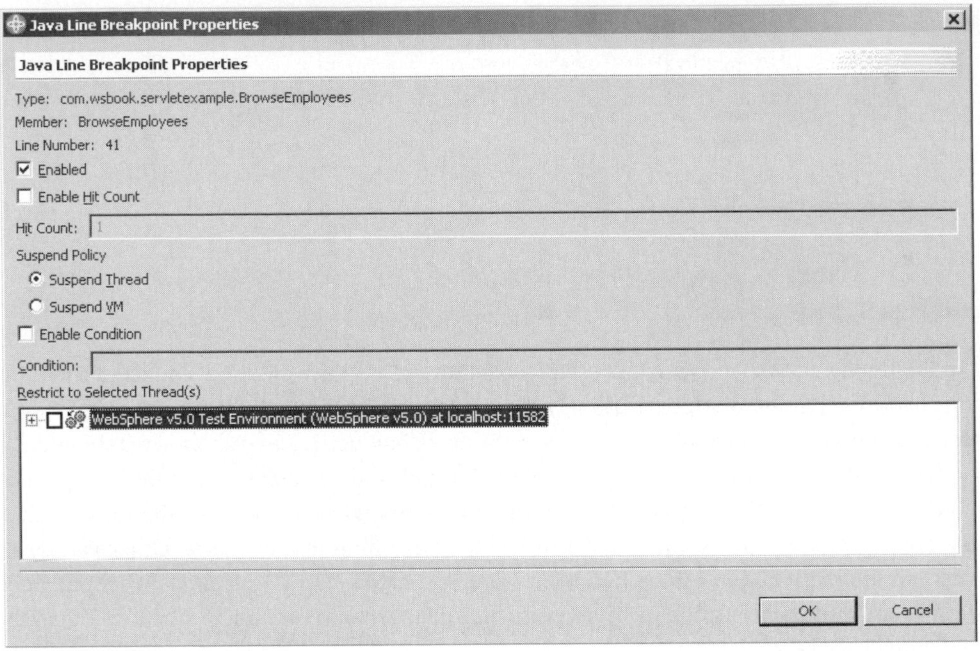

Figure 8.12 Debug properties.

We've already discussed enabling breakpoints and hit count. It is also possible to specify the Suspend Policy. You can suspend either a particular Java thread, or the entire JVM. Generally, you'll only want to suspend a particular thread. However, sometimes when debugging multithreaded applications, it is helpful to be able to suspend all threads. You can specify which threads should have breakpoints enabled by selecting the threads in the Restrict to Selected Thread(s) tree view.

Another very powerful feature is the ability to enable conditions on a breakpoint. The application then stops at the breakpoint if the condition is true when the statement executes in the application. The debugger evaluates the expression in the context at the location of the breakpoint and can reference the same fields that would be visible in the Variables view at that breakpoint.

The Expressions view is an inspector on expressions that you evaluate in the current debug context. You can select any expression in the Source view, right-click, and select *Inspect*. The expression is evaluated and the result will be shown in the Expressions view. You can also use the Display view as a scrapbook for entering and evaluating other expressions including whole fragments of Java code.

Figure 8.11 shows the result of accessing the employee name when the debugger is suspended as shown in Figure 8.10. This should be the first employee in the database. To evaluate an expression in the Display view, type the expression, select it, right-click, and select Display (or use CONTROL+D) to display a string representation of the result (using `toString`), or select Inspect (or use CONTROL+U) to inspect the result in the Expressions view. The variables that are available for use in the expression are the same ones that are visible at the selected point in the debug stack.

The other views in the debug perspective, Registers, Storage, Storage Mapping, Monitors, and Modules are for debugging complied languages such as C++ so we won't cover them further here.

8.2 Summary

In this chapter, you learned how to deploy a simple Web application to the WSAD TE, configure the server, and run the application. You also learned how to debug Web applications using the WSAD debugger. Although the sample application was very simple, other J2EE applications are deployed and debugged using similar techniques.

CHAPTER 9

Managing Session State

Using servlets in complex applications introduces interesting challenges to the developer. Possibly the biggest challenge is to maintain the application state for users as they make multiple trips into your application. We call the information collected and maintained during these trips *session data*. Session data is temporary and only for use across a set of linked pages; transaction data is placed in permanent storage.

Session data is often converted into transaction data within the application. For instance, when a user chooses to save profile information, or checks out a shopping cart, the temporary session data becomes permanent. Correctly maintaining this type of information creates challenges and is a constant problem in servlet- and JSP-based applications. Figure 9.1 shows where the resolution to this problem fits in our architectural road map.

The first challenge comes from the HTTP protocol used for communication between the Web browser and the Web server. As discussed in Chapter 6, this protocol is based upon a request/response model and is stateless. That is, once a request is submitted from the client browser to a Web server, and the server acts upon the request and sends a response back to the browser, the server forgets about the request and the requestor. There is no intrinsic method in the protocol for holding state information about the transaction itself. After a transaction is complete, data not explicitly stored during the interaction is lost.

The second part to this problem comes from the way servlets live in the application server. On a particular application server, a single instance of each servlet class handles all GET and POST requests for its particular URL. In this environment, each HTTP request is handled on a unique thread running the `service()` method of that instance. Since each servlet instance is a shared resource, you can't effectively store the client session data in the instance variables of the servlet itself because data stored by one thread could be overwritten by another. Remember that a servlet is an object shared by multiple simultaneous threads.

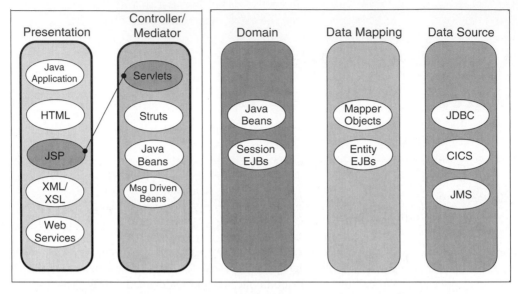

Figure 9.1 Architectural road map position of session management.

You could attempt to use synchronization and an in-memory hash table to manage instance data for each user, but only at a significant cost in effort and performance. The implication to the developer in this case is that there should be no maintenance of state information in the servlet itself, or, more directly, no instance variables—only local variables and parameters!

If instance variables are used there is no guarantee that the state will be reliable at any given time. In this chapter, we will explore the most common approaches to storing session data, and look at the configuration options that are available within WAS.

9.1   Some Client-Side Session Approaches

Before we begin to look at the specific support for session management that WebSphere and the servlet API provide, we will need to review some of the existing solutions that Web sites use to convey and maintain session information. As we will see later, this discussion is germane to understanding both how WebSphere's session management works, and in understanding alternatives to the WebSphere solution.

9.1.1   Using Cookies to Maintain State

The most common way to store session information in the CGI world is through the use of a cookie. Cookies can be used to send information gathered on the server to the client for storage. The server accomplishes this by attaching information to the HTTP response headers. The browser will then automatically return the cookie on the next request by placing the information in the request header sent to the server. The browser maintains a collection of cookies scoped by domain and path. In other words, a browser will only return cookies to those servers within the domain that created it.

It is important to use cookies appropriately. It is not a good idea to store passwords, credit card numbers, date of birth, etc. in cookies since this information is sent back and forth to the browser on every request and thus may be sniffed or (even worse) altered or spoofed.

This information, if provided by a user, is best kept on the server. As a result of abuse of customer privacy by Web sites using cookies inappropriately, many users now routinely configure their browsers to disallow any cookies. Thus, you should be careful about relying on cookies as your only session state storage mechanism.

9.1.2 Hidden Fields

Another option for maintaining session data is through the use of hidden fields. This very simple option involves the use of standard HTML-hidden fields. This solution allows for session sharing between servlets that are linked through the use of HTML forms. To use this, each servlet response that results in an HTML form output writes additional input fields into the form. These additional fields should be defined with the `type="hidden"` parameter. The net result is that the user will not see the field as a visible item on the form, but the resulting GET or POST will send the value along as a request parameter. The servlet that processes the form information can then obtain the session data through the use of the passed parameters.

A major drawback of hidden fields is that as the number of hidden fields grows, the size of the page increases, thus increasing download times. Also, hidden fields suffer from the same security issues as cookies, since sensitive data could be passed back and forth in the clear.

9.1.3 URL Parameters

Similar to the idea of hidden fields, information can also be transmitted from the browser to the server in the HTTP header by placing this information in parameters that are passed in as part of the URL that invokes a CGI or servlet. For instance, if we wanted to pass a user name as part of a URL request, the URL passed to a servlet could look like the following:

```
http://myhost/servlet/TestServlet?userid="Bob Smith"
```

If this URL were sent from the browser, the target servlet (`TestServlet`) could obtain the HTTP parameter named `userid` by using the `HttpRequest.getParameter(name)` method. While URL parameters are useful for passing small pieces of information, they are not appropriate for passing larger sets, since there is a limit to the size of the URL.

9.2 Servlets and Session State

A framework for saving session state is provided in the Java servlet API. The API provides an interface designed specifically for the purpose of maintaining state information in our servlet-based applications. This interface is the `javax.servlet.http.HttpSession`.

The HttpSession interface provides a way to store and manipulate state information that is available to all servlets of the Web application while the session remains valid. In practice, one session is maintained for each user that is interacting with the Web application. The application chooses to establish this session at a point where some state information needs to be maintained, typically very early on in the process, such as at login or authentication time.

As each session is created it is assigned a unique identifier. This identifier is then associated with the user and becomes the key that can be used to locate the appropriate session for subsequent requests. Later, we will discuss the different configurations by which the session identifier can be maintained. After the session is established, it will remain valid until it expires from inactivity, the browser is closed, or is invalidated programmatically. The period of inactivity can be configured through the WAS administrative console or set programmatically.

The `HttpSession` interface provides the basic mechanisms for storing and retrieving application state information. The first thing that needs to be done is to obtain an instance of an `HttpSession`. This can be done through the `HttpServletRequest` interface. The interface method that needs to be used here is `HttpSession getSession( boolean )`.

The servlet specification defines a standard cookie (which must be named JSESSIONID) that acts as a unique key to the user's session data. The boolean argument, if true, creates a session if one is not already present for the JSESSIONID associated with the request. Conversely, if the boolean argument is false, a `null` will be returned if there is not a session already established.

When obtaining a session by using `HttpSession getSession( true )`, it is sometimes desirable to know if the `HttpSession` that was returned was a newly created session or was one that had been established by a previous call. This can be done by using the `HttpSession` interface method boolean `isNew()`. This method simply returns a boolean indicating if the session ID was delivered in the current `HttpServletRequest` object.

It may also be desirable to discard a session. The `HttpSession` interface provides the method `invalidate()` for this purpose. This method simply discards the session, and gives the assurance that the next call to `getSession(true)` will yield a session that is new.

The definition of the `HttpSession` interface is very simple and provides a structure that can be used to store state data in key/value pairs. We can place objects in a session instance by using the `setAttribute( String, Object )` method, and retrieve objects by using `getAttribute( String )`. Note that more than one value can be placed in the session object. The HttpSession structure is similar to that of `java.util.Hashtable` in that any number of elements can be stored by unique identifier and value pairs.

One thing you should note is that (even though the specification doesn't require it) the objects that you place in an `HttpSession` attribute should all implement the `java.io.Serializable` interface. As you will see later in our discussion of WAS's session scalability features, these objects will usually be persisted in a database or transmitted across a network connection. Thus if the object placed in the session attribute is not serializable, it will not be available for access by other servers.

Also, be careful of the size of the objects you place in the session attributes. Remember that there is a finite amount of heap space available to a JVM. If your objects are very large (a large fraction of a megabyte or more) you have placed an upper limit on the number of users that a single server can support. As we will see later, even before this limit is reached, you may encounter performance problems related to making this session information available to other servers. Thus, you should probably restrict your session attributes to small objects, or to keys used to fetch larger objects from permanent storage.

In review, the methods of API we have discussed thus far:

IN HTTPREQUEST:

```
public HttpSession getSession( boolean param1 );
```

IN HTTPSESSION:

```
public boolean isNew();

public void invalidate();

public java.lang.Object getAttribute(java.lang.String param1);

public void setAttribute(java.lang.String param1, java.lang.Object
```
param2);

The following example demonstrates the use of some of these methods. We will construct a hypothetical example from our timesheet domain (introduced in Chapter 2). We want to build a set of servlets comprising an EmployeeEditor that will allow a user to change the attributes of an Employee. The user must first enter an employee ID number on an HTML page followed by an HTML page that shows the current values of the Employee's attributes in editable text fields. After editing, the user can submit the new values. The first servlet invoked is DisplayEmployeeValues, the code of doPost()looks like the following:

```
// First servlet will retrieve employee values and place them in

// in the session

public void doPost ( HttpServletRequest request,

                     HttpServletResponse response )

                throws ServletException, IOException {


   String id = request.getParameter ( "id" );

   Employee emp = Employee.getEmployeeFor(id)

   // Create a new session
```

```
HttpSession session = request.getSession( true );

if( session.isNew() == false ){

        session.invalidate();

        session = request.getSession(true);

}

session.setAttribute( "employee", emp );

// send a response back with a JSP page

. . .

}
```

In the previous example you see how to:

- Create a session. The `true` parameter in the `getSession()` method specifies to create a session if one is not found in the request object.
- Check to make sure that the session is new (useful, for instance, if the possibility that a servlet can be used from a shared terminal exists).
- Add an object to the session, using a key/value pair.

Let's suppose now that the user has finished editing the Employee and now wishes to submit his changes. When Submit is pressed, it invokes another servlet, which will process the changes. Here is the code to do this:

```
// Subsequent servlet being called to process changes to the Employee

public void doPost (

    HttpServletRequestrequest,

    HttpServletResponseresponse

    ) throws ServletException, IOException {


    // Look for an existing session

    HttpSession session = request.getSession( false );
```

```
// check to see if session exists, if does not exist handle error

if ( session == null )

    handleError ();

else {

        Employee emp = ( Employee ) session.getAttribute ( "employee" );

        if ( emp != null ) {

        // Retrieve the values from the Http Parameters

        // and set them into the Employee instance.

        // Next update the employee in the database.

        // Finally invalidate the user session

        session.invalidate ();

                }

    }


    // send a response

    . . .

}
```

Here we see how to:

- Retrieve an existing session from the request object. The false parameter in the `getSession ()` method specifies not to create a session if one is not found in the request object. In that case `null` is returned.
- Handle the error if the session does not exist.
- Retrieve an object from the session. The `getAttribute ()` method return type is `java.lang.Object`, so the value must be cast to the correct type before using it.

This example also shows invalidating the session. When you are finished using a session (e.g., no more servlets will need the session) you should send `invalidate()` to the session to release the objects held in it. A session time-out value is set in the WebSphere Administration Console—when the time-out is reached the session will be invalidated and all objects within it will be garbage collected. However, invalidating the session manually is more efficient, because relying on session time-outs will result in objects remaining in memory unnecessarily long.

In addition, the `HttpSession` interface defines methods to remove a particular name/value pair and to obtain all the names of the values stored in the session. These methods are `remove-Attribute( String )`, and `String[] getAttributeNames()` respectively.

9.2.1 HttpSession Binding

Sometimes objects stored in the session may need to be notified when they are stored or removed from the session. This may be to get an opportunity to do some initialization, cleanup, or another function. Objects requiring this function should implement the `HttpSessionBind-ingListener` interface found in the `javax.servlet.http` package. This interface defines the `valueBound()` and `valueUnbound()` methods. These methods, when implemented, will be called when an object of this type is set and removed from the session respectively. Implementing the interface in this way allows for fine-grain control over what happens as a result of storing and removing objects from a session.

A common use for this listener interface is to provide a trigger that can be used to remove information from a temporary database table when the user either logs out of a Web site, or after the session time-out value expires.

9.2.2 How the Session Is Found

So, now that you've seen how the HttpSession API is used, the next question to ask is how does this work? When the `HttpServletRequest.getSession()` method is called, the application server determines which HttpSession instance belongs to a particular user by examining a session identifier, which is stored by default in a special cookie in the user's browser. For sessions to work with the default settings, cookies must be enabled in the browser. Session cookies are not stored persistently and expire when the browser is closed. The `HttpSession` instances themselves are initially held in-memory within an application server's JVM. Only the identifier is stored in the client browser. This is shown Figure 9.2.

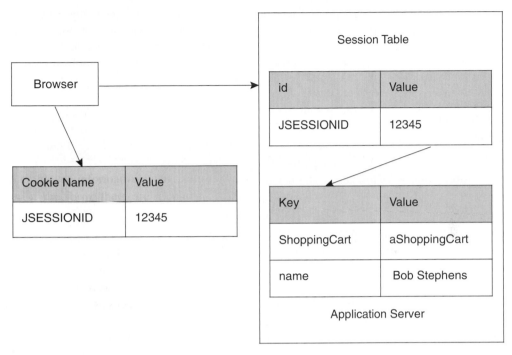

Figure 9.2 HttpSession lookup architecture.

9.3 Choosing the Right Approach

As mentioned earlier, the use of cookies provides the simplest approach for maintaining session identifiers. While it may be the easiest solution, it is not always the most reliable. You cannot always depend on cookies being available. This forces the consideration of alternative methods for session management. In order to truly provide the most flexible solutions possible, you must look at providing multiple mechanisms for the users to obtain unique sessions.

A popular way for achieving this is to combine techniques in order to obtain the most reliable coverage. If you want to provide the most reliable site possible you should use cookies in conjunction with URL rewriting. The good news in this scenario is that as long as cookies are enabled in the client browser, cookies will be the vehicle for transporting the session identifier between the browser and server.

This is good news because this technique is very efficient and easy to implement. The bad news is that the application must be prepared for the case where cookies are not available. That is the place where URL rewriting becomes a useful option.

9.3.1 URL Rewriting

An alternative to using cookies to store the session ID is to use a mechanism called URL encoding or URL rewriting. In order to use URL encoding you need to use the `encodeURL()` or `encodeRedirectURL()` method of the HttpResponse interface. Basically, `encodeURL()` is used to append the unique session ID to the URL in any links that your servlet generates. The `enco-deRedirectURL()` method does the same and is used in conjunction with the `callRedirect()` method. When a user invokes a servlet using this altered URL, the server strips the extra information from the URL and uses it as the session ID to get the session data. The application server must support URL rewriting and you must also enable that option when appropriate. For more information on using the servlet API for URL rewriting, refer to the servlet specification.

There is a perception among some developers that URL rewriting techniques degrade the performance of the Web site across the board. While this may be a valid argument if you are simply comparing it to the use of cookies, it certainly lacks credibility when thinking about the possibility of storing large amounts of data in a back-end data source.

Furthermore, WAS provides some help in this area. However, you must take into account that all URLs that you use in the application that refer to the application must be encoded. This means that some pages that could otherwise be left as HTML pages must instead be made into JSP pages—with a resulting increase in processing requirements.

The implementation of session management in WebSphere allows for both options to be configured. In addition, when cookies are enabled in the browser, all subsequent calls to `enco-deURL( String )` return immediately with no effect. The method itself results in no operation, therefore removing the performance degradation.

As application developers, this gives us the best of both worlds—the ability to plan for the worst-case scenario while not adversely affecting our performance when the best-case scenario is available.

This flexibility comes at a cost. It is quite challenging to add the appropriate `enco-deURL()` methods at every required point in an application. If you miss a single URL, the session is lost, and will not be recovered. Because of this, you need to determine if there is a business need to make the investment for adding URL rewriting to your applications. If the cost of a few lost customers who have disabled cookies is worth it to you, then by all means pursue that option. However, for most cases, making the use of cookies mandatory for your site is an option that is good enough.

Whether you decide to use cookies or URL, rewriting is configured on the session management configuration page of WAS. These settings are also configurable in the server configuration editor of WebSphere Studio.

9.4 Session Persistence

Up to now our discussions of session management have focused on an in-memory storage solution. When sessions are stored in memory, it is very quick and efficient to find an individual HttpSession instance. This mechanism becomes a major complication when we need to scale our application to handle more users and we begin using more than one server running the same Web application. To understand the problems, look at Figure 9.3, which illustrates a common setup for a high-traffic Website of the type we examined in Chapter 4.

In most high-traffic Web sites, the volume of incoming HTTP requests is too great for a single Web server or a single application server to handle. So, a load balancer (either a hardware

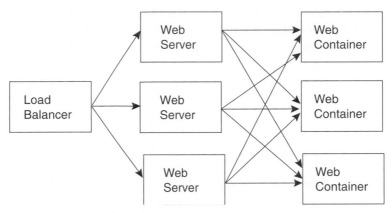

Figure 9.3 Load balancing configuration.

router or a software router, like IBM's Load Balancer) is used to divide the incoming HTTP requests among a number of Web servers. A routing algorithm such as round robin routing or random routing chooses which server will handle each request. This routing among Web servers affects how our application needs to manage session data.

If HttpSessions are stored in memory only on the server where the HttpSession is created, that server must receive *all* future requests from that client. This requirement is called server affinity. This session information will not be available to the servlets running in the other application servers. For some Web sites server affinity may not pose a problem. However, the way in which routers determine server affinity can pose problems in higher volume Web sites.

In many load balancers, a client is assigned to a particular Web server by examining the IP addresses on the incoming request and always assigning requests from a particular client address to a particular server. This is commonly called sticky routing.

The reality of today's Internet is that many ISPs have proxy configurations that make it appear to the router that all packets from that ISP are coming from the same IP address. In the worst case, this means that all packets from a single ISP may end up at the same application server, defeating the purpose of load balancing.

Also, many corporations now assign outgoing IP addresses randomly, so that two requests from the same client are not guaranteed to have the same IP address. In this case, server affinity cannot be guaranteed.

Discounting sticky server affinity at the Web-server level leaves us back where we started with in-memory sessions—how do we guarantee that a user will always return to the same Web container instance for each request? In WAS this is done through a second layer of routing that happens at the Web Server plug-in level.[1] What happens is that WebSphere encodes a unique

---

1.   Remember from Chapter 4 that the plug-in is a piece of code installed in a Web Server to route HTTP requests to
      a set of WAS Web containers.

identifier for the creating Web Container in the session identifier encoded in the JSESSIONID cookie. Whenever a request arrives at any plug-in, it examines the cookie value, then routes the HTTP request back to the Web container identified in the session ID value.

The problem with this solution is that it does not provide for failover. If session data is held only in memory, and that server fails, users being supported by that application server will no longer be able to access their sessions. There are two basic solutions to this: Either you persist the session data in a database that a backup server can obtain it from or you replicate the session data to one or more backup servers over a network as changes are made to the session. That leads us to WAS's mechanisms for session persistence and replication.

9.4.1   WebSphere Persistent Session Management

The majority of the session management issues and techniques described in this section apply to only the WAS ND edition, where more than one server is part of a cluster of servers. This is the situation where server and session affinity come into play. If you are running your applications on a single server, the issue of session management becomes much simpler. In that case, you have two things to consider—how to make sure that the data in the sessions is stored and retrieved in the most efficient manner, and whether you use cookies or URL rewriting to store session ID information.

Once you install WAS ND and start to build clusters of servers to share the load among multiple servers, you also have to start considering your options for session persistence.

In WAS prior to 5.0, there was only one option to persist and share session information; that is, to use a back-end data store, such as a DB2 database, to store and share session data. This approach is still available in 5.0 of the server, although new configuration options have been added to database persisted sessions to make them more efficient, depending on a variety of running environments.

In addition to the database session persistence approach, a memory-to-memory (M2M) replication architecture is offered. The M2M approach does not require the additional expense and headache of maintaining a session database, and eliminates the single point of failure that a session database would introduce.

Let's look at these two different ways to handle session persistence and how to configure the options for each method.

9.4.1.1   Database session persistence

Storing session data in WAS 5.0 is implemented in a way very similar to how it was done in WAS 3.5 and 4.0.

To start using database session persistence, you first must designate a database for storing the sessions. This should be a new database used only for this purpose. If you are using IBM DB2, it is very easy to create a new database—

Open a DB2 Command Window.
Start > Programs > IBM DB2 > Command Window

At the DB2 Command Window enter:

```
DB2 create database SESSDB
```

Or any other name you like.

After the database is created close the window.

A database created with default values will perform well, but if large objects are placed in the session regularly you may want to increase the row size parameter from 4 KB to 32 KB.

Note that for the following steps we assume some level of familiarity with the WAS 5.0 administrative console. You also need WAS ND to be able to make these configuration choices on your machine.

After the database is created you will need to either define a new JDBC provider or use an existing one and create a data source under it. The data source will point to the database that holds your session data, in the case of this example, SESSDB.

Once the database and the data source are defined you can proceed to associate the data source with the session management settings.

Note the link trail at the top of Figure 9.4 that shows you how to get the database settings configuration page. As you can see, you enter the JNDI name of the data source you just created. You also provide a user ID and password for the application server to use when connecting to the database.

Application Servers > **WLM_Server1** > **Web Container** > **Session Management** > **Distributed Environment Settings** >
Database Settings

Database Settings description [i]

Configuration		
General Properties		
Datasource JNDI name:	* jdbc/Sessions	[i] Specifies the JNDI name of the data source from which the Session Manager will obtain database connections.
User ID:	db2admin	[i] The user ID for database access.
Password:	••••••••	[i] The password for database access.
DB2 row size:	ROW_SIZE_4KB ▼	[i] The tablespace page size configured for the sessions table, if using a DB2 database. Possible values are 4, 8, 16, and 32 kilobytes (K). The default row size is 4K.
Table space name:	SESSIONS	[i] Tablespace to be used for the sessions table.
Multi row schema:	☐ Use Multi row schema	[i] Whether to place each instance of application data in a separate row in the database.
Apply OK Reset Cancel		

Figure 9.4 Setting the distributed environment settings for sessions.

This page is also where you can adjust the DB row size. You might want to go to a larger row size if you expect the sessions to contain large amounts of data.

There are two other settings on this page. Table space name lets you specify the name of the table to be used for the session data. Multirow schema is discussed in the next section.

Single vs multirow schema   By default, session management uses a single row schema to store session data in the database. Using the single row schema means that all the data for each session is stored in one row of the database. This has benefits because all the data for the session can be read or written with a single access to the database, which translates into a bit of a performance advantage. It also saves space on the database. The major drawback is the amount of data that can be stored per session—a maximum of 2 MB.

Switching to a multirow schema, as the name implies, means that session data can occupy more than one row per user. Each row can have a maximum capacity of 2MB. Session size is limited only by the total capacity of the system hosting the database. Of course the larger the amount of data, the bigger the performance hit on the overall system and application. It is good practice to limit the amount of data stored in sessions to a reasonable size (on the order of a few tens of kilobytes at the most). If the amount of session data is generally small it is better to stick to the single data schema.

9.4.1.2   Memory-to-memory session replication

We just covered how to use a relational database to share session information between cluster members. Another method to achieve the same goal is the use of M2M session replication which does not involve a session data database.

Instead of using a database, M2M replication (Figure 9.5) involves two or more WASs in the same cluster. You can think of this type of replication as a buddy system. Session affinity ensures that once a session has been created, subsequent requests will be routed to the same server. When the HTTP plug-in routes a request to the server that created the session and that server is not available, the plug-in has information, which identifies the session originator's buddy(ies) and reroutes the request to the next available buddy.

The buddies contain replicas of the sessions created on the original server. Using this buddy system, another server in the cluster can service a request destined to the originator of the session if it is not available.

Which servers back each other up is configured through the administrative console. In clusters where there are not a large number of servers involved, the default configuration where every server backs every other server works well. This method of replication is called N-way peer-to-peer. As you can imagine, in clusters with a large number of servers the overhead of every server backing up every other server's sessions can become very expensive, both in the number of replication operations and the amount of memory required to store session data.

Internally, the replication of sessions is handled by a messaging system similar to JMS. M2M session data is stored within the application server's JVM.

Application Servers > WLM_Server1 > Web Container > Session Management > Distributed Environment Settings >

Internal Messaging

Configuring Memory to Memory session replication. ⓘ

Configuration

General Properties

Replication :	⦿ Select replicator from the following domain	ⓘ Select a replicator to be used for Memory to Memory replication.
	MyCluster ▾	
	Replicators: WLM_Server1 ▾	
	Listen to partition IDs : 1,2,3,4,5,6,7,8,9,10	
	○ Select replicator from another domain	
	IP Address:	
	Port :	
	Listen to partition IDs :	
Runtime mode :	Both client and server ▾	ⓘ Select the mode in which this server has to run: Both, Client and Server, Client Only, Server Only, or Not Shared. The mode implies whether data is only sent (client), only received (server), or both. The default is both.

Apply	OK	Reset	Cancel

Figure 9.5 Setting memory-to-memory replication for sessions.

To reduce overhead in large clusters the session management facility has the ability to partition the servers into groups. The default number of partitions is 10, but the number can be changed. Each server is configured to listen to one or more partitions, reducing the number of overall replications. Servers listening on the same partitions back each other up.

The runtime mode should be set to both client and server, for all variations of the N-way peer-to-peer configurations. If you have determined that neither N-way peer-to-peer nor single replica configurations are appropriate, you can configure a client/server environment for session persistence. In this configuration a single, or multiple, machine(s) are configured so that their sole mission is to be session replication servers. The other machines in the server cluster are configured as client only. If session failover is an absolute requirement you should configure more than one machine in the replication domain as server only.

Other values concerning the replication domain are shown in Figure 9.6.

Environment > Internal Replication Domain

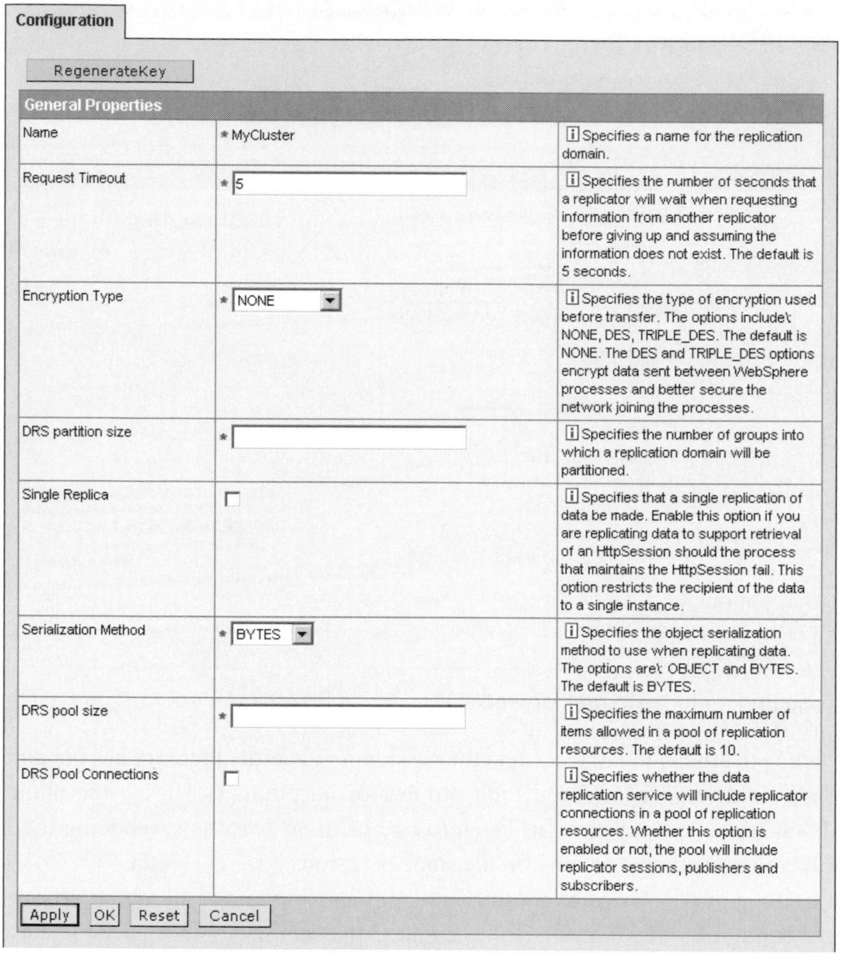

Configuration		
RegenerateKey		
General Properties		
Name	* MyCluster	ⓘ Specifies a name for the replication domain.
Request Timeout	* 5	ⓘ Specifies the number of seconds that a replicator will wait when requesting information from another replicator before giving up and assuming the information does not exist. The default is 5 seconds.
Encryption Type	* NONE ▼	ⓘ Specifies the type of encryption used before transfer. The options include\: NONE, DES, TRIPLE_DES. The default is NONE. The DES and TRIPLE_DES options encrypt data sent between WebSphere processes and better secure the network joining the processes.
DRS partition size	*	ⓘ Specifies the number of groups into which a replication domain will be partitioned.
Single Replica	☐	ⓘ Specifies that a single replication of data be made. Enable this option if you are replicating data to support retrieval of an HttpSession should the process that maintains the HttpSession fail. This option restricts the recipient of the data to a single instance.
Serialization Method	* BYTES ▼	ⓘ Specifies the object serialization method to use when replicating data. The options are\: OBJECT and BYTES. The default is BYTES.
DRS pool size	*	ⓘ Specifies the maximum number of items allowed in a pool of replication resources. The default is 10.
DRS Pool Connections	☐	ⓘ Specifies whether the data replication service will include replicator connections in a pool of replication resources. Whether this option is enabled or not, the pool will include replicator sessions, publishers and subscribers.
Apply OK Reset Cancel		

Figure 9.6 Internal replicator setting.

There are two options on this page that merit special attention:

- The DRS partition size entry defines the number of partitions (set to 10 by default) in the replication domain. This number can be changed depending on the size of the cluster.
- Selecting the single replica check box creates a special case of the N-way peer-to-peer configuration, where only one other server is configured as the buddy for each server. This greatly reduces the number of replication cycles and memory usage, and can increase performance significantly. One disadvantage is that if both the main server and the single buddy are down, accessing the session data will fail.

9.4.2 Comparing Database Persistence to M2M Replication

As we noted earlier, managing M2M session replication can be easier than WAS 5.0 session persistence to a database because M2M doesn't require a database.

Also note that the M2M solution eliminates a single point of failure, without any configuration changes, whereas the database session persistence solution typically entails more expense and complexity beyond installing a database. Also, in many customer sites, different teams manage the application servers and the database servers, making coordination difficult.

On the other hand, what becomes a factor with M2M is the fact that memory utilization increases as the session data that would otherwise be in a database is now spread across the application server JVM heaps. Also, M2M replication is not recommended across geographically distributed server farms because the communication required to synchronize the session caches requires a high-speed LAN connection.

9.4.3 Controlling When Session Data Is Persisted

Whether you use the database or the M2M replication scheme in your server cluster, other factors can affect the performance and reliability of storing session data.

The point when the session data is stored plays an important role. In WAS there are several session update options.

You can define when a session is persisted, what information is persisted, and when to clean up old session data which is no longer in use.

All of these tuning parameters can be updated from the `Distributed Environment -> Tuning Parameters` page (Figure 9.7).

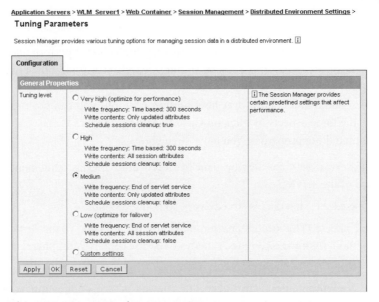

Figure 9.7 Session management tuning parameters.

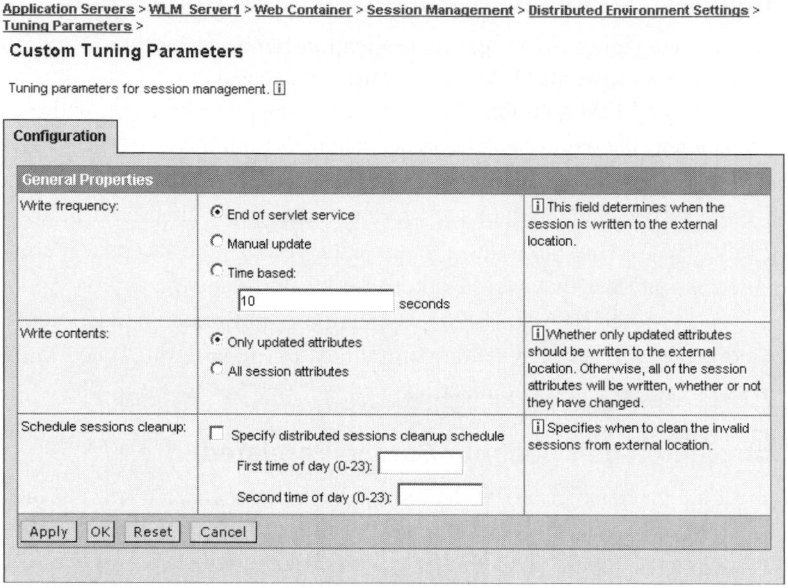

Application Servers > WLM_Server1 > Web Container > Session Management > Distributed Environment Settings > Tuning Parameters >

Custom Tuning Parameters

Tuning parameters for session management. [i]

Configuration

General Properties		
Write frequency:	⦿ End of servlet service ○ Manual update ○ Time based: `10` seconds	[i] This field determines when the session is written to the external location.
Write contents:	⦿ Only updated attributes ○ All session attributes	[i] Whether only updated attributes should be written to the external location. Otherwise, all of the session attributes will be written, whether or not they have changed.
Schedule sessions cleanup:	☐ Specify distributed sessions cleanup schedule First time of day (0-23): Second time of day (0-23):	[i] Specifies when to clean the invalid sessions from external location.

Apply   OK   Reset   Cancel

Figure 9.8 Custom session persistence tuning parameters.

There are four preconfigured settings and each determines:

- **Write frequency**—how often session data is persisted
- **Write contents**—whether all data in the session is written or only changed elements
- **Session cleanup**—whether to schedule removal of invalid session data

These preconfigured settings are rated from very high to low performance. Low performance is not necessarily a bad thing; these settings represent a trade-off between speed and failover protection.

If you need additional control over how session is stored you can customize each of the components for the three aspects by clicking Custom settings (Figure 9.8).

Let's examine these properties. You have three choices:

1. End of servlet service. Session data is stored after the last statement in the service method of the servlet.

2. Time based. Session data is stored every so many seconds.

3. Manual update. This occurs programmatically by the code in the servlet explicitly by calling the `IBMSession.sync()` method. IBMSession is WebSphere's implementation of the HttpSession interface.

The first two mechanisms are under the control of the application server. The third depends on how the servlet is coded.

The reason why the time when the session data is made persistent is important has to do with the transaction that is started when the session is first obtained from the request object. The transaction is not committed until the criterion, specified in the write frequency parameter, is met. If a database is involved, the row containing the session data is locked until the transaction ends. In general, the transaction should be committed as soon as the session has been updated and no more updates are forthcoming.

Using manual update could be the most reliable way of committing the transaction. The developer of the servlet knows when the session data has been updated, in this case the `IBMSession.sync()` method is called and the transaction is committed. However, this puts additional requirements on the developer.

Committing the transaction at the end of the service method is automatic and requires no effort. This requires WAS to perform a database update at the end of every service method—a substantial overhead.

Time-based updates have a different set of trade-offs. Performance tests have shown that writing session data at a 10-second interval provides very good performance with good session reliability. One thing to consider, when selecting the time interval, is the amount of data to be written on every cycle. If the amount of data is large, a short interval can degrade performance considerably. The major drawback of time-based updates is that when a server goes down, all updates to all sessions since the last interval update will be lost. So, if you set the interval too long, you have the possibility of lost data. If the interval is set very short you have the same overhead issues encountered with end of service writes.

9.4.4 Session Management Levels

What is the scope of these settings? It would appear at first glance that applying these choices at the server level is the right choice. That would be true if all the applications running on a particular server shared the same requirements. However, setting the session management choices at the server level has the disadvantage that if you have multiple servers, in a cluster environment, you must repeat the administrative tasks to set all the servers in the cluster with the same values.

It is better to tune session management criteria at the application level. That way, regardless of which server in the cluster the application runs on, the session will be managed the same way, without having to configure each server separately. In fact WAS gives you the flexibility to configure session management parameters at the Web module level for each enterprise application.

To configure session management at the Web module level in an enterprise application level select *Applications > AppName > Web Module > WarFileName > Session Management*.

To configure session management at the server level select *Servers > Application Servers > ServerName > Web Container > Session management*.

9.5 Summary

In this chapter we have examined the basics of servlet session management—we've compared traditional approaches from the CGI world, and seen how WAS implements the HttpSession interface.

We covered the two approaches for persisting session data to a database and memory to memory. We also covered some of the performance implications of the session management configuration options.

This should prepare you to understand some of the more challenging problems that face developers in building applications that must scale across multiple-node and multiple-JVM configurations in WebSphere.

JavaServer Pages Concepts

Most of the content presented to the user as part of a Web application is HTML. These Web pages are easily created and managed using HTML page editors which allow the developer to concentrate on the presentation and content through the use of a WYSIWYG user interface. In previous chapters, we have concentrated on the mechanics of the implementation of server-side logic using servlets. In one example, servlets directly delivered HTML content to the HTTP output stream with string literals in Java. While this gets the job done, few would consider this a best practice.

As an alternative to creating all output on the servlet, one could use the `RequestDispatcher` object, available from the `ServletRequest`, to *include* static HTML from files. This frees the servlet developer from having to deal too much with HTML directly—but fails to allow a page designer to be able to see a complete page's layout at design time because the page must be maintained and managed as smaller page segments rather than as a complete document. A second disadvantage is mixing both controller logic and presentation within the servlet. It is best to keep the presentation (view) separate from the controller logic (model). This way the view can be created and maintained by an individual or team focused only on the presentational concerns of the site or application.

A better solution exists in the form of JSPs. A JSP is a file that contains extended HTML like tags that allow embedding dynamic content (e.g., Java code and special server-side HTML tags) along with standard HTML. In this way, we can develop the presentation of information using any standard HTML editor (like Microsoft FrontPage or the HTML editor that is included in IBM WebSphere Studio). Dynamic content is obtained by the model layer of the application and placed in JavaBeans which are accessible by the JSP in the view layer. This approach not only allows the flexibility to more cleanly separate the back-end generation of dynamic content from the presentation in HTML, but also permits the two development roles, writing HTML and

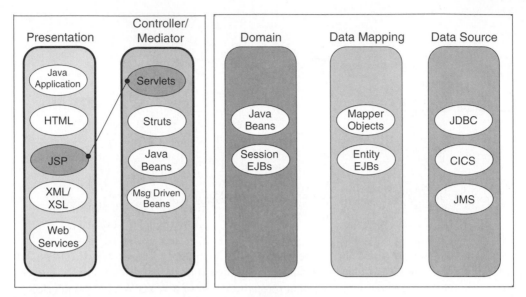

Figure 10.1 Architectural road map position of JSPs.

writing Java, to be split among different team members, each with complementary skill sets. It also makes the process of developing dynamic content simpler, since it is easier to edit and deploy an HTML page than to change HTML within the Java source code of a servlet, and then recompile and redeploy it.

We show the position of JSP within our overall architectural road map in Figure 10.1. If you are already familiar with JSP basics, JSP syntax elements and how JSPs are processed by the Web container you can safely skip this chapter. Chapter 13 provides detailed coverage on how to create, test, and debug JSPs using WebSphere Studio. Otherwise, you should read on to understand how JSPs are built, compiled, and executed, and how you can benefit from using them.

10.1 Page Templates and Server-Side Scripting

A facility that provides page content and can be customized on a per request basis is often called a page template. The created page template does not completely represent a page delivered to the client, but represents the form (layout, style) of the page. It is representative of many instances of the actual page. One such template technology is implemented with JSPs.

To generate an actual page from a page template requires processing. The processing step executes instructions to insert *dynamically* obtained content within the otherwise static HTML stream. For example, consider three different views of an extremely trivial JSP shown in Figures 10.2–10.4.

Figure 10.2 shows a WYSIWYG page editor view of the JSP. For the most part, this looks like a simple HTML file. A placeholder (seen as a box with part of the code) is provided as a hint that JSP-specific content has been defined as part of the page.

Figure 10.2 Building a JSP page.

Figure 10.3 shows the Source view for the page. Here you can see the HTML code representing the page and the specific content that is behind the placeholder in the form of the JSP tag:

```
<%= new java.util. Date() %>
```

This JSP tag appears as if it were an extended HTML tag, similar in formatting to other HTML tags. Figure 10.4 shows the rendered page as viewed by a browser. The page is made up static content, like the color, title, headings, etc. that will displayed the same way every time the page is requested. The dynamic content, the time on the server when the request is made, will be generated on each request and is inserted seamlessly in the resulting page.

```
book_simple.jsp  X
book_simple.jsp
<!DOCTYPE HTML PUBLIC "-//W3C//DTD HTML 4.01 Transitional//EN">
<HTML>
<HEAD>
<%@ page
language="java"
contentType="text/html; charset=ISO-8859-1"
pageEncoding="ISO-8859-1"
%>
<META http-equiv="Content-Type" content="text/html; charset=ISO-8859-1">
<META name="GENERATOR" content="IBM WebSphere Studio">
<TITLE>Simple JSP</TITLE>
</HEAD>
<BODY bgcolor="teal" text="yellow">
<H1 align="center">Thank you for visiting our site</H1>
<H2>You had contact with our server at:</H2>
<center><H2>
<%= new java.util.Date() %></H2>
</BODY>
</HTML>
Design  Source  Preview
```

Figure 10.3 HTML Source view of JSP.

Figure 10.4 Display sent to the browser when the JSP executes.

10.2   A Short History of Java Server Pages

JSP is one of a family of technologies known as server-side scripting.[1] A competing member of this family is Active Server Pages (ASP) from Microsoft. Each technology shares a similar structure, namely a source file that is a mixture of HTML and script code and runtime processing that occurs on the server. ASP is the older technology.

JSP was initially developed by a working group under the supervision of Sun Microsystems. Work began on the technology (under its current name) in late 1997. It was announced at the JavaOne conference in March 1998. The first public specification and reference implementation, Version 0.91, was available in June 1998. One year later, the first true JSP Specification (Version 1.0) was made public.

JSP 1.2 became available in August 2001. With each release of the specification, Sun Microsystems also released a reference implementation.

At the writing of this book, the Java servlet and JSP specifications are developed by Sun Microsystems under the JCP. Reference implementations have been turned over to the Apache group, under the umbrella of the Jakarta Project (for more information see *http://jakarta.apache.org*). The Jakarta Project's reference implementation effort is called Tomcat.

WAS 5.0 provides a runtime for the J2EE 1.3 specification which includes support for JSP 1.2. For backward compatibility, J2EE 1.2, and, therefore, JSP 1.1 are supported.

10.3   Page Compilation—Runtime View

At the heart of JSP technology is the process used to take the JSP source and convert it to a runtime object that executes within a Web container. The specification states that a Java class is to be generated which implements the `javax.servlet.jsp.HttpJspPage` interface. This Java class,

---

1.   Other scripting technologies are PHP, ColdFusion, and CGI.

Table 10.1 Servlet to JSP method mapping.

Servlet Method Name	JSP Method Name
service()	_jspService()
init()	_jspInit()
destroy()	_jspDestroy()

in most cases a servlet, defines a `_jspService()` method which will be called by the Web container to provide the runtime service.

In addition to `_jspService()`, the HttpJspPage class implements the other life cycle methods of a servlet. Table 10.1 shows the mapping between the servlet and JSP methods.

The process of parsing the JSP source, producing the Java class, and compiling it (to make it ready to be loaded into the servlet engine), is known as page compilation. For most Web containers, this page compilation service is provided by a servlet. The level of support is determined by the J2EE level of an installed Web module.

Each page compilation servlet has a number of initialization parameters which affect the behavior of the page compilation. One of the most important of these is the `keepgenerated=true`. Setting this parameter ensures that the generated class's source code is saved to the file system (not just the compiled byte code file). This is useful for the developer to gain a general understanding of how the JSP works and can also be referenced while debugging.

Setting the `keepgenerated` parameter is done using the Web deployment descriptor editor's extension page in WebSphere Studio. An optional parameter is `scratchdir`, which indicates where the source files will be kept.

This page compiler option (Figure 10.5) should be used only during development. It is not a good idea to keep the generated source for the JSPs during production because you could end up with a lot of unnecessary files—and delay page compilation.

To learn more aspects of the class generated from the JSP source, consider the Java source code file shown in Listing 10.1 whose `_jspService()` method created the output for the JSP presented in Figures 10.2 and 10.3.

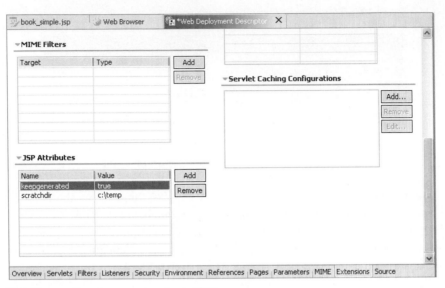

Figure 10.5 Generating Java source from JSPs.

Listing 10.1 Generated servlet source

```
public void _jspService(HttpServletRequest request, HttpServletResponse
response)
  throws java.io.IOException, ServletException {
   JspFactory _jspxFactory = null;
   PageContext pageContext = null;
   HttpSession session = null;
   ServletContext application = null;
   ServletConfig config = null;
   JspWriter out = null;
   Object page = this;
   String  _value = null;
   java.util.Stack _jspxTagObjects = new java.util.Stack();
   try {
```

```
  if (_jspx_inited == false) {

    synchronized (this) {

      if (_jspx_inited == false) {

        _jspx_init();

        _jspx_inited = true;

      }

    }

  }

  _jspxFactory = JspFactory.getDefaultFactory();

  response.setContentType("text/html; charset=ISO-8859-1");

  pageContext = _jspxFactory.getPageContext(this, request, response,

              "", true, 8192, true);



  application = pageContext.getServletContext();

  config = pageContext.getServletConfig();

  session = pageContext.getSession();

  out = pageContext.getOut();
// begin [file="/book_simple.jsp";from=(0,0);to=(3,0)]
  out.write("<!DOCTYPE HTML PUBLIC \"-//W3C//DTD HTML 4.01

      transitional//EN\">\r\n<HTML>\r\n<HEAD>\r\n");

  // end



  // begin [file="/book_simple.jsp";from=(7,2);to=(16,0)]
  out.write("\r\n<META http-equiv=\"Content-Type\" content=\"text/html;
```

```
    charset=ISO-8859-1\">\r\n<META name=\"GENERATOR\" content=\"IBM

      WebSphere Studio\">\r\n<TITLE>Simple

      JSP</TITLE>\r\n</HEAD>\r\n<BODY bgcolor=\"teal\"

    text=\"yellow\">\r\n<H1 align=\"center\">Thank you for visiting our

  site</H1>\r\n<H2>You had contact with our server at:</H2>\r\n<center>

      <H2>\r\n");

  // end



  // begin [file="/book_simple.jsp";from=(16,3);to=(16,25)]

   out.print( new java.util.Date() );

  // end

  // begin [file="/book_simple.jsp";from=(16,27);to=(19,0)]

    out.write("</H2>\r\n</BODY>\r\n</HTML>\r\n");

  // end

} catch (Throwable t) {

  if (out != null && out.getBufferSize() != 0)

    out.clearBuffer();

  if (pageContext != null) pageContext.handlePageException(t);

} finally {

  while (_jspxTagObjects.empty() == false){

    ((javax.servlet.jsp.tagext.Tag)_jspxTagObjects.pop()).release();

  }

if (_jspxFactory != null) _jspxFactory.releasePageContext(pageContext);
```

```
        /* Service Finally Phase */

    }

  }

}
```

The package statement and several import statements were dropped from the file listing, as were the generated `_jspInit()` and `_jspDestroy()` methods. For this simple JSP, everything of interest appears in `_jspService()`. The initial part of this method defines a number of local variables that are later initialized from utility methods on the class, PageContext. Immediately after defining the local variables, one-time behavior (calling `_jspx_init()`) is invoked.

After the initialization of the JSP the service method proceeds to output both the static and dynamic parts of the page interleaving between them as necessary to maintain the structure of the page. The static elements are represented by strings and sent to the output stream using simple `out.write()` methods, where *out* is an object of type PrintWriter. The dynamic part of the page is converted into the appropriate Java code from the original JSP expression or scriptlet.[2] In the case of our example the JSP expression:

```
<%= new java.util.Date() %>
```

was converted to:

```
out.print( new java.util.Date() );
```

There are also a number of comments, inserted by the page compiler, which document the source of the static content for the page, such as the file containing the HTML, including starting and ending row and column position.

The `HttpJspPage` interface also defines two methods—`jspInit()` and `jspDestroy()`. These methods can be overridden if the JSP needs to perform any one-time initialization or termination behavior. When the generated class is a servlet, the superclass (provided by the page compilation service) will override the HttpServlet's `service()` method so that its behavior is to call `_jspService()`. Similarly, the HttpServlet's `init()` method will call `jspInit()` and `destroy()` will call `jspDestroy()`. In this way, the servlet engine's control model gets mapped to the JSP runtime model (as specified in the `HttpJspPage` interface).

Page compilation occurs if no servlet class has yet been generated for the target JSP or if the currently available servlet class' creation date (time stamp) is older than the JSP source file.

---

2.   Scriptlets, along with other elements of JSP syntax, are discussed later in this chapter.

Otherwise, if the servlet class exists, it is invoked if it is already loaded or it is loaded and invoked if it is not currently loaded.

Errors can occur during page compilation at three levels:

1. The JSP tags themselves can be malformed. When using WebSphere Studio, the JSP validator will catch these errors and list them in the Tasks view when the JSP file is saved.

2. The Java class generated during page compilation may produce Java compilation errors and will be reported as such. The JSP validator will catch most of the conditions that can lead up to these types of errors.

3. The JSP can encounter runtime errors, just like any regular Java code. These errors are the most harmful in the user's eyes. If not handled properly ugly and cryptic stack dumps are displayed on the user's browser. These errors are best handled in an error page, which can clean up the original exception and display a meaningful error message to the user.

10.4 JSP Syntax

Three categories of elements make up the JSP syntax:

1. Scripting Elements
2. Directives
3. Action Tags

We will look at the first two groups in this chapter and consider actions in the next chapter.

10.5 Scripting Elements

When writing JSPs, your first interest is in adding code that executes at runtime and can perform server-side functionality. The most direct way to specify the Java code that appears in the generated class is through the use of JSP scripting elements. There are three distinct scripting elements specified for JSP:

1. Scriptlets
2. Expressions
3. Declarations

10.5.1 Scriptlets

Scriptlets are Java code fragments placed as they are directly to the `_jspService()` method. This is the most direct way to write Java code within a JSP. The syntax for a scriptlet is:

```
<% Java code fragment %>
```

At initial glance, allowing any Java code fragment rather than a statement, collection of statements, or expression probably seems odd. But, it should be noted that scriptlets will be intermixed with HTML, and Java blocks will frequently need to be split. For example, consider part of a JSP file that will produce a variable sized HTML table:

```
<Table><Tbody>

    <% PrintWriter out = request.getWriter();3

      for (int i=0; i<a.size; i++) {   %>

    <tr>

      <td><% out.print(i); %></td>

      <td><% out.print(a[i].getAProperty()); %></td>

    </tr>

<% } %>

</Tbody></Table>
```

As you can see the `for` loop is split across a number of scriptlets. It is quite clear that the JSP code in the example is difficult to read, both for HTML page developers and Java programmers. Because of this, we will work to minimize scriptlets when developing JSPs. We put forth this goal despite the fact that scriptlets are the most general-purpose scripting element in JSP.

10.5.2 Expressions

A scripting element is frequently required to supply a runtime value (expression) to the page template. In other words, most of the time we are trying to place dynamic (displayable) data to the HTTP output stream. JSP expressions are a short form of scriptlet to be utilized in these circumstances. The syntax for a JSP expression is:

```
<%= a_Java_expression %>
```

---

3.   The `request` variable used here is one of several implicit objects available to the JSP page. It represents the `HttpServletRequest` object.

The semantics of this tag is to:

- Evaluate the expression
- Convert the result to a string (if non-primitive)
- Output the string (or primitive) to the current output stream

As you will see, JSP expressions are likely to be the most common JSP tag type seen throughout the JSP source file. They are self-contained and rarely split across HTML, so they are easier for the JSP developer and Web designer to recognize and maintain, unlike general scriptlet expressions that can contain any legal Java code.

10.5.3 Declarations

While scriptlets and expressions permit writing code that appears in the `_jspService()` method, Declarations are used to write direct Java code at the class level. The syntax for a JSP declaration is:

```
<%! Java member definitions %>
```

Declarations can be used to define instance variables and static variables as well as define methods. Defining new methods is useful when complex scripts are repeated. This repeated script can be encapsulated in a method body, and the repeated script can be replaced by repeated method call.

More likely however, declarations will be used to override `jspInit()` and `jspDestroy()` when needed. An example declaration is:

```
<%!

private static PropertyResourceBundle environment = null;

public void jspInit() {

  try {

  inputStream stream = getServletConfig().getServletContext().

                       getResourceAsStream("/props.txt");

  environment = new PropertyResourceBundle.(stream);

  } catch (IOException ex) {}

}

%>
```

10.6   Directives

While scripting elements map directly to code within the class that is generated, directives represent direction to the page compiler. These requests include specifying certain properties the class that is created is to have, for how translation occurs, or for how the class will operate during runtime. There are currently three different directives:

1. Page

2. Include

3. Taglib

These directives differ in what they let the JSP developer specify. We will look at both the page and include directives here. The taglib directive is part of the custom tag support required in JSP 1.1. We address JSP 1.1 issues at the end of Chapter 11.

10.6.1   The Page Directive

The page directive is a way to configure a number of operational attributes of the generated JSP. The page directive syntax is:

`<%@ page` *`page_directive_attr_list`* `%>` where *`page_directive_attr_list`* may include any of the items shown in Table 10.2.

Table 10.2 JSP page directive attributes.

Attribute Name	Attribute Value Range	Description
language	Compliant JSP scripting language	Default value is "java"
extends	A Java class which implements HttpJspPage interface	This should not be used without consideration as it prevents the JSP container from providing specialized super classes which provide enhanced quality of service.
import	A comma separated list of fully qualified Java package or type names	The default import list is java.lang.*, javax.servlet.*, javax.servlet.jsp.*, and javax.servlet.http.*. This is the only attribute that may appear in more than one page directive within the page. Multiple import attributes are interpreted as the set union of all listed types and packages.
session	"true" | "false"	Indicates whether the JSP is session-aware or not. The default value is "true."

Table 10.2 JSP page directive attributes. (Continued)

buffer	"none" | size size is something like "12kb"	Specifies the buffering model for the JspWriter opened to handle content output form the page. A specific buffer size guarantees that the output is buffered with a buffer size not less than that specified.
autoFlush	"true" | "false"	Default is "true." If false, the stream is buffered and an exception is thrown when the buffer overflows. If true, the stream is flushed.
isThreadSafe	"true" | "false"	Default is true. If "false" the typical implication is the generated class implements SingleThreadModel.
info	Arbitrary String	This can be retrieved using the Servlet.getServletInfo() method.
isErrorPage	"true" | "false"	Indicates if the page is used to handle errors. If "true," the implicit script variable exception is defined and bound to the offending Throwable from the source JSP page in error.
errorPage	A URL	The JSP will catch all exceptions and forward processing to the names target resource.
contentType	"Type" | "Type; charset=CHARSET"	The default value for type is "text/html"; the default value for the character encoding is ISO-8859-1.

An example page directive is:

```
<%@ page errorPage="TSErrorHandler.jsp" isErrorPage="true"

import="com.workbook.casestudy.domain,com.workbook.casestudy.mediator"%>
```

Note that a page can contain several page directives. With the exception of `import` no other attribute may be specified more than once. Two of the attributes, `session` and `isErrorPage` affect the availability of the associated implicit objects for use by scriptlets and expressions.

10.6.2 The Include Directive

The include directive allows for the translation time composition of multiple files into a single JSP source file. The syntax for the include directive is:

```
<%@ include file="relativeURLspec" %>
```

Execution of the `include` tag at translation time results in the insertion of the text of the specified resource into the JSP source file. Since this is a translation time include, you will not want to use this directive to include resources that change. If you wish to include volatile content, this should be done with a runtime include mechanism like the `<jsp:include>` action.

10.6.3 Implicit Objects

Both scriptlets and expressions result in code being placed in the `_jspService()` method. Several local variables (implicit, or predefined, objects) are guaranteed to be available to these scripting elements by the JSP specification. The implicit objects are shown in Table 10.3.

Both exception and session are only present in particular circumstances, depending on the how the page directive is defined. The exception object is present if the JSP is configured as an error page (`isErrorPage="true"`). The session object is present if the JSP is configured to be session-aware, which is the default. If the page is configured to be session-aware and a session object does not exist when the page is displayed a session object is created.

Table 10.3 JSP implicit objects.

Implicit Object (Local Variable Name)	Java Type	Object Represented by Reference
request	javax.servlet.http.HttpServletRequest	The request associated with this invocation
response	javax.servlet.http.HttpServletResponse	The current response object
out	javax.servlet.jsp.JspWriter	A writer connected to the output stream
session	javax.servlet.http.HttpSession	The current session object for the requesting client
pageContext	javax.servlet.jsp.PageContext	The pageContext (a utility object) for this JSP
application	javax.servlet.ServletContext	The servlet context for this JSP
config	javax.servlet.ServletConfig	The ServletConfig for this JSP servlet
page	java.lang.Object	Usually corresponds to this
exception	java.lang.Throwable	The Throwable that resulted in the error page being invoked

10.7 JSP Documents

JSP documents are JSP pages created using XML style syntax instead of JSP syntax. In this section we cover the XML elements which can be used for constructing a JSP document.

The JSP 1.2 specification describes several reasons of why you would want to use XML style syntax in your JSPs:

- JSP documents can be passed directly to the JSP container; this will become more important as more and more content is authored as XML.
- The XML view of a JSP page can be used for validating the JSP page against some description of the set of valid pages.
- XML-aware tools can manipulate JSP documents.
- A JSP document can be generated from a textual representation by applying an XML transformation, like XSLT.
- A JSP document can be generated automatically, say by serializing some objects.

A JSP written using XML style syntax can include another document, which uses JSP syntax, with the include directive, and vice versa. However, JSP syntax cannot be intermixed with XML syntax on the same page.

JSP pages using XML style syntax use the same file extension as pages using JSP syntax—.jsp. The container can distinguish between JSP and XML syntax pages because the XML syntax page is an XML document with a jsp:root element. JSP syntax pages cannot use the jsp:root element.

Similar to JSP syntax, pages written using XML syntax can use the following elements:

- `jsp:root` is the first element on the page and introduces the namespace for the custom tags on the rest of the page
- JSP directives
- JSP scripting
- JSP actions
- JSP custom actions
- `jsp:text` for static text (template) data

From the semantic perspective, a JSP document is the same as a JSP page. There are static or template elements and elements that produce dynamic context. The document is processed, like any other XML document where the nodes of the document are identified. Nodes containing template information are passed unchanged to the output stream. The remaining nodes are interpreted and their resulting output is passed to the stream.

10.7.1 Examining an XML Style Syntax JSP Document

Let's examine the source for a JSP document. In fact, the output from this JSP is the same as the example you saw in Figures 10.2 and 10.3. The major difference is that in this case we have used XML style syntax.—

```
<jsp:root xmlns:jsp="http://java.sun.com/JSP/Page" version="1.2">

    <jsp:directive.page language="java"

   contentType="text/html; charset=ISO-8859-1" pageEncoding="ISO-8859-1" /

>

    <jsp:text>

        <![CDATA[ <?xml version="1.0" encoding="ISO-8859-1" ?> ]]>

    </jsp:text>

    <jsp:text>

        <![CDATA[ <!DOCTYPE html PUBLIC "-//W3C//DTD XHTML 1.1//EN"

            "http://www.w3.org/TR/xhtml11/DTD/xhtml11.dtd"> ]]>

    </jsp:text>

    <html xmlns="http://www.w3.org/1999/xhtml">

    <head>

        <title>SimpleXMLJSP.jsp</title>

    </head>

    <jsp:text>

        <body bgcolor="teal" text="yellow">

        <h1 align="center">Thank you for visiting our site</h1>

         <h2>You had contact with our server at:</h2>

         <center>

            <jsp:expression>new java.util.Date()</jsp:expression>
```

```
        </center>

        </body>

    </jsp:text>

    </html>

</jsp:root>
```

In the example, note the jsp:root element at the very top of the page. As mentioned before it defines the root of the document and defines the namespace. Also note the use of the `jsp:text` element to enclose static template text. Other differences you may notice are the use of XML style syntax for the page directive and the expression which gets the current date.

10.7.2 XML Syntax Elements

Table 10.3 shows the mapping between the JSP syntax tags and XML syntax elements. JSP standard and custom actions can be used in both JSP and XML syntax pages because they are already expressed in XML terms.

Table 10.4 Mapping between syntax tags and elements.

JSP Syntax	XML Element
N/A	<jsp:root>
<% page *directive* %>	<jsp:directive.page *directive*/>
<%@ include file="*relativeURLspec*" %>	<jsp:directive.include file="*relativeURLspec*"/>
<%! *Some declaration* %>	<jsp:declaration> Some declaration </jsp:declaration>
<% Java code fragment %>	<jsp:scriptlet> Java code fragment </jsp:scriptlet>
<%= Java expression %>	<jsp:expression> Java expression </jsp:expression>
<%@taglib uri="uriVaue" prefix="prefix" %>	Expressed at jsp:root as a xmlns:prefix="uriValue"

10.7.3 Creating an XML Syntax JSP in WebSphere Studio

Creating a JSP, which uses XML syntax with WebSphere Studio is very similar to creating a regular JSP file. There are, however, a couple of choices that need to be selected for the JSP to be created properly.

Start in the Web perspective. Select the Web Content folder of the Web project where you want to create the new JSP. From its context menu, select *New > JSP file*. (Figure 10.6)

In order for the Use XML Style Syntax check box to be enabled, the Markup Language selected has to be either XHTML[4] or XHTML Frameset. From then on, you can continue to define the many other parameters on the wizard. Usage of the New JSP File wizard will be fully covered in Chapter 13.

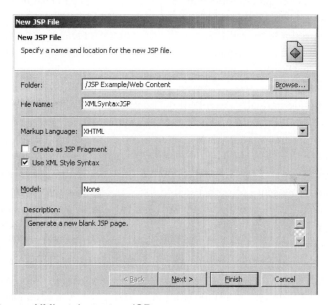

Figure 10.6 Creating an XML style syntax JSP.

10.8 Roles for JSP

JSP is a broad enough specification to support many different programming models and common uses. This potentially broad appeal is both a strength and a weakness of JSPs.

Since it is possible to write a complete general-purpose servlet using JSP scripting elements, some may be tempted to do so. In this role, a JSP is comprised almost entirely of one or

---

4.   Extensible HyperText Markup Language (XHTML™) is a family of current and future document types and modules that reproduce, subset, and extend HTML, reformulated in XML. XHTML document types are all XML-based, and ultimately are designed to work in conjunction with XML-based user agents. XHTML is the successor of HTML. Source: W3C HTML Home page.

more scriptlets and declarations. It provides an opportunity to write an HttpServlet by only specifying, through JSP elements, the content of the `_jspService()` method and perhaps other utility methods. For some, this may be a shortcut over using a Java development environment to
create the complete class declaration. The JSP will be compiled into a servlet the first time it is
requested by a client; from then on its behavior is the same as any other servlet. A disadvantage
in this approach is you lose the benefits that such a development environment affords the developer. This loss probably more than offsets the productivity gain from letting the page compiler
build the class framework.

On the other extreme, a JSP can play the role of HTML page template only. In this mode,
a secondary goal during development is to minimize the Java code that appears in the JSP. JSP-
aware HTML page development tools like IBM WebSphere Page Designer support this role.

A third role is a true mix of HTML and Java code. Although more general, this is perhaps
the most easily abused role for a JSP to play. To see what we mean by this, when a JSP is used in
this way it plays the role of controller and view as well as perhaps part of the model in the MVC
model. In this mode, the JSP is called directly by the user from the browser and the JSP determines what needs to be done and, in some cases, performs the requested action.

These actions are normally the role of the controller and the model layers. After the operation is performed the JSP generates the output back to the user. In addition to not separating
these programming layers (model, view, and controller), the JSP source itself becomes hard to
maintain. It is difficult to sort out what the runtime behavior is when there is a lot of complex
Java logic intermixed with HTML tags. Further, there is likely no good development environment to assist in making sense of such a source file.

It is the authors' strong opinion that JSPs should be kept to one extreme or the other. Currently there are no noteworthy tools available to strongly support the JSP as a faster servlet
development mechanism. (For instance, there is no Java/JSP-based, Microsoft Visual InterDev
style tool on the market.) This leaves us with trying to restrict JSPs to be strictly a page template
technology playing the role of the view (or view engine) in our MVC programming model. We
revisit this issue while discussing JSP programming models in a later chapter.

10.9 Summary

In the introduction to servlets chapter, we looked at the possibility of generating dynamic content directly on the servlets since they had the knowledge and access to the data which needed
to be displayed. This meant generating HTML code to create the static content as well as the
dynamic content in the servlet. This was later considered not a best practice as the servlet provided both the controller and view layers of the application, meaning that there could be no
separation of responsibilities.

In this chapter, we saw how JSPs start from the opposite perspective. That is, instead of
embedding HTML in Java code in a servlet, why not embed small scriptlets of Java code in
HTML? Especially given the goal of eliminating business logic from the presentation layer, this

approach resulted in just a little Java code within the HTML whereas the alternative invariably resulted in lots of HTML in the Java code.

In a later chapter, we will continue this discussion by examining more JSP tags and discussing what tools exist to support JSP development for WebSphere. We will also look at how to reduce the amount of Java code in JSPs by using JavaBeans and JSP tag libraries.

Tag Libraries and Custom Tags

11.1 Introduction

The JSP specification defines a very limited set of standard actions, but it also defines a mechanism to make JSPs extensible. These custom (actions) tags provide an opportunity to design special presentation logic, factored into reusable components and callable from within JSP via a tag, or XML markup, syntax.

One aspect of JSP syntax that is a feature—and, in some ways, a drawback—is the ability to write any arbitrary Java logic, via scriptlets and declarations, commingled with HTML syntax within the same JSP file. This can lead to JSP source that is both hard to read and maintain. We recommend that a JSP should be predominantly HTML.

So while the combination of these syntaxes is easily expressed within a JSP, it is awkward and inefficient to maintain. In addition, a page designer is not likely the right person to be writing and/or maintaining Java code within such JSPs. JSP custom tags address this problem by providing an alternative way of expressing dynamic page content using XML tags so the final syntax will be more suitable for user interface development using HTML.

This chapter, by addressing JSP tag libraries as a mechanism for extending JSP, is addressing only the presentation layer and the JSP technology (Figure 11.1, on the next page).

11.2 Basic Model for Custom Tags

There are three parts to custom tags: The tags, the taglib descriptor, and the tag handler (Figure 11.2).

The tags that are added to a JSP provide the mechanism for how the service of a custom tag is invoked within a JSP.

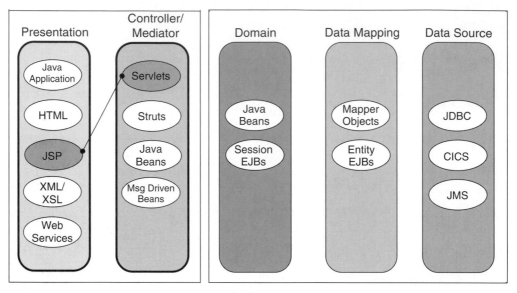

Figure 11.1 JSP custom tags within the road map.

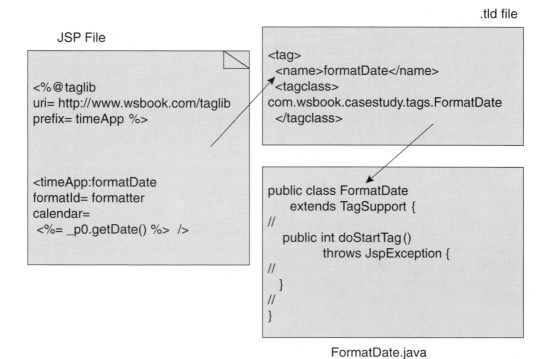

Figure 11.2 Key pieces of JSP custom tags.

The taglib descriptor is a file that provides metadata about a set of custom tags that are packaged within a tag library. The file type is .tld, and is frequently referred to as the tld file. The JSP author will include a taglib directive within the JSP to resolve the source for custom tags used within the page and to associate a prefix (namespace) to be used to refer to that set of custom tags within the page. At translation time, the page compiler uses the metadata within the tld file to validate the syntax of its use within the JSP. The page compiler uses the metadata to perform code generation—actually writing Java code to invoke the appropriate methods on the corresponding tag handlers.

The tag handlers are Java classes that provide the runtime behavior for the custom tags.

11.3 JSTL and Other Widely Used Tag Libraries

One of the immediate benefits of JSP tag libraries is the ability to use them across multiple applications, multiple projects, and multiple organizations. A prime example of this is the Java Standard Tag Library (JSTL). This tag library, available from Sun Microsystems, provides a number of utility services in a collection of easy-to-use custom tags.[1]

JSTL includes simple utility tags and a set of conditional tags—`if` and `choose` (with its companion `when` and `otherwise` tags). There is a powerful pair of iteration (looping) tags, `forEach` and `forTokens`. These are useful in writing display pages without writing scriptlets to supply the looping logic.

JSTL also includes a set of tags for working with Web resources including the `url`, `import`, and `redirect` tags. There is also a large set of tags dedicated to supporting internationalization (I18N) of JSPs including the `fmt:message` tag and a number of format and parsing tags (e.g., `formatNumber` and `parseNumber`). Without a good set of I18N tags, providing support for multiple locales in JSPs is a chore and difficult to maintain.

A greater portion of JSPs are being written using standard utility tag libraries. For example, authors of theme and skins (the branding look and feel elements) for WebSphere Portal Server have their JSPs comprised mostly of custom tags from a single tag library, which provides highly optimized and specialized tags for manipulating presentation objects associated with the portal.

11.4 Writing Tag Handlers

The third piece in Figure 11.2 is the actual Java class that provides the runtime behavior of a custom tag—the tag handler. Such a class must implement one of the three interfaces: `Tag`, `IterationTag`, or `BodyTag`. The interface that your class implements depends upon the context and behavior of the corresponding tag (Table 11.1).

More often than not, tag handlers will be classes that extend one of the convenience support classes, `TagSupport` or `TagBodySupport`. Listing 11.1 shows a tag handler class:

---

1.   *http://java.sun.com/products/jsp/jstl.*

Chapter 11 • Tag Libraries and Custom Tags

Table 11.1 JSP categorizing custom actions.

Characteristic	Behavior Description	Interface
Simple action	Does some logic (within the doStartTag()). May be parameterized by attribute values.	Tag
Actions with a body	Similar to Simple Action but needs to perform logic at the beginning and the end of the body (logic in both doStartTag() and doEndTag()	Tag
Conditionals	Use of return values from doStartTag()	Tag
Iterations	The doAfterBody() method is invoked to determine whether or not to reevaluate the body.	IterationTag
Actions that process their body	Needs a way of diverting the output of a body evaluation for other manipulation. Works with a BodyContent object and uses the setBodyContent() and doInitBody() methods of the BodyTag Interface	BodyTag
Cooperating actions	Interact with other (logically nested) tags—sharing data for instance. Makes use of the setParent() method and the findAncestorWithClass() helper method of TagSupport.	Any
Actions defining scripting variables	Many actions will create server-side objects and make them available to other scripting elements on the page. This is the prime use for the page context. May define implicit objects declared either via the variables element or the tageiclass element in the taglib descriptor.	Any

Listing 11.1 FormatDate tag handler class.

```
package com.wsbook.casestudy.tags;

// various imports omitted for brevity

public class FormatDate extends TagSupport {

    private String formatId;  // attribute with key into session for
                              // DateFormat object

    private Calendar calendar; // attribute - Date to be displayed

    /**Performs the processing of this simple action. */

    public int doStartTag() throws JspException {
```

```java
        String dateString = null;

        Formatter formatter =

        (Formatter)pageContext.getSession().getAttribute(formatId);

        if (formatter == null)

                formatter = Formatter.getDefaultFormatter();

        if (calendar != null) {

                dateString = formatter.format(calendar);

                try {

                        pageContext.getOut().write(dateString);

                } catch (IOException ioe) {

                        throw new JspException(ioe.getMessage());

                }

        }

        return EVAL_BODY_INCLUDE;

    }

    public void setCalendar(Calendar calendar) {

        this.calendar = calendar;

    }

    public void setFormatId(String formatId) {

        this.formatId = formatId;

    }

}
```

This class extends `TagSupport` making it very easy to code. Other than declaring the two attribute fields and the corresponding setters,[2],all of the logic is found in the `doStartTag()` method. This is common for a large set of simple actions. This tag will have no body (or at least one that this tag depends upon). The method retrieves the formatting object from the session using the key value supplied via the `formatId` attribute. There is some logic to handle the case where no such formatter object exists on the session. It then generates the formatted date string using the format object and the other attribute `calendar`. Next, the logic gets access to the output stream and inserts the formatted date string into this stream.

The return value indicates whether or not to continue evaluating the body of the tag (if it exists). This tag does not create or manipulate any scripting variables, making it very simple indeed.

Different return values are available for each of the methods of the tag interfaces. These can cause the tag body to be skipped, evaluated, or reevaluated. There are others that indicate that processing should not continue on the page or that processing should continue.

11.5 Tag Library Descriptor (.tld)

The semantics of custom actions must be validated both at translation time and at runtime. More importantly, the code generator (page compiler) at translation time must know how to convert a "foreign" tag into valid Java code. This is the role of the tag library descriptor (.tld) file. This XML descriptor specifies information about the tag library itself; e.g., its namespace and a description of each tag. For our simple single tag taken from the tag library used in the case study, let's look at the corresponding .tld file, shown in Listing 11.2. This file is commonly located in the WEB-INF\tld folder of a .war file.

Listing 11.2 timeApp.tld descriptor file.

```
<?xml version="1.0" encoding="ISO-8859-1" ?>

<!DOCTYPE taglib PUBLIC "-//Sun Microsystems, Inc.//DTD JSP Tag Library 1.1//

EN"

              "http://java.sun.com/j2ee/dtds/web-jsptaglibrary_1_1.dtd">

<taglib>

    <tlibversion>1.0</tlibversion>

    <jspversion>1.2</jspversion>
```

---

2.   Setter methods are called by the framework before `doStartTag()` is invoked.

```
<shortname>timeApp</shortname>

<uri>http://www.wsbook.com/taglib</uri>

<info>TimeApp application tag library</info>


<tag>

    <name>formatDate</name>

    <tagclass>com.wsbook.casestudy.tags.FormatDate</tagclass>

    <info>displays incoming date using available Formatter</info>

    <attribute>

        <name>calendar</name>

        <required>true</required>

        <rtexprvalue>true</rtexprvalue>

    </attribute>

    <attribute>

        <name>formatId</name>

        <required>true</required>

        <rtexprvalue>true</rtexprvalue>

    </attribute>

</tag>

</taglib>
```

Of importance at the top of the file is the <uri> tag, which specifies a namespace for the tag library. A corresponding mapping to the namespace is then found in the web.xml file to physically locate the .tld file. After that is the declaration of a tag whose name is formatDate that is handled by the FormatDate class. Next is the declaration of the two attributes, calendar and formatId, both of which are marked to be required (enforced at translation time) and can accept runtime expressions for their values. For additional examples and subtleties of the .tld contents, see the JSP specification.

11.6   Taglib Directive and Coding Custom Actions

So we have worked our way back from the tag handler to the tag library descriptor and on to the use of the tags within a JSP. There are two parts to using custom actions within a JSP.

First, at JSP file scope, the page needs to let the translator know which .tld files may need to be interrogated while validating (syntax), then generating code. This is accomplished with the taglib directive. For example, in most of the case study's JSPs you will find the following directive:

```
<%@taglib uri="http://www.wsbook.com/taglib" prefix="timeApp"%>
```

This declares the availability of a tag library to this body of the JSP file. The `uri` attribute specifies a namespace-like `uri`, which should uniquely identify the corresponding .tld file. This is only resolved within the .war file and a taglib map element in the web.xml file.

The second attribute, `prefix`, specifies the prefix to be used (namespace alias) with tags from this tag library. For example the following appears within pending_view.jsp (see Chapters 30 and 31 for full discussion of the case study):

```
<TD align="center">

<timeApp:formatDate formatId="formatter"

calendar="<%= _p0.getDate() %>"/>

</TD>
```

Note the tag is specified as `timeApp:formatDate` where `timeApp` corresponds to the prefix declared in the taglib directive. Thus the validator (page compilation) will expect to find a tag named `formatDate` declared within the .tld file associated with the `uri=" http://www.wsbook.com/taglib"`. Upon locating that declaration, it can verify the tag attributes and generate code that calls the `doStartTag()` method of an instance of the FormatDate class (after invoking the two attribute setters).

The resulting custom tag for our case study provides a simple way for the end user to select how dates should be displayed in the application. The preferred formatter object is stored on the HttpSession. All date displays make use of this `formatDate` tag to provide a consistent, yet customizable, look and feel to date presentation, as illustrated in Figures 11.3 and 11.4.

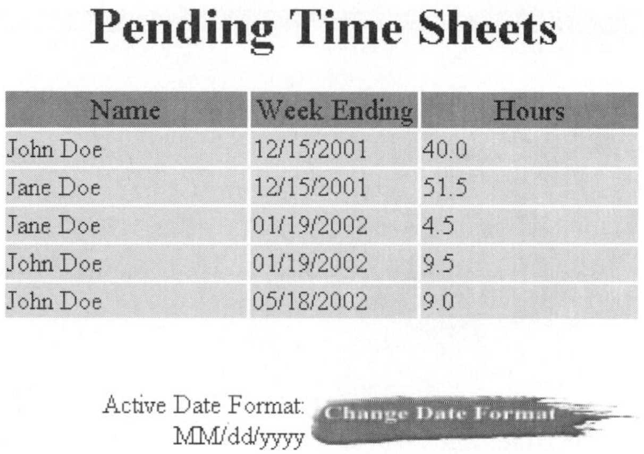

Pending Time Sheets

Name	Week Ending	Hours
John Doe	12/15/2001	40.0
Jane Doe	12/15/2001	51.5
Jane Doe	01/19/2002	4.5
John Doe	01/19/2002	9.5
John Doe	05/18/2002	9.0

Active Date Format:
MM/dd/yyyy   Change Date Format

Figure 11.3 Date display using custom tag.

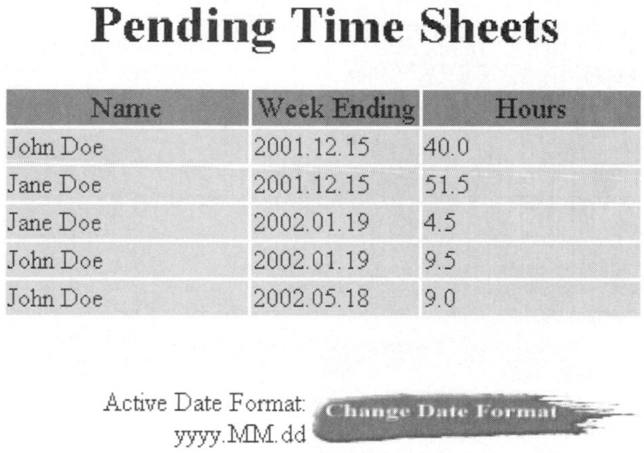

Pending Time Sheets

Name	Week Ending	Hours
John Doe	2001.12.15	40.0
Jane Doe	2001.12.15	51.5
Jane Doe	2002.01.19	4.5
John Doe	2002.01.19	9.5
John Doe	2002.05.18	9.0

Active Date Format:
yyyy.MM.dd   Change Date Format

Figure 11.4 Same page with different preference set for date format.

11.7 Support for Custom Actions

WebSphere Studio has several features that help you work efficiently with tag libraries. The first involves declaratively specifying any of a group of standard tag libraries to be associated with a Web project. Through a simple check box, Studio will add the .tld files to the Web project, add the corresponding entries in the web.xml file, and update the projects Java build path to include the tag library jar file(s) (Figure 11.5, on the next page).

There is also easy support for mapping the tag libraries' URI to a physical .tld file in the Web Deployment Descriptor editor (Figure 11.6). This results in the corresponding entry in the web.xml file (Figure 11.7).

Most of the taglib support is within WebSphere Studio's JSP editor, called the page designer. This allows easy insertion of taglib descriptors as well as the custom tags.

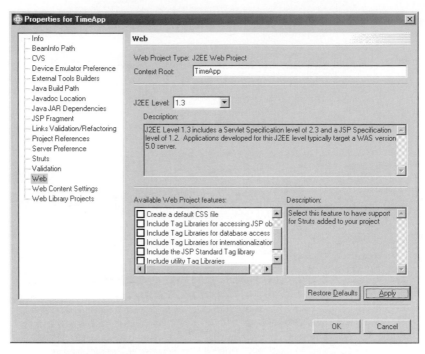

Figure 11.5 Ability to select tag libraries as Web project features.

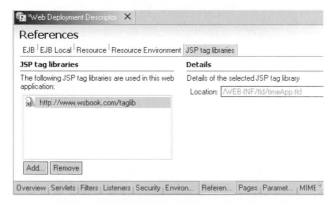

Figure 11.6 JSP tag library references in the Web Deployment Descriptor editor.

```
      <welcome-file>default.jsp</welcome-file>
    </welcome-file-list>
  - <taglib>
      <taglib-uri>http://www.wsbook.com/taglib</taglib-uri>
      <taglib-location>/WEB-INF/tlds/timeApp.tld</taglib-location>
    </taglib>
```

Figure 11.7 JSP tag library reference in web.xml file.

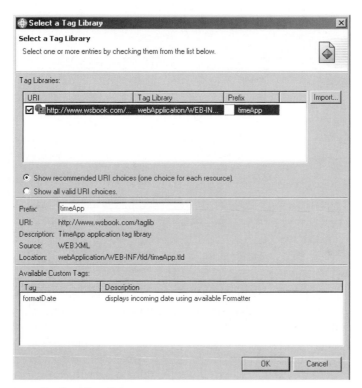

Figure 11.8 Insert taglib directive dialog.

The dialog shown in Figure 11.8 is launched from the page properties dialog after selecting the JSP tab and clicking Add for the selected taglib directive tag. It provides a list of all tag libraries associated with the .war file. You can select any number of the available tag libraries and have the taglib directive(s) written for you. The nice thing about this directive, if your projects are large or complex, is that it shows you the available Custom tags associated with each tag library.

The final piece is the wizard to insert a custom tag. This is accessed via the *JSP > Insert Custom* menu item. It provides a list of all available (for that page) custom tags (Figure 11.9).

The content assist will then provide information about the available custom tag attributes. For more information, see Chapter 13.

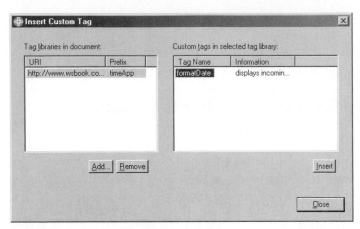

Figure 11.9 Insert custom tag dialog in Page Designer.

11.8 Summary

We have looked at support for building and using reusable presentation and scripting logic within JSPs via a tag extension mechanism known as tag libraries and custom tags. A JSP developer should exploit the available standard tag libraries to aid in the development of his JSP pages. When you are tempted to write custom Java code within your JSPs in the form of scriptlets, contemplate the option of creating one or more custom tags (actions) instead. If done properly (and these are generally simple to write), the resulting code will be a reusable component.

In addition, a JSP with custom tag(s) rather than scriptlet code will be easier to read and easier to maintain. When not done properly, the resulting custom actions will be poorly documented and useful only in the context where used, making readability and maintainability more difficult.

CHAPTER 12

Design Considerations for Controllers

When designing large-scale applications based upon servlets and JSPs, each decision you make should ultimately enhance the reliability and scalability of the application as a whole. You should always strive to reduce the complexity of the application and ease the maintenance process. This chapter will focus on a few simple design considerations that can help you achieve some of these goals.

In this chapter, we will look at design decisions of the controller/mediator layer. In addition, it will address application services (Figure 12.1).

12.1 Where Do Controllers Come From?

Possibly the biggest single hurdle for many developers new to Web-based J2EE technologies is understanding how to divide the behavior of their application among classes. While the basic principles of layering and the MVC pattern may seem obvious to some, they are certainly not readily apparent to many new Web programmers, especially those who come from traditional graphical user interface backgrounds. To begin, we will review the role of the controller within a layered architecture.

Recall from the discussions of five-layer architecture in Chapters 1 and 5 that the controller/mediator layer separates the presentation of information from the domain model that holds the information. The motivation behind this separation is generally to allow more flexibility and reuse when creating or changing the views or presentation, or when making changes to the domain layer of the application.

Applying a layered architecture in this fashion allows for domain classes to be used more flexibly across multiple applications. With this in mind, you can see that the servlets and other associated classes that we write in a Web-based application fall into the controller layer of the architecture.

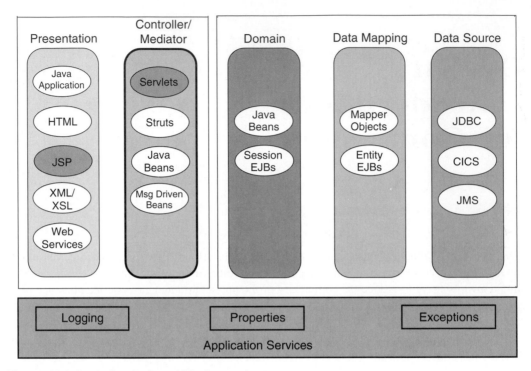

Figure 12.1 Controller design within the road map.

Controllers are responsible for taking parameters passed from the presentation layer, contacting the appropriate business logic classes, and passing the processing on to them, then taking the results and routing the user to the next appropriate screen. Servlets will perform either part or all of this function.

We haven't described how this is done, and how you discover which controllers and views are necessary for a particular application. To teach this process, we will start by examining an example application to see how you can factor it into model, view, and controller aspects.

Let's consider a simple application for managing employees taken from our case study. Our case study is comprised of several use cases for managing and tracking employee time sheets, and reporting on the time sheets submitted. Obviously, you must first have employees in the system to be able to submit a time sheet.

As with any MVC application, the first step in writing our application is to determine the model classes. In this case, this is pretty simple; we only have a single model class, Employee. We'll examine the implementation of this class in later chapters, but as you can guess, it's pretty straightforward. There are attributes for the Employee's name, ID number, age, and address.[1]

---

1. In a more complete design, Address might be split into a second class, but we'll keep this simple so as not to distract from our discussion of views and controllers.

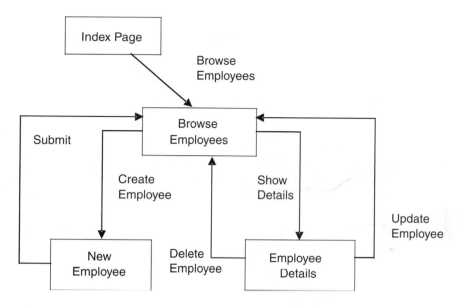

Figure 12.2 Employee management screen design.

Imagine that our users have sketched the partial design for the application shown in Figure 12.2.

In building this kind of Web-based application, users will often start with a set of page designs that have been mocked-up as static HTML. Let's assume that is the case in our application—we will show how to transform a set of Web pages into an MVC application.

How do we proceed from this mock-up showing only the screens to building an application? A simple procedure can help identify the remaining parts of the application.

First, let's identify the views in our application. This is trivial given the diagram in Figure 12.2. We can first assume that we have only JSP pages in our sample application. If there is any dynamic content in a page (meaning content that changes based on the state of the application or a user action) it should be shown in a JSP page. We would find that this means we have three JSP pages in our application:

- Browse Employees
- New Employee
- Employee Details

The index page has no dynamic data, and thus does not need to be a JSP page.

The next thing to look for is the transition between the pages. Transitions arise from what we call Go buttons. A Go button is either an HTML button that submits a form or performs a GET on a URL, or a link between pages. Each Go button that performs a unique function should have its own controller. If two or more buttons refer to the same function and have the same set of parameters (or one is a subset of the other) then the two buttons represent the same transition. Each Go button represents one of two things:

1. An individual function request to present some data (e.g., an HTTP GET)
2. A request to process a particular data stream (e.g., a set of HTTP parameters from the URL or parameters that are POSTed from an HTML form)

In the first case, you would want a unique controller to perform that function since it could not otherwise be determined what set of information the user was requesting.

In the second case, the fact that each form or set of HTTP parameters passed on a URL represents a different data stream (with a different format; e.g., set of parameters and values) would indicate that you would want a different filter for that data stream, and thus a unique controller.

If a transition is dynamic (either the data displayed on the page changes or a particular link or submit button may ultimately direct the user to more than one page) there needs to be a controller that implements the transition to the page.

In this respect, the controller is acting as a filter in a pipes and filters architecture [Buschmann]. Data come in, are processed, and go out in a different form. Think about each controller as filtering a different data stream. Just as you wouldn't attempt to use the same filter to clean the air and the oil in your car, you wouldn't want to process multiple data streams through the same filter. In this context, you can see why you would want a different controller, or filter, for each set of input data.

Here we see that not all transitions in our example meet these criteria—for example, the link from Browse Employee to New Employee does not change the way in which the New Employee page is displayed in any way. Table 12.1 summarizes results from our analysis.

Table 12.1 Action required to get from source to destination.

Source Page	Action Required	Destination Page
index.html	BrowseEmployeeList	browseEmployees.jsp
browseEmployees.jsp	N/A	newEmployee.jsp
browseEmployees.jsp	ShowDetails	employeeDetails.jsp
newEmployee.jsp	CreateEmployee	browseEmployees.jsp
employeeDetails.jsp	UpdateEmployee	browseEmployees.jsp
employeeDetails.jsp	DeleteEmployee	browseEmployees.jsp

What we have on either side of the table are the views of our system. What we have identified in between are the controllers of our system. There is a different controller for each unique, active transition. So, we have identified five potential controllers:

- BrowseEmployeeList
- ShowDetails
- CreateEmployee
- UpdateEmployee
- DeleteEmployee

Deleting an employee involves identifying the employee to be deleted, while updating the employee involves identifying the employee and providing the updated data. In the case study chapters that follow, we'll combine these into a single controller that handles both actions, although you can see how they could have just as easily have remained separate.

12.2 Controller Design Alternatives

Now that we've identified the controllers, how do we implement them? Two approaches we will look at are the page controller approach and the gateway servlet approach.

12.2.1 Page Controller

The easiest approach, and the one that was most often used in the early days of J2EE, was to make each Controller implemented via its own servlet. That would mean that each servlet (which corresponds to its own unique URL) would implement one and only one controller function. [Fowler] refers to this approach as the page controller approach, and we will refer interested readers there for details. We will show a detailed example of using this approach in Chapter 14.

With the role of the servlet clearly defined as a control mechanism within the application, we can quickly identify a very abstract role that it fills. You might even go as far as to say that every servlet within an application follows a similar design or pattern.

Specifically, the role of the servlet is to take a request made over the HTTP, extract any arguments that were passed, initiate a process that is specific to the request, and provide dynamic results based upon the processing that was performed. The results that are returned could basically fall into one of three types: returning HTML directly, forwarding the request to a JSP, or redirecting the request to a new page. As simple and effective as this approach is, it is not always the most appropriate choice, as we will see next.

12.2.2 Gateway servlet

You can make a valid argument for having only one servlet in an application handle all requests and pass the real processing off to a helper class. This single servlet is often called a gateway servlet. This argument is strongly based upon the fact that each call to a servlet results in a very nearly identical set of processing.

The real difference is in the processing performed, and the results returned, but it follows a very simple pattern. The key lies in identifying a unique controller for a particular request—this

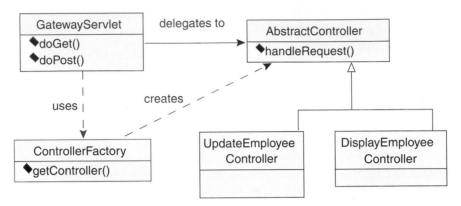

Figure 12.3 Gateway servlet design.

can be easily accomplished by using a polymorphic set of controllers, plus an object factory. In a sense, each controller acts as a strategy for implementing a particular transition of the type shown in Figure 12.2. This is shown in Figure 12.3.

In this simple design (which should only be taken to be representational), we see the basic parts of the architecture. The entry point into frameworks of this type is the gateway servlet, which implements the standard doGet and doPost methods we have seen earlier by using a Con-trollerFactory to create instances of subclasses of an abstract Controller class. The Controller classes are simple POJOs—they are not J2EE components. Usually, the ControllerFactory will use a map of URIs to Controller classes to determine which controller subclass to instantiate. Once the correct controller instance is returned to the gateway servlet, it will delegate the responsibility of handling the request to controller instance. [Fowler] and [Alur] refer to this as the Front Controller approach, and it has become the most common approach for designing Web-based J2EE front-ends.

The benefits of using this design technique are three-fold.

The first benefit is the ability to add functions to your application without requiring reconfiguration of the application server. This is possible because new functions are not defined in individual servlets, but rather by implementing a simple interface or extending an abstract Controller class.

The second benefit stems from the first and is simply that work is not duplicated between classes; rather it is leveraged through a simple abstraction. Note the subtle differences between this design pattern and what has been the traditional servlet approach. Traditionally, the number of application functions that are being supported has determined the number of servlets in an application. In other words, if you need to be able to handle login requests and user profile update requests, you would implement a servlet for each function and configure the application server to recognize both servlets.

In contrast, this solution simply classifies application functions as controllers created by a standard abstract servlet that has the ability to process them abstractly. This gives the ability to add, change, and delete functionality in the application server, without needing to administer the configuration of the server itself.

This design will ultimately make your applications more extensible, and easier to maintain. The Apache Struts framework is built on this model. It is the framework used to build the Web front-end to our case study. We will discuss the specifics of Struts in more detail in Chapter 14, but for the time being, we will only consider the abstract design of the framework in general.

A final advantage that this design conveys is that it makes thread safety less of an issue in servlet development. Since each controller is created individually and will be used only by a single thread you need not be as careful with thread safety issues as you must be when the servlet is acting as the controller. This alone is often enough to make developers, especially those uncomfortable with multithreaded programming, choose this approach. On the other hand, you still must be careful to consider the use of any shared resources accessed by these controllers.

One of the advantages of the page controller approach is that it reuses servlet instances to reduce memory footprint problems and performance issues resulting from creating and destroying controller objects. However, any approach you choose will end up creating and destroying other objects used in processing a request. Since controller objects are usually lightweight, the impact is often minimal.

Two notable disadvantages of the gateway approach are: (1) with anonymous controllers, you cannot utilize performance monitoring tools to identify the distinct behavior of individual controllers; (2) the access control requirements for each controller within your application must be identical as there is only one principal URL upon which you can apply security constraints.

In our full case study implementation, we will use Struts for the controller/presentation layer, thus employing the gateway servlet approach.

12.3 Exception Handling

One of the key elements of delivering reliable software is the ability to recover gracefully from unexpected application errors. In Web-based applications, this is key because you do not want the users of your application to see unpleasant HTTP error returns in their browser.

To ensure that these kinds of errors never reach the client browser, we must have a mechanism in place to intercept any potential application exceptions that are not expected. The following discussion, while brief, provides a simple and straightforward solution to this problem in a way that does not use any application-server-specific features. Later we will examine some WebSphere-specific solutions to the same problem. Which approach you choose is a matter of personal preference and concern for portability.

The basis for this solution is an abstract controller that serves as the root for all of your application controllers. (Note that this feature could just be an intrinsic part of your gateway servlet.) As an example, let's consider the other approach, where each controller is a unique servlet. In this case, this abstract Controller class should be the place that you will implement common behavior across all of the servlets within your application. Part of the common behavior is the ability to handle all uncaught exceptions generically. This has proven to be a convenient way to keep the users of your Web-based applications from ever seeing the result of an unexpected server exception. These exceptions, if left unhandled, result in an HTTP Error 500 that is unpleasant and confusing for the user.

```java
import java.io.*:

import javax.servlet.*;

import javax.servlet.http.*;

public abstract class BaseServlet extends HttpServlet {

      public final void service ( HttpServletRequest request,

HttpServletResponse response ) throws ServletException, IOException {

      try {

             super.service( request, response );

      }

      catch( Throwable aThrowable ) {

             handle( aThrowable, request, response );

      }

      }

      protected abstract void handle( Throwable aThrowable,

HttpServletRequest request, HttpServletResponse response ) throws

ServletException, IOException;

}
```

The implication of this solution is that extensions of this servlet must not override the `service()` method, as this will short circuit the exception handling functionality. This proves to be acceptable as you usually override specific HTTP request methods such as `doGet()` or `doPost()`.

Notice also that the `handle()` method is abstract. This means that concrete servlets extending BaseServlet must provide an implementation for handling exceptions, which allows for application-specific exception handling. The `handle()` method in each subclass would prob-

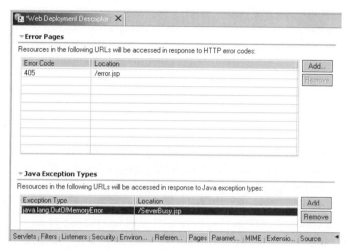

Figure 12.4 Setting error response pages in Web deployment descriptor editor.

ably return a simple error page to the user, indicating what error occurred, as well as providing instructions on how to proceed.

Now that you have seen a generic solution to this problem, we can look at error-page feature of J2EE. This is easiest to set using the Web Deployment Descriptor (web.xml) editor from within WebSphere Studio (Figure 12.4). It can also be set using the Application Assembly Tool.[2] This allows an arbitrary number of application-specific error pages (JSP or servlets) that are forwarded to whenever the corresponding HTTP error code is to be returned to the browser or the corresponding Java exception is thrown and *un*caught by the application.

In the past, this error page solution was proprietary and supported in different ways by different vendors. It is now a standard element of the web.xml file and part of the J2EE specification. In cases where the HTTP error code can be translated into an application response, this mechanism is very useful. For Java exception error handling, although this is a very flexible mechanism, it should only be used and configured for fallback behavior. It is much better to at least initially catch all exceptions and respond in the base controller in an application appropriate manner.

12.4 Logging

As part of any application, it is useful to support application level logging and tracing. Although a low-tech approach for debugging, it is often the most useful mechanism for detecting application misbehavior in production (particularly in a distributed environment).

---

2.   The Application Assembly Tool (AAT) is a tool to build and edit J2EE archive (.WAR and .EAR) files. It is targeted for use by the J2EE deployer role to make modifications to deployment descriptors prior to application deployment.

Any logging framework used by an application needs to have low impact when logging is turned off. In this way, production code can have logging code deployed without incurring a heavy performance cost. Looking forward, J2EE V1.4 which prerequisites J2SE V1.4 requires the use of the `java.util.logging` framework. What to do in the meantime? The most common approach is to use the Logging framework maintained by the Apache group, log4j (see *http://jakarta.apache.org/log4j*).

With log4j, logging behavior is controlled by editing a configuration file, without touching the deployed application binary. One of the distinct features of log4j is inheritance in loggers. Using a logger hierarchy makes it possible to manage which log statements are enabled at an arbitrary granularity by whatever organization the developer desires. A logger has five distinct printing methods, one for each log level. The levels and their order are: DEBUG < INFO < WARN < ERROR < FATAL.

Listing 12.1, a code sample from log4j manual, outlines the use of this hierarchy, the level inheritance, and the corresponding determination of whether or not a statement is enabled:

Listing 12.1 Filtering of Log Messages within log4j.

```
// get a logger instance named "com.foo"

Logger  logger = Logger.getLogger("com.foo");



// Now set its level. Normally you do not need to set the

// level of a logger programmatically. This is usually done

// in configuration files.

logger.setLevel(Level.INFO);



Logger barlogger = Logger.getLogger("com.foo.Bar");



// This request is enabled, because WARN >= INFO.

logger.warn("Low fuel level.");



// This request is disabled, because DEBUG < INFO.
```

```
logger.debug("Starting search for nearest gas station.");


// The logger instance barlogger, named "com.foo.Bar",

// will inherit its level from the logger named

// "com.foo" Thus, the following request is enabled

// because INFO >= INFO.

barlogger.info("Located nearest gas station.");


// This request is disabled, because DEBUG < INFO.

barlogger.debug("Exiting gas station search");
```

As you can see, logging can be organized into whatever logical hierarchy you choose allowing very fine-grained control over enabling and disabling logging. In log4j, the possible target for a log is also very flexible. It can include an OutputStream, a Writer, a remote log4j server, a remote UNIX Syslog daemon, or an NT event logger, among others.

WAS users should find this organization very familiar. It is this same organization that is used by the WebSphere trace facility. In this case, the trace hierarchies are call components. WebSphere also provides JRas extensions, an application API to the WAS trace and logging facility. This can also be used to add messaging and tracing to your WebSphere applications.

12.5 Servlet Filters

One of the themes that runs throughout this book and is integral to J2EE application architecture goals is the goal to build reusable components. One key design philosophy that facilitates reuse is to provide the appropriate granularity of service. Another goal is to provide a mechanism to allow for the composition of services to create more complex and full-featured functionality. New with the servlet 2.3 specification is just such a standardized composition model for Web applications. The composable components in this case are servlet filters (see Figure 12.5).

As we discussed in Chapter 6, a filter is a component called as a wrapper to a request to a Web component (servlet or JSP). A filter can intercept the incoming request prior to delivery to the servlet. In this mode, the filter may provide additional quality of service operations (e.g., encryption, logging, and auditing). The filter can block the request and provide direct response to the client. This might be the case with an authentication or authorization agent. It might also be done if the filter is acting as a caching filter. The filter can also intercept and/or alter the

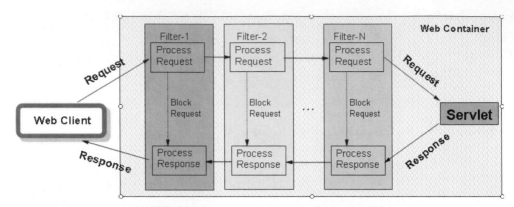

Figure 12.5 Design with servlet filters.

response stream. Data conversion filters—image conversion, XSLT processing, or a MIME-type chain filter—perform this function.

Another characteristic of a servlet filter is that they are associated at deployment time with either a Web resource or a group of Web resources via a URL pattern. Thus, the service composition is not something that needs to be managed programmatically.

A servlet filter is a class that implements the `javax.servlet.Filter` interface. The key method defined in this interface has the signature:

```
public void doFilter(ServletRequest request, ServletResponse response,

FilterChain chain) throws ServletException, IOException;
```

This method is invoked when the filter receives the incoming request stream. In the body of this method, the filter can do whatever processing it chooses. To forward the request to the remaining filters (Web component), the following line of code is called:

```
chain.doFilter(request, response);
```

Should the filter decide that further processing should not happen, this method is not called. If the filter wishes to intercept the response stream, that is available upon return from the `chain.doFilter()` call.

WebSphere Studio has a wizard to create Filter classes. It also has special entries in the Web deployment descriptor editor to manipulate and configure filter chains (see Figure 12.6).

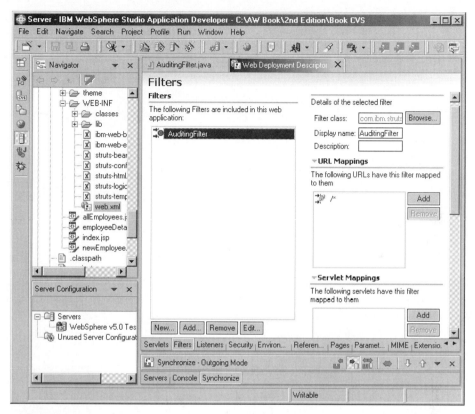

Figure 12.6 Configuring filters in WebSphere Studio's Web deployment descriptor editor.

12.6 Summary

We have covered several advanced topics in Web programming in this chapter. We've discussed how to find and implement controllers in an application, seen how exception handling within an application can be done using both J2EE-error pages and in a generic way, looked at using a standard Logging framework to enhance application maintenance, and examined servlet filters. In the next chapter we'll return to our case study for an end-to-end look at MVC development.

Developing and Testing JSPs in WSAD

In Chapters 6 and 7, you saw how to develop servlets to add dynamic behavior to your Web application. Servlets work well, but at the end of Chapter 7, we explored some difficulties in using servlets alone. Developing good dynamic HTML is hard. Getting the content right, making it look good, and getting HTML to do what you want can be quite difficult. It's even harder when the HTML is buried in Java print statements. In the Java editor, there's no WYSIWYG design view, no HTML content assist, no preview, quotes on attribute values have to be escaped, etc.

When servlets are used to create user interface components consisting of dynamic HTML pages, it's the HTML that is the primary focus, not Java. JSPs allow you to focus on the dominant language, HTML, making the development process much simpler.

Another problem we discussed was mixing control logic and user interface look and feel. By separating these concerns, we can develop JSPs that focus only on the user interface, making them simpler to develop, easier to test, and more reusable. We also discussed error handling which is a special case of separating control logic from user interface page design. In the servlet implementation, we had to catch exceptions and output different HTML based on the exception. JSPs offer a different solution by allowing us to specify error pages directly avoiding all the extra code.

In this chapter, we'll return to the example we developed in Chapter 7 and reimplement some of the servlets as JSPs. In doing so, we'll use the indirect development model based on MVC to provide better separation of user interface, controller, error handling, and model code as shown in Figure 13.1. We'll also introduce the components of WSAD that support JSP development, deployment, and testing. As in Chapter 7, we'll do this by introducing the tools in the context of developing the example JSP-based application.

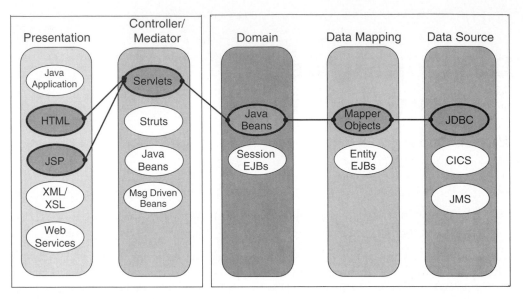

Figure 13.1 Architectural road map.

13.1 Another Look at MVC

Before jumping too far into the discussion of development tools for JSP, we should revisit the developer roles that may play a part in the development and maintenance of JSPs. Many early JSP developers were Java programmers who needed a way to purge their servlets of string literals representing HTML text. For them, any scripting tool or text editor that permits directly editing the HTML/JSP tags is sufficient.

When the Java programmers within an organization build JSPs, the development process typically observed has the static content of the JSPs developed by the Web page developers. These pages, developed to have consistent look and feel with the rest of the Web site, are then handed off to the Java developers to add in the scripting code responsible for providing the dynamic content. The final JSPs are usually returned to the Web page development team for maintenance, under the assumption that the added scripting code will rarely, if ever, need to change.

In general, the Web page development team only modifies the static HTML portions of the JSP source as necessary in order to account for new images, links, text updates, and similar visual updates.

The MVC programming style, particularly the wrapping of dynamic content in one or more JavaBeans, provides the opportunity for a different development model. When page developers build JSP pages, the most burdensome task is placing dynamic content within the page. This difficulty stems from the lack of accessibility to the Java (JSP) syntax.

13.2 JavaBeans, Introspection, and Contracts

The key problem of building JSP pages in an MVC environment is communication. When a team is divided into a set of individuals that develop Web pages and a second set of individuals that are server-side Java developers, lack of communication can create challenges.

Web developers are aware of what content should appear on the page. They must communicate to the server-side developers that certain dynamic content should be displayed on that page. This dynamic content is generally data that results from a client request (whether successful or unsuccessful). It is also possible for the server-side developer to communicate to the Web developer what dynamic content is available for display at a given point based on the information that has been collected from the user and retrieved from the server.

Formalizing the packaging of the dynamic content represents the contract between the JSP developer and the bean providers. Defining one or more types that expose the dynamic content as properties specifies most of this contract. These types are implemented as JavaBeans. JavaBeans have the advantage of being very tool friendly. It is very easy for a tool to introspect on a JavaBean class (and/or an accompanying BeanInfo class) and present to the developer the available properties, events, and methods. For our Display Page JSPs, these JavaBeans only need to deliver dynamic content as bean properties.

The rest of the contract involves the location of the JavaBeans at runtime. In other words, what information must be supplied in the useBean action, to make it possible to locate the JavaBeans (i.e., in what scope and under what ID will the bean be found).

A typical JSP page development tool feature permits browsing a set of JavaBeans to select a property for display on the page. Complexities arise in dealing with indexed properties—primarily with specifying the context for indexing, and nested properties. Nested properties arise when the structure of the dynamic data is complex. For example, consider our TimeSheet object. This object represents a collection of TimeSheetEntries. A TimeSheetEntry contains properties for date and project, neither of which are primitive data. If one wants to display the project name for a particular TimeSheetEntry, the JSP expression would look like:

```
<%= TimeSheet.getEntry(index).getProject().getName() %>
```

This could also be specified by walking the beans and their properties and selecting the leaf property name (TimeSheet, entry(index), project, name). For a tool to facilitate walking nested JavaBean properties, each property must be available in a nontype hiding manner. For instance, in the previous scenario, it is possible to get at the collection of TimeSheetEntries via the method `getEntries()` on the TimeSheet object. This returns a vector of TimeSheetEntry objects.

A vector, however, hides the type information of its contents. All accessors to the contents of the vector only guarantee that they return an instance of the Object class. A tool will not be able to expose the properties of the actual Java type stored in the collection, only the limited properties of `java.lang.Object`. By supplying the indexed property entry in the TimeSheet bean, it is possible to perform recursive introspection and make the project name visible to a developer.

13.3 Building Applications Using JSPs with WSAD

So let's get started with the JSP example. What we're going to do is take the servlet example project we created in Chapter 7 and change it to use JSPs where appropriate. If you don't want to develop the example from scratch, you can use the JSP Example project from the CD-ROM. See Appendix A for instructions on how to load the workspace containing the examples. If you're not familiar with the servlet example, look at section "Building an Example Servlet with WSAD" in Chapter 7 before proceeding. This chapter also assumes you are familiar with the WSAD basics covered in Chapter 7. If not, you might want to read Chapter 7 before continuing.

Create a J2EE Web project called JSP Example. In the Web project features list, select any features you want. We'll be working with the JSP Standard Tag library later in the chapter, so you can select it now. Remember, you can always add new Web project features by editing the Web project's properties or importing tag libraries.

Select Next when you are ready. On the next page of the Create a Web Project wizard, select an enterprise application for deploying the JSP Example (DefaultEAR is fine), set the context root for the Web application to jspExample, and make sure to select J2EE level 1.3. Press Finish to create the JSP example.

The layout of the project will be identical to the servlet example project in Chapter 7, except you might notice a number of Java .jar files were added to the WEB-INF/lib folder if you selected additional Web project features.

The domain model for the JSP example is the same as for the servlet example. Ideally this domain model would be in its own project so it could be shared by many other projects. But for this simple example, we'll copy it from the servlet example project. Copy and paste are a very effective means of instantiating patterns, so we'll be using it a lot.

Go to the servlet example project and select all the contents of the Java Source folder, copy, and then paste into the Java Source folder of the JSP example project. Be sure to copy the application.properties file too since it defines the data source information required to access the database. Edit the Web deployment descriptor (`web.xml` file) and add the CreateEmployee and UpdateEmployee servlets the same as you did in Chapter 7. Select each servlet and add the default URL mapping. You can delete the BrowseEmployees.java and EmployeeDetails.java servlet files in the `com.wsbook.servletexample` package, as we will be replacing those servlets with JSPs. You can also copy the images folder, banner.html, browseEmployees.html, and index.html files from the servlet example project Web Content folder since we'll need very similar files for this example.

Edit the index.html file to indicate the purpose of the Web application. Make sure there is a link on the page to browseEmployees.html. Refer to Chapter 7 if you need any help creating or editing the page. You should have something that looks like Figure 13.2 for file `index.html`.

Now create or edit the browseEmployees.html file and set the `src` attribute of the list frame to browseEmployees.jsp as shown in Listing 13.1. Recall that this link was to the Browse-Employees servlet in Chapter 7. Since this servlet was primarily used to display a list of employees, JSP provides a better solution.

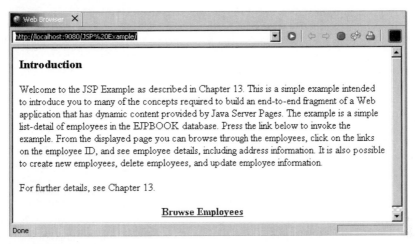

Figure 13.2 index.html.

Listing 13.1 browseEmployees.html

```
<!DOCTYPE HTML PUBLIC "-//W3C//DTD HTML 4.01 Transitional//EN">

<html>

<head>

<meta http-equiv="Content-Type" content="text/html; charset=iso-8859-1">

<title>Servlet Example</title>

</head>

<frameset rows="50,*, 240">

        <frame name="banner" scrolling="no" noresize src="banner.html"

                marginwidth="0" marginheight="0" frameborder="0"/>

        <frame name="list" scrolling="auto" src="browseEmployees.jsp"

                marginwidth="50" marginheight="20"frameborder="1"/>

        <frame name="detail" marginwidth="0" marginheight="20"

                frameborder="0"/>

        <noframes>
```

```
    <body>

    <p>This page uses frames, but your browser doesn't support them.</p>

    </body>

    </noframes>

</frameset>

</html>
```

Now create the browseEmployees.jsp file. Select the Web Content folder, right-click, and select *New > JSP File*. The New JSP File wizard has a number of pages that can be used to customize the creation of the JSP page and make any necessary updates to the Web application deployment descriptor. Press F1 to get a detailed description of all the things you can set. This information is primarily used to initialize information in the JSP file. We'll either be taking the defaults for most entries, or changing them using Page Designer.

Enter the JSP file name, select HTML for the markup language, and press Finish to create the file. This first version of browseEmployees.jsp will be a traditional JSP using Java in scriptlets and expressions. Later we'll see how to use JSP tag libraries as another option for entering dynamic content. Listing 13.2 shows the browseEmployees.jsp file source. Doesn't this look a lot better than the Java source code we created in Listing 7.5?

Listing 13.2 browseEmployees.jsp

```
<!DOCTYPE HTML PUBLIC "-//W3C//DTD HTML 4.01 Frameset//EN">

<HTML>

<HEAD>

<%@ page

    language="java"

    contentType="text/html; charset=WINDOWS-1252"

    import="com.wsbook.servletexample.domain.Employee,

            java.sql.SQLException,java.util.Iterator"%>

<META http-equiv="Content-Type"

    content="text/html; charset=WINDOWS-1252">
```

```
<META name="GENERATOR" content="IBM WebSphere Studio">


<TITLE>Browse Employees (JSP version)</TITLE>

</HEAD>

<BODY>

<h3 align="center">All Employees</h3>

<TABLE align="center" BORDER="yes" CELLSPACING="2" CELLPADDING="0"

      WIDTH="70%">

      <TR>

            <TD>

            <center><b>Id</b></center>

            </TD>

            <TD>

            <center><b>Name</b></center>

            </TD>

            <TD width="40">

            <center><b>Age</b></center>

            </TD>

      </TR>

      <%try {

            Iterator employees = Employee.findAll().iterator();

            while (employees.hasNext()) {

                  Employee employee = (Employee) employees.next();%>

      <TR>
```

```
        <TD><A HREF="employeeDetails.jsp?id=<%=employee.getId()%>"

              target="detail"> <%=employee.getId()%></A></TD>

        <TD><%=employee.getName()%></TD>

        <TD width="40"><%=employee.getAge()%></TD>

    </TR>

        <%}

} catch (SQLException e) {

}%>

<TR>

    <TD colspan="3">

            <A href="employeeDetails.jsp" target="detail">

            Create Employee...

            </A></TD>

    </TR>

</TABLE>

</BODY>

</HTML>
```

The previous example shows how you can easily mix Java and HTML within a JSP page, and how you can use Java iterators to generate table rows in a JSP, a very common practice we'll revisit later. There's one thing that's not quite right about this example. Notice the scriptlet near the end—

```
<%> }

        } catch (SQLException e) {

} %>
```

That scriptlet presents a problem, or rather solves a problem in a brute-force way. The issue is that `Employee.findAll()` can throw an SQLException. If the database is not available for some reason (say it was not created, or DataSource is misconfigured) then `findAll()` will fail and an exception will be thrown. However, in this version of the JSP, the user would not know at all! So, if eating the exception isn't the right approach, what else could you try?

You could try to forward to another page that would display the error, but that won't work. You can't use `RequestDispatcher.forward()` or `RequestDispatcher.include()` if you've sent any output to the client. Doing so would raise an IllegalStateException. Instead, you could change the output that follows to show that an error occurred, but that's not a great solution either—what if the exception occurred 3/4 of the way down a page? The user might not notice that the information he was viewing was incomplete (and thus wrong).

Another option would be to move all of the code that can throw an exception to the very beginning of the JSP, but that's not the best solution either. Then you end up with a bunch of initialization Java code laced with `if` statements and catch blocks before you ever get to the meat of the JSP (the HTML).

Since none of these solutions work, we have to conclude we should try something else. In fact, the right solution is to apply MVC in the way we've already discussed. We'll perform the database lookup in a servlet class that will then forward to our browseEmployees JSP in the case where the database lookup succeeds, or forward to an error page in the case where it doesn't. So, we'll need to change our browseEmployees.jsp to get the employees from the session context that is filled in by the controller servlet instead of invoking the `Employee.findAll` method directly.

Listing 13.3 browseEmployees.jsp

```
!DOCTYPE HTML PUBLIC "-//W3C//DTD HTML 4.01 Frameset//EN">

<HTML>

<HEAD>

<%@ page

    language="java"

    contentType="text/html; charset=WINDOWS-1252"

    import="com.wsbook.servletexample.domain.Employee,

            java.util.Iterator"%>

<META http-equiv="Content-Type"

    content="text/html; charset=WINDOWS-1252">
```

```
<META name="GENERATOR" content="IBM WebSphere Studio">


<TITLE>Browse Employees (JSP version)</TITLE>

</HEAD>

<BODY>

<jsp:useBean id="employees"

        type="java.util.Iterator" scope="request"></jsp:useBean>

<h3 align="center">All Employees</h3>

<TABLE align="center" BORDER="yes" CELLSPACING="2" CELLPADDING="0"

        WIDTH="70%">

        <TR>

                <TD>

                <center><b>Id</b></center>

                </TD>

                <TD>

                <center><b>Name</b></center>

                </TD>

                <TD width="40">

                <center><b>Age</b></center>

                </TD>

        </TR>

                <% while (employees.hasNext()) {

                        Employee employee = (Employee) employees.next();%>

        <TR>
```

```
            <TD><A HREF="ShowEmployeeDetail?id=<%=employee.getId()%>"

                target="detail"> <%=employee.getId()%></A></TD>

            <TD><%=employee.getName()%></TD>

            <TD width="40"><%=employee.getAge()%></TD>

        </TR>

            <% } %>

        <TR>

            <TD colspan="3"><A href="newEmployee.jsp" target="detail">

Create

            Employee... </A></TD>

        </TR>

</TABLE>

</BODY>

</HTML>
```

If you compare the version in Listing 13.3 to the previous one, you'll quickly see what changed. The major difference is that we no longer need the try...catch block because we are no longer calling the findAll() method. Instead, the collection of Employees is being passed in to the JSP through the HttpRequest, which the JSP picks up through using the useBean tag. This is a typical way of using session context to pass information between components in an application. Since the set of employees is no longer fetched in the JSP, the mechanism by which a user requests that the list be displayed is slightly different also. We need to create a controller servlet that accesses the employees and forwards them to the servlet for display.

From the Web perspective, select the Java Source folder in the JSP example project and use the *New > Servlet* menu option from the Context menu to create a servlet. The servlet class will be named com.wsbook.servletexample.BrowseEmployees, and will only implement the doGet() method. The source code for this servlet is shown here:

```
package com.wsbook.servletexample;

...
```

```java
public class BrowseEmployees extends HttpServlet {

    public void doGet(HttpServletRequest req, HttpServletResponse resp)

        throws ServletException, IOException {

            try {

                Collection employees = Employee.findAll();

                req.setAttribute("employees", employees);

                RequestDispatcher rd =
getServletContext().getRequestDispatcher("/browseEmployees.jsp");

                rd.forward(req,resp);

            } catch (SQLException e) {

                RequestDispatcher rd =
getServletContext().getRequestDispatcher("/databaseError.html");

                rd.forward(req,resp);

            }

        }

}
```

This is the elegant solution that we were looking for. This servlet attempts the lookup of the list of employees from the database, and if all goes well, it places the collection in the HttpRequest and forwards the request to the browseEmployees JSP. If a database exception occurs, it forwards the request to an HTML page that informs the user that an error has occurred.

Changing the application flow like this, though, means we'll have to undo a change we made earlier. Edit the browseEmployees.html file and set the src attribute of the list frame to BrowseEmployees. This will set the file back to its previous value, which will invoke the servlet first, which will then delegate display of the page to our new JSP.

13.4   Editing JavaServer Pages

The default editor for JSP pages is page designer. As with HTML pages, page designer supports three views of a JSP page: Design, Source, and Preview. Most JSP editing is done in the page designer Source view, which has many features designed to simplify JSP editing.

You can insert, delete, or edit tags in the source pane in a number of ways:

- Type tags in directly
- Use content assist to prompt for valid tags and tag attributes
- Use the JSP menu items
- Select toolbar buttons
- Select a tag and edit its attributes in the Properties or Attributes view
- Add and remove tags using the Outline view

As with any other HTML tag, you can use content assist to help enter JSP tags. As a convenience, you can also use the JSP menu items on the menu bar to insert common JSP tags into your file. Many of these menu items provide dialogs that assist in setting the attributes and content of the tags. Since they are dialogs, they have F1 help that you can use to get detailed information about permissible values for the tag attributes. You'll also find many common HTML editing functions are available on toolbar buttons.

Another great editing convenience is the ability to navigate around in the JSP, and add tags and attributes from the outline view. You can select a tag in the outline view to position the source and design views at that tag. Use the context menu on the selected item to remove the tag, or add valid children tags either before or after the selected tag. The attributes for the tag are also available from the context menu. Selecting an attribute adds it to the tag with a default value, in many cases. Remember you can always use undo and redo actions to remove or reapply edits no matter how many were made to the document.

The best thing about the page designer source editor for JSPs is that content assist works seamlessly across both HTML and Java. The editor understands the syntax of both languages so it always knows what's possible to include at any point in the source. Content assist eliminates the need for tedious and error-prone typing. You can use content assist to add HTML tags, JSP tags, and tags from tag libraries, attributes of tags, values of some attributes, scriptlets, expressions, access variables available at the current scope, methods and properties of variables, code macros, etc. It's hard to imagine how we got along without content assist.

Invoke content assist anywhere in the source pane by pressing CONTROL+SPACE. Then scroll down the list to see what's available at that point in the code or type prefix characters to automatically search the list for matching contents.

Press ENTER on a selection to have it added to the source. You can also add your own JSP macros to the source editor that can be invoked using content assist. Select *Window > Properties* and navigate to *Web and XML Files > JSP Files > JSP Macros*. You can enter a new macro that will show up in content assist at the enabled location and with the given content. Use the macros provided by WSAD as examples or copy, paste, and update their contents to make your own.

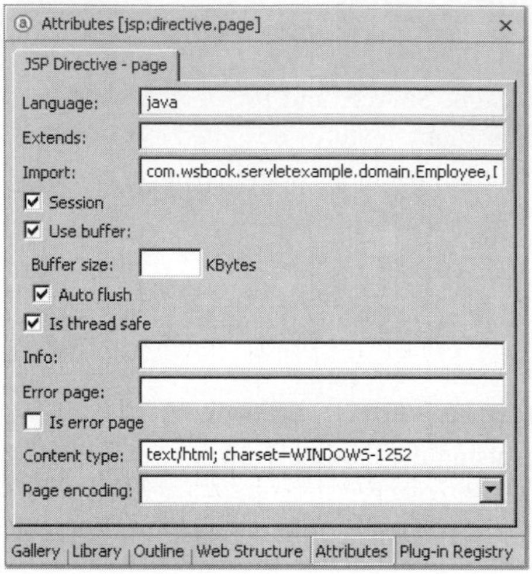

Figure 13.3 JSP page directive attributes.

JSP tags, scriptlets, and expressions are also shown in the Attributes view. For example, select the jsp:page element in browseEmployees.jsp. You can either edit the properties directly in the jsp:page tag using content assist, or use the dialog in the Attributes view as shown in Figure 13.3.

Each has its advantages. We've already discussed the benefits of content assist in the source pane. The Attributes view presents the attributes of the selected tag organized in a dialog. Edit any field and the updated attribute appears in the tag in the source pane. The corresponding attribute will be removed for fields without values. The field labels are often more descriptive than the tag attribute names alone. If you use the Attributes view, you don't have to worry about the appropriate XML syntax for a parameter or quoting attributes since the dialog adds them to the source document for you. And you can always press F1 to get context-sensitive help.

The Attributes view also shows the contents of JSP scriptlets or expressions when selected in either the design or the source pane of the page designer. Figure 13.4 shows the page designer Design view opened on browseEmployees.jsp. The cell under the Name column heading is selected and the expression code is shown in the Attributes view. You can edit the expression directly in the Attributes view without having to switch to the Source view and locate the containing tag. However, content assist is not supported in the Attributes view. Unless the edit is very simple, or you know exactly what to enter, you might want to edit in the source pane instead.

Now, let's return to the example. Referring to Listing 13.3, the JSP contains a page directive that indicates the language is Java and the content type is text/html, and lists the referenced classes that must be imported into the page in order for it to compile and run. The page directive is followed by HTML for defining the table to display the employees. After outputting the header table row, a scriptlet is used to iterate over all the employees in the database and create a

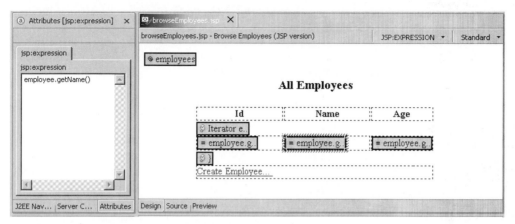

Figure 13.4 Page designer Design view.

table row containing the employee ID, name, and age, the summary information we wanted to display to help select an employee.

The employee ID entry is output in an anchor tag whose `href` attribute references the employeeDetails.jsp file with `id` as an argument. We'll be developing that JSP next. The last row in the table provides an anchor tag with `href` linking to a JSP for creating employees.

Next we'll create a servlet and JSP for viewing the employee details. Recall that in the first version of our browseEmployees JSP we referenced the employeeDetails.jsp in the anchor tag that displayed the employee ID in the table. In the second version, we changed from referencing the employeeDetails JSP to referencing a URL that represents the ShowEmployeeDetail servlet. As in the prior example, start by creating the employeeDetails.jsp file as shown in Listing 13.4.

Listing 13.4 employeeDetails.jsp

```
<!DOCTYPE HTML PUBLIC "-//W3C//DTD HTML 4.01 Frameset//EN">

<html>

<head>

<%@ page

  language="java"

  contentType="text/html; charset=ISO-8859-1"

  import="com.wsbook.servletexample.domain.Employee,

          java.util.Iterator,
```

```
                javax.servlet.jsp.JspException"%>

<meta http-equiv="Content-Type" content="text/html; charset=ISO-8859-1">

<meta name="GENERATOR" content="IBM WebSphere Studio">

<title>Employee Details</title>

</head>

<body>

    <jsp:useBean id="employee"

            class="com.wsbook.servletexample.domain.Employee"

            scope="session">

    </jsp:useBean>

    <h3 align="center">Employee Details</h3>

    <div align="center">

<form name="updateEmployee" target="_top" method="post"

    action="UpdateEmployee">

<table align="center" border="1" cellpadding="0" cellspacing="0"

    width="70%">

    <tr>

            <td width="60">

            <div align="right">Name:</div>

            </td>

            <td><input type="text" name="name" size="70"

                value="<%=employee.getName()%>" /></td>

    </tr>

    <tr>
```

```
        <td width="60">

        <div align="right">Age:</div>

        </td>

        <td><input type="text" name="age" size="70"

              value="<%=employee.getAge()%>" /></td>

</tr>

<tr>

        <td width="60">

        <div align="right">Street:</div>

        </td>

        <td><input type="text" name="street" size="70"

              value="<%=employee.getStreet()%>" /></td>

</tr>

<tr>

        <td colspan="2">

        <table border="0" cellpadding="0" cellspacing="0">

              <tr>

                    <td width="60">

                    <div align="right">City:</div>

                    </td>

                    <td><input type="text" name="city" size="27"

                          value="<%=employee.getCity()%>"/></td>

                    <td width="30">

                    <div align="right">State:</div>
```

```
                              </td>

                              <td><input type="text" name="state" size="6"

                                     value="<%=employee.getState()%>/"></td>

                              <td width="30">

                              <div align="right">Zip:</div>

                              </td>

                              <td><input type="text" name="zip" size="10"

                                     value="<%=employee.getZip()%>" /></td>

                       </tr>

                </table>

                </td>

         </tr>

         <td colspan="2">

         <div align="center">

                <input type="submit" name="submit"

                       value="Update"

                       align="center"/>

                <input type="submit" name="submit"

                       value="Delete"

                       align="center"/>

         </div>

         </td>

         </tr>

  </table>
```

```
</form>

</div>

</body>

</html>
```

The body of the page has a `jsp:useBean` tag that looks for a JavaBean in the session scope that is the selected employee. This bean will be used later to communicate the selected employee to the UpdateEmployee servlet that performs the updates.

In Chapter 7, we used a hidden field in the HTML form containing the employee ID, and used the ID in the UpdateEmployee servlet to look up the employee to be updated. This may be less efficient because the employee may have to be fetched from the database twice. After retrieving the Employee from the session, the rest of the JSP creates an HTML form containing fields for all the employee information. We use JSP expressions to initialize the fields with data from the selected employee. The form action invokes the UpdateEmployee servlet when the Submit button is pressed.

As in the previous example, you will also need to add the ShowEmployeeDetails servlet. The source code for this servlet is shown here—

```
package com.wsbook.servletexample;

...

public class ShowEmployeeDetail extends HttpServlet {

    public void doGet(HttpServletRequest req, HttpServletResponse resp)

        throws ServletException, IOException {

        try {

            String employeeId = req.getParameter("id");

            Employee employee =

                Employee.findByPrimaryKey(employeeId);

            HttpSession session = req.getSession(true);

            session.setAttribute("employee", employee);

            RequestDispatcher rd =
```

```
                    getServletContext().getRequestDispatcher(

                        "/employeeDetails.jsp");

                rd.forward(req, resp);

        } catch (NoSuchObjectException e) {

            RequestDispatcher rd =

                    getServletContext().getRequestDispatcher(

                        "/noSuchEmployee.jsp");

                rd.forward(req, resp);

        } catch (SQLException e) {

            log("***Error attempting to find employee", e);

            RequestDispatcher rd =

    getServletContext().getRequestDispatcher("/databaseError.html");

                rd.forward(req, resp);

        }

    }
```

This servlet is similar to the BrowseEmployees servlet shown earlier. One difference is that when a database exception occurs, it is logged to the servlet log using `Servlet.log()`. These messages are printed to the Console view when using the Web application server within the WTE. This makes it easier to debug your Web application. In a production application server, the messages are logged to the server's log files.

The UpdateEmployee servlet is almost the same as the one we used in Chapter 7. The primary difference is we're now getting the selected employee from the session rather than looking it up again by ID. Notice that the UpdateEmployee servlet also removes the selected employee from the session context once it is done updating. This keeps the memory footprint down by removing context variables that are no longer needed. Listing 13.5 has the details for the UpdateEmployee servlet.

Listing 13.5 UpdateEmployee.java

```java
package com.wsbook.servletexample;

...

public class UpdateEmployee extends HttpServlet {

    public void doPost(HttpServletRequest req, HttpServletResponse resp)
        throws ServletException, IOException {

        // Update the employee and address information and
        Employee employee =
            Employee)req.getSession().getAttribute("employee");
        // see what button the user pressed
        String action = req.getParameter("submit");
        if (action.equals("Delete")) {
            try {

                employee.delete();
            } catch (SQLException e) {
                log("***Error deleting an employee: "+e);
            } catch (MappingException e) {

            }
        } else {
            employee.setName(req.getParameter("name"));
```

```java
        try {

            employee.setAge(

                Integer.parseInt(req.getParameter("age")));

        } catch (NumberFormatException exc) {

                log("***Error, employee id must be a number");

        }

        employee.setStreet(req.getParameter("street"));

        employee.setCity(req.getParameter("city"));

        employee.setState(req.getParameter("state"));

        employee.setZip(req.getParameter("zip"));

        try {

                employee.update();

        } catch (MappingException e) {

                log("***Error, couldn't save employee or
address");

        } catch (SQLException e) {

                log("***Error updating employee: ", e);

        }

    }

    req.getSession().removeAttribute("employee");

    // refresh the employee's list so it shows the updates

    resp.sendRedirect("BrowseEmployees");

    }

}
```

13.5   Validating the JSP Page

In WSAD 5.0, all you need to do to check a JSP page is save it. The J2EE validator run, and finds any HTML or JSP tag errors, and any Java errors in scriptlets or expressions. Custom tags can also specify their own validators, which are also run. You can control what gets validated in all projects by editing the workspace preferences. Select `Window> Preferences` and then select `Validation`. Figure 13.5 shows the available preferences. You can also override workspace validation preferences by setting the Validation preferences for the properties of an individual project.

JSP validation actually runs the page compiler and then the Java compiler. The only errors that could remain are runtime (logic) errors which appear as exceptions in the Console view or Web application server logs, but the line number where the error occurred is that of the JSP file. There is little reason to ever look at the generated Java code, although you can if you want.

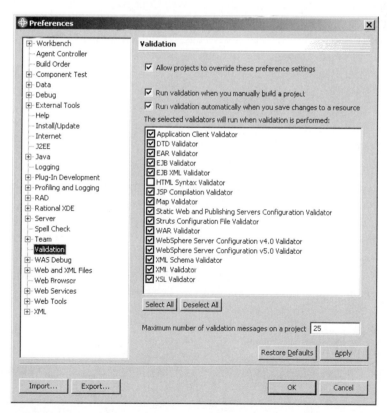

Figure 13.5 Validation preferences.

13.6 Running on the Server

We're now almost ready to test the JSP. If you haven't done so, edit the JSP Example project Web deployment descriptor and add the BrowseEmployees, ShowEmployeeDetail, UpdateEmployee, and CreateEmployee servlets. You'll also need to add the jdbc/EJPBOOK data source reference as described in Chapter 7. Then, if you didn't select an EAR for your sample application when you created it, do so now by selecting an EAR project and adding your application as a module to its deployment descriptor.

You'll also need to deploy the EAR to a server configuration, and configure the server to support the EJPBOOK data source as described in Chapter 7. And you'll also want to create the noSuchEmployee.jsp error page to display a message indicating the employee could not be found in the database. Check the Task view for broken links or any other problems and fix them as needed.

Now select the JSP Example project, or the Web Content/index.html file, and select the Run on server choice from its context menu. You'll see the index.html file displayed in a Web browser in a Workbench editor pane. Navigate to the link you added to invoke browseEmployees.html. You should see the same output you saw when running the servlet example in Chapter 7. If you have any trouble, review the sections on editing the Web application and enterprise application deployment descriptors and setting up the server configuration covered in Chapter 7. Everything should be the same except for using both JSPs and servlets to split the work of display.

13.7 Debugging the JSP

Debugging JSPs is just as easy as debugging servlets. The debugger supports source level debugging directly in the JSP. There is no need to save the generated Java from the JSP page compiler and debug using the generated Java source. To debug a JSP using the TE server, first make sure the server is started in debug mode. From the Web perspective, select the Servers view. Locate the server instance that is configured to run the EAR project for your Web application module. You should see that it is started in debug mode as shown in Figure 13.6.

If the server is not started in debug mode, select it, right-click, and select *Stop*. After the server stops, right-click again and select Debug. The server will be started in debug mode and you will be able to debug JSPs and servlets.

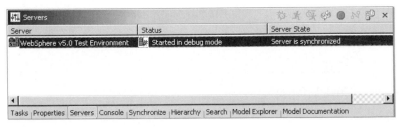

Figure 13.6 Starting the TE in debug mode.

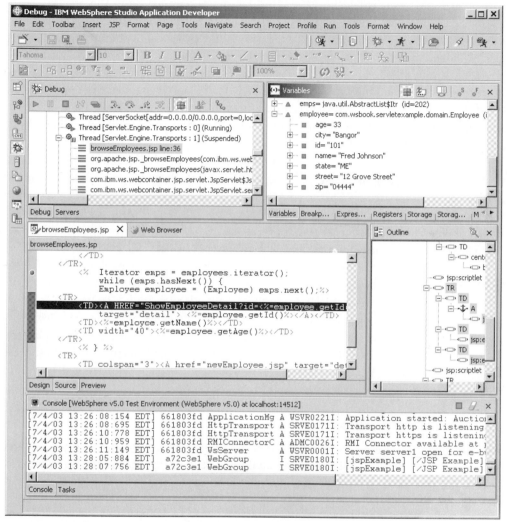

Figure 13.7 Debugging a JSP BrowseEmployees, ShowEmployeeDetail.

Next, open the JSP you want to debug with the Page Designer editor, and go to the Source view. You can set a breakpoint on any line that contains Java source. Open the browseEmployee.jsp file, and set a breakpoint on the line that gets an Iterator over all the employees in the database as shown in Figure 13.7. Set the breakpoint by double-clicking in the margin to the left of the line of code. A breakpoint will be set, and you'll see the breakpoint marker in the left margin.

Now select index.html, right-click, and select either *Run on Server...* or *Debug on Server....* You can select either because we already started the server in debug mode. If the server weren't running, and you wanted to debug a JSP, you could simply select Debug on

Server…, and the server would be started in debug mode automatically. You should see the browser open in the Workbench with index.html displayed. Select the link that invokes the browseEmployee.html file. This file will invoke the browseEmployees.jsp in order to fill in the table in the list frame.

If the step-by-step debugging dialog is displayed, disable step-by-step debugging and go to the debugger view and press F8 to continue. We don't want to use step-by-step debugging because we have specifically set a breakpoint at the point we want to debug the application. Recall that you can turn off step-by-step mode for all Web projects by setting the preference in the WAS Debug preferences.

Once the application has halted at the breakpoint, press the *Step* button or F6 three times. You should see something like Figure 13.7, showing the JSP stopped at the line that is putting the employee ID as an argument to the employeeDetails.jsp link. Notice that debugger stopped at a line containing HTML that contained a JSP expression. If the HTML does not contain any Java, it is skipped when you step to the next executable line. At this point, you can examine variables in the JSP such as the employee variable shown in the Variables view.

Clear the breakpoint by removing it from the Breakpoints list or by double-clicking the marker in the browseEmployees.jsp file and press *Run* or F8 to allow the JSP to finish displaying the employee list. See the WSAD Help for further information on debugging Web applications including how to debug using a remote WAS. Open the Help contents, and browse to *Web developer information > Debugging applications*. You can also develop and debug J2EE application using a remote WAS. However, developing and debugging J2EE applications is easiest using the built-in WTE server. The WTE uses a WAS 5.0 server, so your applications will behave just as they would when running inside an external WAS.

13.8 Simplifying JSPs

Earlier in the chapter, we discussed the separation of Web and Java developer roles, and how MVC helps separate business logic and user interface concerns. This enables the Web developer to concentrate on HTML and a consistent user interface. Recall that the Web content developer is concerned with the best presentation and flow for the Web application, not the implementation issues that are required when programming in Java. When HTML and Java are combined, content developers are drawn into evolution and maintenance issues that they would prefer to avoid. JSPs help solve these problems by allowing the focus to shift from Java to HTML. But the JSPs we've developed so far still have Java code in the expressions and scriptlets.

In this section, we'll explore using custom JSP tags, and the JSTL to eliminate the use of Java in JSPs. This may sound like a reasonable ideal, but it isn't without cost. We'll explore the issues that arise, and a hybrid approach may provide a reasonable compromise.

WSAD 5.0 also supports JSPs written using either Java or JavaScript. If you have Web content developers who are familiar with JavaScript, creating JSPs using JavaScript may be another option.

13.8.1 Java Standard Tag Library

The JSTL provides a number of custom JSP tags to eliminate the need to use Java for most common operations in a JSP. JSTL supports the following custom tags:

- out—Output expressions to the output stream
- set—Set variable properties in storage scopes (page, request, session, application)
- remove—Remove variables from storage scopes
- if—Conditional execution tag
- choose, when, otherwise—choose among many options when test conditions are met
- forEach, forTokens—Iterate over collections of objects or tokens in a string
- url—Support for parsing URL strings
- import—Import text from other files
- redirect—Redirecting output to another page

In addition, JSTL supports two modes of operation. You can use either Java expressions to specify tag attribute values or the JSTL Expression Language (EL) which provides easy access to variables in the storage scopes and a simple grammar for arithmetic and logical expressions. For details, see JSR-52, "JavaServer Pages Standard Tag Library" available from *http://www.jcp.org*. The tag library comes in two versions, runtime (RT) and EL. The RT version supports Java expressions while the EL version supports the JSTL Expression Language.

Each version is stored in a different tag library with a different XML namespace prefix. You can also use both versions in the same JSP by using the proper namespace prefix. However, it is not possible to mix Java and EL syntax in the same tag. Use EL syntax in EL tags, and Java syntax in RT tags.

To use custom tags in a JSP, you must first add the tag library to your Web project. The easiest way to do this for JSTL is to edit the Web project's properties, and add JSTL as a Web project feature. Select the JSP example project, right-click, and select Properties. Then select the Web properties page. Under Available Web Project features: select Include the JSP Standard Tag library as shown in Figure 13.8. This will include all the tag library definitions and .jar files needed by your application to use JSTL. You should now see files `jstl.jar` and `standard.jar` in the WEB-INF/lib folder of the Web project.

13.8.2 JSTL Expression Language

Now let's edit browseEmployees.jsp to use JSTL and its EL. You can add custom tags to a JSP using the Insert Custom Tag dialog shown in Figure 13.9. From the menu bar, select *JSP >Insert Custom...* to bring up the dialog. The dialog shows the tag libraries that are currently imported into our JSP as jsp:taglib directives. If there are no tag libraries in the document, the list will be empty. To insert JSTL, click *Add...* to invoke the Select a Tag Library as shown in Figure 13.10.

The tag libraries that are available for selection are those that have been imported into the Web project. If the tag library you want isn't available in the list, press the *Import...* button to import it into the project as a tag library .jar file. You can also specify a URI for the tag library,

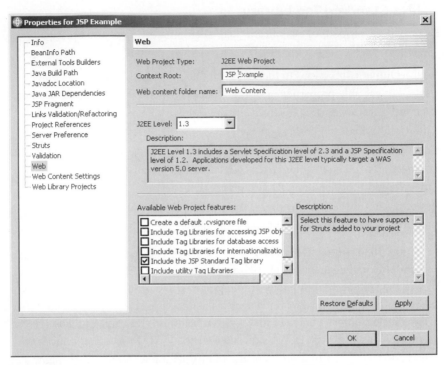

Figure 13.8 Adding the JSP Standard Tag Library feature to a Web project.

which will place an entry in the Web application deployment descriptor mapping the URI name to the tag library location so the Web application server can find the required classes.

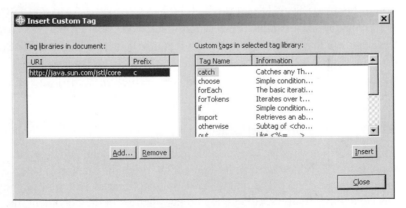

Figure 13.9 Adding a custom tag to a JSP.

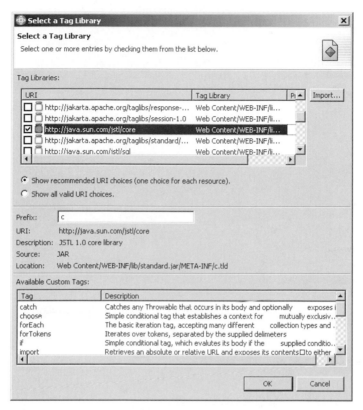

Figure 13.10 Adding a tag library to a JSP.

JSP 1.2 tag library .jar files contain the .tld files directly in the .jar file eliminating the need for additional entries in the deployment descriptor. Since we added the JSTL feature by updating the Web properties, the tag libraries we need are already in the Web application.

Select a tag library by clicking its URI to see the tags and tag descriptions that are in that tag library, and the namespace prefix required for using them. This is very helpful in identifying the tag libraries you need. Select the tag library with URI *http://java.sun.com/jstl/core* by clicking the check box to the left of the tag library URI as shown in Figure 13.10. Notice the Prefix field. You'll need to use this prefix when accessing tags from this library. Click *OK* on the Select a Tag Library and you'll see the selected tag libraries in the Insert Custom Tag dialog, which also shows the tag library URI, prefix, and available tags. Notice that JSP taglib directives were inserted at the beginning of the JSP indicating the tag library URI and prefix available for use in the JSP. Now you can insert custom tags into the JSP by selecting the tag library URI in the Insert Custom Tag dialog to display the tags in that library and then select a tag to insert it into the document.

Alternatively, you can type the tag library prefix followed by a colon and invoke content assist to see what tags are available in the library.

Listing 13.6 shows another version of browseEmployees.jsp called browseEmployees3.jsp that uses JSTL EL.

Listing 13.6 browseEmployees3.jsp – Using JSTL EL

```
<!DOCTYPE HTML PUBLIC "-//W3C//DTD HTML 4.01 Frameset//EN">

<%@taglib uri="http://java.sun.com/jstl/core" prefix="c"%>

<HTML>

<HEAD>

<%@ page

        language="java"

        contentType="text/html; charset=WINDOWS-1252"

        import="com.wsbook.servletexample.domain.Employee,

java.util.Collection, java.util.Iterator"%>

<META http-equiv="Content-Type"

        content="text/html; charset=WINDOWS-1252">

<META name="GENERATOR" content="IBM WebSphere Studio">


<TITLE>Browse Employees (JSP version)</TITLE>

</HEAD>

<BODY>

<jsp:useBean id="employees" class="java.util.ArrayList" scope="request">

</jsp:useBean>

<h3 align="center">All Employees</h3>

<TABLE align="center" BORDER="yes" CELLSPACING="2" CELLPADDING="0"

        WIDTH="70%">
```

```
    <TR>

        <TD>

        <center><b>Id</b></center>

        </TD>

        <TD>

        <center><b>Name</b></center>

        </TD>

        <TD width="40">

        <center><b>Age</b></center>

        </TD>

    </TR>

    <c:forEach var="emp" items="${employees}">

    <TR>

        <TD><A HREF="ShowEmployeeDetail?id=<c:out value="${emp.id}"/>"

            target="detail"> <c:out value="${emp.id}"/></A></TD>

        <TD><c:out value="${emp.name}"/></TD>

        <TD width="40"><c:out value="${emp.age}"/></TD>

    </TR>

    </c:forEach>

    <TR>

        <TD colspan="3"><A href="newEmployee.jsp"

target="detail">Create

        Employee...</A></TD>

    </TR>
```

```
</TABLE>

</BODY>

</HTML>
```

This version uses the jsp:useBean tag to declare a bean for the employees list. Remember that all variable accesses using JSTL EL are variables in some storage scope. It is not possible to access regular Java variables using JSTL EL. In addition, any local variables JSTL creates, such as the one specified by the `var` attribute of the c:forEach tag, will be created as variables in the page scope. This will be important to remember when mixing Java and JSTL expressions in the same JSP because it determines how to access the variables.

JSP browseEmployees3.jsp shows a couple of important simplifications of the browseEmployees.jsp. The first improvement is in iterating over the employees in the database. The c:forEach tag specifies a `var` attribute that names a variable in the page scope that iterates over the collection obtained from the `items` attribute. In this case, the items obtained from the employees variable we initialized in the jsp:useBean tag.

We then use the `emp` variable to output the employee properties in the HTML table using the c:out JSTL tag. You can't use a JSP expression here because JSTL EL variables are only valid in the EL version of JSTL. Using the c:out tag instead of a JSP expression also unifies the JSP editing because everything is handled as an XML tag. Notice that the employees variable is type hiding as it is a collection that only knows it contains objects.

However, we didn't have to do anything for the JSTL EL to know the `emp` variable represented an employee and had `id`, `name`, and `age` properties. This is because JSTL EL uses Java reflection to access the attributes of the bean through its `getProperty` methods. For example, the EL expression `${emp.name}` would result in the same value as the JSP expression `<jsp:getProperty name="emp" property="name"/>`.

Using JSTL EL did result in removing the JSP expression and scriptlet tags, and did simplify the JSP, especially in the area of exception handling and iterating over collections. However, it raises some issues:

- Any tag library introduces new language elements that Web developers have to learn. Those that achieve common use will be well understood, but others could create confusion. Good tag library documentation integrated with WSAD is helpful.
- Tag libraries use potentially verbose XML syntax in some situations where Java is actually simpler. For example, outputting the employee name using a JSP expression is `<%=employee.getName()%>`. The same thing using JSTL EL would be `<c:out value="${employee.name}"/>`
- JSTL EL can only access properties of a bean. It cannot use methods and events that are also defined on the bean. This significantly limits its ability to access computed

attributes or simple business logic. It does, however, help keep business logic out of JSP pages and supports our goal of using JSPs exclusively for user interfaces.

- JSTL EL has to lookup a variable reference in a storage scope and then uses reflection to access the reference attribute. This will be slower than calling an accessor method directly on a Java variable but does eliminate the need to cast variables to the proper type in cases where the type is hidden by a container.
- JSTL potentially adds to the complexity of the Web application through the use of additional tag libraries and contributes to runtime overhead.
- Content assist is not currently supported for JSTL EL.
- Page designer does not currently support Attribute dialogs for JSTL tags although content assist does work for all custom tag libraries.
- Custom tags may not have a meaningful appearance in the page designer Design view limiting their utility in WYSIWYG editing.
- The JSP debugger does not currently allow setting breakpoints on JSTL statements. In addition, it is more difficult to examine variables during debugging because they are inside the JSP context variables instead of being simple Java local variables.

13.8.3 Mixing JSTL RT with JSP Expressions

Some of these issues will be addressed by future enhancements to WSAD. Others can perhaps be addressed by taking a hybrid approach using the JSTL RT tag library. Listing 13.7 shows another version of the browseEmployees.jsp called browseEmployees2.jsp. This version uses JSTL just for handling exceptions and iteration. Everything else is done using standard JSP tags or Java in JSP expressions and scriptlets.

To use the RT version of JSTL use the Insert Custom Tag dialog to add a jsp:taglib directive to the JSP. From the menu bar, select *JSP > Insert Custom...* to display the Insert Custom Tag dialog. Press *Add...* to display the Select a Tag Library dialog. Scroll down the list of tag libraries available in the Web project and select the one with URI *http://java.sun.com/jstl/core_rt* This is the RT version of the JSTL tag library. Notice that is uses prefix c_rt instead of just *c* for the EL version of JSTL. Using different prefixes allows you to use both Java and JSTL EL in the same JSP, although not in the same tag.

Listing 13.7 browseEmployees2.jsp – Using JSTL RT

```
<!DOCTYPE HTML PUBLIC "-//W3C//DTD HTML 4.01 Frameset//EN">



<%@taglib uri="http://java.sun.com/jstl/core_rt" prefix="c_rt"%>

<HTML>

<HEAD>
```

```
<%@ page

       language="java"

       contentType="text/html; charset=WINDOWS-1252"

       import="com.wsbook.servletexample.domain.Employee,

                  java.sql.SQLException,java.util.Iterator"%>

<META http-equiv="Content-Type"

       content="text/html; charset=WINDOWS-1252">

<META name="GENERATOR" content="IBM WebSphere Studio">


<TITLE>Browse Employees (JSP version)</TITLE>

</HEAD>

<jsp:useBean id="employees" class="java.util.ArrayList" scope="request">

</jsp:useBean>

<BODY>

<h3 align="center">All Employees</h3>

<TABLE align="center" BORDER="yes" CELLSPACING="2" CELLPADDING="0"

       WIDTH="70%">

       <TR>

              <TD>

              <center><b>Id</b></center>

              </TD>

              <TD>

              <center><b>Name</b></center>

              </TD>
```

```
                    <TD width="40">

                    <center><b>Age</b></center>

                    </TD>

            </TR>

            <c_rt:forEach var="emp" items="<%=employees%>">

                    <%Employeeemp=(Employee)pageContext.getAttribute("emp");%>

                    <TR>

                            <TD><A

                                    HREF="ShowEmployeeDetail?id=<%=emp.getId()%>"

                                    target="detail"> <%=emp.getId()%></A></TD>

                            <TD><%=emp.getName()%></TD>

                            <TD width="40"><%=emp.getAge()%></TD>

                    </TR>

            </c_rt:forEach>

            <TR>

                    <TD colspan="3"><A href="ShowEmployeeDetail"

target="detail">Create

                    Employee...</A></TD>

            </TR>

</TABLE>

</BODY>

</HTML>
```

As we've done in the previous versions of this example, we begin by pulling the employees ArrayList from the request scope with a jsp:usebean tag. Remember all variables used by JSTL tags are in some storage scope. So we have to declare a local Employee variable called emp. We access the emp attribute from the page context, casting it to an Employee. Then we can use the emp variable in other JSP expressions and scriptlets. This approach isn't that much more complicated than using JSTL EL, and it is more flexible and faster. At the same time, it retains the JSTL facilities for handling exceptions and iterating over collections.

13.9 XML compliance

A number of JSP tags have an alternative XML syntax. Web content developers may find these tags more familiar. In addition, emerging tools may be able to take advantage of XML to provide further enhancements and validation. Both the JSP directives and JSP scripting tags have an alternative form.

For the JSP directives, the XML compliant syntax is:

```
<jsp:directive.directivename directive_attributes />
```

For example `<jsp:directive.page isErrorPage="true"/>`.

The scripting elements are block tags. They are:

```
<jsp:declaration> declaration goes here </jsp:declaration>

<jsp:scriptlet> code fragment goes here </jsp:scriptlet>

<jsp:expression> expression goes here </jsp:expression>
```

The following expressions have the same result:

```
<jsp:scriptlet>employee.getName()</jsp:scriptlet>

<%=employee.getName()%>
```

13.10 Summary

JSP offers an extremely productive tag language to develop server-side Java logic. Its greatest value-add is in the development of Web pages that include dynamic content. JSPs make it possible to eliminate the need for servlets to ever write content to an HTTP response stream. By using JavaBeans as mediators to factor all business logic and data translation out of both servlets and JSPs, the resulting set of server-side assets have a very clean division of responsibility. Servlets are simple controllers, JSPs are simple page templates, and everything else is facilitated by the remaining server-side layer(s) in the application.

With JSP-aware page development tools like WSAD Page Designer, it is further possible to easily develop and maintain JSPs within these tools. This allows developers in the right roles using the right tools to produce the right assets for the enterprise application.

CHAPTER 14

Apache Struts as an MVC Framework

Deciding which path to take is one of the hardest decisions a servlet and JSP developer faces. Since J2EE exploded onto the programming scene we have been given a plethora of API choices, but precious little guidance on how best to make use of these options.

Luckily, some order is beginning to emerge from the chaos, mostly thanks to the dedicated work of a few individuals pooling their knowledge and efforts through the Apache Software Foundation. In particular, we want to introduce you to one of the simpler and more useful frameworks to emerge from the Apache effort, the Struts framework for developing Web-based applications using the MVC architecture. In this chapter, we'll cover how Struts implements the MVC architecture, what benefits it conveys to a servlet developer above and beyond the standard J2EE APIs, and how the tooling for Apache Struts can be used in WSAD.

14.1 Road Map

This chapter concentrates on the controller/mediator layer and the use of the Struts framework to implement this layer. The simple example is built using only Web container services. Figure 14.1 shows the technologies used within the example presented in this chapter. However, the entire focus is on the presentation and controller/mediator layers. It is only in the full code sample that the other three layers are represented.

14.2 Why Do You Need a Framework?

You may be asking "Isn't J2EE already a framework to solve these problems?" Yes, in a way. Lots of development organizations have successfully applied the following mapping of J2EE APIs to the three roles in the MVC pattern as we've shown in the preceding chapters:

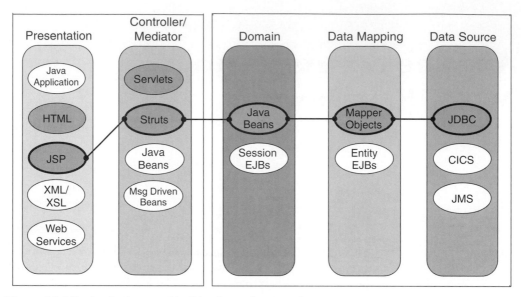

Figure 14.1 Technologies used in this chapter's example.

- Model—JavaBeans and EJBs
- View—JSPs
- Controller—Servlets

In this approach, servlets act as controllers and are the recipients of HTTP POST requests, and are responsible for passing POSTed data to the model and selecting which JSP page will be invoked to display results. This is often called the Model II JSP architecture and we've already discussed it at length. However, even though these J2EE APIs make it possible to develop Web-based applications that implement the MVC pattern, there are a number of common problems that must be solved in every servlet project:

- **Mapping HTTP Parameters to Java Beans**—One of the most common tasks that servlet programmers have to do is to map a set of HTTP parameters (coming in from the command line or from the POST of an HTML form) to a JavaBean for manipulation. This can be done using the `jsp:usebean` and `jsp:setProperty` tags, but this arrangement is cumbersome as it requires directly invoking the JSP to handle the HTTP request, something that is not encouraged in a Model-II (MVC) architecture.
- **Validation**—There is no standard way in Servlet/JSP programming to validate that an HTML form is filled in correctly. This leaves every servlet programmer to develop her own validation procedures—or not, as is far too often the case. Far too often, the servlet programmer neglects to handle it at all.
- **Errors**—There is no standard way to handle the display of error messages in a JSP page or the generation of error messages in a servlet.

- **Message Internationalization**—Even when developers strive to keep as much of the HTML as possible in JSPs, there are often hidden obstacles to internationalization spread throughout servlet and model code in the form of short error or informative text messages. While it is possible to introduce internationalization with the use of Java Resource Managers, this is rarely done due to the complexity of adding these references.
- **Hard-Coded JSP URIs**—One of the more insidious problems in a servlet architecture is that the URIs of the JSP pages are usually coded directly into the code of the calling servlet in the form of a static string reference used in the `ServletContext.getRequestDispatcher()` method. This means that it is impossible to reorganize the JSPs in a Web site (or even change their names) without updating Java code in the servlets.

Programmers are too often faced with reinventing the wheel each time they begin building a new Web-based application. Having a framework to do this kind of work for them would make developers more productive and allow them to focus more on the essence of the business problems they are trying to solve, rather than on the accidents of programming caused by the limitations of the technology.[1] Solutions are often captured in best practice patterns that specify how to use a collection of enabling technologies like J2EE in the context of a particular architecture. What's needed is a way to codify these best practices so they can be easily used by developers.

14.3 What Is Struts?

Simply put, Struts is an open-source framework for solving the kind of problems described earlier. Information on Struts, a set of installable .JAR files, and the full Struts source code is available at *http://jakarta.apache.org/struts*. Struts has been designed from the ground up to be easy to use, modular (so that you can choose to use one part of Struts without having to use all the others), and efficient. It has also been designed so that tool builders can easily write their tools to generate code that sits on top of the Struts framework.

14.4 A Simple MVC Struts Example

To illustrate how MVC and Struts can help solve problems, let's revisit the simple JSP example presented in Chapter 13. During this process, we will refactor the design and explore a number of aspects of designing and developing a Struts-based Web application.

We will begin by creating a Web project, one which we target for building Struts-based code.

As you can see in Figure 14.2, we have checked the Web project feature, Add Struts support. This will include a number of Struts .JAR and .tld files into the project.

---

1.   [Brooks]

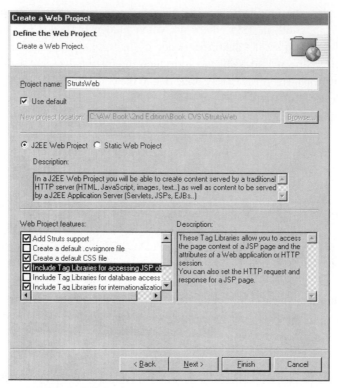

Figure 14.2 Web project with Struts support.

Remember from Chapter 12 that our employee management example has the following JSPs:

1. allEmployees.jsp—The page displays all employees. For each employee there is a hyperlink to select in order to show complete details on that particular employee. It also provides a link to allow for the creation of an employee.

2. employeeDetails.jsp—This page shows the complete employee data in a form that can be updated. There are two separate operations that are selectable: (1) update employee data to reflect changes made on the form and (2) delete the employee from the database.

3. newEmployee.jsp—This page supplies the entry form to create a new employee.

There is also the initial index.jsp page. You will also recall that we identified the actions (Table 14.1) associated with transitions between the pages in the example.

Table 14.1 Actions associated with transitions.

Source Page	Action Required	Destination Page
index.jsp	AllEmployees	allEmployees.jsp
allEmployees.jsp	FindEmployee None (create link clicked)	employeeDetails.jsp newEmployee.jsp
employeeDetails.jsp	AlterEmployee followed by AllEmployees	allEmployees.jsp
newEmployee.jsp	CreateEmployee followed by AllEmployees	allEmployees.jsp

14.4.1 Building the Model (Form Beans)

Looking at our application, we can easily determine that we can start with one model class, the Employee class. In the Struts environment, we will create an associated JavaBean that is populated from the form found on the newEmployees.jsp page. We will let Struts automatically handle the association between this bean and the HTML form. To accomplish that, our new EmployeeForm class will extend ActionForm (Listing 14.1).

Listing 14.1 EmployeeForm ActionForm Bean

```java
public class EmployeeForm extends ActionForm {

    private String id = "";

    private String name = "";

    private int age = 0;

    private String street = "";

    private String city = "";

    private String state = "";

    private String zip = "";

}
```

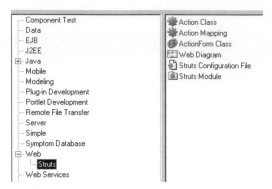

Figure 14.3 WebSphere Studio new wizards for Struts-based application development.

In most respects, this is a standard JavaBean that extends the ActionForm class. This class (among other things) implements the `Serializable` interface, allowing our class to meet the requirements of being a JavaBean, so long as it implements the appropriate no-argument constructor and implements setter and getter methods for the attributes shown in the table. Our class would implement these methods, but we will not show the implementation here.

14.4.2 Building the Actions

Building a controller layer in Struts is a little different than building one with the standard Model-II JSP architecture. The biggest difference is that each Struts Web application will contain only a single servlet (an `ActionServlet`). The Struts framework delegates the work of mediation (picking the next JSP) and adapting model objects to the JSP (view) protocol to a lower layer of objects, the Action objects.

You can quickly build a skeleton for an Action by choosing one of the Struts creation wizards in Studio (Figure 14.3). (Note that we could have also used the wizard to create the Action-Form class, EmployeeForm.)

Let's look at the definition of an Action object in Listing 14.2:

Listing 14.2 CreateEmployeeAction class definition

```
/** This class adds new Employees  */


public class CreateEmployeeAction extends Action {


}
```

Notice that this class extends the `Action` class from the Struts framework. Action classes normally override a single method defined in the Action class, the `perform()` method. An example of this method, which is analogous to the `service()` method in a servlet, is shown in Listing 14.3.

Listing 14.3 Action class' perform() method

```
public ActionForward perform(ActionMapping mapping,

    ActionForm form, HttpServletRequest request,

    HttpServletResponse response)

    throws IOException, ServletException {



    ActionErrors errors = new ActionErrors();

    ActionForward forward = new ActionForward();

    EmployeeForm employeeForm = (EmployeeForm) form;

    Employee employee = new Employee(

        employeeForm.getId(), employeeForm.getName(),

        employeeForm.getAge(), employeeForm.getStreet(),

        employeeForm.getCity(), employeeForm.getState(),

        employeeForm.getZip());

    try {

        employee.create();
```

```
} catch (Exception e) {

    // Report the error using the appropriate name and ID.

    errors.add("id", new ActionError("error.id.duplicateid"));

}

if (!errors.empty()) {

    saveErrors(request, errors);

    // Forward control back to the entry form

    forward = mapping.findForward("error");

} else {

    // Forward control to the appropriate 'success' URI
//(change name as desired)

    forward = mapping.findForward("displayAll");

}

// Finish with

return forward;

}
```

This method deserves a lot of attention, as it introduces a couple of key concepts in Struts. The first is the notion of an ActionForward. Returning an `ActionForward` object is the way in which a Struts Action class's `perform()` method indicates which JSP page will be invoked as a result of the logic being performed. Here we see that only a single ActionForward can be returned. We will look at the findForward mechanism later; however, this will set the corresponding page or action to forward to upon completion (success or failure) of the Employee creation. The actual URI to forward to is externalized into the struts configuration file. In this way, your code does not have to hard code the specific URI(s).

The second concept to introduce is the idea of an ActionForm. Struts will automatically perform the mapping of HTTP parameters to fields in an ActionForm. You do not need to code this mapping yourself. As you can see, this makes it easy to obtain and manipulate the objects corresponding to the HTTP parameters—in most cases all you need to do is perform a cast and begin using the object as we have done here.

14.4.3 ActionForm Validation

One thing that probably will strike most experienced servlet programmers as odd about the `perform()` method (Listing 14.3) is how short it is. As we have noted, there is no code necessary to extract out the HTTP parameters from the `HttpServletRequest`, so that is missing, but you may also have noticed that there is no code to perform any validation on the resulting form. It is not that the code is not needed, but rather that the Struts framework has already handled it. To enable this validation, the programmer must do two things: (1) add a `validate()` method to an ActionForm class (EmployeeForm) and (2) indicate which HTTP requests are to result in validation taking place. Let's start with looking at the validate method for Employee-Form (Listing 14.4).

Listing 14.4 EmployeeForm's validate() method

```
public ActionErrors validate(ActionMapping mapping,

HttpServletRequest request) {

ActionErrors errors = new ActionErrors();

// Validate the fields in your form,

// adding each error to this.errors as found, e.g.

if ((id == null) || (id.length() == 0)) {

errors.add("id", new ActionError("error.id.required"));
```

```
}

try {

    int checkage =

    Integer.parseInt(request.getParameter("age"));

} catch (NumberFormatException e) {

    errors.add("age", new ActionError("error.age.integerval"));

}

return errors;

}
```

First note the `ActionErrors` object. This object, which is returned from the validate method, serves a couple of purposes. If the returned object does not contain any `ActionError` objects, validation is assumed to have succeeded. If one or more `ActionError` objects are added to the ActionErrors collection, validation failed. The collection of errors can be displayed using the Struts form tag library. If validation fails, control will not be passed to our Action. This implies that in the `perform()` method of the CreateEmployeeAction class where we access the `EmployeeForm` (`ActionForm`) object we know that it has been populated from the input HTML form and has passed validation (a very powerful model.).

The rest of the `validate()` method contains simple checks on the values of Employee-Form's properties and/or looking at the source form parameters. If a check fails, an `ActionError` object is created. The first argument to the ActionError's `add()` method is the name of the property for which validation failed. The second argument to the `add()` method is an ActionError. The argument to the ActionError constructor is a String that matches a property value in the ApplicationResources.properties file. This will correspond to an error message. By moving the message out to a property file, internationalization is easily supported. To connect the dots, a subset of our ApplicationResources.properties file is shown in Listing 14.5.

Listing 14.5 Entries in ApplicationResources.properties

```
error.id.required=<li>The id field is required!

error.age.integerval=<li>Age must be an integer value.
```

The last piece of the validation puzzle opens up the discussion of the struts-config.xml configuration file.

14.4.4   Putting it all Together in the struts-config.xml file

The action servlet needs to be able to instantiate the appropriate action to handle an incoming request. In addition, the framework needs to know about which `ActionForm` objects to populate for an incoming request. These and other configuration properties are established in the struts-config.xml file in the WEB-INF folder of your Web project (i.e., WAR module). The struts configuration file editor has a number of views or tabs to view and update the data.

Figure 14.4 shows the four actions associated with this application. Looking at the configuration for the CreateEmployeeAction, the class is selected on the top of the right hand side. The Action is associated with an ActionForm (employee) which is selected via a drop-down choice. (The ActionForm was previously configured as shown in Figure 14.5. The ActionForm is specified to be placed into the request scope. Next you can see that the validate attribute is set to yes, indicating that the framework should invoke the ActionForm's `validate()` method. We noted

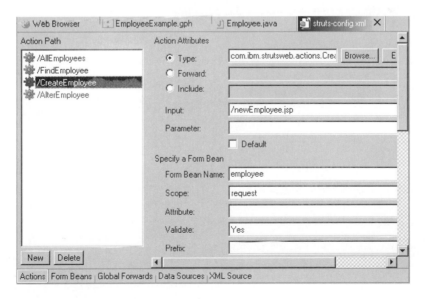

Figure 14.4 Struts-config.xml editor.

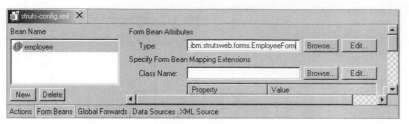

Figure 14.5 ActionForm (Form Beans) configuration.

that if validation fails, control is not passed to the Action. Control is instead forwarded back to the input page, specified here as /newEmployee.jsp.

Let's take a look at the Form Beans tab where the EmployeeForm ActionForm is configured. There is not much to this. The ActionForm class is specified and a name (employee in this case) is associated with it.

14.4.5   HTML Form Tags

Struts provides a form handling tag library to facilitate working with Form Beans and in particular dealing with validation errors. Listing 14.6 is the JSP source code for newEmployee.jsp.

Listing 14.6 Input Form JSP source.

```
<!DOCTYPE HTML PUBLIC "-//W3C//DTD HTML 4.01 Frameset//EN">

<%@taglib uri="/WEB-INF/struts-html.tld" prefix="html"%>

<html:html><head><title>Employee Details</title></head>

<body>

<P align="center"><IMG border="0" src="images/banner.jpg" width="309"

height="50"></P>

<h3 align="center">Create Employee</h3>

<b><font color="red"><html:errors /></font></b>

<div align="center">
```

```
<html:form action="CreateEmployee.do">

<table align="center" border="1" cellpadding="0" cellspacing="0"

    width="70%">

    <tr><td width="60"><div align="right">Id:</div></td>

        <td><html:text property="id" /></td>

    </tr>

    <tr><td width="60"><div align="right">Name:</div></td>

        <td><html:text property="name" /></td>

    </tr>

    <tr><td width="60"><div align="right">Age:</div></td>

        <td><html:text property="age" /></td>

    </tr>

    <tr><td width="60"><div align="right">Street:</div></td>

        <td><html:text property="street"/></td>

    </tr>

    <tr><td colspan="2"><table border="0" cellpadding="0"

cellspacing="0">

                <tr><td width="60">
```

```
                        <div align="right">City:</div></td>

                        <td><html:text property="city" /></td>

                        <tdwidth="30"><divalign="right">State:</div>

                        </td>

                        <td><html:text property="state"/></td>

                        <td width="30"><div align="right">Zip:</div>

                        </td>

                        <td><html:text property="zip"/></td>

                  </tr></table></td></tr>

         <td colspan="2">

         <divalign="center"><inputtype="submit"name="submit"value="Submit"

                  align="center"></div></td>

         </tr></table>

</html:form>

</div></body></html:html>
```

The second line of this Struts page is a tag library directive indicating that this page will use the tag library described in /WEB-INF/struts-html.tld. Four tag libraries are included with Struts:

   • The HTML tag library, which includes tags for describing dynamic pages, especially
     forms.

- The beans tag library which provides additional tags for providing improved access to JavaBeans and additional support for internationalization.
- The logic tag library which provides tags that support conditional execution (if…else…) and looping.
- The template tag library for producing and using common JSP templates in multiple pages.

Our newEmployee.jsp file includes the HTML tag library. The tags in this library all begin with the tag library identifier html. Note the line that includes the `html:errors` tag. This tag will display the contents of the `ActionErrors` object if not empty. Next, consider the `html:form` tag. A normal HTML form tag could be used, but this requires the use of special input tags. For example, look at the `html:text property="id"` tag. The nearly equivalent HTML tag is commented out on the previous line. This text field is associated with the Form Bean's `id` property. Further, if an `EmployeeValue` object is available on the page at runtime, the text field will display the `id` property as the initial value.

It is time to consider how this all fits together at runtime. Then we will revisit some of loose ends, like the ActionForward declarations.

In Figure 14.6, you can see the very normal looking HTML page displayed. The input values entered as shown will trigger both validation errors. Clicking Submit will trigger the population of the Form Bean, followed by a call to `validate()`. Validation will fail and control will be returned to the input page as shown in Figure 14.7.

The details of the error message are again encoded in the ApplicationResources.properties file. Note the default of preceding each displayed error with the `<li>` tag. That is to accommodate the following:

Figure 14.6 newEmployee.jsp, inputting invalid data.

Create Employee

You must correct the following error(s) before proceeding

- Age must be an integer value.
- The id field is required!

Id:	
Name:	John Smith
Age:	0
Street:	

City:		State:		Zip:	

Submit

Figure 14.7 Input page with ActionErrors displayed.

```
errors.header=You must correct the following error(s) before proceeding<ul>

errors.footer=</ul>
```

14.4.6 Local Forwards

So what happens if we succeed in validation? Back in Listing 14.2, after retrieving the EmployeeForm Form Bean, we create an Employee model bean and make a call to its `create()` method. This makes the JDBC call to add the new Employee record. Note that it is possible that the insert fails due to a duplicate `id` value. The way to handle this situation is the same as validation failing. So we create an ActionError to the `ActionErrors` object. In this case, we must explicitly save this object into the request scope (the call to saveErrors). The remainder of the `perform()` method is to invoke the `findForward()` method on the `ActionMapping` object. If the create was successful, we will forward to the symbolic name displayAll. If we fail, we will forward to the symbolic name error.

Back in the struts-config.xml editor, if you scroll further down the page for our CreateEmployee Action, you will see the two defined local forwards (see Figure 14.8).

So displayAll, maps to one of our other actions, AllEmployees. This action retrieves all of the employees from that database and then forwards to allEmployees.jsp to show the summary of each employee. A forward can map to any URI. You can easily imagine how each action mapping might have at least two local forwards (success and failure pages, for instance) and how the application would have a global error page, as well as perhaps a start page that you could always reach in a serious error condition. Figure 14.9 shows the results of entering valid data.

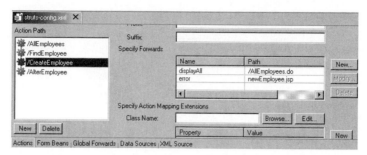

Figure 14.8 Local forwards for an action.

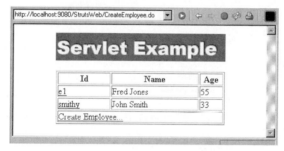

Figure 14.9 Result of adding a new Employee.

Figure 14.10 Studio Outline view when editing struts-config.xm.

The complete struts-based version of this sample application can be found on the CD as SimpleStruts.ear. Figure 14.10 shows the outline of our application showing the actions with their ActionForwards.

WebSphere Studio provides support for building and testing Struts-based applications. For those who are more graphical in their approach to Web application design, there is a Web diagram editor (Figure 14.11) that lets you compose the relationship between your actions, Form Beans and JSP. You can even kick off the specialized creation wizards from this tool (e.g., adding an Action node and then double-clicking the icon within the diagram will launch the create Action wizard).

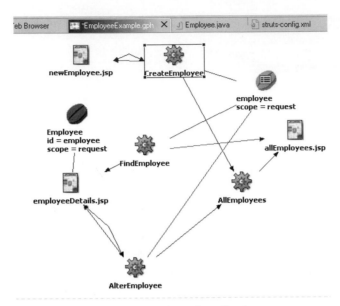

Figure 14.11 Web diagram for a simple struts-based application.

14.5 Struts Best Practices

Of all the common design principles for using Struts that have emerged over the past few years, the most widely applicable one is the idiom of separating Struts Actions into Processing and Display-specific actions. For instance, in our simple application, we have a page, allEmployees.jsp, that displays the employees and provides links to enable creating, updating, and removing employees. In our earlier discussion we looked at the CreateEmployee action. When this action completes (inserts a new employee record) the user should be returned to the view displaying all employees.

The AllEmployees action is a very typical Display action. It has no interaction with any input parameters. It retrieves the current list of employees from the model layer and forwards to the allEmployees.jsp to display them. Both AlterEmployee and CreateEmployee are Processing actions; FindEmployee is another Display action.

Figure 14.12 shows the very typical control flow with Processing and Display actions. You can see the error path that returns to the action page (our newEmployee.jsp page). On success of the processing action, we forward to the display action, AllEmployees, which in turn forwards to the display page.

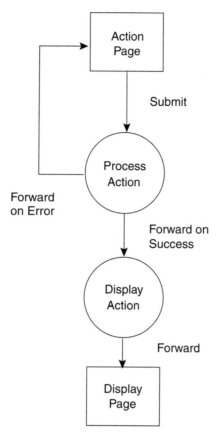

Figure 14.12 Interaction between processing and display actions.

14.6 Summary

Struts is a very powerful and yet simple open-source MVC framework for building Web applications. It concentrates on coordination between the controller and presentation layers. Struts greatly assists in processing and validating form data, managing and displaying errors, externalizing URIs, and supporting internationalization. Combined with the tools in WebSphere Studio, this is an attractive framework upon which to build your Web applications.

CHAPTER 15

XML/XSL Web Interfaces in WSAD

Building on our knowledge of using JSPs with servlets to create robust Web interfaces, in this chapter, we will introduce an alternative way (also a part of J2EE) of creating Web-based interfaces using XML and XSL. We will also cover several tools in WSAD that can be used to create XML/XSL interfaces. We will focus on how to use XML and XSL within a J2EE application rather than discuss the basics of XML/XSL. We will cover:

- A strategy for using XML/XSL for Web Interfaces
- An example static XML and XSL interface
- An example enhanced XSL file
- An example dynamic XML and XSL interface
- When to use XML/XSL for Web interfaces

This chapter will advance your knowledge of the fundamental concepts of XML and XSL as a Web interface alternative. We will focus mostly on the servlet container with a short discussion on the domain layer in the ejb container (see Figure 15.1) and demonstrate the use of XML/XSL in Java using the Apache Xalan-J transformer from within WebSphere Studio.

15.1 Strategy for Using XML/XSL for Web Interfaces

XML and XSL can be used for many purposes. The primary purpose of XML is to represent data in a self-describing way. XML is not a programming or a logic-based language but one created to represent data with the metadata information included in the XML document. XSL is an XML-based language used by a transformer program (Apache Xalan-J, for example) to transform XML documents into other forms. When looking at XML and XSL, it is not obvious that these technologies can be used to build Web interfaces. However, using them together can

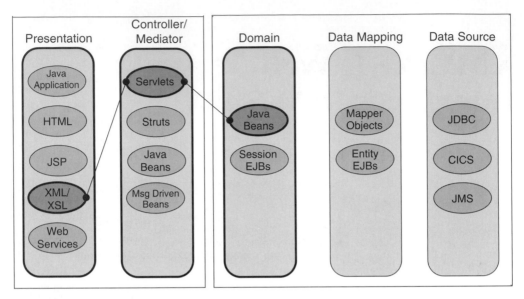

Figure 15.1 Where XML/XSLT fits into the road map.

greatly enhance separation of the presentation layer from the controller layer, as well as increase developer productivity.

The basic technique for creating Web interfaces using XML and XSL is to use a Java class to generate an XML stream, which can then be transformed into HTML using XSL. The domain objects and mediators use this XML Generator to generate a concise and complete XML document as output from some servlet request or Struts action. Figure 15.2 shows how this technique fits into the MVC architecture.

In Figure 15.2, the interaction controller is responsible for obtaining the request and returning the HTML response. The interaction controller uses mediators and domain objects to service the request and then calls the XML Generator to generate the XML based on the data result returned from the domain model. Finally, the interaction controller calls the XSL Transformer to transform the XML into HTML as a response to the request.

Let's consider a set of requirements that we provide a Web interface for Time Sheet detailed data as well as Time Sheet Summary Information as shown in Figure 15.3.

In the sections that follow, we will discuss the MVC components shown in Figure 15.2, using the Time Sheet Information in Figure 15.3.

15.1.1 Interaction Controller

The interaction controller is the gatekeeper to the function that is requested from a Web page URL. The interaction controller can be implemented as a servlet, a JSP, or as a Struts Action. The interaction controller has no logic in it except to process a request, delegate to other objects, and return a response.

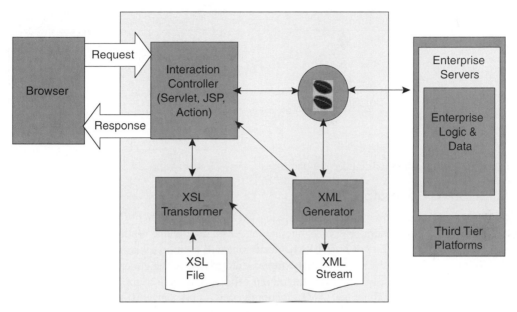

Figure 15.2 XML/XSL Web interface MVC diagram.

Figure 15.3 Time Sheet information.

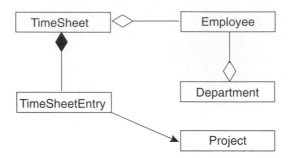

Figure 15.4 Time Sheet partial domain model.

15.1.2 XML Generator

The job of the XML Generator is to generate an XML DOM (Document Object Model), JDOM, or stream. While the generator could generate an XML document, rendering it in a persistent form is not necessary. The generated XML document will contain dynamic data, which is only valid for the duration of the request. Many implementations save the generated XML to a file for debugging purposes and turn this extra file output off when moving to production.

The structure of a generated XML document must represent what is needed for the Web interface rather than that of the domain model or data model. In a domain model, domain objects contain other domain objects. In a data model, foreign keys are used to relate multiple tables. In a Web interface, the data is derived from several domain objects and database tables. The generated XML document should contain preresolved relationships and references. The job of coding the XSL is a painting—not a programming—exercise, which we will cover shortly.

In order to create a Web interface, we need application data to drive the interface. The application data will almost always ultimately come from a database and the data it provides will be instantiated in some domain object. Consider a portion of the domain model for the time sheet case study (covered in its entirety later) in Figure 15.4.

We have a requirement to generate Web interfaces, which show the summary, detail, and combined information for a time sheet. We need data from each of the five domain objects pictured in Figure 15.4. However, it would not be prudent to generate an XML document from all the data contained in the domain model. The structure of a generated XML document must represent what is needed for the Web interface rather than that of the domain or data model.

The following XML document, timesheet.xml, gives us the needed data to meet the Web interface requirements for displaying a time sheet:

```xml
<?xml version="1.0" encoding="UTF-8"?>

<TimeSheet weekEnding="4/25/2003">
```

```xml
      <Employee id="257899" name="Leonard, Elouise"
deptName="Programming"/>

      <Entries>

            <Entry>

                  <Date>4/21/2003</Date>

                  <Hours>8.5</Hours>

                  <Project id="4567" name="ACME AP"/>

            </Entry>

            <Entry>

                  <Date>4/22/2003</Date>

                  <Hours>5</Hours>

                  <Project id="4567" name="ACME AP"/>

            </Entry>

            <Entry>

                  <Date>4/22/2003</Date>

                  <Hours>5</Hours>

                  <Project id="2345" name="ACME HR"/>

            </Entry>
```

```
        ...


    </Entries>

    <Summary totalHours="45.5" overTimeHours="5.5">

        <ProjectTotals>

        <Project id="4567" name="ACME AP" totalHours="37.5"/>

        <Project id="2345" name="ACME HR" totalHours="8"/>

        </ProjectTotals>

    </Summary>

</TimeSheet>
```

This XML document represents a time sheet for a single employee working on multiple projects. As you review the timesheet.xml file you will notice that the employee information as well as the detailed time sheet entries are included. Also, notice that Employee contains a dept-Name attribute instead of a subelement for Department with a name attribute. Since there is really no additional information needed from the Department besides its name, it is better to simplify the XML so that the XSL can be more easily coded. Additionally, notice that the XML document contains a summary element, which contains hourly totals by time sheet and project. This summary information could have been derived from the detailed information; however, it is a best practice to compute derived values in Java code, in the XML Generator, instead of in XSL. Java is a much more powerful language than XSL and therefore should be used to compute derived values.

15.1.3 XSL

XSL is essentially the paint for the Web interface. XSL is a combination of three other APIs:

- XSLT—XSL Transformations
- XPath—XML Path Language
- XSL FO—XSL Formatting Objects

XSLT supports conditional logic and looping constructs; however, the basic construction element in XSLT is the template, a block of XSLT code in many ways like a Java function. Templates can be named to act more like a function call or they can be set up to match an element in the XML data file.

XPath is the mechanism used in XSL to find elements and attributes in the XML data file. The XPath expression `TimeSheet/Employee/@id` gives a path from the current location in the XML document to the attribute `id` on the subelement Employee which is a part of the element TimeSheet. This is a very simple XPath expression but should show you right away that XSL was designed to make it very easy for programmers to find data in an XML document. XPath is used to locate things in an XML document. If we were to say that XML is like a database, we would also say that XPath is like SELECT in SQL.

XSL FO is an API and set of elements that allow an XSL developer to transform XML into other things besides XML, text, or HTML. XSL FO allows XML to be transformed into print streams and, even more importantly, PDF output.

In the previously provided XML document, we have an element named TimeSheet. As such, we can create a template in the XSL file, which matches TimeSheet. Listing 15.1 shows an XSL file, which contains a basic template to create summary time sheet information:

Listing 15.1 timesheet1.xsl

```
<?xml version="1.0" encoding="UTF-8"?>

<xsl:stylesheet xmlns:xsl="http://www.w3.org/1999/XSL/Transform"

    version="1.0" xmlns:xalan="http://xml.apache.org/xslt">

  <xsl:strip-space elements="*" />

  <xsl:output method="html" />

    <xsl:template match="TimeSheet">

        <H1>Time Sheet</H1>
```

```
        <TABLE border="0">

            <TR>

                <TD><B>Week Ending:</B></TD>

<TD><xsl:value-of select="@weekEnding"/> </TD>

                <TD> </TD>

                <TD> </TD>

            </TR>

            <TR>

                <TD><B>Employee:</B></TD>

<TD><xsl:value-of select="Employee/@name"/> </TD>

                <TD></TD>

                <TD><B>Total Hours:</B></TD>

<TD><xsl:value-of select="Summary/@totalHours"/>

</TD>

                </TR>

                <TR>

                <TD><B>Department:</B></TD>

<TD><xsl:value-of select="Employee/@deptName"/> </TD>
```

```
                              <TD> </TD>

                              <TD><B>Total Overtime Hours:</B></TD>

                              <TD>

<xsl:value-of select="Summary/@overTimeHours"/>

</TD>

                              </TR>

                    </TABLE>

          </xsl:template>

</xsl:stylesheet>
```

This XSL file, timesheet1.xsl, contains a single template for the TimeSheet element. This XSL file is almost 90 percent HTML with the few XSL statements in bold typeface. With exception to the first five and the last two lines in Listing 15.1, the XSL statements are concerned with obtaining the data from the XML document. For example, the line

```
<TD><xsl:value-of select="@weekEnding"/> </TD>
```

will cause the value of the weekEnding attribute of the TimeSheet element to be placed inside the HTML TD element. Notice that the XPath expression "@weekEnding" is used to access the "weekEnding" attribute of the current element (TimeSheet). Also, the line

```
<TD><xsl:value-of select="Employee/@deptName"/> </TD>
```

will cause the value of the deptName attribute of the Employee element of the TimeSheet element to be placed inside of the HTML TD element.

When the timesheet1.xsl file is applied to the timesheet.xml file, the result will resemble Figure 15.5.

15.1.4 Pulling It All Together

Figure 15.5 represents a portion of the time sheet output that we would like to build in XML and XSL. We will add additional templates and expressions to the XSL so that we obtain the Web

Figure 15.5 Time sheet summary only.

interface shown in Figure 15.3. We will not have to change the XML document as it contains all of the necessary data. For now, it is important to understand that while we are using a static XML document in this discussion so far, in our completed application the XML Generator will generate an XML stream with dynamic data and then it will be transformed with our XSL.

15.2 Example XML/XSL Web Interface with WSAD

In this section, we will build the example shown in Figure 15.3 using the static XML document, timesheet.xml. In the next section, we will add a servlet and an XML Generator in order to show you how to use Java to do the transformation. WSAD provides many tools to help create, test, and debug XML and XSL. We will use the tools provided in WSAD to enhance our development efforts. Most of our time will be spent in the Web perspective and the XML perspective. You will follow these steps in implementing the XML/XSL Example using WSAD:

1. Open the XML perspective

2. Create a Web project

3. Create a sample XML file containing a time sheet (use timesheet.xml)

4. Create an XSL file to display the time sheet (use timesheet1.xsl)

5. Use WSAD tools to apply XSL to XML

6. Debug XSL

15.2.1 Creating a Web Project

In Chapter 7, we learned how to create a Web project. We will primarily use the XML perspective instead of the Web perspective to view this project in this section. Open the XML perspective by selecting *Window > Open Perspective > Other...* from the menu bar. Select XML from the list of available perspectives (Figure 15.6).

Next, create a new Web project by selecting *File > New > Web Project*. This will bring up the Create a Web Project wizard. Enter the Project Name of XMLXSLExample and specify that this is a J2EE project. Uncheck any checked items for creation. Specify the DefaultEAR project as your enterprise project and enter a Context Root of XMLXSLExample (no spaces). Finally, select J2EE 1.3. Refer to Chapter 7 for details on each of these settings.

Figure 15.6 Select perspective.

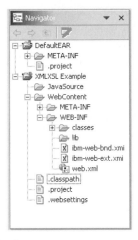

Figure 15.7 XMLXSL Example project.

Let's look at what was created.

Figure 15.7 shows the DefaultEAR and XMLXSL Example projects that were created by the Create a Web Project wizard in the Navigator view. To avoid typing, you can import the rest of the files for the example XML/XSL Web interface from the CD. If you do the import, you can skip "Creating the XML file" and "Creating the XSL file" sections and go directly to the "XSL Debugging and Transformation" section. See Apppendix A for instructions on importing examples.

15.2.2   Creating the XML file

XML and XSL files do not have to be on the HTTP path in order to be used in a Web application. The HTTP path is a path that is accessible to the Web browser through a URL. We will discuss this in detail later but for now create the XML file in a folder that is not on the HTTP path. Create a folder named XMLSource as a subfolder of the main project folder, XMLXSL Example by first selecting the XMLXSL Example project and then selecting the *File > New > Folder* menu option. In the wizard, enter the folder name of XMLSource.

Previously, we worked with the timesheet.xml file. Now we need to bring this file into WSAD so that we can use the WSAD tools to test it with our XSL files. Select the XMLSource folder and then select the *File > New > Other...* menu to display all of the types of files that can be created, as shown in Figure 15.8.

Select XML from the list on the left and XML again from the list on the right. Press the *Next* button to move on to the next screen in the wizard (Figure 15.9).

This wizard screen gives several ways to create an XML file. If you had a DTD or XML Schema file, you could generate a sample XML file from either of those. Also, we will see later that you can generate a DTD or XML Schema from an XML file. Select the *Create XML file from Scratch* radio button. Press the *Next* button to move on to the next screen in the wizard as shown in Figure 15.10.

Enter the name of the XML file as timesheet.xml and press the *Finish* button to complete the creation of the XML file. The navigator view of WSAD will now resemble Figure 15.11.

Additionally, the XML file will be opened in the editor area with the minimal lines for an XML file. You will need to enter the code from the timesheet.xml file as shown earlier in this chapter or import the one from the CD-ROM. Once you have entered the code, save the file and close it.

15.3   Creating the XSL File

As we have said previously, the XSL file is the paint for our Web interface. The first XSL file that we created previously, timesheet1.xsl, needs to be brought into WSAD. Select the XML-Source folder and then select *File > New > Other...* to display all of the types of files that can be created as shown in Figure 15.12.

Select XML from the list on the left and XSL from the list on the right. Press the *Next* button to move to the next screen in the wizard as shown in Figure 15.13.

Enter the name of the XSL file as timesheet1.xsl. Press the *Next* button to move to the next screen in the wizard as shown in Figure 15.14.

Select the timesheet.xml file as shown in Figure 15.14: Associate an XML file14. Then press the *Finish* button to complete the creation of the XSL file. The navigator area of WSAD will now resemble Figure 15.15.

Additionally, the XSL file will be opened in the editor area with the required lines for an XSL file. Also notice that the editor color codes elements of the XSL file to aid in your recognition of the parts of an XSL file. Additionally, the Outline view shows a hierarchical tree structure

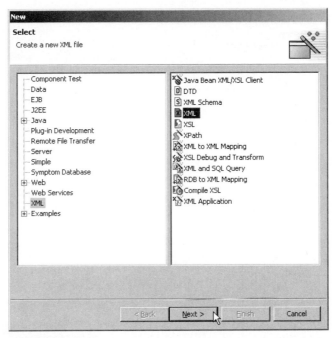

Figure 15.8 Creating an XML file.

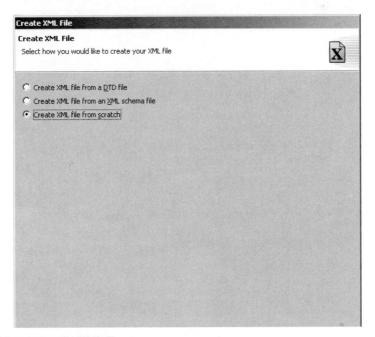

Figure 15.9 How to create XML file.

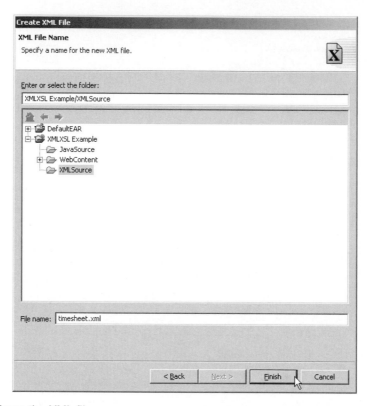

Figure 15.10 Name the XML file.

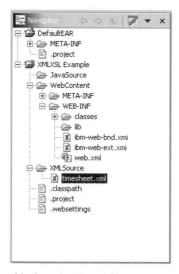

Figure 15.11 XMLSource folder with timesheet.xml file.

Figure 15.12 Creating an XSL File.

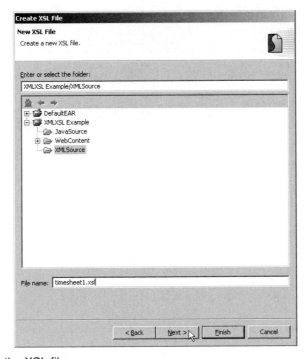

Figure 15.13 Name the XSL file.

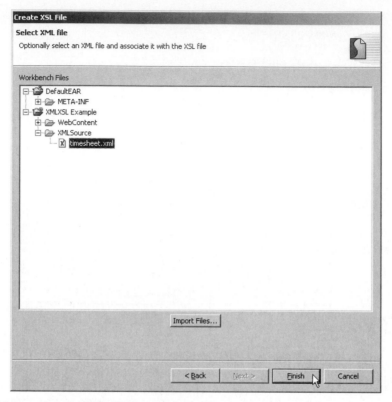

Figure 15.14 Associate an XML file.

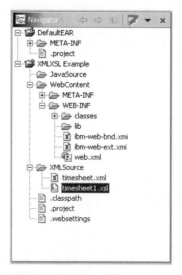

Figure 15.15 XMLSource folder with timesheet1.xsl file.

of the elements contained in the XSL file. Enter the code from the timesheet1.xsl file as shown earlier in this chapter. Once you have entered the code, save the file and close it.

15.3.1 XSL Debugging and Transformation

You can use the XSL editor to create an XSL file. To test your XSL file, use the XSL debugging and transformation tool to apply the XSL file to a source XML file and create a new HTML, XML, or text file. You can open the new HTML, XML, or text file in a Web browser from the Sessions view in the XSL debug perspective.

The XSL debugging and transformation tool records the transformation that is generated by the Apache Xalan-j processor, an XSLT processor that transforms XML files into HTML, text, or other XML file types. It implements the World Wide Web Consortium (W3C) recommendations for XSLT and XPath. For more information on the Xalan processor, refer to *http://xml.apache.org/xalan-j/*.

15.3.1.1 Transforming XML files

A transformation describes rules for transforming a source tree (logically a DOM tree) into a result tree. The transformation is achieved by associating patterns with templates. A pattern is matched against elements in the source tree. A template is instantiated to create part of the result tree. The result tree is separate from the source tree and the structure of the result tree can be completely different from the structure of the source tree. In constructing the result tree, elements from the source tree can be filtered and reordered, and arbitrary structures can be added.

To transform the timesheet.xml file using the timesheet1.xsl file, select both files from the Navigator view in the XML perspective. Next, right-click and select *Apply XSL > As HTML*. This is shown in Figure 15.16.

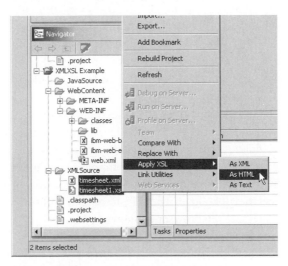

Figure 15.16 Applying XSL to XML.

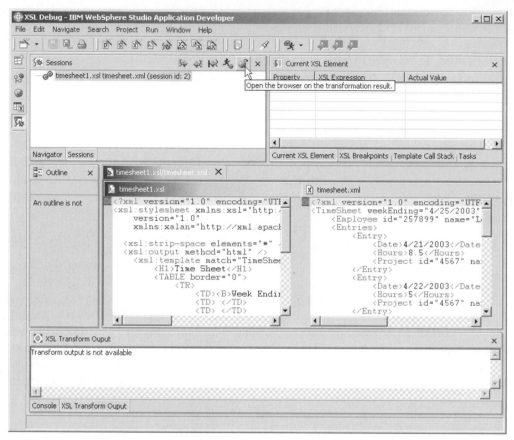

Figure 15.17 XSL debug perspective.

The Xalan-j processor will be initialized and then the XSL debug perspective will be launched with a session for the timesheet.xml and timesheet1.xsl files. The processing will be halted at the root tag in the XML file as shown in Figure 15.17.

Notice that this perspective shows the current sessions in the top left-hand corner and the current XSL element in the top right-hand corner. Also, notice that the XML file and XSL file are side by side in the middle, and the output (HTML, in this case) is located at the bottom. This perspective is set up to allow a developer to step through each line in the XML and XSL so he can debug the file. However, if you want to do a quick transform and view the resulting HTML page, simply select the globe icon. The transformation will occur and the result will be displayed in the WSAD internal Web browser as shown in Figure 15.18.

The transformation output is saved in an HTML file in the same folder as the XSL file. Notice the newly created timesheet_timesheet1_transform.html file in the XMLSource folder. Before leaving this perspective, close the Web browser and end the session. Select the session, right-click, and select Terminate. Close the perspective.

Figure 15.18 Result of transformation.

15.3.1.2 Debugging XSL and XML files

Return to the XML perspective, select the timesheet.xml and timesheet1.xsl files again and restart the debug session by selecting *Apply XSL > As HTML*. When the XSL debug perspective displays, begin stepping through the XSL and XML by selecting the step icon as shown in Figure 15.19.

As you step through the XSL transformation script, information about the XSL element being used is shown in the **Current XSL Element** view. The **XSL Breakpoints** view shows the breakpoints set in the input XSL file. The **Tasks** view shows a list of any errors that occurred during the transformation.

After you make any changes, you can select the session in the **Session** view and right-click to select **Relaunch**. This will apply the XSL file to the XML file again and let you see what impact your changes had. You can terminate the session and close the perspective.

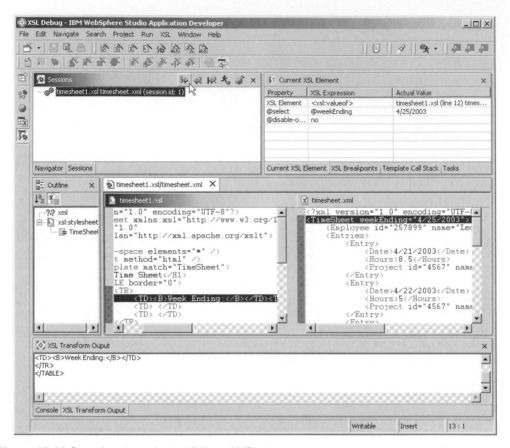

Figure 15.19 Stepping through the XML and XSL.

15.3.1.3 Options for Debugging and Transforming XSL files

There are two ways you can debug and transform XSL files:

1. Select the XSL and XML files you want to work with and select **Apply XSL** from the pop-up menu as we just did

2. Use the XSL Debugging and Transformation wizard.

If you want to quickly apply an XSL file to an XML file and transform it, use the pop-up menu to transform your XML file. If, however, you want to specify information about the transformation (e.g., the location of the output file), use the XSL Debugging and Transformation wizard.

If you are transforming and debugging any XSL files that call external Java programs, you should use the XSL Debugging and Transformation wizard. In the wizard, you can select the **Remote XSL Application** option to specify a class path for the external Java program.

15.4   Enhanced Example of XML/XSL Web Interface with WSAD

Now that you have learned how to use WSAD to transform and debug simple XML and XSL files, it is time to introduce some new XSL concepts that will help you to use XSL within WSAD on a future project. We will continue to work with a static XML file at this point, timesheet.xml, as this is the best way to build XSL interfaces in the real world. Later, we will dynamically generate the XML from Java and then apply the XSL to the XML stream using JAXP and Apache Xalan-j Java API. In the code samples that follow, each point of interest has been highlighted with a bold typeface.

You will follow these steps in implementing the XML/XSL Example project enhancements using WSAD:

1. Review timesheet1.xsl

2. Refactor 1: Decompose into templates

3. Refactor 2: Add time sheet entry detailed information

The sections that follow will cover these steps. If you previously imported the XMLXSL Example project, you will not need to create any of the files in this section.

15.4.1   Review timesheet1.xsl

Currently, the timesheet1.xsl file does not fulfill our requirements to display timesheet summary and detailed information. Listing 15.2 is a review of timesheet1.xsl.

Listing 15.2 A review of timesheet1.xsl

```
<?xml version="1.0" encoding="UTF-8"?>

<xsl:stylesheet xmlns:xsl="http://www.w3.org/1999/XSL/Transform"

    version="1.0" xmlns:xalan="http://xml.apache.org/xslt">

  <xsl:strip-space elements="*" />

  <xsl:output method="html" />

      <xsl:template match="TimeSheet">

          <H1>Time Sheet</H1>

          <TABLE border="0">
```

```
                    <TR>

                        <TD><B>Week Ending:</B></TD>

<TD><xsl:value-of select="@weekEnding"/> </TD>

                        <TD> </TD>

                        <TD> </TD>

                    </TR>

                    <TR>

                        <TD><B>Employee:</B></TD>

<TD><xsl:value-of select="Employee/@name"/> </TD>

                        <TD></TD>

                        <TD><B>Total Hours:</B></TD>

<TD><xsl:value-of select="Summary/@totalHours"/>

</TD>

                    </TR>

                    <TR>

                        <TD><B>Department:</B></TD>

<TD><xsl:value-of select="Employee/@deptName"/> </TD>

                        <TD> </TD>
```

```
                         <TD><B>Total Overtime Hours:</B></TD>

                         <TD>

<xsl:value-of select="Summary/@overTimeHours"/>

</TD>

                    </TR>

             </TABLE>

      </xsl:template>

</xsl:stylesheet>
```

The timesheet1.xsl file only shows summary information at this point. We need to re-factor the code into several templates and also add templates to handle the Entry elements so that we can show detailed information. Let's refactor the file to use more templates, then we'll handle adding Entry templates to handle the details.

15.4.2 Refactor 1: Decompose into Templates

Create an XML file in the XMLSource folder named timesheet2.xsl. The XML in Listing 15.3 is the first refactor.

Listing 15.3 First refactoring of timesheet1.xsl

```
<?xml version="1.0" encoding="UTF-8"?>

<xsl:stylesheet xmlns:xsl="http://www.w3.org/1999/XSL/Transform"

     version="1.0"

     xmlns:xalan="http://xml.apache.org/xslt">

  <xsl:strip-space elements="*" />
```

```xsl
<xsl:output method="html" />

    <xsl:template match="TimeSheet">

        <H1>Time Sheet</H1>

        <TABLE border="0">

            <TR colspan="2">

                <TD><B>Week Ending:</B><xsl:text>
</xsl:text>

<xsl:value-of select="@weekEnding"/>

</TD>

                <TD></TD>

            </TR>

            <TR>

            <TD><xsl:apply-templates select="Employee"/></TD>

            <TD><xsl:apply-templates select="Summary"/></TD>

            </TR>

        </TABLE>

    </xsl:template>

    <xsl:template match="Employee">
```

```
                    <TABLE border="0">

                        <TR>

                            <TD><B>Employee:</B></TD>

<TD><xsl:value-of select="@name"/> </TD>

                        </TR>

                        <TR>

                            <TD><B>Department:</B></TD>

<TD><xsl:value-of select="@deptName"/> </TD>

                        </TR>

                    </TABLE>

            </xsl:template>

            <xsl:template match="Summary">

                    <TABLE border="0">

                        <TR>

                            <TD><B>Total Hours:</B></TD>

<TD><xsl:value-of select="@totalHours"/> </TD>

                        </TR>

                        <TR>
```

```
                     <TD><B>Total Overtime Hours:</B></TD>

<TD><xsl:value-of select="@overTimeHours"/> </TD>

                         </TR>

                 </TABLE>

         </xsl:template>

</xsl:stylesheet>
```

Paste this code into the timesheet2.xsl file. Notice that the single template, TimeSheet has been broken into two other templates: Employee and Summary. One of the reasons for this refactoring is to simplify the XPath expressions. Notice that in the timesheet1.xsl file (the first version) has an XPath expression such as `"Employee/@name"`. In the revised version, the timesheet2.xsl file's XPath expression is simply `"@name"` because the code is now inside of the Employee template instead of TimeSheet. Another reason for this refactoring is to break up the logic into manageable pieces. Additionally, if you create a separate template per XML element in the XML data file then you can reuse the templates in various ways. Notice the TimeSheet template uses the `xsl:apply-templates` element to first call the Employee, then the Summary template. Now that we have this logic in separate templates, we can show the summary information ahead of the employee information by simply changing two lines of code. We would change the following lines from:

```
<TR>

                 <TD><xsl:apply-templates select="Employee"/></TD>

                 <TD><xsl:apply-templates select="Summary"/></TD>

         </TR>
```

to:

```
         <TR>

                 <TD><xsl:apply-templates select="Summary"/></TD>
```

```
<TD><xsl:apply-templates select="Employee"/></TD>

</TR>
```

If you apply the new timesheet2.xsl file against the timesheet.xml file, the result will be unchanged. The output will be identical.

15.4.3 Refactoring 2: Add Time Sheet Entry Detailed Information

The next refactoring is to add the detailed information (time sheet entries) to the output. To do this, we need to add templates and update some. First, let's add templates to the file.

15.4.3.1 Entries Template

The Entries template matches the "Entries" element in the timesheet.xml file. The "Entries" element contains "Entry" elements. This is the perfect place to put HTML output that only needs to occur one time for all "Entry" elements. Listing 15.4 shows the Entries template.

Listing 15.4 The Entries template

```
<xsl:template match="Entries">

        <TABLE border="1" cellpadding="0" cellspacing-"0"
width="100%">

            <TR>

                <TH>Date</TH>

                <TH>Hours</TH>

                <TH>Project</TH>

            </TR>

        <xsl:apply-templates select="Entry">

            <xsl:sort data-type="text"
```

```
order="descending" select="Date"/>

        </xsl:apply-templates>

    </TABLE>

  </xsl:template>
```

Add this template to your timesheet2.xsl file. There are a couple of things to note about the Entries template. First, we are displaying the time sheet entries in an HTML table. We need to supply TH (table heading) elements for the entire table only one time for the table. Next, we are using an `xsl:sort` element in this XSL file. The `xsl:sort` element must be specified as a nested element in the `xsl:apply-templates` element and it allows the developer to specify how the data given to the applied templates will be sorted. Normally, the data is given to the applied templates in the order they appear in the XML document. In this case, the `"Entry"` elements will be sorted by the `"Date"` child element in descending order.

15.4.3.2 Entry Template

The Entry template matches the `"Entry"` element and has the sole purpose of generating a row in the HTML table using data from the `"Entry"` element in the timesheet.xml file. Listing 15.5 shows the Entry template.

Listing 15.5 The Entry template

```
<xsl:template match="Entry">

    <TR>

        <TD><xsl:value-of select="Date"/></TD>

        <TD><xsl:value-of select="Hours"/></TD>

        <TD><xsl:value-of select="Project/@name"/></TD>

    </TR>

</xsl:template>
```

Add this template to your timesheet2.xsl file. The only thing to note here is that for an "Entry" element, we would like to display the project name. The "Project" element is nested within the "Entry" element and had two attributes – "name" and "id." All we are interested in is "name." The XPath expression "Project/@name" points to the "name" attribute in the child element of the current element "Project." When writing XSL, remember that the current element is the one that matched the template you are writing the code in. The current element in the Entry template is "Entry."

15.4.3.3 Integrating with Existing Templates

In order to cause the Entries and Entry templates to be used, we need to update the TimeSheet template to use the xsl:apply-templates XSLT element to call the Entries template. Add the following code to the bottom of the TimeSheet template just before the </xsl:apply-templates> end tag:

```
<HR/>

<xsl:apply-templates select="Entries"/>
```

This will add a horizontal rule (a line) to the HTML output and then it will call the Entries template.

15.4.3.4 Testing the New Templates

Once you have made these updates, apply timesheet2.xsl to the timesheet.xml file. The generated HTML should create a Web page as shown in Figure 15.20.

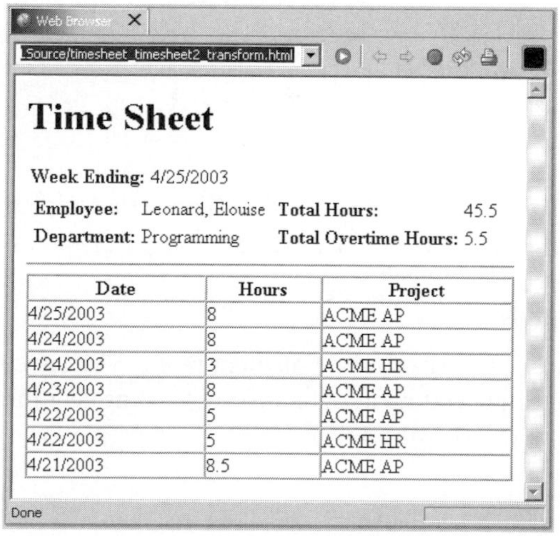

Figure 15.20 Refactoring 2—time sheet output.

15.4.4 Refactoring 3: Add Project Summary Information

The next refactoring will add the project total information to the output. In order to do this, we need to add more templates and update others.

15.4.4.1 ProjectTotals template

The ProjectTotals template matches the `"ProjectTotals"` element in the XML document. The ProjectTotals template, shown in Listing 15.6, is very similar to the Entries template where it handles the one-time-only items such as table headers.

Listing 15.6 The ProjectTotals template

```
<xsl:template match="ProjectTotals">

    <TABLE border="1">

        <TR>

            <TH>Project ID</TH>

            <TH>Name</TH>

            <TH>Hours</TH>

        </TR>

        <xsl:apply-templates select="Project"/>

    </TABLE>

</xsl:template>
```

Add this template to the timesheet2.xsl file. We'll create a template to handle the layout of the results returned from the highlighted `<xsl:apply-templates>` tag in the next section.

15.4.4.2 Project Template

The Project template matches the `"Project"` element in the XML document. The Project template has the sole purpose of generating a row in the table of project information displaying the information specific to a project (Listing 15.7).

Listing 15.7 Project template

```
<xsl:template match="Project">
```

```
    <TR>

        <TD><xsl:value-of select="@id"/></TD>

        <TD><xsl:value-of select="@name"/></TD>

        <TD><xsl:value-of select="@totalHours"/></TD>

    </TR>

    </xsl:template>
```

15.4.4.3 Integrating with Existing Templates

In order to invoke the ProjectTotals and Project templates, we need to update the TimeSheet template to use the `xsl:apply-templates` XSLT element to call the ProjectTotals template. Modify the TimeSheet template so that it resembles the code in Listing 15.8.

Listing 15.8 Modifying the TimeSheet template

```
    <xsl:template match="TimeSheet">

        <H1>Time Sheet</H1>

        <TABLE border="0">

    <TR colspan="2">

        <TD><B>Week Ending:</B><xsl:text>   </xsl:text>

<xsl:value-of select="@weekEnding"/></TD>

            <TD></TD>

        </TR>

        <TR>
```

```
                    <TD><xsl:apply-templates select="Employee"/></TD>

                    <TD><xsl:apply-templates select="Summary"/></TD>

        </TR>

        </TABLE>

        <HR/>

        <TABLE border="0">

    <TR colspan="2">

            <TD><B>Project Totals</B></TD>

            <TD></TD>

    </TR>

    <TR>

                        <TD><xsl:apply-templates

select="Summary/ProjectTotals"/>

</TD>

            <TD></TD>

    </TR>

            </TABLE>

            <HR/>
```

```
        <xsl:apply-templates select="Entries"/>

    </xsl:template>
```

The `<HR/>` tag will add a horizontal rule (a line) to the HTML output and then it will call the ProjectTotals template.

15.4.4.4 Testing the New Templates

Once you have made these updates, apply the timesheet2.xsl to the timesheet.xml file. The generated HTML should create a Web page as shown in Figure 15.21.

15.5 Dynamic Example XML/XSL Web Interface with WSAD

The only thing that remains to be done with our sample is to add Java code to make the Web interface dynamic. Using a static XML document as we did in the previous sections is the preferred way to create the initial XSL Web interfaces because you only have to debug your templates, not the Java code as well. However, at some point, the XSL has to be used in an application that dynamically generates XML. To add the dynamic nature to our sample, we will

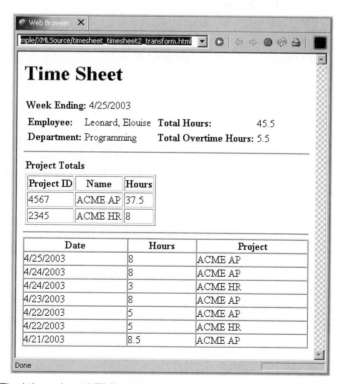

Figure 15.21   Final time sheet HTML output.

first create JavaBeans representing our domain model. Next, we will need an XML Generator to generate the XML. Additionally, we need to create a servlet to handle the Web interaction and XSL transform and a utility class that implements the javax.xml.transform.URIResolver interface to find the XSL files on the classpath.

You will follow these steps in implementing the XML/XSL dynamic example using WSAD:

1. Create a Java package

2. Create an XML Generator

3. Update project classpath to find Xalan-j and the XSL files

4. Create a URIResolver to resolve XSL files on classpath

5. Create a servlet to process requests

6. Test and debug on WSAD TE

The sections that follow will take you through these steps. If you previously imported the XMLXSL Example project, you will not need to create any of the files or Java packages that are mentioned in this section, rather you can simply browse them as you read along.

15.5.1 Create a Java Package

The first thing you will do is to create a Java package named com.wsbook.xmlxsl.sample. Create this package in the XMLXSL Example project under the JavaSource folder. If you are unsure how to create a Java package, refer to Chapter 7.

15.5.2 Create an XML Generator

The XMLGenerator is the class that creates the dynamic XML. In most cases, this class interacts with mediator and domain layers to extract data for the generated XML. In order to focus on the Java generation of XML, we will simplify the problem and use hard-coded data to render the XML. The XML Generator contains one method, generateXML(String showDetails). If the showDetails string is equal to "on" then the TimeSheet details will be displayed. The XML Generator is called TimeSheetXMLGenerator.java and the source code is shown in Listing 15.9 (Note: Some redundant source code has been omitted).

Listing 15.9 TimeSheetXMLGenerator.java source code

```
package com.wsbook.xmlxsl.sample;

import java.util.Properties;

import javax.xml.parsers.DocumentBuilderFactory;

import org.w3c.dom.Document;
```

```java
import org.w3c.dom.Element;

import org.w3c.dom.Node;



public class TimeSheetXMLGenerator {

    public Document generateXML(String showDetails) {

        Document doc = null;

        try {

    doc = DocumentBuilderFactory.newInstance().

    newDocumentBuilder().newDocument();

        } catch (Exception e) {

        System.out.println("Exception occurred - " + e);

        Return null;

        }



        //      <TimeSheet weekEnding="4/25/2003">

        Element timeSheetElem = doc.createElement("TimeSheet");

        doc.appendChild(timeSheetElem);

        timeSheetElem.setAttribute("weekEnding", "04/25/2003");
```

```
//          <Employee id="257899" name="Leonard, Elouise"

//              deptName="Programming"/>

            Element employeeElem = doc.createElement("Employee");

            timeSheetElem.appendChild(employeeElem);

            employeeElem.setAttribute("id", "257899");

            employeeElem.setAttribute("name", "Leonard, Elouise");

            employeeElem.setAttribute("deptName", "Programming");



            if (showDetails.equalsIgnoreCase("on")) {

                // <Entries>

                Element entriesElem = doc.createElement("Entries");

                timeSheetElem.appendChild(entriesElem);



                // Entry 1

                //          <Entry>

                Element entryElem = doc.createElement("Entry");

                entriesElem.appendChild(entryElem);
```

```
//                       <Date>4/21/2003</Date>

Element dateElem = doc.createElement("Date");

Node textNode = doc.createTextNode("4/21/2003");

dateElem.appendChild(textNode);

entryElem.appendChild(dateElem);



//                       <Hours>8.5</Hours>

Element hoursElem = doc.createElement("Hours");

textNode = doc.createTextNode("8.5");

hoursElem.appendChild(textNode);

entryElem.appendChild(hoursElem);

hoursElem.setNodeValue("8.5");



//           <Project id="4567" name="ACME AP"/>

Element projectElem = doc.createElement("Project");

entryElem.appendChild(projectElem);

projectElem.setAttribute("id", "4567");
```

```
            projectElem.setAttribute("name", "ACME AP");


        // ... Additional entries not shown

    }



//          <Summary totalHours="45.5" overTimeHours="5.5">

    Element summaryElem = doc.createElement("Summary");

    timeSheetElem.appendChild(summaryElem);

    summaryElem.setAttribute("totalHours", "45.5");

    summaryElem.setAttribute("overTimeHours", "5.5");


        //                <ProjectTotals>

    Element projectTotalsElem =
doc.createElement("ProjectTotals");

        summaryElem.appendChild(projectTotalsElem);


//                <Project id="4567" name="ACME AP"

//                    totalHours="37.5"/>
```

```
        Element project1Elem = doc.createElement("Project");

        projectTotalsElem.appendChild(project1Elem);

        project1Elem.setAttribute("id", "4567");

        project1Elem.setAttribute("name", "ACME AP");

        project1Elem.setAttribute("totalHours", "37.5");


//                      <Project id="2345" name="ACME HR"

//                            totalHours="8"/>

        Element project2Elem = doc.createElement("Project");

        projectTotalsElem.appendChild(project2Elem);

        project2Elem.setAttribute("id", "2345");

        project2Elem.setAttribute("name", "ACME HR");

        project2Elem.setAttribute("totalHours", "8");


        return doc;

    }

}
```

The generator's main purpose is to generate a Document. As we said before, this sample uses hard-coded data so that the focus of the sample can be on how to use the JAXP API to create a `Document` object. JDOM can also be used in the XML Generator if your team is familiar with that API.

Notice that the XML Generator conditionally generates the `"Entries"` element. One of the nice things about XSL is that if you want to exclude a part of the output, you can simply omit the XML elements without having to make a change to the XSL document. Also, notice that the JAXP API allows for text nodes to be added to elements to give them their data as shown in the creation of the `"Date"` and `"Hours"` elements. JAXP also provides the `setAttribute()` method to add attributes to an element as a key/value pair.

15.5.3 Update Java Classpath

The XMLXSL Example project classpath must be modified to find the xalan.jar and the XSL files. The xalan.jar file contains the Apache Xalan-j Java classes needed to perform an XSL transform. When we use the WSAD tools to do a transformation as we did in the previous sections, the xalan.jar file is automatically placed on the classpath. However, for our Java project, we must explicitly add this JAR file to the project build classpath. To do this, select the XMLXSL Example project and then select the Properties selection from the right-click menu. The dialog window as shown in Figure 15.22 will be displayed.

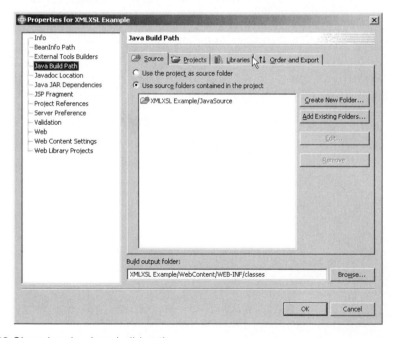

Figure 15.22 Changing the Java build path.

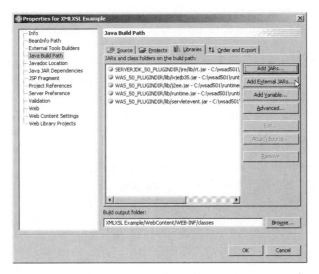

Figure 15.23 Libraries tab.

Select the Libraries tab so that we can add the jar file. The dialog will change to resemble Figure 15.23.

From the Libraries tab, select the Add External Jars button to display the file selection dialog. Navigate to the [wsad-install-dir]/runtimes/base_v5/lib directory. Select the xalan.jar file from the list of files and then press the Open button to make the selection. The Libraries tab will now resemble Figure 15.24.

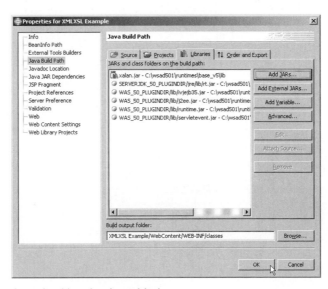

Figure 15.24 Libraries tab with xalan.jar added.

Select the *OK* button to close the dialog and update the Java classpath change. Now the Apache Xalan API will be available to any Java source code created in the XMLXSL Example project.

When using XSL in a Web application, the XSL will not interfere with making the distributed WAR file portable. A portable WAR file is one that can be moved from one application server to another without having to be rebuilt. At the heart of this issue is how the XSL files are found by the XSL transformer. If the XSL files are found using file IO, then a relative or absolute path must be given to the Web application in a properties file or servlet initialization parameter. While this will work, it leads to many development-time and runtime errors that can be easily avoided. Additionally, it can render the WAR file nonportable.

The way to avoid this situation is to set up the XSL transformer to find the XSL files on the Java classpath. In a Web application, the WEB-INF/classes directory is always on the Java classpath. We want our XSL files copied to that directory. In the next section, we will discuss how to set up the transformer to find the XSL files on the Java classpath. To add the XSL files to the WEB-INF/classes directory, we need to once again modify the XMLXSL Example projects Java build path. Open the Properties dialog again and select the Libraries tab as shown in Figure 15.25.

Select the Advanced button to open the dialog shown in Figure 15.26.

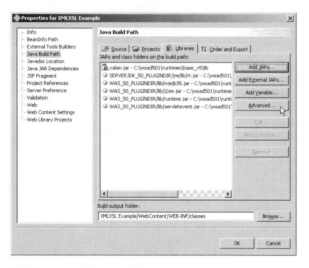

Figure 15.25 Adding XMLSource - Libraries tab.

Figure 15.26 Advanced Add Classpath Entry.

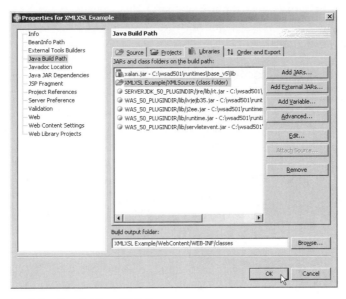

Figure 15.27 Libraries tab after Adding XMLSource.

Select the *Add Existing Class Folder* radio button and then select the *OK* button. When the dialog appears, drill down into the XMLXSL Example project and select the XMLSource folder. Select the *OK* button to return to the Libraries tab as shown in Figure 15.27.

Select the *OK* button to close the dialog and finish the classpath update. Notice that in the Navigator view, the XSL files have been copied from the XMLSource folder to the WEB-INF/ classes directory as shown in Figure 15.28.

Figure 15.28 XSL files have been copied to WEB-INF/classes folder.

Whenever the project goes through a rebuild, the contents of the XMLSource folder will be copied to the WEB-INF/classes directory. To force this copy to happen, use the *Project > Rebuild Project* menu option.

15.5.4   Create a URIResolver Implementation

Now that the XSL files are on the classpath we need to create a class called a URIResolver, which will be used by the transformer to find the XSL files. The `javax.xml.trans-form.URIResolver` is an interface in JAXP which contains one method named `resolve(String    href,    String    base)` and returns a `javax.xml.trans-form.stream.StreamSource` object which is also a part of JAXP. Our URIResolver is named ClassPathURIResolver.java and the source code is shown in Listing 15.10.

Listing 15.10 ClassPathURIResolver.java source code

```
package com.wsbook.xmlxsl.sample;

import java.io.InputStream;



public class ClassPathURIResolver implements

javax.xml.transform.URIResolver {



     public javax.xml.transform.Source resolve(String href,

          String base)

          throws javax.xml.transform.TransformerException {

          javax.xml.transform.stream.StreamSource result = null;

          String path = href;

          try {

               InputStream inputStream = getClass().
```

```
        getResourceAsStream(path);

            System.out.println("ClassPathURIResolver.resolve() path = "

                + path);

                if (inputStream != null) {

                result = new

                        javax.xml.transform.stream.StreamSource();

                result.setInputStream(inputStream);

                }

        } catch (Exception exc) {

                System.out.println(" Exception on --> href = "

                                + href + " base = " + base

                                + " Exception = " + exc);

        }

        System.out.println("resolved path = " + path + " href = "

                                + href + " base = " + base );

        return result;

    }

}
```

The heart of the URI resolver is the statement:

```
InputStream inputStream = getClass().getResourceAsStream(path);
```

This statement uses the Java classpath to find the file represented by the `path` variable and places that file in an `InputStream` object. This is the same method that java.util.ResourceBundle uses to find *.properties files, which are also typically located on the classpath. This saves us the time and trouble of having to write code to search the classpath ourselves.

15.5.5 Create a Servlet

The servlet handles the request, parses any parameters, calls any business or mediator logic, calls the XML Generator, and transforms the XML into HTML. Our servlet, TimeSheetX-SLServlet.java does not call any business or mediator logic so that we can shorten the sample. The TimeSheetXSLServlet.java servlet has three methods, `doGet()`, `render()`, and `dumpXML()`.The `doGet()` method handles the GET HTTP request and parses parameters from the request. The `doGet()` uses the XML Generator to generate the XML and then calls the `render()` or `dumpXML()` methods, depending on the value of the transform HTTP parameter. The TimeSheetXSLServlet.java is shown in Listing 15.11.

Listing 15.11 TimeSheetXSLServlet.java

```
package com.wsbook.xmlxsl.sample;


import java.io.IOException;


import java.io.Writer;


import java.util.Properties;


import javax.servlet.ServletException;


import javax.servlet.http.HttpServlet;


import javax.servlet.http.HttpServletRequest;


import javax.servlet.http.HttpServletResponse;


import javax.xml.transform.Source;
```

```java
import javax.xml.transform.Transformer;

import javax.xml.transform.TransformerFactory;

import org.apache.xalan.serialize.SerializerToXML;

import org.w3c.dom.Document;

public class TimeSheetXSLServlet extends HttpServlet {

    public static final String XSL_FILE = "/timesheet2.xsl";

    public void doGet(HttpServletRequest req,

    HttpServletResponse resp)

        throws ServletException, IOException {

        String showDetails = req.getParameter("showDetails");

        if (showDetails == null) {

            showDetails = "off";

        }

        String transform = req.getParameter("transform");

        if (transform == null) {

            transform = "off";

        }
```

```
        TimeSheetXMLGenerator generator = new

            TimeSheetXMLGenerator();

        Document xmlDoc = generator.generateXML(showDetails);

        if (transform.equalsIgnoreCase("on")) {

            render(req, resp, xmlDoc, new Properties());

        } else {

            dumpXML(xmlDoc, resp.getWriter());

        }

    }

    public void render(HttpServletRequest req,

    HttpServletResponse resp,

        Document xmlDoc, Properties xslParms) {

        try {

            Source src = new

                javax.xml.transform.dom.DOMSource(xmlDoc);

            TransformerFactory tFactory =

                TransformerFactory.newInstance();

            tFactory.setURIResolver(new

                ClassPathURIResolver());
```

```
           Transformer transformer =

           tFactory.newTransformer(tFactory.getURIResolver().

                       resolve(XSL_FILE, null));

           javax.xml.transform.Result result = new

               javax.xml.transform.stream.StreamResult(

               resp.getWriter());

           transformer.clearParameters();

           java.util.Enumeration parmNames = xslParms.keys();

           while (parmNames.hasMoreElements()) {

               String parmName = (String)

                   parmNames.nextElement();

               String parmValue = (String)

                   xslParms.get(parmName);

                   transformer.setParameter(parmName,

                   parmValue);

           }

           transformer.transform(src, result);

       } catch (Exception e) {
```

```
                    System.out.println(

                        getClass().getName() +

                        " Exception occurred - " + e);

                    e.printStackTrace();

            }



    }



    public void dumpXML(org.w3c.dom.Node xmlTree, Writer writer) {

        try {

            SerializerToXML s2x = new SerializerToXML();

            s2x.setWriter(writer);

            java.util.Properties props = new
                        java.util.Properties();


            props.setProperty(javax.xml.transform.OutputKeys.INDENT,

                        "yes");

            s2x.setOutputFormat(props);
```

```
                    s2x.serialize(xmlTree);


            } catch (IOException ioExc) {


            }


        }


}
```

Notice that URIResolver is used in the statements:

```
        tFactory.setURIResolver(new ClassPathURIResolver());


    Transformer transformer =


    tFactory.newTransformer(tFactory.getURIResolver().


    resolve(XSL_FILE, null));
```

First, ClassPathURIResolver is assigned to the transformer factory. This guarantees that any `<xsl:include/>` or `<xsl:import/>` elements found in the XSL file will be obtained using ClassPathURIResolver. Then, ClassPathURIResolver is used to get the stream for the timesheet2.xsl file. Using ClassPathURIResolver helps to ensure that using XSL does not in any way make the war file nonportable.

15.5.6 Test and Debug

You can create a simple index.html file in order to more easily test TimeSheetXSLServlet.java. This HTML file will resemble Figure 15.29 when shown in the browser.

Using this index.html file allows us to test the dynamic nature of our servlet, XML, and XSL more easily. This index.html file should be placed in the XMLXSL Example project in the WebContent folder. Listing 15.12 shows the source for index.html.

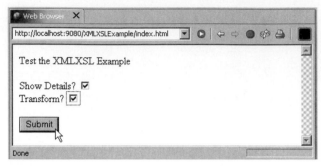

Figure 15.29   Index.html.

Listing 15.12 Source for index.html

```
<!DOCTYPE HTML PUBLIC "-//W3C//DTD HTML 4.01 Transitional//EN">

<HTML>

<HEAD>

<TITLE>index.html</TITLE>

</HEAD>

<BODY>

<P>Test the XMLXSL Example<BR>

<BR></P>

<FORM action="/XMLXSLExample/TimeSheetXSLServlet"

name="XMLXSLTransformer" target="_blank">

Show Details?

<INPUT type="checkbox" name="showDetails" checked="true">
```

```
<BR>

Transform?

<INPUT type="checkbox" name="transform"  checked="true">

<BR>

<BR>

<INPUT type="submit" name="Submit" value="Submit">

</FORM>

</BODY>

</HTML>
```

To test your work, simply run index.html on a WebSphere 5.0 TE server. Select the index.html file and then from the context menu, select *Run on Server*.

15.6   When to Use XML/XSL for Web Interfaces

At this point you might be thinking, "I have JSPs, why would I want to use XML and XSL?" JSPs are indeed an effective way to develop dynamic HTML interfaces and with the addition of taglibs, a JSP can be crafted to keep the view code separated from the controller code. However, in many cases XML and XSL is a better choice for creating Web interfaces.

One of the first arguments usually leveled against using XML and XSL is that the performance of using XSL is inadequate. As in any endeavor, performance measurements vary with the application. However, in our tests, we have seen that the performance of an XML and XSL interface doing the same function as a JSP interface is often very comparable. Additionally, Xalan provides a way to compile the XSL into Java using its translet technology to achieve even faster interfaces. There is some measurable difference in the speed of JSP and XSL interfaces, but this only becomes a factor in the most demanding interfaces.

At development time, a JSP can be very cumbersome since it has to be continually re-compiled before testing the latest change. On the contrary, XSL is interpreted so a change to XSL is realized on the next HTTP request. Another development-time advantage is that XSL contains no Java code. XSL provides a way to create dynamic Web interfaces that separates Java-based controller code from view-based XSL instructions. JSPs, even with the use of taglibs, often end up including scriptlets, which are Java code. This means that a Java developer is needed to maintain the JSP pages. With XSL all that is needed to develop the actual Web interface is a sample XML document and an XSL transformer.

Being able to develop the Web interface using only a sample XML document is a key point. It means that the Web interface developer does not have to know Java, does not have to have a database connection, and does not have to have an application server handy in order to be productive.

Additionally, due to the fact that the Java code in the XML Generator is focused on generating XML, the XML can be used for other purposes later in the lifetime of the application. For instance, if the application needed to work on a PDA, a different set of XSL files could be used to render smaller, more concise output. If the application needed to be called as a SOAP service, the generated XML could be used as part of the SOAP envelope. In fact, this flexibility is probably the single best reason to use XML with XSL. XSL has the distinct drawback that it is a rules-based language; this is something that many developers have difficulty understanding when compared to a simple procedural approach like JSP. It is not entirely clear that if you are only building a single, HTML-based interface, that there is much of an advantage to using XML with XSL. However, when you are in a situation where you require multiple application interfaces that each vary from each other in fixed, repeating ways, XSL transformation is a very attractive option for your user interface development.

There are several frameworks, which can be used in conjunction with the techniques described in this chapter. One such framework, Struts for Transforming XML with XSL (stxx) is an extension of the struts framework to support XML and XSL without changing the functionality of struts. Stxx supports Struts 1.0 and 1.1. You can read more about stxx at *http://stxx.source-forge.net/*.

15.7 Summary

In this chapter we have covered the basics of XSL, Java, and XSLT and how to use XSL in WSAD. XML and XSL can be used to build robust Web interfaces that can be easily repurposed.

CHAPTER 16

Developing and Testing the Domain Model

In Chapter 1, we introduced the concept of layers that can be used to partition the overall enterprise application architecture into separate concerns in order to simplify development and maintenance. Recall that the presentation layer provides the application user interface, the domain layer, the business semantics, and the data source layer persistence and integration with existing applications. Additional layers map between the core layers: the controller/mediator layer that maps the presentation to the domain, and the data mapping layer maps the domain layer to the data sources.

In this chapter, we'll take a closer look at the domain layer to see what role it plays in the enterprise application, how it is created, how it is integrated with the data source layer, and how it is tested.

Getting the domain model right is critical to the success of the enterprise application as it captures the semantics of the problem to be solved in a manner that greatly affects the ability to modify the application to meet changing business needs. Developing and validating the domain model early in the development life cycle of an application provides a good foundation for all other aspects of development. Figure 16.1 shows what we're covering in the layered architectures.

16.1 The Domain Model Layer

The domain model layer represents an abstraction of the business application problem space. It formalizes the knowledge discovered about a particular subject area of interest to the business, and provides the foundation for the business applications. A powerful domain model focuses attention on the problem being solved and improves communication among developers and users of the system. Establishing a solid domain model provides a foundation for incremental development and evolution of software systems that more closely support customer needs.

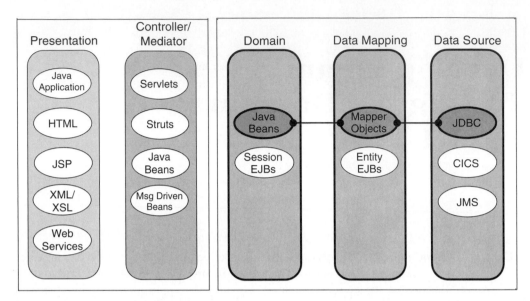

Figure 16.1 Layered architecture road map.

Eric Evans defines the domain model layer as that which "…serves to capture knowledge, enhance communication, and provide a direct path to implementation and maintenance of functional software" [Evans]. A domain model structures knowledge about a particular subject area while abstracting away extraneous detail. The business value of your application is derived from this layer.

In a seminal paper [Brooks], Fred Brooks once made a distinction between "essence" and "accidents" in software engineering. The essence of a problem is what makes it intrinsically interesting or hard. This may be finding the right formula for calculating a value, or developing an algorithm to solve a complex problem efficiently. Accidents of implementation stem from inadequate languages or tools, or from a limited understanding of the capabilities of the tools and languages you have.

We want to handle domain complexity separately from IT complexity in order to focus on the problem domain and not the implementation domain. In other words, you want to be able to concentrate on the essence of your business problem, and not overly concern yourself with the accidents of a particular implementation technology.

To this end, the specific purposes of the domain model are:

- To rigorously and unambiguously capture, maintain, and evolve knowledge about the business problem domain;
- To provide a common, shared language to enhance communication about the problems being solved;
- To provide a solid foundation for the implementation and maintenance of software that provides the intended business value.

Business applications are often subject to many different dimensions of change. There are changes in how the application should be viewed to support different stakeholder roles and client devices. There are changes in how the data is accessed from data sources. There are changes in the runtime deployment architectures to support nonfunctional characteristics, or to enable integration with other applications. But most importantly, there are changes in the market forces that drive the business processes the applications are intended to support.

Since the domain model represents that portion of the business domain that is automated and, therefore, constitutes the business value of the application, and since it is often subject to rapid change, it is important to build the application in a way that minimizes coupling with other application layers. The domain model separates business logic from views or persistence mechanisms so they can all vary independent from each other. You need to be able to modify, build, and test quickly to enable change. Separation of concerns is the primary mechanism for managing complexity, facilitating reuse, and enabling change.

16.1.1 Service Layer

The controller/mediator layer separates application and business domain logic and is useful for implementing coordinated application logic involving multiple, loosely coupled, transactional domain model objects. The controller/mediator layer is especially useful when the application must accomplish some task or use case accessed by multiple clients. It provides a layer for abstracting common user interface and application controller logic that can be shared across many user interface implementations.

The domain model provides the foundation for developing the rest of the enterprise application. However, it is possible that the same domain model may be used for many purposes in an application, or reused in different applications. Each use satisfies some aspect of the business problem. Often these different purposes will require a different perspective on the domain model. This could be as simple as using different names for the same information or behavior, or abstracting lower-level functions into some other behavior more focused on a particular domain.

You can try to incorporate these functional views into the domain model directly, but sometimes it is better to factor them into separate packages and classes. The Service Layer pattern [Fowler] is a means of providing multiple interfaces to the same domain model to better suit particular needs, views, or use cases. Use this pattern to provide APIs for particular purposes so that the domain model does not become overcomplicated with different functional views. Service layer methods often model specific use cases or business processes and can represent transactional boundaries. Service layers aren't always necessary, but they can be very useful when the same domain model is used for different purposes.

16.1.2 Approaches to Domain Modeling

There are many approaches to organizing domain logic, including process modeling, functional decomposition, data-centered design, and object modeling. All are useful in different circumstances, but using an object model for the domain model has many advantages, even for simple problems.

Functional decomposition does a good job capturing anticipated functions, but does not capture the overall domain in a manner that facilitates changing functions or adding unanticipated functions. This is because each function focuses attention on one particular activity that must be accomplished. Indeed, one of the measures of software quality is high functional cohesion and low coupling. However, it's often hard to see how all the functions fit together.

As we said earlier, enabling rapid change is one of the primary results of a good domain model. Functional decomposition often results in duplicated code and high coupling in calls/ called relationships, plus it spreads state and logic throughout the application and only handles one dimension of complexity (function).

Data-centered designs are useful for simple CRUD (create, read, update, delete) applications since they often allow record sets obtained from relational databases to be displayed and manipulated directly by user interface components. However, this tightly couples the presentation, domain, and data store layers making it difficult to change any of them. This may be fine for simple CRUD applications that are data-centered, stable, and/or short lived. It doesn't scale well to complex domains because of the increased complexity of handling a UI, domain, and relational database that are all managed together. In addition, a number of useful OO techniques such as inheritance, strategies, and other patterns that can simplify application development and maintenance are not directly supported by relational technology; making development more challenging.

Object modeling addresses many of these issues by providing a rich language for capturing broad domain knowledge. The primary advantage of object modeling results from encapsulation of knowledge through grouping behavior with the state it needs. This reduces complexity by keeping closely related state and behavioral knowledge together, avoids duplication, and reduces data coupling between objects. There are also many approaches to domain object modeling from simple intuitive approaches such as CRC (Class, Responsibility, and Collaborator) cards all the way up to the RUP (Rational Unified Process). We won't cover them all here, but we will take a look at one simple approach to domain modeling based on the notion that domain models are more often discovered than designed.

Iterative development based on exploration with your customer, implementing, mapping to the data source layer, and testing proves particularly useful for developing complex domain models. The whole process is oriented around change from the beginning. What follows is an oversimplification of what can be a very complex topic. However, we have found it useful for capturing a wide variety of domain models. For a more complete treatment of domain modeling, see [Evans].

16.1.3 The Mini-Max Approach to Domain Modeling

Start by having your customers tell you a story about their business or your end users about how they want to use your application. Focus on observable, existing, or anticipated business processes or functions, scenarios, and use cases. Don't worry too much about data at this point— there's more knowledge and value in the business processes. Data comes later as you determine what's required to implement the functions that support the business' processes. Also, spend time thinking out of the box in order to discover new business opportunities and processes that support them. You don't want to develop something the customer already has.

The business processes can be captured in text, use-case scripts, pseudocode, or UML interaction or collaboration diagrams. At this stage, it isn't necessary to be too formal. You want to focus on discovering knowledge about the domain, not requirements or modeling tools. A white board is often the best CASE tool at this stage. Avoid using tools that focus the attention on the computer or tool, not the business. You also want to be able to easily interact with the participants in the business. This can be hard to do when the view port is a 1024 x 768 screen.

Try to identify logical subsets of the business domain that are more or less independent and use this as a guide when you partition the domain into separate packages to manage complexity. These packages can be UML or Java packages, folders in the file system, or sections in a document. The implementation doesn't matter at this point. The goal is to identify different functional areas in the domain that can be handled more or less independently.

For each distinct business process that you have discovered, identify participating objects and assign responsibilities. The objects are often identified by nouns in the descriptions while the functions are verbs describing the processing, but this is only a guideline, not a rule. Some verbs may ultimately become service or domain controller objects.

One good place to find domain objects is in the customer's organization charts. Departments and employees often have well-defined roles and responsibilities supporting business objectives. This is a rich source of domain information that focuses on the customer's core value proposition and the responsibilities of the key stakeholders. Moreover, the players and processes that make up a business domain rarely change independent of evolutions in technology.

Today every business has customers, accounts, suppliers, and so on; years from now that will still be true. It is likely that the means to access them and their abilities to interact with each other more fluidly will evolve in time; however, the basic business rules that underlie this interaction will remain principally unchanged. All the more reason to focus on these immutable facts of doing business than the tools and technologies that support their implementation.

Examine each responsibility and determine what other information and operations are required to support it. As you discover new information and behavior, examine each existing domain object starting from concrete examples; avoid worrying too much about abstraction or generalizations at this early stage and instead focus where the new knowledge best fits. If it doesn't fit anywhere, create a domain object and put it there. Name the objects based on the role they play in the business, not how they are implemented in the application or database. Once you identify an object that should own the new information or behavior, try to push the information or behavior up the class hierarchy to the highest point possible by asking the same question about each superclass. We call this the mini-max approach to class hierarchy design. It pushes information and behavior up the class hierarchy as high as it can go without compromising cohesion. This results in a shallow class hierarchy that minimizes coupling between objects and maximizes the behavior of each participating object.

Next, map the domain objects to their underlying data store layer in order to support persistence. This is the subject of the rest of this chapter. Doing this early ensures the domain model is consistent with the (often existing) data sources layer early in the development cycle, avoiding potential big surprises later.

Don't let existing databases dictate the domain model. They may be out of date, or designed to solve a different problem. Get the database administrators involved in discovering the domain model; they will often know the data very well. You can try to get them to update the schema to better fit with the domain model, but this may be very difficult to do. Instead, you can use the data mapping layer to allow the domain model and relational schema to evolve more independently.

Finally, take the business functions you started with and that were used to define the domain layer, and then turn them into test cases to run against the newly implemented subset of the domain model. This validates the domain model based on the original requirements.

After you've completed these steps, iterate. Do incremental development driven by test cases that match anticipated functions, scenarios, and use cases that were used to develop the model. During each development iteration, try to implement specific functions that were identified as system requirements. Refactor as needed to incorporate new knowledge.

Implement the domain model first and then map it to a persistent store. The original functional requirements are implemented as test cases that can be used to ensure the domain model actually solves the intended problems. This provides complete feedback between requirements, domain model, and testing early and often in the development life cycle, ensuring the extended team understands the business problem as it is discovered and evolves. Keep in mind a customer often doesn't know precisely what she *wants* until you show her something that *isn't it*. Continuous and iterative refinement of the domain model through the full life cycle can avoid more unpleasant surprises, missed expectations, and unsatisfied customers.

16.1.4 Issues with Domain Modeling

There are some issues with domain modeling that should be taken into consideration. One of the most significant is that stakeholders often can't discern their original business process or use cases; they're hidden in a web of collaborating objects. This is a hard issue to address completely, but there are some things that can help.

First, presenting more abstract views of the domain model using UML use case, interaction, and collaboration diagrams can focus attention on the essence of the domain model. If you're working at the programming level, using a good program development environment can make navigating the domain model implementation simple and easy, making it easier to figure out how things relate and how well the implementation matches your initial design thoughts. The Java development tools in WSAD are stellar in this regard. You can pretty much put the cursor over anything and get hover Help showing its specification or JavaDoc if available. Press F3 to immediately open its definition.

You can select interfaces and methods and see how they are used or where they are implemented to find out how to implement or customize them. Search is based on Java semantics, not just strings, and is extremely fast. Another technique is to put breakpoints at interesting points in the application and then run it under control of the debugger. When the breakpoint is reached, the stack trace in the debug perspective will tell you how you got there, effectively a view of a process instance. Just double-click on any entry in the stack trace to view the Java source at that point. Then, single step to see where you might go next.

There are even applications that can introspect the information collected by the application profiling tools and recreate the original process models. We won't cover those here, but tools like Rational XDE Professional can be useful in this regard.

Another problem is that developers can find it hard to realize known and anticipated functions in an object model. This requires a kind of abstract thinking and a semantic shift that some people find difficult. You start out following a specific sequence of steps in a function, but then have to abstract domain knowledge about not only that function, but all the other parts of the domain it interacts with. Abstracting meaning out of simple steps in a particular function requires a thorough knowledge of the domain, something many programmers don't have. One approach to addressing this problem is through pair-programming where team members who have a functional world view are paired with someone else who can deal effectively with OO abstractions, resulting in a better domain model than either could have created by themselves.

Rich domain models can take longer to build and cost more in their initial development. However, they can reduce overall cost when applications are changed or extended. It is hard to achieve a balance between these conflicting goals, especially when your customer doesn't know what unanticipated functions the team is going to come up with, and isn't willing to pay for the increased development costs. You can always start out with a simple, limited domain model with lots of function calls implementing the system behavior. Then, as the application gets more complicated, use the knowledge obtained up to that point to help develop a better domain model for subsequent releases. This can result in a lot of refactoring and redeveloping, but it might be better than other alternatives.

There is also increased risk if the team is not experienced in OO development. In this case it may be useful to hire consultants to participate in pair-programming teams to help mentor the development team. This is often cheaper and faster than sending the developers off to a number of classes since they learn the techniques while working with an expert to solve the problem in the context of their own business instead of general programming exercises. It may seem costly in the short term; however, one good mentor can boost the productivity of a larger group more than enough to offset the additional cost (if not, they are not a good mentor, in the authors' shared opinion).

16.2 The Data Mapping Layer

This layer provides the persistent data from a technology-specific data store for the domain layer, which in turn provides this data in a more natural and accessible format for other domain objects. These data sources could be anything—existing applications, façades encapsulating existing applications, object databases, real-time sensors. But very often the data source layer is a relational database.

The data mapping layer is the gateway that maps between the domain layer and the data sources layer. In Chapter 7, we developed a very simple model and persisted the domain objects in a relational database using the Active Record pattern. This works well for simple object models that closely match tables in the database. But the pattern doesn't scale well for more complex domain layers, primarily because the domain model is responsible for the mapping, which results in tighter coupling between the domain and data source layer. This coupling limits data mining flexibility and inhibits change in both the domain model and database schema.

Larger domain models will be permeated with mapping code throughout its many domain objects, making it harder to maintain as domain model and relational schemas change due to refactoring and schema migration. Also, this coupling makes it difficult to test the domain model without a database.

Two important principles of software development are encapsulation and separation of concerns. This typically means factoring out the things that change so they can be implemented independently—and clients don't need to be aware of, or dependent on, implementation details. This enables reuse and isolates change to minimize maintenance overhead. The encapsulation of persisting data is a common example of managing variability. There are numerous different object models to persist and ways to persist them using many different database technologies or even the same technology. So when mapping between the domain and data source layers, we want to define interfaces that are independent of the actual domain model as well as the data store technology choices. This means that the interfaces can be implemented using a variety of techniques, each having different nonfunctional or quality-of-service characteristics.

There are two points of variability we need to manage: The data source architecture and the actual data to be managed as specified by the domain model. The mapping layer manages variability in both of these dimensions while keeping the domain and data source layers decoupled.

See [Fowler] for an excellent treatment of object/relational mapping and implementation details on each of the patterns used.

Why are we covering this much detail in the mapping layer? POJOs and JDBC are very effective for implementing and persisting domain models, but sometimes developers start out with simple domain models and simple mappings that work very well, and don't have to deal with all the concerns below. Then as the application grows, and adds more concurrent users, new problems crop up that can't be easily handled without a more complete persistence solution. Thus, without ever intending to, development shops can end up building their own persistence framework.

The result is additional unplanned work, missed schedules, and cost overruns. We highly recommend that you avoid this trap by using a commercial object-to-relational mapping tool to generate as much of this code as possible. Or better yet, skip ahead and see how you can use entity EJBs to do the work for you. If you're still intent on building the mapping layer yourself, the following sections will introduce concerns you may want to address.

16.2.1   Object-to-Relational Mapping

Object-to-relational mapping can be quite complex due to a number of factors:

- There is an impedance mismatch resulting from different programming models. For example, procedural Java vs. declarative SQL.
- Identity is generally handled transparently in domain object models through references maintained by the underlying programming language runtime. In relational schemas, identity must be implemented explicitly in the schema often using business data for primary and secondary keys.
- Objects can have one-to-many and many-to-many associations with other objects through collections while relational schema normalization prevents a column from having multiple values.
- The object and relational programming models have different type systems often requiring transformations from one to the other.
- Relational schemas do not directly support inheritance.
- The domain model and schema definition often evolve independently.
- There can be many domain models on the same data sources through data mining techniques.
- The transformation from the domain model layer to and from the data source layer results in data redundancy between in-memory representations being manipulated by applications, and data stored in a potentially shared repository. Unless carefully managed, this data redundancy can result in stale data or lost updates, especially when dealing with concurrent applications.
- Object models do not have native support for transaction semantics.
- Object models present a natural programming interface to the domain model, but they can introduce performance overhead depending on how the mappings to the data sources are implemented, and how close the data source schemas correspond to the typical uses cases supported by the domain model. Often it is easier to create an optimized query that returns exactly what is needed for a function without requiring an object model to provide further abstraction.

As a result there are many issues involved in object-to-relational mapping schemes. We'll introduce the issues and discuss possible solutions, in particular, one similar to that used for the case study discussed in Chapters 2 and 31. This solution is based on patterns taken from [Fowler] which provides a more detailed treatment and explores other mapping alternatives that may be appropriate for other situations. We are going to focus on Data Mapper and its associated patterns.

To facilitate the discussion, we'll refer to an example taken from the case study model described in Chapter 2, as shown in Figure 16.2. This simple example provides most of the modeling issues we need to cover. There is a one-to-many, bidirectional association between department and employee. We've shown the employee address as a one-to-one association nav-

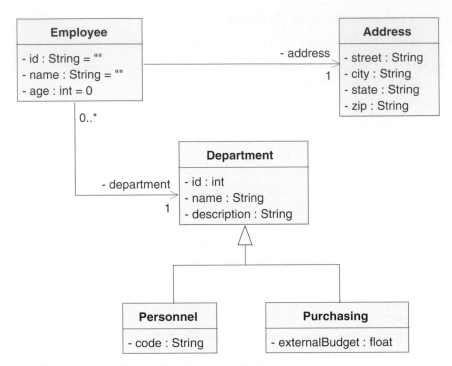

Figure 16.2 Example model taken from the case study.

igable in only one direction. There are two subtypes of department, personnel, and purchasing to show simple inheritance. There are other modeling issues, but these are the basics in every domain model.

16.2.1.1 Mapping Architecture Overview

Figure 16.3 gives an overview of the primary classes used in a typical mapping. The complete implementations of these classes, and the example domain model given in Figure 16.2, are provided in the Data Mapper Example project on the CD. See Appendix A for instructions on how to load projects from the CD.

We use the Separated Interface [Fowler] pattern to create a Mapper interface that captures the common mapping behavior that is independent of both the domain model and the persistence technology. JDBCMapper is an abstract implementation of this interface for JDBC. This class provides an implementation of mapping behavior specific to JDBC but independent of any particular domain object being mapped.

Other abstract implementations could be created for other data source layers, including different mappers in the same application for different domain objects. For example, in the section on testing the domain layer, we'll explore using a simple in-memory mapper to verify the domain model before implementing an object/relational mapping. Finally, there is a concrete instance of the JDBCMapper for each domain model object that maps that object to its relational data source.

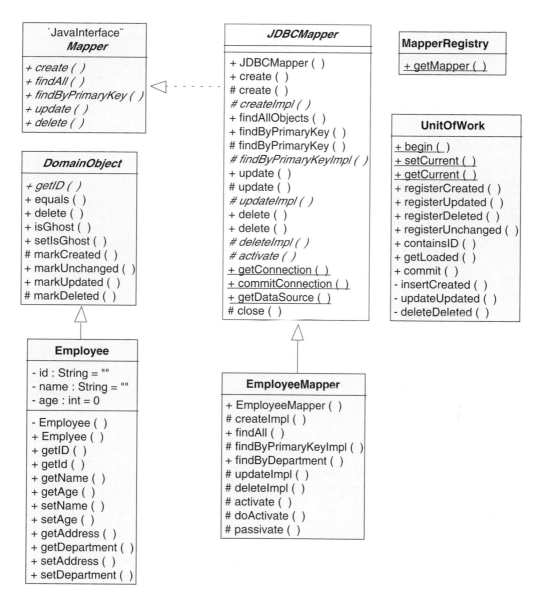

Figure 16.3 Object-to-relational mapping overview.

For example, EmployeeMapper maps an `Employee` domain object to the EMPLOYEE table in a relational database.

The Mapper interface shown in Figure 16.3 specifies the methods that a particular mapper must have for any domain model object and data source. These methods correspond to the typical CRUD operations that are required to persist and update objects instances in their data source.

The two methods are used to find all instances of a domain object, or to find a particular instance given its object identifier. You'll see a similar pattern when we introduce EJB home interfaces.

JDBCMapper provides an abstract implementation of the Mapper interface that is specific to JDBC. The implementation of each Mapper method is broken into two methods. The first, the one with the same name as the method in the Mapper interface, implements the JDBC-specific behavior, primarily connection management and JDBC exception handling. This method then calls an abstract method of the same name but with an Impl suffix that represents the domain model object-specific behavior. It is these abstract Impl methods that the domain object-specific mapper must implement to create, read, update, and delete instances of that object in the relational database (Listing 16.1).

Listing 16.1 Implementing a Mapper method

```
public void update(DomainObject domainObject) throws

                NoSuchObjectException {

    Connection conn = null;

    try {

        // get a connection

        conn = getConnection();

        updateImpl(conn, domainObject);

    } catch (Exception e) {

        System.out.println("Exception " + e +

            " caught in update()");

        throw new NoSuchObjectException("Wrapped Exception
 " +
                    e + " caught in update()");

    } finally {
```

```
                    close(conn);


              }


        }
```


```
     protected abstract void updateImpl(Connection conn,

          DomainObject anObject)

          throws SQLException, MappingException;
```


The abstract `activate` method is implemented by domain object-specific subclasses to move data from the data source layer to the attributes of the domain object. We'll cover this in more detail later. JDBCMapper also manages connections to the underlying database. A Java.properties file is used to externalize the specific data source and schema information, as was done in Chapter 7.

At last we have a concrete implementation of the JDBCMapper for each domain model object. Each abstract data source mapper requires a concrete implementation for each domain model object. For example, EmployeeMapper contains the SQL statements required to do the CRUD operations. These statements are prepared and used in the implementations of the abstract `Impl` methods specified in the JDBCMapper superclass. The `createImpl` method creates a row in the database and maps the attributes of the `Department` instance to columns in the row. The `findByPrimaryKeyImpl` method executes a query having a `where` clause specifying an expression that matches the primary key of the table to the value of the identifier for the domain object. The `updateImpl` method updates an existing row in the database with values from a modified `Employee` instance. And the `deleteImpl` method deletes an existing row in the EMPLOYEE table whose primary key matches the employee's identifier. Except for the SQL statements, and the assignment to and from domain object attributes and statement parameters, this code follows a similar pattern for all domain objects.

16.2.1.2 Accessing Object-Specific Mappers

Clients often need to interact with the data source layer, directly or indirectly, through existing domain objects. This means there must be some well-known way to find the mapper class for any given domain object. An easy way to do this is to use the Registry pattern [Fowler] to provide a well-known object that can be used to locate objects and services.

The MapperRegistry class, shown in Figure 16.3, provides access to the mappers to be used for each object in the domain model class. MapperRegistry can use an entry in the Java .properties file for the application that specifies what data source layer to use. It then fills in a table of the correct mapper to use for each domain model object keyed by its class. This can be useful for switching between development with an in-memory null mapper (one that doesn't use any data source layer) and a deployment time data source layer to facilitate testing.

The `getMapper` method looks up the mapper instance to use for the given domain object class. Note, in Listing 16.2, that the mapper instances are all singletons—a single instance of a mapper class handles the mapping for all instances of that class.

Listing 16.2 Mapper instances are singletons

```
String dataSource =

ApplicationProperties.getProperty("com.wsbook.mapping.datasource");

if (dataSource.equals("jdbc")) {

    registry.put(Employee.class, new EmployeeMapper());

    registry.put(Department.class, new DepartmentMapper());

} else { // assume "memory"

    registry.put(Employee.class, new TransientObjectMapper());

    registry.put(Department.class, new TransientObjectMapper());

}
```

16.2.1.3 Mapping Objects to Relational Tables

The first step in modeling an OO domain model to a relational database is to map each domain model object to one or more relational tables. There are three possible strategies for mapping an OO domain model to a relational database—top-down, bottom-up, and meet-in-the middle.

In the top-down strategy, the object model is used to derive the schema for the database. No existing schema elements are used. In the bottom-up strategy, the opposite occurs. The domain object model is derived from the relational schema. Meet-in-the-middle is used when, for some reason, the domain model and relational schema don't match well. This is often the case when there is an existing domain model and an existing database schema, both of which need to be reused. Meet-in-the-middle is a more realistic strategy since there is often an existing, at least partial, relational schema, and a domain model needs to mine that data and extend it to support new functions. Top-down strategies often result in databases that are not well normalized or are difficult to optimize. A good object model is not necessarily a good database schema. Conversely, the bottom-up strategy often does not result in the best object model. Relational schemas are often influenced by normalization and performance requirements or similar technology-related needs of a database and thus may not represent ideal object models, so the bottom-up strategy might only be useful for creating an initial domain model from an existing schema. The classes created from the schema could then be refactored to provide a domain model that better captures the semantics of the domain.

We'll focus on meet-in-the-middle since it is the most general approach and it provides additional flexibility by allowing the domain model and schema to evolve more independently. This strategy can use the Mapper [Fowler] pattern to bridge between the domain and data source layers.

16.2.1.4 Handling Object Identity

Object identity is a critical concept in object technology. It must be possible to uniquely identify an instance of something that encapsulates state and behavior. Generally object identity is handled by the underlying programming language through a memory reference or pointer and the application developer does not need to deal with its implementation details. However, this is not the case for relational database schemas which have to provide information about columns that make up primary (or secondary candidate) keys, and foreign keys that are used to link rows in the database. These keys often consist of data that is meaningful in the business domain, such as employee ID numbers for identifying individuals.

The domain model needs to provide a way of mapping object identity to identity in the data source layer. Since all domain objects must have an identifier, an implementation could introduce a Layer Supertype [Fowler] called DomainObject that is the supertype of all domain model objects, and implement identity management there. Then the other domain model objects can inherit identity management behavior from the layer supertype.

The identifier for an object can often be a single primitive value like an integer or string, or it could be a combination of attributes that make up a composite candidate identifier. An Identity Field [Fowler] can be used to simplify identity management so that the identifier is always an instance of an object. This way the same identity handling code can be used regardless of the actual implementation of the identifier for any particular domain model object.

The DomainObject layer supertype can provide an abstract method `getID` that returns the identifier for a domain model object. Concrete subclasses implement this method by returning an object that contains their key. DomainObject can also implement the `equals` method by checking to see if the referenced values compared are of the same type and have the same identifier.

Two references are considered identical if they reference the same domain object. For domain objects having identity, this means the referenced domain objects are of the same type and have the same identifier. Other aspects of DomainObject will be covered in a later section.

It is a good idea to avoid using business data for identifiers because this data is subject to change, making it difficult to update all references from other objects. For similar reasons, avoid identifiers that contain foreign key components (ID dependency) as this causes the identifier of one object to depend on an association with other object, resulting in increased coupling. Changing the association would result in an unintended change in the identity of the participating objects.

Object identifiers, and database primary keys need to be Globally Unique Identifiers (GUIDs) that, once assigned to an object instance, are never changed or reused on any other object instance. Otherwise they wouldn't uniquely and unambiguously identify a specific object instance. Identifiers should also be simple primitive values in order to make them easy to compare, resulting in faster queries.

Other candidate identifiers that have more specific business meaning can be used as arguments to finder methods as described later. Identifier values can be provided by a GUID generator or by using sequenced attributes supported by the underlying database management system (DBMS). Sequenced attributes are convenient, but they are not standard SQL types and can introduce undesirable DBMS dependences. Another option is to create a key table in the database indexed by key domains, and whose values are simple integers that are incremented every time a new GUID is needed.

16.2.1.5 Mapping Object Attributes

The attributes (properties or fields) of a class can be partitioned into a number of categories that determine how they should be mapped. The simplest category consists of attributes that have primitive types like `int` or `java.lang.String`. Examples of such attributes are the employee `name` and the department `description`. These fields can be mapped directly to columns of the table of the corresponding domain object. The column name is often similar to the name of the attribute while its type is the corresponding SQL type. Any differences between the Java and SQL type systems are handled in the domain object-specific mapper. Identity attributes that are primitive types also fall into this category.

The second attribute category consists of Value Object [Fowler] attributes that are non-primitive types, but are objects that contain primitive types and are treated as a single value. That is, these objects have no identity of their own (they are referentially transparent—references to different instances of the same value cannot be distinguished) and it is not necessary to distinguish one instance from another other than by values. Common examples are `Integer`, `Money`, `Date`, `Time`, etc. These types generally should not have a corresponding table of their own, but instead, should use an embedded value [Fowler] to map the object to fields of the table corresponding to the object that contains the attribute.

Domain object identifiers that are composite objects are value objects and should be mapped using an embedded value so the identifier can be treated as a single object. You can also use an embedded value for simple, one-to-one containment associations. Using an embedded value simplifies the relational schema and eliminates joins that might be required to access an instance of the containing object. A final reason for using an embedded value is when you have to map to an existing database schema that embeds more than one object into a single table, and the embedded objects don't have a separate identity. The domain model might want to separate the embedded objects to provide a better object model.

The EmployeeMapper, doActivate, and passivate methods actually perform the mapping to and from the results or reading or updating the database (Listing 16.3). We'll cover setting the employee's department when we cover associations and lazy load.

Listing 16.3 The doActivate method

```
protected void doActivate(DomainObject domainObject, ResultSet rs)

    throws SQLException, MappingException {

    Employee emp = (Employee)domainObject;

    emp.setName(rs.getString(2));

    emp.setAge(rs.getInt(3));

    emp.setAddress(new Address(emp));

    emp.getAddress().setStreet(rs.getString(4));

    emp.getAddress().setCity(rs.getString(5));

...

}



protected void passivate(DomainObject domainObject, PreparedStatement ps)

    throws SQLException, MappingException {

    Employee emp = (Employee)domainObject;
```

```
ps.setString(1, emp.getId());

ps.setString(2, emp.getName());

ps.setInt(3, emp.getAge());

if (emp.getAddress() != null) {

        ps.setString(4, emp.getAddress().getStreet());

        ps.setString(5, emp.getAddress().getCity());

    ...

    }

}
```

16.2.1.6 Finding Objects

Obviously, application code needs to be able to access object instances in order to manipulate them. However, there are often only a few, top-level objects that the application needs to access directly. The rest are accessed through navigable associations from these few root objects. Finder methods are used to access these root object instances. The application would have a different root-level object for each independent portion of the domain layer that it needs to manipulate. An application would use finder methods to locate root-level objects given some query criteria, often the identifiers of the objects. But other search criteria can be supported too.

In order for applications to use finder methods, they must be able to, well, find them. Since the finder methods eventually have to query the data sources and return domain model objects, they can be implemented in the mappers, and can therefore be located through MapperRegistry as described in the section "Accessing Object-Specific Mappers."

The domain object specific-mapper should have at least one finder method. Finder methods should be static since they do not require an instance of the mapper to function. Each domain object should have a method that finds that object by its identifier. The abstract method findByPrimaryKeyImpl does this for all JDBCMappers.

Domain object specific-mappers implement this method by executing an SQL query that searches the corresponding table for a row whose key column matches the object's identifier. Other finder methods can be provided as needed by the application. For example, a mapper for the department can be used to find all employees in that department. These methods can also be used by the mapper layers themselves to load objects referenced through associations.

Since finders are usually implemented by querying the database, they may not return object instances the application has added to the in-memory domain model as part of a transaction until after the transaction is committed. So it's a good idea to call finder methods early in the transaction in order to ensure a more consistent state across the whole domain model in the transaction.

Database queries can be expensive. Therefore, it is best to err on the side of accessing too much data and filtering in the finder methods or mapping layer instead of doing lots of little queries in multiple finder methods.

Different use cases may benefit from using finder methods that return more than one object type. These finders can fill in certain associations in the domain model because you know you'll need them in a particular situation. These finder methods can use a join instead of multiple queries to reduce database accesses. They can be coordinated with data clustering and indexes in the data source layer for efficient access.

The `findByPrimaryKey` method for EmployeeMapper is quite simple. It prepares the SQL statement for looking up an employee by its primary key, executes the statement, and calls the activate methods to put the data into the `Employee` domain object (Listing 16.4).

Listing 16.4 The EmployeeMapper findByPrimaryKey method

```
protected static final String _readString =

    "SELECT ID, NAME, AGE, STREET, CITY, STATE, ZIP, DEPTID FROM "+

    authId+ ".EMPLOYEE " +

    "WHERE ID = ?";




protected DomainObject findByPrimaryKeyImpl(Connection conn, Object id)

    throws SQLException, MappingException {

        PreparedStatement ps = conn.prepareStatement(_readString);

        ps.setString(1, (String)id);

        ResultSet rs = ps.executeQuery();
```

```
      rs.next();


      return activate(rs);


}
```

16.2.1.7 Maintaining Consistent State

In any application, it is important that the domain model is always in some known, consistent state. Transactions can be used to ensure the domain model is in a consistent state when it is persisted in the data source layer, but it is also important to maintain consistent state in the in-memory version of the domain model while a transaction is executing.

One way to avoid consistency problems is to ensure that there are no duplicate instances of domain model objects. Otherwise the application may make partial updates in more than one instance where they derive from the same data, resulting in an inconsistent state. A mapping layer can use the Unit of Work pattern [Fowler] to mark the beginning and ending of transactions, and an Identity Map [Fowler] in the unit of work to ensure any object is only loaded once. Abstract class JDBCMapper findByPrimaryKey method shown in Figure 16.3 and Listing 16.5 gets the current unit of work, and checks to see if it already contains an object identified by the given identifier. If so, it returns that object and there is no further access to the database.

Listing 16.5 JDBCMapper findByPrimaryKey method

```
public DomainObject findByPrimaryKey(Object id) {


      UnitOfWork current = UnitOfWork.getCurrent();


      if (current.containsID(id)) return current.getLoaded(id);


      Connection conn = null;


      DomainObject object = null;


      try {


            conn = getConnection();


            object = findByPrimaryKeyImpl(conn, id);
```

```
    } catch (Exception e) {

    ...

    } finally {

        close(conn);

    }

    return object;

}
```

When a new instance is activated and filled in from the data source, it is marked as unchanged and added to the unit of work so that other accesses to an object with the same identifier return the same instance. The identity map in the unit of work also provides a cache for all objects read regardless of how or when they were accessed by the application. This can simplify application development and result in much better performance because the client does not need to worry about avoiding extra, unnecessary, or redundant database reads (Listing 16.6).

Listing 16.6 Unit of work identity map

```
protected DomainObject activate(ResultSet rs) {

    try {

        String id = rs.getString(1);

        UnitOfWork current = UnitOfWork.getCurrent();

        if (current.containsID(id)) return current.getLoaded(id);

        Employee emp = new Employee(id);

        doActivate(emp, rs);
```

```
        emp.markUnchanged();


        return emp;


    } catch (SQLException se) {


        …


    }


}
```

16.2.1.8 Mapping Associations

Mapping associations between objects to a relational database is one of the more complex aspects of object-to-relational mapping. A number of issues must be considered:

- Creating object references in the data sources
- Association multiplicity
- Navigability
- Composition
- Type-safe collections
- Referential integrity
- Deletion semantics

Even the simple example in Figure 16.2 requires an implementation addressing many of the listed issues.

Associations between objects in the domain model are supported through object references in the underlying programming language. These object references have to be mapped to the mechanism supported by the data source layer. For relational database systems, that's foreign keys. Our example used an identity field for every domain object. The identity fields are mapped to the domain object's primary key in their corresponding tables. These identity fields can also be used to provide values for the foreign keys necessary to map the associations between domain objects.

Different mapping options are required for one-to-one, one-to-many, and many-to-many associations. For one-to-one associations, you can use an embedded option. But if the domain objects participating in the association also participate in associations with other domain objects, or can stand alone, foreign key mapping [Fowler] supports more flexible mappings.

A foreign key mapping is also very good for one-to-many associations. Take a look at the association between Employee and Department shown in Figure 16.2. A department has many employees, and an employee knows his department. Since the association is navigable in both directions, the Employee class has a method called `getDepartment` that returns the employee's department, and the Department class has a method called `getEmployees` that returns a Java collection containing employee references.

Relational databases require tables to be normalized, meaning the department table cannot have a repeating group; in this case, a list of employees. As a result, the implementation of associations in relational database is reversed from what it is in a domain object model.

The employee table has a department column containing a department ID that is a foreign key reference to a row in the department table. The department table has no reference to any employee. Instead, a query is required to determine the employees who belong to a particular department. This query is implemented in the Employee `findByDepartment` finder method which is used by the Department class when the `getEmployees` method is invoked. Lazy Load [Fowler] is used to avoid executing the query unless the `getEmployees` method is actually called. We'll cover the details in the "Lazy Load" section.

Updating bidirectional associations presents additional problems. The association must be updated in both participating objects, regardless of which participant was used to set the association. For example, the Employee `setDepartment` method must remove the employee from the current department, set the department field, add the employee to the new department, and mark the employee as updated.

Similarly, Department `addEmployee` method must set the employee's department. This way the client application can set the association between a department and employee either by setting the employee's department, or adding an employee to a department. The semantics are the same.

Many-to-many associations present additional problems because they would require a repeating group in both participating tables which is not allowed for normalized databases. Instead, mappers can use Association Table Mapping [Fowler] to introduce an additional correlation table that converts the many-to-many association into two one-to-many associations that can be handled using a foreign key mapping. This table only contains two columns made up of foreign key references to the associated tables. If the association itself requires additional information, this is generally modeled as an associative object in the domain model which can be used to formalize the association as well as contain data for the association itself. In this case, the identifier for the associative object must consist of the identifiers from the domain objects participating in the association.

Bidirectional associations are navigable in both directions and have an accessor method in both participating objects. This can be implemented as a foreign key in both tables, or in one of the tables requiring a query to navigate the association in the other direction. Unfortunately, one-to-many associations often result in bidirectional navigability even though it is not specified in the model. That's because of the reference/foreign key implementation reversal noted earlier and the mappers must be able to get and set the information when doing the mapping, causing the accessors to be public. If desired, a state variable can be used to protect these methods so they can only be called while loading and unloading. All other invocations, although visible, would throw an exception.

Containment associations have additional implementation implications. If an employee were contained in her departments, adding an employee to another department would require removing her from the current department. It may also be necessary for an employee to always belong to some department. These additional semantics can be implemented in the accessor methods that add and remove members from their containers. Containment associations also have additional deletion semantics where deleting the container also implies deleting all its members. This can be done in the domain model directly by iterating over the members of a containment association and deleting them. Alternatively, the implementation could rely on cascade deletes through foreign key constraints to let the database delete the members.

Another issue results from using Java collections model the many side of a one-to-many association. Java collections are strongly typed, but their members are always Objects. One way to avoid this problem is for the Department to be responsible for managing its employees through `addEmployee` and `removeEmployee` methods, which are type-safe because their arguments are Employee references. However, a client application could call the `Department` `getEmployees` method and directly add and remove objects from the underlying collection. This would, of course, not be a good practice because any integrity maintained by the domain supporting the semantics of employees belonging to departments would not be maintained.

Another option is to create type-safe collections that understand containment semantics and ensure the items added to the collection are of the correct type.

16.2.1.9 Inheritance

Relational data sources do not directly support inheritance so we need to put the translation from an inheritance hierarchy to data in the database in the mapping layer.

There are three approaches to implementing persistence inheritance and three corresponding patterns:

1. Single Table Inheritance [Fowler] represents an inheritance hierarchy as a single table whose columns contain all the fields of all the classes in the hierarchy, plus an extra column for a type indicator.

2. Class Table Inheritance [Fowler] has a separate table for each class.

3. Concrete Table Inheritance [Fowler] is somewhere in the middle. This pattern uses a table for each concrete subclass in the hierarchy.

The patterns for persistence inheritance are not mutually exclusive. It is possible to use different patterns on different parts of the same hierarchy. This technique can be used to minimize the effect of compromises that might fit better in one part of the hierarchy than another. We cover inheritance mappings in Chapter 25.

16.2.1.10 Lazy Load

A domain model is often a highly connected graph of objects. Client applications use finder methods to access distinguished objects in the domain model to initiate their work and then traverse associations in the domain model to visit other objects. It is entirely possible that accessing a single root object could end up loading the whole database in order to satisfy references between associated objects. This, of course, would be prohibitive due to poor performance and large memory footprint. It would also be very inconvenient for the client application to be required to invoke finder operations and realize every association in the domain model—that's the domain model's job.

Ideally, the application would only read what it actually uses. However, we don't want the client application to deal with this because what it needs to read may vary depending on the semantics of the domain and events that occur outside the system. Lazy Load [Fowler] provides just the solution we need. Finder methods return the requested object, but the associations that object has with other objects are not filled in from the database, avoiding the additional queries. Instead, the associations are filled in with a proxy that doesn't contain the domain object, just an identifier for how to get it. Then, when the client invokes an accessor method on one of these proxies, a finder method is automatically invoked and the proxy is filled in with the real domain object.

As a consequence, queries are only executed, and associations between domain objects realized, only if they are actually used. A secondary benefit is that the client application doesn't have to be aware of how or when things are read from the data source layer.

It is possible that making use of lazy load for every association will result in too many small queries for associations that are always navigated in frequent use cases on the domain model. For these situations, you might want to use lazy load on distinguished accesses, but use finder methods in other cases that realize more than one association in the domain model in anticipation of their use. These custom finder methods can use joins and other more complex queries to access data for more than one domain object in a single query.

An employee has a navigable association with his department. When the EmployeeMapper `doActivate` method activates a new `Employee` instance from information in the database, it checks to see if the department is a valid ID, and if so, creates a `Department` instance, sets its ID, and the sets the employee's department (Listing 16.7).

Listing 16.7 Creating a Department instance

```
if (deptId != 0) {

    Department dept = new Department(rs.getInt(8));

    dept.setIsGhost(true);
```

```
        emp.setDepartment(dept);


}
```

The Department is not actually read at this time. Instead, it is marked as a ghost, an object instance that knows its identifier, but nothing else. When an application accesses the department with the Employee `getDepartment` method, the department is read from the database (Listing 16.8). If the department is never accessed, it is never read.

Listing 16.8 Accessing the Employee getDepartment method

```
public Department getDepartment() {

    if (department != null && department.isGhost()) {

        Mapper mapper = MapperRegistry.getMapper(Department.class);

        department =

            (Department)mapper.findByPrimaryKey(department.getID());

    }


    return department;


}
```

16.2.1.11 Keeping Track of Changes

Client applications can make arbitrary changes to domain model objects at any time. This creates a problem when mapping to a data source layer because we don't want to update the database every time something changes in the domain model. Making many such update requests would have a very negative effect on performance, and even if this weren't an issue, the data source layer should only be updated at points when the domain model is known to be in a consistent state.

To keep track of changes, mappers can use Units of Work [Fowler]. We already introduced unit of work when maintaining the domain model in a consistent state by using an identity map to avoid duplicate object instances. This section looks at the same problem from the standpoint of data source updates.

A typical client application would create a unit of work, create, read, update, and delete some domain model objects in the context of that unit of work, and, at some point, where the unit of work represents a consistent state of the domain model, the application commits the unit of work. This pattern is repeated throughout the client application. Listing 16.9, for example, is a fragment of client code that creates an employee called "Fred Johnson."

Listing 16.9 Creating a client

```
{


        UnitOfWork.begin();


        emp = new Employee("757174");


        emp.setName("Fred Johnson");


        emp.setAge(33);


        emp.delete();


        UnitOfWork.getCurrent().commit();


}
```

Data mappers must ensure the unit of work is never shared across multiple threads which may introduce consistency problems. The `begin` method creates an instance of a `UnitOfWork`. As shown in the listing, a DomainMapper `activate` method gets the current unit of work and checks to see if the instance being activated is already in the identity map maintained in the `UnitOfWork`. If it is, the instance is returned and the method is complete. If not, the row from the database is transformed into a new domain object instance, and that instance is marked as unchanged.

`UnitOfWork` is responsible for:

- Containing all the objects read from the data source in a unit of work.
- Seeing if a domain object is already in the unit of work and returning instances of already loaded objects.
- Registering a domain object just mapped from the data source layer as unchanged.
- Maintaining a list of objects that were newly created and/or deleted in the unit of work.

- Maintaining a list of objects that were updated in the unit of work. Domain model set accessor methods update the state of their domain model object and mark it as updated in the current unit of work.

Java does not have a method for deleting an object instance and freeing its memory. It uses automatic garbage collection instead. Although it is possible to create a custom finalizer that would mark the object as deleted in the unit of work when it is garbage collected, it would not be possible to predict when this might occur. The object might not be deleted until after the unit of work was committed, in which case it wouldn't be deleted from the data source layer. So DomainObject provides an explicit `delete` method that marks the object as deleted in the current unit of work.

After executing any desired business logic in a unit of work, the client application calls `UnitOfWork.getCurrent().commit()` to commit the unit of work. This method iterates through the collections in the unit of work and, using the appropriate mapper instances, inserts created objects, updates changed objects, and removes deleted objects in order to update the data source layer. See the Data Mapper Example on the CD for the complete code listings.

Note that `commit` also has to clear the current unit of work. This means that the read cache in the previous unit of work is lost and the client application will have to reread the domain model in the next unit of work. This is important to ensure the domain objects in memory are consistent with their corresponding data in the data source layer, especially when the database could be accessed by many concurrent applications. Otherwise, the application might be working with stale data across transaction boundaries.

As a result, client applications should not hold on to references to domain object instances across unit of work boundaries as these objects have not been read in that unit of work. Implementations should raise an exception when an update is applied to a domain object that is not in the current unit of work.

16.2.1.12 Transaction Management

Unit of work is also a great place to handle transactions since it already marks the beginning and ending of some logical unit of work in the application. The transaction could be started in the `begin` method, and committed in the `commit` method. You probably noticed that these method names were, in fact, chosen to correspond to the usual transaction semantics.

The great thing about unit of work is that it keeps deciding when to read and write the database and transaction management out of the domain model and out of the client application. This greatly simplifies client application development and ensures the domain model and data source layers are consistent. A common practice is to begin and commit a unit of work in service layer or controller/mediator methods that support application use cases as they often correspond to transaction boundaries.

16.2.1.13 Odds and Ends

There are a number of other concerns that may be applicable to your applications:

- Scalability through load balancing
- Transactions (based on domain model semantics, not the database schema)
- Access control (based on domain model semantics, not the database schema)
- Distribution (in those cases where it is needed)

These issues introduce enough complexity that it is best not to even try to address them with the same roll-your-own approach that you can use for object persistence. We will cover a much more complete set of solutions to these problems when we discuss Enterprise Java Beans.

16.3 Testing the Model

The domain model is the foundation of application development since it contains knowledge about the business problem being solved. As a result, it is important to design, implement, and test the domain model early and often in the application development life cycle. To facilitate this development, and to focus on domain semantics, it is useful to be able to build and test the domain model without having to have a complex user interface, or dealing with other systemic concerns like performance, distribution, transactions, persistence, and security. These can come later once the domain semantics have been captured.

JUnit (*http://www.junit.org*) provides a simple framework for developing and running suites of test cases. This can be very helpful in early domain model development by formalizing the expected semantics in repeatable tests. In fact, it is often useful to develop the test cases first based on the expected domain model behavior, and then develop the domain model until the tests run. The test cases can often be based on use cases or end-user business processes since they have the most visible value to the customer. We will examine JUnit in Chapter 17.

It would be useful to be able to test some of the domain semantics before creating all that mapping code. One way to do this is to use a different mapper layer that doesn't require an object-to-relational mapping. For example, `TransientObjectMapper` shown in Listing 16.10 is a Mapper that doesn't do anything. The domain data is simply kept in memory during a test case and then thrown away. If the test cases require some domain objects to be persisted beyond a test suite so they can be reused, a simple Mapper that serialized the domain objects as Java objects or XML files could be used. This would take some coding, but it wouldn't require creating the database schema or installing and connecting to a database. Having to do all this while trying to discover and validate the domain model can be difficult and moves attention away from the customer's problem and onto the computer.

Listing 16.10 TransientObjectMapper

```
package com.wsbook.mapping;

import java.util.ArrayList;
```

```java
public class TransientObjectMapper implements Mapper {

public void create(DomainObject anObject) throws MappingException {

}



        public ArrayList findAll() {

                return null;

        }




        public DomainObject findByPrimaryKey(Object anObject)

                throws NoSuchObjectException {

                return null;

        }




        public void update(DomainObject anObject) throwsNoSuchObjectException

        {

        }
```

```
public void delete(DomainObject anObject) throws NoSuchObjectException

{


}


}
```

There are a number of ways to specify the mapping layer to use, including factory methods, a registry, or a Plugin [Fowler]. MapperRegistry could be responsible for determining which mapper to use for each domain object.

Using test suites is especially important for regression testing when both the domain model and relational schema are changing during development. Resist the temptation to avoid refactoring a domain model to keep from having to change the mapping or data source layers. The work you save may get lost many times over every time an ineffectively designed domain model is used. Since the mapping between the domain model and the data source layers is isolated in the data mapping layer, it's easy to know what to update when things change. However, this is tedious code, and it's easy for errors to creep in. Repeatable regression testing will make it easy to discover them before they appear in front of a customer.

16.4 Summary

This chapter covered the domain model layer and data mapper layers in the layered architecture. You saw the importance of the domain model in establishing the foundation for applications that provide business value, enabling effective communication between the customer and development team members, and providing a means of verifying application requirements. We also introduced the concerns that have to be addressed when mapping the domain model onto data sources through the data mapping layer. This represents a lot of the work involved in developing the domain model and applications that use it, work that might be better spent on the customer's problem.

Fortunately, object-to-relational mapping follows a number of repeating patterns making it possible for commercial products to generate much of the mapping code. Using such products may reduce risks and development time on your projects.

Another possibility is to use local entity beans and object-to-relational mapping tools that are part of WSAD to automate the generation of the mapping code. J2EE covers all of the issues discussed in this chapter and more. This is the subject of Chapters 24, 25, and 26.

provide several mechanisms to aggregate classes into larger functional units like EJBs. So, for our purposes we'll consider unit testing to encompass component testing as well.

- **Functional testing (which includes integration testing)**—The testing of aggregated functions or whole use cases. Functional tests aim to show that the combination of components function as expected. Functional tests look for things like consistent data representations, consistent data validation, and proper sequencing of calls.
- **System testing**—The testing of complete scenarios that span multiple components of the application to complete a full story. System tests can be run on only a complete system; this includes tests for the nonfunctional requirements of a system, or the "-ities" (security, reliability, accountability, recovery, etc.)
- **Performance testing**—A special case of system testing aimed at determining if performance requirements are met. This deserves special consideration for two reasons: (1) It requires special testing techniques (such as repeated, concurrent test runs to determine the behavior of a system under load) and testing tools to measure the performance of the system. (2) Performance is one of the "-ities" that has the most obvious effect on a system (people may ignore parts of a system that are complex or difficult to use, but everyone notices when a system is slow) but usually receives the least amount of attention until too late in the development cycle to do anything about it.

In this book, we will only concern ourselves with unit and functional testing, and ways of making them easier. In this chapter, we'll look at simple strategies for automated testing suitable for applications that will run on WebSphere. We will discuss the JUnit testing framework as well as provide a simple example of how to use JUnit to write automated unit test cases. Later in the case study, we will revisit JUnit and show some advanced techniques for using JUnit with J2EE applications.

First, we need to examine more large-scale issues. It's not enough to simply know what you want to do; a test plan is not enough for success. A test plan must be supported by the selection of appropriate test tools, coding standards, and overall testing strategies.

17.1.1 Tool Selection

Tool and framework selection for testing is important and there are many commercial packages and open source tools to select from. Tools and frameworks should be selected for:

- **Unit test**—The tool selected for unit test should be capable of testing public interfaces without polluting domain or application classes. The code written to support the unit test should generally not be deployed with the application to avoid polluting the application with test code and unnecessarily increasing the code bulk of your system. Also, test code deployed into production can create security holes, or have an adverse effect on performance if left in place. So, your unit test tool should allow you to keep test code separate from application code, and also to avoid deploying test code into production.
- **Functional test**—Tools selected for functional test should be able to test component public interfaces as well as component user interfaces. The code written to support

functional testing should not be deployed with the application for the same reasons as described in the unit test section.

- **Systems test**—The tool selected for system test should be able to simulate user functions that fulfill use cases tasks. This could be the same tool selected for function test, but may need to include extensions to support other styles of testing.
- **Performance test**—The tool selected for performance test should be able to simulate a population of users to gain an understanding of the application load limitations. There are a number of commercial options to choose from. Some of the tools have scripting languages to build test scripts and simulate system load and reporting.

17.1.2 Coding Standards

Establishing and enforcing coding standards can enhance application development team communications, reduce coding efforts, and simplify testing. Establishing coding standards should include:

- **Setting naming standards**—Following common naming standards for classes, interfaces, members, and methods can lead to a better understanding of the code by developers and testers alike. This better understanding will result in less repeated code and more reusable classes. This will reduce the number of identical or nearly identical tests that are necessary in the overall system. Common naming standards will also make refactoring easier and public interfaces more predictable.
- **Institute message protocol standards**—Chaining messages in a long cascading list can produce code that is difficult to understand, debug, and test. Individual methods can be reduced in size, simplified, and made clearer by establishing rules that limit the number of messages that can be chained.
- **Setting application layer guidelines**—As we've discussed, establishing application layers and determining layer interfaces can place behavior in appropriate layers, strengthen component public interfaces, and simplify testing.
- **Establish common services**—Defining common services such as exception handling, tracing, and logging can increase reuse and simplify testing. It is much easier to look for log messages in one location and to read a common format, than it is to search several different files and understand multiple formats.

17.1.3 Testing Strategies

Establishing the right coding standards and picking the right tools are necessary but not sufficient conditions for making testing successful. If a company doesn't train its people or organize its testing appropriately, the best tools will remain shelfware that adds no value to the development process. Here are some strategies for adopting test practices to make your testing more successful—

- **Identify class public interfaces to test early.** Make sure that the development team has 100 percent coverage of public interfaces; class public interfaces should be identified and plans put in place to exercise the public interfaces as soon as they are identified.

- **Put the right people on the job.** Developers should be responsible for testing their own classes, while the team as a whole should review the unit test plan. Attempts to create special test teams to develop and execute tests of component-level software often results in spotty tests and conflict between developers and testers due to lack of communication or incomplete communication.

17.1.4 Why Unit Test?

Unit testing is one of the most important contributors in preventing software defects. Unit testing is also an excellent way to determine if there is sufficient understanding of the domain model and its behavior. In fact, many developers prefer to develop the test cases first, essentially as the implementation of application use cases, and then develop the domain model sufficiently to execute the tests. This is sometimes called needs-based programming or test-driven development.

Unit tests do not typically validate user interface functions or verify system level features, although you can expand the definition to include these concepts. They are instead most often concerned with validating that the application's domain and infrastructure classes function as expected. Use cases are often a good source of test cases as they focus on the functionality that has value to the customer. However, such tests wouldn't necessarily have to include user interface considerations.

With a set of unit tests in place, you can be confident that adding a new function or changing anything will not wreak havoc on the function you have implemented. What is necessary to achieve this level of comfort is a tool that allows you to easily create tests for new functions, and also easily rerun tests on existing functions. Luckily, we have that in WebSphere Studio in the JUnit framework, as we will see in the next section.

17.2 What Is JUnit?

The JUnit Test Framework is an open source unit test framework for Java available from junit.org. The idea behind JUnit (expressed in [Beck]) is that if regression testing is made simple enough, developers will find that creating automated test cases is no harder than running test cases manually. This framework supports:

- The creation of unit test cases with no change in application code. Unit test cases can be created with no impact on the application.
- The ability to automate regression unit testing.
- The ability to create reusable test fixtures (sample data).
- The ability to create test cases without modifying the application.

You should write JUnit tests to validate your public interface methods, not to test trivial code like getters and setters. JUnit test cases are best suited to decide questions such as whether

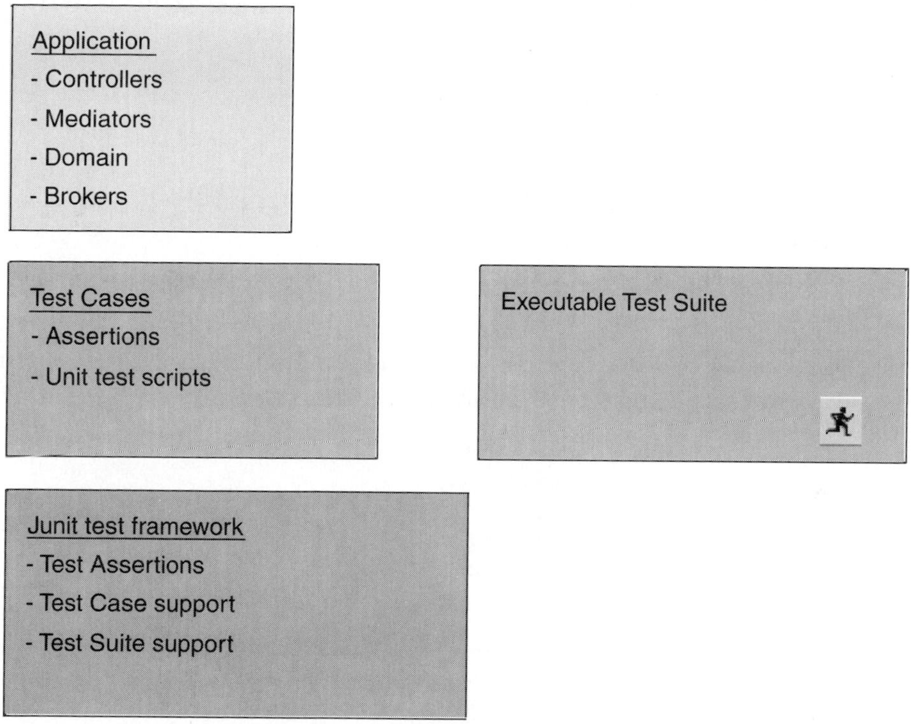

Figure 17.1 JUnit Test Framework and application.

domain objects can be created and traversed properly, if exceptions are thrown and handled correctly, or if persistent data retrieval and update is handled in the right way.

The JUnit test cases and executable test suites are not embedded in the application. The executable test suite can be modified to regression test portions of the application. The JUnit Test Framework is shipped with IBM WSAD and contains support for test assertions, test cases, test suite development, and test reporting (Figure 17.1).

The JUnit framework API is fairly easy to use. The three primary packages that you will use are:

- **junit.framework**—contains classes and interfaces to support test assertions and test cases
- **junit.extensions**—provides additional support for test setup and exception handling
- **junit.textui**—supports an executable suite of test cases

The `junit.framework` package contains most of the classes and interfaces you will use to unit test your application:

- **Assert**—class that contains a set of test assertion methods
- **Test**—interface to run test cases and collect results
- **TestCase**—class fixture to run one or more tests
- **TestResult**—class that collects results of executed test case
- **TestSuite**—class that collects test cases
- **AssertionFailedError**—exception thrown when test assertion fails
- **TestListener**—class that listens for test progress

The Assert class is particularly helpful as it provides assertion methods that your test cases can use to check your application. The methods of the Assert class are shown in Figure 17.2.

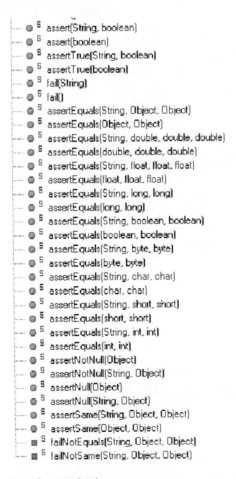

Figure 17.2 Assert class assertion methods.

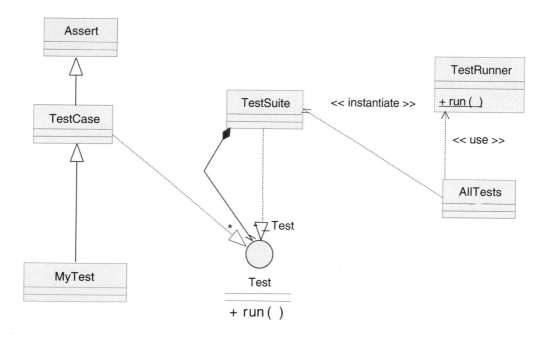

Figure 17.3 Class hierarchy and implementation.

A closer look at the API shows that the TestCase class uses the Assert class to provide the assertions to test your application. In your test cases you extend TestCase, which is an abstract class, (for example, MyTest). You will also create a class that identifies and runs the test suite, (for example, AllTests). See Figure 17.3.

17.3   A Simple Example

The following simple example illustrates the process required to write JUnit test cases. The first step is selecting a class or classes to write test cases for. Figure 17.4 depicts a simple Department class that holds a collection of Employee objects.

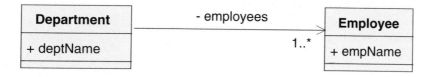

Figure 17.4 Application classes.

Listing 17.1 shows the Department domain classes.

Listing 17.1 The Department class

```java
package com.ibm.junit.domain;

import java.util.Enumeration;

import java.util.Vector;


public class Department {

static int noEmployees = 0;

private String departmentName = null;

private String departmentType = null;

private Vector employees = null;


public Department() {

        super();

        employees = new Vector();

}


public String getDepartmentName() {

        return departmentName;

}
```

```java
public void setDepartmentName(String vehicleName) {

    this.departmentName = vehicleName;

}



public String getDepartmentType() {

    return departmentType;

}



public void setDepartmentType(String deptType) {

    this.departmentType = deptType;

}



public Vector getEmployees() {

    return employees;

}



public void setEmployees(Vector emps) {

    this.employees = emps;

}



public static int getNoEmployees() {
```

```
        return noEmployees;

}



public static void setNoEmployees(int noEmp) {

        noEmployees = noEmp;

}



public void addEmployee(Employee anEmp) {

        getEmployees().add(anEmp);

}



public void removeEmployee(Employee anEmp) {

        getEmployees().removeElement(anEmp);

}



public boolean hasEmployee(String empName) {

        Vector emps = this.getEmployees();

        Employee emp = null;

        if (emps.isEmpty())

                return false;

        Enumeration e = emps.elements();
```

```
    while (e.hasMoreElements()) {

            emp = (Employee) e.nextElement();

            if (emp.getEmpName().equals(empName)) {

                    return true;

            }

    }

    return false;

}



public boolean hasAllEmployees(Vector emps) {

    Employee emp = null;

    Enumeration e = emps.elements();


    while (e.hasMoreElements()) {

            emp = (Employee) e.nextElement();

            if (!this.hasEmployee(emp.getEmpName())) {

                    return false;

            }

    }

    return true;

}
```

```java
public String toString() {

    return "(" + this.getDepartmentName() + "/" +

                this.getDepartmentType() + ")";

}


public boolean equals(Object o) {

    Department dep = (Department) o;

    Vector emps = dep.getEmployees();


    if (this == dep){

        return true;}

    else {

        (ifthis.getDepartmentName().equals(dep.getDepartmentName()))

        &&this.getDepartmentType().equals(dep.getDepartmentType()))

        && this.hasAllEmployees(emps))

            return true;

    }

    return false;

}
```

}

Listing 17.2 shows the Employee class.

Listing 17.2 The Employee class

```
package com.ibm.junit.domain;

public class Employee {


    private String empName = null;

    public Employee() {

        super();

    }


    public String getEmpName() {

        return empName;

    }


    public void setEmpName(String aName) {

        this.empName = aName;

    }

}
```

You will want to create a new Java Project for the purposes of this example named MySimpleHRProject and add these classes to that project. In this example, these two classes represent the classes that will be tested. After selecting the classes to be tested, you should:

- Implement a subclass of TestCase to define the test case assertions. A TestCase is a class that runs the test (TestCases subclass the class TestCase).
- Define application class instances that store the application state.
- Initialize the test case fixtures by overriding the `setup()` method. A "Fixture" is an attribute in that class that is used to hold an object under test, or an object a tested object can be compared to.
- Implement the test case methods.

WSAD comes with tools to help you create JUnit test cases and suites, tasks which can be done in four easy steps. Figures 17.5 and 17.6 illustrate two stages of the process.

1. Create a project for the JUnit TestCase and TestSuite classes. Name it MySimpleHRTestProject.

2. Make sure this project contains the MySimpleHRProject in the classpath. Set the junit.jar as a variable in the classpath as well. Select *project > Properties menu > Java Build property > Variables* tab. Click the *Add Variable* button (Figure 17.5).

3. Select the JUNIT variable and click *OK*. You will be prompted to rebuild the projects. Click *Yes*.

4. If the junit.jar variable does not exist in the variables list, select *Edit* to add it to the list. Name the variable and click the *File* button to find the junit.jar file where you installed WSAD (Figure 17.6). Click *OK* and go back to step 3.

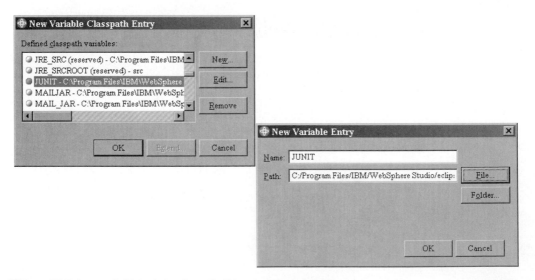

Figure 17.5 (upper left) junit.jar Java Build properties variable.

Figure 17.6 (lower right) Obtain new variable.

Figure 17.7 JUnit TestCase Wizard.

To build the DepartmentTest class, you can use the JUnit TestCase wizard (Figure 17.7):

1. Open the new wizard dialog by either pressing CTRL+N or selecting *File > New > Other* from the menu bar or pressing the Open the New Wizard toolbar button.

2. Select *Java > Junit* in the left pane and TestCase in the right pane.

3. Click the *Next* button. Next you will specify the test case class (Figure 17.8).

4. Name the test case class `DepartmentTest` and subclass the `junit.framework.TestCase` class. Put the `DepartmentTest` class in the package `com.ibm.junit.test`. Select `Department` as the Test class (the class to be tested).

5. Click the `main()`, `setup()` and `teardown()` methods to let the wizard generate them for you. After clicking `main()` also check "Add TestRunner statement for text ui"

6. Click the *Next* button. You will now specify the methods you want to test in Department (Figure 17.9).

7. Check the `getDepartmentName()`, `setDepartmentName()`, `getEmployees()`, and `setEmployees()` checkboxes to generate test method stubs for these Test class methods. The wizard will generate `testGetDepartmentName()`, `testSetDepartmentName()`, `testGetEmployees()`, and `testSetEmployees()` TestClass method stubs. Click the *Finish* button.

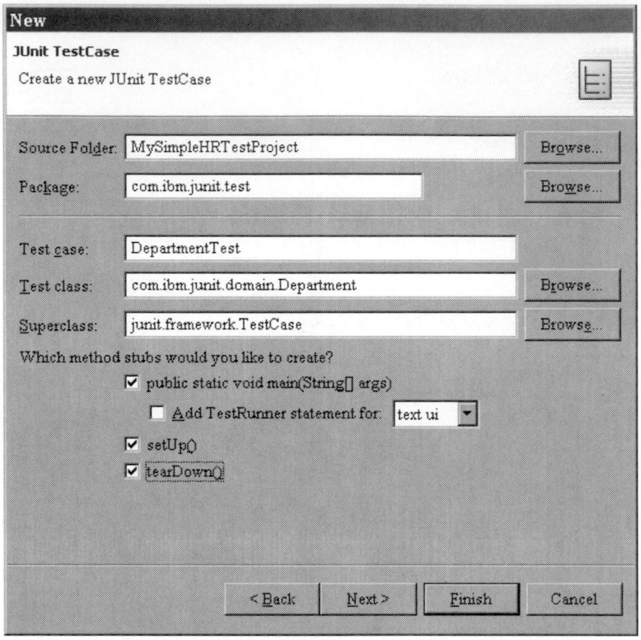

Figure 17.8 Specify the TestCase class.

Figure 17.9 Specify Test class methods to test.

As you would expect from a wizard, the JUnit TestCase wizard only generates the stubs of the setup, teardown and test methods. You need to fill in the implementation of the methods in the `DepartmentTest` class as shown in Listing 17.3.

Listing 17.3 DepartmentTest class

```
package com.ibm.junit.test;

import java.util.Vector;

import com.ibm.junit.domain.Department;

import com.ibm.junit.domain.Employee;


import junit.framework.TestCase;

public class DepartmentTest extends TestCase {

Department dept = new Department();


public DepartmentTest(String arg0) {

        super(arg0);

}



public static void main(String[] args) {

        junit.textui.TestRunner.run(DepartmentTest.class);
}



protected void setUp() throws Exception {

        super.setUp();

        dept = new Department();

        dept.setDepartmentName("Quality");
```

```java
        dept.setDepartmentType("Management");

        Vector emps = new Vector();

        Employee emp1 = new Employee();

        emp1.setEmpName("David Pitt");

        emps.add(emp1);


        Employee emp2 = new Employee();

        emp2.setEmpName("Greg Hester");

        emps.add(emp2);


        Employee emp3 = new Employee();

        emp3.setEmpName("Russ Stinehour");

        emps.add(emp3);


        dept.setEmployees(emps);
    }



    protected void tearDown() throws Exception {

        super.tearDown();
    }



    public void testGetDepartmentName() {

        String dName = "Quality";

        assertEquals(dName, dept.getDepartmentName());
```

```
}


public void testSetDepartmentName() {

        String dName = "Engineering";

        dept.setDepartmentName(dName);

        assertEquals(dName, dept.getDepartmentName());

}


public void testGetEmployees() {

        Department d1 = new Department();

        d1.setDepartmentName("Sales");

        d1.setDepartmentType("Overhead");

        Vector emps = new Vector();

        d1.setEmployees(emps);

        assertEquals(d1.getEmployees().size(), 0);

}


public void testAssertDepartmentHasEmp() {

        String empStr = "Kyle Brown";

        String failMsg =

        "\n \t The Department " + dept + " does not have the Component (" +

                empStr + ")";

        assertTrue(failMsg, dept.hasEmployee(empStr));

}
```

```
public void testSetEmployees() {

        Department d1 = new Department();

        d1.setDepartmentName("Sales");

        d1.setDepartmentType("Overhead");

        Vector emps = new Vector();

        Employee e1 = new Employee();

        e1.setEmpName("Russ Stinehour");

        emps.add(e1);

        d1.setEmployees(emps);

        assertEquals(d1.getEmployees().size(), 1);

}

}
```

Next you will need to write an executable class to run the test suite. This class will send the `run()` message to the TestRunner class. The `run()` method will be passed the test suite object to execute the `testXXX()` public methods. You can specify test methods using the `addTest(...)` method. This allows you to specify the specific test methods and their order. You can use the TestSuite wizard (Figure 17.10) to generate the Test suite class for you.

1. Open the new wizard dialog by selecting *File > New > Other* from the menu bar.
2. Select *Java > Junit* in the left pane and TestSuite in the right pane.
3. Click the *Next* button. Next you will specify the TestSuite class (Figure 17.11).
4. Specify the MySimpleHRTestProject project and `com.ibm.junit.test` package. Specify the Test suite class name as AllTests. Check the `main()` checkbox and the "Add TestRunner statement for text ui" checkbox. Click the Finish button. The wizard generates the AllTests class (Listing 17.4).

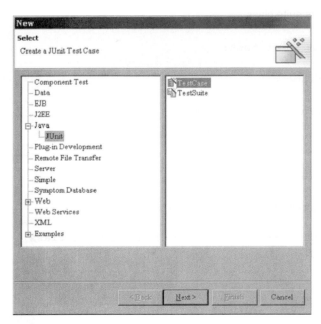

Figure 17.10 TestSuite wizard.

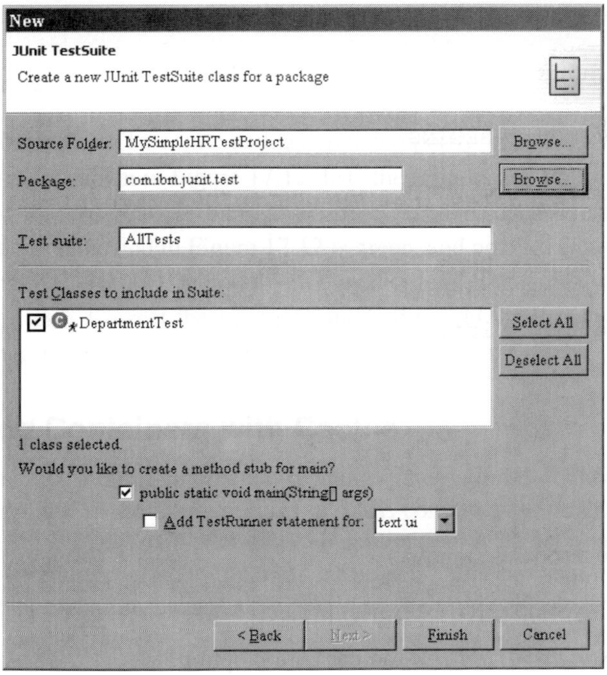

Figure 17.11 Specify the TestSuite.

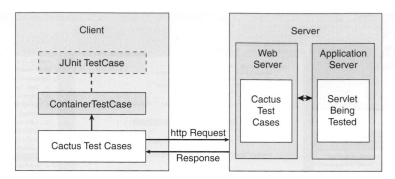

Figure 17.13 Client and server Cactus.

Unfortunately, simulation objects cannot completely unit test domain objects. Another method of unit testing domain objects within J2EE containers is to write test case code within the container objects themselves. This methodology could test domain and container interaction, but the domain and container objects would include test code. This pollution of the domain and container objects is, in many cases, unacceptable.

The Apache Software Foundation Jakarta project has created the Cactus framework, (*http://jakarta.apache.org/commons/cactus/index.html*). Cactus is an open-source testing framework that provides container testing services for servlets, JSP custom tag libraries, filters, and EJBs. Cactus provides redirector objects that serve as points of entry to container services and access to container objects. Cactus uses the JUnit testing framework to make test assertions and report results. Cactus differs from HttpUnit in that Cactus tests behavior between domain and container objects while HttpUnit tests responses from specific containers. HttpUnit contains support for examining the DOM and is probably better used for functional testing.

Cactus contains both client and server-side testing components (Figure 17.13). The container test case classes exist on both the client and server. Care must be taken to keep these classes in synch and that the classpaths include JUnit and Cactus JAR iles.

17.4.1 Cactus API

The `org.apache.cactus` package contains the classes the test case developer will use to test container integration:

- **AbstractTestCase**—the base class from which server-side test case classes are derived
- **ServletTestCase**—subclasses AbstractTestCase and has methods to test servlets
- **JspTestCase**—subclasses AbstractTestCase and has methods to test JSP custom tags
- **FilterTestCase**—subclasses AbstractTestCase and has methods to test filters
- **ServletURL**—supports URL
- **ServiceDefinition**—supports communications between client and server redirector
- **Cookie**—supports cookie objects

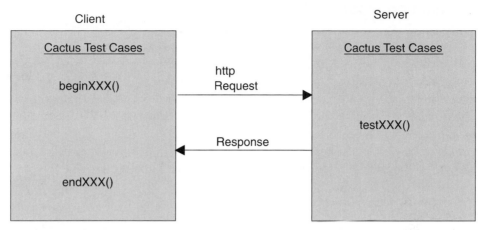

Figure 17.14 Client and server TestCase instances.

- **WebRequest**—encapsulates all the HTTP request data sent from the client to the server TestCase
- **WebResponse**—represents a client-side view of the TestCase server's response (Figure 17.14)

The testXXX() method, where XXX is the name of the test, executes the test logic. The beginXXX() method initializes variables and passes control to the redirector servlet. The redirector servlet instantiates the TestCase object and uses reflection to execute the testXXX() method. After the testXXX() method has executed, a WebResponse is passed back to the client where the endXXX() method is executed. The endXXX() method can make test assertions against the WebResponse and report the results.

As the open source community adds new support to Cactus for different containers, the ability to enhance unit test will be greater. Cactus, along with HttpUnit, will offer more flexibility to unit test. They should be used together in order to gain an in-depth unit test.

17.5 Function Testing Applications in WSAD

Providing automated regression testing of end-user interaction ensures that the Web application continues to work while the view layer and components of the system are refined. End-user interfaces can change dramatically during the application development process. Automated test cases validate that the system fulfills functional and system level requirements in spite of change. Not taking the time to write automated functional test cases leaves the door open for hard-to-find bugs derived from user experience issues, subcomponent interaction, and server configurations. Function-level testing is difficult because of the number of permutations associated with end-user interaction with the application. In this section we'll look at function-level testing strategies. We will also discuss the HttpUnit testing framework as well as provide a simple example of how to use HttpUnit to write automated functional test cases.

17.6   Function Testing

As a reminder, function testing tests end-user interaction and system functionality of Web applications. It does not typically test or verify individual class public interfaces.

Function testing begins with a test plan. Application development teams must document Web application navigation, dynamic content possibilities, and error handling. Naming standards for frames, tables, and form content should be established. View, controller, and mediator layer interaction should be standardized to help simplify functions and make Web application interaction more predictable. Tool and framework selection for function testing is important. There are many commercial packages and open source tools to select from. Tools and frameworks selected for function test should be able to simulate user functions that fulfill use cases tasks.

17.7   What Is HttpUnit?

The HttpUnit Test framework is an open source functional test framework available from SourceForge. This open framework supports:

- Sending requests to the Web application
- Receiving responses from the Web application
- Maintaining Web client state

The HttpUnit test cases and executable test suite are not embedded in the application. The executable test suite can be modified to regression test portions of the application. The HttpUnit Test Framework is shipped with IBM WSAD. HttpUnit uses JUnit to hold the individual test cases (Figure 17.15).

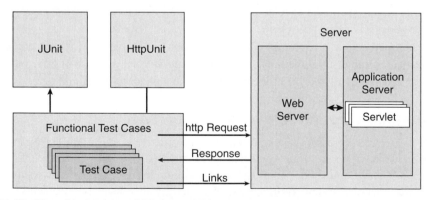

Figure 17.15 Class hierarchy and implementation.

17.8 The HttpUnit API

HttpUnit provides two primary packages for simulating Web application functions:

- **com.meterware.httpunit**—contains classes for testing http server systems
- **com.meterware.servletunit**—contains classes for unit testing servlets and providing internal access to running servlets using a standard servlet container

WebClient is an abstract class with a concrete class implemented for your use. WebClient maintains context for a series of requests, manages cookies, computes relative URLs, and presents a single object interface for sending requests and receiving responses from/to a server. The WebConversation class takes the place of a Web browser talking to a Web site. A concrete class, WebConversation provides a number of convenience methods to help with Web application functional testing:

- **addCookie()**—adds a name/value pair to the list of application cookies
- **getCookieNames()**—returns an array of cookie names
- **getCookieValue()**—returns cookie value for a given name
- **getFrameContents()**—returns WebResponse for a specified frame
- **getFrameNames()**—returns an array of strings of frame names
- **getHeaderFields()**—returns a dictionary of active headers
- **getRequest()**—returns a WebResponse from a URL or WebRequest

WebConversation is responsible for maintaining session context. To use the WebConversation, you must create a WebRequest and ask for a WebResponse.

```
WebConversation wc = new WebConversation();

WebRequest req = new GetMethodWebRequest(

"http://www.meterware.com/testpage.html" );

WebResponse resp = wc.getResponse( req );
```

A convenience method is provided to help simplify the process:

```
WebConversation wc = new WebConversation();

WebResponse resp = wc.getResponse("http://www.meterware.com/testpage.html");
```

The WebResponse has many methods to access information about a page and its contents:

- **getForms()**—returns an array of forms
- **getFormWithId()**—returns a form with an ID
- **getFormWithName()**—returns a form with a name
- **getLinks()**—returns an array of links
- **getLinkWith()**—returns first link with user clickable text
- **getLinkWithImageText()**—returns first link with image alt text
- **getTables()**—returns an array of top level tables
- **getTableStartingWith()**—returns first table starting with specified text in the first row and column
- **getTableStaringWithPrefix()**—returns first table starting with prefix text in the first row and column
- **getTableWithSummary()**—returns first table containing the summary
- **getTableWithId()**—returns the first table containing the ID

17.9 Following Links

URL links defined in HTML documents are the simplest and most common form of navigation among Web pages. HttpUnit allows users to find links by the specifying text within them, and to use those links as new page requests (Listing 17.5).

Listing 17.5 Following page links

```
WebConversation wc = new WebConversation();

// read the page

WebResponse resp = wc.getResponse(

"http://httpunit.sourceforge.net/doc/Cookbook.html" );

// find the link

WebLink link = resp.getLinkWith( "response" );

// convert it to a request

WebRequest req = link.getRequest();

// retrieve the referenced page

    WebResponse jdoc = wc.getResponse( req );
```

Login Page

Please enter your User ID and Password and click the Submit button.

User ID [   ]

Password [   ]

[Submit] [Reset]

Figure 17.16 Simple form.

17.10 Working with Forms

A Web form can be accessed with the following methods:

- **getName()**—returns string of name attribute of form
- **getDOMSubtree()**—returns DOM node of form
- **getID()**—returns string of ID attribute of form
- **getParameterNames()**—returns names of all input parameters of form
- **getParameterValue()**—returns default parameter value
- **getRequest()**—returns a request that simulates a submission (has many forms with arguments)

A dynamic Web site tends to have many HTML forms that contain various controls. The HTML for these controls varies widely but HttpUnit makes them look the same. Common functional testing activities of form definitions are bulleted here:

- Verify the control contents and their default value
- Submit the form with varied input

Accessing the form in Figure 17.16 can easily be done as shown in Listing 17.6.

Listing 17.6 Accessing form controls

```
// select the first form in the page

WebForm form = resp.getForms()[0];

// assert that the form has parameters

assertEquals(form.getParameterName("userId" ) );

assertEquals("MYPASSWORD", form.getParameterName("password") );
```

HttpUnit uses JTidy (which is an HTML syntax checker and pretty-printer) to parse HTML. JTidy will not parse any HTML that does not follow the HTML specifications (even if browsers do). More forgiving browsers will accept poorly formed HTML, but not HttpUnit. Use thestaticmethod`HttpUnitOptions.setParserWarningsEnabled(true)`beforerequestinga page and it will send warnings to System.out when poorly formed HTML is encountered

In order to test a form submission, first obtain the form from WebResponse. Then, assert that key parameters are on the form.

Next, obtain the Submit button from the response and then establish a WebRequest with the Submit button (Listing 17.7).

Listing 17.7 Testing a form submission

```
//Obtain the form from the WebResponse

WebConversation wc = new WebConversation();

WebResponse wr = wc.getResponse("http://localhost:8080/example");

WebForm wf = wr.getFormWithName("myForm");

//Assert that key parameters are on the form

assertEquals(wf.getParameterName("userId");

//Obtain the submit button

SubmitButton sb = wf.getSubmitButton("submit", "Continue");

//Establish a WebRequest with the submit button

WebRequest wreq = wf.getRequest(sb);



wr = conversation.getResponse(wreq);
```

17.11 Working with Tables

A table in a page is a discrete element. Elements in a table can be accessed from the retrieved table.

Accessing a table on a page can be done with methods to obtain text or table cells:

- **asText()**—returns entire table as 2-dimensional string array
- **getCellAsText()**—returns string of given cell
- **getTableCell()**—returns TableCell for position

Individual table cells can be accessed:

- **getText()**—returns table cell contents as a string
- **getColSpan()**—returns table cell `colspan` attribute
- **getRowSpan()**—returns table cell `rowspan` attribute
- **getDOM()**—returns DOM of table cell

As you can see in Listing 17.8, accessing rows and columns is straightforward.

Listing 17.8 Accessing table items

```
WebConversation wc = new WebConversation();

String url = "http://httpunit.sourceforge.net/doc/Cookbook.html"

// get the 1st table

WebTable wt = wc.getResponse(url).getTables()[0];

// test for 3 rows

assertEquals(3, wt.getRowCount());

// test for 4 columns

assertEquals(4, wt.getColumnCount());

//test to see if there is a single link in the last column

//in the first row

assertEquals(1, wt.getTableCell( 0, 2 ).getLinks().length );
```

In most cases, HttpUnit is used to test for text within a table cell (Figure 17.17).

First Name	Last Name	ID
Greg	Hester	100
Russ	Stinehour	115
Joe	Smith	123

Figure 17.17 A simple table.

Tables can be accessed with the WebResponse `getTableStartingWith()` method. Table cells can be accessed with the `purgeEmptyCells()` method sent to a `Table` object. The `asText()` method accesses only the cells and returns the text in the cells. The JUnit assertion methods can be used to test for specific text content within cells (Listing 17.9).

Listing 17.9 Accessing table cells

```
WebConversation wc = new WebConversation();

String url = "http://www.mysource.com";

WebResponse resp = wc.getResponse(url);

//purge cells with images and graphics

// Test to see if the cells are correct

String [][] cells =

resp.getTableStartingWith("First Name").

purgeEmptyCells().asText();

assertEquals( "First Name",cells[0][0]);

assertEquals( "Last Name", cells[0][1]);

assertEquals( "Greg", cells[1][0]);

assertEquals("Hester", cells[1][1]);
```

17.12 Working with Frames

If you need to access a frame or set of frames, send a message to WebConversation to receive an array of frame names or a frame with a specific name (Listing 17.10).

Listing 17.10 Accessing frames

```
String [] frameNames = conversation.getFrameNames();



List fList = Arrays.asList(frameNames);
```

```
//get the body frame with the link

response = conversation.getFrameContents("_parent:Help Body");

String s

= response.getText();



//assert that the frame has the text

// "EmployeeInputForm.html - input employee id"

assertTrue("Contents not found",

s.indexOf("EmployeeInputForm.html - input employee id")>-1);
```

17.13 Working with a Document Object Model (DOM)

HttpUnit provides the ability to inspect an HTML DOM. DOM is a World Wide Web consortium standard (*http://www.www3.org/DOM*) which allows programmatic access to HTML. As mentioned earlier, HttpUnit uses JTidy to create an HTTP response into an in-memory DOM. DOM programming can be difficult; however, it can access information that HttpUnit cannot provide directly (e.g., table captions). DOM programming should be used only if there is no other way of obtaining information about a WebResponse. As an example of using DOM, we'll look at two ways to test for the src image attribute. The two ways follow and are shown in Listing 17.11.

- Use the DOM to find and evaluate the src image attribute
- Search the WebResponse for the src image attribute

Listing 17.11 Two ways of accessing table information

```
//1. Use the DOM to find and evaluate the image src

//   attribute

//Get the top level table

WebTable firstTable = response.getTables() [0];

//Get the first cell - which should be the image

TableCell pictureCell = firstTable.getTableCell(0,0);
```

```
//Get the DOM for the cell <td>

Node node = pictureCell.getDOM();

//Get the first child node <img>

node = node.getFirstChild();

//Get the attributes of the <img> tag

NamedNodeMap nnm = node.getAttributes();

//Get the node for the src attribute

Node na = nnm.getNamedItem("src");

//Get the src attribute value

s = na.getNodeValue();

assertEquals("Incorrect image",

s,"./Images/Cl-TroyTolle.jpg");

//2. Search the response for a String of

//   the image source

String s = response.getText();

assertTrue("Image incorrect",

s.indexOf("./Images/Cl-TroyTolle.jpg") >-1);
```

17.14 Functional Test Design Considerations

The HttpUnit framework can be complicated at times. Keep in mind:

- Keep the tests simple—checking for text rather than searching DOM nodes
- HttpUnit does not work with poorly formed HTML
- Give forms names and IDs to simplify testing and access of items
- Keep the context of the test context known by passing WebConversation from page to page to simplify navigation testing

Test classes are subclassed from `junit.framework.TestCase`. Each test case can be executed stand-alone or executed from a main test case class. Tests should be written to test for:

- Navigation
- Broken links
- Dynamic content
- Form default parameter values
- Error handling
- Authentication for login

17.15 Summary

Testing is critical to any application development effort and selecting the appropriate tools and test methodology is important to any testing effort. JUnit is the best choice for building reusable test cases that do not pollute application classes when testing domain classes, controllers, and mediators. JUnit is so successful at this that it has become a defacto Java standard and is supported directly in WSAD. On the other hand, Cactus is the tool of choice for testing Web and EJB containers. Likewise, HttpUnit can be used to test detailed user interfaces. In any case, automating test cases to regression test program modules is crucial if application quality is to be achieved.

CHAPTER 18

Supporting Enterprise Applications

So far we've demonstrated how you can effectively use Java servlets and JSPs together with Java-Beans to build a server-side MVC architecture that can solve real-world programming problems. Now we want to take a broader look at some of the systematic IT concerns that application developers face, and look at some of the challenges to large-scale enterprise application development.

We'll do this by summarizing where we are so far in using J2EE to develop distributed applications. Then we will take a more detailed look at systematic concerns like transaction management, distribution, security, and persistence, and explore how the technologies we've discussed address them. We'll see a number of concerns that are either unaddressed, or insufficiently addressed, to support enterprise scale applications for many users distributed over wide geographic regions. In the process, we'll set the stage for the last of the major J2EE technologies that make up the heart of the WAS—EJBs.

But first, let's review what we've covered so far, and provide a context in which to discuss enterprise development with EJBs.

18.1 Another Look at the *n*-Tier Architecture

Previous chapters introduced you to layered architectures and how they help separate concerns to facilitate application development and maintenance. We also looked at how these layers are typically deployed to *n*-tiered architectures to support application performance and availability requirements. This section looks at the *n*-tier architecture from the perspective of available technologies you can use to address application scalability. Figure 18.1 shows the overall interaction between the logical (and often physical) roles of the typical 4-tier distributed enterprise application.

The typical application scenario starts with the client, often a Web browser, initiating a request for some service. The request is sent through a communication channel using an agreed

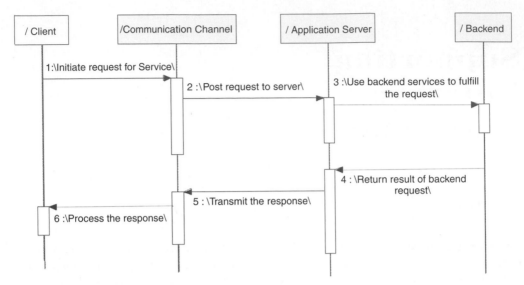

Figure 18.1 Interactions in a 4-tier architecture.

upon protocol to the application server. The server attempts to fulfill the request executing any necessary business logic. The implementation of the service will often require delegation to back-end or legacy systems which provide services required to complete the business logic or access and update persistent data. The back-end system returns its results to the requesting application server which finishes any remaining business logic and then transmits the response, again through the communication channel, back to the requesting client where it is processed and/or displayed.

Figure 18.2 shows some of the typical technologies that can be used to implement each of the roles involved in an *n*-tier distributed application. This is not an exhaustive list, but it should provide enough to indicate that there is a lot you have to know in order to build scalable distributed applications.

As you can see, there are a lot of technology choices available to build the same Web application. Horizontal slices through the technologies in each role define various application architectures. Different slices provide different functional capabilities and nonfunctional characteristics that affect how the application is developed, and how it performs. Figure 18.2 shows such a slice that includes the J2EE technologies we have discussed so far.

Another thing that makes application development more difficult is that as you add new function points to an application, or scale up the number of users, performance requirements, database size, etc., you may be forced to use a more powerful set of technology choices. Unfortunately, these technologies do not always seamlessly merge into integrated, layered architectures. Instead, the technologies often represent quite different programming models which can result in significant technology changes for a relatively modest change in application require-

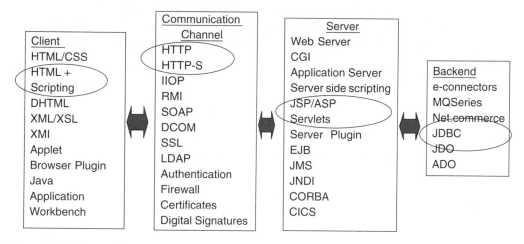

Figure 18.2 Technologies for each architectural role.

ments. As a result, applications often cannot easily include capabilities from higher level technologies without making significant design changes.

This can also result in the need for additional development tools and training, all of which can slow development, and discourage evolving applications from meeting changing business needs. Having an extensible integrated development environment, such as WSAD, helps because the tools for all the technologies are integrated into the same IDE. Model-driven development may also help by allowing application developers specify platform-independent models of their business applications, and then translate them to a platform-specific model for deployment.

As the application outgrows one choice of deployment technologies, the same platform-independent model can be translated to a different platform-specific model that provides the necessary capabilities. However, J2EE also provides a solution because it consists of a complete, standard programming model that supports a wide range of application needs.

In the following sections, we'll look at some of the systematic IT concerns that applications have to address and how they are supported by the J2EE technologies we have looked at so far. In subsequent chapters, we'll see how EJBs provide even more capabilities to help develop scalable, integrated applications.

MODEL DRIVEN ARCHITECTURE

Model Driven Architecture (MDA) is a set of standards managed by Object Management Group Inc. (OMG) for defining the scope, contents, creation, and usage of models in a development process. MDA raises the level of abstraction of application development by capturing the domain and application information in high-level models instead of low-level code. This allows a broader community of people to participate in the development process, in particular business analysts who are domain experts and the primary stakeholders (and purchasers) of the deployed applications.

> The MDA process specifies the creation of PIMs which are translated into PSMs applicable for some Platform Models (PMs). A PM is a model of a particular platform, such as J2EE. This translation process is similar to high-level language compilers and the mediators and mapper patterns that map the presentation, domain, and data source layers as described in this book.
>
> MDA supports separation of concerns by allowing PIMs and PMs to be developed and evolve separately, and then a PIM-to-PSM translator is used to map the PIM to something suitable for a particular platform. This minimizes the coupling between the business and the IT systems, making it easier to update the business application to a new version of the platform model, or perhaps an entirely different platform model. For further information, see *http://www.omg.org/mda*.

18.2   Why Aren't HTML, Servlets, and JSPs Enough?

The first question you have to ask is "Why do I need yet another Java API?" You've already seen that standard Java classes and JavaBeans can be effective in acting as the domain model layer in the MVC architecture, and you've also discovered how you can develop persistence and other application services for Java in a layered architecture.

The answer is that while we can write classes that can do these things for us, there are ways in which they can be done better. Java is wonderful in that it is a general-purpose language—you can use it to build just about anything. However, when you start facing the problems of building a robust, distributed, persistent application you start to notice that some problems are harder than others. To understand why we need EJBs let's focus on the following five problems:

- Distribution
- Application integration
- Persistence
- Transactions
- Security

In this chapter, you will learn that the goal of J2EE is to manage these problems in a standard way, and to do so without requiring the developer to spend his time explicitly programming these aspects of enterprise-level programming.

18.3   Object Distribution

The first of the problems addressed by EJBs is that objects in an enterprise-scalable system need to be *distributed*. In short, this means that the parts of your program should be able to be deployed to as many different physical machines and in as many separate operating system processes as appropriate to achieve the performance, scalability, availability, and reliability goals of your system.

Another reason to distribute objects is to take a system that is logically layered and implement the layering as physical tiers—in this way a set of distributed objects can be accessed from multiple, independently developed systems so long as those objects provide a single, common, networked API for the new systems to build on.

In the previous chapters, applications handled distribution by either HTTP or a remote connection to a database management system. HTTP provides a very simple, stateless means of accessing coarse-grained distributed resources. This works well for HTML pages and other document-centered resources, but it does not support the rich semantics that are often required for distributed business applications.

HTTP is one of a number of distribution technologies today, but in the Java world, two technologies stand out as especially widespread and important: OMG CORBA object distribution model and Sun Java Remote Method Invocation (RMI) protocol.

Not coincidentally, they are the two that form the core of the distribution solution for EJBs. Since this book is not about either CORBA or RMI, we refer the reader to other works like [Orfali] that provide a more detailed overview of these technologies.

We do need to look at a couple of the pros and cons of each technology to understand why the EJB model has evolved as it has. Along the way, we will point out areas that we will cover more in-depth as we begin to examine the EJB distribution model.

18.3.1 A Quick Overview of CORBA

CORBA was developed by a consortium of companies during the early 1990s to provide a common language and vendor-neutral standard for object distribution. CORBA has been well accepted since its inception, with a number of products and vendors supporting the CORBA standard, and a long history of successful projects developed using it.

The heart of CORBA is the idea of a special-purpose piece of software, an ORB that facilitates communication between object spaces. The CORBA model requires an ORB on both ends of the distributed system. The ORB is responsible for handling the marshaling of parameters from outgoing method invocations to a CORBA proxy, and responsible for receiving messages on the other end of a conversation and turning them into local messages to a CORBA stub that can then act on the received message and return a response to the calling object.

There are two more major pieces of the CORBA model: IDL, the language in which CORBA interfaces are defined; and CORBA Services, which provide standard ways for CORBA objects to interact. CORBA Services include things like naming, transactions, etc., which we will see are major parts of building a distributed system. By default, CORBA uses IIOP for low-level communication between ORBs.

CORBA is a robust and complete set of technologies that are both mature and well understood. Some of the advantages of CORBA are:

- It is a standard interface. This makes it possible for multiple vendors to implement their own products based on the standard, and makes it possible for these products to interoperate.
- It is computer language neutral. CORBA clients and servers can be written in a variety of computer languages, including Java, C++, C, Smalltalk, and Ada. The only

requirement is that the remote interfaces for CORBA-distributed objects be written in CORBA IDL, which is translated into classes in the target implementation language through a postprocessor (a CORBA compiler).

• It provides a specification of common services that are required by most distributed applications, simplifying application development by eliminating the need for each program to recreate its own implementation.

However, the technology cannot be all things to all people. Two disadvantages to using CORBA to build distributed systems in Java are:

• Developers must use two languages: IDL and Java
• Very few vendors implement all of the optional services like security and transactions, making it difficult to buy a complete infrastructure.

As a result, CORBA has not made the great inroads into corporate Information Systems (IS) departments that its originators had hoped. Instead, developers started to look for simpler solutions, but solutions that perhaps were not as flexible and powerful. Out of that search grew the interest in Java RMI.

18.3.2   A Brief Overview and History of RMI

Java RMI is a standard part of the Sun JDK 1.1 and the Java 2 platform. RMI is an all-Java distribution solution. Its primary advantages are that it features a very simple programming model that does not require programming in two languages (Java and IDL) like CORBA, and does not require you to purchase additional ORB and CORBA tools.

RMI's programming model is very simple. It has the notion of a remote object and a remote interface as its two primary constituents. A remote object is an object whose methods can be invoked from another JVM, potentially on a different host. A remote object is described by one or more remote interfaces, which are Java interfaces that declare the methods of the remote object. RMI is the action of invoking a method of a remote interface on a remote object.

Remote interfaces are standard Java interfaces that extend `java.rmi.Remote`.

Remote objects can be any class of objects that implement a remote interface, although more often than not remote objects extend `java.rmi.server.UnicastRemoteObject`.

An advanced feature in RMI that is not in CORBA is distributed garbage collection. A feature that is not directly supported in CORBA is the notion of pass-by-value objects. In RMI, any Java object that implements `java.io.Serializable` can be passed as a method parameter to a remote object, and it will be serialized on the client end, and deserialized on the server end, allowing the server to operate on a local copy of the parameter.[1]

---

1.   Java serialization is a technology that is often poorly understood. For an explanation of serialization, see [Horstmann]

While RMI is very powerful, it doesn't support multiple languages, nor does it support all of the services that CORBA supports. For instance, RMI includes a naming service, but not other CORBA Services like transactions or persistence.

Also, there is a perceived lack of security in systems using RMI. While RMI includes a security manager that allows applets to use RMI, its lack of authentication and other security protocols, and the lack of support for RMI in corporate firewall systems have made its introduction more problematic than that of CORBA, which does not have these perceived problems. These reasons lead to the combination of the two technologies (RMI over IIOP).

RMI over IIOP combines the best features of RMI with those of CORBA. Like RMI, RMI over IIOP allows developers to develop purely in Java. Developers do not have to develop in both Java and IDL. Like RMI, RMI over IIOP allows developers to write classes that pass any serializable Java object as remote method arguments or return values. However, RMI over IIOP uses IIOP as its communication protocol, so it is interoperable with other CORBA applications. The combination of these two technologies forms an unbeatable combination of power and ease of use.

18.3.3 Some of the Remaining Holes

So, RMI makes distributed programming a much simpler proposition for Java programmers, and RMI over IIOP gives programmers the ease of use of RMI combined with the interoperability of CORBA. However, there are still many hard problems left in building distributed systems. In particular, RMI did not include direct support for a common distribution idiom that had initially emerged to circumvent a drawback for CORBA. One of the CORBA Services that had been proposed, partially to deal with the fact that CORBA had no facilities like distributed garbage collection, was the CORBA Lifecycle Service. At the heart of this service specification was the idea of a factory[2] object that served as a source of other distributed objects. The factory created objects and retrieved existing instances where appropriate. Most CORBA systems had evolved into using this idiom, even where the Lifecycle Service was not fully implemented.

18.3.4 Where This Leads Us

Luckily, developers can now take advantage of both of these useful pieces of technology that have addressed the prior issues of CORBA and RMI. EJBs use RMI over IIOP as their base distribution technology. Likewise, in J2EE, the EJB home interfaces play the role factory objects, incorporating object lifecycle management. We will examine these issues in more depth when we introduce the EJB programming model in Chapter 19.

18.4 Integration Styles and Messaging

So far, we've considered the issue of object distribution, and have shown how the most common mechanisms in Java have solved this problem. However, as we discussed at the beginning of the chapter, there are many ways to handle program-to-program communication in Java. The gen-

---

2. A factory object's job is to create other objects. The Factory Method and Abstract Factory Design Patterns [Gamma] are specializations of this more general pattern.

eral problem of program-to-program communication has been a constant and ongoing source of research, development, and heartache almost since the dawn of the computer age. In particular, five different ways of program integration have risen to the forefront as the most commonly implemented solutions to this problem. Let's examine them so that we can understand the most common, and attractive, alternatives to object distribution in particular situations.

- *File transfer*—This was the original means of program-to-program communication, and is still the basis of many mainframe systems. In it, each program works on a physical file (stored, perhaps, on a hard disk, a tape drive, or a stack of punched cards) and then another program will take that file as its input and produce a new file, or modify the file if the storage medium allows it. While this has proven effective for solving many problems, issues of latency and resource contention have usually made it unattractive for today's high-speed, high-volume applications.

- *Shared database*—Another popular mechanism derived from the file transfer mechanism is the shared database system. In this solution, database software handles some of the resource contention issues by providing mechanisms for locking and unlocking the data appropriately, and also provides standard mechanisms for creating, deleting, searching, and updating information. However, the latency issue remains even in this solution: Before one program can use information, it must be written to a database (a physical file) by the other program. Shared databases are still a key part of the J2EE standard. It is only through shared databases that we can achieve the scalability of J2EE by allowing entity beans in different JVMs (perhaps in a cloned environment such as is possible in WAS ND) to handle transactions against the same tables simultaneously.

- *Raw data transfer*—In this scheme, different programs use a mechanism like a network data transfer protocol (such as TCP/IP sockets) or a physical transfer mechanism (e.g., shared memory) to communicate information between different programs. The drawback of this popular solution is that it requires synchronous communication—each program must wait on the other to complete its request before processing a response. While it is possible to temporarily disconnect the systems, this involves adding significant complexity to the overall system, and leads to programming issues that few programmers are competent to deal with. For example, it is up to the programmer to decide how to guarantee that a message is properly sent and received; the developer must provide retry logic to handle all the cases where the network link is severed, or the request or response was lost in transmission. You might think that raw data transfer is not a part of the J2EE standard, especially since the EJB specification specifically restricts the use of Java sockets within EJBs. However, if you consider that the HTTP protocol fits this definition, you can see that this approach is still a key part of J2EE.

- *RPC*—Remote Procedure Call is a way of reducing the complexity of the raw data transfer approach by wrapping the network protocols within a layer of code libraries so it appears to the calling and called programs that a normal procedure call had taken place. RPC is extremely popular, and is the basis of modern systems like CORBA, RMI, and EJB. However, the basic issues of synchronicity and guaranteed delivery still remain, which lead us to the need for yet another data transfer mechanism.

• *Messaging*—Messaging is a means of providing high-speed, asynchronous, program-to-program communication with guaranteed delivery. This particular solution is often implemented as a layer of software called Message-Oriented Middleware (MOM).

As compared to the other four communication mechanisms, relatively few developers have had exposure to messaging and MOMs, and developers in general are not familiar with the idioms and peculiarities of this communication's platform. As a result, we have seen many programmers try to use messaging in an inappropriate way, or to develop systems that do not take advantage of the capabilities and strengths of messaging.

18.4.1 JMS and MOMs

A simple way to understand what a messaging system does is to consider voice mail (as well as answering machines) for phone calls. Before voice mail, when someone called, if the receiver could not answer, the caller hung up and called back later to see if the receiver would answer. With voice mail, when the receiver does not answer, the caller can leave a message; later, the receiver (at his convenience) can listen to the messages queued in his mailbox. Voice mail enables the caller to leave a message now so that the receiver can listen to it later, which is often a lot easier than trying to get the caller and the receiver on the phone at the same time. Voice mail bundles (at least part of) a phone call into a message and queues it for later; this is essentially how messaging works.

In enterprise computing, messaging makes communication between processes reliable, even when the processes and the connection between them are not.

J2EE defines a standard API for messaging. This is the JMS. There are a number of products available for embedding messaging into and between applications. One of the oldest and best-known messaging products is IBM's WebSphere MQ. WebSphere MQ implements the JMS API. WAS includes a limited version of MQ Series, called WebSphere Embedded Messaging, that allows WebSphere application servers to communicate with other WebSphere application servers, and also allows Java application clients to communicate with WebSphere servers. However, WebSphere Embedded Messaging does not support connection to other programs, such as legacy systems. For that, you should use the WebSphere MQ product, which is fully compatible with WAS.

Besides WebSphere MQ, many other products implement the JMS API, and it is possible to use these products with WAS, but the details of managing that integration are beyond the scope of this book. However, we will discuss how WebSphere EJBs interact with the JMS messaging API in Chapter 27 and show you how to take advantage of asynchronous communication with EJBs.

18.5   Object Persistence

Of all of the problems of OOP, few have generated as much interest, or as much confusion, as the problem of object persistence. When reduced to its bare essentials, object persistence is not difficult to understand—making an object persistent means its state (the values of its variables) can be preserved across multiple invocations of a program that references that object. This can be accomplished in any number of ways, the easiest of which for Java programmers is probably the Java serialization mechanism that is part of the basic JDK.

It's not persistence per se that gives programmers and architects nightmares. The problem is not that people want objects to be persistent, but that they want to store the information in the objects in a particular format and access it in a controlled manner. In most cases, this format is a relational database (RDB). Unfortunately, there is a serious impedance mismatch between objects and RDBs.

The relational (table) model is a simple model, built upon a sound mathematical foundation that has been its key strength. It is a technology that has been used very successfully for a number of years and is consequently well understood. Since new applications are seldom built in a vacuum, relational technology is commonly used in new applications for the following reasons:

- Information often exists in legacy databases that must be used by new systems.
- RDBs have strong query and report-writing capabilities. Even in the brave new world of Web interfaces, people still want to see paper reports.
- Relational technology provides built-in data integrity constraints in the form of database transactions and integrity rules.
- There are well-known procedures for backing up and restoring database after catastrophic failures. This level of safety provides comfort and peace of mind to the customers that pay for new systems development.

The drawbacks of using a relational database with an object system are:

- RDBs have limited modeling capabilities. Behavior, object containment, and inheritance are not easy to define in an RDB when compared to Java or an object database.
- There is no way of representing true Java object identity in an RDB. When programming in an OO language like Java, you must interact with an object that contains a copy of the persistent data. There are always two spaces at work in a problem, the data space in the relational database and the object space in Java. Keeping these two spaces in sync is one of the primary problems persistence implementations must address.
- There is a semantic mismatch between Java and SQL. SQL data types do not match Java data types, leading to conversion problems.

In many cases, up to 50 percent of application code bulk is devoted to the mechanics of connecting application objects with the relational database. As we saw in Chapters 8 and 16, it requires considerable care and diligence to ensure a good design and implementation when combining the two architectures. Luckily for Java programmers, many commercial persistence frameworks have evolved to fill the gap and provide a mapping between an object model and a relational database that address the previous issues. The disadvantage is that each vendor's API is proprietary, and there is no standardization of the capabilities of these solutions. However, as we will see, even this is not the whole story. J2EE container-managed entity beans can handle persistence for your applications in a standard way. We will examine WebSphere's support for CMP in depth, and demonstrate how it provides flexible, robust object persistence support in Chapters 23 through 25.

18.6   Objects and Transactions

Even die-hard Java persistence programmers begin to roll their eyes when the subject of object transaction management comes up. After all, persistence frameworks have solved the hard part of object-to-relational mapping, so what could be so hard about transactions? This attitude stems more by the experience of the majority of Java programmers than from a close examination of the details of large-scale Java systems.

Most Java systems that use a database only read or write data to databases provided by a single database vendor. In cases like this, the transaction features provided by JDBC are enough. While a Java program may use many database tables, usually an application will use one of Oracle, Sybase, or DB2, but not all three together, or even two of three. Even experienced Java programmers have seldom worked with multidatabase systems. However, the small minority of programs that do use multiple persistence stores can cause a disproportionate number of headaches for the programmers that build them.

To illustrate, let's review some details of JDBC. In JDBC, the primary point of contact between the Java program and the database lies with an interface named `java.sql.Connection`. Each Connection represents a live conversation with one database, be it an Oracle Database, a DB2 database, or whatever.

The problem here is that each Connection object represents a single database. Say you are building a system that uses both DB2 and Oracle. This is common in enterprise systems where one group may manage a local, workstation-based departmental database, while another may manage a global, enterprise-wide mainframe system. So how can you build a system with JDBC so that all SQL statements are either fully committed or fully rolled back to both databases at once?

The short answer is you can't, not without adding another layer of software. Synchronizing multiple data sources like this is a complex problem and solving it has historically been the role of a system called a Transaction Processing Monitor (TP Monitor for short), like IBM's CICS or Encina products. As Java becomes more prevalent in this kind of system, it becomes necessary to absorb some of the roles of a TP Monitor into our enterprise programs. This is exactly what the EJB container in WebSphere provides. Understanding how this works is crucial to understanding some of the more complex, and powerful features of J2EE and EJBs. We will examine this in depth in Chapter 28.

18.7   Security in Enterprise Applications

Another consistent problem in building enterprise applications in Java has been the lack of a set of common APIs that enable developers to handle the basics of application security. Simply put, the problem of application security lies in determining:

- Who should be allowed access into a system, and how is their identity verified (authentication)?
- What access to the different parts of a system should be granted to which individuals (authorization)?

CORBA defines a Security model, but ORB vendors rarely implement it. Neither HTTP nor Java RMI contains any provisions for application level security. As a result, most distributed object programmers have ended up creating a roll-your-own security model, resulting in a plethora of incompatible and incompatible implementations, with varying capabilities. As you will see in Chapter 29, J2EE provides a standard way of addressing security issues.

18.8   Summary

In this chapter, we looked at the systematic IT concerns developers of scalable applications have to address, and summarized how the J2EE architectural components we have discussed so far support them. Although it is possible to develop fairly scalable, distributed business applications with just HTML, Servlets, JSPs, and JDBC, as we have seen in this and previous, chapters, there are a lot of concerns that are not addressed and others that limit application scalability. In the next chapter, we'll be taking a look at another significant part of the J2EE architecture—EJBs—and see how they provide much better transparent, portable, and scaleable support for these systematic IT concerns and scaleable applications that must address them.

Basic EJB Architecture

In the previous chapter, we examined the common problems that all scalable applications must address. Now that you have a firm understanding of the issues at hand, we will begin to demonstrate how EJBs solve these problems. In the three years since we wrote the first edition of *Enterprise Java Programming with IBM WebSphere*, several things have changed on the Java development landscape. When we wrote the first edition, EJBs were a brand-new technology (the specification was at the 1.0 level). Few developers had encountered EJBs, and even those that had used the technology were not necessarily familiar with all of its capabilities.

Now as we write this, the commonly accepted version of the EJB specification is the 2.0 level and the 2.1 specification is in the public draft stage. Even though many things have changed, and many more developers are familiar with the benefits that EJBs grant to them, the basic ideas underlying the EJB specification haven't changed. EJBs still provide the best API to enable Java developers to write secure, scalable, distributed applications. We show their central position as we return to our architectural road map in Figure 19.1.

In this chapter, we'll begin with an overview of core EJB concepts, explore what is new in the EJB 2.0 specification, and investigate fundamental patterns and best practices for using EJBs.

19.1 Core EJB Concepts

Two key core concepts of the EJB 2.0 specification have been carried over from the EJB 1.0 and EJB 1.1 specifications. They are the component/container architecture, and the EJB runtime deployment architecture.

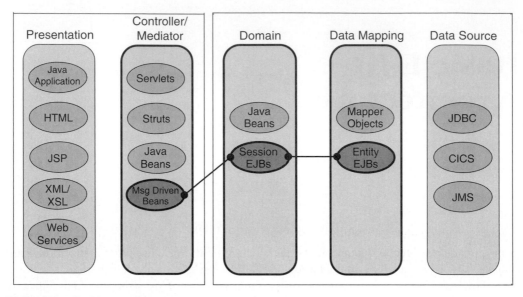

Figure 19.1 Architectural road map.

19.1.1 Components and Containers

An EJB is a component that implements business logic in a distributed enterprise application. By a component, we mean that an EJB is a logical concept that is spread across several physical Java classes and interfaces.

An EJB container is where EJBs reside; multiple EJB classes are deployed (or run) within a single EJB container. The EJB container is responsible for making the EJB available to the client—you can't use an EJB without a container. The EJB container provides security, concurrency, and transaction support and memory management (by swapping unused EJBs to secondary storage and by managing a pool of EJB instances). The container is transparent to the client in the respect that the client itself never interacts with it directly; the client only interacts with the container through proxies[1] to the EJB.

19.1.2 Deployment

All EJBs are deployed into an EJB container within the context of an EJB-JAR file. Each EJB-JAR file can contain one or more EJBs. The EJB-JAR file consists of the class files that the specification requires the developer write for each EJB, as well as the classes that are generated by the container to support distribution, persistence, transactions, and security. A set of entries in an XML file called a deployment descriptor describe each EJB in an EJB-JAR file and inform the container how to handle details like transaction support and persistence. This XML file is always

---

1.   As in the Proxy pattern from [Gamma].

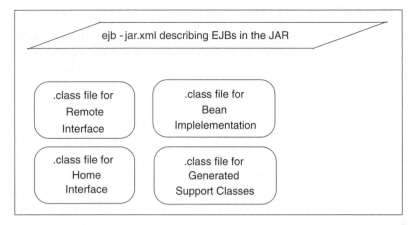

Figure 19.2 EJB-JAR file structure.

named ejb-jar.xml and must be located within the META-INF directory of the EJB-JAR file. This structure is shown in Figure 19.2.

19.2 The EJB Types

Earlier, we discussed problems in building scalable applications: the need for object distribution, the need to support object persistence, and the need to handle enterprise messaging. The EJB specification does not provide a single magic bullet that solves all of these problems in one component. Instead, it provides several component types that you can use together to help build support scalable, secure, distributed applications. Now, we'll explore the functions of the EJB types and how each contributes to our goal of building scalable, secure, distributed applications.

Figure 19.3 shows the types of EJBs defined in the EJB 2.0 specification.

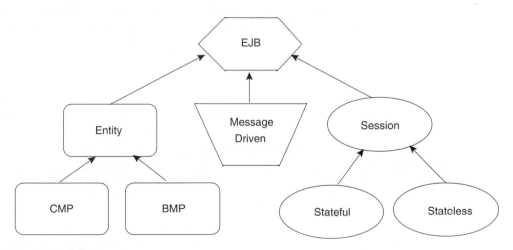

Figure 19.3 EJB Types.

In general, all EJBs share two key attributes:

- All EJBs are transactional objects. This means that any EJB can participate in an existing transaction or manage a new transaction, either declaratively (meaning that the transaction boundaries are declared in the deployment descriptor and the transaction will be started and committed for you automatically) or programmatically using classes defined in JTA. You will learn more about this in Chapter 28.
- All EJBs participate in EJB security. For session and entity EJBs, this means that the EJB will pass on a security context containing information about the user (such as his identity and the security roles that he can take on) to other EJBs, and that you can declare in the EJB deployment descriptor what methods of that EJB may be invoked by users in a particular role. Message-driven beans are an exception to this latter rule; we will discuss the security complications arising from their differences in Chapter 29.

The similarities between the bean types end with these attributes. In the following section, we'll examine each bean type in more detail.

19.2.1 Session EJBs

A session EJB is a nonpersistent object that provides access to business logic on the server. In most cases, a client accesses a session EJB's logic through a remote interface over the network although (as we will see later) EJB 2.0 defines a mechanism for accessing that logic locally (in the same JVM) as well.

The wire protocol that session EJBs[2] use to provide this remote access is RMI over IIOP. This means that there is a well-defined, standard mapping of EJB interfaces to CORBA IDL. These two together assure the interoperability of systems written in an EJB compliant server to external CORBA systems.[3] It also ensures that systems that have evolved to accommodate CORBA (like firewalls) can support EJB systems.

Other than the new provision of optimized local access, session beans function almost identically to the way that they have functioned since EJB 1.0, so if you have written applications using session beans before, you will find that few or no code changes are necessary to update them to work in WebSphere 5.0.

Session EJBs can be either stateful or stateless. Stateful session beans exist for the duration of a single client/server session. Likewise, the client has a reference to a stateful session bean that is potentially valid for the lifetime of the client. Because a stateful session bean may have state, and may last a long time, the container is responsible for passivating (or storing) and activating (or retrieving) the stateful session EJB state. This allows the container to manage the total amount of memory that is in use at any time; if a stateful bean is still active (e.g., it hasn't

2.   Entity beans can also be distributed, but this is rarely a good idea, as we will see later.

3.   WAS fully supports interoperability with most CORBA ORBs. For details on how to use WebSphere together with CORBA systems, refer to the WebSphere InfoCenter.

been removed by the client) but has not been in use for some time, the container can passivate it to disk storage to make room for newer, more active instances.

When a client has a reference to a stateless session bean, it is not necessarily holding a reference to any particular session bean. The EJB container may pool stateless session beans to handle multiple requests from multiple clients. Compare this to the case with stateful beans.

If we had 1,000 clients all making requests of a stateful bean type, we would have to simultaneously keep 1,000 instances in memory, since each client has a connection to a unique stateful bean. On the other hand, if we implemented the same logic in a stateless bean, then all 1,000 clients could be serviced by 100, or 10, or conceivably even 1 bean instance, resulting in significantly lower memory use.

The easiest way to think about session beans is that they provide the client's view of the business logic of an application. They are the function of the application if you prefer to think of it that way. Since session beans represent the function of the application, there should logically be something else to represent the data of the application. The EJB model provides for that (among other mechanisms) through entity EJBs.

19.2.2 Entity EJBs

An entity EJB is a persistent object that represents an object view of information stored in a persistent data store. Each entity EJB is unique in that it carries its own identity—entity EJBs of a particular type must be uniquely identifiable by a specific primary key. Entity EJBs that manage their own persistence are called BMP entity beans. Entity EJBs that delegate the management of their persistence to the EJB container are called CMP entity beans.

An entity EJB represents some set of data in a database (e.g., is persistent), can participate in transactions, and allows shared access from multiple users. An EJB server like WebSphere provides a scalable runtime environment for a large number of concurrently active entity EJBs.

The major difference between entity beans as they existed in previous versions of Web-Sphere (implementing the EJB 1.0 and EJB 1.1 specifications) and the entity beans that exist in WebSphere 5.0 (using the EJB 2.0 specification) is that the container-managed entity bean portion of the specification was nearly completely rewritten to accommodate many of the capabilities that have been part of WebSphere's CMP implementation since WebSphere 3.5. In particular, entity bean relationships are now a standard part of the EJB 2.0 specification. You will learn about how CMP relationships are created and used in WebSphere in Chapters 23 and 25.

19.2.3 Message-Driven Beans

Message-driven beans are a new EJB type that was first introduced in the EJB 2.0 specification. An MDB is a special object that acts as a receiver of JMS messages from a JMS queue or topic. MDBs implement a single method that is not part of the standard EJB life cycle—the `onMessage(Message m)` method. This method is invoked in response to the receipt of a JMS message from the topic or queue that the MDB is configured to listen on and then may, optionally, begin a transaction that includes the message receipt.

An MDB is not the same as a JMS MessageListener (a class that implements the `javax.jms.MessageListener` interface) in that, since it is an EJB, it begins an EJB transaction prior to the receipt of the message. In this case, the message receipt is included as part of the transaction that is started. So, if an exception is thrown later in the handling of the message (say, by an entity EJB that writes to a database table) that causes the EJB transaction to roll back, and then the message is placed back on the queue automatically for reprocessing.

This unique ability to include the message receipt in the same transaction as other work performed by the bean is the major reason why MDBs were introduced in the EJB 2.0 specification.

While this survey has covered a lot of ground, it's okay if you don't understand everything yet. We will be covering these topics in much more detail in succeeding chapters. Also, you may want to consult [EJB] or a book like [Monson-Haefel] for additional perspective on this complex issue.

19.3 Introducing the EJB Programming Model

Now that you understand a little bit about the different types of EJBs, you are ready to start examining the EJB programming model. In fact, there are two distinctly different programming models for EJBs—one for session beans and entity beans, and another one for MDBs. We'll begin by looking at the way in which session and entity beans are developed and used, and then take a look at how the MDB approach differs from that base.

First, let's remember that EJBs are components. Each EJB is composed of a number of different classes—some provided by you the developer, and some provided by the EJB container. An example of this is how session and entity EJBs use the factory idiom for creating objects.

Since an EJB is a component, you can't simply use the `new` operator in Java to create on. The code that creates the EJB may not be running in the same JVM as the actual EJB, and, beyond that, the EJB container may want to pool EJB objects and reuse them to reduce the overhead of object creation. Instead, an EJB programmer must create a Java interface, called a home interface, which defines the ways in which the EJB will be created. The EJB factories that implement these interfaces (whose implementation is provided by the container) are called EJB homes.

So how, then, does a client obtain an EJB home? The client cannot use the new operator, since then she would simply be back in the same position we were in earlier. Clients locate EJB homes through a standard naming service that supports the JNDI API. JNDI is simple to use (like the RMI naming service) but it supports many of the advanced features of the CORBA naming service (like support for directory-structured names).

When you deploy a session or an entity bean, you give it a unique JNDI name; clients can then look the implementation of the home up through that unique name.

Once an EJB client obtains a home and uses it to look up or create and EJB, what does it receive in return? EJBs take the RMI approach of only requiring that the programmer define a simple Java interface that declares a remote object's external face to the rest of the world. In EJB terminology, this is called the remote interface, and it declares the externally accessible methods the remote object will implement. What the client receives, then, is another class provided by the container that implements this interface. This object acts as a proxy to the actual EJB implementation class, which is the final piece of this EJB that the developer is required to implement and provide to the container within the EJB-JAR file.

By applying the factory and proxy patterns in this way, the EJB specification avoids some of the problems that plagued CORBA and RMI. Since remote and home are Java interfaces, we avoid the need to program in both IDL and Java as in CORBA. Since EJB deployment automatically registers EJB homes in the JNDI namespace, we avoid the bootstrapping problem of RMI, since RMI required the developer to manually insert distributed objects into the RMI registry.

As we said earlier, starting in EJB 2.0 there are two ways to define homes and proxies for your EJBs, depending on whether or not the client knows it will be deployed within the same JVM as the EJB. In addition to declaring a home interface and a remote interface, EJB providers can declare a local home interface and a local interface. If the EJB client and the EJB are in the same JVM, then the client can choose to look up the local home rather than the remote home from the JNDI provider. The client will receive an object that implements the local interface from any of the local home's factory methods. In most other respects, using the local interface is the same as using a remote interface. We'll discuss what this means to the design of your EJB programs in the next section.

Finally, we come to the programming model of MDBs. This model is significantly simpler than the programming model for entity or session beans, since MDBs do not have clients that invoke specific methods on those beans. A MDB responds to any messages that are sent to the JMS destination that it monitors, regardless of how that message arrived at that destination. So, this simplifies the interface of the MDB down to a single method—onMessage(Message aMsg). All MDBs implement this same interface, although each will respond differently to the message that is received. Likewise, since there is no need to look up an MDB from JNDI, there is no home or local home interface for the MDB.

19.4 EJBs—Distributed or Not?

Up until the introduction of EJB 2.0 (first implemented by IBM in WAS 5.0), all WebSphere EJBs were alike in two respects—not only were they transactional components, but they were always, by their very nature, distributed components.

In the EJB 1.0 and EJB 1.1 specification, there was only one way that you could access the methods of an EJB—by calling methods in a remote stub that implemented the remote interface. This had some ramifications on every call to an EJB; regardless of whether or not the EJB was in the same JVM as the EJB stub, the method parameters passed to the call and the return value brought back from the call were serialized on one end and deserialized on the other.

This was done to preserve the illusion of local/remote transparency; if every client has to use the same interface, and the semantics of every call are pass-by-value (e.g., always serializing and deserializing parameters), then it doesn't matter to the EJB client whether the EJB the client is calling is in the same container or in a remote container.

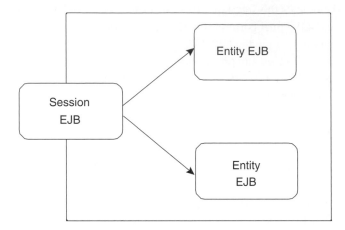

Figure 19.4 Distributed Façade Design pattern.

While local/remote transparency is a cool idea in theory, in practice it turns out not to be quite as useful as you might imagine. In fact, when you are designing an EJB system, you are nearly always aware as to whether or not the EJB you are calling is located in the same JVM as you are. To understand why this is true, let's examine some principles of layering in EJB systems.

You've already seen how there are three basic types of EJBs: session beans, entity beans, and MDBs. As we discussed earlier, session beans provide the access to the business logic in your EJB server. In fact, there's even a special way of using session beans in this manner that has become so ubiquitous that only rarely would we recommend using them in any other way—session beans act as distributed façades onto the business logic of your application.

The heart of the Distributed Façade pattern (as described in [Fowler], also called Session Façade in [Alur]) is a simple idea. You don't want to expose the details of how your application implements its business logic or handles implementation details like persistence to the application's clients; you want to hide these details so that EJB clients are only aware of how the business logic is invoked, not what the business logic does. The ramification of this idea is that clients only ever see session beans; any entity beans in your application are hidden behind a protective layer of session beans, as shown in Figure 19.4.

There are other ramifications of this pattern, but we will examine those in detail in Chapter 30, when we will show a detailed implementation of this pattern in our case study.

19.4.1 The Local EJB Idea

While the Distributed Façade pattern has proven to be extremely useful in practice, there's a problem inherent in its use. Sometimes bean deployers separate the Web container and EJB container into separate tiers, or JVM instances, to facilitate reuse and enable additional load balancing flexibility. However, it is often the case that the client to the session beans is a servlet or JSP codeployed in the same JVM as the session EJB. In that case, the additional overhead from the serialization required by the pass-by-value semantics is unnecessary.

This overhead becomes particularly unnecessary where entity beans are concerned. If all entity beans are wrapped in a layer of session beans, there is never any reason to incur the overhead required by remote access to an entity bean. In recognition of these scenarios, the EJB 2.0 specification added a new approach to both entity and session beans: a local interface and local home interface that parallel the remote and home interfaces discussed earlier.

19.4.2 Differences Between Local and Remote EJBs

There are two differences between using a local interface and a remote interface that you have to keep in mind when developing with EJBs.

First, parameters to a local interface are pass-by-reference, and not pass-by-value. One of the ramifications of this is that you can't reuse a parameter inside your EJB; that is, you shouldn't update a value of an object parameter inside of a session EJB (which would be a Java programming practice in any case). While this would work with a remote interface (because the object instance that is passed in would be a different copy than the one that was created in the client), with a local interface the same object would be used, perhaps leading to unexpected behavior later in the client.

Second, the actual interfaces used by the client application are different. If an EJB has both local and remote interfaces, client applications will choose different JNDI references and home interfaces to access them. In short, to create or find a local EJB, a client must use an EJB local reference (which we will cover in detail in the following chapter) and then use the local home interface. However, to create or find a remote EJB, the client may either look up an EJB remote home reference, or look up a JNDI name directly, and then use the remote home interface. This is a subtle point that many people miss when first learning about remote and local EJBs. We will investigate this in more detail in Chapters 20 and 22.

19.5 Basic Architectural Patterns for EJBs

So, how do you practically apply this information to your EJB designs? There are two simple rules that we will show you how to apply in our case study, and that you can apply to your own designs that can help you take best advantage of the capabilities of EJB 2.0:

- When you are using session beans as session façades, provide both a remote and a local interface for your session bean. That allows you to take advantage of the remote capability of the session bean if you separate the EJB container from the Web container, and also allows you to take advantage of the performance benefit of local interfaces if you do codeploy the Web and EJB containers. The WebSphere 5.0 Performance Report [Willenborg] shows that codeployment and the use of local interfaces can provide up to a 21 percent performance increase in many situations over calling a remote EJB method.
- Always create only local interfaces for entity beans. Do not allow access to entity beans remotely, and only use them in the context of the Session Façade pattern. We will cover the reasons for this restriction in Chapter 30.

There is one more pattern you should consider applying with regard to local and remote interfaces. Let's consider how you use MDBs. You might remember that we've only discussed remote and local interfaces when applied to session and entity beans. This is because MDBs do not have either remote or local interfaces (or even homes, for that matter). This is because a client doesn't create an MDB or invoke its methods—as discussed earlier, the `onMessage()` method is invoked whenever a JMS message arrives on the queue or topic with which the MDB is associated. However, there is a useful variation on the Distributed Façade pattern to apply when you are building MDBs.

The issue here is that if you have business logic that you need to run asynchronously when a message is received by an MDB, there is a good chance that you also need to run that same logic synchronously at some point.

Let's say we're in a bank and that we have a system that processes requests to transfer money from one banking account to another as they come in from a queue. This might happen if the requests are received from a non-J2EE system like a telephone voice response system.

One possibility is to implement the order processing logic directly in the MDB, or in a Java class called by the MDB. Another, better approach would be to place a session bean (another façade) between the business logic implementation and the MDB. You would then use an EJB local interface to the session bean in the MDB. This allows you to also synchronously process transfer requests—something you might want to do if you had tellers who also needed to be able to do the same thing, but need to complete the transaction while the customer is standing directly in front of them in the bank. This approach is shown in Figure 19.5.

This arrangement, whereby the methods of a Session Façade may be invoked either by synchronous clients or upon the asynchronous receipt of a message, has been referred to as the Service Activator pattern by [Alur].

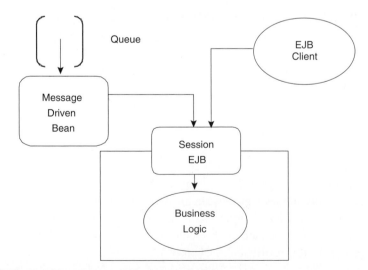

Figure 19.5 Message-driven beans with session beans.

19.6   The Role of Persistence

One of the most contentious parts of designing systems that use EJBs is determining how object persistence will be handled. There is almost no area of EJB design that can cause more religious arguments and flame wars than debating the merits of persistence options. The problem is that many of the most strongly held opinions are expressed by those with the least amount of experience with the different technologies; often people will generalize from a bad experience with one tool or application server and use that broad brush to paint an entire technology (like entity beans) as not being useful. While we will examine many of these technologies in more detail in later chapters, gaining a basic understanding of how the different options function can be useful in making an informed decision about which technology best fits in each situation.

19.6.1   Mapper Layers

In Chapter 7, we examined one way of connecting objects (used in servlets and JSPs) to a relational database through an implementation of the Active Record pattern described in [Fowler]. Active Record pattern is a simple way to retrieve objects from a database, and then update the objects in the database.

Active record has drawbacks, as we discussed earlier. It doesn't handle object relationships very well. Imagine if we were trying to load a TimeSheet for an Employee from the database that contained TimeSheetEntries with different tasks and the hours worked on those tasks. There's no good way to fetch the set of contained objects using the Active Record pattern. The Active Record pattern also includes database access queries (in this case SQL) directly in the domain model code. This is often derisively referred to as sprinkling SQL and can become a maintenance problem as developers find they must go to several objects to make a simple change like changing a table name.

In fact, very few projects end up using the Active Record pattern. Instead, a more useful approach, described in Chapter 16, and one that we will use in our case study, is called the Data Mapper pattern, sometimes referred to as Data Access Objects (DAO) in [Crupi]. [Fowler] describes the heart of this pattern as "A layer of Mappers that moves data between objects and a database while keeping them independent of each other and the mapper itself."

Moving the database access logic into a separate class away from the domain object allows you to more easily centralize your SQL code (making maintenance easier). It also allows you to define object relationships by creating networks of mappers that rely on other mappers to create objects of the right type. In our earlier case, you could imagine that the TimeSheet mapper might call on the TimeSheetEntry mapper to create the entries for a particular TimeSheet.

The great thing about the Data Mapper pattern is that it works equally well either outside or inside an EJB. It can also work with any arbitrarily complex SQL statement, and it can handle things like views, calculated columns, and joins. As a result, it's the basis of many of the persistence schemes used for most J2EE applications. However, as discussed in Chapter 16, the Data Mapper pattern is not perfect. Even though mappers can handle complex SQL and odd relational structures, the fact is that *you*, the programmer, are responsible for writing this logic. This can be time-consuming and error-prone, especially if you are not intimately familiar with SQL and

JDBC. You can instead choose to use an open-source Data Mapper framework (like Apache Castor) or a commercial framework like Oracle TopLink, but this introduces yet another API you must master and puts you at the mercy of the capabilities of that particular tool.[4]

Finally, there are a number of very complex, and subtle issues involved in building complex object/relational (O/R) mapping layers. For one, it is difficult to correctly implement capabilities like caching, which can have an enormous impact on the overall performance of your mapping layer. So, in many cases, it's useful to look at the built-in persistence scheme for WebSphere—CMP entity beans.

19.6.2 Container Managed Entity Beans

There have been two major complaints made in the J2EE community about CMP entity beans: (1) Some assert that CMP entity beans have such poor performance that they're too slow for any real application and (2) some assert that CMP entity beans are so limited in their support of O/R mapping that they're not useful in the real world. Like most complaints, these accusations have their basis in truth. In fact, in some very early application servers, the O/R mapping support for CMP beans was extremely limited. This has never been the case of CMP beans in WebSphere. Even WAS 3.5 had sophisticated, albeit proprietary, O/R mapping support that supported object relationships EJB inheritance supported in a relational database; and even mapping to a relational database in a top-down, bottom-up or meet-in-the-middle approach. All of this support has improved substantially, and aspects of it have even become part of the J2EE standard, as you will see when you examine these features in Chapters 23, 24, and 25.

The performance complaint also had an element of truth in it at one point. In prior versions of WebSphere, there were substantial differences between the performance of CMP EJBs and other approaches like raw JDBC. However, that difference has narrowed significantly. With the improved caching techniques in WebSphere 5.0 and the introduction of features like CMP preloading, the performance of CMPs in WebSphere 5.0 is acceptable for most applications. CMP preloading uses an SQL JOIN to load a set of EJB's when a parent EJB in a relationship is loaded. For example, the TimeSheetEntries for a Timesheet can be loaded whenever a TimeSheet is loaded, saving one or more SQL statements to load the individual TimeSheetEntries. What's more, the ease of development makes it an excellent choice for application developers with tight time constraints. CMP preloading will be discussed in more detail in Chapter 25.

So, are CMP entity beans right for you? In most cases, they should be your first choice for object persistence. If your need to use highly complex SQL that a CMP bean can't handle, then use data mappers. It doesn't have to be either/or. In fact, most applications can successfully use a mix of the two approaches, using the most appropriate tool in each situation. The important thing to remember is that finely crafted persistence mechanisms are costly to develop and difficult to maintain when the domain model changes. Since many applications have lifetimes mea-

---

4.   Note, even with a third-party O/R framework, you may still decide to apply the Data Mapper pattern to minimize the impact of external APIs on your business logic.

sured in Web-years,[5] it may make better sense to use the automated tools and focus more development resources on the actual business problem.

19.6.3 Other Options

The major problem with picking technologies to use in a large-scale system is that Java technology doesn't stand still for long. A decision made on the merits of a technology may be invalidated six months later, when a new technology emerges, or when an old technology is revitalized in a new version. The same is certainly true of persistence technologies. There are several interesting technologies that aren't yet mature enough (or supported) for us to recommend at this point, but that may well become useful in the near future. Foremost among these is the Java Data Objects (JDO) standard. JDO is a technology for successfully hiding the persistence mechanism behind a set of POJOs. In this way, you get the best of both worlds. You don't have to think about coding the details of your object persistence (as when you use CMP EJBs) but the objects that are persisted are regular Java objects, and not heavier weight components like CMP entity beans (an advantage of data mappers).

The most serious issue with JDO is that its connection to the J2EE architecture has not been well-defined. It is not part of the J2EE standard, and it is not clear how the transaction support in JDO will work with the transaction support provided by EJB containers. So, in the future, JDO (or a technology like it) may prove to be the best choice for object persistence in WebSphere, but for the time being, it should probably be set aside. You may also find that local CMP beans provide additional services, such as security, that simplify the overall application development problem while reducing the overhead associated with the EJB container.

19.7 When Do You Need EJBs?

While EJBs provide a complete, scalable solution for large-scale distributed Java programming, the technology is not appropriate for every project. Next will consider questions that project teams may ask if they are toying with moving to EJBs from other technologies, or considering a new project that may use EJBs.

19.7.1 Some Technical Questions to Ask

Let's begin by examining questions that can be used to determine if EJBs are an appropriate technology for your situation. If you can answer yes to any of these questions, EJBs may be an appropriate technology in your situation. If these questions do not apply, other technologies may be more appropriate.

Is there a need now, or may there be a need in the foreseeable future, for access to enterprise data and shared business logic from multiple client types or multiple application clients?

Whenever an application needs to be used from multiple client types (e.g., Web browser, pervasive devices like cell phones and PDAs, Java client applications, etc.) EJBs are often a

---

5.   A Web-year is like a dog year, but far shorter.

good solution to provide a common platform for shared business logic and data. EJBs provide a distributed infrastructure on which multiple client applications written using a number of technologies (servlets and JSPs, Java clients, and CORBA clients) can be layered.

Another, very common situation where the distributed aspect of EJBs becomes extremely useful is when you are building applications that must have an application client written using Java Swing. In this case, you want to separate the reusable, common business logic from the strict GUI logic of the application in order to avoid falling into the fat-client trap where precious server-side resources (like database connections) are monopolized by client programs. In this case, writing your common business logic as a set of EJBs that are shared across all of the client applications allows for the best use of both client-side display power and server-side resources.

What is perhaps the most common case is where you need to layer your business logic. Often you can find that you can provide abstract business services that other applications can reuse. Providing this logic as a component that can be managed, deployed, and versioned separately from the rest of the application can provide a number of benefits over and above lower-level forms of code reuse such as copy-cut-and-paste or including common libraries in your applications.

Is there a need for concurrent read and update access to shared data?

Traditional, fat-client solutions require the application to manage access to shared data at the database level. This often results in highly complex schemes to deal with database locking and concurrency, or alternatively, loss of data integrity when these issues are not considered.

CMP entity EJBs automatically handle these complex threading and simultaneous shared-data issues. As mentioned previously, the EJBs control the access to the back-end data and manage the current transactions and database locking internally. This reduces the total programming effort by reducing the amount of effort spent in writing database control logic, while ensuring the consistency and validity of the data.

Is there a need to access multiple disparate data sources with transactional capabilities?

Many applications require the ability to access multiple data sources. For instance, a program may update data in both a middle-tier Oracle database and a mainframe CICS or IMS system accessible through WebSphere MQ The key is that some applications require that this access be fully transactional—that data integrity be maintained across the data sources. For example, an application may demand that placing a user order will consist of storing the detailed order information in an Oracle database and simultaneously placing a shipment order with a CICS system through WebSphere MQ. If either the database update or the MQ enqueuing fails, the entire transaction should roll back.

In the past, the only choices to build systems like these were transaction monitors like Encina, CICS, or Tuxedo, which used nonstandard interfaces and required development in languages like COBOL, C, or C++. However, now EJBs in WAS 5.0 support multiple concurrent transactions with full commit and rollback capabilities across multiple data sources in a full two-phase commit-capable environment. Some data sources are only supported with one-phase commit semantics. We'll discuss this in Chapter 28.

Is there a need for method-level object security seamlessly integrated with security for HTML documents, servlets, JSPs, and client logins?

Certain types of applications have security restrictions that have previously made them difficult to implement in Java. For instance, certain insurance applications must restrict access to patient data in order to meet regulatory guidelines. Until the advent of EJBs there was no way to restrict access to an object or method by a particular user. Previously, restricting access at the database level, and then catching errors thrown at the JDBC level, or by restricting access at the application level by custom security code would have been the only implementation options.

EJBs now allow method-level security on any EJB or method. Users and user groups can be created which can be granted or denied execution rights to any EJB or method. In Web-Sphere, these same user groups can be granted or denied access to Web resources (servlets, JSPs, and HTML pages), and the user IDs can be seamlessly passed from the Web resources to the EJBs by the underlying security framework.

19.8 Summary

In this chapter we've examined some of the basic concepts inherent in the EJB architecture. We've looked at the types of EJBs available in WebSphere 5.0, seen where they are appropriately used, and examined some patterns for dealing with questions of object persistence and application layering. In the process, you've seen how EJBs can be the answer to many of the systematic IT concerns we looked at in the previous chapter. In particular, we briefly examined:

- How object distribution with session façades avoids the multiple programming-model pitfalls of CORBA, and provides object distribution at the right level of granularity.
- How the declarative security of EJB addresses the security concerns of RMI.
- How all EJBs are transactional objects, and how you can use this fact to build systems that are transactionally aware.
- How CMP entity beans can provide a mechanism for flexible and efficient object persistence.

In the next chapter you'll begin building your own EJBs and learn about the capabilities for EJB development that are in WSAD.

CHAPTER 20

Developing EJBs with WSAD

Up to now you've seen how EJBs are structured and how the J2EE technology makes use of them. Now we are ready to give an explanation of how EJBs are created within WSAD. We will begin by looking at creating and using session beans which fall within the domain layer as shown in Figure 20.1. Before we delve into the details of how this is accomplished, we will provide a foundation of how the WSAD environment operates in connection with EJBs and other J2EE artifacts.

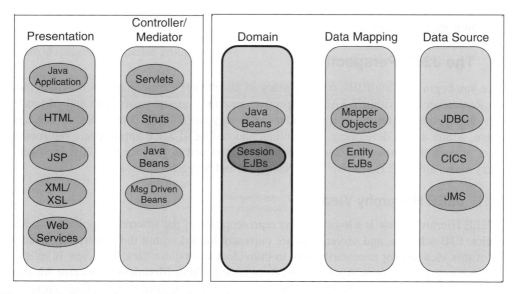

Figure 20.1 Session beans within the road map.

20.1.2 J2EE Navigator View

The J2EE Navigator view is a tabbed tree view in the same pane of the J2EE perspective as the J2EE Hierarchy view. Unlike the J2EE Hierarchy view, the J2EE Navigator view shows the underlying resources that exist on disk for each of the J2EE projects in the workspace. We will go into more detail about J2EE projects later in this chapter. Figure 20.4 shows a portion of the expanded J2EE Navigator view with the TimeSheetGroup project which was also shown in Figure 20.3 but in the J2EE Hierarchy view.

Think of this view as a combination of the base Navigator view and the Java Package Explorer. Like the traditional Navigator view, the J2EE Navigator view shows all projects within the workspace and their contained resources.

Like the Java Package Explorer, the J2EE Navigator view displays all Java projects with their package structure exposed. The view also has unique J2EE features such as the specific deployment descriptor entry placed within the root of the project. This is used as a convenience mechanism to quickly open the deployment descriptor editor for the J2EE project. The view also contains specialized filters so that you can filter out projects that are not J2EE projects.

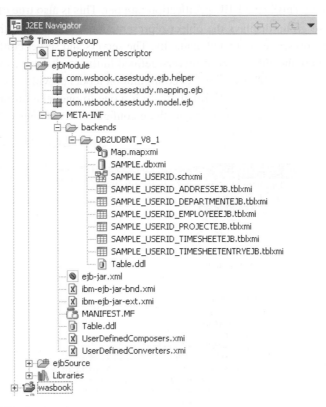

Figure 20.4 J2EE Navigator view.

20.1.3 Servers View

The Servers view is simply a view that has a listing of the defined local and remote application servers. Within this view you can start a particular server in one of three different modes: normal, debug, and profiling. Other actions available in this view include restarting a server, stopping a server, disconnecting from a server, and publishing to a server. When testing EJBs, you will typically like to start the UTC. The UTC can be launched from the Server view by selecting the Run universal test client context menu for a particular running server. Consult the WSAD documentation for more details on each of these actions.

20.1.4 DB Servers View

The DB Servers view, shown in Figure 20.5, is a view of live database connections which allows you to view the tables in a database, view the data in a table, and import database tables to a folder in the workbench. Consult the WSAD documentation for more information about creating database connections or use the F1 Help provided for this view.

One of the most important features of this view is the ability to import databases, schemas, and/or tables to a specific folder. For example, if you select a specific table, you can import that table definition into an EJB project by selecting the Import to Folder context menu action. This action will open a dialog, shown in Figure 20.6, to enter the folder in which you want to import the table definition. If you are importing to an EJB project, just browse for the EJB project and ensure that the Use default schema folder for EJB projects is checked. This will ensure that the table definitions are imported to the proper back-end folder location so that they can be used by the EJB module. An EJB project stores its table definitions in a specific folder under the ejbModule/META-INF/back-ends folder. Table definitions outside of this location cannot be used for object-to-relational (O/R) mappings for CMPs.

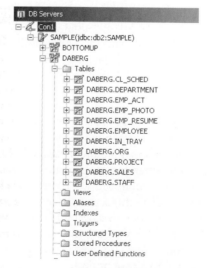

Figure 20.5 DB Servers view.

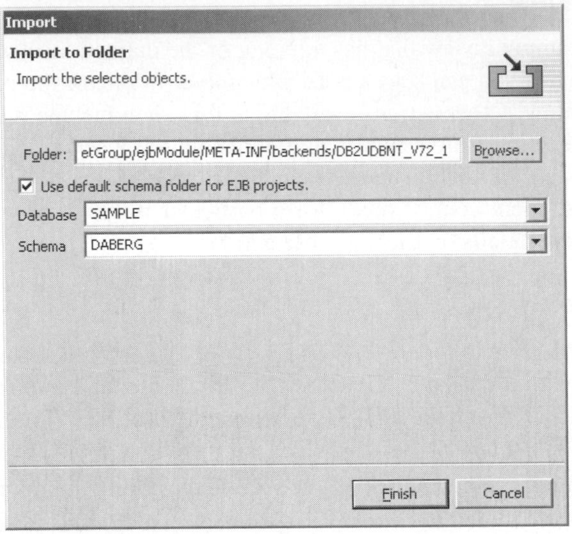

Figure 20.6 Imports to folder dialog.

If you would like to import database tables to an existing back-end folder within an EJB project, deselect the Use default schema folder for EJB projects check box and browse to the specific back-end folder. If you do not deselect this check box, a new back-end folder will be created within the EJB project for the tables that you have selected to import. This means that the table definitions for the selected tables will be imported into a new back-end folder for the EJB module. If the option is deselected, you can then import the table definitions of the selected tables into an existing back-end folder that exists for the EJB module.

Importing a database into the back-end folder creates a subfolder and populates it with a number of XML Metadata Interchange (XMI) files that contain information about the database connection, the database itself, its schema, and the tables in the database. These files will be used when mapping CMP beans to a relational database.

20.2 J2EE Projects

Before we can talk about J2EE projects, let us present a gentle reminder of what a project is. As described in Chapter 7, a project is a structure in the workbench that is used to store resources. It actually maps to a physical directory on disk in any location that you wish. A project can be a simple project which is nothing more than just a container or it can have specific behavior. An example of a specific type of project within the workbench would be a Java project. A Java project is a simple project with specific actions and behaviors for dealing with Java files. For example, a Java project will have the notion of a Java build path or classpath. Also, a Java project can have one or more source folders that contain .java files that are to be compiled when one of them changes or a build is performed. The compiled .class files will be copied to the projects output location which is also specific to a Java project.

J2EE projects, like Java projects, are specialized projects that have additional semantics that map to concepts from the J2EE specification. For example, an enterprise application project maps to an enterprise application in the J2EE specification. The other J2EE projects include EJB projects, application client projects, Web projects, and connector projects. Each project type is represented as a group within the J2EE Hierarchy view. Also, all of these projects, except for the enterprise application project, are Java projects because they may contain .java files. The enterprise application project does not contain any .java files so it is not a Java project.

J2EE projects have specific behaviors for dealing with the deployment descriptor and its contents. To ensure that there are no problems with the contents of these projects validations are performed on the contents. The validations are done by specialized objects called validators and each knows how to validate a specific object. This validation may be syntax validation or semantic validation. For example, the EJB validator will validate the semantic of the EJB deployment descriptor but the EJB XML validator will validate the syntax of the EJB deployment descriptor based on the ejb-jar.dtd. Validators run during each build of the workbench which usually happens after saving changes to an editor. It may be desirable to disable one or more validators if you are not concerned with the results of the validation. This can be done by changing the `Validation` property for a specific project. You may also disable validators for all projects by changing the *Window > Preferences > Validation* preferences.

Let's take a simple example of how to create an EJB project. We will go through the steps of creating the TimeSheetGroup EJB project that was used in the case study.

1. Select *File > New*. Select EJB from the left list of the New wizard and select EJB Project from the right list.

2. Click the *Next* button to proceed to the EJB Project wizard.

3. Select Create 2.0 EJB Project to create a 2.0 EJB module. Each EJB project and all other J2EE projects, are associated with a deployment descriptor specification version.

4. Click the *Next* button.

5. Enter TimeSheetGroup for the Project name as shown in Figure 20.8. The Directory is the one on your system that will physically contain the contents of the EJB project. By default, a new directory with the same name as your project is created in your current workspace directory.

6. Select *New* for the enterprise application project and enter wasbook for the New project name. This is the enterprise application project that this new EJB project should be added to. You must either create an enterprise application or use an existing one to associate the new EJB project or any J2EE module project. This is required since an EJB project or any other module project must be tested within the context of an enterprise application.

Click *Finish*. Two new projects will be created, TimeSheetGroup and wasbook, both of which will appear in the J2EE Navigator view and the J2EE Hierarchy view with their specific icons and versions. Note that the enterprise application version is 1.3 since this is the lowest J2EE version that supports the new 2.0 EJB project that was created.

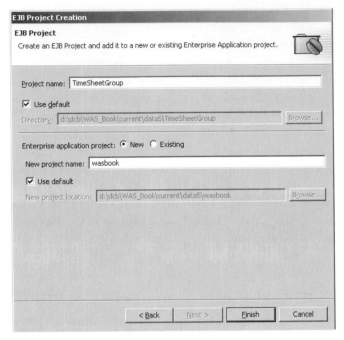

Figure 20.7 EJB project wizard.

Figure 20.8 Enterprise applications group.

When you expand the wasbook enterprise application from the J2EE Hierarchy view, as shown in Figure 20.7, the TimeSheetGroup.jar EJB module appears under the modules tree group. This EJB module maps directly to the TimeSheetGroup EJB project that was just created. If you select the TimeSheetGroup.jar entry, you can then select the Go to deployment descriptor context menu item which will move the current selection to the TimeSheetGroup entry under the EJB Modules group. This is a convenience action to find the actual module within the J2EE Hierarchy view so that you may edit its contents or open the deployment descriptor editor.

When this new EJB project is added to the enterprise application as an EJB module, the module URI used is derived from the name of the project. This module URI will then be used when the enterprise application is exported to create the module JAR file. To change the module

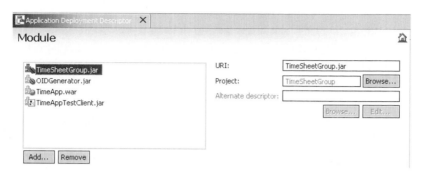

Figure 20.9 Enterprise application editor modules.

URI, you will need to open the enterprise application deployment descriptor editor. Do this by expanding the enterprise application from the J2EE Hierarchy view and double-clicking on the EAR Deployment Descriptor entry to open the editor. On the **Modules** page of the deployment descriptor editor, you will notice a list of all the modules.

Figure 20.9 shows the upper portion of the module page. If you select the TimeSheet-Group.jar module, detail information for the URI and the project is displayed in the text areas to the right. You can now update the URI to another name that you would like to use. If for some reason you need to change the project that the selected module represents, you can do so by clicking on the *Browse* button next to the project text field. You will be presented with a list of the J2EE projects that exist in the workbench that correspond to the same type of module that is selected. So, for example, if the TimeSheetGroup.jar module is selected, the list will only contain other EJB projects within the workbench.

The module section shown in Figure 20.9 allows you to add or remove modules from the enterprise application. To remove a module from the enterprise application, select the desired module from the list and click the *Remove* button. This will not delete the corresponding module project but it will remove the reference to this module project from the enterprise application project. Remember that the application defines the modules which will need to be installed on the server. If you click the *Add* button, you will be presented with a list of J2EE module projects that exist in the workbench. Selecting one of these module projects will result in a new module reference being created within the enterprise application and it will be linked to the selected module project.

20.2.1   Java Utility JARs

According to the J2EE 1.3 specification, you are allowed to place JAR files that are not represented as a module within an EAR. These JAR files are typically called utility JAR files since they contain supporting Java code that is used by the other modules defined within the EAR (see the sidebar for more information). In WSAD, you can add a JAR directory to the enterprise application project using the basic file system import wizard that is a part of the base workbench.

More often you are developing the utility JAR contents yourself and have an actual Java project in WSAD for building the JAR file.

Ideally, you would like to use this Java project to create the JAR file that is to be added to the EAR. In WSAD, we have added a concept called a project utility JAR to designate a simple Java project as a utility JAR within an application.

UTILITY JARS WITHIN ENTERPRISE APPLICATIONS FOR CODE SHARING

Within an enterprise application there are specified EJB and Web modules. When developing an application, there is often a common set of Java files used by multiple portions of the application. For example, in our case study, we have application-specific exception classes. When packaging a module, you can easily place all Java files that it requires within the module JAR file. This would work, but if multiple modules require the same Java files, they would have to package them within their module JAR file as well. This means you will have duplicate sets of the same Java files in the enterprise application. This is where utility JAR files become useful.

According to the J2EE specification, you can have any number of JAR files packaged within the EAR. Many of these JAR files are specified as module files within the deployment descriptor. Any JAR file that is not defined as a module is considered a utility JAR file. This means that these JAR files are available to be referenced by any module within the EAR within their MANIFEST file as a Class-Path entry. Thus, you are able to share code among modules without duplication of Java files. This is a best practice because it encourages code sharing and it helps to minimize size and improves maintainability of the enterprise application.

The case study is structured in this manner. The enterprise application structure is shown next. Each module depends on the TimeSheet-AppLogic.jar utility JAR file.

wasbook (EAR)
> **TimeSheetGroup.jar (EJB module)**
> **TimeApp.war (Web module)**
> **TimeAppTestClient.jar (Application Client module)**
> **TimeSheet-AppLogic.jar (utility JAR)**

Figure 20.10 shows the project utility JARs section from the modules page of the enterprise application editor for the wasbook enterprise application. This section allows you to add a Java project as a utility JAR to an enterprise application much like you can add a J2EE project as a module in the module section on the same page. Like a module, a utility JAR has a URI and a Java project. When the enterprise application is exported, the projects defined as utility JARs will be "jarred" up and added to the exported EAR using the URI defined in the enterprise application editor. The benefits of this mechanism are that you can debug your utility JARs using breakpoints in the project Java files. You can also add the same Java project to multiple enterprise applications easily. This nicely supports team development since you do not have to explic-

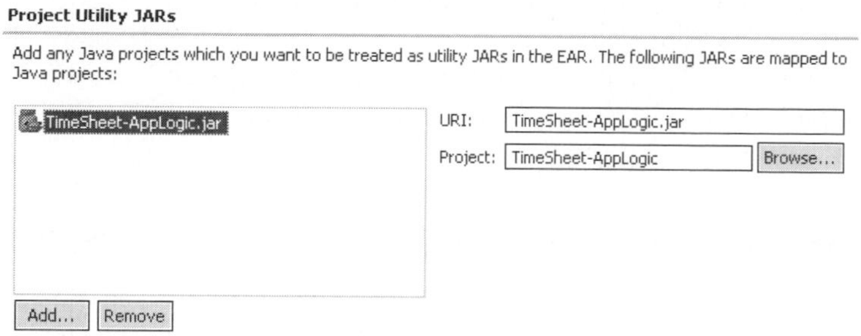

Project Utility JARs

Add any Java projects which you want to be treated as utility JARs in the EAR. The following JARs are mapped to Java projects:

TimeSheet-AppLogic.jar		URI:	TimeSheet-AppLogic.jar	
		Project:	TimeSheet-AppLogic	Browse...

[Add...] [Remove]

Figure 20.10 Project utility JARs.

itly create the JAR that is to be added to the EAR after each change, and it eliminates the need for redundant copies of the Java files that are contained in the utility JAR during development.

EJB CLIENT JAR

There is an optional ejb-client-jar element for the ejb-jar element within the EJB deployment descriptor. This element defines the location of a JAR file within the application relative to the deployment descriptor which contains all of the class files that a client program needs to use the client view of the EJBs contained within the ejb-jar file. The class files within the ejb-client-jar will be the home and component interfaces as well as other classes that these interfaces depend upon.

The ejb-client-jar is then packaged within the same application as the ejb-jar element that defines it. The ejb-client-jar may then be referenced as a Class-Path entry of other modules within that enterprise application. The ejb-client-jar file will need to be copied to another enterprise application if a module in the other application references the client view. For example, if the deployment descriptor for ejb1.jar defines an ejb-client-jar which is referenced by web1.war, since web1.war references the client view of ejb1.jar, it includes a class path reference to the ejb1_client.jar. A second application has a Web module, web2.war, also reference the ejb1_client.jar in a Class-Path entry. Notice that the ejb1_client.jar is copied to the second application.

```
application1.ear:

        META-INF/application.xml

        ejb1.jarClass-Path:  ejb1_client.jar

        <ejb-client-jar>ejb1_client.jar</ejb-client-jar>
```

(The following line is in the deployment descriptor.)

```
ejb1_client.jar
```

```
web1.warClass-Path:  ejb1_client.jar


application2.ear:


META-INF/application.xml


ejb1_client.jar


web2.warClass-Path:  ejb1_client.jar
```

WebSphere Studio does not currently have support for EJB client JARs; however, an EJB project can be assigned as a project utility JAR within an enterprise application. This will add the EJB project as a utility JAR within an enterprise application that does not define that same EJB project as a module. This is very similar to using an EJB client JAR except that the JAR that is created will contain all of the contents from the EJB project, whereas an EJB client JAR would only contain the client interfaces and stubs necessary for RMIs.

20.2.2 J2EE Project Dependencies

A well-factored enterprise application will have modules and utility JARs that are dependent upon each other without introducing cyclical dependencies. Modules define their dependencies on other modules or utility JARs within the EAR by specifying the dependent JARs with the Class-Path entry in the MANIFEST.MF file in the META-INF folder. This is how the runtime classpath is specified for a particular module which is used within the server. Here are the contents of the MANIFEST.MF file for the TimeSheetGroup EJB module used in the case study.

```
Manifest-Version: 1.0

Class-Path: TimeSheet-AppLogic.jar
```

Notice that its classpath entry includes the TimeSheet-AppLogic.jar utility JAR that was added in the enterprise application editor.

Setting the MANIFEST.MF Class-Path is required in order to test the module on the server but it does not help with developing and compiling the Java code within J2EE module projects. In this case, the development classpath is maintained by updating the Java build path for each module project. Remember that a module project is also a Java project. As you can see, two classpaths—the development time classpath and the runtime classpath—must be maintained and in synch at all times. This can be very confusing and frustrating for developers because they can get their code to compile but they have a difficult time getting the same module to run on the server. To alleviate this, WSAD has created the JAR dependency editor and the Java JAR dependencies property page.

20.2.3 JAR Dependency Editor

The JAR dependency editor is used to update both the runtime MANIFEST.MF classpath as well as the development time Java build path; therefore, you should avoid using the Java build path for a module project. If you use the Java build path to update the development time classpath, the runtime classpath will not be modified and there is a good chance that the module will not operate properly when deployed to the server.

The JAR dependency editor can be opened by selecting the module in the J2EE Hierarchy view and then selecting *Open With > JAR Dependency Editor* from the context menu. This editor can also be opened by double-clicking on the MANIFEST.MF file from the J2EE Navigator view. There is also a project property page with the same information and functionality. This property page is opened by selecting the module or J2EE project and selecting *Properties > Java JAR Dependencies* from the context menu.

The JAR dependency editor, shown in Figure 20.11, is opened on the MANIFEST.MF file for the TimeApp Web project used in the case study. The editor has two pages—a dependencies page and a source page. The dependencies page has several fields and a list used to edit the

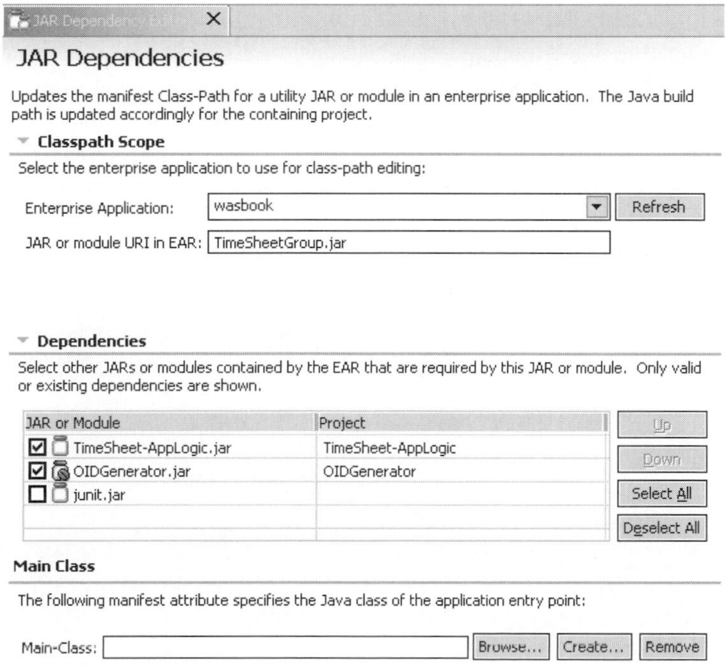

Figure 20.11 JAR dependency editor.

dependencies among modules and utility JAR files within a specified enterprise application. The source page is the raw text associated with the MANIFEST.MF file. A change to the source page will update the dependencies page and vice versa.

The classpath scope section is a read-only section that is used to set which enterprise application to use when setting the classpaths. The enterprise application combo box will default to the first available application that the given module is contained within. Remember that a module project may be added to one or more enterprise application projects. The JAR or module URI in EAR text field is a read-only field that shows the URI for the selected module project within the selected enterprise application. In this case, the module URI is TimeApp.war for the TimeApp module project within the wasbook enterprise application. Changing the enterprise application will drive changes to the dependencies table (Table 20.1).

The dependencies section will show all available JARs or modules contained within the selected enterprise application which are valid dependencies for the selected module. If a JAR file you need is not in the list, go back to the EAR application that contains the module, and add it to the Project Utility JARs. The table shows the URI for the module or utility JAR file as well as the project that the file maps to within the workbench. Any JAR that does not map to a project is contained directly within the enterprise application project as an actual JAR file. Table 20.1 shows the valid dependencies across the top and the selected module or utility project along the left side. Any combination that is not valid will not appear as a possible JAR dependency in the list. Note from Table 20.1 that no other module or utility JAR can depend upon either a Web module or an application client module.

When you set up your MANIFEST classpath, you may be tempted to select all the available JARs and modules within the enterprise application because you may be uncertain about your final application structure. Avoid doing this because it leads to cyclical project dependencies which fail to build within WSAD. You can eliminate this problem by carefully setting up

Table 20.1 Valid JAR dependency combinations.

	EJB Module	Web Module	Connector Module	Application Client Module	Utiiity JAR
EJB Module	X		X		X
Web Module	X		X		X
Connector Module	X		X		X
Application Client Module	X		X		X
Utility JAR	X		X		X

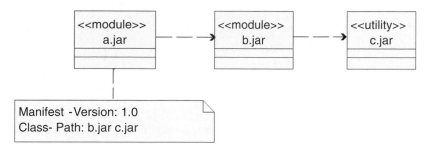

Figure 20.12 Implicit module classpath dependencies.

modules and utility JARs within an enterprise application such that there are no bidirectional dependencies (e.g., JAR A depends on JAR B and JAR B depends on JAR A). Also, you should only add required JARs or modules that are not already required by the existing utility JARs or modules in the dependencies list to the Java JAR Dependencies. For example, if you have a module a.jar, which has a dependency on module b.jar and utility JAR c.jar, and b.jar already depends on c.jar, you will only need to add b.jar as a dependency since you will also pick up c.jar through b.jar (see Figure 20.12).

To make our example a bit more interesting, we are going to select the junit.jar from the Dependencies list shown in Figure 20.11. Here are the contents from the source page where you can see that both JARs on specified in the Class-Path. Note that WSAD will split each entry on a new line to make it easier to read.

```
Manifest-Version: 1.0


Class-Path: TimeSheet-AppLogic.jar


 junit.jar
```

After saving the changes in the editor, you can select the TimeSheetGroup from the J2EE Hierarchy view and select Properties from the context menu. Then select Java build path to see how the development time classpath is affected by the changes.

Figure 20.13 shows the order and export page of the Java build path. Notice that there is an entry for the TimeSheet-AppLogic project which maps to the TimeSheet-AppLogic.jar entry in the enterprise application. There is also an entry for the junit.jar file which is located in the was-book project. This is a direct reference to the JAR file since there is not a mapping to a project within the workbench. Both entries are exported so that any other Java project that requires the TimeSheet-AppLogic project will also pick up these entries on their classpaths. These Java build path entries directly map to the entries that were saved in the MANIFEST.MF file so that the runtime and development time classpaths are in synch.

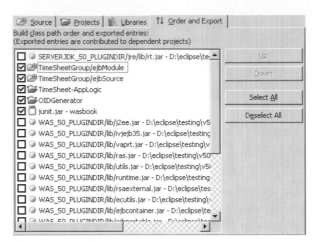

Figure 20.13 Java build path.

20.3   Creating a Session Bean

Now that you have seen how to create an EJB project as well as how to set up dependencies from an EJB project to other modules and utility JARs within the enterprise application, you are ready to create an enterprise bean. Creating an enterprise bean within WSAD is accomplished by using the enterprise bean creation wizard. You will use this wizard to add an enterprise bean entry to the ejb-jar.xml deployment descriptor. It also has the capability of generating, if necessary, the JavaBean classes and interfaces required to support the enterprise bean. We will start by providing details of how to create both stateless and stateful session beans. Later chapters will provide additional details for creating entity beans and MDBs.

Start by creating an EJB project named UtilitiesGroup which belongs to a new EAR project named UtilityEAR. We will use this EAR and EJB project for the rest of this example. Once you have done so, you are ready to create a session bean that will be used to create random integer values. This could be a useful class if you do not have a natural key value for your object model. For example, a person will have a Social Security number as a natural key value but a LineItem may not have a natural key value. In this case, any unique value would be adequate. Note that this is a simple example of a session bean and you would probably not use this example as a way to produce unique IDs because random integers are not guaranteed to be unique.

A much better option for automatic ID generation will be described in Chapter 23 when container-managed entity beans are described.

20.3.1   Using the EJB Creation Wizard

Like many other actions within WSAD, opening the EJB creation wizard can be accomplished many ways. The most basic way to open the wizard is to select *New > EJB > Enterprise Bean* from the File menu bar. This path is available anywhere within WSAD. When working in the J2EE perspective, which is the desired perspective to operate within when working with enterprise applications and EJBs, there are many methods to open this wizard. For example, it can be opened using the context menu on an EJB module selection in J2EE Hierarchy view. Refer to the online documentation for other shortcuts to opening the EJB creation wizard.

Select *File > New > EJB > Enterprise Bean* from the menu bar to open the Enterprise bean creation wizard. Figure 20.14 shows the first page of this wizard where it is necessary to select an EJB project in which you would like to create the new enterprise bean. For this example, we will select the UtilitiesGroup EJB project from the combo box. This page will not appear for all open actions because the selected project may already be known and cannot change.

The second page of the EJB creation wizard, shown in Figure 20.15, contains choices for the basic settings of the new enterprise bean. Near the top of the page is a series of four radio buttons for each type of enterprise bean. In this example, we are creating a session bean. The name of the session bean that we are going to create is RandomIDGenerator and it is entered in the Bean name text field. The Source folder, which defaults to ejbModule, is a folder within the EJB project in which the newly created bean is placed. You may select another existing source folder or enter a new folder name and it will be created for you. You may wish to select a different source folder other than ejbModule since this is the location used when generating deploy code. Choosing another source folder will allow you to keep your bean classes and deploy code completely separated. We will enter source so that we can demonstrate the difference from using the default. The default package will be the package name used for the bean class and interface names that are set on the next page of the wizard.

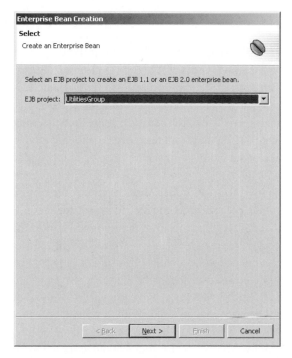

Figure 20.14 EJB creation wizard page 1.

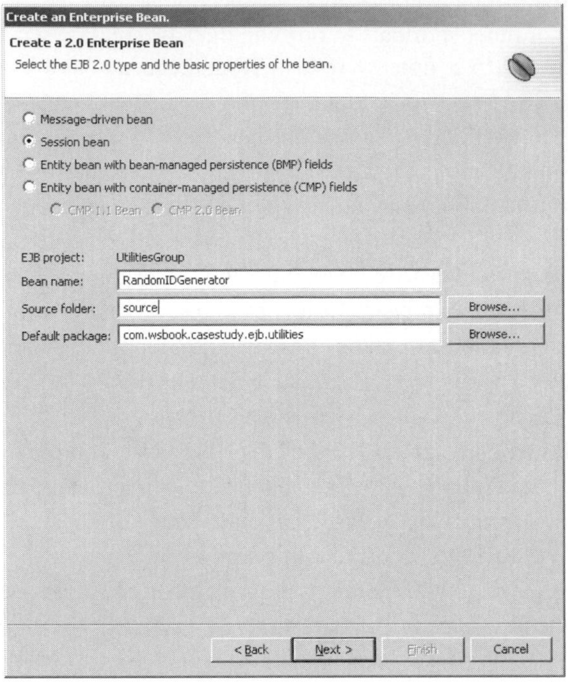

Figure 20.15 EJB creation wizard page 2.

The third page of the EJB creation wizard, shown in Figure 20.16, is used to set deployment descriptor details for the session bean. The first section of the page is where you specify whether or not the session bean is stateful or stateless. With a stateful session bean, conversational state must be retained across methods and transactions. This is accomplished within the EJB container by serializing each method call to ensure that the state is preserved between method invocations. A stateless session bean does not contain any conversational state between method calls. Therefore, any session bean instance may be used by the container since state is not preserved.

The next section is used to specify the transaction type which can be either container or bean. This setting determines whether the session bean will have container-managed or bean-managed transaction demarcation. When the transaction type is set to Container, the transaction demarcation is controlled by the container and is governed by transaction settings on the methods of the session bean client interfaces. With a transaction type of Bean, the session bean is required to create, commit, and rollback the user transactions itself and no transaction attributes should be set for the client interface methods. See Chapter 28 for more details on transactions.

The next field is the bean supertype. This combo box will contain the names of other session beans already created in the EJB project. You can select one of these bean names to define an EJB inheritance hierarchy. You will learn more about EJB inheritance in Chapter 25. The

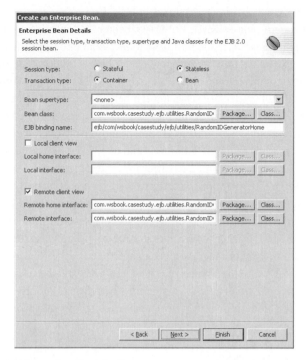

Figure 20.16 EJB creation wizard page 3.

bean class text field is the name of the new session bean's EJB class. The default EJB class name is the bean name and the default package name from the previous page. You may change the name or you may browse for another existing Java bean class or just an existing package name. If you select an existing bean class, the text in the field will change to blue if Java source code is detected and red if only a Java binary file exists for the class name.

Note: A bean class will only be generated upon finish if the selected Java class name does not already exist because it is possible to create a session bean definition from a set of existing bean classes.

The EJB binding name is the JNDI name that will be bound to the session bean within WebSphere. In this example, the default JNDI name is set to ejb/com/wsbook/casestudy/ejb/utilities/RandomIDGeneratorHome which is derived from the fully qualified name of the default home interface name. This JNDI name is specified at bean creation time since it is required for testing purposes.

The last section of this wizard page is for the client views. You can choose to create a local and/or remote client view by selecting the Local client view and Remote client view check boxes respectively. Using a remote client view indicates that a remote client interface and a remote home interface will be created for use by remote clients. Remote clients use RMI for accessing the enterprise bean. Using a local client view indicates that a local client interface and a local home interface will be created for use by local clients (i.e., clients on the same JVM). Local method invocation does not require RMI. Refer to Chapter 22 for more detail about EJB clients and Chapter 30 for deciding when is the best time to use local client interfaces.

For session beans, the Remote client view check box is selected by default but you may decide to create a local client view or both. Just like the bean class, the remote home interface and remote interface default values are set using the bean name and default package name from the first page. The name of the remote home interface adds Home to the end of the default Bean class name (e.g., com.wsbook.casestudy.ejb.utilities.RandomIDGeneratorHome). Also, like the bean class name, you can change the default name and choose an existing class name. Again, the Java interface will only be generated if an existing Java interface name is not selected.

The last page of the EJB creation wizard gives you some control over the generated bean class and client interfaces that will be generated. The EJB Java Class Details page, shown in Figure 20.17, has three sections for affecting the generated classes and interfaces. The Bean superclass field allows you to specify another Java class for the new bean class to extend. This is normal Java inheritance and not EJB inheritance. If a bean supertype is specified from the previous page, this field will have the fully qualified name of the supertype bean's bean class and it will be disabled. It is disabled since you are unable to change the superclass if an EJB supertype is specified. This field will also be disabled if you have selected an existing bean class on the previous page.

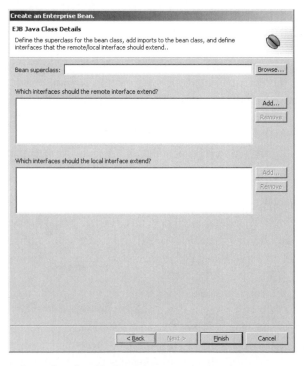

Figure 20.17 EJB creation wizard page 4.

The second section is a list of Java interfaces that the new remote interface should extend. This section will be disabled if you have not selected to generate a remote interface or you have selected an existing remote interface. The last section is very similar to the second section except that it allows you to specify other Java interfaces that the local interface should extend. This section will be disabled if you have not selected to generate a local interface or you have selected an existing local interface.

After you press the *Finish* button, three new Java classes will be generated under the Source folder.

- com.wsbook.casestudy.ejb.utilities.RandomIDGenerator
- com.wsbook.casestudy.ejb.utilities.RandomIDGeneratorBean
- com.wsbook.casestudy.ejb.utilities.RandomIDGeneratorHome

A new enterprise bean entry will be entered into the deployment descriptor for the new RandomIDGenerator session bean.

```
<session id="RandomIDGenerator">

  <ejb-name>RandomIDGenerator</ejb-name>

  <home>com.wsbook.casestudy.ejb.utilities.RandomIDGeneratorHome</home>

  <remote>com.wsbook.casestudy.ejb.utilities.RandomIDGenerator</remote>

  <ejb-class>com.wsbook.casestudy.ejb.utilities.RandomIDGeneratorBean

  </ejb-class>

  <session-type>Stateless</session-type>

  <transaction-type>Container</transaction-type>

</session>
```

20.4 Testing the New Session Bean

Before we can test anything, we first need to provide some behavior on our new RandomIDGenerator session bean. This bean will be responsible for generating a new random integer that may be used for setting IDs on other beans. So, we will add the following methods and field to the RandomIDGeneratorBean Java class using the editor provided by WSAD. You can open this bean class in a number of different ways including double-clicking on the RandomIDGenerator bean from the list on the Beans page of the EJB deployment descriptor editor. Remember that the implementation of the `getRandom()` method will not guarantee a unique integer but rather a random integer. Chapter 23 will describe a mechanism to obtain a truly unique integer.

```
private Random random;

...


public int calculateID() {

  return getRandom().nextInt();

}


private Random getRandom() {

  if (random == null)

    random = new Random(System.currentTimeMillis());

  return random;

}
```

The method `calculateID()` will not be accessible to a remote client unless we add it to the remote interface of our session bean. You can do this from the Java editor for the RandomID-GeneratorBean class. Select the `calculateID()` method from the outline and select the *Enterprise Bean > Promote to Remote Interface* menu action. You will notice that a small *R* will appear in the outline next to the method to indicate that it appears on the remote interface.

20.4.1 Testing the Session Bean with the Universal Test Client

There are a number of different ways to test our new session but we have chosen to use the UTC for our initial testing. In Chapter 22 you will create an application client to do the testing for you. Before we can test this new session bean, it is necessary to generate the deployment code. The deployment code will contain the concrete beans as described by the EJB 2.0 specification as well as the necessary stubs and ties for all EJBs that have remote client interfaces. To generate the deployment code, select the UtilitiesGroup EJB module from the J2EE Hierarchy view and click *Generate > Deploy* and *RMIC Code* from the context menu that is opened using the right mouse button. This will open the generate deploy and RMIC code wizard.

Ensure that all of the EJBs are selected that you want to have deployment code generated and click the *Finish* button. Note, all of the generated deployment code will be generated to the

Figure 20.18 Run UTC and server.

ejbModule folder. As mentioned earlier, you may want to generate your enterprise bean classes to a different folder to keep the code separated from the deployment code.

Now that the deployment code has been generated, the session bean is ready to be tested with the UTC. To begin, select the RandomIDGenerator bean in the J2EE Hierarchy view of the J2EE perspective. From the context menu select *Run on Server* as shown in Figure 20.18.

If there are no servers defined, you will be presented with a Server Selection dialog to specify the type of server that you would like to create. We will select WebSphere v5.0 Test Environment and click *OK*. This will automatically create a server and configuration with the UtilityEAR added to the new server; it also starts the server. Once you've either created or selected a server, the server will start. The Console view will show the progress of the server startup sequence. Look for a line similar to the following:

```
[4/7/03 21:42:47:700 EDT] 660cfc3b WsServer A WSVR0001I: Server server1 open

for e-business
```

When this line appears your server has started normally without any errors. However, that line won't be the last line in the console. There will be a set of lines containing the text [IBM Universal Test Client] that will follow the open for e-business message that will indicate that the UTC is starting. At the end of this sequence, you will see the new page contained in a new Web Browser tab as shown in Figure 20.19.

This page shows the UTC opened to your new EJB. The UTC is a Web application that allows you to test both EJBs and Web services. It consists of two different views: a references view that allows you to select objects like EJBHomes and EJB instances, and methods within those objects, and a Parameters pane that allows you to set parameters for the methods, invoke

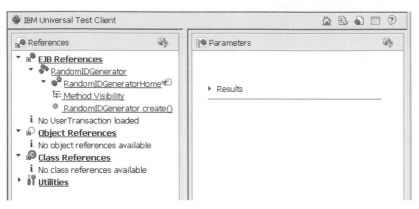

Figure 20.19 Universal test client.

the methods, and examine the results. We'll examine some more of its capabilities later. For the time being, we're simply going to use the UTC to:

- Obtain a reference to the EJB home for the `RandomIdGenerator` EJB
- Create an instance of the `RandomIdGenerator` EJB
- Send the `calculateId()` message to the new instance

If you have not done so, expand the RandomIDGenerator tree view under EJB References to show both the RandomIDGenerator bean icon and the icon for the RandomIDGenerator-Home. Under method visibility you will see an entry for the `create()` method in RandomID-GeneratorHome (the only method in the home interface). Select that method and the parameters pane will change to show a button allowing you to invoke that method. Press the *Invoke* button. This will invoke the `create()` method and return a remote reference to a RandomIDGenerator bean. Your Parameters page should look like Figure 20.20 after pressing the Invoke button.

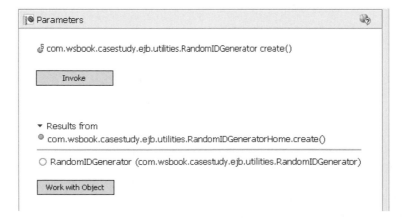

Figure 20.20 Parameters pane of UTC.

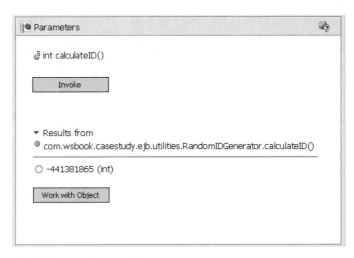

Figure 20.21 Random ID generator results.

As you see, you have a reference to a RandomIDGenerator available. Since we want to send other messages to this object, press the Work with Object button, which will add the RandomID-Generator reference to the references tree view. The remote reference will be labeled RandomID-Generator 1. Expand the reference and now you'll see a list of the methods available on the remote interface. As you might expect, the list will only contain one entry (`int calculateID()`) since that is the only method in the remote interface. If you select the `int calculateID()` method in the References pane, again you'll see an *Invoke* button in the Parameters pane. Press the *Invoke* button and you'll see your random number. Your Parameters pane should then look something like Figure 20.21.

Note that your random number obtained from invoking the `calculateID()` method will be different from this one—it is random after all! So, now you've seen the basics of using the UTC you might want to experiment with sending the `calculateID()` message several times, or seeing what happens if you try to send `create()` a second time. This experimentation (and reading the appropriate online Help available by clicking the question mark icon at the top right of the UTC page) should make you familiar with the operation of the UTC, and able to use it to test your EJB methods.

20.5 Summary

This chapter provided the first introduction to the J2EE perspective and its basic usage for developing and testing enterprise applications. The chapter discussed the structure of J2EE artifacts within WebSphere Studio and it provided information about packaging and enterprise application and setting of class paths for J2EE modules. A simple example of creating and testing a session bean was then provided to provide the basic understanding of how EJBs are created and tested using WebSphere Studio.

The next several chapters will build upon this foundation to provide more details about testing and debugging EJBs, creating enterprise bean clients, creating and mapping container-managed entity beans, creating bean-managed entity beans and MDBs, container transactions, J2EE security, and, lastly, a wrap-up of the best practices for an EJB architecture.

Testing and Debugging EJBs in WSAD

In Chapters 7 and 8 we explored how to develop and test servlets using a simple example that updates employees in a relational database. In Chapter 13, we modified the example using JSPs to simplify dynamic page generation. In Chapter 16 we extended the example domain model and implemented the data mapping layer using Martin Fowler's Data Mapper pattern. Recall that in the summary section of Chapter 16 we discussed a number of issues that weren't covered by the data mapper pattern including domain specific transaction management and security. Data mapper relies on the underlying database management system to provide transaction management and access control through JDBC. Migrating capabilities that are equivalent to these database mechanisms into domain model policies can be a difficult task. In Chapter 18 we discussed how EJBs help by providing a framework for managing the various systematic concerns that must be addressed in building scaleable distributed business applications. In Chapter 20 we covered how to build EJBs in WSAD. In this chapter, we'll be taking a look at the rest of the development lifecycle, in particular deploying and testing EJBs. We'll modify the example from Chapters 13 and 16 by introducing a *Service Layer* between the servlets and JSPs that handle HTTP requests and responses, and the employee domain model. This Service Layer will be implemented by a simple J2EE Session Bean that provides an API for use cases involving typical employee management functions. By using a session bean, we can introduce transaction management and access control at the method level in the bean. This simplifies application development by exploiting the J2EE container to do a lot of the work that would ordinarily have to be built in your own application logic.

21.1 Developing the Service Layer

We'll start by changing the example developed in Chapters 13 and 16 to use a session bean to mediate between the server-based presentation logic and the domain model.

21.1.1   Creating and Configuring the Example Projects

Create a new J2EE 1.3 Enterprise Application project called *EmployeeManagement* containing an EJB module and a Web module. The Enterprise Application Project Creation wizard will create three projects in the WSAD workspace called *EmployeeManagement* for the Enterprise Application (EAR project), *EmployeeManagementEJB* for the EJBs (EJB project), and *EmployeeManagementWeb* for the Web resources including the HTML and servlets that access the EJBs (Web project). The EJB and Web projects are also automatically deployed to the EmployeeManagement EAR. If you want to avoid developing the example from scratch, these WSAD projects are available on the CD. You'll also need the Data Mapper Example project for the domain model and the database mapping using JDBC. See Appendix A for instructions on loading the examples from the CD.

Follow these steps to configure the projects:

1. Edit the EmployeeManagement EAR Deployment Descriptor and add the Data Mapper Example package as a Project Utility JAR as described in Chapter 20, section "Java Utility JARs". The EmployeeManagementEJB project needs to be able to access domain model classes in this project. By including the Data Mapper Example project as a Project Utility JAR, these classes will be available to the modules within the enterprise application when it is deployed and run.

2. Open the properties for the EmployeeManagementEJB project. Select the Java Build Path, and add a source folder called src to the project source folders. Leave the build output folder to EmployeeManagementEJB/ejbModule. We'll be putting all the EJBs we create in packages in the src folder instead of the ejbModule folder so we can keep our code separate from the code generated during deployment as described in Chapter 20.

3. While the EmployeeManagementEJB project properties are open, select the Java JAR Dependencies tab. From the available dependent JARs, select the *Data_Mapper_Example.jar* from the Data Mapper Example project that was added as a project utility jar to the EmployeeManagement EAR in step 1. See Chapter 20 for more details about setting classpaths and the use of project utility JARs within WSAD. This will allow the EmployeeManagementEJB project to reference classes in the Data Mapper Example project during development and runtime.

4. Edit the *References* page of the EJB Deployment Descriptor editor opened on the EmployeeManagementEJB EJB module and add a Resource Reference to the EmployeeManagement EJB called *jdbc/EJPBook*, to a javax.sql.DataSource resource with Application Authentication, Shareable scope, and JNDI name: `jdbc/EJPBOOK`. This will allow the project to use the EJPBook database required to persist the domain model in the Data Mapper Example project.

21.1.2   Creating the Session Bean

Next we'll create the `EmployeeManagement` session bean in the EmployeeManagementEJB project. Select *File>New>Other...>EJB>EnterpriseBean* to open the EJB Creation wizard (see

Chapter 20 for more details). Create a stateless session bean named *EmployeeManagement* in the *src* folder, and in the package *com.wsbook.acme.management* with both a local and remote client view. We'll be using the local client view (interface) to invoke the bean functions from servlets running on the server. The remote interface can be used by other Java client applications. It is of course possible to use the remote client view from the server too, but it is much more efficient to use the local client view.

21.1.3 Add the Service Layer Methods

The employee management use cases we want to implement in the session bean include creating new employees, accessing a collection of existing employees, updating employee data, and removing employees. These are pretty simple use cases that are also directly supported by the domain model and mapping layer. But by using a session bean, we can create methods supporting the client's view of the domain model, and provide the proper transaction management and access control. Different client applications accessing the same domain model may have different views on that model, or use different interfaces to it. These different interfaces can be both a convenience to client developers, providing a interface specific to their needs, and enable more flexible access control through different session bean methods that access the domain model.

Add the methods shown in Listing 21.1 to the *EmployeeManagementBean.* Note that the extra set of curly braces enclosing the begin and end of the unit of work appear to be superfluous, but they ensure the instance variables used inside the unit of work are not visible after the unit of work has been committed, and will be garbage collected appropriately. This convention helps ensure the application does not access stale data outside a unit of work. `UnitOfWork` is discussed in Chapter 16. Later on we'll see how to use J2EE to handle this important aspect of application development.

Listing 21.1 EmployeeManagementBean

```
public Collection findAll() {

    Collection employees = null;

    try {

        UnitOfWork.begin(); {

        EmployeeMapper mapper =
        (EmployeeMapper)MapperRegistry.getMapper(
         Employee.class);

        employees = mapper.findAll();

        } UnitOfWork.getCurrent().commit();

    } catch (MappingException e) {
```

```java
                e.printStackTrace();

        }

        return employees;

}



public Employee getEmployee(String id) {

        Employee employee = null;

        try {

                UnitOfWork.begin(); {

                EmployeeMapper mapper =
                    (EmployeeMapper)MapperRegistry.getMapper(

                 Employee.class);

                employee = (Employee)mapper.findByPrimaryKey(id);

                } UnitOfWork.getCurrent().commit();

        } catch (MappingException e) {

                e.printStackTrace();

        }

        return employee;

}



public void update(Map args) {

        try {

                UnitOfWork.begin(); {
```

```
                    EmployeeMapper mapper =
                      (EmployeeMapper)MapperRegistry.getMapper(
                      Employee.class);

                    Employee emp = (Employee)mapper.findByPrimaryKey(

                     getParameter(args, "id"));

                    emp.setName(getParameter(args, "name"));

                    emp.setAge(Integer.parseInt(
                     getParameter(args, "age")));

                    emp.getAddress().setStreet(

                     getParameter(args, "street"));

                    emp.getAddress().setCity(

                     getParameter(args, "city"));

                    emp.getAddress().setState(

                     getParameter(args, "state"));

                    emp.getAddress().setZip(

                     getParameter(args, "zip"));

              } UnitOfWork.getCurrent().commit();

        } catch (MappingException e) {

              e.printStackTrace();

        }

  }


public void createNewEmployee(Map args) {

      try {

            UnitOfWork.begin(); {
```

```java
            EmployeeMapper mapper =
              (EmployeeMapper)MapperRegistry.getMapper(

              Employee.class);

            Employee emp = new Employee(

              getParameter(args, "id"));

            emp.setName(getParameter(args, "name"));

            emp.setAge(Integer.parseInt(

              getParameter(args, "age")));

              new Address(emp);

            emp.getAddress().setStreet(

              getParameter(args, "street"));

            emp.getAddress().setCity(

              getParameter(args, "city"));

            emp.getAddress().setState(

              getParameter(args, "state"));

            emp.getAddress().setZip(

              getParameter(args, "zip"));

        } UnitOfWork.getCurrent().commit();

    } catch (MappingException e) {

        e.printStackTrace();

    }

}


public void deleteAnEmployee(String id) {
```

```
    try {

        UnitOfWork.begin(); {

            EmployeeMapper mapper =
            (EmployeeMapper)MapperRegistry.getMapper(

              Employee.class);

          Employee emp = (Employee)mapper.findByPrimaryKey(id);

          emp.delete();

        } UnitOfWork.getCurrent().commit();

    } catch (MappingException e) {

        e.printStackTrace();

    }

}


public String getParameter(Map map, String id) {

    String value = null;

    String[] values = (String[])map.get(id);

    if (values != null && values.length > 0) {

        value = values[0];

    }

    return value;

}
```

Each of the methods dealing with employees creates a new unit of work, gets the `Employ-eeMapper` from the `MapperRegistry`, and creates, reads, updates, and/or deletes the employee data. The map that is passed in for arguments comes from the servlet request. Each key is a request parameter name while the value is a list of strings. The *getParameter* method is a convenience method for accessing a parameter value from the map. Note that there will be some information messages in the Tasks view indicating that `java.util.Collection` and `java.util.Map` must be serializable at runtime in order to be passed as arguments to the distributed methods in the remote client view. The Collection returned by the `findAll` method returns an `ArrayList` which is `Serializable` as is the `Hashmap` used for the parameters, so these errors can be ignored. A better solution would be to encapsulate these parameters in a class in order to have simpler and more reliable access. Struts form beans play this role. But we won't bother with that refinement in this simple example. We also didn't address data validation, or appropriate exception handling in the above code in order to simplify the example.

21.1.4 Promoting the Service Layer Methods to the Local and Remote Interfaces

So far we've implemented the session bean methods, but they aren't visible to the client. To make them available for invocation by clients, we have to promote the methods to the local and/ or remote client views. While the EmployeeManagementBean.java class is open, select the `findAll`, `getEmployee`, `update`, `createNewEmployee`, and `deleteAnEmployee` methods in the outline view. Right click and select *EnterpriseBean>Promote to Local Interface* context menu action and the *EnterpriseBean>Promote to Remote Interface* context menu action. Now the methods are available in both the local and remote client views. You might want to edit the EmployeeManagement.java interface (the remote interface), and EmployeeManagementLocal.java add JavaDoc for the new methods since these interfaces are the client views.

21.1.5 Developing the Client View

Next we'll update the HTML pages and servlets from the JSP Example project described in Chapter 13. First edit the properties of the EmployeeManagementWeb project, select the Java JAR Dependencies tab, and add the EmployeeManagementEJB as a dependent JAR. This will make the EJBs in the EmployeeManagementEJB project visible both during development time for compiling servlets and JSPs, and at runtime when the classes need to be loaded. Recall that using JAR dependencies ensures that both the development time classpath, and the deployment classpath information is kept in sync and only has to be specified in one place.

Next edit the Web Deployment Descriptor and add the CreateEmployee, BrowseEmployees, ShowEmployeeDetail, and UpdateEmployee servlets along with their default URL mappings. Without this, the servlets will appear as broken links when referenced in other HTML or JSP pages.

Listing 21.2 gives the changes to the BrowseEmployees.java servlet.

Listing 21.2 BrowseEmployees.java

```
package com.wsbook.acme.management;

import java.io.IOException;

...
```

```java
public class BrowseEmployees extends HttpServlet {

    public void doGet(HttpServletRequest req, HttpServletResponse resp)

        throws ServletException, IOException {

        try {

            InitialContext context = new InitialContext();

            EmployeeManagementLocalHome emh =

                (EmployeeManagementLocalHome) context.lookup(

                    "java:comp/env/ejb

EmployeeManagementLocal");

            EmployeeManagementLocal em = emh.create();

            Collection employees = em.findAll();

            req.setAttribute("employees", employees);

            RequestDispatcher rd =

                getServletContext().getRequestDispatcher(

                    "/browseEmployees.jsp");

            rd.forward(req, resp);

        } catch (Exception e) {

            RequestDispatcher rd =

                getServletContext().getRequestDispatcher(

                    "/remoteAccessError.html");

            rd.forward(req, resp);

        }

    }

}
```

This is only slightly different than the implementation in Chapter 13 that went directly to the domain model. The servlet looks up the `EmployeeManagementLocalHome` and uses it to create an instance of the `EmployeeManagementLocal` interface which it then uses to add the collection of employees to the servlet request session data. The JSPs from Chapter 13 hardly have to change at all other than of course to use the new *com.wsbook.acme.Employee* domain model. The other servlets and JSPs have similar changes.

Now that the coding is done for our enterprise application, the next thing to do is to test the modifications.

21.2 Overview of the Testing Process

Before proceeding with testing your EJBs we'll need to cover some of the built-in testing tools in WebSphere Studio Application Developer (WSAD). Just as we developed EJBs by following a step-by-step approach in the previous section, we'll use a similar approach to deploy, test, and debug EJBs. In short, the necessary steps are:

1. Generate the EJB Deployment classes in the EJB projects used in the EAR

2. Create and configure a Server instance and add the EAR project

3. Publish and start the Server Instance

4. Test an EJB with the Universal Test Client and the client Web module

5. Debug the EJB code (if necessary) using the WSAD debugger

6. Publish the enterprise application to an external WebSphere server

7. Debug the published application using the distributed debugger

So start up WSAD and work through each of these steps.

21.2.1 Step 1: Generate the EJB Deployment Classes for an EJB Project

Before we begin this step, we'll need to review some basic EJB concepts in order for you to understand what's happening. Remember that an EJB is a *software component*. In the previous sections, we've been concentrating on developing the user-developed part of entity and session EJBs (the Home, Local, and Remote Interfaces, and the bean implementation class). However, these classes are not the entire EJB. An EJB will also consist of classes that are provided by the container that handle the distribution, transaction, thread safety and (optionally) persistence aspects of the EJB component. Obviously, different EJB types will support different aspects of these features (for example, only the CMP Entity bean container handles persistence). We can call these classes *deployment* classes, since generating them is part of the EJB deployment process that is outlined in the EJB specification. In addition, the remote interfaces require proxy stubs to be generated that implement the remote interfaces on the client through remote procedure calls to the enterprise beans on the server. These interfaces are generated by the Java rmic (Remote Method Invocation Compiler) utility as part of the deployment code.

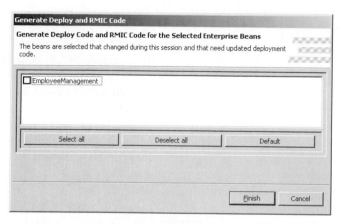

Figure 21.1 Technologies used in this chapter's example.

To generate the deployment code, select the *EmployeeManagementEJB* project, right click, and select *Generate>Deploy and RMIC Code...* . The *Generate Deploy and RMIC Code* dialog is displayed as shown in Figure 21.1. Select the enterprise beans you want to deploy and click **Finish**. By default, only the enterprise beans that have changed and require new deployment code are selected. But you can select any other beans you want to refresh their generated code.

The deployment process that is executed after choosing this menu item can last anywhere from a few seconds to take several minutes, depending upon the speed of your processor and the number of EJBs selected.

The classes generated for deployment are placed in the *ejbModule* folder in the EJB project as specified by the J2EE specification. This is why we recommend creating a separate src folder (also discussed in Chapter 20) for user contributed code in order to keep user code and deployment code separate. Another good reason to keep the code separate is that you often don't need to maintain versions of the generated deployment code in the repository since it can be easily generated from the enterprise beans. For instance, to keep deployment code out of a CVS repository, select the root packages (often com and org) in the *ejbModule* folder, right click, and select *Team>Add to .cvsignore*. Don't add the META-INF or databases folders to the .cvsignore file as you will probably want to version the deployment descriptors and database configuration information contained in these folders[1].

21.2.2 Step 2: Create and Configure a Server Instance and Add the EAR Project

In order to run the deployed code, we must first deploy the *EmployeeManagement* EAR to a server instance. The easiest server instance to use is the WebSphere version 5.0 Test Environment server that's built into WSAD. So create a WebSphere version 5.0 Test Environment for the

---

1.   Note: These files and most other generated EJB files are excluded from source control by default.

server and configuration, giving the server a name you can easily recognize as a server for testing purposes. Server instances and configurations are usually automatically created in a project called *Servers*. Each server has a <server name>.wsi XML file that contains the information about the WebSphere Server Instance. Each server configuration is contained in a <server name>.wsc folder that contains a number of XML files that describe the server configuration including enterprise applications that have been deployed to that server, available data source resources, ports, etc. Generally you never need to look at these files as the server configuration editor provides an integrated editor for all the information. However, knowing the files involved can simplify sharing servers and server configurations with your team members by committing them to your shared team repository. These resources can be versioned in the repository and shared across projects like any other. In particular, definitions of environment variables, MIME type mappings, data sources, EJB references, JAAS authentication entries, etc. are captured separately from the server instance. This allows the same configuration to be used by many different servers. To change the configuration for a server, select the server in the *J2EE Hierarchy* view, right click, and select *Switch Configuration*. The configurations that are compatible with that server are displayed in a submenu with the current configuration checked. Select some other configuration to change the server configuration.

In order to test our enterprise application, we need to add it to the server configuration, and then edit the configuration to specify all the resource needed by the application. You can add the *EmployeeManagement* EAR to the test server configuration by selecting the configuration, right clicking, and selecting *Add*. A submenu is displayed that shows all the available enterprise applications in your workspace that are not already added to this server. Alternatively, you can double click on the server instance in the *J2EE Hierarchy* view to open the server configuration editor, and select the *Applications* tab to add the application. You can open the server configuration editor from either the server or its configuration. The only difference is that opening the editor from the server instance causes the editor to include an extra *Server* tab for editing the server instance information. For a summary of the server configuration editor, see Chapter 8.

Note: If you're using more than one server instance, and want to run them at the same time, you'll have to edit the server configuration and select the *Ports* tab to select different ports. Multiple servers cannot run on the same ports at the same time.

The only other thing we need to edit in the server configuration is to add a data source for the database used to persist the domain model. This is the same data source that was used in Chapter 16. Open the *Server Configuration* editor on the server instance and select the *Data source* tab. Add a *DB2 JDBC Provider* if there isn't one already in the server configuration. Select the DB2 JDBC provider and add a data source called *EJPBook* with JNDI name *jdbc/ EJPBOOK*. This creates a JNDI binding to the database using the same name we used for configuring the EJB resource reference above. Select the data source, and edit its properties to set the *databaseName* to *EJPBOOK*, the DB2 database we've been using for the employee management examples in Chapter 7, 8, 13, and 16. Save the server configuration and close the editor.

21.2.3 Step 3: Publishing and Starting the Server Instance

Now that the server instance has been created and configured with the desired applications and resources, we're now ready to start the server. But first, the applications that are to be run on the server must be published to the server. This step copies files from the application into the locations required by the server in order for the application to run. For the WebSphere built in test environment, this does not do much because the application files are directly referenced from your WSAD workspace by the test environment. But for remote servers, this results in any changes that have been made to the application to be published or re-published to the server. Generally the server instance knows that data it depends on has changed in the workspace and needs to be re-published. In these cases, the server will automatically publish its configured applications when it is started or restarted.

To publish and start the server, we need to go to the *Servers* view in the J2EE perspective. Select the test server and right click to display the menu shown in Figure 21.2.

Before we publish and start the server, let's take a quick look at some of the other things you can do with a server instance. The *Debug* menu item starts the server up in debug mode so you can debug servlets, JSPs, and EJBs that are running on the server. *Start* starts the server without debug capability. *Profile* starts the server and collects profile information for evaluating performance. *Restart* restarts an already running server. Use this menu item if the server configuration changed as this requires restarting the server. *Stop* stops the running server. *Disconnect* terminates a remote debug session and disconnects WSAD from a remote server. *Publish* publishes the applications configured for this server by copying any necessary files to locations required by the server. *Restart Project* displays a submenu of the projects belonging to the applications that are running on this server. You'll need to restart a project whenever any of its configuration information changes. *Run universal test client* starts up the UTC which can be used to

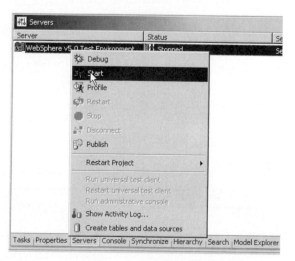

Figure 21.2 Server menu.

test your EJBs. The UTC is discussed in the next step and in Chapter 20. *Run administrative console* starts the WebSphere admin console which can be used to configure a WebSphere server. Note that to enable *Run administrative console*, you have to enable the administration console on the *Configuration* page of the server configuration editor. Running the admin console is sometimes useful because the WSAD server configuration editor doesn't handle every possible configuration; while the full admin console lets you control every aspect of the server.

Select the *Start* menu item to start the server. The server is automatically published if necessary. Take a look at the *Console* tab to view the server logs. Make sure there were no problems starting up the server applications, or accessing any of the data sources. When the server says it is "open for e-business" in the *Console* log, you're ready to start testing.

21.2.4   Step 4: Test Your EJB with the Universal Test Client and Client Web Module

At this point we're ready to try the application using a couple of options. You can go ahead and just run the Web application by selecting the *EmployeeManagementWeb* project, right click, and select *Run on server...*. This will display the welcome page configured for the application as specified on the *Pages* tab of the Web deployment descriptor editor. In this case, *index.html* will be displayed. Click on the *Browse Employees* link to display the employees in the database. Click on an employee ID to see the employee details as shown in Figure 21.3.

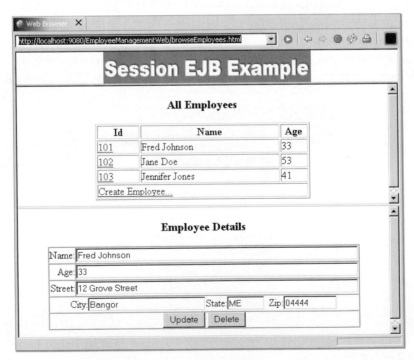

Figure 21.3 Employee list and details using a Session EJB.

If the application doesn't work the first time, it may be useful to break the testing down into smaller pieces in order to figure out what is wrong. The best place to start testing is the domain model because if it's wrong, then nothing in the application is going to work. Since we already developed the domain model in the Data Mapper Example, we can assume it's correct and focus testing on what we changed or added in this example. That would be the session EJB used to provide a distributed service layer to client applications.

The easiest way to test EJBs is to use the Universal Test Client (UTC). There are a number of ways to start the UTC including selecting the server in the *Servers* view and invoking *Run universal test client* as described in the previous section. You can also open a Web browser on URL *http://localhost:9080/UTC/* to run the UTC outside WSAD. The port is whatever port you set in the server configuration. But the easiest way to test is to simply select an EJB within an EJB Module in the J2EE Hierarchy view which is in the J2EE perspective, right click, and select *Run on Server....*

The UTC details were covered in Chapter 20 so we'll go quickly through using it to for initial testing of our *EmployeeManagement* bean. The *JNDI Explorer* allows you to navigate and explore the elements in you JNDI server. Note that there is also an entry *[Local EJB beans]* that allows you to also explore EJBs with local interfaces that do not have an EJB Local Ref in the WebSphere Application Server. Go ahead and use the *JNDI Explorer* to lookup an the *EmployeeManagementHome* EJB, or navigate the JNDI *ejb* namespace to the bean, or, even easier, select the *EmployeeManagement* EJB in the *J2EE Hierarchy* view and select *Run on server....* Expand the *EJB References* and then the *EmployeeManagement* bean to see the home interface and it's *create* method. If the method isn't visible, click on *Method Visibility* under *EmployeeManagementHome* and make sure the methods for the bean are selected to be visible. Select the *create* method and press *Invoke* to create an instance of an *EmployeeManagement* session bean. Press *Work with Object* to add an instance of the *EmployeeManagement* bean to the *EJB References*. Then expand the *EmployeeManagement* reference to see the session bean methods. Select the *getEmployee* method and fill in a parameter for an employee. The value you enter will be the ID of any employee you created when running the examples in Chapter 16. If there are no employees in the database, use the *EmployeeManagementWeb* application to create some. Then press *Invoke* to invoke the *getEmployee* method followed by *Work with Object* to add the *Employee* to the *Object References*. Then select the *Employee* object in the object references and try invoking any of its methods. The returned results are displayed in the UTC (using their *toString* methods), and you can use *Work with Object* to see the details. Note the *Employee* is a simple JavaBean from the Data Mapper Example. If you don't remember any of the employee IDs, try invoking the `EmployeeManagementHome.findAll` method first. This will return a java.util.Collection. Press *Work with Contained Objects* to add the employees to the Object References. In this cause you use the contained objects instead of the container because you want to work with the employees, not the Java collection. You can then invoke the getId method on any of the employee references to get its ID.

21.2.5 Step 5: Debugging EJBs Using the WSAD Debugger

One of the greatest advantages of WSAD is that debugging a J2EE application, like any other Java application, can be done in-place using in the Java debugger and the built-in WebSphere Test Environment. There is no need to create all the application JAR files and deploy before debugging. Debugging EJBs can be done using the standard WSAD debugger to:

- Set and clear breakpoints in EJB code and client code
- Step over code, step into code, or jump to the next breakpoint
- Examine values of variables in EJB code and client code and change the values while the code is running
- Make changes to the code and save them. The enterprise application is automatically restarted in order to pick up the code changes.

You never need to leave WSAD to do any of these things. There is no separate deployment or compilation required, or debug step you have to perform to run the debugger. If you set a breakpoint and run the application server in debug mode, then the debugger will halt the currently running thread at the breakpoint you set, and wait for your intervention to continue.

Covering all of the features of the WSAD debugger is something that is beyond the scope of this book. However, you can get a feel for how easy it can be to debug your EJBs through the following example debug scenario. Additional information is also available in Chapter 8.

Imagine that we're having trouble updating the employee information. The *City* field on the form is always coming up `null`. The *EmployeeManagementBean update* method is shown in Listing 21.1, but let's change it as shown in Listing 21.3 in order to create the error. We've simply misspelled city (shown in bold) when getting the parameter value from the form data resulting in the employee city always being set to null. This is actually a common error because the parameters are accessed by string names which are not checked by the compiler. Of course constants can be used to define these strings in one place, but we didn't do that for our simple example. Now let's say that no matter how much we studied the code study, we couldn't find the error. Let's use the debugger to see if we can figure out what's causing the problem.

Listing 21.3 EmployeeManagementBean update method with error

```
public void update(Map args) {

    try {

        UnitOfWork.begin(); {

            EmployeeMapper mapper =
                (EmployeeMapper)MapperRegistry.getMapper(

            Employee.class);
```

```
Employee emp = (Employee)mapper.findByPrimaryKey(
    getParameter(args, "id"));

emp.setName(getParameter(args, "name"));

emp.setAge(Integer.parseInt(

    getParameter(args, "age")));

emp.getAddress().setStreet(

    getParameter(args, "street"));

emp.getAddress().setCity(

    getParameter(args, "cith"));

emp.getAddress().setState(

    getParameter(args, "state"));

emp.getAddress().setZip(getParameter(args, "zip"));

} UnitOfWork.getCurrent().commit();

} catch (MappingException e) {

    e.printStackTrace();

}

}
```

In order to debug anything running on the server, the server must first be started in debug mode. If the server is already running, stop it and start it back up in debug mode as described in step 3. WSAD automatically switches to the debug perspective.

Open the *EmployeeManagementBean.java* file, and scroll down to the *update* method. Set a breakpoint on the line that creates the *EmployeeMapper*. Now to run the *EmployeeManagementWeb* project, select an employee by clicking on the employee id link, and attempt to update the employee details. If the *Step-by-Step Debug* dialog is displayed, select *Disable step-by-step mode* and press *OK*. Then go to the Debug view, select the currently suspended thread in the Test Environment server process, and press the *Resume* button, press F8, or right click and select

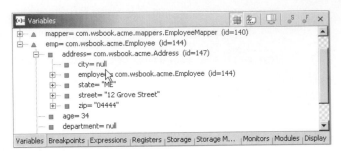

Figure 21.4 Debugging the EmployeeManagementBean–Variables view.

Resume. Step-by-step mode is on by default. You can change this default by turning off *Use step-by-step debug mode* on the *WAS Debug* preferences.

Now, single-step (press F6) through the code until you reach the line that sets the city field of the employee's address. You can examine the *emp* variable in the debugger *Variables* view. Expand the *emp* variable and its *address* field as shown in Figure 21.4 to see the *city* is currently null.

Single step again and notice that the *city* field didn't change in the *Variables* view. Let's see if we can figure out what's wrong. We'll start by seeing what value is being used in the *setCity* method. In the *EmployeeManagementBean.java* editor window, select the expression *getParameter(args, "cith")*, right click, and select *Display.* The debugger will switch to the *Display* view and display the selected text and the evaluated value. Notice it is still null. Maybe it was wrong in the arguments from the HTML form. You can see the arguments, but it's a little tricky. Go back to the debugger *Variables* view and expand the *args* field. You can see it's a Java Hashtable which makes it a little harder to see the values, but it's still possible. Expand the *table* field and look through the entries, expanding each one, until you see one whose key is "city." Then expand the *value* field as shown in Figure 21. 5 and note that it is "Bangor" as expected, not null.

This looks right. If it wasn't, or if you couldn't find the entry, then we might expect that the field name was wrong on the form and there is no city argument. So what's wrong? Go back to the debugger *Display* view and look at the expression. There it is! City is spelled wrong. Correct the spelling in the Display view to getParameter(args, "city"), select the text, and press the display button, or right click and select *Display.* You should see the result *(java.lang.String) Bangor* as expected. Now go back to the code for *EmployeeManagementBean*, and fix the spelling there too. Notice that when you saved the file, the server stopped the EmployeeManagement application, as well as its associated EJB jar and Web module. That's because the code changed. Now go back to the *Web Browser* and press the *Update* button on the employee details form again. Now you should see that the City: field on the employee details form is updated correctly.

The WSAD debugger has many more features, but we've only shown the basics that are generally useful for typical application debugging. The good news is that it's the same debugger that's used for any Java application. The turnaround time for finding and fixing a bug using the debugger isn't significantly increased just because we're debugging EJBs.

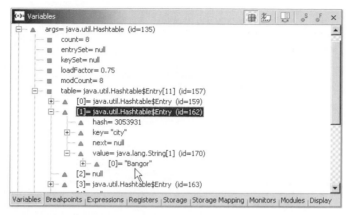

Figure 21.5 The args variable.

21.2.6   Step 6: Publish the enterprise application to an External WebSphere Server

Now you've completed the application and you've tested it to ensure it works. The next step is to publish the application to a remote production server where it can be accessed by others.

Using a remote WebSphere application server isn't much different than using the built in Test Environment. You just need additional information when creating a server instance and configuration that is specific to the remote installation. There are also considerations for starting and stopping a production server, or one that is used by more than one person. Otherwise the deployment process is the same: create a server instance and configuration, add the enterprise application to the server, configure any server resources such as data sources, publish the server, start it up, and run the application.

21.2.6.1   Create a Server Instance and Configuration

From the *J2EE Hierarchy* view, select the *Servers* or *Server Configurations* group, right click and select *New>Server and server configuration*. Enter a server name, expand *Server type: WebSphere version 5.0* and select *Remote server*. Click *Next*, enter the host name for the remote server, and click *Next* again. The next wizard page, shown in Figure 21.6, is used to specify the settings for the remote server. You will need to get this information from your server administrator. All pathnames on this wizard page are relative to the remote host. You will need to know the WebSphere installation directory shown as *D:\WebSphere\AppServer* in Figure 21.6. You can select *Use default WebSphere deployment directory*, but this is generally not a good idea when more than one user is deploying applications to the same server. This is because the original server configuration will be replaced by the configuration you are creating when the server is published, causing any applications that have been published by others to be removed. Your fellow developers won't like this very much. Instead, use a separate *WebSphere deployment directory* associated with either the set of applications you are deploying, or your user ID. This folder must

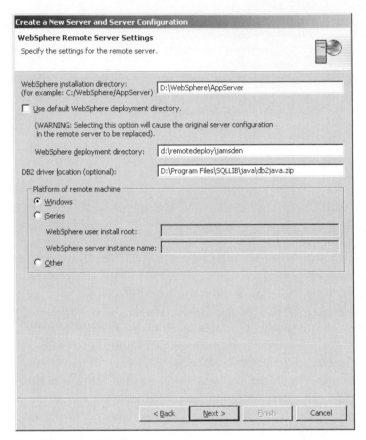

Figure 21.6 WebSphere Remote Server Settings.

exist on the server machine at the specified path. Since our application also uses DB2, you will also need to fill in the *DB2 driver location*. Enter all the required information and press *Next*.

In order to publish the application, WSAD needs to be able to copy files from projects in your local workspace to their corresponding location on the remote machine. This publish step is also used for publishing the built in Test Environment server, but most of the files don't need to be copied as they are accessed by the server in their original workspace locations. The next wizard page specifies a *Remote File Transfer Instance* that tells WSAD how to copy files from the local workspace to the server. You can either create a new file transfer instance, or use an existing one if the configuration is the same. There are two ways files can be copied: by using a remote file system mount and regular file copy facilities provided by the operating system, or by using ftp. Since we're going from a Windows client to a Windows server, we'll select the *Copy file transfer mechanism*, and press *Next*. The next wizard page, shown in Figure 21.7, is used to specify the particular settings for the file transfer mechanism. Fill in the *Remote file transfer name* to be a name that describes the source and target destinations and then fill in the *Remote*

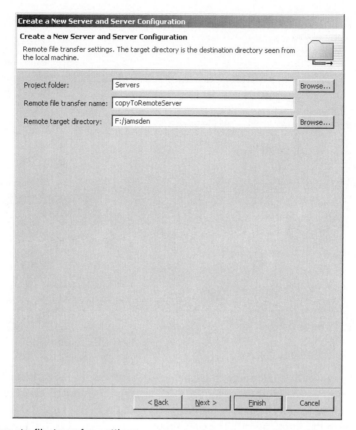

Figure 21.7 Remote file transfer settings.

target directory. This directory is the pathname to the directory on the local machine that is mounted to the *WebSphere deployment directory* specified in the WebSphere remote server settings as shown in Figure 21.6.

These mechanisms are stored in a project in the workspace in XML files called <*remote file transfer name*>.*rft*. By default, all server instances, configurations, and file transfer mechanisms are stored in a project called *Servers*, but you can put them in any project you want by creating a new *Server Project* or by creating a server instance and configuration in any other project.

21.2.6.2   Add the Enterprise Application to the Server

You can add enterprise applications to the server instance by selecting the remote server's configuration and invoking the *Add* menu. A submenu is displayed listing all the enterprise applications in the workspace that are not already added to the selected server instance. You can also add enterprise applications from the *Applications* tab in the server configuration editor.

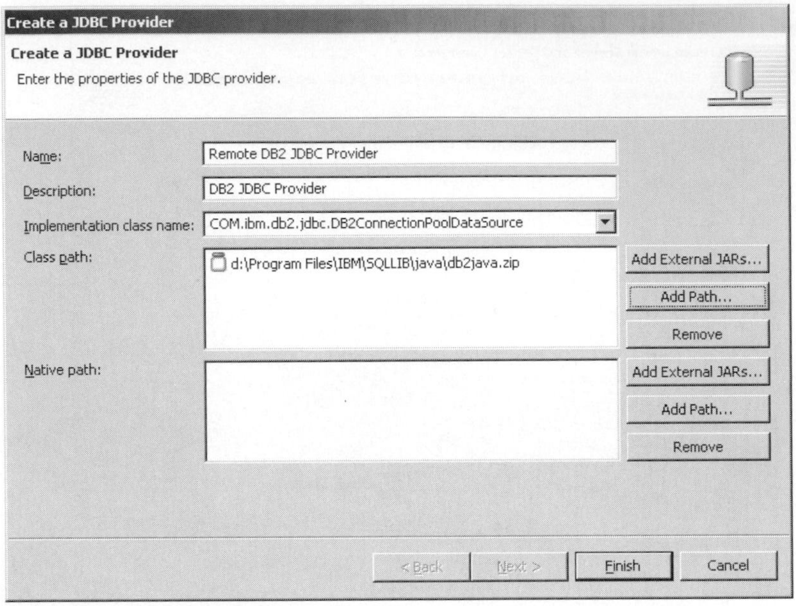

Figure 21.8 JDBC provider properties.

21.2.6.3 Configure the server

For our example, we need to configure a data source for accessing the EJPBOOK data source. Create the database on the server as described in Chapter 16. Then create a data source in the remote server configuration as described in Chapter 8, section "Configure the WSAD Test Environment and Publish the Application". The only thing that is different is that the classpath for the JDBC provider for DB2 needs to be specified as the location on the server, not the client machine. Make sure the classpath information is correct for your server implementation as shown in Figure 21.8. The *Class path* includes a path entry for *db2java.zip* to its location on the remote server. You can add this entry by pressing the *Add Path...* button and entering the correct path information as obtained from your server administrator.

21.2.6.4 Publish the Server

Generally there is no need to explicitly publish the server as WSAD detects changes in the enterprise applications that have been added to a server and automatically republishes as necessary. You can control this behavior in the *Server* preferences. Select *Window>Preferences...* and select *Server*. The preferences shown in Figure 21.9 are displayed. Make sure *Automatically publish before starting servers* is selected. You may also want to make sure *Automatically restart servers when necessary* is not checked to avoid unnecessarily restarting shared servers until all configuration changes have been completed.

You can also publish the server manually. Select the remote server in the *Server Configuration* view, or the *Servers* view, right click, and select *Publish*. WSAD will use the configured remote file transfer mechanism for that server to copy files associated with applications that have

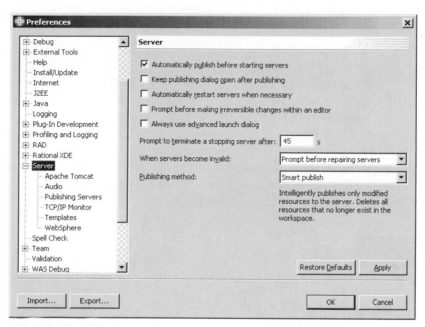

Figure 21.9 Server Preferences.

been added to that server configuration to their corresponding locations on the remote server, including any required dependent projects corresponding to utility JAR files.

21.2.6.5 Start Up the Server

You can start the remote server from the *Servers* view, just like you started the Test Environment. However, it is more likely that a production server will be managed by a server administrator in order to coordinate the activities of many developers and end users, all using the same server.

21.2.6.6 Run the Application

When using the menu item *Run on Server...* for a Web or EJB module, you will need to edit the project's *Server Preference* property and select the remote server as the default server, or select *Prompt for server before running* to select the server each time the project is run. Then just select the *EmployeeManagementWeb* project, right click, and select *Run on server...* . The index.html file is displayed in the integrated Web browser. Click on the *Browse Employees* link to see the employees in the database as shown in Figure 21.3. If you just created the database, the list will be empty. Create a few employees and view their details to ensure the enterprise application works as expected.

21.2.7 Step 7: Debug the Published Application Using the Distributed Debugger

Sometimes it is necessary to debug an application running on a remote server. This would be the case if you were running the application on an application server that is not integrated with WSAD. You can still use the built-in test environment to do most of the debugging, and then deploy to the remote server when the application appears to be working. This will save a lot of time because you can use source level debugging without needing to republish and restart the server on every change. However, there may be bugs that only show up when running on a remote server, so it's nice to be able to debug there too.

To debug on the remote server, simply restart the remote server in debug mode as described in Step 5: "Debugging EJBs Using the WSAD Debugger" above. Then debug exactly the same as you did for the built-in Test Environment.

21.3 Summary

In this chapter we've seen how to introduce a Service Layer into the application architecture to provide a more convenient API for client applications, and to provide better transaction management and access control based on the client use cases. We've covered how to deploy and test Enterprise JavaBeans using the WSAD. We've discovered how to start and stop servers and run test clients. Finally, we've covered how to use the powerful debugging tools built into the WSAD for Java environment to debug your EJBs. In the next chapters, we'll be exploring other ways we can exploit the J2EE architecture to simplify application development. In particular, we see how Container Managed Entity Beans can be used to eliminate all the tedious code we had to develop to implement the Data Mapper pattern for persisting our domain model.

CHAPTER 22

EJB Client Development

You've now seen many of the parts of building a system with J2EE and WebSphere, and some of the pieces may be starting to come together in your mind. You've seen how servlets and JSPs work, and you've even seen how EJBs can be used to provide remote access to business logic. What we haven't talked about are the ways to access that remote business logic, and under what conditions each would be used. While we've shown an example of using a servlet as an EJB client, we have not yet examined any other options for building EJB clients.

In this chapter we'll explore those other options and show you an example of building an additional type of J2EE module, a J2EE client application, and show you one way of deploying that client to use WAS. We show the parts of the architectural road map we touch on in this chapter in Figure 22.1.

However, before we delve into the details of building EJB clients, we'll need to backtrack and reexamine some basic J2EE concepts in order to set the stage for explaining when to use the J2EE client options. Remember that one of the key organizing principles of J2EE is that it is composed of two fundamental types of objects: Containers and components. Figure 22.2, adapted from the J2EE specification, shows the kinds of containers present in a J2EE application environment, and the components that are deployed in those containers.

One of the major choices you'll have to make in designing your applications is deciding what kind of client GUI you will be providing for your users. Making the right choice in this decision is the key to avoiding headaches later. The three basic choices you have for WebSphere are the same as in any J2EE application server: Servlets, Java client applications, and applets. You'll notice from Figure 22.2 that all three types of clients may access shared logic implemented as an EJB. We'll look at each of these in turn, and discuss the situations where they provide the most appropriate choice for a user interface to your back-end EJB logic.

465

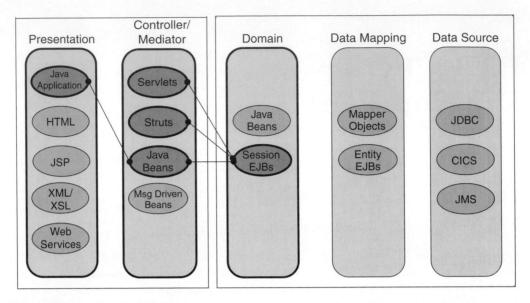

Figure 22.1 Architectural road map.

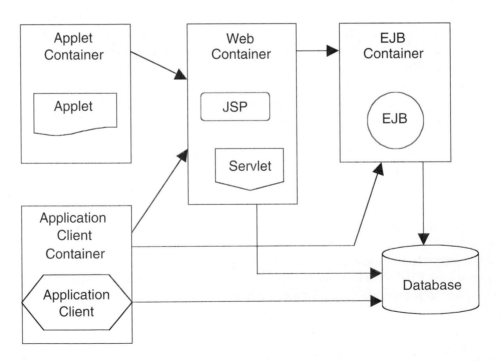

Figure 22.2 Containers and components.

22.1 Using Servlets as EJB Clients

While all three EJB client types are supported within WebSphere, the most common application architecture is when you use both servlets and EJBs to bring the full power of J2EE to bear on your business problem. As a result, WebSphere is highly optimized to take maximum advantage of servlets as EJB clients. While any of the three client types may work, developers usually choose servlets for one or more of the following reasons:

- Most computer-literate users expect applications to run in a browser and many user requirement documents are often written to the effect that it is assumed that the client presentation will be through a Web page. It is usually an uphill fight to convince users and business analysts that other client choices may, in fact, be better for a particular application.
- Browsers are ubiquitous, and nearly all of them will work with a standard, servlet-based Web application, although different browsers may have problems with applets, or application distribution mechanisms like WebStart due to different levels of support for Java or the Java plug-in.
- Servlets communicate to end-client browsers through HTTP. More firewalls support HTTP than any other protocol, making it easier to configure your corporate network to use a servlet client rather than an IIOP client like a Java application.
- In order to make a Java application client work with WebSphere, you must distribute a large set of WebSphere JAR files along with the files that make up your application. The mechanism for distributing these files differs based on the deployment method you choose (described later), but the size and difficulty of distributing them remains an issue.

So, as you can see, it is often easiest to build your clients as Java servlets. This is the approach we have taken in our case study, and it should be encouraged whenever possible. Nonetheless, there are some good reasons for building Java application clients, as you will see in the next section.

Now, you may be wondering, "What about JSPs?" We do not recommend ever using JSPs as EJB clients for two basic reasons:

1. JSPs are best thought of as view components only, as you may recall from our earlier discussions on MVC. If you try connecting to an EJB from a JSP then it is taking on model- or controller-like behavior. This kind of mixture of roles leads to maintenance difficulties.
2. A key problem with calling any type of back-end logic from a JSP is how to handle exceptions correctly. Basically, if you try to call an EJB remote method from a JSP scriptlet (or even from a tag library) you will find you will have to wrap that call in a `try...catch` block in order to catch the `RemoteException` that all remote methods must be able to throw. Likewise, you would have to catch exceptions from the EJB home, and any application-specific exceptions the EJB may throw—adding greatly to the complexity of the scripting code.

We recommend that only servlets (and helper classes called from servlets) call EJB methods. Handle any possible exceptions before calling the JSP so that you can know ahead of time exactly which page—results or error—to display.

22.2 Building Java Application Clients

If servlets make such a good clients, why would you ever want to build a Java application? There are some situations under which a desktop Java application is the best option:

- Regardless of how sophisticated you make your HTML and JavaScript, there are some styles of user interface that are simply impossible (or at least extremely difficult) to build using servlets and JSPs. In particular, applications that require drag-and-drop, direct-manipulation interfaces, or applications that require significant graphic display are not suited for HTML-based interfaces.

- Application clients can take advantage of some sophisticated performance features like prefetching and caching data that has not yet been displayed, but that will be displayed in the future. Also, application clients can take advantage of multithreading, and can be displaying one set of data while simultaneously fetching another.

- Applications that must be run in a disconnected mode when a network is not available are not well-suited for an HTML user interface based on servlets or JSPs. Examples of this kind of application include field data-entry applications (such as one an insurance agent might use when selling a new customer an insurance policy) and applications that allow users to look up data from a local database (such as a knowledge-base of auto repair information).

- Sometimes you need to run a business process on a schedule. For instance, you may have an account reconciliation process that needs to run every day at midnight. While it is possible to build this kind of application into the Web container (perhaps by starting a thread in a `Servlet.init()` method and then using `Thread.sleep()` to force the thread to sleep until time to run the reconciliation) that is usually not the best way to schedule a timed process. UNIX-based systems have the ability to start timed processes using the cron utility. Under Windows-based systems you can use the System Scheduler. In either case, it is often easiest to build a Java application client that has no user interface, and then invoke that client from the appropriate system utility.

If you are in any of these situations, you may want to use an application client. Building an application client would be substantially easier than trying to make a Servlet/JSP-based solution work in these instances.

22.3 Applet Clients in WebSphere

Few parts of Java emerged with as much hype, or disappeared with as little fanfare, as the Java applet. Once considered to be a crucial part of Java technology, movement in the Java technology space has lately delegated it to the status of an "also-ran" among Java programming models.

While initially heralded for its ability to provide easily accessible client code that was "write once run anywhere" and for innovative features like the built-in security sandbox, in fact, the Java applet has become a seldom-used part of the J2EE developer's tool box.

There are a few basic reasons for this, most of which derive from the difference between the perceived needs of the Web community and the actual needs of corporate developers. In short, they are:

- Applets were initially envisioned as being a way to provide rich client interfaces that HTML alone could not provide. However, in the intervening years since the release of Java 1.0, it has become clear to most developers that very rich user interfaces can be developed using HTML and JavaScript. As a result, often the same results can be achieved with less overhead (and at a lower cost) using these technologies than can be achieved using Java applets.

- The promise of "write once, run anywhere" was torpedoed by Microsoft's abandonment of Java on the browser and its subsequent refusal to upgrade its JVM beyond the antiquated 1.1.3 level. While the Java language has continued to evolve and improve its standard class libraries, the reality of having to work with a back-level environment has made it difficult for developers to conceive of writing applets that will run on Internet Explorer, by far the most popular Web browser. While this can be mitigated through the use of the Java Plug-in,[1] which provides an improved JVM to the browser, the perceived benefits of applet code downloading become faint when compared to the real worry of having to periodically upgrade the Java Plug-in across thousands of client desktops.

- The very abilities that business customers most want from their rich-client desktop applications, such as the ability to print to local printers, to save temporary data files to a disk, or to connect to more than one back-end machine for obtaining corporate data, are the very abilities that are most difficult to provide in an applet environment. While you can relax the security sandbox restrictions through signed applets, this remains an annoyance that many developers don't want to deal with.

As a result of these drawbacks, most corporate users have abandoned applets in favor of application clients. However, if you believe you can live within the limitations of an applet, and you are convinced that it is your best client programming option, how can you connect to back-end EJB resources in WebSphere from an applet? WebSphere supports applets that connect to EJBs only through a special version of the Java Plug-in, referred to as the WebSphere applet client. The WebSphere applet client provides the special environment necessary to allow applet clients to communicate to WebSphere servers via RMI-IIOP. No other Java Plug-in version can provide the necessary environment. The WebSphere plug-in must be installed on a client

---

1.   The Java Plug-in is an installation option for most JREs and JDKs, including the IBM JRE that comes as part of WebSphere.

browser either from the WebSphere installation CD or from a remote network location. Once you have installed the WebSphere applet client, there are some further restrictions that you must live within:

- The WebSphere applet client only works on some levels of browsers (Internet Explorer 5.0 and above, and Netscape Navigator 4.7 and above), and only in Windows NT and Windows 2000.[2]
- The WebSphere applet client is limited in that it does not support Secure Sockets Layer, which means that authentication information must pass in clear text.
- There are a number of runtime parameters that may need to be set up in the WebSphere applet client control panel before you can use the applet (see the InfoCenter for more details).
- As with all other applets developed using the Java Plug-in, you have to use the Object embed tag to load your applet (instead of the standard <applet> tag) and set up the properties file correctly.

In the end, this turns out to be a lot of work for the developer and probably not worthwhile unless you're primarily developing intranet applications where you completely control the client desktop. Since application clients don't solve the client update problem, and since applets are so limited in what they can do, what is a developer of Internet or extranet applications supposed to do?

Here is an option that may work. Instead of using RMI-IIOP to connect from your applet or application to your EJBs, consider communicating over HTTP using SOAP. In many respects this is probably an easier choice, since there are fewer restrictions, and it will work with nearly any JDK/browser combination. We will cover this option in more depth in Chapters 30 and 31.

If you do choose to write an application client that uses SOAP over HTTP, you can solve the download and update problem in a simple way by using one of a number of new technologies, like Sun's Java WebStart, that implement the Java Network Launch Protocol (JNLP) standard. Java WebStart provides you with the ability to dynamically download and update a standard application client program that does not suffer from the restrictions of an applet. Java WebStart is a feature of Sun's JDK 1.4; since WAS 5.0 is currently based on Java 1.3.1 it's not supported yet by IBM as an official WebSphere client technology. However, there is nothing to prevent you from using Sun's JDK 1.4 to develop your client applications (even inside WebSphere Studio, which allows you to configure the JDK for each Java project) and then simply package the applications with the necessary SOAP jar files.

---

2.   As of the time of this writing, the applet client was not yet certified to run on Windows XP.

22.4   Naming and the WebSphere Namespace

The EJB architecture formalizes how EJB clients obtain and effect remote references and local object (nonremote) instances from the server. Client access to EJB objects consists of the following steps:

- Obtain an initial naming context
- Look up an EJB home from the initial context using an EJB reference
- Use the home interface (creating, finding, or removing EJBs)
- Use the EJB

Before we move on to showing you how to write an EJB application client and how to deploy it in WebSphere, let's look at the first two steps (obtaining an initial naming context from JNDI and performing a name lookup) and discuss some issues on how to refer to JNDI in your applications.

JNDI (JAVA NAMING DIRECTORY INTERFACE)

Directory services have proven to be a convenient way to organize and partition information about user, resources, networks, machines, security information, and, in the case of Java, objects. In an attempt to make access to directory services independent of a specific service implementation, Sun, along with other leading industry vendors, defined the JNDI specification and reference implementation. Currently version 1.2 of the specification is available for download at the Java software Web site.

The JNDI implementation provides a standardized access API to directory service into a JNDI naming manager. This naming manager controls access to specific directory service implementations such as RMI, COS (CORBA Object Services) naming, or LDAP (Figure 22.3).

The JNDI service provider interface (SPI) allows directory/naming implementations supplied by different providers to be installed and accessed from Java in a neutral fashion. Java developers commonly access directory services through the interfaces defined in the `javax.naming` package. Context is a core interface in this package; it provides operations to maintain name-to-object bindings. The `javax.naming.directory` package supplies the ability to create directory objects and attribute objects that can be examined through the use of the DirectoryContext interface.

For more information regarding the JNDI specification, visit *http:// java.sun.com/jndi*.

J2EE product providers are responsible for supplying an interface to their particular distribution solution through JNDI. WebSphere has provided a particular implementation (SPI) that stores references to home objects in a potentially distributed naming service. The naming service exists within each managed server within a WAS deployment. In WebSphere ND this means each application server, each node agent, and the deployment manager.

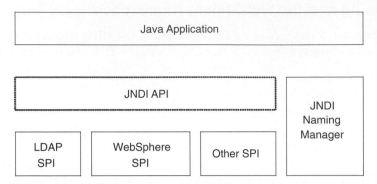

Figure 22.3 JNDI API.

These remote reference/name pairs are even shared across servers in a cluster through clustering in WebSphere ND. This is related closely to WebSphere's EJB load-balancing scheme. If an application server fails, WebSphere's node agent process will automatically restart the server and allow it to pick up the values of the registered home objects from the XML files when it comes back up.

When writing an EJB client the developer is responsible for obtaining a JNDI InitialContext which will be used to perform the lookup operation.

The recommended syntax for obtaining an InitialContext within J2EE application code is:

```
InitialContext initialContext = new InitialContext();
```

In previous versions of WAS, one would provide two properties to the InitialContext constructor (via a Properties object), `URL_PROVIDER` and `INITIAL_CONTEXT_FACTORY`. The `URL_PROVIDER` supplied a hostname and port to a particular naming server. In WebSphere 5.0, developers are discouraged from hard-coding a particular `URL_PROVIDER`. When an InitialContext is created with no parameters, WebSphere will automatically connect the application code to an appropriate name service. For applications running on WebSphere core, the naming service listens on Port 2809[3] within the application server. On WebSphere ND, the node agent listens on 2809 while the individual application servers listen on sequential ports starting with 9810 (see Figure 22.4).

Programmers with experience in other application servers, sometimes worry that client code needs to know a magic name server host to hook into WebSphere. In fact, any name server in the WebSphere cell will suffice. Within WebSphere, the naming service within an application server upon which an EJB is deployed is where the actual name/object reference is bound.[4] Be

---

3.   These ports numbers are the default values provided by WebSphere but can be changed if desired.

4.   If an EJB is installed within a cluster, the binding is replicated on each cluster member application server.

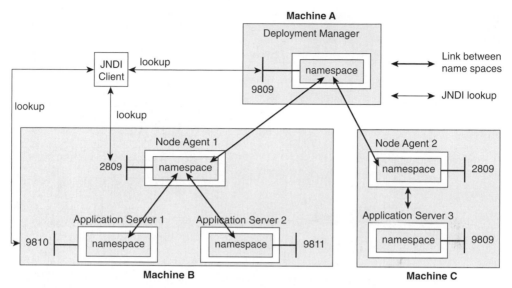

Figure 22.4 WebSphere ND namespace topology.

aware that when you are running in a clustered environment, your client code should be resilient enough to withstand the failure of a naming server. If your EJB client code runs within the application server, the naming service you will connect to will always be the one running in the same application server JVM as the servlet or JSP. Thus, you don't have to worry about naming server failure. If the naming service has failed, then so has your client code!

When you are writing a J2EE client application, then, you must provide additional information. With a J2EE client application, there must be a bootstrap server that the client will use as the initial naming service. This can be provided at the command line, or it can be provided using the URL_PROVIDER property to the InitialContext discussed earlier. What if the bootstrap server is itself not available? WebSphere provides a mechanism to deal with this. You can provide a set of application server hostnames and ports in the standard corbaloc format in the URL_PROVIDER property. So, in a J2EE application client designed to access EJBs running in a clustered environment, the recommended way to obtain an InitialContext is to use the following code:

```
import java.util.Hashtable;

    import javax.naming.Context;

    import javax.naming.InitialContext;

    ...

    Hashtable env = new Hashtable();
```

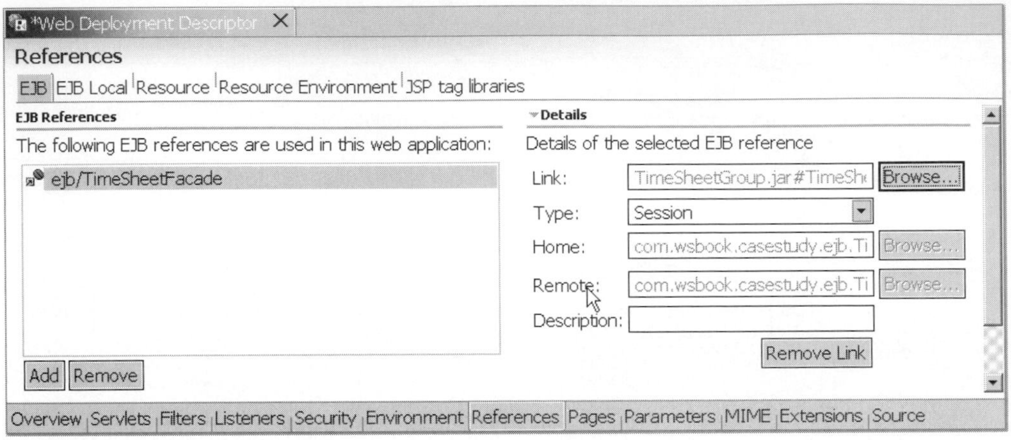

Figure 22.5 Creating an EJB Reference for Servlet Client.

```
   env.put(Context.INITIAL_CONTEXT_FACTORY,

"com.ibm.websphere.naming.WsnInitialContextFactory");

   env.put(Context.PROVIDER_URL, "corbaloc::host1:9810,:host2:9810");

   Context initialContext = new InitialContext(env);
```

Note that all of the servers for which you provide host name and naming port numbers must be members of the same cluster. Otherwise, unexpected results may occur. What will happen in this case is that the client will attempt to use the first host in the list as its bootstrap server. If it cannot be contacted, it will then try to use the second entry in the list.

What JNDI names are supplied by the developer within a ejb-jar.xml file and what are the runtime qualified names within WebSphere name service? What name or reference should a developer use in the EJB client code to look up an EJB home?

22.4.1 Names and Name Resolution

EJB clients should look up EJB homes via locally managed EJB references. EJB and resource references are component-local names for resources and are populated in the component local namespace which is prefixed with java:comp/env.

Figure 22.6 shows the Web deployment descriptor editor in WebSphere Studio. The References tab has been selected and a new EJB reference has been added. The name given is ejb/TimeSheetFacade and a link was selected to the TimeSheetFacade session bean. This selection prefills the entries for home, remote, and WebSphere bindings. A servlet Client in the TimeSheetWeb.war file would look up and use a reference to this session bean, using the following code:

```
InitialContext context = new InitialContext();

Object tsObj = context.lookup("java:comp/env/ejb/TimeSheetFacade");

TimeSheetFacadeHome tsHome = (TimeSheetFacadeHome)

    PortableRemoteObject.narrow(tsObj, TimeSheetFacadeHome.class);

TimeSheetFacade facade = tsHome.create();
```

Lookup is performed by the local application server's name service which then resolves the local reference to the JNDI name, in this case, ejb/com/wsbook/casestudy/TimeSheetFacadeHome.

EJB references can be created for each EJB client type. Figure 22.6 shows the Reference tab in WebSphere Studio's client deployment descriptor editor.

Within WebSphere Studio when EJB references are created, the JDNI binding is set. This can later be changed using WebSphere Studio, the WebSphere AAT, or from the WebSphere administration clients during deployment.

Then the real namespace name resolution will start to take place. For that discussion we will need to talk about names within the WebSphere naming service.

In the previous example, the TimeSheetFacade bean's home is bound into the JNDI namespace with a relative name, ejb/com/wsbook/casestudy/TimeSheetFacadeHome. This name is relative to the naming context associated with the application server(s) that the EJB is deployed to. The qualified name contains topological information as a naming prefix. For exam-

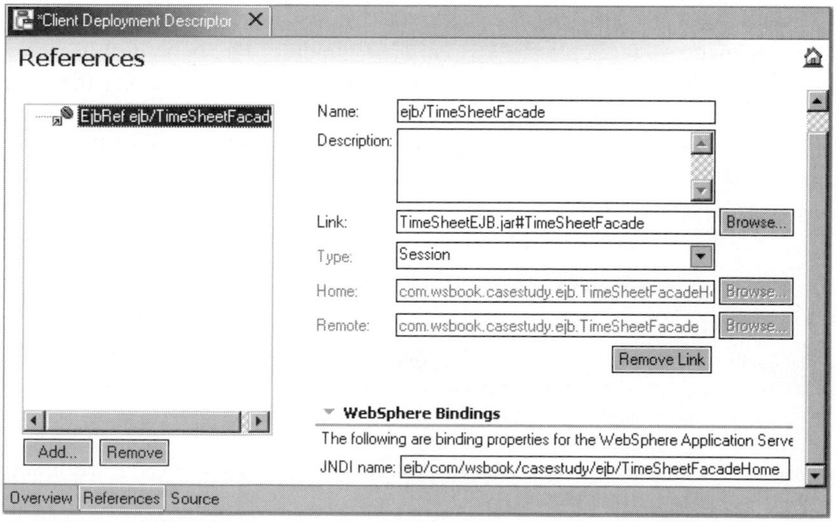

Figure 22.6 Creating EJB reference for application client.

ple, in a core installation, with the EJB installed on server1, running on a node called WSNode, the qualified name will be *cell/nodes/WSNode/servers/server1/ejb/com/wsbook/casestudy/TimeSheetFacadeHome*.[5] (Quite a mouthful, eh?)

Qualified names become important in an WebSphere ND deployment where the namespace is distributed. Consider a view on the WebSphere namespace shown in Figure 22.7. This shows the federated, distributed namespace rooted at *cell*. A cell, you recall earlier, is a grouping of nodes and corresponding managed servers for common administration.

Figure 22.7 is complex. The lower right-hand segment, labeled server roots, is where all of the application objects are bound. These transient bindings are initialized when the corresponding servers are started. The upper left-hand segment is a set of static bindings or links that represent the cell's topology and the atypical link(s) to foreign cells. These static bindings are available to *all* name servers in the cell.

Consider a deployment topology with an application client being launched on node *Y* connecting to an EJB deployed to ServerA running on Node Z. The application client container will have its BootstrapHost set to node Z[6] and the BootStrapPort set to the naming service port (P) of ServerA. The EJB reference will typically be bound to the qualified JNDI name for the EJB, e.g., *cell/nodes/Z/servers/ServerA/ejb/com/wsbook/casestudy/TimeSheetFacadeHome.* Here the JNDI name is resolved and the corresponding object is returned to the application client. Note that in the WebSphere ND environment, the lookup will not resolve unless the EJB reference is bound to the qualified name.[7]

22.5 Creating a Test Client

Now that you've seen the different types of available EJB clients, and you understand the situations in which each can be used, you're ready to start building your first application client in WebSphere Studio. Remember from the earlier description that each application client will be packaged into its own special application client J2EE module. The benefit of an application client module is that you can set up references scoped to the application using the capabilities of the application client deployment descriptor. A special requirement of an application client is that it requires that there be a Main class defined within the MANIFEST.MF file. That means there is a Java class with a `static void main(String[])` method that will be invoked when the application client is executed.

---

5.   A similar qualified name structure is used to access cluster members. For example, if TimeSheetFacadeHome were deployed to a cluster named ClusterE, then its qualified JNDI name would be: *cell/clusters/ClusterE/ejb/com/wsbook/casestudy/TimeSheetFacadeHome*.

6.   The syntax to run a J2EE client is: launchClient –CCBootstrapHost Z –BootstrapPort P MyClientApp.jar.

7.   There is a second type of name that can be used that will also always resolve. These are CORBA names. See WebSphere 5.0 InfoCenter for more details on CORBA name.

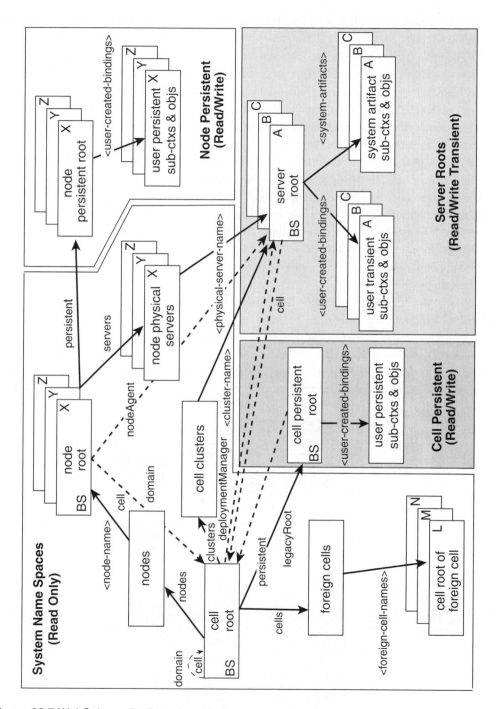

Figure 22.7 WebSphere distributed and federated namespace.

For this example, you'll build a simple application client for the RandomIDGenerator EJB you built in Chapter 20.

To begin you need to create an application client project. Do so by selecting *New > J2EE > Application Client Project*. On the first page of the application client project wizard, choose to create a J2EE 1.3 application client project. The creation wizard is very similar to the one shown in Figure 18.7. On the second page, enter the new project name, IDGeneratorClient, and select the existing enterprise application project UtilityEAR. You could press Finish at this point but your example will be referencing the UtilitiesGroup EJB project so you need to set up dependencies on the next page. On the next page, click the UtilitiesGroup.jar check box option as shown in Figure 22.8. This will cause the Java build path for the newly created IDGeneratorClient project to include the UtilitiesGroup project and it will update the MANIFEST.MF ClassPath entry for this new project to include the UtilitiesGroup.jar. This JAR is the module definition for the UtilitiesGroup project within the enterprise application. Thus, both the development time and runtime classpaths will be updated. After selecting Finish, the IDGeneratorClient project is created and it is added as a module to the UtilitiesEAR application.

Remember that an application client requires the definition of a Main class within the MANIFEST.MF file. This is quite easy to do and you can create the Java class and set it in the MANIFEST.MF file at the same time. To do so open the JAR dependency editor by selecting the IDGeneratorClient application client module from the J2EE Hierarchy view and select *Open With > JAR Dependency Editor* from the context menu. In the Main Class section at the bottom of the editor, click the *Create* button. This will launch a new Java Class wizard to create the Main class. The default source folder will be that of the application client project (e.g., IDGener-

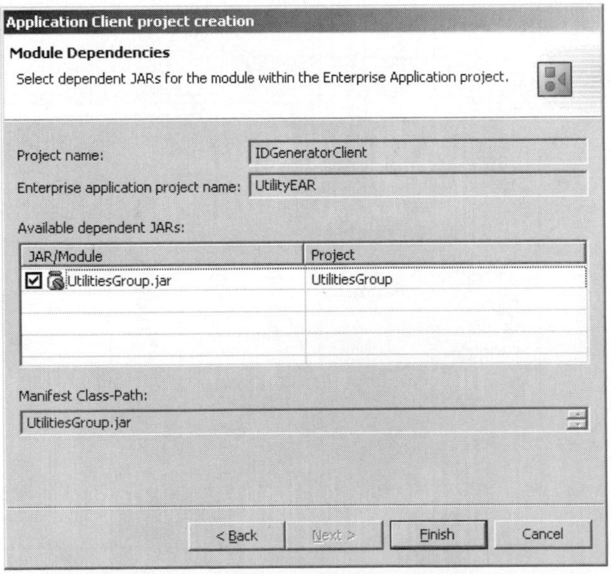

Figure 22.8 Module dependencies for a new application client.

atorClient/appClientModule) and we will enter the package as com.wsbook.casestudy.test. The name for the class will be IDGenerator test. After pressing finish, the IDGeneratorTest class is created and the Main Class field has com.wsbook.casestudy.test.IDGeneratorTest entered. Now you can save the JAR dependency editor.

To test the RandomIDGenerator Session bean from our new application client, your client will need to do a lookup of the home for the session bean. We could use the JNDI name defined for the RandomIDGenerator but that would require that we hard code the name in our main class. This is usually not a good idea since Java code would need to be updated whenever the JNDI name of the bean was changed. A better practice is to define an EJB reference to the session bean from the application client. Then the EJB reference name is unique to the application client and we can use this name for the lookup of the session bean's home. Then, if the JNDI name of the session bean changes, we only need to update our EJB reference and not Java source code.

To define the EJB reference open the application client deployment descriptor editor by selecting the IDGeneratorClient application client module from the J2EE Hierarchy view and select *Open With > Deployment Descriptor Editor*. Turn to the references page of the editor that is opened. Click the Add button to open the References wizard shown in Figure 22.9. We will select the EJB reference option to create an EJB reference. On the next page of the wizard, shown in Figure 22.10, enter the name for the reference as ejb/IDGenerator. We recommend you start the name with ejb because this is suggested by the EJB specification.

Next you will set the link. This is optional but if you know the exact EJB that you want to reference it is a good idea to set it to eliminate the need to fill in the rest of the fields on the wizard page. To do so, click the Browse button to open the link selection dialog shown in Figure 22.11. Select the RandomIDGenerator session bean from the UtilitiesGroup module within the

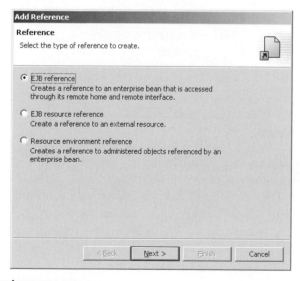

Figure 22.9 Create references page.

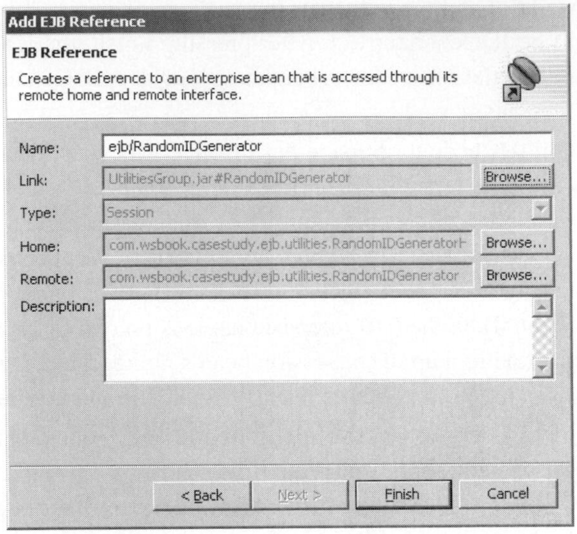

Figure 22.10 EJB Reference wizard page.

Figure 22.11 Link selection dialog.

UtilityEAR. You can only select an EJB to reference from within an EJB module for the same enterprise application that the application client belongs.

Notice that once a link is specified, the type, home, and remote are automatically entered based on the selected EJB. These fields are also disabled since you cannot change them unless you remove the link. After pressing the Finish button, the following EJB reference entry is added to the deployment descriptor of the application client. Now you can save the editor to commit your changes.

```
<ejb-ref id="EjbRef_1045965714288">

<description></description>

<ejb-ref-name>ejb/IDGenerator</ejb-ref-name>

<ejb-ref-type>Session</ejb-ref-type>

<home>com.wsbook.casestudy.ejb.utilities.RandomIDGeneratorHome</home>

<remote>com.wsbook.casestudy.ejb.utilities.RandomIDGenerator</remote>

<ejb-link>UtilitiesGroup.jar#RandomIDGenerator</ejb-link>

</ejb-ref>
```

Now you are ready to update your main class to add behavior to test the session bean. You now need to update the main method of the IDGeneratorTest class to the following:

```java
public static void main(String[] args) {

    try {

        InitialContext ctx = new InitialContext();

        //Lookup the home using ejb reference name

        RandomIDGeneratorHome home;

        Object ref = ctx.lookup("java:comp/env/ejb/IDGenerator");

        home = (RandomIDGeneratorHome)
PortableRemoteObject.narrow(ref,

        RandomIDGeneratorHome.class);

        //Create a RandomIDGenerator.

        RandomIDGenerator generator = home.create();

        //Print out 10 random IDs.

        for (int i = 0; i < 10; i++)

            System.out.println(generator.calculateID());
```

```
        } catch (NamingException e) {

            e.printStackTrace();

        } catch (RemoteException e) {

            e.printStackTrace();

        } catch (CreateException e) {

            e.printStackTrace();

        }

}
```

Before we move on, let's examine some of the salient points of this example. Remember from our earlier discussions that there are four steps to using an EJB:

- Obtain an initial naming context
- Look up an EJB home from the initial context using an EJB reference
- Use the home interface (creating, finding, or removing EJBs)
- Use the EJB

In our example, we're using the simplest form of the first step; obtaining the initial context with its default, no-argument constructor. When we run this client inside WebSphere Studio, this will point the bootstrap host and port to the WTE so the naming server used will be the one inside the application server running in the WTE.

In the second step, we're looking up the EJB remote reference we declared in the client deployment descriptor by using the name java:comp/env/ejb/IDGenerator. The JNDI prefix java:comp/ indicates that you are referring to a reference declared in the deployment descriptor as opposed to a JNDI name that comes from the naming service.

Another issue worth pointing out is found in this line of code:

```
home = (RandomIDGeneratorHome) PortableRemoteObject.narrow(ref,

RandomIDGeneratorHome.class);
```

Recall that in Chapter 20 we used a local home interface to access our EmployeeManagementHome from within our servlet. As we've stated several times, local homes and local interfaces should be the preferred way to access EJBs from servlets due to the performance improvements provided by local EJBs. However, here we are building a J2EE client. We cannot use a local interface since the client code will not be running within the same JVM as the EJB. Instead, we must use a remote home and a remote interface.

Remote homes require an additional step (mandated by the EJB specification) to clarify how to treat the reference obtained from JNDI. Since the reference is a remote object, the `Por-tableRemoteObject.narrow()` method is required to obtain a true proxy that implements the home interface. Thus, in addition to casting the result to RandomIDGeneratorHome, we must also narrow the result to that type using `PortableRemoteObject.narrow()`. This is required in every instance where you obtain a remote EJB reference from JNDI. Avoiding this is yet another advantage of using local interfaces where that is possible.

After casting and narrowing the home, it is a simple matter of creating the EJB with the `create()` method, then using the EJB reference. The only thing to note is that (as we showed in the previous chapter) you must remember to catch all of the checked exceptions that can be thrown by the methods used.

Now that you are done creating all of the classes that are necessary for the enterprise application, you must generate the deploy code before running on the server. The deploy code generation will create all required EJB deploy code as well as the necessary RMIC code for accessing from a remote client. To do this, select the UtilityEAR enterprise application from the J2EE Hierarchy view and select *Generate Deploy Code*. This will generate deploy code for all contained EJB modules. You can also generate deploy code for individual EJB modules or even individual EJBs.

It's now time to run your UtilityEAR within a WebSphere 5.0 server. To do so, select the UtilityEAR enterprise application from the J2EE Hierarchy view and select *Run on Server*.

To test your application client, use an application client launcher to run it. Why can't you just select the *Run on Server* item from the context menu as you have done in the past to test servlets, JSPs and EJBs? Put simply, the client does not run on the server; it runs in a separate JVM and must be invoked separately. Why can't you run your new class as a standard Java application? Because we need to run our application as a J2EE application client within the WebSphere client container. Properly setting up the client container is what the application client launcher does.

To set up an application client launcher select *Run > Run* from the menu bar. This launches the Launch Configurations wizard shown in Figure 22.12. Select WebSphere 5.0 application client from the list and click the *New* button. Then set the Name of your launcher to IDGeneratorTest and specify the UtilityEAR as your enterprise application. To pass arguments to the main class, set them on the Arguments tab of the launcher. Now click the *Run* button to launch the application client for the UtilityEAR enterprise application.

Listing 22.1 is the sample output from our run. The first portion is the startup information output by the application client environment. The last 10 integers are the results of the actual test as it printed out 10 IDs that were calculated from the RandomIDGenerator session bean. Compare your output to this and make sure that this is what you see.

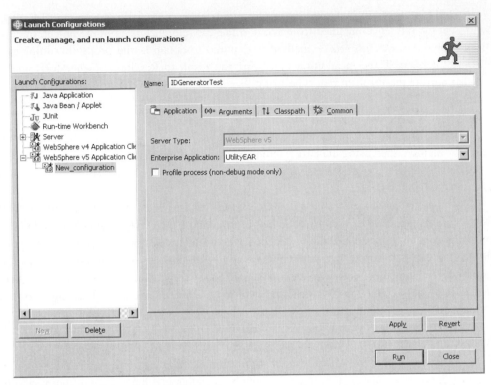

Figure 22.12 Launch configuration wizard.

Listing 22.1 Random IDGenerator sample output

```
IBM WebSphere Application Server, Release 5.0

J2EE Application Client Tool

Copyright IBM Corp., 1997-2002

WSCL0012I: Processing command line arguments.

WSCL0001I: Command line, property file, and system property arguments

resolved to:

        File to launch        = D:/dcb/WAS_book/current/data/UtilityEAR

        CC Property File      = null

        Client Jar File       = <default>

        Alternate DD          = null
```

```
        BootstrapHost              = BERGT30

        BootstrapPort              = <default>

        Trace enabled              = false

        Tracefile                  = null

        Init only                  = false

        Classpath Parameter        = null

        Security Manager           = disable

Security Manager Class  = Not used. -CCsecurityManager=disable

Security Manager Policy = Not used. -CCsecurityManager=disable

        Exit VM                    = false

        Soap Connector Port        = null

Application Parameters  =

WSCL0013I: Initializing the J2EE Application Client Environment.

WSCL0025I: Binding EJB reference object:

JNDI name: ejb/IDGenerator ==> ejb/com/wsbook/casestudy/ejb/utilities/

RandomIDGeneratorHome @ corbaloc:iiop:BERGT30

Description:

WSCL0031I: The object was bound successfully.

WSCL0600I: Binding HandleDelegate object.

WSCL0031I: The object was bound successfully.

WSCL0900I: Initializing and starting components.

WSCL0910I: Initializing component:

com.ibm.ws.activity.ActivityServiceComponentImpl

WSCL0911I: Component initialized successfully.

WSCL0901I: Component initialization completed successfully.
```

```
WSCL0035I: Initialization of the J2EE Application Client Environment has

completed.

WSCL0014I: Invoking the Application Client class

com.wsbook.casestudy.test.IDGeneratorTest

1102768142

2146514068

263242487

1850530316

856817741

76407504

1979926623

1080449668

304490551

1460207340
```

22.6 Deploying Application Clients in WebSphere

Now that you've built and tested an application client inside WSAD, you're ready to learn how to deploy and invoke an application client outside of WSAD. WebSphere provides three different ways of deploying application clients: the J2EE client container, the pluggable application client, and the thin application client.

The J2EE client container is a full-featured client container that, as the name suggests, is fully compatible with the J2EE 1.3 specification for application clients. You install it on a client machine through an installation option on the WebSphere application client CD. J2EE compliance means that your application client program must be packaged within an application client JAR file with the appropriate application client deployment descriptor, and that that JAR file must be located within an EAR file. WebSphere's J2EE client container is invoked through the launchClient command. launchClient is simply a .bat file that invokes a Java program that can start J2EE application clients placed in deployed .ear files .

One of the key features of the J2EE client container is that it includes IBM's JRE—which (as mentioned earlier) contains all of the classes necessary to communicate with an EJB deployed in WAS over RMI-IIOP.

The pluggable application client is more lightweight than the application client container and also downloadable (which is not true of the application client container). It is comprised of a set of JAR files you can copy to the client. (To obtain these JAR files you must install them initially off of the WebSphere installation CD.) The pluggable application client is meant to install on top of Sun's JRE. The assumption is that if a client machine already has Sun's JRE installed on it, then this will be a smaller installation than that of the full J2EE application client container. What it allows you to do in your application client is to connect to EJBs directly through the use of RMI-IIOP. It does not, however support the use of local references in the application since it is not a full J2EE client container and thus does not contain an application client deployment descriptor.

Finally, the thin application client is much like the pluggable client but includes the IBM JDK. You do not have to have Sun's JRE already installed on the client machine. The same programming model restrictions apply, however. Likewise, when developing for the pluggable application client, your application client code must provide the InitialContext factory class name and location directly—there are no defaults. Thus you have to fully specify paths to JNDI-named objects like EJB homes.

For more information on using the pluggable application client or the thin application client, refer to the WebSphere InfoCenter. We will discuss the J2EE client container more in-depth in the following section.

22.7 Deploying and Running the EJB Client to the WebSphere Client Container

In order to run your EJB client outside of WSAD you'll need to first install the WebSphere client container. This is shipped as a separate part of the WebSphere installation; it's not installed unless you explicitly choose to do so.

In a development system, you will normally install the application client to the same root directory where WebSphere is installed. That is, it will be installed to <Install Root>/WebSphere/AppClient if WebSphere is installed to <Install Root>/WebSphere/AppServer. If you're installing the application client on a client system, then it would install to the same directory, although there would be no corresponding AppServer directory.

Earlier we described how the J2EE application client module can be packaged inside an EAR file. You've also seen how when we created the IDGeneratorClient application client project in WSAD that we associated it with the UtilityEAR enterprise project, which was also the enterprise project with which the UtilitiesGroup EJB project was associated.

As you can surmise from your experience with J2EE packaging, this association defines a containment structure for an EAR file that can be exported to disk for deployment in WAS. What confuses some people is the fact that the very same EAR file (containing both the application client JAR file and the EJB-JAR file) is what is used by the WebSphere application client container to run the application client itself. This strikes some as overkill—why deploy the entire EJB-JAR file to a client machine? The fact is that WebSphere does this because the J2EE specification doesn't leave any other options. For instance, in VisualAge for Java, IBM used to provide a menu option to generate an EJB client JAR which contained only the remote stubs and the home and remote interfaces from an EJB-JAR file, and did not include the implementation classes. This function was provided outside of the EJB specification.

When application clients were officially introduced in J2EE 1.2, the IBM tooling moved to what was the only J2EE-supported configuration, which was packaging an application client JAR with the entire EJB-JAR inside an EAR. That rather heavyweight solution (although specification-compliant) is why the other two client deployment options (thin clients and pluggable clients) were developed. Be warned that those are WebSphere-specific and provide features outside the J2EE specification.

This problem of delivering client-side EJB code was addressed in EJB 2.0. WSAD currently does not support the creation of EJB client JARs. It does, however, support defining an EJB project as a Java project utility JAR within the EAR containing the application client. This is a poor man's support of an EJB client JAR. The issue with this approach (as with placing the entire, standard EJB-JAR in the EAR with the client) is that it contains more than the client JARs.

Now that you understand what you'll be using to run the application client, you're ready to export the UtilityEAR project and run its contained application client using the WebSphere client container. But first we need to decide where to export our EAR file. Unlike installing an EAR file into WebSphere application server, where there is a standard installedApps directory to hold your applications, there is no such standard directory for clients. So, for our purposes, we will create a directory called WebSphereClients from the root of your hard drive to hold the EAR file containing your application client.

So, begin by selecting the UtilityEAR project in the J2EE perspective and then select *File > Export*.[8] In the Export selection dialog, select EAR file and press Next. This will bring up the EAR Export page. In the drop-down under What resources do you want to export? select UtilityEAR. Finally, in the combo box under Where do you want to export resources to? type <Install Root>/WebSphereClients/Utility.ear (substituting your root drive [e.g., C:] or root directory for <Install Root>). Then press Finish. WebSphere will create the WebSphereClients directory and the Utility.ear file and place it in that directory.

Before you can launch your application client, we need to make sure that the EJB container that you will connect to is running. Select the Servers tab at the bottom-right corner of the J2EE perspective. Examine the status of the WTE that you created in Chapter 20. If it is not running, press the Run button (with the running-man icon) to start the server. Make sure that the open for e-business message appears before you move on to launching your client.

Launching an application client with `launchClient` is easy to do. You simply change your directory to the <Install Root>/WebSphere/AppClient/bin directory and type launchClient at the command prompt, followed by the name of a deployed *.ear* file. Other command-line options

8.   You can also select the enterprise application in the J2EE Hierarchy view and select the Export EAR File… context menu.

allow you to specify which of multiple application client *.jar* files contained in an *.ear* file to use. If you invoke the .bat without any parameters it will display the list of options.

Note that `launchClient` is case-sensitive. If you see an error message stating it can't find the client *.jar* file, unzip your deployed application *.ear* file and verify that the capitalization of the client *.jar* file name on the command line is the same as it is in the *.ear* file.

To complete your exercise, open a windows command prompt and change your current directory to <InstallRoot>/WebSphere/AppClient/bin. Then type `launch Client <Install Root>\ WebSphereClients\Utility.ear` and watch the console output. It should be almost exactly the same as what was shown in the previous section when you ran the application client inside WSAD.

22.8 Some Design Points about EJB Clients

One of the easiest traps for a developer new to a technology like servlets or EJBs to fall into is to assume that the way a simple example is built is the same way all programs using that technology *should* be built. Hopefully we've been able to convince you so far in this book that this is not true—you need to plan your architecture ahead of time to deal with issues of scalability, performance, and maintainability.

There are a few general points that we should make about the last example that you should *not* do in your own EJB client code:

- Don't create an InitialContext for every home lookup. Creating an InitialContext is a fairly slow operation. While an InitialContext cannot be shared among multiple threads of execution (at least according to the Sun specification), you should try at the very least, to limit the number you create to one per thread by passing it around as necessary through method parameters or a ThreadLocal variable. However, a better solution is to locate and cache the home references all at once to simply avoid the issue.
- You don't want to create and drop an EJB home reference after one use. Unlike InitialContexts, home references can be shared among multiple object types or threads of execution, so you should consider using the Singleton pattern[9] to share them. Although these are cached within the container in WebSphere 5.0, it is a good practice to not repeatedly look up (and narrow) the home objects.
- Try to avoid generically catching Exception . Your code should usually trap and handle each potential exception type individually—often you will want to do something different for each type of exception that may occur. Resort to catching Exception only when the total code bulk of trapping each exception type becomes too unwieldy, or when you really do want to do the same thing no matter what exception is thrown. If you have too many of your own exceptions, consider making them descend from a special root exception class for your project or company and trapping that instead. If you do

9.   From [Gamma]

that, you should consider the idiom of wrapping exceptions, by which you write an abstract MyException class that can contain another exception. When you throw the new wrapped exception you add the previous exception into the new one. Your exceptions then subclass this new class. This allows you to preserve the original stack trace. Note that this feature has been added to J2EE 1.4 (which will not be supported until WAS 5.1) and that WebSphere's internal exception classes already implement this idiom.

- Don't try to do all of the client steps (obtaining the initial context, getting the home, creating the EJB, sending messages, etc.) in a single method. Use functional decomposition to split these steps into multiple methods so that each does only a single thing. This will make maintenance and debugging simpler.

- Last, but certainly not least, don't do *everything* in *one* class. Follow the MVC architecture that splits the responsibility for presentation, user request handling, and model behavior into different classes. The same layering principle applies to EJB clients as well. In a later chapter we will describe how to build layered systems that hide the EJB implementation details from the objects manipulated by the servers.

22.9 Summary

Now you've seen the pros and cons of building the different types of EJB clients. You've also seen examples of a servlet EJB client (in Chapter 21) and a trivial EJB application client in this chapter. You've learned about the different ways to deploy your application clients, and also seen some best practices for writing EJB clients, regardless of their type. In the next chapter you'll move on to learning about the next major portion of EJB development—learning about how CMP works.

CHAPTER 23

Simple CMP Entity Beans

In Chapter 19 you read that there are three types of EJBs supported by WebSphere—MDBs, session beans, and entity beans. You have already learned a lot about how session beans work, and how they are developed in WebSphere Studio for deployment into WAS. Now it is time to discover another part of the puzzle—how CMP entity beans work, and how they provide access to persistent data stored in a relational database.

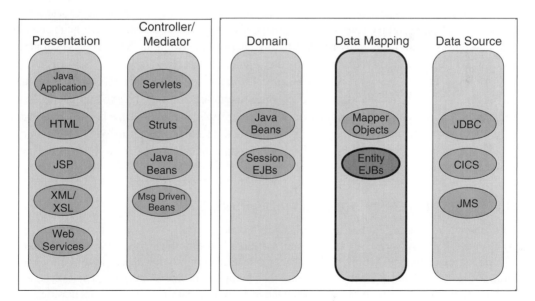

Figure 23.1 Container managed entity beans within road map.

23.1   Entity Bean Basics

Earlier, in the chapter on EJB architecture, we discussed how entity beans could provide access to data sources like a relational database such as DB2, or a transaction processing system like CICS or IMS. Remember that there are two basic types of entity EJBs: BMP (sometimes called self-managed persistence EJBs) and CMP.

CMP entity beans handle the details of the mapping between the object representation of your data (the EJB attributes) and the way in which your persistent data are stored (for example, as columns in a relational database table) themselves. They can accomplish this because they are generated by a tool set that has knowledge of both the data source that you want to use, and the structure of the data in that data source (like a table schema).

Because they handle this mapping themselves, they are easier to build, since most of the work is done by code generated by the EJB container. The trade-off for this ease of use comes in the fact that each EJB container (like WebSphere) supports only predetermined data sources. For instance, in WebSphere 5, CMP beans support Cloudscape, IBM DB2, Informix, Oracle, Microsoft SQL Server, and Sybase database types.

BMP entity beans make handling the details of mapping to a particular data source the responsibility of the bean developer. The BMP specification provides a set of hooks that user-defined code can tie into. These hooks are implemented as a set of callback methods in the Bean class. The developer of a BMP bean is guaranteed that these methods will be called at particular points in the EJB life cycle, but is responsible for providing the implementation of these methods, which will store and retrieve data from the persistent store. As a result, BMP beans can be written to retrieve data from and store data to any data source available through Java, but at the cost of more effort spent in programming by the bean developer.

As EJBs mature, more tools will become available to support a wider variety of data sources through CMP. So, a valid design decision is to employ a mix of the two approaches in an application. As time goes on, beans that must today be implemented as BMP beans can be later implemented as CMP beans. For example, CMP beans developed today in WebSphere Studio can be made to connect to a much wider variety of data sources and perform much better than those EJBs created with earlier versions of the tools.

23.2   CMP in WebSphere and WebSphere Studio

Part of the magic of CMP comes from the fact that code generation tools can take advantage of knowledge of the structure of both the persistent data and the objects that map to that data to generate mapping code. However, with that sophistication comes hard choices in tool implementation. Defining a sophisticated object-relational mapping is not something that everyone is capable of. It requires a high level of knowledge in both relational database technology and object design to make the mapping work in the best way.

The EJB specification defines three roles applicable to the development of an EJB:

- The enterprise bean provider, who designs the EJB interfaces and writes the business logic in the EJB.
- The application assembler, who combines EJBs into applications and subsystems to meet specific user requirements.
- The deployer, who deploys the enterprise beans in a specific operational environment.

IBM has developed a suite of tools that provides considerable flexibility to developers acting in each of these three roles. You have to understand each role in order to understand how IBM's tool strategy for CMP EJBs works.

For instance, an EJB deployer is expected to have knowledge of a particular operational environment, including what relational databases are available to store EJB data. On the other hand, an enterprise bean provider or application assembler is expected to have much more detailed information on what database schemas exist that may need to be mapped to EJBs.

To address these two roles and their goals and expectations, IBM has provided two ways of developing CMP EJBs:

- WAS provides a simple CMP implementation that maps an entity EJB to a single relational database table with a straightforward column to attribute mapping (top-down mapping which is described in Chapter 24).
- WebSphere Studio provides tools that allow more complex CMP mappings from columns in multiple relational database tables to a single entity EJB. It also supports EJB inheritance.

Both WebSphere Studio and WAS support association relationships between entity EJBs using Container Managed Relationships (CMRs) as defined in the J2EE 1.3 specification. More details on CMRs later in this, and in the following chapters.

In an environment where all that is needed is a very simple entity bean mapping, WebSphere's basic CMP entity bean support is adequate. An enterprise bean provider can deliver an ejb-jar file containing only the basics parts of the entity bean (the remote and home interface, the bean implementation class, the key class, and the deployment descriptor). The deployer can then take this jar file and use WebSphere's built-in deployment tools to automatically generate the necessary persistence code and automatically create a database table to contain the bean information.

In a more complex environment where multiple-table mappings, associations, relationships, or inheritance is needed, the enterprise bean provider or the application assembler will have to work within the WebSphere Studio tool suite to provide a mapping between the EJBs and the relational database tables in which the EJB's data is stored. The developer will then deliver a jar file, which contains the code for the EJBs already generated for the deployer, who will then install the jar file without having to generate the deployment code.

 The deployment tool within WAS is identical to the deployment mechanism in WebSphere Studio. Therefore, any complex mapping generated in WebSphere Studio 5.0 can be deployed within WAS 5.0. You also have the option of generating the deployment code in WebSphere Studio and installing the enterprise application in WAS without any further assembly.

In this and succeeding chapters, you will learn about both types of mappings—simple and complex, and how WAS and WebSphere Studio interoperate to make CMP beans work.

23.3 Creating a CMP EJB Using WebSphere Studio

As you saw in Chapter 20, WSAD has a first-class EJB development environment. The mechanics of creating a CMP EJB are not much different than those for creating a session bean, with the exception, of course, of the need to identify CMP fields and how the key for the bean will be constructed.

In this section we will go through the steps for creating the DepartmentEJB CMP bean that is discussed later in the chapter.

Since you are just beginning to experiment with EJBs, we suggest that you start with an empty workspace and follow along as we create and test the DepartmentEJB bean. This bean is included as part of the case study implementation application in the CD.

We will assume that you have WSAD started on an empty workspace and can follow along. If you don't, you can still read along and follow the process.

Some of the directions to create the EJB will be somewhat terse, as you have already read about the basics; if you get stuck refer to Chapter 20 for detailed instructions.

As you saw in Chapter 20, EJBs are created in EJB projects and EJB projects are part of an enterprise application project. This is part of the J2EE module containment hierarchy and Web-Sphere Studio will enforce it.

The first thing to be done is to create an EJB project named LearningEJB. This project should be under an EAR project named LearningEAR.

To create the EAR project and EJB project select: *File > New > Enterprise Application Project* from the main menu. On the first page of the wizard make sure you click Create J2EE 1.3 Enterprise Application Project, then Next.

Name the EAR project LearningEAR and the EJB Module LearningEJB. Uncheck the Application client module and Web module check boxes (see Figure 23.2). Click *Finish*.

Switch to the J2EE perspective. The J2EE Hierarchy view should now show the new enterprise application and EJB module you just created (Figure 23.3).

Under EJB Modules select the LearningEJB module, from its context menu click: *New > Enterprise Bean*. This is the same wizard you used before when you created the Session bean. The first and second pages of the wizard are identical. However, on the second page select the last radio button, Entity Bean with container-managed persistence (CMP) fields. Also select CMP 2.0 Bean. Name the bean DepartmentEJB.

In order to keep the generated EJB code separate from the developer's code, the source folder should be different than ejbModule. Enter source for Source folder. Enter `com.wsbook.casestudy.ejb` for the package name. Click *Next* (Figure 23.4).

From this point on the wizard is different than that of the session bean. The main difference on this page is at the bottom where the CMP fields, or attributes, are defined and displayed. See Figure 23.5.

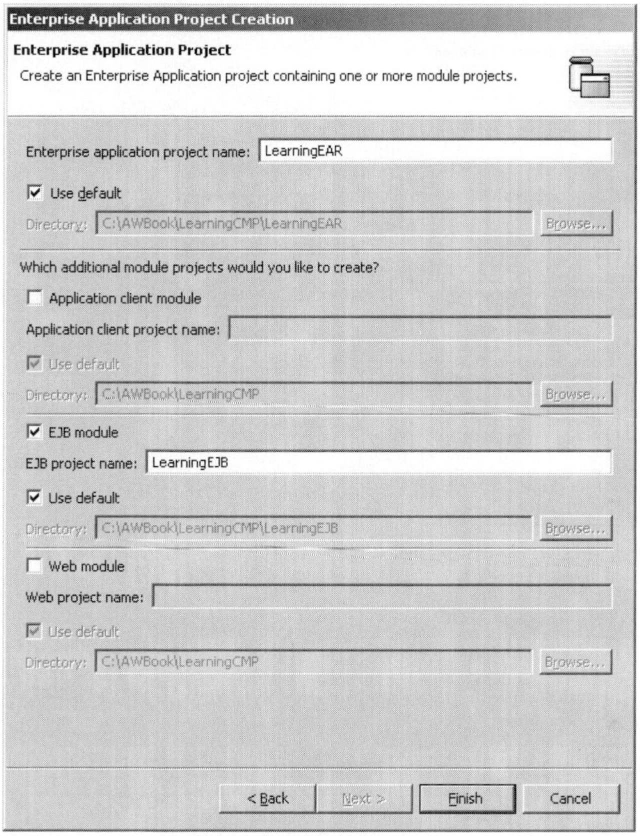

Enterprise Application Project Creation

Enterprise Application Project

Create an Enterprise Application project containing one or more module projects.

Enterprise application project name: LearningEAR

☑ Use default

Directory: C:\AWBook\LearningCMP\LearningEAR   Browse...

Which additional module projects would you like to create?

☐ Application client module

Application client project name:

☑ Use default

Directory: C:\AWBook\LearningCMP   Browse...

☑ EJB module

EJB project name: LearningEJB

☑ Use default

Directory: C:\AWBook\LearningCMP\LearningEJB   Browse...

☐ Web module

Web project name:

☑ Use default

Directory: C:\AWBook\LearningCMP   Browse...

   < Back   Next >   Finish   Cancel

Figure 23.2 Creating the EAR and EJB projects.

J2EE Hierarchy   ×

- Enterprise Applications
  - LearningEAR
    - Modules
      - LearningEJB.jar
    - Project Utility JARs
    - Utility JARs
- Application Client Modules
- Connector Modules
- Web Modules
- EJB Modules
  - LearningEJB
- Databases
- Servers
- Server Configurations

Figure 23.3 J2EE Hierarchy view with new projects.

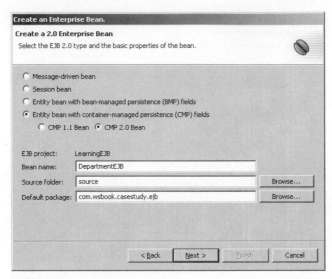

Figure 23.4 Defining the DepartmentEJB.

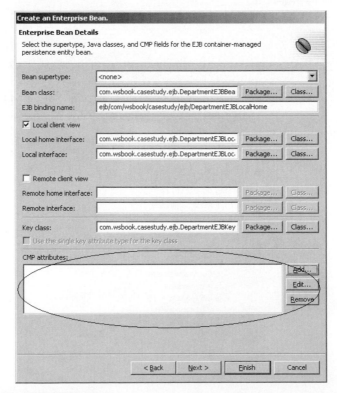

Figure 23.5 Adding CMP attributes.

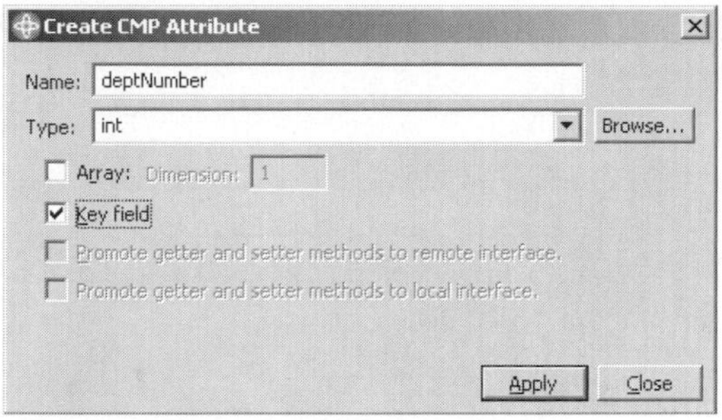

Figure 23.6 Defining the key for DepartmentEJB.

The DepartmentEJB has two CMP fields:

- int deptNumber
- String name

The EJB key is `deptNumber`. Let's define these CMP fields. Click *Add*. The create CMP attribute wizard opens, Figure 23.6.

CMP attributes are defined one at the time; you select a name and a type for each one. If this particular attribute is part of the key for the EJB, you also check the Key field check box. Define the `deptNumber_`attribute as a key field as seen in Figure 23.6. Click *Apply*, which leaves the wizard open to facilitate entering more attributes.

Create a CMP attribute of type String with a Name of name, which is not part of the key. When defining a nonkey attribute you are given a chance to promote the getter and setters for the attribute to the remote or local interfaces, this can save your doing this later in the development process. Only the check boxes for the interfaces you chose in the previous page of the wizard will be enabled here (Figure 23.7).

Since this is the last attribute we need, click *Apply*, then *Close*. In Figure 23.8 you can see the attributes on the create an enterprise bean wizard.

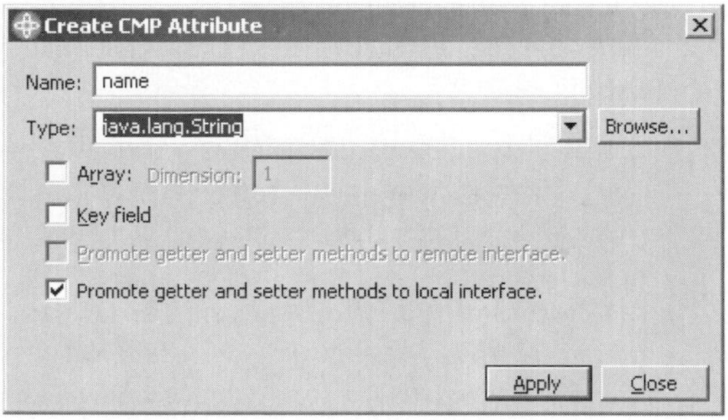

Figure 23.7 Defining nonkey attributes for DepartmentEJB.

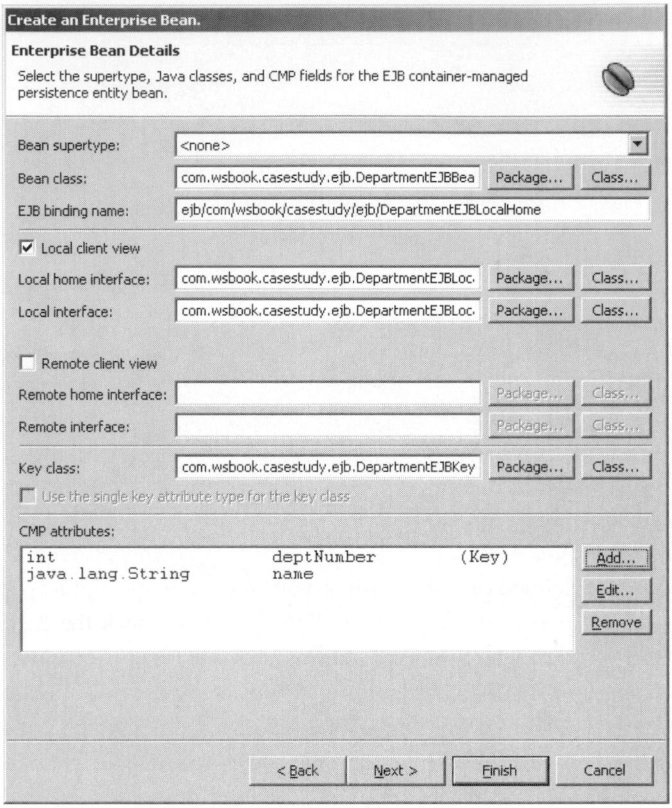

Figure 23.8 Wizard ready for code generation.

Notice that we are following the best practice to have only a local client view of the EJB by generating local and a local home interfaces. Click *Finish*.

At this point the generation of the code for the bean takes place. When generation completes the classes shown in Figure 23.9 are available to us.

We will look at the generated code for each of these classes later in the chapter.

A few things to note in Figure 23.9:

- On the J2EE Hierarchy view the DepartmentEJB is shown as a logical entity, with the components (classes) that make it up shown below it. Also the CMP fields are shown here. The key icon, to the left of deptNumber, makes it clear that this field is the key of the EJB.
- A separate class, DepartmentEJBKey, to represent the key was created. Having a separate class to represent the key gives you additional flexibility should the requirements for the key change later on; for example, adding another field.

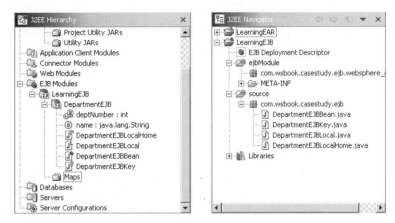

Figure 23.9 Generated files after wizard completion.

- On the J2EE Navigator view you see the generated classes organized by package name. Notice that, in addition to `com.wsbook.casestudy.ejb` package under the source project, another package under the ejbModule project was also created. This and other packages under ejbModule will hold the classes generated as a result of mapping the EJB to the back-end store and generating the deployed classes.

Default `ejbCreate(int)` and `ejbPostCreate(int)` methods were generated by the wizard. These are required to create departments using a department number. We would also like to be able to create fully populated departments using the department number and the department name. To do this we need to manually create methods `ejbCreate(int, String)` and `ejbPost-Create(int, String)`. You can create as many pairs of `ejbCreate()` and `ejbPostCreate()` methods as necessary for a particular EJB. In the case of DepartmentEJB, no other create methods are necessary.

The completed new pair of methods would look like the code in Listing 23.1:

Listing 23.1 ejbCreate() methods

```
public com.wsbook.casestudy.ejb.DepartmentEJBKey ejbCreate(

    int deptNumber, String deptName) throws javax.ejb.CreateException {

    setDeptNumber(deptNumber);

    setName(deptName);

    return null;

}
```

```
public void ejbPostCreate(int deptNumber, String deptName)

    throws javax.ejb.CreateException {

}
```

The `ejbCreate()` method in CMP beans needs to initialize the CMP fields.

Because we want the new `ejbCreate()` method to be part of the client view of the EJB, we need to promote it to the local home interface. To accomplish this, select the method on the Outline view, and from its context menu select: *Enterprise Bean > Promote to local > home interface*. On this context menu, the choices available depend on the selections you made in the original wizard. In this case, we only selected local interfaces, so that is the only choice enabled (Figure 23.10).

After promoting the method, a decoration is added to the method name in the Outline view to indicate that the method is now part of the local home interface; such a decoration can be seen in Figure 23.10 in the `ejbCreate(int)` method. Promoting a method to the local home interface, actually creates a corresponding `create(int, String)` on that interface. From the

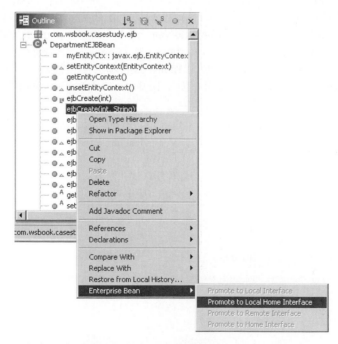

Figure 23.10 Promoting method to local home interface.

EJB client's point of view, only methods exposed on the home and remote interfaces are available to be used.

For each `ejbCreate()` in the Bean class of the EJB there is a corresponding `create()` with the same number and type of parameters (in the same order). It is the `create()` method that is called by the client using the home of the EJB. This call later percolates to the Bean class's `ejb-Create()` method. In the case of an entity bean, the record on the persistent store is created by the container at the end of the call to `ejbCreate()`.

23.3.1 What's Left to Do

The next steps to complete the EJB so it can be used in an application follow:

Step 1   A CMP entity bean needs to have a mapping between the CMP attributes and the column on the database table to where the EJB will be persisted. To create the mapping, select the EJB module and from its context menu select *Generate > EJB to RDB Mapping*, see Figure 23.11.

Since you have not imported a database (you'll use a new one for this example), you are asked whether or not to create a back-end folder (Figure 23.12). Back-end folders contain database-related information. If you had imported any database connections, you would see them listed under the existing back-end folders list. Click *Next*.

Since this is a very simple example to show the mechanics of mapping the CMP entity bean, you will map the EJB to the database using the top-down approach. In this case, each attribute of the EJB is mapped to a column of the same name in the database table (Figure 23.13). Ensure that Top Down is selected. Click *Next*.

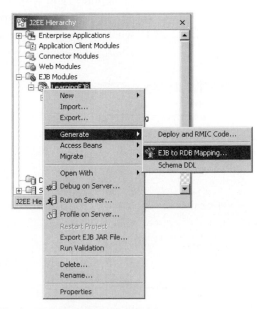

Figure 23.11 Mapping the DepartmentEJB to a database.

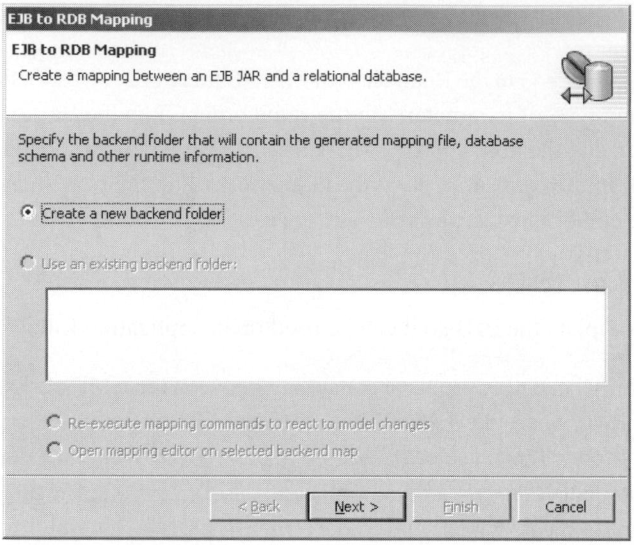

Figure 23.12 Creating a back-end folder.

The last thing to do is to select the database type. To keep this example simple, you will use a Cloudscape database. Name the database DEPARTMENT. Take the defaults for the rest of the settings (Figure 23.14). Click *Finish*.

At this point, WebSphere Studio generates the mapping. The mapping editor opens. From this editor you can manipulate and fine tune the mappings (you will not do this in this chapter, but we'll defer that to Chapter 24). Take a look around the mapping editor, but do not change anything. Pay special attention to Figure 23.15 where you can see how the EJB attributes align to the database table columns.

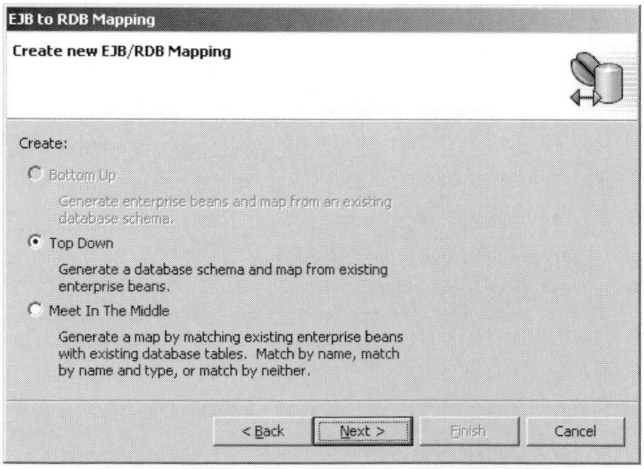

Figure 23.13 Generating database schema based on EJB attributes.

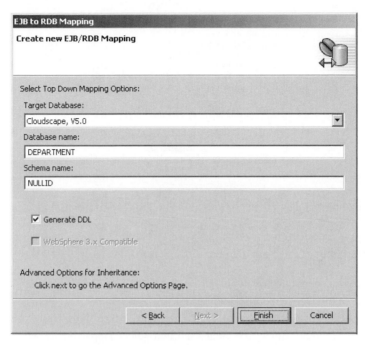

Figure 23.14 Selecting target database and database name.

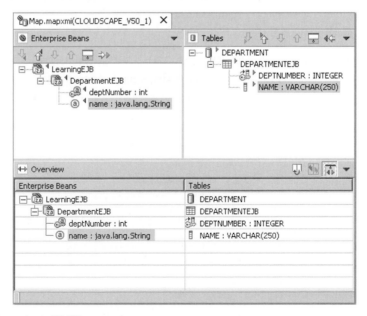

Figure 23.15 DepartmentEJB's mappings.

Figure 23.16 Generated files resulting from mapping the DepartmentEJB.

Close the mapping editor. Switch to the J2EE Navigator view and see the files that were generated as the result of the mapping operation (Figure 23.16).

Step 2   Before you generate the deployed code, set up the deployment descriptor to indicate which data source the DepartmentEJB will use.

Double click LearningEJB in the J2EE Hierarchy view. This will open the deployment descriptor for the module. Select the Beans tab and select DepartmentEJB. Under WebSphere Bindings enter jdbc/testds for the CMP container factory JNDI name (Figure 23.17). Save the file.

If all entity beans on the module used the same data source, you could save yourself work and define the default data source for all the beans. These can be overridden on and bean by bean basic if required. This is done on the Overview tab under WebSphere Bindings.

Step 3   Generate the deployed code. This creates the rest of the classes needed for the EJB. This step is similar to generating the deployed code already covered in the chapter dealing with session beans. The mechanism is the same, the generated classes are different. From the J2EE

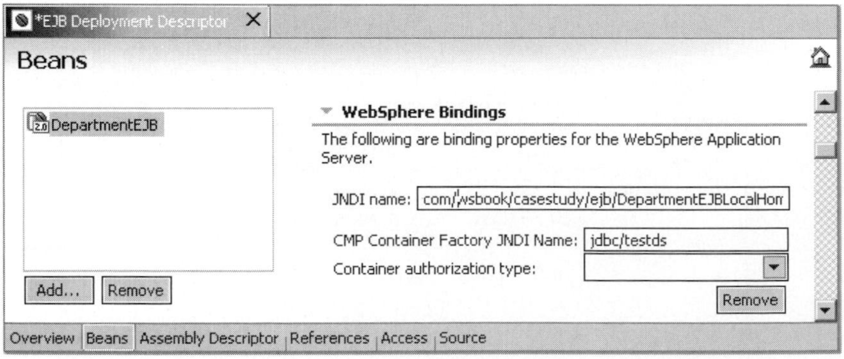

Figure 23.17 Defining the JNDI name for the data source used by the CMP.

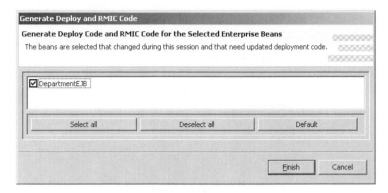

Figure 23.18   Generating deploy code for DepartmentEJB.

Hierarchy view, select the Learning EJB module and from its context menu select Deploy and RMIC Code. See Figure 23.18. Ensure DepartmentEJB is selected and click *Finish*.

On the J2EE Navigator view you can see the generated code in packages `com.ibm.wsbook.casestudy.ejb`, `com.ibm.wsbook.casestudy.ejb.websphere_de ploy`, and `com.ibm.wsbook.casestudy.ejb.websphere_deploy.CLOUDSCAPE_V50_1`. You normally do not pay too much attention to these generated classes, although studying the generated code can provide an insight into how EJBs are truly implemented. Sometimes during debugging it might be useful to step into these classes to inspect intermediate results.

Step 4   Switch to the server perspective and create a server and configuration. Take all the defaults. You did this when testing the session bean; refer to that chapter if you require more details. Add the LearningEAR project to the server configuration.

Step 5   Create the database, table, and data source. From the server perspective, select the server you just created (under the Servers tab). From its context menu, select *Create tables and data sources*, see Figure 23.19. All the information required to perform this step has been defined. The JNDI name of the data source and the back-end folder contain this information.

Step 6   The last step, before integrating the EJB into the rest of the application, is to perform unit testing using the UTC. From the J2EE perspective, select DepartmentEJB under LearningEJB and from its context menu select *Run on Server*. Click *Finish* to use the server you created in Step 4.

Step 7   The UTC starts and automatically does a lookup on the DepartmentEJB bean. Expand DepartmentEJBLocalHome and click the `create(int, String)` method. Enter a number for the key and a department name, and then click *Invoke* to insert a record on the database. See Figure 23.20.

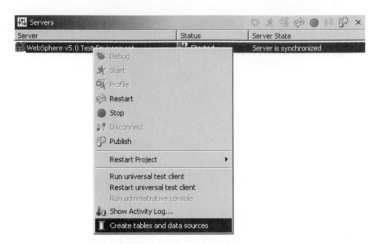

Figure 23.19 Creating the tables and data sources for the bean.

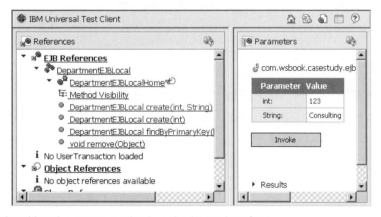

Figure 23.20 Invoking the create method on the home interface.

Step 8   The method executes and makes available the object just created. Click *Work with Object* (Figure 23.21). This adds the DepartmentEJBLocal entry to the References panel. From there you can exercise the methods on the local interface.

Step 9   From the References pane of the UTC, select and expand the DepartmentEJBLocal entry. Select the getName() method and click *Invoke*. You should now see the value of the cmp-field, Consulting, displayed on the Parameters pane (Figure 23.22).

Step 10   Change the department's name invoking the setName() method, and then verify that the change took place.

     This concludes unit testing the DepartmentEJB entity bean.

     Now let's take a detailed look at the parts that make up a CMP bean.

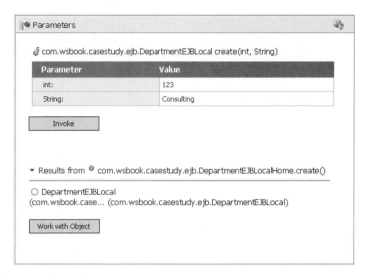

Figure 23.21 Results of invoking the create method.

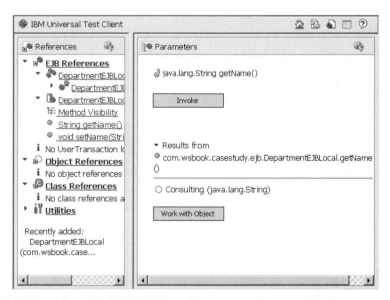

Figure 23.22 Results of invoking the getName() method on the local interface.

23.4   The Parts of an Entity Bean

To understand how entity beans work, you need to review what the EJB specification says about entity beans.   There are significant differences between entity and session beans, so first examining them can help in understanding the examples that follow. To set the stage, consider the following example.

23.4.1   Local Interfaces

The case study (the time entry system) needs a way to store information for the different departments in a company. A department consists of an integer departmentNumber (which is unique) and a department name (like Engineering or Consulting). As we discussed in Chapter19, best practices recommend that entity beans only use local interface methods to expose their function. So, if you are implementing entity EJBs using the EJB 2.0 specification (as part of J2EE 1.3), you should not use remote interfaces, opting instead to access entity beans through their local interfaces as part of a Session Façade implementation.

Therefore, DepartmentEJB has been defined as having only a local public view. No remote or home interfaces are generated. Instead you find local and a local home interface generated by WebSphere Studio (Listing 23.2).

Listing 23.2 Getter and setter methods in local interface

```
package com.wsbook.casestudy.ejb;

public interface DepartmentEJBlocal extends javax.ejb.EJBlocalObject {

    public java.lang.String getName();

    public void setName(java.lang.String newName);

}
```

The local interface in Listing 23.2 defines two types of methods: getters, which return the value of an attribute of the entity bean; and setters, which allow clients to change the value of an EJB attribute. Attributes that have both getter and setter methods are referred to as entity bean properties. Entity bean properties can be either cmp-fields or cmr-fields which will be described in more detail later and in Chapters 24 and 25. The only thing even slightly unusual about this local interface is the fact that there are no methods to access deptNumber. This is because deptNumber is treated as a special key field, as you will see later.

23.4.2   Local Home Interfaces

In this section we will specifically discuss the local home interface of the DepartmentEJB, but all of the concepts covered also apply to remote home methods of the type we used to implement using the EJB 1.x specification. The main difference is that life cycle methods on the remote home interface must also be declared to throw `java.rmi.RemoteException`.

Like session beans, entity beans also must define a local home interface that describes the factory responsible for creating them. However, there are additional features that entity home interfaces must define that session beans do not. To understand the differences, look at Listing 23.3, defining a DepartmentEJBLocalHome interface.

Listing 23.3 DepartmentEJB local home interface

```
package com.wsbook.casestudy.ejb;

public interface DepartmentEJBLocalHome extends javax.ejb.EJBLocalHome

{

    public DepartmentEJBlocal

        create(int deptNumber) throws javax.ejb.CreateException;

    public DepartmentEJBlocal create(int deptNumber, String name)

            throws javax.ejb.CreateException;

    public DepartmentEJBlocal findByPrimaryKey(DepartmentEJBKey

        primaryKey)

        throws javax.ejb.FinderException;

    public java.util.Collection findAll() throws

            javax.ejb.FinderException;

}
```

This simple EJBLocalHome defines two `create()` methods, which differ in two ways from the `create()` methods you have seen in the example stateless session EJB that was covered earlier.

- `create()` methods for entity EJBs (and stateful session EJBs) can take arguments. These arguments will be used by `ejbCreate()` methods to set the values of the EJB's attributes when it is created.
- Notice that we have defined two `create()` methods, each with a different number of arguments. In this respect, `create()` methods are like class constructors in Java—you can have as many as you like, so long as they differ in parameter type and/or order. This allows you to create entity beans in different ways depending upon the situation. You will learn more about why you would want different `create()` methods as we work through the details of this example.

The next thing to notice about this local home interface is the presence of a new type of method. This is called a finder method, and you can identify it in a local home interface because it always begin with the lowercase letters "find." In this example, there is a single finder method, `findByPrimaryKey()`.

```
DepartmentEJB findByPrimaryKey(DepartmentEJBKey key)

  throws javax.ejb.FinderException;
```

Clients use finder methods to locate an existing instanceóor a set of instancesóof an entity EJB. Correspondingly, finder methods can return either a single instance of the entity bean (a `findByPrimaryKey()` does) or they can return a collection of entity beans which can be iterated over by the client, to obtain the set of instances.s

Every home interface for an entity bean must define a `findByPrimaryKey()` method. The argument is always an instance of another class that must be especially defined for this entity beanóa primary key class. Understanding why this method (and this class) must be defined requires explanation. Remember that an entity bean represents persistent data. This means that there must be some way of matching a particular entity bean instance with the corresponding data in the data source. There are two ways to specify a primary key:

- A primary key that maps to a single cmp-field in the container-managed entity
- A primary key that maps to multiple cmp-fields in the container-managed entity

A primary key that maps to a single cmp-field can use the primkey-field deployment descriptor tag to indicate a cmp-field that contains the primary key. This means that the fieldís type must be the primary key type. The type of the primary key must be ajava.lang.Object type that is serializable. This means that Java primitive types cannot be directly used as the primary key. Therefore, cmp-fields with Java primitive types cannot be used in the primkey-field element.

In the case study, we use `java.lang.String` as the primary key of the EmployeeEJB. Listing 23.4 is an excerpt from the deployment descriptor for the EmployeeEJB. You should notice that the primkey-field is set to empId which is typed to `java.lang.String` which is the same as the `prim-key-class`.

Listing 23.4 EmployeeEJB deployment descriptor segment

```
<entity id="EmployeeEJB">

      <ejb-name>EmployeeEJB</ejb-name>

      <local-home>com.wsbook.casestudy.ejb.EmployeeEJBhome</local-home>

      <local>com.wsbook.casestudy.ejb.EmployeeEJB</local>

      <ejb-class>com.wsbook.casestudy.ejb.EmployeeEJBBean</ejb-class>
```

```
    <persistence-type>Container</persistence-type>

    <prim-key-class>java.lang.String</prim-key-class>

    <reentrant>False</reentrant>

    <cmp-version>2.x</cmp-version>

    <abstract-schema-name>EmployeeEJB</abstract-schema-name>

    <cmp-field id="CMPAttribute_6">

            <field-name>empId</field-name>

    </cmp-field>

    <cmp-field id="CMPAttribute_14">

            <field-name>name</field-name>

    </cmp-field>

    <cmp-field id="CMPAttribute_1044593764765">

            <field-name>office</field-name>

    </cmp-field>

    <primkey-field>empId</primkey-field>

    ...

</entity>
```

When a primary key maps to multiple cmp-fields, or if the key is represented by a Java primitive type, you must define a custom key class. This class has public fields with the same name and type as the key cmp-fields in the bean. In this situation, the primkey-field tag is not used since the primary key class is used to define the key cmp-fields by name. The next section will walk through one of the case study CMP beans that define a custom key class.

ENTERPRISE BEAN CREATION WIZARD LOGIC

In WebSphere Studio, the enterprise bean creation wizard is logic for deciding whether to create a new key class or use the cmp-field as the key class itself depends on the two factors:

1) Is the type of the cmp-field designated as the key, a Java primitive type? If so, generation of a key class that wraps the primitive type is automatic and the developer has no options to consider.

2) If the type of the cmp-field designated as the key is a Java class, the developer has a choice to make. Use the cmp-field's class as the key directly; as we did with the string empId in Listing 23.4 or let WebSphere Studio create a key class which will wrap the cmp-field. This decision is controlled by the selection of the Use the single key attribute type for the key class check box on the wizard (Figure 23.7). This check box is enabled and disabled depending on the make up and type of the cmp-field(s) designated as being part of the key. If the check box is selected, a key class will *not* be generated and the type of the cmp-field will be used instead.

Note that compound keys, regardless of the types which make them up, will always have a key class created by the wizard.

23.4.3 Key Classes

Now that you understand why you must define a key class for an entity bean, you are ready to examine the key class for our DepartmentEJB (Listing 23.5):

Listing 23.5 DepartmenEJBKey class implementation

```
package com.wsbook.casestudy.ejb;

public class DepartmentEJBKey implements java.io.Serializable {

    static final long serialVersionUID = 3206093459760846163L;

    public int deptNumber;

    public DepartmentEJBKey() {

    }

    public DepartmentEJBKey(int deptNumber) {

        this.deptNumber = deptNumber;

    }

    public boolean equals(java.lang.Object otherKey) {

        if (otherKeyinstanceof

            com.wsbook.casestudy.ejb.DepartmentEJBKey) {

                com.wsbook.casestudy.ejb.DepartmentEJBKey o =
```

```
                    (com.wsbook.casestudy.ejb.DepartmentEJBKey)

                otherKey;

            return ((this.deptNumber == o.deptNumber));

        }

        return false;

    }

    public int hashCode() {

        return ((new java.lang.Integer(deptNumber).hashCode()));

    }

    public int getDeptNumber() {

        return deptNumber;

    }

    public void setDeptNumber(int newDeptNumber) {

        deptNumber = newDeptNumber;

    }

}
```

The only requirement that is placed on a key class by the EJB specification is that it must be serializable. However, the container used by WAS and WebSphere Studio put a few more restrictions on the key class. the class must implement `equals()` and `hashCode()` so that instances of the class can be compared with each other.

23.4.4 Uniqueness of Primary Keys

Since each entity bean represents a row in persistent storage, such as a database, and each row must be unique, the primary keys in the entity bean must also be unique. Generation of unique primary keys has to be dealt with at some level. Some databases, such as IBM DB2, implement a special type of numeric column of type Identity, whose value is filled by the database manager each time a row is created, thus ensuring unique values; this column can be used to contain the primary key for the table. Unfortunately WebSphere Studio does not, at this time, take advantage of Identity columns, mainly because not all supported database types implement this feature.

In the case study, we propose a simple solution to this problem whose implementation can be found in its own module called OIDGenerator. Basically in the `ejbCreate()` method(s) for the entity bean you are working with, you make a call similar to:

```
public com.wsbook.casestudy.ejb.DepartmentEJBKey

    ejbCreate(String deptName) throws javax.ejb.CreateException {

        int id = OIDGeneratorHelper.getNextId("DEPT_JB");

        setDeptNumber(id);

         setName(deptName);

        return null;

}
```

OIDGeneratorHelper is a POJO which interfaces with the rest of the module. The string passed to `getNextId()` must be unique for each type of entity bean. OIDGenerator is implemented using the session and entity beans accessing a locked table schema.

For a complete example of how to use this autokey generation feature, please see the TimeSheetEntityEJBBean example implemented for the case study of the book.

23.4.5 Bean Implementation Classes

In order to understand the code (Listing 23.6) for the DepartmentEJBBean implementation class of DepartmentEJB, you will need to review a few concepts that are true about all entity beans. See Figure 23.23 for a diagram showing the entity bean life cycle.

- All entity beans must implement `ejbActivate()` and `ejbPassivate()`, which are hooks (methods called by the container at predetermined times) for special behavior that needs to happen when a bean is swapped to or retrieved from secondary storage.
- All entity beans must implement the `ejbRemove()` hook method, which is called before the EJB is destroyed, so that you can execute any necessary cleanup code.
- All entity beans must implement a set of `ejbCreate()` methods that correspond to the `create()` methods on the home interface of the EJB. For each `create()` method defined in the home interface, there will be a corresponding `ejbCreate()` method that matches it in number, type, and order of parameters.
- All entity beans must implement a set of `ejbPostCreate()` methods that correspond to the `ejbCreate()` methods. For each `ejbCreate()` method defined, a corresponding `ejbPostCreate()` method matches it in number, type, and order of parameters. This method is a hook that is called after any `ejbCreate()` method is called. You can use it

to do any additional generic setup that must be done before a bean instance is ready for use. The EJB Object itself (e.g., the object that controls transaction and thread safety) is not available until after `ejbPostCreate()` is invoked, so you do not want to invoke remote business methods as part of EJB creation until that point.

There are a few new life cycle methods that are specific to entity EJBs that you haven't seen before (Figure 23.23). They are:

- The methods `getEntityContext()`, `setEntityContext(EntityContext e)`, and `unsetEntityContext()`. These methods are meant to handle the management of the EntityContext, an object that provides access to some of the underlying EJB framework features like the Transaction framework and the EJBObject that manages much of the transaction, threading, and distribution for the bean's implementation. There was a corresponding `setSessionContext()` method in the previous stateless session bean.
- The methods `ejbStore()` and `ejbLoad()`. These two methods are hooks that will be called before the data in the entity bean is written to a persistent store by the container, and after new data has been read in respectively. They are useful if you need to do any conversion from data types that cannot be stored in a relational database to those that can. You will learn more about how these two methods are used in BMP beans in the chapter on BMP as well.

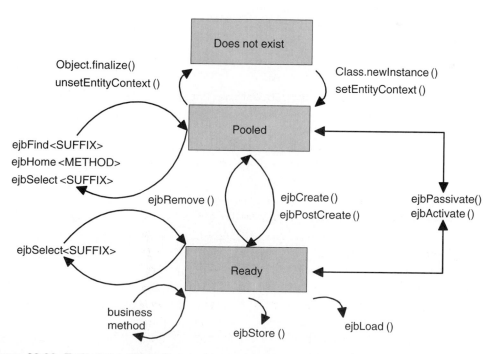

Figure 23.23 Entity bean life cycle.

The final methods needed to complete the EJB implement the local, or remote, interfaces. Now that you've been introduced to the different methods that are necessary to implement a CMP entity Bean class, you are ready to examine the implementation of the Bean class as a whole (Listing 23.6). Afterwards, we will revisit some of the methods in more depth to point out some noteworthy features of the implementation.

Listing 23.6 DepartmentEJBBean class implementation

```java
package com.wsbook.casestudy.ejb;


public abstract class DepartmentEJBBean implements javax.ejb.EntityBean {


    private javax.ejb.EntityContext myEntityCtx;


    public void setEntityContext(javax.ejb.EntityContext ctx) {

        myEntityCtx = ctx;

    }


    public javax.ejb.EntityContext getEntityContext() {

        return myEntityCtx;

    }


    public void unsetEntityContext() {

        myEntityCtx = null;

    }


    public com.wsbook.casestudy.ejb.DepartmentEJBKey

        ejbCreate(int deptNumber) throws javax.ejb.CreateException {
```

```
            setDeptNumber(deptNumber);

        return null;

    }


    public com.wsbook.casestudy.ejb.DepartmentEJBKey

        ejbCreate(int deptNumber, String name)

            throws javax.ejb.CreateException {

            setDeptNumber(deptNumber);

            setName(name);

            return null;

    }


    public void ejbPostCreate(int deptNumber) throws

            javax.ejb.CreateException

    {       } //nothing to implement on this EJB


    public void ejbPostCreate(int deptNumber, String name)

            throws javax.ejb.CreateException {

    }


    public void ejbActivate() {

    }//nothing to implement on this EJB


    public void ejbLoad() {
```

```
    }//nothing to implement on this EJB


    public void ejbPassivate() {

    }//nothing to implement on this EJB


    public void ejbRemove() throws javax.ejb.RemoveException {

    }//nothing to implement on this EJB


    public void ejbStore() {

    }//nothing to implement on this EJB


    public abstract java.lang.String getName();


    public abstract void setName(java.lang.String newName);


    public abstract int getDeptNumber();


    public abstract void setDeptNumber(int newDeptNumber);

}
```

Now you are ready to take a closer look at some of the individual features of this class.

First notice that a great many of the methods in the class—ejbActivate(), ejbPassivate(), ejbRemove(), ejbLoad(), and ejbStore()—have an empty implementation. They don't do anything. The reason is that this class is simple enough that there is no need to take advantage of any of these hooks to perform special processing. In general, most of the life cycle methods in your EJB implementation classes will be empty like this.

The method hooks must be implemented because they are defined in the javax.ejb.Entity-Bean interface, which the Bean class implements. These methods don't require any implementation unless the bean has some special requirements. This may seem like a waste of programming effort, but it is for a good reason: You always want to have the option to implement these methods to deal with unusual circumstances when/if the time comes. In the meantime, you have two good options for implementing all of these empty method bodies:

1. WebSphere Studio will automatically generate the empty method bodies when you create an entity bean in the EJB development environment. This way you don't have to worry about doing the typing yourself.

2. If you aren't using WebSphere Studio to develop EJBs for WebSphere (as you should), then you can take advantage of an idiom defined in [Monson-Haefel] called Bean-Adapters. A BeanAdapter is a class that implements javax.ejb.EntityBean or javax.ejb.SessionBean that provides default do-nothing implementations of the EJB life cycle methods. Your classes will extend this class, and thus inherit the method implementations. This way you will need to override a life cycle method only when you need the additional implementation details.

There are a few life cycle methods that must not have an empty implementation. In particular, the methods managing the EntityContext must set or return an instance variable of the type EntityContext. The container uses this instance in managing the life cycle of the bean, so it is important that you remember to implement these methods accordingly. These implementations give you all of the information you need to implement these methods in your own beans. Again, if you are using WebSphere Studio to write your beans, these methods' implementations are automatically generated.

This leaves the declaration of the Bean class and two sets of methods to examine—the `ejbCreate()` methods, and those that implement the corresponding local or remote interfaces methods. To understand the implementation of these methods, first look at this fragment of the class definition:

```
public abstract class DepartmentEJBBean implements javax.ejb.EntityBean {

     private javax.ejb.EntityContext myEntityCtx;

...


     public abstract java.lang.String getName();


     public abstract void setName(java.lang.String newName);
```

...

}

One of the significant changes in EJB 2.0 is that the Bean class is declared as abstract. Along with the class definition, note that the CMP fields name and deptNumber are not declared in the class. Furthermore, the getter and setter methods for the CMP fields are also abstract. The declaration of the CMP fields and implementation of these methods will be generated by the container. This gives the container provider greater flexibility when generating the implementation classes to include improvements in performance through caching by customizing how CMP fields are really implemented by the container.

Let's consider the `ejbCreate()` methods in Listing 23.7:

Listing 23.7 Code segment of ejbCreate() methods

```
public package com.wsbook.casestudy.ejb ejbCreate(int deptNumber)

        throws javax.ejb.CreateException {

                setDeptNumber(deptNumber);

                return null;

        }



        public com.wsbook.casestudy.ejb.DepartmentEJBKey

            ejbCreate(int deptNumber, String name)

                throws javax.ejb.CreateException {

                setDeptNumber(deptNumber);

                setName(name);

                return null;

        }
```

Both of these methods show how you initialize the values of the cmp-fields from the arguments of a `create()` method. Different `create()` methods provide different ways of initializing the fields. For instance, often you will have a `create()` method that does not take any arguments corresponding to the properties of a bean. You will instead set some of them to a default, or calculated value.

One more last detail, again regarding the EJB 2.0 implementation; `ejbCreate()` methods are declared to return the key type for the EJB, in our case DepartmentEJBKey. They must, however return a value of null.[1]

There is nothing more in this example that we need to examine from a code perspective. The variable setters and getters for the properties are simple, and work exactly as they would in any Java class. Instead, now is the time to examine how to create and test entity EJBs in WebSphere Studio, and how to deploy them in WebSphere.

23.5 Deployment Descriptor

In this section we will look at several aspects of CMP entity beans that require little or no programming effort, yet add a tremendous amount of function to the Bean. These features are defined in the EJB deployment descriptor (EJB DD).

The EJB DD is an XML file, called ejb-jar.xml. It describes the features of one or more EJBs in an EJB JAR file. The EJB container uses the information in this file to correctly generate the code for the EJBs. There is one EJB DD for each EJB JAR file.

Listing 23.8 DepartmentEJB deployment descriptor segment

```
<entity id="DepartmentEJB">

    <display-name>DepartmentEJB</display-name>

    <ejb-name>DepartmentEJB</ejb-name>

    <local-home>

        com.wsbook.casestudy.ejb.DepartmentEJBLocalHome

    </local-home>

    <local>

        com.wsbook.casestudy.ejb.DepartmentEJBlocal

    </local>

    <ejb-class>
```

---

1.   [EJB 2.0 Specification 10.5.2] The requirement is to allow the creation of an entity bean with BMP by subclassing an entity bean with CMP.

```
        com.wsbook.casestudy.ejb.DepartmentEJBBean

    </ejb-class>

    <persistence-type>Container</persistence-type>

    <prim-key-class>

        com.wsbook.casestudy.ejb.DepartmentEJBKey

    </prim-key-class>

    <reentrant>False</reentrant>

    <cmp-version>2.x</cmp-version>

...

</entity>
```

In the portion of the EJB DD in Listing 23.8, you see how it defines the name of each EJB (in our case the DepartmentEJB), the names of the types representing the local, local home interfaces and Bean class, the type of persistence (CMP or BMP), the class implementing the key, the CMP version,[2] etc. There will be a group of definitions for each EJB contained in the JAR file. The acceptable elements and values for the EJB DD are defined on the document type definition (DTD) file for EJBs found at *http://java.sun.com/dtd/ejb-jar_2_0.dtd.*

There are three features we will introduce in this section. In later chapters you will get a chance to become better acquainted and to dig deeper into their details. The three features are:

- Container-managed fields
- CMRs
- Finders and selectors using EJB QL

Aside from these three features, which we will cover here, there are quite a few other definitions in the EJB DD; for example, EJB security, transactional attributes, etc. They will be covered in later chapters.

---

2.   Since EJB 2.0 deployment descriptors can define both EJB 1.1 and EJB 2.0 EJBs, each entity element must define the version of the EJB it describes. If the EJB being described is CMP and cmp-version is 2.x, the deployment descriptor for the bean must also include the abstract-schema-name element for the bean.

23.5.1   Container Managed Persistence Fields

CMP fields are defined in the EJB DD; these are the attributes that will be persisted to the back-end data source by the container. Getter and setter methods, for these fields, are defined as abstract methods in the EJB Bean class. Any getter and setter methods, which need to be exposed to the EJB client, need to appear in the local (or remote) interfaces. The implementation of getters and setters is generated by the container when deploying the EJB. Before you can generate the deployed code for a CMP EJB, you need to map the CMP fields to the corresponding database columns. The mapping process is covered in Chapter 24.

Listing 23.9 shows how CMP fields are defined in the EJB DD.

Listing 23.9 DepartmentEJB deployment descriptor segment defining CMP fields

```
<entity id="DepartmentEJB">

...

    <abstract-schema-name>DepartmentEJB</abstract-schema-name>

    <cmp-field>

        <field-name>name</field-name>

    </cmp-field>

    <cmp-field>

        <field-name>deptNumber</field-name>

    </cmp-field>

...

</entity>
```

Note that there is no mapping information in the EJB DD. This is because the EJB 2.0 specifications do not yet prescribe how to define this type of information. Only elements defined by the specification appear in the DTD and can therefore be included in the EJB DD file, ejb-jar.xml. Each tool provider (IBM, BEA, Sun, etc.) is free to define attributes to extend the formal EJB DD and include specialized information required by their tools.

In WebSphere there are several other files which are used to further define the EJB's features, so that the EJB containers in IBM products can extend the function defined by the specification. Some of EJB DD extender files used by WebSphere are:

- ibm-ejb-jar-bnd.xmi
- ibm-ejb-jar-ext.xmi
- map.mapxmi (does not exist until mapping is done)

These files can be found, along with ejb-jar.xml, under META-INF folder of the ejbModule folder.

23.5.2 Container Managed Relationships (CMR)

Relationships between EJBs are very common. A relationship, or association, between EJBs is defined by several factors:

- Multiplicity
- Navigability
- Roles

CMRs were introduced with the EJB 2.0 specification. Before EJB 2.0, IBM and other tool providers managed relationships between entity beans using their own proprietary approach. This resulted in EJBs that would run on only a particular server type. Entity beans developed with VisualAge for Java or WebSphere Studio Classic, which contained relationships, would not run on another tool provider's server; they would only run on WAS.

As the specification evolves, so does interoperability. EJB 2.0-compliant entity bean relationships are now portable between different EJB 2.0 compliant application servers.

Using WSAD makes defining entity bean relationship very easy. You will see the details about defining CMRs using WebSphere Studio in Chapter 25.

23.5.3 EJB Query Language (EJB QL)

Before the EJB 2.0 specification, different tool providers came up with their own customized support for finder methods. Finder methods are part of the home interface and are used to find one or more of entity beans, which match a specified criteria. A special finder method, findBy-PrimaryKey(), is mandatory and is produced by WebSphere Studio. Other finder methods are generally required in your entity beans. For example, on the DepartmentEJB there is a method to find all departments.

Starting with EJB 2.0, the way queries are defined in entity beans has changed. In the past we used SQL, a database-centric query language. Now we use a new query language called EJB Query Language, or EJB QL. It is an EJB-centric query language where queries are not expressed in terms of tables and columns in a database, but in terms of entity bean schemas and attributes. The creation of EJB QL queries will be covered in more detail in Chapter 24 and Chapter 25 will cover more advanced EJB QL statements that may be necessary for your application.

23.6 Summary

In this chapter we covered the basic structure of CMP entity EJBs. You've walked through a code example showing the classes that a bean provider must write to implement a CMP EJB.

You created and tested an entity bean and you started to learn about CMRs and how the EJB QL is used with finders and select methods.

CHAPTER **2 4**

CMP Mapping
Strategies and
Mapping in WSAD

In Chapter 14, we described several different mapping patterns demonstrating how to write your own JDBC code to persist a domain model to a relational database. The problem with roll-your-own persistence is the large amount of code that you must update whenever the domain model or the relational database changes. This can become a maintenance nightmare and it discourages refactoring of the domain model.

Chapter 23 introduced container-managed entities which have the benefit of using container-managed transaction demarcation, built-in security support, and automatic JDBC code generation for finding and persisting container-managed entities. This provides more efficiency developing the application because there is no need to develop JDBC code, a transaction framework, and to build in security into your domain layer.

In this chapter you will learn how to map your domain model, in the form of container-managed entities, to a relational database using the mapping tools provided in WSAD.

Figure 24.1 shows how mapping of container-managed entities fits into the entire application architecture. We will describe the major mapping strategies the tools use, and we will show how easily you can change the mapping to suit refactoring of either the domain model or the relational database. You will see the mappings the tools in WSAD use to automatically generate and update relational database access code of the type that was touched on in Chapter 14. This chapter will also show simple examples to illustrate the solutions to situations when a domain attribute type does not map directly to a relational column type and how to map dependent values that are embedded in a domain object. Also, we will provide an introduction to generating finders for container-managed entities.

The mapping files and supporting mapping code (e.g., converter and composer classes which will be described later) are outside the scope of the EJB specification and are specific to

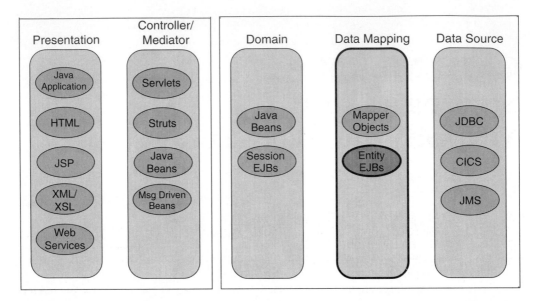

Figure 24.1 Container-managed entity mapping within the road map.

WebSphere. You should be aware that this code will not work outside of a WAS. This mapping code is not intended to be portable to other application servers.

24.1 Databases, CMPs, and Maps

Now that you've discovered what the basic object model of our case study looks like, you're ready to look at how that object model relates to the objects in a relational database. Before we begin, however, we need to review some basic relational technology terminology.

In a relational database, data is stored in tables as rows and columns. A table is a single entity that represents a particular record layout. You define a table by stating the names, data types, and (optionally) sizes of the columns that comprise the table. The database has groupings of schematas which are used to provide qualification to the table names. For example, a table named TEST.FOO has TEST as the schema name. Each schema has a set of tables that are defined as members of that particular schema. A table can belong to only one schema and each schema belongs to one database. So a database is the root object that contains a complete set of schematas and their associated tables.

In short, what we need to do is define how our objects (container-managed entity beans) map to a set of database tables. Thus we have to define a mapping between our container-managed entities within the EJB JAR and the tables within a database. To do this, you need to be able to view, and perhaps manipulate, both sides of the coin—the database tables and the object model.

WSAD contains a set of tools that allow you to do precisely this. In WSAD, you can define a database mapping to an EJB module in one of three ways:

- A "top-down" mapping will automatically create a new database and tables from a set of container-managed entity beans by following some simple mapping rules.
- A "bottom-up" mapping will create a new set of container-managed entity beans to a matching set of database tables.
- A "meet-in-the-middle" mapping allows you to create a set of container-managed entity beans and database tables separately and then define the mapping between the two using some simple name and type matching rules.

24.1.1 Top-Down Mapping Example

To demonstrate a top-down mapping, we will use the TimeSheetGroup EJB module from the case study. To begin, launch the EJB to RDB mapping wizard by selecting the TimeSheetGroup EJB module from the J2EE Hierarchy view within the J2EE Perspective and select *Generate > EJB to RDB Mapping* from the context menu (Figure 24.2) opened by right-clicking.

The first page of the EJB to RDB mapping wizard (Figure 24.3) requires you to either create a new back-end folder or use an existing back-end folder. In WSAD 5.0, there is support for multiple EJB to RDB mappings for the same set of container-managed entities within a 2.0 EJB module. The metadata files associated with the database and its tables are all stored in subfolders of the folder named Backend.

Each subfolder is an existing back-end folder that is displayed in the wizard. Later in this chapter we will discuss multiple back-end support in WSAD. In our example, no database or mapping exists for our EJB module, so only the create a new back-end folder option is available at this time.

The second page of the mapping wizard (Figure 24.4) provides options for each of the three mapping approaches: bottom-up, top-down, meet-in-the-middle. For our top–down mapping example, we will keep the default Top Down selection. This option will create a database

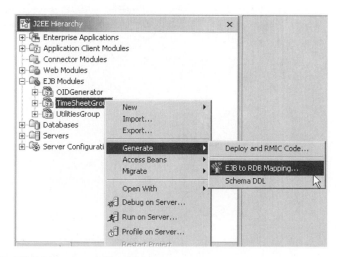

Figure 24.2 EJB to RDB Mapping Action.

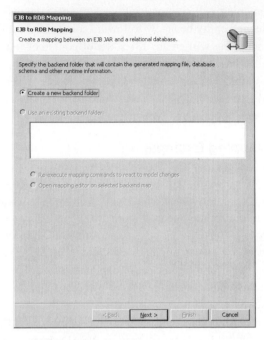

Figure 24.3 Select back-end folder wizard page.

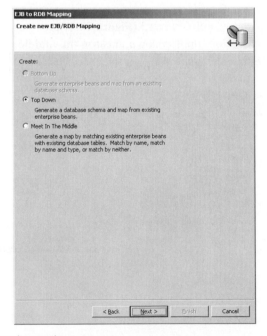

Figure 24.4 Select mapping option page.

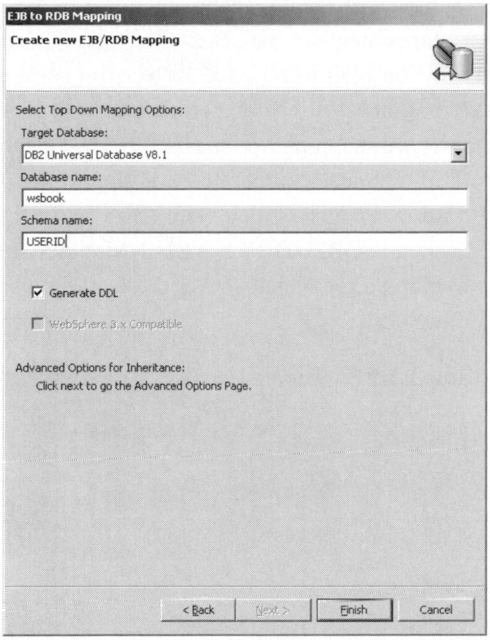

Figure 24.5 Top-down mapping options.

and schema, and tables for each container-managed entity bean within our EJB module. The tables will be named with the same name as that of the container-managed entity and each column will be named based on the corresponding cmp-field within the container-managed entity.

Any cmp-fields that have been added to the key of the container-managed entity will have its associated column added to the primary key of the new table. A mapping will be defined for each of the container-managed entity beans to the table that was created on its behalf.

Click the *Next* button to move the top-down mapping options page shown in Figure 24.5. The first and most important option is Target Database. Table 24.1 shows the databases currently supported by WSAD 5.0. We will be using DB2 8.1 for our example. Database name will be the name of the target database. The Schema name is the name of the schema that you want all new tables to be a member of. This schema name will be used as the qualifier for the generated SQL. So, a table named EMPLOYEE that had the schema name set to TEST would appear in the generated SQL as fully qualified, (i.e., TEST.EMPLOYEE). If you want to control the qualification of the queries based upon a login ID (this is the common case with DB2 that the default schema name used within a query will be the user's login name if one is not supplied) you should enter NULLID for the Schema name. This name is treated special by the SQL generator so it will not add the schema qualification to the tables within the SQL queries. Therefore if the query being executed is being done using a DB user ID of "bob," then the fully qualified table name would become "bob.EMPLOYEE."

The Generate DDL option will create a table.ddl file for the newly generated database which can be used to export the contents to the actual database. The WebSphere 3.x Compatible option should only be used if you plan to target a 3.x version of WebSphere. This option will adjust the type mappings so that they will be compatible for this version of WebSphere.

Now that all of the top-down mapping options have been set, the last thing to do is to click the *Finish* button. This will automatically generate a top-down mapping based on the selected options and the rules for top-down mapping that were described earlier. The mappings will be stored in the META-INF/backends/DB2UDBNT_V81_1/Map.mapxmi file. Figure 24.6 is the resulting overview from the map editor which shows the new tables and their associated mappings to container-managed entities.

Table 24.1 Supported WSAD 5.0 databases.

Cloudscape, V5.0
DB2 Universal Database V6.1
DB2 Universal Database V7.1
DB2 Universal Database V7.2
DB2 Universal Database V8.1
DB2 Universal Database for OS/390, V6
DB2 Universal Database for OS/390, V7
DB2 Universal Database for iSeries, V4R5
DB2 Universal Database for iSeries, V5R1
Informix Dynamic Server, V7.3
Informix Dynamic Server, V9.3
Informix Dynamic Server.2000, V9.2
Microsoft SQL Server 2000
Microsoft SQL Server, V7.0
Oracle8i, V8.1.7
Oracle9i
SQL-92
SQL-99
Sybase Adaptive Server Enterprise, V11.9.2
Sybase Adaptive Server Enterprise, V12
Sybase Adaptive Server Enterprise, V12.5

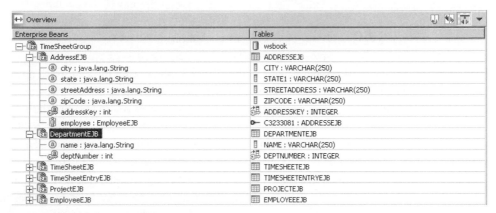

Figure 24.6 Top-down mapping results.

24.1.2 Bottom-Up Mapping Example

A bottom-up mapping is used when there is a new EJB project without any EJBs defined within it and you have a set of database tables that you would like to access with container-managed entity beans. In this case, WSAD creates a container-managed entity bean for each table within the database for the back end selected on the previous page. Also, WSAD adds a cmp-field to the key of the newly created container-managed entity for each column within the primary key of the table.

For this example, we will be using the DEPARTMENT table shown in the DDL in Listing 24.1. If you wish to follow along with this example, you will need to execute the following DDL against your database (i.e., DB2). Refer to your database documentation for instructions to execute the DDL.

Listing 24.1 EMPLOYEE DDL

```
CREATE TABLE BOTTOMUP.EMPLOYEE

  (EMP_NO INTEGER NOT NULL,

  FIRSTNME VARCHAR(50),

  MIDINIT CHARACTER(1),

  LASTNME VARCHAR(50),

  PHONE VARCHAR(25),

  HIREDATE DATE);
```

```
ALTER TABLE BOTTOMUP.EMPLOYEE

  ADD CONSTRAINT EMPLOYEE_PK PRIMARY KEY (EMP_NO);
```

Start by creating an EJB project named BottomUpExample and set the enterprise application to a new application named BottomUpExampleEAR. Refer to Chapter 20 for instructions on
creating an EJB project. Now follow the steps from the top-down example to open the EJB to
RDB mapping wizard on the new BottomUpExample EJB module. Select the new back-end
folder option as in the top-down mapping example. Click *Next* to go to the mapping options page
shown in Figure 24.4 and this time only the Bottom Up option is available and it is selected.

Click *Next* to continue to a page that is dynamic based upon whether you already have a
logical database defined within your EJB project. In this example, the logical database does not
exist. This means it is not necessary to already have a logical database defined within the EJB
project in order to use the Bottom Up option. So, you can immediately use this wizard to create
container-managed entity beans based upon an existing set of database tables with just the EJB
project created.

The next bottom-up mapping page, assuming no existing database within the EJB project,
allows you to specify information to create a database connection as shown in Figure 24.7. This
is required because bottom-up mapping requires that logical database to exist within the EJB
project. We will not go into details for every field on the connection page. If you need help, refer
to the online documentation or the help for this page by clicking on F1.

One other thing on this page that should be pointed out is the last option, Use existing connection. When this is selected, you can choose from database connections that have been created
by using the Data perspective or the DB Servers view of the J2EE perspective (Figure 20.6).
Click the *Next* button to proceed to the next page where the database tables can be selected.

The next page shows a Tree view of all tables defined within the specified database. They
are grouped based on the schema for which they were defined as shown in Figure 24.8. You
should select the BOTTOMUP schema for this example. Figure 24.8 also shows another schema
named DABERG which has multiple tables associated with it. Selecting the DABERG schema
would automatically select all of the tables associated with this schema. You are not required to
select tables from the same schema grouping nor are you required to import all of the tables
from a given database. Doing so would create an EJB module that would be unmanageable due
to its large size. Note, some tables may be imported even though you did not select them because
the mapping tool requires target tables of foreign key relationships to be imported as well.

Click *Next* to move to the next page which provides details for the generated container-
managed entities as shown in Figure 24.9. The first option, Select a specification level, allows
you to choose the level of EJB you would like to create, either 1.1 or 2.0. Note, with the 2.0
specification option, only local client view interfaces will be created, in accordance with our best
practice of only using local interfaces for container-managed entities.

The Package for generated EJB classes option provides the ability to determine the package for which the newly generated Java files will be defined.

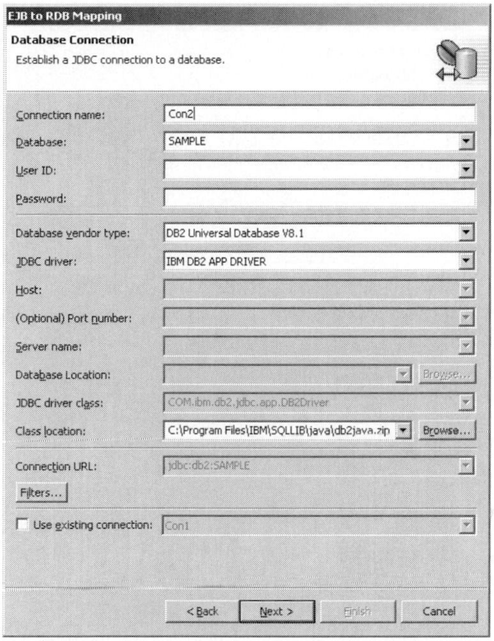

Figure 24.7 Database connection wizard page.

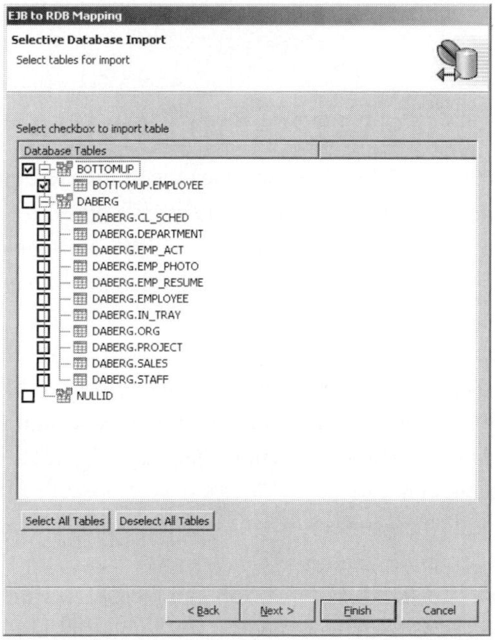

Figure 24.8 Selective database import wizard page.

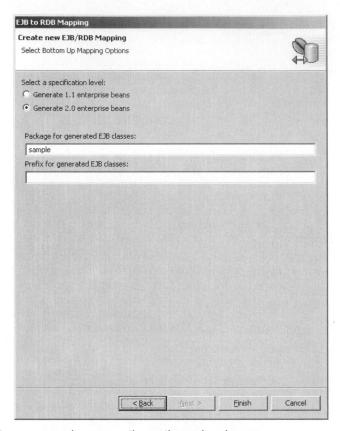

Figure 24.9 Bottom-up mapping generation options wizard page.

The Prefix for generated EJB classes provides the ability to define a prefix to be added to each EJB Java class name that is used to create a new Java class. If you enter a string it will be prefixed to the database table name to form the name of the associated Java class. If no prefix is specified this value is ignored. Note that this page would appear instead of the previous two if a database had already existed within the EJB project.

Now that all of the bottom-up mapping options have been set, the last thing to do is to click the *Finish* button. This will automatically import the selected BOTTOMUP.EMPLOYEE table into the BottomUpExample EJB project, an Employee container-managed entity will be generated for the table, and new mappings will be generated between the imported table and the generated container-managed entity.

The mappings will be stored in the META-INF/backends/DB2UDBNT_V81_1/ Map.mapxmi file in the BottomUpExample EJB project. Figure 24.10 shows the overview section of the mapping editor for this example. You can clearly see the naming of the container-managed entity and its fields reflects the table name and column names.

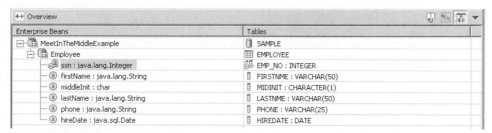

Figure 24.10 Bottom-up mapping results.

24.1.3   Meet-in-the-Middle Mapping Example

The meet-in-the-middle mapping approach only applies if container-managed entity beans and a logical database and its tables already exist within an EJB project. With this approach, only mappings are created and nothing more (i.e., no container-managed entity beans are created nor are database tables). The mappings created will use simple name and type matching rules for matching tables to container-managed entities and columns to cmp-fields. With WSAD, there are independent type mapping rules for each supported database vendor (see Table 24.1). These type mappings are not made accessible for modifications and they are mostly derived from common sense.

For this example, you will need to start by creating another EJB project named Meet-InTheMiddleExample using the same steps as in the Bottom Up mapping example. Next a container-managed entity needs to be created within this project. Refer to Chapter 23 for details on creating a container-managed entity. Set the following information for the container-managed entity using the EJB Creation wizard and use all other default values to create the container-managed entity.

Bean name: Employee
Default package: meet.in.the.middle.example
CMP attributes:

```
ssn : java.lang.Integer     (Key)
firstName : java.lang.String
middleInit : char
lastName : java.lang.String
phone : java.lang.String
hireDate : java.sql.Date
```

Now follow the steps from the top-down example to open the EJB to RDB mapping wizard on the new MeetInTheMiddleExample EJB module. Select the new back-end folder option as in the top-down mapping example. Click *Next* to go to the mapping options page shown in Figure 24.4. Again both the Top Down and Meet in the Middle options are available. Select the Meet in the Middle option and click the *Next* button.

You are now presented with the same connection page as in the bottom-up example in Figure 24.7. At this point you can use the same connection you used in the previous mapping example. This page appears since a logical database does not exist in the EJB project. If one had existed, you would not see this or the next page. Click the *Next* button to select the tables to import. The select Database Import page, shown in Figure 24.8, appears. Select the BOT-TOMUP.EMPLOYEE table and click the *Next* button.

The next page, shown in Figure 24.11, has three simple mapping rules that are available: None, Match by Name, and Match By Name and Type. Selecting None creates a new (empty) mapping between the database and the EJB JAR within the EJB project but it does not map any of the container-managed entities. The Match by Name option will do the same as the None option except it will attempt to create a mapping for each container-managed entity. It creates an entity mapping if the name of the container-managed entity matches one of the simple names of a database table (ignoring case). For example, if you have an EJB named Address, it will create a mapping if a database table is found with the name Address or ADDRESS or any other case combination. This option also applies when creating mappings for cmp-fields which are mapped to database table columns with the same name. The last option, Match By Name and Type, is

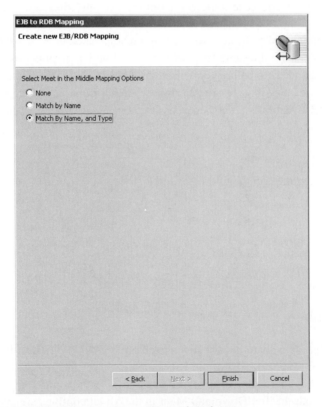

Figure 24.11 Meet-in-the-middle mapping options wizard page.

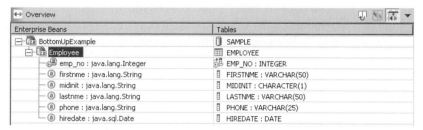

Figure 24.12 Meet-in-the-middle mapping results.

nearly the same as the previous one except that when mapping cmp-fields to columns, both the name and type are used to determine if a mapping should be created. The name must match and the types must be compatible according to the type mapping rules for the selected database.

Select the Match By Name and Type option and click the *Finish* button. This will import the BOTTOMUP.EMPLOYEE table to a new back-end folder within the MeetInTheMiddleEx-ample EJB project and it will create mappings between the Employee container-managed entity and the imported table. Also, all cmp-fields are mapped to the correct columns in the EMPLOYEE table even though the names were not an exact match. The mapping rules were applied and the best matches were found. The mapping editor opens to reveal the resulting map-pings shown in the Overview section of the mapping editor in Figure 24.12.

24.1.3.1 Existing Back-end Folder Options

Now that you have seen an explanation of the mapping options within the EJB to RDB mapping wizard, we can return to Figure 24.2 to provide descriptions of the remaining two mapping options. These options should now be enabled since you have created at least one back-end folder by using this wizard. With at least one back-end folder available, the Use an existing Backend folder is enabled. If you select this option, the back-end folder list in Figure 24.2 is enabled. When you select one of the existing back-end folders from the list, the two radio but-tons under the list are enabled.

The first option, Re-execute mapping commands to react to model changes, is used to re-execute the mapping commands that were used to create the map file. For example, if you cre-ated the map file using the top-down mapping option, this option will re-execute a top-down mapping command to pick up any changes that were made to the EJB module and reflect them in the database tables. Be forewarned that this option will delete and recreate the mapped data-base tables in this scenario. Also note in this example, if you made changes to one of the data-base tables or the database in any way, this option will not have any effect since the mapping was created using the top-down mapping option.

The same is true if you first created the map file using the bottom-up mapping option. This option will re-execute the bottom-up commands to react to changes made to the database and reflect them in the EJB module. Warning: This will delete all cmp-fields and relationships as well as the methods that support them. The action will then re-create the cmp-fields and relationships and their associated methods in the container-managed entities based on the database tables.

It should now be apparent that you cannot mix mapping approaches. Once you have decided upon one, you must continue to use it or switch to using the meet-in-the-middle mapping approach if you want to make changes to both the container-managed entities and the database tables.

The second option, Open mapping editor on selected backend map, opens the mapping editor for the selected back-end folder without running any commands or making any modifications to the file. This is a convenience option for opening the mapping editor for multiple back-end folders. You can do the same by double-clicking the desired backend mapping under the Maps section within an EJB module from the J2EE Hierarchy view (see Figure 20.3).

24.1.4 EJB Mapping Editor

Now that we have described how to use the EJB to RDB mapping wizard to create a mapping for your EJB module, you are ready to learn the basics of using the EJB mapping editor. This is opened after running the EJB to RDB mapping wizard. Figure 24.13 shows the contents of the EJB mapping editor that was opened after creating a top-down mapping for the TimeSheetGroup EJB project used within the case study. You would use this editor if you are required to make manual changes to a top-down or bottom-up mapping or if you simply use the meet-in-the-middle mapping approach.

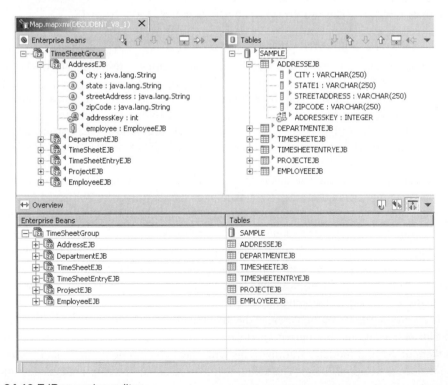

Figure 24.13 EJB mapping editor.

Table 24.2 EJB to RDB mapping editor action buttons.

Action Name	Button Icon
Create a new mapping	
Create mappings for children with matching names	
Create mappings for children with matching types	
Re-execute Mapping Commands	
Overview filter mapped objects	
Overview flip orientation	

The EJB mapping editor is divided into three major areas: the Enterprise Beans list, the Tables list, and the overview as shown in Figure 24.13. The Enterprise Beans list is a tree view of the EJB JAR, its contained container-managed entities, and their CMP and CMR fields. The Tables list is a tree view of the database, its contained tables, and their columns and foreign keys. These two lists work together to create the desired mappings. In order for the map to be free of validation errors, you must map each element in the Enterprise Beans list to an element in the Tables list.

The actions in Table 24.2 are easy to carry out. To create a mapping between a container-managed entity bean and a database table, select the desired container-managed entity bean from the Enterprise Beans list and the database table that you would like to map to from the Tables list. Next, click one of the mapping toolbar buttons in order to create the mapping. The mapping buttons function as follows:

- The *Create a new mapping* button creates a mapping between the CMP bean and the selected table and nothing more.
- The *Create mappings for children with matching names* button does the same as the simple mapping button as well as creating mappings for each cmp-field to a table column where there is a column with the same name, ignoring case, within the selected table.
- The *Create mappings for children with matching types* button will do the same as the simple mapping button and also create mappings for each cmp-field to a table column where there is an unmapped column with a type that can be mapped to the cmp-field type.

The last two actions may be used even after a simple mapping has been applied as long as there is an unmapped cmp-field and there is an available column that can be mapped by the action. Note that any simple mapping can also be accomplished by simply dragging and dropping a member from the Enterprise Beans list to the Tables list and vice versa.

Figure 24.14 Mapping list button bar.

Both the Enterprise Beans list and the Tables list have the same button bar (shown in Figure 24.14). The actions associated with these buttons are merely convenience actions to make traversal through the lists easier.

The first two actions, starting at the left, change the current selection to the next mapped object and the previous mapped object correspondingly. The third and fourth buttons are similar to the first two except that they change the current selection to the next unmapped object and the previous unmapped object. The fifth button, which looks like a window shade, is used to filter the list so that only unmapped objects are displayed when the button is pressed. The last button has the same action for both lists but it points in the opposite direction for each list. This button will select the mapped object(s) from the other list for the currently mapped selection. For example, if the city cmp-field was selected for the AddressEJB from the Enterprise Beans list and this button was selected, the CITY column for the ADDRESSEJB table in the Tables list will be selected.

The Overview section of the mapping editor provides a view of the current mappings from the point of view of either the enterprise beans or the tables. By default the view is with respect to the enterprise beans and it shows only mapped members. To see the unmapped objects as well, you can click the overview filter mapped objects button shown in Table 24.2. The view is divided into two lists Enterprise Beans and Tables similar to the other lists. The way to read this view is to look at an object from the left list like the AddressEJB and then look directly at the object to the right to see which object(s) it maps to (i.e., ADDRESSEJB table). If the Overview filter mapped objects button is selected, the object to the right will be empty if the object to the left is not currently mapped. You can change or create a mapping by selecting the element in the right list and selecting from the available unmapped elements (tables or columns in this case) drop-down tree list.

Remove Mapping, *Match by Name*, and *Match by Type* are all available from the overview context menu for the element selected in the right list. You might have noticed by now that we continue to refer to the lists as right and left as opposed to Enterprise Beans list and Tables list. The reason is that the Enterprise Beans list is not necessarily always on the left. Remember that the right list is the master showing the mappings for these elements. The default is to show the container-managed entity beans but you can switch the lists such that the tables are on the right and enterprise beans are on the left. This is accomplished with the Overview flip orientation button shown in Table 24.2. This is useful if you like to create or view mappings based on the database definition.

The mapping editor also has an outline view, shown in Figure 24.15, which is used to navigate between existing mapped objects. The outline shows all of the mappings that have been created between container-managed entity beans and database tables. Notice that the selections are all linked within each view. So, if you select a mapping from the outline, the corresponding EJB object is selected from the Enterprise Beans list, the corresponding database object is

Figure 24.15 Mapping editor outline.

selected from the Tables list, and the mapping is also selected within the overview. The outline contains the same context menu actions as the overview where a mapping exists.

There is one additional mapping action that we have yet to mention which appears in virtually all of the context menus and the workbench toolbar. This is the Re-execute mapping commands action which has an associated toolbar button shown in Table 24.2. This action is equivalent to using the Re-execute mapping commands to react to model changes from the first page of the EJB to RDB mapping wizard as shown in Figure 24.2. This action is useful if you make a change to the EJB module after performing a top-down mapping. This action will cause the top-down mapping command to be re-executed, which would cause a database artifact to be created and mapped to the new features in the EJB module. The same is true if you did a bottom-up mapping and you changed the database tables or if you did a meet-in-the-middle mapping and you changed either the EJB module or database tables, or both.

24.1.5   Re-executing Mapping Commands

The *Re-execute Mapping Commands* action accomplishes its task by re-executing the persistent commands that were serialized within the Map.mapxmi file. This is the same action that would be executed if you had selected the Re-execute mapping commands to react to model changes option from the EJB to RDB mapping wizard shown in Figure 24.2.

When a mapping command is performed, it is tracked and added to the persistent commands list that is saved with the file. So you can perform a meet-in-the-middle mapping initially and then map a cmp-field that was not automatically mapped by the command to a database column. If you later select the *Re-execute Mapping Commands* action, this last mapping command is also executed since it was tracked and added to the persistent command stack. Only commands that create mappings are tracked. Delete mapping commands are not tracked.

We should re-emphasize a point that was made earlier when describing this option in the EJB to RDB mapping wizard. If you select the *Re-execute Mapping Commands* either from the toolbar or the context menu, and the Top Down mapping option was used to create the map, all database tables will be deleted and recreated based on the container-managed entities in the EJB module. Also, if you use the Bottom Up mapping option to initially create a map, the Re-execute

Mapping Commands option will delete all of the cmp-fields and relationships in the mapped container-managed entities.

Re-executing the mapping command will also cause all of the methods that were created on the entity to be removed. Then new cmp-fields and relationships will be created based on the table that the container-managed entity is mapped. All methods that were added by the user will be maintained and not be deleted. Any table that is removed will cause the corresponding container-managed entity to be deleted from the EJB module.

24.1.6 Re-execute Mapping Commands Alternative

We have just seen how you can use the Re-execute Mapping Commands option to create mappings to pick up changes to either the database or to the EJB module, but not both. So you have a problem if you used the Bottom Up mapping option to create the map and later you update one or more of the container-managed entities that were generated and possibly add a new database table. The problem is that you want to use the Re-execute Mapping Commands action to pick up the changes to the database (i.e., the new table) but that will delete all of the container-managed entity generated methods, cmp-fields, and relationships and recreate only the ones based on the table. This is not the desired effect because you want to preserve your changes to the container-managed entities.

This can be solved by two different methods. First, you could create a container-managed entity for the new table and then use the meet-in-the-middle mapping approach to map the new container-managed entity and its cmp-fields to the new database table and its columns. This seems like a lot of work just to keep your modifications to the container-managed entities. The good news is that there is a much simpler solution. Let's use a very simple example to show how this would work.

We start by creating a database and one table, TABLEA, or you could simply import a table from an existing database. Next we use the EJB to RDB mapping wizard to generate a new bottom-up map which would create a Tablea container-managed entity. So far we have done nothing new. Now, let's assume that you wanted to add business logic to the ejbCreate method generated on the Tablea container-managed entity. Now the Tablea container-managed entity has been modified beyond the point of its generation using the mapping wizard.

Next, you might update the database by adding a new table, TABLEB. You would like to have a new container-managed entity created for TABLEB and have a new mapping defined for this table and bean. At first guess you think about using the Re-execute Mapping Commands action to pick up the database changes. Remember when re-executing a bottom-up mapping command, the cmp-fields and relationships of the container-managed entries are deleted (this also updates the ejbCreate method) and new ones are created to reflect the current shape of the database and its tables (the ejbCreate method is recreated at this point). This is not the desired effect because you have modified the Tablea bean.

This is where our second alternative comes in. From the mapping editor (shown in Figure 24.13) you can select the new database table, TABLEB, from the Tables list. Now you can drag the table to the EJB JAR (the root object in the tree view) in the Enterprise Beans list. Once you drag the table over the EJB JAR, the icon will switch to a plus (+) symbol indicating that it can be dropped. This is only possible because you created the map using the bottom-up mapping option so you can drag and drop tables to the EJB JAR.

If you drop the new TABLEB on the EJB JAR, WSAD creates a Tableb container-managed entity with cmp-fields for each column in the table. It also creates a mapping for the new container-managed entity and the table as well as for each cmp-field and its associated column. This is what you want since the new table will get a new container-managed entity created for it while leaving the other container-managed entities intact. Also, if just one or more columns were added to TABLEA, you can drag and drop the column to the Tablea container-managed entity to have a new cmp-field created and mapped.

IMPORTING CHANGES FROM THE DATABASE

It is very common for individuals to import all tables for a specific schema within the database and then map it to a set of container-managed entities. At a later time changes may be made to the physical database and you will want to import those changes back into your EJB project. You will often not be aware of the specific changes so it is safer to import the entire set of tables within the schema and/or database. This causes a problem with WSAD 5.0.1 which will manifest itself as a loss of all of your mappings.

This loss of mappings takes place because the map file has references to the logical database tables and columns. Each of these tables and columns has a generated ID to ensure that they are unique. When the tables are imported a second time, new files are created to store the metainformation and, therefore, new IDs are generated. These new IDs are different than the ones in the map file, thus causing the problem. A more in-depth discussion of the problem and a new feature to correct the problem can be found in "Importing Database Table Changes into an EJB Module in WebSphere Studio While Preserving References" at *http://submit.boulder.ibm.com/wsdd/library/techarticles/0305_berg/berg.html* .

This example was for bottom-up mapping but there is a corresponding option when using top-down mapping. In this case, you created the map using the Top Down mapping option and then made changes to the database tables. If you create a container-managed entity, you will want a new table to be created for the bean but do not want to re-execute the top-down mapping command because that would delete the current database tables. This means that you will lose any changes that were made to the database tables. Instead, you can open the map editor and drag the new container-managed entity from the Enterprise Beans list and drop it on the database from the Tables list. This will create a database table, create columns for each cmp-field, and create new mappings for each of these, all without deleting any of the existing database tables. Also, if just one or more cmp-fields were added to Tablea, you can drag and drop the cmp-field to the TABLEA table to have a new column created and mapped.

> **MAPPING DIRECTIONS**
>
> Every map that is created has a direction associated with it. This direction indicates whether it was created using the top-down or bottom-up approach. These are the only two directions. If the meet-in-the-middle approach were used, the mapping will indicate the top-down direction by default. This will dictate the direction that objects can be created. For example, if bottom-up were used to create the mapping, you will be able to drag and drop changes to the database or tables onto the corresponding EJB JAR or container-managed entity but you will *not* be able to drag and drop container-managed entity changes to the database. The opposite is true for the top-down direction.

24.1.7 Defining and Using Converters

By default, complex EJB properties (i.e., subclasses of `java.lang.Object` which are not Java primitive type wrappers) that are serializable are serialized and mapped to an appropriate binary database column. While this does allow for properties of arbitrary Java types, it is not an optimal solution. Since the column is binary, it is impossible to query this column using standard SQL query tools. Likewise, the performance of serializing and deserializing an object into a binary large object (BLOB) can be poor. In order to improve the mapping options for these types, WSAD has the concept of converters. These helper classes provide an open framework for converting between object types and database types used by the mapping and deploy code specific to WebSphere. If you used the EJB development environment in VisualAge for Java in the past, the converters in WSAD are very similar those used in VAJ.

WSAD provides a number of common converters for use by the EJB to RDB mapping editor within any EJB project; however, you may need other types of conversion. If this is the case, you will need to create your own converter class and define this converter so that the EJB mapping framework will be aware of it.

This is done by using the converter or composer wizard. To help demonstrate how to define and use a converter, change the date cmp-field of our TimeSheetEntryEJB CMP bean from the TimeSheetGroup EJB module from a java.lang.String object type to a java.util.Date using the edit action on the Beans page of the EJB deployment descriptor editor. Also change the typing of the DATE1 column in the TIMESHEETENTRYEJB table from DATE to VARCHAR using the Table editor.

First we begin by defining and creating a converter class. Start by selecting *New > Other > EJB > Converter or Composer* from the workbench menu bar. This will open the EJB converter or composer wizard shown in Figure 24.16. Select the Converter radio button to create a converter and then enter the EJB project in which the converter will be defined. Then provide a fully qualified name for the converter class (`com.wsbook.casestudy.ejb.DateToStringConverter`) and its supertype name. The supertype is a combo box because you must select an already defined converter class. If you do not have a need for a specific supertype, use the default `com.ibm.vap.converters.VapAbstractConverter`.

Lastly, define the target type of the converter. This is the Java type that the database type will be converted to. In this example, we choose `java.lang.String`. Note that the Generate a

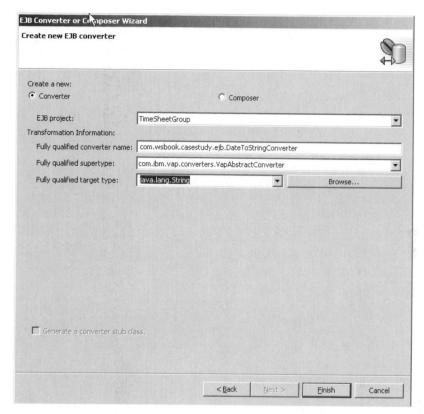

Figure 24.16 EJB converter wizard.

converter stub class option is checked by default. If the converter class name specified already exists, you should deselect this option in order to create a converter definition using the existing converter class. This option will automatically generate the new converter class for you leaving only two methods to be implemented.

When the wizard finishes, notice that it has created a file in the EJB project named User-DefinedConverters.xmi. This file contains the definition of converters that were defined specifically for this EJB project. If you would like to share these definitions with other EJB projects, you will need either to redefine the converter within each EJB project that you would like to use it or copy this file to the other EJB projects. You will also need to ensure that the converter class is accessible to the other EJB projects by putting it on both the development time and runtime classpaths. One way to do this would be to put the converters in a separate project and treat them as utility JAR files (see Chapter 18 for more details about configuring J2EE projects).

There is also a new Java class defined within the TimeSheetGroup EJB project. If you open a Java editor on the `com.wsbook.casestudy.ejb.DateToStringConverter` Java class you will see that the converter class is stubbed in for you. The only thing left to do is to implement the `dataFrom(Object)` and `objectFrom(Object)` methods. The data-From(Object) method is used to convert the `java.lang.String` object type that is passed to a `java.sql.Date` type to be used when writing to the database.

```
public Object dataFrom(Object anObject) {

        //date in format "mm-dd-yyyy"

        Date date = null;

        try {

                String dateString = (String) anObject;

                DateFormat formatter = new SimpleDateFormat(

                        "MM/dd/yyyy");

                java.util.Date parsed =

                        formatter.parse(dateString);

                return new java.sql.Date(parsed.getTime());

        } catch (ParseException e) {

                // can't do anything, so eat the exception

        }

        return date;

    }
```

The `objectFrom(Object)` method is used to convert the `java.sql.Date` database type that is passed to a java.lang.String type to be used when reading from the database.

```
public Object objectFrom(Object aField) {

        //return a String in format "mm-dd-yyyy"

        java.sql.Date date = (java.sql.Date) aField;
```

```
        String value = null;

        DateFormat formatter = new SimpleDateFormat("MM/dd/yyyy");

        value = formatter.format(date);

        return value;

    }
```

Now that we have defined our converter, we are ready to use it within our map. Return to the EJB to RDB mapping editor for the TimeSheetGroup EJB project. Select the date cmp-field from the TimeSheetEntryEJB within the Overview section. Notice that the Properties view has changed to show the properties for the current field mapping. You could achieve the same results by selecting the field mapping from the Outline view.

24.1.8 Defining and Using Composers

In the Properties view, select the Transformation value field. It should change to a combo box. Scroll to the bottom of the list to see the new user defined converters. Select the new `com.wsbook.casestudy.ejb.DateToStringConverter`. Now this field mapping has a converter defined for it and this converter will be used when the deployed code is generated.

Composers, much like converters, are another mechanism for serializing a custom Java type to the database without using a BLOB column to accomplish this task. This is common with container-managed entities when using dependent values which are defined as concrete Java classes that are serializable and can be the type of a cmp-field. The internal structure of dependent values is not defined in the deployment descriptor.

Composers are unique to the mapping framework used by WSAD and the deploy code specific to WebSphere. A composer will take a single cmp-field type and map it to multiple database table columns, thus the table columns compose the object type used by the cmp-field. For example, a common composer type provided with WSAD is a composer for joining title, first-Name, and lastName database columns into a single name attribute in a container-managed entity. In order to use a composer, we must first define it using many of the same steps that we did when creating the converter.

First, open the EJB Converter or Composer wizard following the same steps used to create a converter. Now select the composer radio button. The wizard page changes to display the contents for creating a composer as shown in Figure 24.17. Several of the fields are shared with the creation of a converter. First, specify the EJB project in which the composer will be defined. Then enter the fully qualified name of the composer class, (`com.wsbook.case-study.ejb.OfficeLocationComposer`). Like the converter, we must select a supertype for our composer from the list of already defined composers. If there is not a known supertype, use the default `VapAttributeComposer` type. Enter the qualified Java target type for the composer

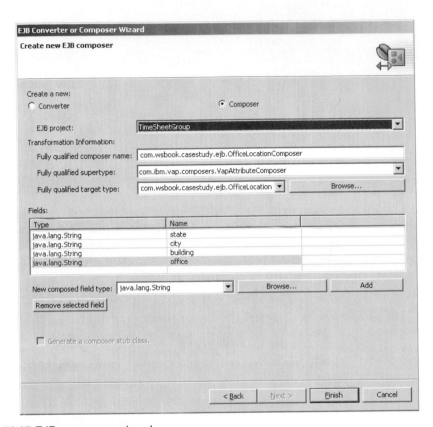

Figure 24.17 EJB composer wizard.

(`com.wsbook.casestudy.ejb.OfficeLocation`). The type does not need to exist and probably will not exist at this time.

The Fields section is where the composer differs from the converter. In this section, it is necessary to define the fields within the target type (i.e., `com.wsbook.case-study.ejb.OfficeLocation`) that will be mapped to individual database columns. For this example we added four columns that are used to compose a person's unique office location. This was done by selecting a composed field type from the combo box and clicking the *Add* button. This adds the field to the table. We then can select the Name column entry and type in a new name of the field. Again the generation option, Generate a composer stub class, appears at the bottom of the wizard. With this option selected, a new composer class and the target type will be generated. Upon finish the composer class and the target type class are generated and the composer is defined in the new UserDefinedComposers.xmi file.

The target type that is generated is just a data structure that is free of compile errors and is ready to be used, but you may make changes to suit your needs. Just as with the converter, you will need to implement the `dataFrom(Object)` and `objectFrom(Object[])` methods. The

`dataFrom(Object)` method takes the target type (`com.wsbook.casestudy.ejb.Office-`
`Location`) and returns an `Object` array with composed fields in the order that they are defined
in the `getAttributeNames()` method (e.g., the order that they were defined within the wizard).

```
public Object[] dataFrom(Object anObject) {

    Object[] anArray = new Object[4];

    if (anObject != null) {

      OfficeLocation location = (OfficeLocation) anObject;

        anArray[0] = location.getState();

        anArray[1] = location.getCity();

        anArray[2] = location.getBuilding();

        anArray[3] = location.getOffice();

    }

    return anArray;

}
```

The `objectFrom(Object[])` method receives the database column types passed within
the `Object[]` in the order in which they appear in the `getAttributeNames()` method. It
must return an instance of the `com.wsbook.casestudy.ejb.OfficeLocation` class with its
attributes appropriately set.

```
public Object objectFrom(Object[] anArray) {

      OfficeLocation location = new OfficeLocation();

      location.setState((String) anArray[0]);

      location.setCity((String) anArray[1]);

      location.setBuilding((String) anArray[2]);

      location.setOffice((String) anArray[3]);
```

```
    return location;

}
```

In order to use this new composer first add a new office cmp-field to the EmployeeEJB using the EJB deployment descriptor editor on the Beans page within the CMP Fields list of the selected bean. Set the type to be the new composer target type (com.wsbook.case-study.ejb.OfficeLocation). Also add four new columns, all typed to VARCHAR to the EMPLOYEEEJB table: STATE, CITY, BUILDING, and OFFICE. Do this using the Table editor by selecting the NULLID.EMPLOYEEEJB table from the TimeSheetGroup database under the Databases section in the J2EE Hierarchy view and selecting the Open action from the context menu, then adding the columns.

Now open the EJB to RDB Mapping editor for the TimeSheetGroup EJB project so that you can map the new office cmp-field. Select the office cmp-field from the EmployeeEJB from the EnterpriseBeans list and select the STATE, CITY, BUILDING, and OFFICE columns from the EMPLOYEEEJB table from the Tables list. Then select the Create Mapping context menu option or button from the workbench toolbar. This will open the EJB Composer wizard shown in Figure 24.18 since you are mapping one cmp-field to multiple database columns.

First select the new composer from the drop-down list (i.e., com.wsbook.case-study.ejb.OfficeLocationComposer). This populates the table with the attributes defined when you created the composer. For each attribute, select one of the four columns selected in the mapping to be directly mapped to the attribute. The new mapping is defined after pressing Finish. If you look in the Overview section, you will see that the office cmp-field is now mapped to

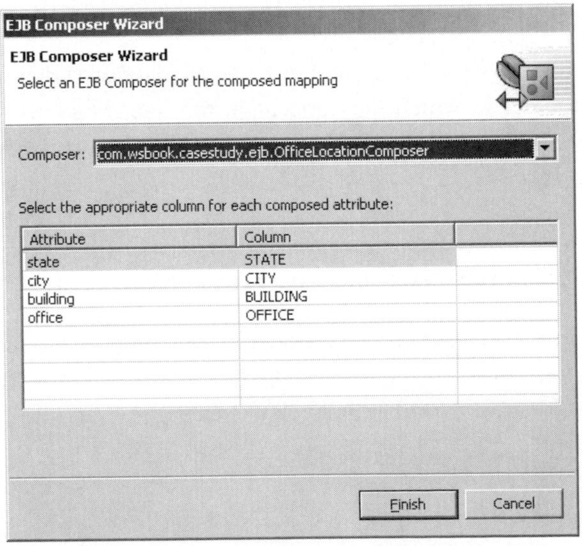

Figure 24.18 EJB composer wizard.

Figure 24.19 Back-end folder structure.

four columns. If you need to change the composer, you can do so from the Properties view when the mapping is selected from the Overview or the Outline views. Clicking on the button for the Transformation class will launch the EJB composer wizard once again.

24.2 Multiple Mapping Back-end Support

We first touched on the mapping back-end support when we were describing the EJB to RDB mapping wizard. The first page of this wizard (Figure 24.2) provided options for creating a back-end folder or using an existing back-end folder when creating or making changes to the map file. When we created the top-down mapping for our TimeSheetGroup EJB module a new back-end folder was created based on the type of the database. Since we first mapped to a DB2 8.1 database, a back-end folder was created with the name DB2UDBNT_V81_1. The last number will be incremented if we create another back-end mapping to the same database type. Figure 24.19 shows the TimeSheetGroup EJB project structure within the J2EE Navigator provided with WSAD. Notice that the location of all back-end folders will be within the META-INF/back-end folder.

At this point you are probably asking what it means to have multiple back-end folders. Whenever you generate the deploy code for an EJB project that contains multiple back-end folders, deploy code is created for each back-end folder. For example, you might find it convenient to use DB2 UDB as a back-end for unit testing, while your target production environment is DB2 zOS. You can create a back-end mapping for both and have the deployed code generated for both at the same time. This means that the deploy code would be exported to the EJB JAR

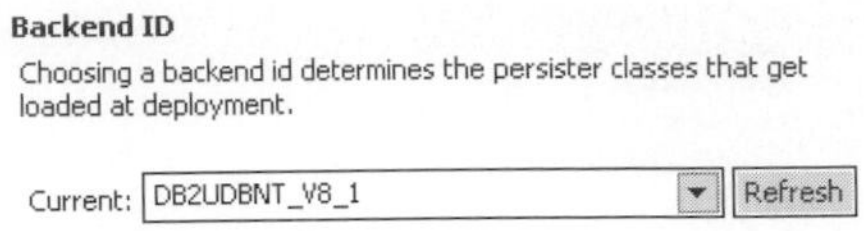

Backend ID

Choosing a backend id determines the persister classes that get
loaded at deployment.

Current: [DB2UDBNT_V8_1   ▼] [Refresh]

Figure 24.20 Current back-end section.

file during export. That means that a JAR can be deployed once and run against many different
database environments.

Only one back end is used by a running application server. Determining which one to use
is accomplished by setting the current back end within the EJB deployment descriptor editor.
When you open the EJB deployment descriptor editor, scroll to the bottom of the Overview
page. Here you will see the Backend ID section as part of the larger WebSphere bindings section
(shown in Figure 24.20). The drop-down box in this section will contain an entry for each back
end that has been created for the project. The current back end will be set automatically during
deploy code generation if it has not already been set.

24.3   Exporting Database Tables

Once you have created your mappings for the EJB project, you must export the logical database
model to a relational database in order to do any testing of the EJB module. This is assuming
that you did not first import the database model from a relational database when doing a bottom-up or a meet-in-the-middle mapping. There are two ways to export the logical database
tables to a relational database: export the database directly or execute the table.ddl file. Both
methods are simple to use but, depending on your needs, one method may be better. Typically
the production database is tightly controlled and you will not be able to export the logical database to the physical database. However, you may have a private database that serves as a testing
ground prior to making changes on the production database. This is where the following export
options are useful.

The simplest approach is to export the logical database model directly to the relational database by using a wizard that generates dynamic SQL statements that are executed against the database. This is accomplished from the J2EE Hierarchy view within the J2EE perspective (see
Figure 20.2). Expand the Databases group so that you can see each of the models that have been
defined. Once you find the database that you want to export, select the *Export to server* context
menu action which opens the Data Export wizard shown in Figure 24.21. The first page of the
wizard displays a tree check box view starting with the root object selected and all of its children
expanded. So in this example the wsbook database contains one NULLID schemata which in turn
contains several tables. Only the selected objects are exported to the relational database.

Note that you can select any database component within the J2EE Hierarchy view and still
select the *Export to server* context menu action. If you select the NULLID schemata from the
J2EE Hierarchy view and select the *Export to server* action, the first page of the data export wizard starts with the NULLID schemata and includes only its child components.

Figure 24.21 Data export wizard.

The second page of the wizard, shown in Figure 24.22, provides options that you can choose when exporting to the database. The first three options allow you to control when the export transaction is committed. By default, the Commit changes only upon success option is selected.

The last three check boxes are probably the most interesting because they control the contents of the SQL statements that will be executed on the database:

- Generate fully qualified names indicates whether you want to include the schemata name for each table (e.g., SCHEMANAME.TABLENAME). You want to ensure that this is not selected since we are not using fully qualified statements in our SQL queries; we want to export the tables without fully qualified names as well.
- Generate delimited identifiers will add quotation marks around the created objects within the statement (e.g., CREATE TABLE "TEST.TABLEA"). Use this option with column names that contain spaces.
- Generate associated DROP statements will add DROP TABLE statements for each table being created as well as DROP SCHEMA statements for each schema. This is

extremely useful when you already have existing databases and you want to overwrite them with a new definition.

The last wizard page is the Database Connection page which is the same page that was used during the bottom-up and meet-in-the-middle mapping approaches earlier in the chapter (see Figure 24.5). You can go back to the previous sections to learn more detail about these sections but they are basically used to provide detailed information for making a connection to the database you wish to use as the target of this export. You can either supply the information to create a connection, or select from an existing connection that has been defined. You should be careful to use the same user ID in this connection page as you plan to use for the datasource that will be defined in the server configuration. This is necessary because the tables will automatically use the user ID for the schema name if one is not supplied during this export. Also, any SQL statements that are not fully qualified will use the user ID of the datasource for the schema qualification of the tables within the statement.

The second method to export the tables to the database is to execute the Table.ddl file which contains SQL statements to create the database, schema, and tables. This file was generated when running the EJB to RDB mapping wizard if you had the Generate DDL option selected (Figure 24.4). If you did not have this option selected at the time that you created the mapping, you can always select the EJB module from the J2EE Hierarchy view and then select the *Generate > Schema DDL* context menu option. This will produce the static Table.ddl file within the current back-end folder. This file is convenient because you can make modifications to suit your needs. The Table.ddl that is generated does not contain foreign key statements since referential integrity sorting (the sorting of SQL statements to ensure database table constraints are not violated) is not maintained by the generated SQL or the WebSphere EJB container.

Remember that these options are typically used to export to a private database for the purpose of testing. You can use the generated DDL file to request changes to your DBA on the production database.

To export tables to the database using the Table.ddl file, select the file from the appropriate back-end folder within the J2EE Navigator view. Next, select the *Run on Database Server* context menu action. This will open the Run Script database wizard shown in Figure 24.23. The first page of this wizard contains a check box list of each statement within the script file. You have the option of deselecting any statement which you do not want to be executed at this time. The second page of the wizard has the same three commit options as displayed in the Data Export Options wizard page shown in Figure 24.22. The last page is the same Database Connection page used in the previous data export wizard and the EJB to RDB mapping wizard.

24.4 EJB Query Language

Thus far you have seen several basic mapping techniques for mapping container-managed entity beans to relational database tables. These basic mappings provide the necessary information for generating the deployment classes which have SQL statements used to access a set of database tables. The SQL queries that are generated support CRUD actions for the container-

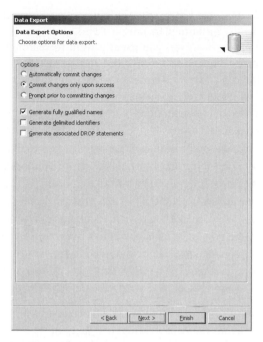

Figure 24.22 Data export options wizard page.

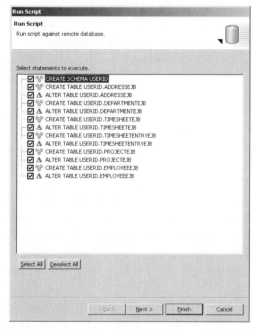

Figure 24.23 Run script wizard.

managed entity beans but there are many situations where you would like to add additional queries to one of these beans. In particular, only a `findByPrimaryKey` method is provided based on the EJB specification. However, you usually want to search by other criteria as well. This is accomplished using EJB queries written with EJB QL, which is a newly defined concept in the EJB 2.0 specification.

EJB QL is used to define queries in terms of persistent properties of the container-managed entity which makes the query definitions portable. EJB QL allows for the selection of entity objects or other values based on its abstract schema types and relationships. The abstract schema of a container-managed entity bean is a persistence representation of the bean that is based on the persistent properties (cmp and cmr fields) and not on the actual database table mappings. This is what allows EJB QL queries to be portable.

The abstract schema names specified by the abstract-schema-name elements in the deployment descriptor are used to denote the abstract schema types in EJB QL. Within WSAD, the abstract schema name of a container-managed entity is defaulted to the name of the bean at creation time. The abstract schema name can be modified in the Abstract schema text field when the bean is selected on the Beans page of the EJB deployment descriptor editor. There are two types of EJB QL queries that can be specified within the deployment descriptor:

1. Finder queries are used for selecting entity objects using finder methods on the home interface. Finder methods may be exposed to clients of the entity bean.

2. Select queries are used for selecting entity objects or values derived from an entity bean's abstract schema type using select methods defined on entity bean class. Select methods defined on the entity bean class are not exposed to the clients of the entity bean.

EJB QL uses a syntax very similar to SQL which explains why each statement string must contain a `SELECT` clause and a `FROM` clause and it may contain a `WHERE` clause. The `SELECT` clause is used to determine the type of the objects or values to be selected. The `FROM` clause is used to designate the domain for which the expressions specified by the `SELECT` and `WHERE` clauses of the query apply. The optional `WHERE` clause restricts the results returned by the query.

WSAD provides tools for creating, editing, and deleting EJB QL queries, their statements, and the query methods. We will walk through a couple of examples where we will create a finder query and a select query. Along the way we will provide more details regarding the query methods and the EJB QL statements.

We will start by adding a finder method to the DepartmentEJB entity from our case study. You will need to open the EJB Deployment Descriptor editor by selecting the TimeSheetGroup EJB module from the J2EE Hierarchy view and selecting the *Open With > Deployment Descriptor Editor* context menu action. Turn to the Beans page and select the DepartmentEJB entity from the list of defined beans. The Queries section, about three quarters of the way down the page, displays EJB QL queries defined for the selected entity bean.

From the Queries section, we are going to create a finder query by clicking the *Add* button to launch the add finder descriptor wizard shown in Figure 24.24. The Method set of radio buttons allows you to choose whether you want to define an EJB QL query element for an existing

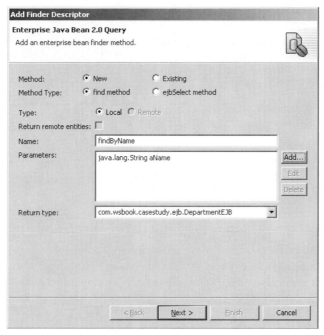

Figure 24.24 EJB QL query method wizard page.

query method or if you would like to create a query method for the new EJB QL query element. The Method Type group provides two radio buttons to indicate which type of query element and method you would like to create. You can either create a new find method which will be defined on the home interface or an ejbSelect method that will be defined on the bean class.

The Type entry is enabled for find queries only. It indicates whether the new finder query method is defined on the local home interface or the remote home interface. The possible return type values are limited based on the home interface type that is selected for the find query. For example, if the find query is defined on the local home interface, the resulting return value or values must be of the local interface type.

For ejbSelect queries, the return value type can be any Java type but if a collection of client interfaces is returned you may need to select the Return remote entities check box. This check box is only enabled for ejbSelect queries and it maps directly to the `result-type-mapping` element in the deployment descriptor. If the check box is selected, it is assumed that the returning objects in the collection will be the remote interfaces of the selected container-managed entity. If the check box is not selected, then local interface types are assumed.

The remaining field values on this wizard directly affect the new method that is about to be generated. If the Existing method option were selected, a list of methods based on the Method Type would appear for selection with the EJB QL deployment descriptor element. The Name field is the name of the method. As defined by the specification, the method name must begin with find if the find method type is selected and ejbSelect if the ejbSelect method type is

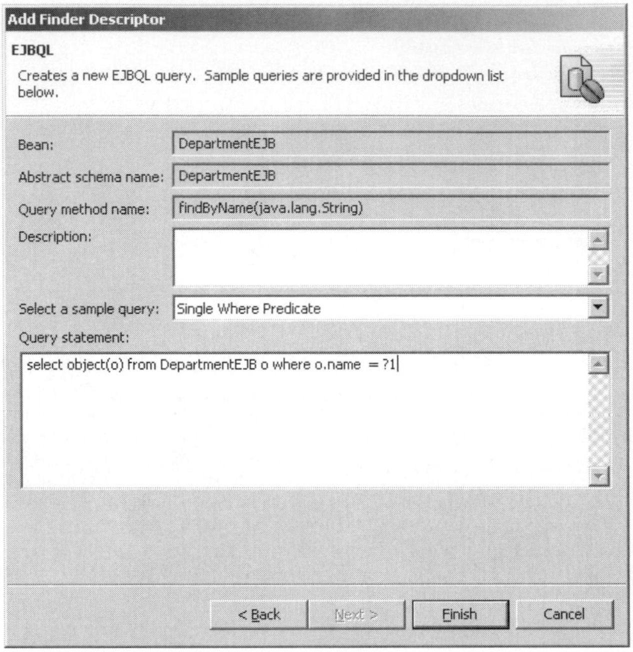

Figure 24.25 EJB QL statement wizard page.

selected. You may add Java parameters to the Parameters list by clicking the Add button to the
right of the list. There must be a parameter for each input parameter within the query statement
in the same order that they are defined in the statement. The Return type is the resulting return
type of the method. See the previous paragraphs for restrictions on this field's value.

Now that enough information has been gathered to create the method, it is now necessary
to enter the actual query statement written in EJB QL. The second wizard page, shown in Figure
24.25, has several read-only text fields that are used for informational purposes only. This
includes the Bean name for which the query is being defined, the Abstract schema name as
defined within the deployment descriptor, and the Query method name which is the actual signature of the query method. You can then enter a Description for this query element which will
appear in the deployment descriptor.

The most important field is the Query statement because this is where the query statement
is defined. To help with creating this statement, WSAD provides a Select a sample query drop-
down box. This drop-down box contains a number of predefined query statement patterns. When
a sample query statement is selected, a valid EJB QL statement is entered in the Query statement
field for the specified bean. For example, a Single Where Predicate sample query would enter the
following statement for our DepartmentEJB.

```
select object(o) from DepartmentEJB o where o.name  is null
```

The statement uses the abstract schema name, DepartmentEJB, to select instances of the bean. The WHERE clause compares fields using the cmp-field name. In most situations it will be necessary to modify the sample query to suit your needs. In this example, we will modify the statement to take an input parameter which will be compared with the name cmp-field. Here is the modified statement:

```
select object(o) from DepartmentEJB o where o.name  = ?1
```

Input parameters are designated by a question mark (?) followed by an integer indicating the parameter position in the method definition we created earlier. The conditional expression may also contain literals such as strings or integers. The statement that we have defined will return the instance of the DepartmentEJB bean that has its name cmp-field equal to the String parameter value passed to the query method. After clicking the *Finish* button, the following query element is defined in the EJB deployment descriptor.

```
<query>

    <description></description>

    <query-method>

        <method-name>findByName</method-name>

        method-params>

        <method-param>java.lang.String</method-param>

      </method-params>

    </query-method>

    <ejb-ql>select object(o) from DepartmentEJB o where o.name = ?1</

ejb-ql>

</query>
```

The findByName(java.lang.String) method shown next is also generated on the DepartmentEJBHome interface.

```
public java.util.Collection findByName(java.lang.String aName) throws

javax.ejb.FinderException;
```

EJB QL queries are powerful since they can be written in terms of the schema types so that they are portable. This portability does not come without a price however. EJB QL statements are not as flexible as typical SQL statements since EJB QL statements are written in terms of bean properties that must be translated into SQL statements. This means that not all SQL statements are supported in EJB QL. Chapter 11 of the Enterprise Java Bean 2.0 specification provides more detailed information for defining EJB QL query statements.

24.5 Summary

In this chapter we have shown you the basic techniques for mapping container-managed entity beans to a set of database tables. We described the three main techniques used by the WSAD EJB to RDB mapping wizard:

- Top-down mapping
- Bottom-up mapping
- Meet-in-the-middle mapping

We have provided a general overview of the functions provided by the EJB mapping editor so you can create, update, and delete mappings for container-managed entity beans to database tables. When a direct mapping is not possible, we demonstrated how to create converters and composers and how to use them within the EJB mapping editor. Once a mapping is created to a logical database model, we described steps to export this logical database model to an actual relational database. Finally, we introduced the query concept of EJB QL as a means to add additional query statements that are beyond the CRUD query statements generated for all container-managed entities. Chapter 25 continues by providing more advanced EJB structures and how to map them using the tools described in this chapter.

CHAPTER 25

Advanced CMP Mapping

In previous chapters we covered the basics of the WSAD J2EE tooling development environment. Chapter 24 showed you how to use the basic mapping approaches in WSAD to map container-managed entity beans to relational database tables in a simple one-to-one way. However, most OO application model designs are more complex than the examples used in Chapter 24. For example, many OO model designs incorporate relationships and inheritance.

This chapter:

- Describes how to incorporate these complexities within an object model composed of container-managed entity beans.
- Provides an overview of the EJB 2.0 specification for relationships.
- Shows how to create relationships between two container-managed entities and map to relationship database tables.
- Explains how the EJB tooling in WSAD has extended the EJB 2.0 specification to include EJB inheritance and the approaches available to map an inheritance structure among container-managed entity beans to a set of relational database tables.
- Provides an in-depth look at EJB QL and how relationships can be used within its statements.

25.1 Simple Mapping Rules

You have seen that WSAD and WebSphere provide a simple mechanism for mapping container-managed entity beans to database tables. This simplicity arises from the assumption that each attribute in an EJB maps to a single column in a single table in a database. This mapping is done by type—String in Java maps to VARCHAR in SQL, int maps to INTEGER, etc.

However, out of the entire set of mapping rules, one sticks out like a sore thumb. All objects that are not convertible to standard SQL types are instead mapped to a BLOB of a maximum size of 1 MB. This rule would apply to any type derived from Object in Java—in other words, every class you might create.

This provides a simple solution for storing objects in a relational database. Objects are serialized into a binary form and then stored into a single column in a table. However, this approach has the following drawbacks:

- BLOBs are not readable from other applications (e.g., reporting tools).
- BLOBs cannot be queried from SQL, making data mining and table maintenance difficult to do.
- BLOBs may not be readable from later versions of the application that created them. This is a tough problem that requires a deep knowledge of how Java serialization works and careful planning to avoid.

These drawbacks have led developers to prefer an alternative approach where objects are mapped to relational databases in such a way that object relationships are preserved in the relational database schema. This approach has been well documented in several places, such as [Fowler]. Let's quickly review this approach to see how it applies to container-managed entity beans in WSAD.

25.2 Object-Relational Basics

In the most common mapping approach, object relationships are represented by foreign-key relationships in the database. To understand how this works, consider the following relationships, drawn from our case study (Figure 25.1).

There is a relationship between TimeSheet and Employee representing the approving relationship, and another relationship between TimeSheet and Employee representing the submitting relationship. As you look deeper at our example, you find another kind of relationship that must be represented. A TimeSheet contains a collection of TimeSheetEntries, as shown in Figure 25.2, which illustrates a multivalued relationship.

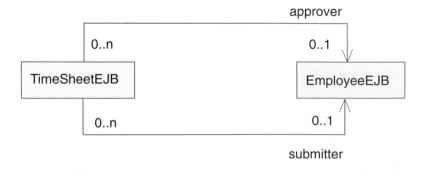

Figure 25.1 Object associations.

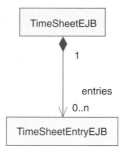

Figure 25.2 One-to-many association.

Normally the approver and submitter associations are represented by having a TimeSheet have two instance variables of the Employee type. Likewise, you might have each TimeSheet hold an array of TimeSheetEntries or a collection containing TimeSheetEntry objects. However, this simple solution won't quite work for entity EJBs. It also doesn't quite map directly to a relational database. Before you see how the former problem is solved, you first need to understand a little about the latter.

As [Fowler] discusses, relationships like we have in the first case (TimeSheet to Employee) are represented in a Relational database by foreign keys that point from the owning table to the owned table. Tables 25.1 and 25.2 illustrate this method. In the tables PK indicates that the column is a part of the primary key constraint for that table.

Table 25.1 TimeSheet table.

TimeSheet Table

TimeSheetId (PK)	State	Approver_EmpId	Submitter_EmpId
1000	NC	3015	2013

Foreign Key Constraints

Name	Columns	Owned Table
ApproverFK	Approver_EmpId	Employee
SubmitterFK	Submitter_EmpId	Employee

Table 25.2 Employee table.

EmpID (PK)	Name	Job Title
2013	Bob Smith	Programmer
3015	Sue Wong	Manager

Table 25.3 Foreign key in one-to-many relationship.

TimeSheet Table

EntryId (PK)	TimeSheet_TimeSheetID	Hours	Date
1011	1000	8.0	2/13/99
1012	1000	8.0	2/14/99

Foreign Key Constraints

Name	Columns	Owned Table
TimeSheetFK	TimeSheet_TimeSheetId	TimeSheet

The ApproverFK and SubmitterFK foreign key constraints of the TimeSheet table have one column that is equal in type to the primary key column in the Employee Table. Thus, each TimeSheet row will contain what are in effect pointers to the two Employee rows. Using foreign keys that point the other way, you can also store 1-*N* (multivalued) relationships. Each contained row has a foreign key pointer to the row that contains it. Table 25.3 illustrates this procedure.

The two TimeSheetEntry rows we have shown in our example both have a foreign key pointer (TimeSheetFK) to the TimeSheet table that provides the link from the two entries (1011 and 1012) to the previously seen TimeSheet having a primary key value of 1000. You can now see the basic outlines of our solution. If we want to map from our object model in Java to a relational database, we must have some way of creating and reconstituting these foreign key relationships. In a nutshell that is what WSAD's relational mapping does.

25.3 Concepts in EJB 2.0 Relationships

So what you want is the best of both worlds. You want to be able to represent object relationships like you do in standard Java classes, but you also want to take advantage of the automatic persistence, distribution, and transaction features that you get from EJBs. The EJB 2.0 specification provides a solution by defining entity EJB relationships within the specification. This section explains how relationships are defined between entity beans within the deployment descriptor.

The EJB 2.0 specification allows for relationships to be defined between two entity beans with CMP. This is accomplished with the definition of a new type called an `ejb-relation` in the EJB deployment descriptor that contains two `ejb-relationship-roles` where each role has a reference to an entity bean by name within the `ejb-role-source` element. Each `ejb-relation` element is defined within the `relationships` tag of the deployment descriptor. These relationships can have multiplicities of one-to-one, one-to-many, and many-to-many. The multiplicity of a relationship role is defined in terms of the number of instances of the source entity with respect to the relationship.

Entity bean relationships can be bidirectional or unidirectional. This means that a relationship can be navigated from both entities if it is bidirectional and navigability can be restricted to only one entity if it is unidirectional. Navigability between entities defined in a relationship is controlled by defining a CMR field (cmr-field) on the relationship role that you would like to traverse. Thus this cmr-field will be implemented on the source entity bean for the relationship role.

A cmr-field is very similar to a cmp-field in that both have to be valid Java identifiers and they obey the same generation rules for the entity. This basically means that there must be get and set accessor methods defined for each cmr-field which will be used for traversal and update of relationships. Also, the cmr-field type must be either the local interface of the other relationship role's source entity within the relationship or a collection (i.e., `java.util.Collection` or `java.util.Set`). If the cmr-field type is a local interface, it represents a cardinality of 0..1 within a relationship. If it is of a collection type, it represents a cardinality of 0..N in a relationship.

CMRs are defined in terms of local client views of the related beans. This means that accessor and setter methods for the cmr-fields can only appear on the local interface. Remember, the type of a cmr-field must be a local interface, `java.util.Collection`, or `java.util.Set`. Therefore, an entity bean that does not have a local client view can only have unidirectional relationships from itself to other entity beans. The lack of a local client view restricts navigation to the entity bean from another related entity.

Chapter 16 touched on what it would take to add relationships by hand to your application but it did not go into detail about maintaining referential integrity. There are two types of referential integrity: relational database constraints and container-managed entity bean integrity. The strict definition of referential integrity within a relational database is that each foreign key value must have a corresponding primary key value. This is accomplished by creating foreign key constraints which define a set of columns within the owning table that match in order, size, and type of the columns in the primary key of the owned table. Defining foreign key constraints on a database can slow performance and force the application to insert and delete rows into database tables in the proper order so that the foreign key constraints are not violated (i.e., the row in the owned table must exist before the row in the owning table).

Among container-managed entity beans, maintaining referential integrity means maintaining references between two objects that have been related. For example, we could have an Employee who is the submitter of a collection of TimeSheets as shown in Figure 25.1. If a TimeSheet were added to the collection of timesheets for an Employee, referential integrity mechanisms would ensure that the TimeSheet also refers to the Employee to which it was just added. The CMR support handles referential integrity among container-managed entities for you. EJB modules running in WebSphere cannot run with foreign key constraints defined since the insert and delete queries within a transaction are not ordered in such a way that ensures that the foreign key constraints are not violated.

We will go into more detail about CMRs when we discuss relationship support in WSAD.

25.4 Associations in UML

Before we embark upon our investigation of the relationship support in WSAD 5.0, let's review associations in UML. This may seem like a sidetrack, but it really does help in understanding some of the decisions behind the relationship support in WSAD 5.0.

In UML, a solid line between the two classes represents an association between two classes. An association in UML simply represents instances of links between objects, but it does not imply anything about the implementation of that link; in fact it is intentionally vague in order to allow for multiple implementation strategies. An association can carry along with it information about the relationship between the objects that are linked. In our case, we are only concerned with binary associations (links between two classes) so we can limit our discussion to that.

Each end of an association can have certain information associated with it:

- Navigability which is represented in UML by an open ended arrow on an association end. Navigability means that you can traverse the link in the direction of an arrow. An association with no arrows is navigable from either end.
- Role name which is the view of the object from the other end. It is the name by which each object is known to the other object in the relationship.
- Multiplicity which specifies how many values an association end may have. This can be a number (1, 2…) or a range (0..1), or it may be the unbound expression (*) which means zero or more.

Figure 25.3 shows these basic decorations used in UML. In this figure, *A* is related to many instances of *B* through the theB association end. Inversely, B is related to zero or one instance of A through the theA association end.

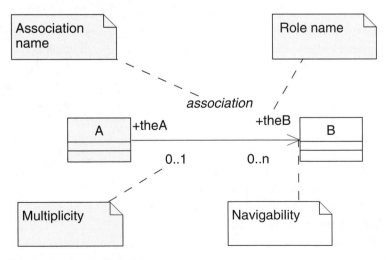

Figure 25.3 UML notation for associations.

25.5   Relationships in WSAD V5.0

Now that you have seen how relationships are represented in the 2.0 EJB specification and how they are represented within UML, you are ready to dive into the relationship support in WSAD 5.0. But first we should explain how relationships are presented within WSAD.

As discussed earlier, the place to look for relationships is within the EJB deployment descriptor editor. This editor displays all EJB 2.0 relationships defined in a deployment descriptor within the Relationships 2.0 section of the Overview page. This is not the only location to view relationships however. On the Beans page, you can select a container-managed entity and scroll down to the Relationships section to see a list of relationships in which the entity bean participates (Figure 25.4) for the EmployeeEJB bean. Also, the Outline view of the editor displays a tree view of all of the EJBs.

Under each container-managed bean, there may be zero or more relationship roles. These are the relationship roles that have the selected bean defined as a source EJB. In other words, the relationship roles that are displayed here are owned by the selected entity. A similar tree view is also shown in the J2EE Hierarchy view under each EJB module.

All relationships are created in WSAD using the relationship wizard. This wizard can be launched from each location by using the *New > Relationship* context menu action for a selected container-managed entity in one of the tree views (i.e., EJB editor outline or J2EE Hierarchy view) or the Add button from the sections within the EJB deployment descriptor editor.

The relationship wizard has two pages. The first (shown in Figure 25.5) requires you to select the two container-managed entities that you would like to relate as well as an optional name and description for the new relationship. When you open the wizard from any of the actions described earlier, except for that associated with the Relationships 2.0 section on the Overview page of the EJB deployment descriptor editor, the first container-managed entity is already selected based on the current selection in the view.

The second page of the relationship wizard (Figure 25.6) is where the specific relationship role information is set. We will look at a case study relationship example between EmployeeEJB and AddressEJB to help us explain the structure of the second page of the wizard. The first thing you will notice on this page is that it is divided into a UML view and an EJB specification view. Only the EJB specification view is updatable and it describes the relationship roles for the rela-

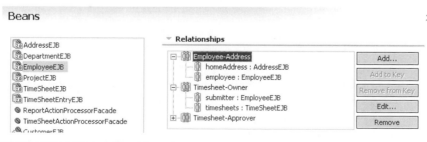

Figure 25.4 Relationships defined for a bean.

Figure 25.5 EJB relationship wizard Page 1.

Figure 25.6 EJB relationship wizard Page 2.

tionship in terms of the EJB specification. Changes made to the EJB specification view will update the UML view.

The UML view illustrates the EJB relationship in terms of UML semantics. When editing a relationship role, blue dotted lines will surround the elements in the UML view that will be updated based on the role you are changing. This is helpful since EJB 2.0 relationships are not defined in terms of UML.

Let's take a closer look at the first relationship role which has EmployeeEJB defined as the Source EJB. Notice that the Source EJB cannot be changed since it was first selected on the previous page and changing one of the container-managed entity beans defined in a relationship changes the entire meaning of the relationship. The next field, Role name, is an optional name for the relationship role. Next we have the Multiplicity field which can be either One or Many. Multiplicity, as defined by the EJB 2.0 specification, is described in terms of the relationship and not the source EJB. So, in this simple example, the One multiplicity for the homeAddress relationship role indicates that there is one instance of the EmployeeEJB source EJB within the relationship. Notice that in the UML view, the blue dotted line appears around the multiplicity for the homeAddress relationship role. This is because multiplicity within UML is in terms of the bean itself. So, in the example, this multiplicity indicates that the EmployeeEJB has one instance of an AddressEJB.

The Navigable check box is not a direct setting in the EJB specification but it does affect the next set of fields. If this check box is selected, the CMR field text field will be enabled and it will be required to have a value which defaults to the role name. Remember from our earlier discussion that a relationship role is navigable if a cmr-field is defined.

Next we have the CMR field type drop-down list. This list is disabled unless the role is navigable and the other relationships role has a multiplicity of Many. When the drop-down list is enabled, you are required to select either java.util.Collection or java.util.Set as one of the types for the cmr-field. The Cascade delete check box when selected will set the cascade-delete option for the relationship role. Cascade delete indicates that when the other relationship role's source EJB is removed, the instances of the current source EJB within the relationship will also be removed. This check box is only enabled if the other relationship's role multiplicity is set to One and is not already checked (only one relationship role can have cascade delete defined).

Finally we have the foreign key check box. This option will require a bit more explanation since it is not explicitly defined in the EJB 2.0 specification. When selected, it indicates that if the source EJB were mapped to a simple table (e.g., TimeSheet in Table 25.1) that table would own the foreign key used in the relationship between the two tables. This option is disabled if any multiplicity is defined as Many since the foreign key must be defined on the relationship role with the Many multiplicity because the mapped table to the source EJB must contain the foreign key when there are multiple rows returned in the relationship (see Table 25.3). This option is used by the mapping wizard when creating tables used in a top-down mapping strategy.

Next we will walk through two common relationship examples, single- and multivalued relationships. Within these examples, we will show how the relationship wizard is used to generate real world EJB relationships.

25.6 Creating a Single-Valued Relationship

For the single-valued relationship example we are going to examine the relationship between EmployeeEJB and AddressEJB from the case study. In this scenario, each Employee has a home address that is being modeled with this relationship. To create this relationship, first open the EJB relationship wizard using any method described earlier in this chapter. Next, ensure that the EmployeeEJB and AddressEJB are selected in the left and right EJB lists shown in Figure 25.5. Also set the Relationship name to Employee-Address.

The second page, shown in Figure 25.6, contains the details of our relationship roles. For the relationship role with the Source EJB defined as EmployeeEJB, set the Role name to `homeAddress` and the Multiplicity to `One`. We want the AddressEJB to be accessible from the EmployeeEJB so we keep the Navigable check box selected. This automatically keeps the CMR field enabled and it is defaulted to the same name as the Role name. We will keep `homeAddress` as the CMR field. Finally, select the Foreign key option to indicate that the table mapped to EmployeeEJB will contain the foreign key reference to the table mapped to AddressEJB.

For the relationship role with the Source EJB defined as AddressEJB, set the Role name to `employee`, leave the Multiplicity as `One`, and leave the default CMR field name as `employee`. Also select the Cascade delete option since it is desirable to have the AddressEJB instance removed when the EmployeeEJB instance in the relationship is removed. After clicking the *Finish* button, you will see the relationship (Listing 25.1) defined in the deployment descriptor.

Listing 25.1 One-to-One relationship

```
<ejb-relation>

  <description></description>

  <ejb-relation-name>Employee-Address</ejb-relation-name>

  <ejb-relationship-role id="EJBRelationshipRole_1034826147916">

    <ejb-relationship-role-name>homeAddress</ejb-relationship-role-
name>

    <multiplicity>One</multiplicity>

    <relationship-role-source>

      <ejb-name>EmployeeEJB</ejb-name>

    </relationship-role-source>

    <cmr-field>
```

```
      <cmr-field-name>homeAddress</cmr-field-name>

   </cmr-field>

 </ejb-relationship-role>

 <ejb-relationship-role id="EJBRelationshipRole_1034826301797">

   <ejb-relationship-role-name>employee</ejb-relationship-role-name>

   <multiplicity>One</multiplicity>

   <cascade-delete />

   <relationship-role-source>

     <ejb-name>AddressEJB</ejb-name>

   </relationship-role-source>

   <cmr-field>

     <cmr-field-name>employee</cmr-field-name>

   </cmr-field>

 </ejb-relationship-role>

</ejb-relation>
```

Also, the following methods have been created on the local interfaces and the bean classes to support the cmr-fields defined in this relationship.

EmployeeEJB

```
public com.wsbook.casestudy.ejb.AddressEJB getHomeAddress();

public void setHomeAddress(com.wsbook.casestudy.ejb.AddressEJB

aHomeAddress);
```

EmployeeEJBBean

```
public abstract com.wsbook.casestudy.ejb.AddressEJB getHomeAddress();
```

```
public abstract void setHomeAddress(com.wsbook.casestudy.ejb.AddressEJB
aHomeAddress);
```

AddressEJB

```
public com.wsbook.casestudy.ejb.EmployeeEJB getEmployee();
public void setEmployee(com.wsbook.casestudy.ejb.EmployeeEJB
anEmployee);
```

AddressEJBBean

```
public abstract com.wsbook.casestudy.ejb.EmployeeEJB getEmployee();
public abstract void setEmployee(com.wsbook.casestudy.ejb.EmployeeEJB
anEmployee);
```

25.7 Creating a Multivalued Relationship

For the multivalued relationship example we will examine the relationship between TimeSheetEJB and TimeSheetEntryEJB from the case study. In this scenario, each TimeSheet has a collection of TimeSheetEntries. To create the relationship, first open the EJB relationship wizard using any method described earlier in this chapter. Next, ensure that the TimeSheetEJB and TimeSheetEntryEJB are selected in the left and right EJB lists similarly shown in Figure 25.5. Also set the relationship name to TimeSheetEntries.

The second page, shown in Figure 25.7, contains the details of our relationship roles. For the relationship role with the Source EJB defined as TimeSheetEntryEJB, set the Role name to `timesheet` and the Multiplicity to `Many`. Remember that Many for this multiplicity means that there are many instances of the TimeSheetEntryEJB within the relationship. We want the TimeSheetEntryEJB to be accessible from the TimeSheetEJB so keep the Navigable check box selected. This automatically keeps the CMR field enabled and it is defaulted to the same name as the Role name, thus the CMR field will be `timesheet`.

For the relationship role with the Source EJB defined as TimeSheetEJB, set the Role name to `entries`, leave the Multiplicity as `One`, and leave the default CMR field name as `entries`. Also select java.util.Collection for the CMR field type since the `timesheet` role has a multiplicity of `Many`. This makes sense since the TimeSheetEJB has a reference to many TimeSheetEntryEJBs. You do not have the option of changing the Foreign key setting since one of the roles has a multiplicity of `Many`. Remember that the EJB 2.0 specification allows for Many-to-Many rela-

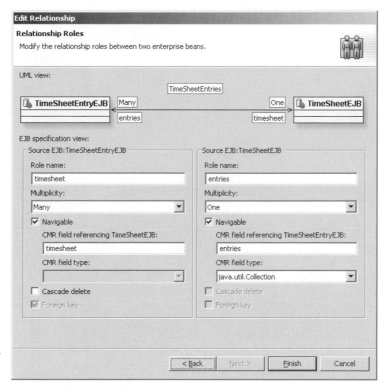

Figure 25.7 Multivalued relationship settings.

tionships. This would appear exactly the same as this relationship except that both roles would have a `Many` multiplicity and they would both define a CMR field type if they are navigable.

After clicking the *Finish* button, you will see the relationship in Listing 25.2 defined in the deployment descriptor. Notice that there are no methods generated on TimeSheetEJBBean for adding or removing from the multivalued relationship. Adding and removing from the relationship should be done directly with the Collection returned from the `getEntries` method.

Listing 25.2 One-to-Many relationship

```
<ejb-relation>

  <ejb-relation-name>TimeSheetEntries</ejb-relation-name>

  <ejb-relationship-role id="EJBRelationshipRole_1034826269180">

    <ejb-relationship-role-name>timesheet</ejb-relationship-role-name>

    <multiplicity>Many</multiplicity>
```

```
    <relationship-role-source>

      <ejb-name>TimeSheetEntryEJB</ejb-name>

    </relationship-role-source>

     <cmr-field>

        <cmr-field-name>timesheet</cmr-field-name>

    </cmr-field>

  </ejb-relationship-role>

  <ejb-relationship-role id="EJBRelationshipRole_1034826301787">

    <ejb-relationship-role-name>entries</ejb-relationship-role-name>

    <multiplicity>One</multiplicity>

    <relationship-role-source>

      <ejb-name>TimeSheetEJB</ejb-name>

    </relationship-role-source>

    <cmr-field>

      <cmr-field-name>entries</cmr-field-name>

      <cmr-field-type>java.util.Collection</cmr-field-type>

  </ejb-relationship-role>        </cmr-field>

</ejb-relation>
```

The following methods have also been created on the local interfaces and the bean classes to support the cmr-fields defined in this relationship:

TimeSheetEntryEJB

```
public com.wsbook.casestudy.ejb.TimeSheetEJB getTimesheet();

public void setTimesheet(com.wsbook.casestudy.ejb.TimeSheetEJB

aTimesheet);
```

TimeSheetEntryEJBBean

```
public abstract com.wsbook.casestudy.ejb.TimeSheetEJB getTimesheet();

public abstract void setTimesheet(com.wsbook.casestudy.ejb.TimeSheetEJB

aTimesheet);
```

TimeSheetEJB

```
public java.util.Collection getEntries();

public void setEntries(java.util.Collection anEntries);
```

TimeSheetEJBBean

```
public abstract java.util.Collection getEntries();

public abstract void setEntries(java.util.Collection anEntries);
```

25.8 Read Ahead Hints

WebSphere 5.0 extends the EJB 2.0 relationship description with additional information that can be used to optimize navigation. The concept is known as read ahead hints (see Figure 25.8). The basic idea is to perform a single SQL query, a relational join, to load an entity bean and a number of related entity beans that would have normally taken several distinct SQL query statements to perform.

On the next page, you must select an entity bean from the EJB module for which this access intent will be defined (Figure 25.9). When the Read Ahead Hint option is selected from the first page, you can only select one container-managed entity on this page because a read ahead hint can only be defined for one container-managed entity at a time.

On the third page of the wizard (Figure 25.10), you must select the element that describes the methods from the selected container-managed entity from the previous page for which this access intent applies. Since the Read Ahead Hint option was selected from the first page, you will only see the possible method elements for the remote and local home interfaces. In reality, however, only the findByPrimaryKey(...) method supports read aheads. In the future, this restriction may be lifted. For now, select the findByPrimaryKey(...) method element from the list.

Figure 25.11 shows where the preload path used in the read ahead hint is defined. This path is built using the cmr-fields of the selected container-managed entity. This path can have both breadth and depth, meaning that you can select multiple cmr-fields for the entity (breadth) and then you can traverse into each cmr-field's type (depth). For this example, we will only

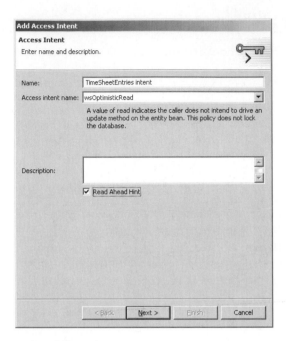

Figure 25.8 Access intent wizard Page 1.

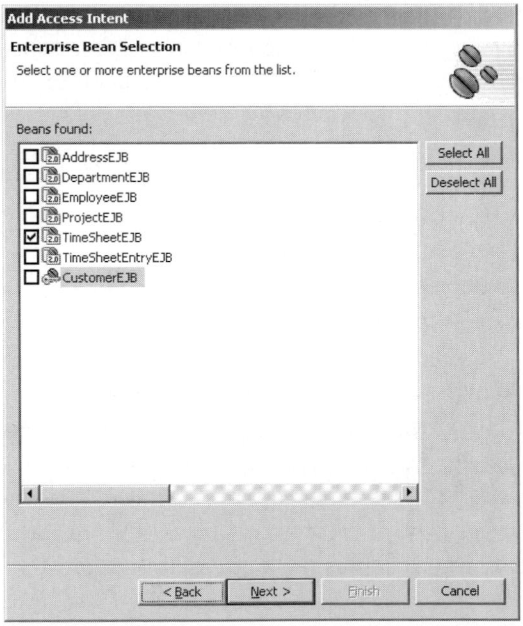

Figure 25.9 Access intent wizard Page 2.

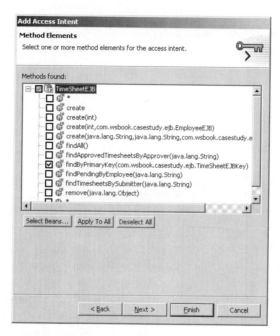

Figure 25.10 Access intent wizard Page 3.

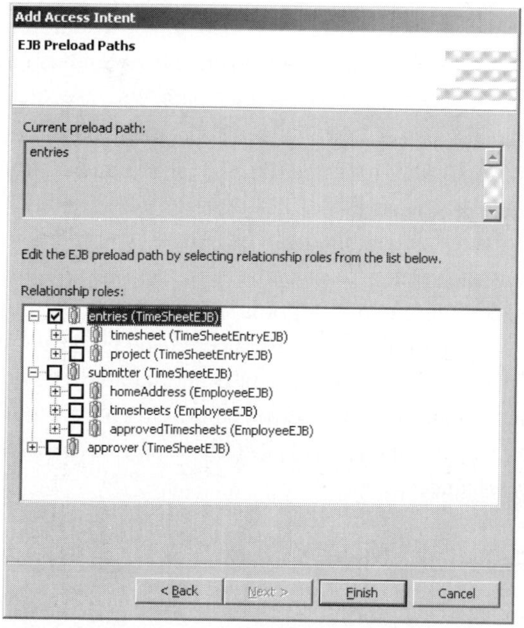

Figure 25.11 Access Intent wizard page 4.

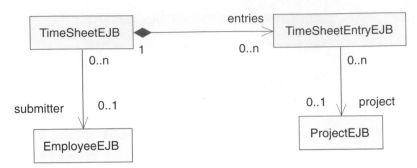

Figure 25.12 TimeSheetEJB related objects.

select the entities cmr-field so that all related TimeSheetEntryEJBs will also be loaded during the find. This creates the simple preload path: `entries`.

We could have defined a more complex preload path. Figure 25.12 shows the related container-managed entities for the TimeSheetEJB. Notice that the relationship role directly owned by TimeSheetEJB (entries and submitter) would constitute the breadth of the path and any relationship roles off of related types would constitute the depth. In Figure 25.12, the breadths paths from TimeSheetEJB would include entries and submitter since these relationship roles are directly associated with the TimeSheetEJB itself. The project relationship role would indicate depth in the read ahead path since it is a relationship role from TimeSheetEntryEJB which is a related entity bean to the TimeSheetEJB entity bean. So, if we wanted to load all related objects shown in Figure 25.12 when a TimeSheetEJB is loaded, we would have to define the following preload path: `entries.project submitter`. Notice that depth is indicated with a period and breadth is indicated with a space. So this preload path will execute one SQL statement that would normally take four.

You may be asking why don't we just specify a read ahead hint for the entire graph of related beans? You would not want to do this because the single SQL query statement, even though it is only one access to the database, can be extremely large and complex. Also, if you do not use the related entities each time you do a find, you are preloading too much information and wasting time and space. So, there comes a point when the defined preload path is so large that you actually start to lose any optimization gains. There is no hard rule when this point is reached because it depends on the complexity of your EJB and database designs (i.e., EJB inheritance defined later in this chapter) and the number of cmp-fields for the entities in the preload path. The gains, however, can be substantial for well-defined preload paths where you almost always use the preloaded entity instances.

25.9 Mapping Relationships

You have seen how to create relationships between two entity beans so now you are ready to map these relationships to a relational database. Remember Tables 25.1–25.3 where we showed how relationships are depicted between database tables? The tables indicated that a foreign key,

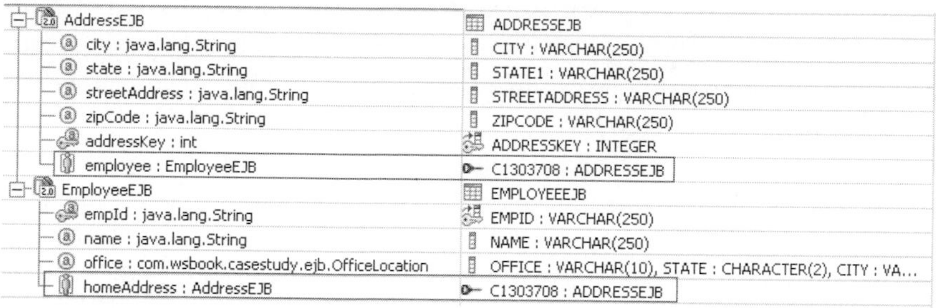

Figure 25.13 Mapped relationship.

which contains a reference to one or more of the table columns, is used to represent a relationship to another table. So, it would make sense that the relationship would map some way to the foreign key reference within the table. Let's step through the mapping of our single valued relationship example.

Begin by opening the EJB to RDB mapping editor by double-clicking the wsbook: DB2UDBNT_V81_1 map under the Maps section for the TimeSheetGroup EJB module. A one-to-one relationship between EmployeeEJB and AddressEJB needs to be mapped to the EMPLOYEEEJB and ADDRESSEJB tables.

First let's take a look at our tables. The EMPLOYEEEJB table has one primary key column, EMPID and the ADDRESSEJB table also has one primary key column, ADDRESSKEY. There is a foreign key defined on the EMPLOYEEEJB table, C3233081, that contains the HOMEADDRESS_ADDRESSKEY column; its target table is the ADDRESSEJB table. Now, to map the relationship you will need to map the homeAddress relationship role to the C3233081 foreign key. This is done by selecting the homeAddress role from the Enterprise Beans list and dragging it to the C3233081 foreign key in the Tables list. You will now see that the homeAddress relationship role is mapped (Figure 25.13) and you should also notice that the other relationship role, employee on the AddressEJB, is mapped as well. This is because only the forward relationship role needs to be mapped within the relationship and the opposite role is done automatically.

A common mistake is to map foreign key columns to cmp-fields on the entity bean. The problem is that it is error prone since there could be multiple columns within a foreign key and if they were each mapped to a cmp-field you would need to ensure that the values of these fields always mapped to a valid foreign key. This can be quite difficult depending on how complex your database model may be.

Another problem with this solution is that you are forcing knowledge of your database design into your object model. For example, if a column were added to a foreign key, this means that another cmp-field would need to be added to the entity bean. The solution used in WSAD does not have this problem since you are mapping relationship roles to foreign keys. As a result, the object model will not need to change at all when you add or remove columns from the foreign key.

This simple example shows how to map a one-to-one relationship but what about a one-to-many relationship? The nice thing is that the mapping is identical in both cases because all that is required to map either a one-to-one or a one-to-many relationship is that the forward relationship role gets mapped to the foreign key.

What about a many-to-many relationship? This is a bit different due to the way that a many-to-many relationship is defined in the database. Tables 25.4–25.6 depict a many-to-many relationship implementation within a database for students and courses. A student can take many courses and a course can have many students. From these tables you can see that student 111-11-1111 has three courses, PHY101, CALC101, and ENG101. Also, course CALC101 has two students, 111-11-1111 and 222-22-2222.

Table 25.4 STUDENT table.

SSN (PK_	NAME	AGE	GPA
111-11-1111	Bob Smith	19	3.00
222-22-2222	Sue Wong	20	3.75

Table 25.5 COURSE table.

COURSE_NUMBER (PK)	NAME	DESCRIPTION
PHY101	Physics 101	
CALC101	Calculus 101	
ENG!)!	English 101	
MHIST202	Modern History 202	

Table 25.6 STUDENTS_COURSES intermediate table.

COURSES NUMBER (PK)	STUDENTS SSN (PK)
PHY101	111-11-1111
CALC101	111-11-1111
ENG!)!	111-11-1111
MHIST202	222-22-2222
CALC101	222-22-2222
PHY101	222-22-2222

Table 25.6 STUDENTS_COURSES intermediate table. (Continued)

Foreign Key Constraints

Name	Columns	Owned Tables
COURSE FK	COURSE NUMBER	COURSE
STUDENT FK	STUDENT SSN	STUDENT

A many-to-many relationship between database tables is accomplished by creating two relationships to a third intermediate, or correlation, table. This intermediate table, STUDENTS_COURSES, is typically small, consisting of only primary key columns for both tables. The intermediate table contains two foreign key references to each table involved in the relationship and all of the columns are part of the primary key for the intermediate table. If this intermediate table has other columns that are not part of the primary key, you don't have a true many-to-many relationship. Instead, the intermediate table is actually another domain object and you have two one-to-many relationships to this intermediate object. So, if there are nonkey columns on your intermediate table, you should model this table as a domain object.

Let's take a very simple example where we have a many-to-many relationship between Student and Course and we have the same database structure as in Tables 25.4-25.6.

Figure 25.14 shows the structure in the EJB to RDB mapping editor (the primary key columns have already been mapped to the key cmp-fields). The same rules will apply in this case for mapping the relationship roles. We must map the forward relationship role in the relationship. For many-to-many relationships, both roles will be forward from the point of view of the intermediate table. So, both relationship roles will need to be mapped to the appropriate foreign key on the intermediate table.

Figure 25.14 displays red arrows which indicate the foreign key that each relationship role in the relationship needs to be mapped. Drag the courses relationship role to the COURSE_FK foreign key and drag the students relationship role to the STUDENT_FK foreign key. It is hard to get this wrong since the mapping editor will not allow you to map the relationship role to the wrong foreign key.

Now is a good time to explain how the other mapping strategies, top-down and bottom-up, handle relationships. The top-down mapping strategy will automatically create the appropriate foreign key columns and foreign key necessary to map both one-to-one and one-to-many relationships. It will then use these foreign keys when creating the maps with the relationship roles. For many-to-many relationships, the top-down mapping strategy will automatically create the intermediate table and map the foreign keys within this table to the relationship roles defined in the relationship. The bottom-up mapping strategy will always create a one-to-many relationship for every foreign key defined within the database.

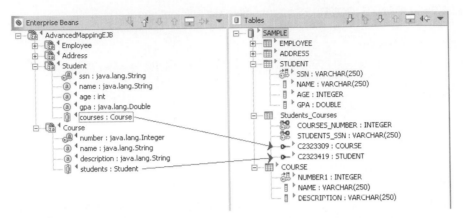

Figure 25.14 Mapping a many-to-many relationship.

Since every relationship in the database is defined exactly the same way, it is impossible to determine the true multiplicity of any relationship by examining only the database schema. The multiplicity is determined by its use within the application.

25.10 Weak vs. Strong Entities

We have already shown that two container-managed entities can be related using a relationship. We have also indicated that relationship roles are mapped within the EJB to RDB mapping editor to foreign keys defined on a database table. We stressed that it is not a good choice to map the individual foreign key columns to cmp-fields since this can cause referential integrity issues and the fields are redundant with the defined relationship roles. An issue we have yet to address, however, is that the situation becomes much more complex when the foreign key columns are also members of the primary key.

The issue is one of weak entity types. This is when you include as a foreign key the primary key attributes of the defining relation and then compose a primary key from the foreign key plus partial attributes of the weak entity relationship.

On the other side is the strong entity (i.e., owner or parent entity) which is an entity that exists on its own, independent of other entities. The weak entity (i.e., dependent or child entity) has an existence which depends on another entity. This situation is most common with one-to-many relationships where the cardinality is a required one for the weak entity. In this situation, the primary key of the owner entity is used as part of the primary key of the dependent child entity.

Consider the common concept of an order comprised of a set of order line items. You would not want to have an OrderLineItem exist outside an Order. In that case, Order is a strong entity, but OrderLineItem is a weak entity. You would probably never construct a query for a set of OrderLineItems except in those cases where you were searching for line items belonging to a particular order, so it makes sense to include the primary key of the Order in the primary key of the OrderLineItem. Weak entities are typically the best choices for using the cascade delete

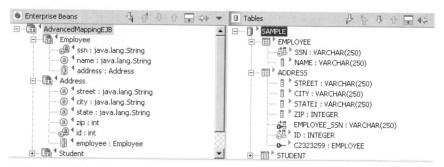

Figure 25.15 Employee to address mapping.

option for the relationship role (Figure 25.6). In this situation, you want the weak entity instances to be deleted when the entity that it depends on is removed.

WSAD supports the concept of strong and weak entities and this can be seen best by walking through an example. In the AdvancedMappingEJB EJB project we defined two container-managed entities Employee and Address. These beans are similar to the ones defined in the case study, but they are less complex to keep this example simple so that you can easily see what is generated by the WSAD tools. For this example a bidirectional one-to-one relationship between Employee and Address where the Address source EJB holds the foreign key option has been defined. The Employee entity has an SSN cmp-field in the key and the Address entity has an ID key field defined. So both entities are strong entities since they can exist on their own. The top-down mapping option is used to generate the tables and maps associated with this example (shown in Figure 25.15).

Now, our DBA has decided that the ADDRESS table should have its ID column removed and the EMPLOYEE_SSN column should be added to the primary key. In other words, he decided that Address is a weak entity, and that Employee is a strong entity. This removes unneeded columns, eliminates the need to generate a unique primary key value for each address, and makes it clearer which address corresponds to which employee. Figure 25.16 shows the structure of the ADDRESS table after the modification.

Now we need to modify the Address entity bean to remove the ID cmp-field since it is no longer needed. Also we need to define key cmp-fields for our Address entity. You could simply define an `employee_ssn` cmp-field, which would map to the foreign key column EMPLOYEE_SSN on the Address entity and set it as a key field. This would work to make

Figure 25.16 Modified ADDRESS table.

Address a weak entity but it would create redundant information because the `employee` cmr-field maps to the foreign key which has the EMPLOYEE_SSN column as its member, and this new `employee_ssn` cmp-field would also be mapped to the EMPLOYEE_SSN column. So, both persistent fields would be mapped to the same column. This is a simple example but you can imagine how complex this situation would be if the foreign key had multiple member columns. Also, each time you add a column to the foreign key, you would be required to add a new cmp-field to the entity and map it to the new column.

Instead, there is a better solution to this problem for container-managed entity beans. In WSAD you can add the weak entity's relationship role to the strong entity just like you can add cmp-fields. In this example, instead of creating an `employee_ssn` cmp-field and mapping it to the foreign key EMPLOYEE_SSN column, you should add the `employee` relationship role to the key of the Address entity. Doing so basically means that Address container-managed entity requires an Employee instance for its identity which is the definition of a weak entity. This in turn indicates that the foreign key columns that are used to map to the `employee` relationship role should belong to the primary key of the ADDRESS table. This alleviates your having to model and map the foreign key columns as cmp-fields.

Using relationship roles (i.e., cmr-fields) in the key of a container-managed entity. It also means that no additional mapping changes are necessary. This can be accomplished anywhere that a relationship is displayed within the J2EE perspective or the EJB deployment descriptor editor. For example, you can expand the Address entity in the Outline of the EJB deployment descriptor editor for the AdvancedMappingEJB module, select the `employee` relationship role, and select the Add to Key context menu action (Figure 25.17). This action is only enabled if the opposite relationship role in the relationship has a multiplicity of `One` and the selected relationship role has the foreign key option selected, because a weak entity must map to a table with the foreign key column and its UML multiplicity must be one (i.e., the other relationship role in the EJB 2.0 specification must be `One`). This means that the *Add to Key* action is only available for a relationship role that returns a single valued object and the table that the source container-managed entity maps to contains the foreign key constraint.

After selecting this action, you will notice a key icon now appears on the relationship role. This change also updates the home, bean, and key classes as well as the deployment descriptor for the Address entity.

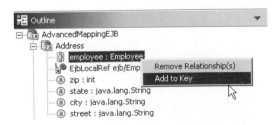

Figure 25.17   Add to Key action.

Now is a good time to take a small side trip to describe some issues with the EJB 2.0 specification. Since the specification is not very clear on the use of cmr-fields on the key class, it is agreed that only cmp-fields can exist on the key class. So what does that mean when you add a relationship role to the key of an entity bean? This means that cmp-fields are derived from the relationship role (`employee`) and the key fields of the role's source entity (i.e., `ssn`). This is necessary to support the fact that the specification does not spell out that cmr-fields can appear in the key class of the entity. This helps to explain the change in the deployment descriptor of the Address entity to include the following cmp-field.

```
<cmp-field>

  <description>Generated to support relationships.  Do NOT delete.</
description>

  <field-name>employee_ssn</field-name>

</cmp-field>
```

This will now help to explain the structure of the AddressKey class (Listing 25.3).[1]

Listing 25.3 The AddressKey class structure

```
/**

 * Key class for Entity Bean: Address

 */

public class AddressKey implements java.io.Serializable {

        static final long serialVersionUID = 3206093459760846163L;

        /**

         * Implementation field for persistent attribute: employee_ssn

         */
```

---

1.   Only the key portions of the AddressKey class are displayed here. This is not the fully generated class from WSAD.

```java
public java.lang.String employee_ssn;



/**

 * Creates a key for Entity Bean: Address

 */

public AddressKey(advanced.mapping.example.EmployeeKey

                  argEmployee) {

    privateSetEmployeeKey(argEmployee);

}

/**

 * This method was generated for supporting the relationship role

 * named employee.

 * It will be deleted/edited when the relationship is deleted/

 * edited.

 */

public advanced.mapping.example.EmployeeKey getEmployeeKey() {

    advanced.mapping.example.EmployeeKey temp =

        new advanced.mapping.example.EmployeeKey();

    boolean employee_NULLTEST = true;

    employee_NULLTEST &= (employee_ssn == null);

    temp.ssn = employee_ssn;
```

```
            if (employee_NULLTEST)

                    temp = null;

            return temp;

    }

    /**

      * This method was generated for supporting the relationship role

      * named employee.

      * It will be deleted/edited when the relationship is deleted/

      * edited.

      */

    public void privateSetEmployeeKey(

            advanced.mapping.example.EmployeeKey inKey) {

            boolean employee_NULLTEST = (inKey == null);

            employee_ssn = (employee_NULLTEST) ? null : inKey.ssn;

    }

}
```

Notice that the constructor takes another EmployeeKey as an argument. This is true since the Address entity's key shape is described by its owner key (i.e., Employee). There is one field in the AddressKey class for each field within the EmployeeKey class. Each corresponds to a cmp-field that was added to the deployment descriptor to support relationships (i.e., employee_ssn). Next, let's examine the create methods that is added to the AddressLocal-Home class.

```
public advanced.mapping.example.AddressLocal create(

            advanced.mapping.example.EmployeeLocal argEmployee)
```

```
      throws javax.ejb.CreateException;


public advanced.mapping.example.AddressLocal create(

      java.lang.String employee_ssn)

      throws javax.ejb.CreateException;
```

The first `create` method in the example should be the most widely used method for creating a new Address entity. This method takes one argument which is the local interface of the Employee entity (i.e., its parent entity). This method is generated since it was indicated that the `employee` relationship role is to be part of the key for the Address entity so an Address instance must have a reference to an Employee bean to be created. Notice that a second `create` method was generated which has the derived fields for the `employee` relationship role (namely `employee_ssn`). The second `create` method is generated for those reluctant to use the parent entity instance to create the weak entity and would rather pass all of the required field values.

Now we are ready to examine the changes to the AddressBean class to support the `employee` relationship role in the key. The following methods were either added or updated after adding the `employee` relationship role to the key.

```
/**

 * Get accessor for persistent attribute: employee_ssn

 */

public abstract java.lang.String getEmployee_ssn();

/**

 * Set accessor for persistent attribute: employee_ssn

 */

public abstract void setEmployee_ssn(java.lang.String newEmployee_ssn);
```

These two methods were generated to support the new cmp-field `employee_ssn` added to support the `employee` relationship role being added to the key of the entity. This is required by the EJB 2.0 specification for all cmp-fields; however, these two methods are not exposed on the local interface since we do not want clients to have access to them. The clients should use the `getEmployee()` and `setEmployee(EmployeeLocal)` methods instead.

```
public advanced.mapping.example.AddressKey ejbCreate(

      advanced.mapping.example.EmployeeLocal argEmployee)

      throws javax.ejb.CreateException {

      advanced.mapping.example.EmployeeKey argEmployeePK =

            (advanced.mapping.example.EmployeeKey)

                       argEmployee.getPrimaryKey();

      setEmployee_ssn(argEmployeePK.ssn);

      return null;

}

/**

 * ejbPostCreate

 */

public void ejbPostCreate(

      advanced.mapping.example.EmployeeLocal argEmployee)

      throws javax.ejb.CreateException {

      setEmployee(argEmployee);

}
```

These two methods must be created to support the first create method from the home interface in the example code. These methods take as an argument the EmployeeLocal interface since it appears in the create method on the home interface. However, there are a couple of aspects from the EJB 2.0 specification which must be explained in order to understand their implementation. First, the specification indicates that the key shape for the entity bean should be fully defined within the ejbCreate method. Second, it mentions that cmr-fields can only be set within an ejbPostCreate method.

So, in this ejbCreate method, it is ensured that the key shape is fully defined by extracting the ssn field from the EmployeeKey which is obtained from the EmployeeLocal instance passed as an argument. This value is set using the setter method for the new cmp-field shown earlier. Note that if there were multiple fields in the `EmployeeKey` class, the signature of this method would not change but the implementation would now have to set multiple fields that it obtained from the key class. You will notice in the `ejbPostCreate` method that the employee reference is finally set as described by the specification.

```
/**

 * ejbCreate

 */

public advanced.mapping.example.AddressKey ejbCreate(

       java.lang.String employee_ssn)

       throws javax.ejb.CreateException {

       setEmployee_ssn(employee_ssn);

       return null;

}
/**

 * ejbPostCreate

 */

public void ejbPostCreate(java.lang.String employee_ssn)

       throws javax.ejb.CreateException {

}
```

The methods above are generated in support of the second `create` method on the local home interface but it is also generated to support remote client interface. This is necessary if the weak entity has a remote client interface because the first `ejbCreate` cannot be promoted to a remote home interface because there is a reference to a local client interface. This `ejbCreate` method will set the private cmp-field values that are necessary for the key shape of the Address entity. The problem with this method is that it will change as the key shape of the Employee entity changes.

Now you should understand why you would want to add relationship roles to the key of an entity as opposed to mapping individual cmp-fields directly to the columns within the primary key and foreign key. The main benefits are that it makes the object dependency more apparent between the entities, it eliminates referential integrity issues, and it simplifies the code since you do not have to be aware of the shape of the underlying fields that support the relationship role when using the local client view.

25.11 EJB Inheritance in WSAD

So far, you have seen a lengthy discussion about one of the two types of relationships (associations) defined in UML, and how associations between EJBs can be implemented in WSAD.

The second type of relationship is generalization. There are two types of generalizations that we can discuss—the inheritance relationship, which corresponds to the notion of implementation inheritance (extends in Java) and the realization relationship, which corresponds to the notion of interface inheritance (implements in Java). We will need to keep these two notions clear as we navigate the sea of what generalization means to EJBs.

The EJB specification is a little vague on the subject of inheritance. There are only two clear indications in the EJB specification about what inheritance means in the context of EJBs.

First, the EJB 2.0 specification states, "The remote interface is allowed to have super interfaces. Use of interface inheritance is subject to the RMI-IIOP rules for the definition of remote interfaces."[2] It also states "The remote home interface is allowed to have super interfaces. Use of interface inheritance is subject to the RMI-IIOP rules for the definition of remote interfaces."[3] The specification indicates requirements of only the remote interfaces, it does not state any inheritance requirements for the local interface or the local home interface.

There are only two other places in the 2.0 specification that refer to inheritance. In both the session bean and entity bean scenarios, all three of home and remote interfaces and bean implementations are shown in a generalization relationship to other respective interfaces and implementations. However the spec is vague on how this can be accomplished.

For instance, in the entity bean scenario in Chapter 15, it states "…tools can use inheritance, delegation, and code generation to achieve mix-in of the two classes [participating in the generalization relationship]."

The EJB 2.0 specification clarifies this situation in its FAQ. It specifically states that component inheritance (i.e., how an entire EJB descends from another EJB) is beyond the scope of the specification due to the complexities involved in component inheritance. However, it discusses how developers can take advantage of the Java language support for inheritance as follows:

• *Interface inheritance.* It is possible to use the Java language interface inheritance mechanism for inheritance of the home and remote interfaces. A component may derive

2.   [EJB 99], p. 194.

3.   ibid, p. 194.

its home and remote interfaces from some "parent" home and remote interfaces; the component then can be used anywhere where a component with the parent interfaces is expected. This is a Java language feature, and its use is transparent to the EJB Container.

- *Implementation class inheritance*. It is possible to take advantage of the Java class implementation inheritance mechanism for the enterprise bean class. For example, the class `CheckingAccountBean` class can extend the `AccountBean` class to inherit the implementation of the business methods.

So the specification seems to give quite a bit of latitude to tools and container implementers when it comes to how to implement component inheritance between EJBs. It is good to keep this in mind when we look at the implementation of EJB inheritance in WAS AE 5.0 and WSAD 5.0. The development teams of these products have sought to create a sensible, consistent implementation of both interface inheritance and implementation class inheritance, while staying within the context of the specification. They have taken upon themselves to defining some aspects of component inheritance. This has proven to be challenging, but, as we will see, it has been possible.

25.11.1 Interface Inheritance for Sessions and Entities

Perhaps the easiest inheritance feature to understand is the direct support for inheritance of methods defined in local interfaces. For instance, what if in our Timekeeping example system we need to add subclasses of our EmployeeEJB as shown in Figure 25.18.

Our goal here is to have two subclasses of EmployeeEJB—SalariedEmployee and Hourly-Employee, with each type of Employee being paid differently. The first task is to define how the local interfaces (which specify the externally available methods of the entity) are related. This

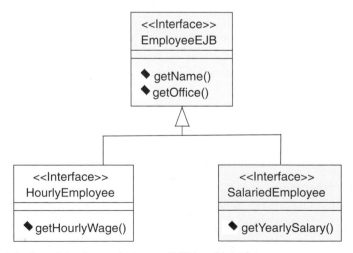

Figure 25.18 Interface inheritance between EJB local interfaces.

turns out to be just as simple as you might think, as the following two code snippets show (from now on, we'll only deal with one of the subclasses for the sake of space):

```
public interface EmployeeEJB extends javax.ejb.EJBLocalObject {

...

}



public interface SalariedEmployee extends EmployeeEJB {

...

}
```

In WSAD and WebSphere, any local interface can inherit from any other local interface, so long as the entire tree is rooted in `javax.ejb.EJBLocalObject`. The part that is more interesting than inheriting local interfaces (which, as we saw, were clearly defined in the specification) is in the inheritance of bean implementations that realize those interfaces.

Figure 25.19 shows how inheritance is used in WebSphere and WSAD. While the example is that of an entity EJB, the principles discussed apply just as well to session beans. This figure is showing inheritance of just the local interfaces but the same is also true for the remote interfaces.

As you can see, there is a parallel hierarchy of EJB implementation classes to match that of the local interfaces. The following two code snippets show how this is done:

```
public class EmployeeEJBBean implements EntityBean {

...

}



public class SalariedEmployeeBean extends EmployeeEJBBean {

...

}
```

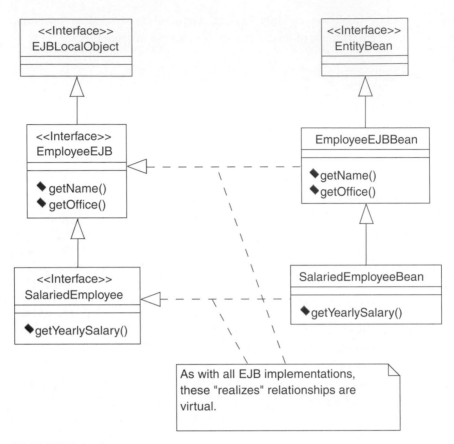

Figure 25.19 EJB inheritance.

The implementation of the subclass entity bean within WSAD will contain only the methods to support the cmp-fields defined for the bean plus the bean life cycle methods (e.g., `ejbRemove()`, `ejbStore()`, etc.). It will not contain any `ejbCreate(...)` or `ejbPostCreate(...)` methods since these methods are defined in one of the superclasses.

There are a few rules that govern EJB inheritance in both WSAD and WebSphere:

- Entity bean implementations cannot inherit from session bean implementations and vice versa.
- You cannot mix and match stateless and stateful session beans with session bean implementations—the type of the parent must match the type of all of its descendants.
- A child entity bean must have the same client views as the parent entity bean. This means that you cannot have a child entity with both a remote and local client view that extends another entity bean with only a local client view.

25.11.2 Building Inherited Beans in WSAD

Now that we've seen what inheritance of local interfaces and bean implementations look like in EJBs, we can understand the support that WSAD provides developers in building EJBs with these relationships. To create an entity bean that inherits from another entity bean, you need to first open the EJB creation wizard by selecting the EJB module from the J2EE Hierarchy view and then select *New > Enterprise Bean* from the context menu. This first page is prefilled with the selected EJB project (i.e., TimeSheetGroup). The second page is shown in Figure 25.20.

The third page, Figure 25.21, is where you define the client view, the bean class name, cmp-fields, and the bean supertype. Notice that the key class defaults to that of the selected Bean supertype and it cannot be changed because all beans within the inheritance structure must share the same key class definition. Also, on the last page of the wizard you can define the bean super-class. This entry field is also preselected to the bean class of the selected bean supertype and you cannot change this value.

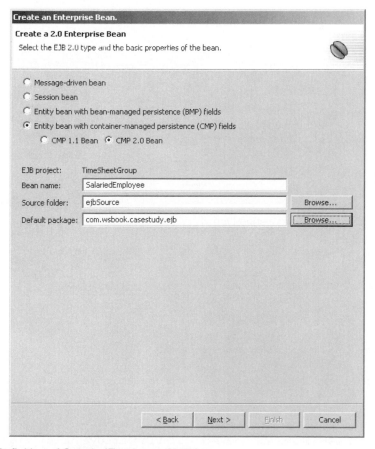

Figure 25.20 Definition of SalariedEmployee CMP bean.

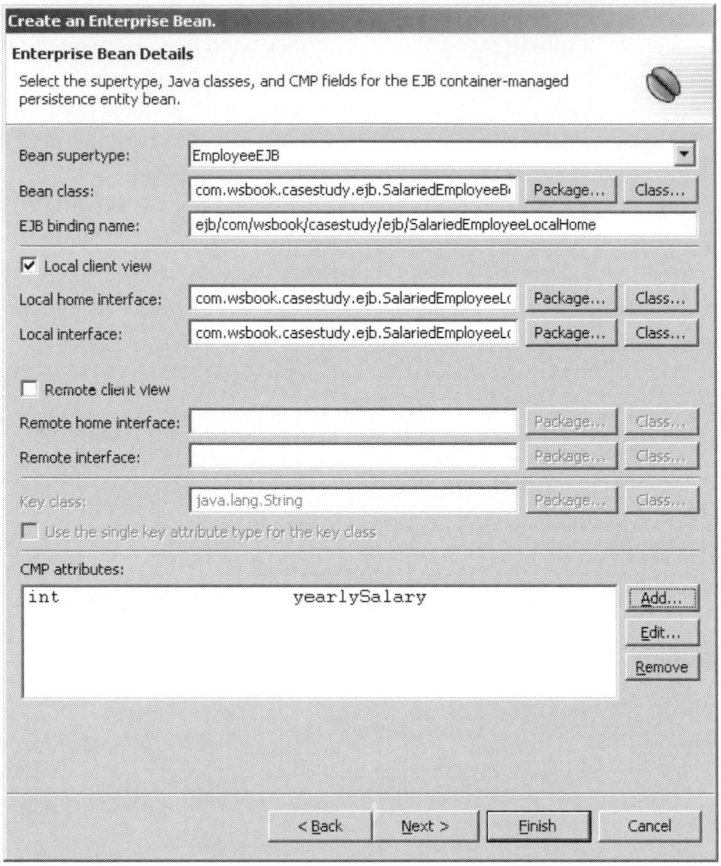

Figure 25.21 Defining the bean supertype.

After selecting *Finish*, the entry in Listing 25.4 is added to the deployment descriptor.

Listing 25.4 SalariedEmployee definition in the deployment descriptor

```
<entity id="SalariedEmployee">

  <ejb-name>SalariedEmployee</ejb-name>

  <local-home>com.wsbook.casestudy.ejb.SalariedEmployeeLocalHome</

local-home>

  <local>com.wsbook.casestudy.ejb.SalariedEmployeeLocal</local>

  <ejb-class>com.wsbook.casestudy.ejb.SalariedEmployeeBean</ejb-class>
```

```
<persistence-type>Container</persistence-type>

<prim-key-class>java.lang.String</prim-key-class>

<reentrant>False</reentrant>

<cmp-version>2.x</cmp-version>

<abstract-schema-name>SalariedEmployee</abstract-schema-name>

<cmp-field>

  <field-name>empId</field-name>

</cmp-field>

<cmp-field>

  <field-name>name</field-name>

</cmp-field>

<cmp-field>

  <field-name>office</field-name>

</cmp-field>

<cmp-field>

  <field-name>yearlySalary</field-name>

</cmp-field>

<primkey-field>empId</primkey-field>

<ejb-local-ref id="EJBLocalRef_1047267616925">

  <ejb-ref-name>ejb/AddressEJB</ejb-ref-name>

  <ejb-ref-type>Entity</ejb-ref-type>

  <local-home>com.wsbook.casestudy.ejb.AddressEJBHome</local-home>

  <local>com.wsbook.casestudy.ejb.AddressEJB</local>

  <ejb-link>AddressEJB</ejb-link>
```

```
    </ejb-local-ref>

    <ejb-local-ref id="EJBLocalRef_1047267616935">

      <ejb-ref-name>ejb/TimeSheetEJB</ejb-ref-name>

      <ejb-ref-type>Entity</ejb-ref-type>

      <local-home>com.wsbook.casestudy.ejb.TimeSheetEJBHome</local-home>

      <local>com.wsbook.casestudy.ejb.TimeSheetEJB</local>

      <ejb-link>TimeSheetEJB</ejb-link>

    </ejb-local-ref>

</entity>
```

Notice there is more in this entry than you defined in the wizard. All of the entries in bold face have been copied from the bean supertype. This is done to satisfy the specification, and it allows the deployment descriptor to remain portable.

After an EJB is created, you can change its EJB inheritance structure at anytime by using the EJB deployment descriptor editor. On the Overview page of the editor, there is an inheritance section which is a part of the larger WebSphere Extensions section since this is not supported by the EJB specification. To change the EJB inheritance, select the desired EJB from the list and click the *Edit* button. This will open an Edit inheritance hierarchy wizard that will allow you to select the Inherits from supertype option which allows you to select another valid EJB from the module to inherit from or you can select the Does not inherit (make root) option that will remove the selected EJB from the current inheritance structure. If you select the second option, you will need to define a new key class for container-managed entities. This wizard will not only change the inheritance of your EJB but it will also refactor the Java classes so that the proper Java inheritance is in place after the edit. Also, the proper key class and create methods will be propagated appropriately.

25.11.3 Inheritance of Home Interfaces

At this point, inheritance of home interfaces cannot be supported while maintaining compliance with the EJB specification. As the EJB 2.0 FAQ suggests, this is mostly due to the required method signatures for find by primary key methods. Each home interface must include a method `findByPrimaryKey(Key inKey)` which returns an instance of its EJB class. If a parent class and subclass tried to define these methods, a signature conflict would be created in the subclass.

For example:

```
public interface EmployeeEJBHome extends javax.ejb.EJBLocalHome {

EmployeeEJB findByPrimaryKey(String primaryKey)...;

}

public interface SalariedEmployeeHome extends EmployeeEJBHome {

SalariedEmployee findByPrimaryKey(String primaryKey);

}
```

Method SalariedEmployeeHome.findByPrimaryKey cannot override the superclass method based on return type only because this would result in ambiguous method invocations in Java. Even though the home interfaces and implementations do not have a formal inheritance relationship, they do participate in the implementation of the inheritance of their EJB classes. When a user defines a generalization relationship, the expectation is that the members of that relationship may be instances of the root class or any of its subclasses. In order to satisfy this requirement, the finders on homes in inheritance hierarchies will answer a mixed collection containing instances of the root EJB class and its subclasses.

25.11.4 Database Inheritance Strategies

Now that we've investigated what it means for an EJB to inherit from another EJB, we have to address a second question that arises in the context of an entity EJB: How are generalization relationships preserved in the database that makes up the bean's persistent store?

There are two different schemes by which inheritance can be represented in a relational database. These schemes and their relative advantages and disadvantages have been described at length in [Fowler], and Chapter 14. The two schemes are:

- Single-table inheritance—by which all the attributes of all of the classes in a hierarchy are stored in a single table, with special SQL `select` statements taking out only those attributes that are appropriate for any particular class.
- Root-leaf inheritance—in which each class in a hierarchy corresponds to a table that contains only those attributes actually defined in that class, plus the key columns that are shared by all members of the hierarchy. An n-way SQL join is required to assemble any particular instance of a class from its corresponding table and all the tables above it in the inheritance hierarchy.

The major advantage of the first scheme is speed, while its major disadvantage is the size of the table (i.e., the number of null columns). The major advantage of the second scheme is its close correspondence to the object model, while its major disadvantage is the time it takes to do the necessary joins.

25.11.5 Mapping an EJB Inheritance Structure

Both of the inheritance schemes mentioned are supported in WSAD for container-managed entities to one degree or another. Which scheme a programmer chooses depends on balancing the benefits and liabilities in the context of how their application uses the data.

In Chapter 24, the EJB to RDB mapping wizard was first introduced to produce a top-down mapping. The top-down mapping options wizard page in Figure 24.5 indicates that there are advanced options if there is an inheritance structure but in Chapter 24 the example did not use inheritance. The *Next* button on this wizard page is only enabled if EJB inheritance is used among the container-managed entities.

The last page, shown in Figure 25.22, will display each inheritance structure within the EJB module. By default, a single-table inheritance strategy is employed when doing a top-down

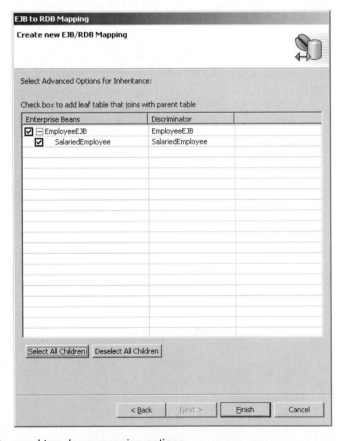

Figure 25.22 Advanced top-down mapping options.

mapping. You can override the default to root-leaf inheritance by selecting container-managed entities on this page. Each container-managed entity that is selected will have its own table generated for it, and a foreign key pointer will be added that joins to the parent table (i.e., the table that is mapped to the root container-managed entity in the inheritance).

Notice that you can mix both root-leaf inheritance and single-table inheritance strategies using this page. This is done by selecting some of the entities and not others. This may be a desired outcome if you have some of the entities with very few cmp-fields so it is more efficient to have those entities mapped with a single table inheritance strategy while other entities have many cmp-fields and would require their own table.

In a bottom-up mapping approach in which container-managed entities are generated from the columns and tables available in a database schema, inheritance cannot be reliably inferred from a database schema, so no inheritance mapping is applied by default. This is why you get one container-managed entity created for each database table that is defined. However, in the meet-in-the-middle mapping approach, where schema and EJB design are developed independently and then mapped into each other, both inheritance schemes are supported.

To map a child entity to one or more database tables, you would use the same mapping tools to create a mapping from the EJB to the database table. For example, if we use our SalariedEmployee example, we could create a mapping from the SalariedEmployee entity to the EMPLOYEEEJB table.

First we need to look at how the EMPLOYEEEJB table is defined. It will contain a new discriminator column which is used to store a string value that will be inserted as a value in the database row that is unique for each entity in the inheritance structure. This is used when reading a row from the database so the correct type of entity is instantiated. Figure 25.23 shows the properties for the mapping of the EmployeeEJB to the EMPLOYEEEJB table. Notice that you must select a discriminator column and a discriminator value. Only the root entity will have the discriminator column but all mappings to each entity in the inheritance will require a discriminator value which automatically defaults to the name of the entity. The discriminator column is used to uniquely distinguish each subtype in the database.

When you add the mapping from SalariedEmployee to EMPLOYEEEJB, a single-table inheritance mapping strategy is set up. This requires a discriminator value to be defined for this mapping (Figure 25.24).

Now, if you want to use a root-leaf inheritance strategy, you would need to map the SalariedEmployee to another table (e.g., SALARIEDEMPLOYEE). Now you can map the cmp-fields from SalariedEmployee to columns on the SALARIEDEMPLOYEE table. The properties

Properties		🏷 ⇒ 📑 ×
Property	Value	
⊟ Bean to Table Strategy	EMPLOYEEEJB_DISCRIM = "EmployeeEJB"	
Discriminator Column	EMPLOYEEEJB_DISCRIM : VARCHAR(32)	
Discriminator Value	EmployeeEJB	

Figure 25.23 Properties for root entity mapping.

Properties	⏩ ⏩ ⏩ ×
Property	Value
⊟ Bean to Table Strategy	🔷 EMPLOYEEEJB_DISCRIM = "SalariedEmployee"
Discriminator Value	ᵃ⌐ SalariedEmployee
InheritedStrategy	🔷 EMPLOYEEEJB_DISCRIM = "EmployeeEJB"

Figure 25.24 Properties for a single-table inheritance mapping.

Properties	⏩ ⏩ ⏩ ×
Property	Value
⊟ Bean to Table Strategy	🔷 EMPLOYEEEJB_DISCRIM = "SalariedEmployee"
Discriminator Value	ˢ⌐ SalariedEmployee
InheritedStrategy	🔷 EMPLOYEEEJB_DISCRIM = "EmployeeEJB"
Join Key - SALARIEDEMPLOYEE	⬦ C5704035 : EMPLOYEEEJB

Figure 25.25 Properties for a root-leaf inheritance mapping.

for this mapping are slightly different than that for a single-table inheritance strategy. Figure 25.25 shows the properties for a root-leaf inheritance mapping. The difference is that this mapping requires a join key to be defined. This is a foreign key on the SALARIEDEMPLOYEE table that joins it to the EMPLOYEEEJB table.

25.11.6   Wrapping Up EJB Inheritance

We don't have a good reason to employ EJB inheritance in the TimeSheet management case study application. Most cases for EJB inheritance stem from having inheritance in the Object model and wanting this directly reflected in your EJB implementation, particularly where there is benefit to the root home interface finder methods returning heterogeneous collection of EJBs. The other big benefit of object inheritance in general, decoupling between client type dependence and runtime type implementation, is supplied with all EJBs through the two local interfaces.

25.12   Advanced EJB QL

In the previous chapter you were first introduced to EJB QL query definitions for a container-managed entity. You learned how to define both find and ejbSelect queries as well as how to generate the methods necessary to support these queries. At that time you were introduced to the EJB QL finder wizard (Figure 24.24). Now, after learning how to create relationships between container-managed entities, we are ready to explore more complex EJB QL queries.

This section will concentrate on specific EJB QL statements and not necessarily the tools to create the queries or the query definitions within the deployment descriptor. We will start with more detailed information for each of the main clauses of the EJB QL query statement, SELECT clause, FROM clause, and WHERE clause. At the end of this section are a number of example find and ejbSelect query statements that could be created for the case study. You may want to refer to these examples while reading through the rest of this section to see more complex statements that can be built with EJB QL.

Before we begin talking about these clause sections of the EJB QL statement, we must first explore identifiers which span all three clauses. An EJB QL identifier must follow the same rules as Java identifiers. A start identifier will be a character for which `Character.isJavaId-` `entifierStart` returns true (e.g., `'_'` and `'$'`) and a part character is a character for which `Character.isJavaIdentifierPart` returns true. Note the question mark (?) is a reserved character and cannot be used as an identifier. Here is a list of reserved identifiers in EJB QL: `SELECT`, `FROM`, `WHERE`, `DISTINCT`, `OBJECT`, `NULL`, `TRUE`, `FALSE`, `NOT`, `AND`, `OR`, `BETWEEN`, `LIKE`, `IN`, `AS`, `UNKNOWN`,[4] `EMPTY`, `MEMBER`, `OF`, and `IS`.

25.12.1 The FROM Clause

We will start by explaining the `FROM` clause since it is where identification variables are defined and used within the other two clauses. Here is the syntax of the `FROM` clause as defined by the EJB 2.0 specification:

```
from_clause ::=FROM identification_variable_declaration [,

identification_variable_declaration]*

identification_variable_declaration ::= collection_member_declaration |

range_variable_declaration collection_member_declaration ::= IN

(collection_valued_path_expression) [AS ] identifier

range_variable_declaration :: abstract_schema_name [AS ] identifier
```

An identification variable is used to designate instances of a specific abstract schema type of an entity bean. There may be multiple identification variables within the `FROM` clause separated by a comma. Identification variables cannot be a reserved identifier or the abstract schema name or the bean name. Let's look at an example of an EJB QL that could be defined for our case study.

```
SELECT OBJECT(o)

FROM TimeSheetEJB o, IN(o.entries) e
```

In this example the identification variable `e` will evaluate to a TimeSheetEntryEJB that is directly reachable from TimeSheetEJB. The cmr-field `entries` represents a collection of the abstract schema type `TimeSheetEntryEJB` and the variable `e` refers to one of the items in the collection. Note that clauses are evaluated form left to right. This is why the second variable declaration, `e`, in this `FROM` clause can utilize the first variable, `o`.

---

4.   Not currently used but reserved for future use.

From this example you can see that an identification variable can refer to a single abstract schema type instance (a range variable) or one element from a collection of abstract schema type instances (a collection member identification variable). That is, an identification variable always refers to a single value.

In the example, o is a range variable and it could optionally be defined with the AS operator (i.e., `TimeSheetEJB AS o`). Range variables are convenient for designating a reference point for objects which may not be reachable by navigation.

The e variable in the example is a collection member identification variable. A collection member identification variable is always declared using the reserved identifier IN within a functional expression and it takes a collection values path expression as a parameter. A path expression is a representation of the navigation of cmr-fields within the entity's abstract schema type. A path expression is defined as an identification variable followed by the navigation operator (.) and a cmp-field or cmr-field. Path expressions can be further composed of another expression if it ends with a single-valued cmr-field. A path expression that ends with a cmp-field or a multivalued cmr-field cannot be further composed.

For example, if range variable t designates a TimeSheetEJB, the following paths are valid: `t.state`, `t.entries`, `t.submitter.name`. The following would be an invalid path expression: `t.entries.date`. This is an invalid path because the `entries` cmr-field resolves to a collection. Collection member identification variables must be used to reference a particular member of the collection. We could fix the invalid expression by declaring the variable e in the FROM clause as `IN(t.entries)` e and then the expression could be correctly written as `e.date`.

25.12.2 The SELECT Clause

The SELECT clause is used to designate the query result. For a finder query, the clause can only contain a single range variable or a single valued path expression that is typed to the abstract schema type of the container-managed entity bean for which it is defined. For select queries, the SELECT clause can contain the same values as a finder query except that the single valued path expression can evaluate to any arbitrary type. These arbitrary types can be the entity bean's abstract schema type or the abstract schema types of other entity beans or values of cmp-fields.

Below is the syntax of the SELECT clause as defined by the EJB 2.0 specification:

```
select_clause ::=

SELECT [DISTINCT ] { single_valued_path_expression |OBJECT

(identification_variable)}
```

The select clause has a number of rules. First, the OBJECT identifier must be used to select values of identification variables defined within the FROM clause. Also, any path expression used within the SELECT clause must be a single valued path expression and not a many valued expression. Finally, the DISTINCT key word is used to remove duplicates from the query result when the return type is a java.util.Collection. The DISTINCT key word is not required if the return type is java.util.Set.

Let's look at simple examples from the case study. A very common query would be one that returned all available instances of a given entity (i.e., findAll query). The following statement will return a collection of EmployeeEJB instances.

```
SELECT OBJECT(o) FROM EmployeeEJB o
```

The following statement will return a collection EmployeeEJB instances which are the submitters from the EmployeeEJB's timesheets.

```
SELECT t.submitter FROM EmployeeEJB AS e, IN(e.timesheets) t
```

The following statement is invalid because the SELECT clause must use only single-valued expressions if expressions are used at all.

```
SELECT t.entries FROM EmployeeEJB AS e, IN(e.timesheets) t
```

25.12.3 The WHERE Clause

The WHERE clause provides the ability to restrict the result of the query. This is done by using a conditional expression as shown in this syntax:

```
where_clause ::=WHERE conditional_expression
```

The WHERE clause may use any identification variable defined within the FROM clause. The conditional expression may also contain Java literals such as strings, numbers, and Boolean literals. String literals are represented by single quotes and the use of a single quote in the literal is escaped by using two single quotes. The Boolean literals are TRUE and FALSE.
Example:

```
WHERE o.name = 'Bob'

WHERE o.isActive = TRUE
```

Path expressions are another construct that is valid with the WHERE clause. There is, however, one exception: empty_collection_comparison_expression or collection_member_expression. We will talk about these expressions in just a moment. Note that the path expression will be unknown if it is composed by using an identification variable that designates an unknown value.

These constructs are important features of the WHERE clause but probably the most important method to restrict the query result would be the use of input parameters within the conditional expression. Input parameters are designated with a question mark (?) and a number starting from 1 (e.g., ?1, ?2, ?3). The number of distinct input parameters cannot exceed the number of parameters specified in the query method signature. However, the query itself does not need to make use of all the parameters from the method. The type of the input parameter will evaluate to the corresponding parameter from the query method.

In the next example, the ?1 variable will have a String type as it corresponds to the aName parameter.

```
public EmployeeEJB findByName(String aName);

SELECT OBJECT(o) FROM EmployeeEJB o WHERE o.name = ?1
```

We have already shown that the WHERE clause is made up of a conditional expression but it can also be made of multiple conditional expressions that are composed of one another. For example, you can use two conditional expressions where both must evaluate to True by using the AND identifier to join both expressions. You could also use two conditional expressions where only one evaluates to True by using the OR identifier to join the expressions. Any evaluation of a given conditional expression or composition of expressions can be negated with the NOT identifier preceding the expression. The ordering of the expressions within the WHERE clause can be controlled by using parentheses [()] to group expressions.

Here is a list of operators that may be used within a conditional expression in order of decreasing precedence as given in the EJB 2.0 specification.

- Navigation operator (.)
- Arithmetic operators:
  +, - unary
  *, / multiplication and division
  +, - addition and subtraction
- Comparison operators: =, >, >=, <, <=, <> (not equal)
- Logical operators: NOT, AND, OR

Table 25.7 provides additional operators that are used within specific expressions in the WHERE clause.

Table 25.7 Specific-expression operators.

Type	Syntax	Description

BETWEEN	`arithmetic_expression [NOT]`
	`BETWEEN arithmetic-expr AND arith-`
	`metic-expr`
		A shortcut instead of using >= and <= tests.

IN	`single_valued_path_expression`
	`[NOT] IN (string-literal [,`
	`string-literal]* )`
		A shortcut for testing of containment or noncontainment within a group of Strings instead of using multiple OR statements.

LIKE	`single_valued_path_expression`
	`[NOT] LIKE pattern-value [ESCAPE`
	`escape-character]`
		The path expression must evaluate to a String. The pattern-value can use an underscore (_) for single characters and a percent (%) for a sequence of characters. ESCAPE defines the escape character to be used when you want to escape the meaning of the underscore and percent in the pattern.

NULL	`single_valued_path_expressionIS` `[NOT ] NULL`	Test for a NULL value within a single valued-path expression.
EMPTY	`collection_valued_path_expression` `IS [NOT] EMPTY`	Test for no elements or some elements from a collection returned in a collection valued path expression.

MEMBER	`{single_valued_navigation |`
	`identification_variable |`
	`input_parameter }`
	`[NOT] MEMBER [OF]`
	`collection_valued_path_expression`
		Tests whether a single object is or is not contained within a given collection.

There are some built-in functions for both Strings and arithmetic in EJB QL. The String functions include:

- CONCAT(String, String) returns a String
- SUBSTRING(String, start, length) returns a String (the start and length are int positions within the String)
- LOCATE(String, String [, start]) return an int (start is an int position within the String)
- LENGTH(String) returns an int

25.12.4 Examples

Here are several EJB QL example statements that reference EJBs defined in the case study.

25.12.4.1 Find Query Examples

1. Return all EmployeeEJB instances.
```
SELECT OBJECT(o) FROM EmployeeEJB o
```

2. Find all states that have a TimeSheetEJB.
```
SELECT DISTINCT t.state FROM TimeSheetEJB t
```

3. Find all TimeSheetEJBs for all 'Smith' submitters.
```
SELECT OBJECT(t) FROM TimeSheetEJB t
WHERE t.submitter LIKE '%Smith'
```

4. Find all TimeSheetEJBs within one of the following states, WV, VA, NC, or SC.
```
SELECT OBJECT(t) FROM TimeSheetEJB t
WHERE t.state IN ('WV', 'VA', 'NC', 'SC')
```

5. Find all ProjectEJBs with a project number between 1000 and 1100.
```
SELECT OBJECT(p) FROM ProjectEJB p
WHERE p.projNumber BETWEEN 1000 AND 1100
```

6. Find all TimeSheetEJBs that have TimeSheetEntryEJBs.
```
SELECT DISTINCT OBJECT(t) FROM TimeSheetEJB t
WHERE t.entries IS NOT EMPTY
```

7. Find all EmployeeEJBs where they have a time sheet in a state different from their home state.
```
SELECT DISTINCT OBJECT(e) FROM EmployeeEJB e, IN(e.timesheets) t
WHERE e.homeAddress.state <> t.state
```

8. Find all EmployeeEJBs that live is the given city and state.
```
SELECT OBJECT(e) FROM EmployeeEJB e
WHERE e.city = ?1 AND e.state = ?2
```

9. Find all TimeSheetEJBs for a given project name.
```
SELECT DISTINCT OBJECT(t) FROM TimeSheetEJB t, IN(t.entries) e
WHERE e.project.name = ?1
```

25.12.4.2 Select Query Examples

1. Select the distinct city names of all EmployeeEJBs.
```
SELECT DISTINCT e.homeAddress.city FROM EmployeeEJB e
```

2. Select the names of all EmployeeEJB that have time sheets within a given state.
```
SELECT DISTINCT e.name FROM EmployeeEJB e, IN(e.timesheets) t
WHERE t.state = ?1
```

3. Select the AddressEJB for an EmployeeEJB with a given name.

```
SELECT e.homeAddress FROM EmployeeEJB e
WHERE e.name = ?1
```

4. Select the employee names for all employees within a particular state with a submitted time sheet entry that is greater than eight hours for a particular project.

```
SELECT e.name FROM EmployeeEJB e, IN(e.timesheets) t,
IN(t.entries) l
WHERE l.hours > 8.0 AND
e.homeAddress.state = ?1 AND
l.project.name = ?2
```

5. Select a distinct set of Project names from the employee's approved time sheet entries where the employee's state is the same as the TimeSheet state for a particular employee ZIP code.

```
SELECT DISTINCT l.project.name FROM EmployeeEJB e,
IN(e.approvedTimesheets) t, IN(t.entries) l
WHERE e.homeAddress.state = t.state
AND e.homeAddress.zipCode = ?1
```

25.13 Summary

In this chapter we covered how to take advantage of EJB 2.0 relationships and inheritance to introduce realistic dependencies among the EJBs within your object model. We provided detailed information of how EJB relationship and inheritance is created as well as how it is implemented. You have seen how the top-down and bottom-up mapping strategies support these dependencies. We also covered detailed information of how to use meet-in-the-middle mapping to map both EJB relationships and inheritance when the domain model and database are maintained independently.

Finally, we expanded on the introduction of EJB QL from the previous chapter with further details on the EJB QL statement constructs including the SELECT clause, FROM clause, and WHERE clause. We also provided several examples of EJB QL based on our case study which you can use as patterns for your own queries.

CHAPTER 26

Bean-Managed Persistence

In earlier chapters you have seen how the EJB specification provides for persistence management in EJB implementations. While data can be stored and retrieved from a database by both session and entity EJBs, you have learned that the primary component type defined in the specification for persistent data storage and retrieval is the entity EJB.

You have seen how the specification describes using one of two options for entity beans: CMP or BMP. CMP implicitly applies persistence to enterprise beans, relieving the bean developer from having to code for it. A detailed discussion of the implementation of CMP EJBs in WAS and WebSphere Studio can be found in Chapters 23, 24, and 25. BMP enables the bean developer to implement persistent operations within bean class methods. The goal of this chapter is to help you understand the basics of writing BMP beans that work in J2EE 1.3 and WAS.

26.1 Applying BMP

Recall that entity beans encapsulate an underlying data source or application, and as such require access to them (Figure 26.1). To ensure that the state of an active entity bean is consistent with the state of the underlying resource is the basis for the entity bean life cycle. Whenever a developer needs more complete control in managing the data persistence than is provided by CMP, the alternative is BMP entity beans (Figure 26.2).

The data access calls necessary to store the state of a BMP entity bean in a persistent store are defined in methods implemented to satisfy the entity bean component contract in Table 26.1.

We will see how these methods are used in the following sections. Bean developers can use the JDBC API, or any other vendor-supplied framework, such as an object relational (OR) mapping product, to access data sources. We will begin with examining this approach, and also investigate some of the ramifications.

613

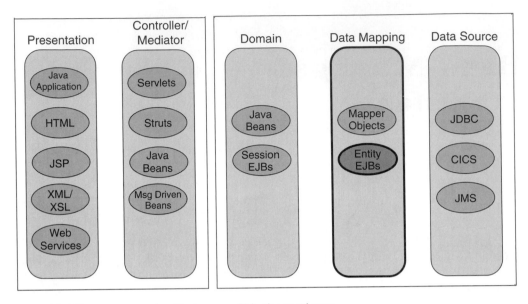

Figure 26.1 Bean-managed entity beans within the road map.

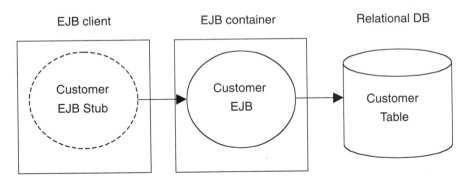

Figure 26.2 Entity bean data source relationship.

Table 26.1 Data access calls for a BMP entity bean.

ejbCreate()	Insert entity bean state into a data source.
ejbRemove()	Remove entity bean from an underlying data source.
ejbFind<method>()	Retrieve entity bean instances based upon the finder method signature.
ejbLoad()	Refresh entity bean state from the data source.
ejbStore()	Update data source attributes with the entity bean state.

At first, simply nesting JDBC calls in entity bean methods might seem like a reasonable approach to implementing persistence. However, a more flexible and reusable design can be produced if requests are forwarded to a mapping class, similar to the mapping design described in Chapters 16 and 30. We will cover that approach at the end of this chapter.

26.2   A Simple BMP Bean

We will go ever so slightly outside the bounds of our example to investigate how BMP beans are written, and their advantages. So far we have only dealt with one aspect of our business domain; the time sheet aspect of an HR system. However, any large company will have other systems as well. Let's imagine that we are building our system for an airline or travel agency. Let's further imagine that we are dealing with a frequent-traveler program. In this sort of program, one of the primary objects involved will be a Customer. Viewing Customer information and making modifications to it constitutes the bulk of the activity in this system. So, we can imagine that we have a Customer as a BMP entity bean. This bean will manage its own state (fields) and we will need to implement each of the entity bean life cycle methods to interface with the persistent datastore.

Listing 26.1 Local interface for Customer.

```
package com.wsbook.casestudy.ejb;

import com.wsbook.casestudy.ejb.CustomerKey;



public interface CustomerLocal extends javax.ejb.EJBLocalObject {

        public int getAccountBalance();

        public String getCustomerName();

        public void setAccountBalance(int accountBalance);

        public void setCustomerName(String customerName);

        public int getCustomerNumber();

}
```

Listing 26.1 shows a simple local interface that defines a customer consisting of a unique customer number, a customer name, and an account balance. The customer number will actually be contained within a separate primary key class, CustomerKey. This makes it easier to modify the key mapping, if necessary, in future revisions. The LocalHome interface for the EJB is likewise simple and straightforward (Listing 26.2):

Listing 26.2 LocalHome Interface for Customer

```
package com.wsbook.casestudy.ejb;

public interface CustomerLocalHome extends javax.ejb.EJBLocalHome {

    public CustomerLocal create(int customerNumber, String customerName)

        throws javax.ejb.CreateException;

    public CustomerLocal findByPrimaryKey(CustomerKey primaryKey)

        throws javax.ejb.FinderException;

}
```

In this case we are taking a very simple approach where we have defined the simplest home interface possible—a `create()` method taking as its arguments a new customer number and customer name, and a `findByPrimaryKey()` method. Now that you've seen the external definition of our EJB, we can move into the meat of the example, the bean implementation class.

Rather than walk through the entire EJB class, we'll look at some selected parts of the EJB and see how it was written using WSAD, and how it can be tested there and used in WAS. First, let's examine the class definition of our Customerbean (Listing 26.3).

Listing 26.3 Class declaration for Customerbean

```
package com.wsbook.casestudy.ejb;

import java.sql.*;

import javax.ejb.*;

import javax.naming.*;

import javax.sql.DataSource;

public class Customerbean implements javax.ejb.entitybean {

    private javax.ejb.entityContext myentityCtx;
```

```
    private String customerName;

    private int accountBalance;

    private CustomerKey key;



    public static final String LOAD_STRING =

        "SELECT cNum, cName, acctBal from USERID.Cust WHERE cNum = ?";

    public static final String FIND_BY_PRIMARYKEY_STRING =

        "SELECT cNum from USERID.Cust WHERE cNum = ?";

    public static final String UPDATE_STRING =

        "UPDATE USERID.Cust SET cName = ?, acctBal = ? WHERE cNum = ?";

    public static final String INSERT_STRING =

        "INSERT INTO USERID.Cust(cNum, cName, acctBal) VALUES (?, ?,

?)";

    public static final String REMOVE_STRING =

        "DELETE from USERID.Cust where cNum = ?";

    /* Create SQL is CREATE TABLE Cust (cNum INTEGER NOT NULL,

            cName VARCHAR(60), acctBal INTEGER) */

    private DataSource ds;

    public static final String DATASOURCE_NAME = "java:comp/env/jdbc/
DS_Ref";
```

The first few lines declare the class as being an implementer of the entity bean interface, and declare the entityContext instance variable. The new enterprise bean wizard in WSAD generated that much for us. You've seen this wizard in use several times in this book, so we won't cover that topic again. The only difference in the initial generation of this EJB was that we choose the EJB to be an entity bean with BMP fields, a choice we have not previously made. Likewise we added three instance variables—key, customerName and accountBalance—and then promoted the getters and setters for each of these variables to the local interface. The primary key is accessible via getPrimaryKey() which returns the CustomerKey object. The CustomerKey object exposes the customerNumber via getCustomerNumber(). We did not promote the setter for the key to the local interface since we don't want clients to be able to change the primary key of a Customer.

Note that unlike the CMP counterpart, this bean class is not abstract. The BMP entity bean class is responsible for managing its own attributes.

The next few lines declare several final static String variables to hold SQL statements—this is the SQL that our persistence methods will execute to store or retrieve our bean data from the database. We will look at some of these more in-depth later.

Finally, we declare an instance variable of type DataSource, and declare a final static String value that names a DataSource. The name of the DataSource is a resource reference that has been defined in the EJB deployment descriptor. To set this up, open the ejb-jar.xml file for the EJB module (Figure 26.3).

In WebSphere Studio, the ejb-jar.xml editor has tabs to organize the deployment descriptor elements. On the References tab, you can add references for a specific EJB. Launch the add reference wizard by selecting the Customer and clicking the *Add* button (Figure 26.4).

The first page of the wizard lets you choose the type of reference to create. In this particular case, we are interested in creating an EJB resource references. On the second page of the wizard (Figure 26.5), you will select the object referenced to be of type javax.sql.DataSource.

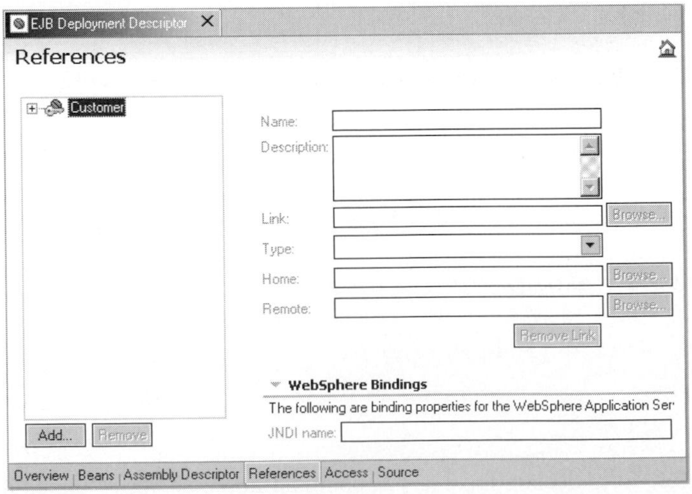

Figure 26.3 Setting resource reference for Customer.

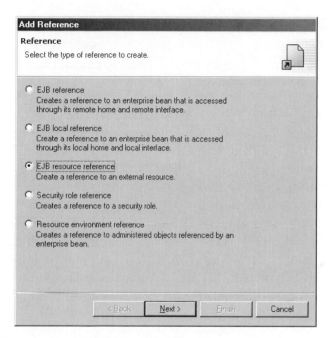

Figure 26.4 Add reference wizard, Page 1.

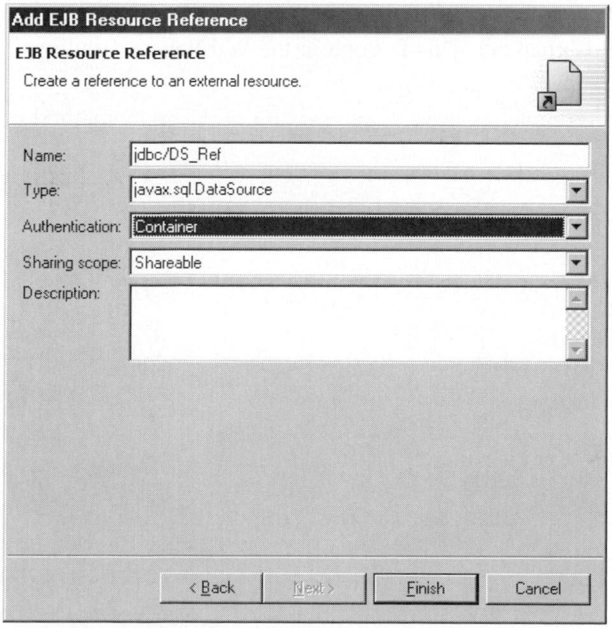

Figure 26.5 Add reference wizard, Page 2.

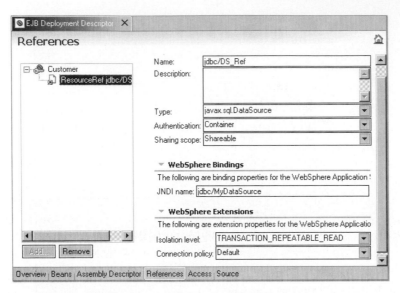

Figure 26.6 Binding resource reference to JNDI name for testing.

The name jdbc/DS_Ref will be added to the java:comp/env local namespace for Customer, java:comp/env/jdbc/DS_Ref. The container-based authentication will be supplied by a JAAS security alias. For testing purposes, the resource reference is bound to the global JNDI name jdbc/MyDataSource for the DataSource (we visit creating the DataSource in the test server configuration later in this chapter). This is done in the WebSphere Bindings section on the References tab after reference is created (Figure 26.6).

This resource reference is used in the getConnection() method of our Customer BMP bean (Listing 26.4).

Listing 26.4 getConnection() utility method

```
    protected Connection getConnection() throws SQLException,

NamingException

    {

        if (ds == null) {

            InitialContext initContext = new InitialContext();

            ds=(DataSource)initContext.lookup(DATASOURCE_NAME);

        }
```

```
        return ds.getConnection();

}
```

We will use this `getConnection()` method in each of the persistence methods in our EJB. The data source itself will be created pointing to our EJPBOOK database utilizing an XA-compliant JDBC driver. Like your CMP beans, you will want your BMP beans to be able to participate in 2-PC distributed transactions. Even though the BMP beans manage obtaining a connection to the data source it is still the EJB container, and not the bean implementation class, that is responsible for committing the changes to the database.

When a connection is retrieved to access an XA resource, the resulting statements executed using that connection will join the distributed XA transaction. The EJB container handles committing the distributed transaction or rolling back the transaction if the EJB transaction aborts (see Chapter 28 for more details).

26.3   Examining BMP Persistence

Now that the preliminaries are out of the way, we can begin investigating how the persistence methods defined in a BMP entity EJB are implemented. This involves looking at each of the persistence methods described earlier.

26.3.1   Writing ejbCreate() Method in BMP beans

We will start by examining the `ejbCreate()` method in our example. Remember from Chapter 23 that each `create()` method in a home interface will correspond to an `ejbCreate()` method with the same parameters in the bean implementation class. However, this is where the similarity ends. While in an CMP EJB the `ejbCreate()` method is only responsible for setting the values of the container-managed instance variables to the values passed in as arguments to the `create()` method, in a BMP EJB the `ejbCreate()` method is also responsible for creating a persistent representation of the object in the data source. In our simple case, this means that it must INSERT a row into the SQL database. The code for the sample `ejbCreate()` method is shown in Listing 26.5.

Listing 26.5 ejbCreate method

```
publicCustomerKeyejbCreate(intcustomerNumber,StringcustomerName)

    throws CreateException {

    CustomerKey key = new CustomerKey(customerNumber);

    this.setCustomerName(customerName);
```

```
this.setAccountBalance(0);



Connection jdbcConn = null;

PreparedStatement sqlStatement = null;

try {

        jdbcConn = getConnection();

        sqlStatement =

                jdbcConn.prepareStatement(INSERT_STRING);

        sqlStatement.setInt(1, customerNumber);

        sqlStatement.setString(2, customerName);

        sqlStatement.setInt(3, accountBalance);

        if (sqlStatement.executeUpdate() != 1) {

                throw new CreateException(

        "Failure in ejbCreate() -- duplicate Customer number");

        }

        return key;

} catch (NamingException e) {

        throw new CreateException(

                "Failure in ejbCreate() -- " + e.getMessage());

} catch (SQLException se) {

        throw new CreateException(

                "Failure in ejbCreate() -- " + se.getMessage());
```

```
        } finally {

            // close statement and connection

            close(sqlStatement, jdbcConn);

        }

    }
```

This method begins much as the corresponding method in a CMP implementation would—it sets the values of the instance variables `customerNumber` and `customerName` to the values passed in to the method. However, the lines following that section of code are unique to a BMP. What happens next is that the method creates a PreparedStatement from the database connection it obtains from the `getConnection()` method we discussed earlier. The PreparedStatement will execute the following SQL, defined in the `INSERT_STRING` constant:

```
INSERT INTO Cust(cNum, cName, acctBal) VALUES (?, ?, ?)
```

Here we substitute the `customerNumber`, `customerName`, and `accountBalance` values for the parameters (`?`s) in the SQL statement. Finally the method executes the SQL statement and checks to see that only one row was added to the database. The final statement in the main branch of the method is to then return a new instance of CustomerKey created from the newly assigned customer number.

A `try...catch` block handles possible exceptions that may occur. Pay particular attention to the `finally` clause in this method. It ensures that the PreparedStatement is always closed and that the JDBC connection is closed, In the case of a JDBC connection obtained from a DataSource, this means that the connection is returned to the pool, rather than being deallocated and destroyed.

26.3.2 Writing BMP Finder Methods

Now that you've seen how BMP EJBs are created, we can move on to the process of finding a BMP EJB, or a set of BMP EJBs, and loading their state from the database. This process starts with the execution of a finder method on the EJB home, which in BMP EJBs will correspond to an `ejbFind...()` method in the EJB bean implementation class. Note that this is different from CMP EJBs, where the finder implementation was entirely handled in the generated EJB home, with only the EJB QL provided by the developer in the deployment descriptor.

In our case, we only have one finder method in our EJB home interface, `findByPrimaryKey(CustomerKey)`. This corresponds to the `ejbFindByPrimaryKey(CustomerKey)` method whose code is shown in Listing 26.6.

Listing 26.6 ejbFindByPrimaryKey method

```
public CustomerKey ejbFindByPrimaryKey(CustomerKey key)

        throws FinderException {

    boolean wasFound = false;

    boolean foundMultiples = false;

    Connection jdbcConn = null;

    PreparedStatement sqlStatement = null;

    try {

        jdbcConn = getConnection();

        sqlStatement =

            jdbcConn.prepareStatement(FIND_BY_PRIMARYKEY_ST

        RING);

        sqlStatement.setInt(1, key.getCustomerNumber());

        ResultSet sqlResults = sqlStatement.executeQuery();

        wasFound = sqlResults.next();

        foundMultiples = sqlResults.next();

    } catch (NamingException e) { // DB error

        throw new FinderException(

    "Database Exception " + e + "caught in ejbFindByPrimaryKey()");

    } catch (SQLException se) { // DB error

        throw new FinderException(

    "Database Exception " + se +

    "caught in ejbFindByPrimaryKey()");
```

```
        } finally {

                close(sqlStatement, jdbcConn);

        }

        if (wasFound && !foundMultiples) {

                return new CustomerKey(key.getCustomerNumber());

        } else {

                throw new FinderException(

"Multiple rows or no rows found for unique key in ejbFindByPrimaryKey().");

        }

    }
```

The flow of this method is simple, but surprising. All this method does is create a Pre-paredStatement executing the following SQL:

```
SELECT cNum from Cust WHERE cNum = ?
```

Now, this is a strange piece of SQL—we are selecting only one column. Why? The reason lies in the way in which BMP EJBs are instantiated from the database. When a finder method is called on an EJB home, the container selects (more or less at random) an instance of the bean implementation class to run the `ejbFind...` method on. When the `ejbFind...` method executes, it must return either a single Primary Key object, or a Collection of Primary Keys (for finders that should return multiple objects). The container will then retrieve from the instance pool, or create, as many entity bean instances as necessary, and set these Primary Key(s) in the entityContext of those beans.

It will then invoke `ejbLoad()` on these EJBs so that the latest values of the data can be loaded from the database. So, in this way the `ejbFind...` methods are more or less disconnected from the rest of the EJB implementation, and do not operate on any of the instance variables of the bean class, but instead only use the arguments of the method as arguments to the SQL. Since all the SQL needs to do is run a `SELECT` to find the primary key columns of the table based on the parameters, this is why we only select a single column in our example.

Since this is a single-valued EJB finder method, we only need to return a single Primary Key object. For this reason, we also want to make sure that only one row exists in the table for this particular primary key value, which is why we check for additional rows being returned.

Now, we could do this by executing a COUNT function in the SQL, but this approach is probably just as easy, and as efficient.

26.3.3 Writing the BMP ejbLoad() Method

Now we are ready to move on to writing our ejbLoad() method. The source code for this method is shown in Listing 26.7.

Listing 26.7 ejbLoad method

```
public void ejbLoad() {

        boolean wasFound = false;

        boolean foundMultiples = false;

        key = (CustomerKey) getentityContext().getPrimaryKey();

        Connection jdbcConn = null;

        PreparedStatement sqlStatement = null;

        try {

                jdbcConn = getConnection();

                sqlStatement=jdbcConn.prepareStatement(LOAD_STRING);

                sqlStatement.setInt(1, key.getCustomerNumber());

                ResultSet sqlResults = sqlStatement.executeQuery();

                wasFound = sqlResults.next();

                if (wasFound) {

                        this.setCustomerName(sqlResults.getString(2));

                        this.setAccountBalance(sqlResults.getInt(3));

                }

                foundMultiples = sqlResults.next();

        } catch (NamingException e) { // log details
```

```
System.out.println(

        "Database Exception " + e + "caught in

ejbLoad()");

    throw new EJBException(e);

} catch (SQLException se) { // log details

    System.out.println(

        "Database Exception " + se + "caught in

ejbLoad()");

    throw new EJBException(se);

} finally {

    // close statement and connection

    close(sqlStatement, jdbcConn);

}

if (wasFound && !foundMultiples) {

    return;

} else {

    System.out.println(

    "Multiple rows found for unique key in ejbLoad().");

    throw new EJBException(

"Multiple rows found for unique key in Customer:ejbLoad().");

}

}
```

The logic of this method is similar to the one in `ejbFindByPrimaryKey()`, but with a few key differences. First, the primary key information used in the `WHERE` clause of the `SELECT` statement is obtained from the EntityContext. This is important as none of the state values of this bean instance can be trusted at this point in the life cycle. Only the EntityContext is known to be valid. Second, the `SELECT` statement itself retrieves values for all the columns in the table as you can see next:

```
SELECT cNum, cName, acctBal from Cust WHERE cNum = ?
```

After retrieving the row from the ResultSet, the method sets the values of the instance variables in this EJB to be those obtained from the corresponding rows in the result set. Note that this may involve some data type conversions or other translations. While WSAD and WebSphere provide helpful converter classes for converting data types (such as changing VARCHARS with "yes" or "no" to Booleans, or converting Dates to Strings with a nonstandard format), these are only available in CMP beans. If there is any data conversion to be done in a BMP bean, you must implement it yourself.

26.3.4 Writing the ejbStore() method for BMP Beans

The next method to investigate is `ejbStore()`. This is the method that the container calls at the end of a transaction or business method to record the state of the EJB to the database. The implementation of this method (Listing 26.8) is much like the implementation of the other methods you've seen.

Listing 26.8 ejbStore method

```java
public void ejbStore() {

        Connection jdbcConn = null;

        PreparedStatement sqlStatement = null;

        key = (CustomerKey) getentityContext().getPrimaryKey();

        try {

                jdbcConn = getConnection();

                sqlStatement =

                        jdbcConn.prepareStatement(UPDATE_STRING);

                sqlStatement.setString(1, customerName);
```

```
                    sqlStatement.setInt(2, accountBalance);

                    sqlStatement.setInt(3, key.getCustomerNumber());

                    if (sqlStatement.executeUpdate() != 1) {

                            System.out.println(

                                "No rows added -- failure in ejbStore()");

                            throw new EJBException("Customer:ejbStore() failed");

                    }

            } catch (NamingException e) {

                    System.out.println(e.getMessage());

                    throw new EJBException(e);

            } catch (SQLException se) {

                    System.out.println(se.getMessage());

                    throw new EJBException(se);

            } finally {

                    // close statement and connection

                    close(sqlStatement, jdbcConn);

            }

    }
```

In many ways this method is the inverse of the `ejbLoad()` method we examined earlier. The SQL executed for this method is the following:

```
UPDATE Cust SET cName = ?, acctBal = ? WHERE cNum = ?
```

As you can see, we set the SQL statement parameters to contain the values of the `customerName`, `accountBalance`, and `customerNumber` variables. Just as in the case of `ejbLoad()`, if there is any data type conversion to be done, you must do it in this method.

The implementation of the `ejbRemove` method follows a similar pattern. See the source code on the CD in BookBMP project for the details.

WHY USE PREPAREDSTATEMENTS?

When using JDBC you have three options for your statements: (1) A Statement is a class that can execute an arbitrary SQL String passed in to it. (2) A PreparedStatement refines a Statement by adding substitution parameters, and by separating the SQL compilation process from the execution of the Statement. (3) A CallableStatement takes away the SQL compilation process entirely by executing a SQL stored procedure. Normally, a PreparedStatement is used in a case where you may reuse the same PreparedStatement and execute it multiple times. So, why have we used PreparedStatement rather than Statement in each of our examples, where this is not the case? The reason is that WebSphere implements a PreparedStatement cache on its JDBC connection pooling mechanism. It entirely skips the compilation process for any statement that matches one that it has stored in its cache. This can provide a significant performance boost at runtime, even though it might not appear from reading the code that any performance gain would be evident.

26.4 BMP vs. CMP

So, what is the best approach for implementing persistence? BMP builds data access within the bean source. CMP keeps persistence requirements independent of the bean itself. However, CMP may be limited to data sources supported by a vendor container mapping tool. The decision lies in data access requirements, and in an EJB container's support of these requirements. In this section we examine some questions you can ask yourself about your particular project to help you determine which choice (BMP, CMP, or neither) is right for a particular requirement.

Is there a set of objects (perhaps constituting a logical subsystem) that are both read and updated relatively frequently, with complex relationships between them changing rapidly?

In a nutshell, this is the case for CMP entity EJBs. When a set of complex relationships exist between different entity beans the complexity of the programming of the relationship management becomes a key driver in choosing a solution. CMP entity EJBs are a compelling solution to this problem. When a tool can generate this code, rather than it being laboriously hand-coded, it allows a system to be more easily adapted to changes in the requirements or the underlying data model.

Another feature of CMP that makes it attractive is its ability to manage optimization of the set of SQL calls that must be made in order to read or write the persistent state of an entity bean. For instance, the CMP model in WebSphere allows a set of entity EJBs to be read from a relational database in a `find()` method with only a single SQL `SELECT` call—much more efficient than the default BMP case, which requires $N + 1$ SQL calls (e.g., 1 SQL select for the `ejbFindBy` call, and N selects, one for each `ejbLoad`) to do the same thing (see Chapter 25 for more on read aheads).

Note that this is exactly the opposite of what some so-called EJB experts will tell you to do. There is an impression in the industry that CMP is somehow less efficient than BMP. In fact, one of the early Sun blueprints advocated an approach called the Composite Entity pattern that advocated large-grained BMPs drawn from several relational tables and representing many logical entities. With the advent of EJB 2.0, and especially with the development of sophisticated and efficient mapping tools like those in WSAD, this pattern has become an antipattern. It is now far easier (and more efficient in most cases) to let WSAD write your SQL code than it is for you to write it in 80 percent of all cases.

Is there a set of objects that are updated VERY infrequently, but whose state is frequently read?

Almost every program has at least some examples of this sort of object. For instance, insurance applications have a number of codes for different medical procedures that change very rarely, perhaps only once a year. Another, more common type of object like this, is a political entity like a county or a state. These change exceedingly rarely, but the list of them may be expanded if an application must be made to work internationally.

Here we have a problem that might sound like it could be solved in the same way as the previous case, or that might also suggest a BMP bean, but instead, this is usually best done by a stateless session bean that returns JavaBeans (e.g., dependent objects) whose state is read once, usually on first use or program startup. So why not use the previous solution and let a BMP entity manage these? The reason is that these objects are not transactional—they are read-only. While it depends upon the caching option used by the EJB container, usually a BMP's state is read once per transaction. In this case, the state will always be the same, regardless of the transaction. So, if we read the state once and hold it in memory for the lifetime of the stateless session bean we will save a large number of needless calls to the back-end storage mechanism.

Do you need to display and scroll through a large (>50 elements) list in your application?

Many applications need to be able to display large lists of data in order to let a user select from that list. In general, this should be avoided because scrolling through a large list is a poor user-interface design choice, but there are times where it is the only option.

When you are retrieving data to display in a list, you generally only need a small subset of data—often lists only contain a unique identifier and some sort of user-readable representation of the list element. In this case, using a custom finder method to retrieve a large set of entity EJBs, only to then use a few data elements in each EJB, is a huge waste of resources. So, instead of retrieving a collection of EJBs and then iterating over the collection, create a simple stateful session EJB that can retrieve only those pieces of data that are necessary through a very minimal

SQL query. You can then return the information in a very simple form like a hash table of key values to the Strings that will be displayed in the list.

Once the user has selected a particular selection from the list, you can use an entity EJB to retrieve and operate on only that selected object by finding the entity EJB with a `findByPrimaryKey()` method using the key value that corresponds to the selected element. In practice, we have found this solution to be over twice as fast as iterating through a collection of entity EJBs in most circumstances, and to generate less references that need to be garbage collected as well. This approach has been documented in detail as the Fast Lane Reader pattern in [Marinescu]. We refer interested readers to there or [Brown00] for an implementation.

Do you need to use stored procedures to access and manipulate your persistent data?

Some applications require the use of stored procedures to access the persistent data. This may be for performance reasons or it may be the only mechanism exposed via a legacy configuration. Unlike any of the previous cases, this is a situation that requires BMP entity beans. The BMP entity bean implementation of the container callback methods (`ejbStore`, `ejbLoad`, ...) can use existing stored procedures. Currently, CMP strategies can not exploit stored procedures.

26.5 Summary

We've only scratched the surface of BMP in this chapter. We have examined what the EJB API provides for BMP entity beans or even investigate obtaining BMP EJBs from data sources other than a relational database.   However, this discussion should ground you in the principles necessary to understand how to move on to these more advanced options when necessary.

CHAPTER 27

Introduction to Message-Driven Beans

So far we have taken a fairly extensive look at entity and session beans. A common thread running through the design of all the EJBs that we have examined so far is that they all respond synchronously to local Java or RMI-IIOP calls. With the EJB 2.0 specification, a new EJB bean was introduced that allows business logic to be invoked asynchronously. MDBs are EJBs, which listen for JMS messages. In this chapter, we will introduce you to some core JMS and MDB concepts. We will begin by examining an overview of JMS, then introduce why MDBs are required, and finally examine two examples and how to execute them in the WSAD environment. Figure 27.1 shows how MDBs fit in our road map.

27.1 Java Messaging Service

As discussed in Chapter 3, JMS is a J2EE standard that provides a vendor-neutral way of sending and receiving asynchronous messages in a distributed environment. JMS provides an API for accessing MOM systems such as IBM WebSphere MQ. J2EE 1.3 requires that an application server must provide a JMS provider. In compliance with this, WAS provides a simple messaging provider (WebSphere Embedded Messaging) that is derived from WebSphere MQ, but does not provide all of the features of WebSphere MQ, such as clustering or advanced queue management facilities.

In addition to supporting development on both WebSphere Embedded Messaging and WebSphere MQ, WSAD provides the MQ Simulator for Java (MQ Simulator). MQ Simulator supports point-to-point (P2P) and publish-and-subscribe (pub/sub) with persistent and nonpersistent messages, but only within a single TE server instance. MQ Simulator is a useful addition to WSAD that will allow us to test our MDB and JMS clients within WSAD.

Java applications that use JMS are called *JMS clients*. Just as WebSphere requires a Java database driver for connection to a database, WebSphere also requires a Java connection to an

633

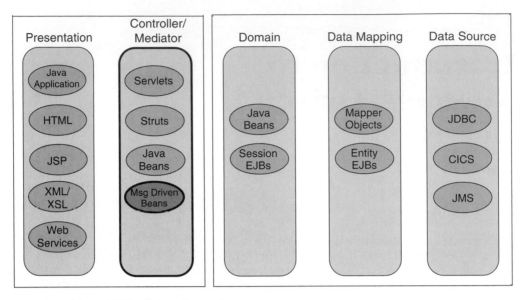

Figure 27.1 Where MDBs fit into the road map.

underlying MOM that is called the *JMS provider*. A JMS client that sends a message is called a *producer* and a JMS client that receives a message is called a JMS *consumer*. It is possible for a single JMS client to be both the producer and the consumer of a message.

27.1.1 JMS Is Asynchronous

At the heart of JMS is the fact that it allows for asynchronous messaging. This means that a JMS client can send a message without having to wait for a reply. This is quite different from the synchronous messaging of Java RMI and similar technologies. RMI is an excellent choice for creating transactional components. Each time a client invokes a bean's method the current thread on the client is blocked until the method is finished. However, this creates a time-based dependency on the EJB server. If the EJB server is unavailable, the method will not complete successfully. Further, if the traffic to your EJB is bursty (meaning it has very high peaks and long periods of quiescence), then your server will be underutilized at times and perhaps overwhelmed at times. These two factors lead to a tight coupling between the client and server. This coupling is relaxed because JMS is asynchronous.

In JMS, a client can fire and forget. A JMS client can put a message on a queue or publish a message to a topic and go on to other important work. Topics and queues are referred to as *destinations*. In this way, clients sending messages are decoupled from clients receiving them.

When using a JMS destination, the JMS client can be assured that the message will be delivered even if downtime occurs. This durability of messages can be optionally specified on both queues and topics. The durability feature of JMS is probably the second most attractive aspect of using JMS for solving certain enterprise situations.

27.1.2 JMS Messaging Models

Two messaging models are available in JMS: pub/sub and P2P. Pub/Sub is intended for a one-to-many broadcast of messages; P2P is intended for one-to-one delivery of messages. In talking about messaging, the creator or sender of the message is referred to as the producer and the receiver of the message is called the consumer.

27.1.2.1 Publish-and-Subscribe

In pub/sub, a single producer sends a message to many consumers through a virtual channel called a *topic*. The producer is unaware of how many consumers, if any, might receive the message. Consumers can only receive the message if they have subscribed.

27.1.2.2 Point-to-Point

P2P messaging allows JMS clients to send and receive messages both synchronously and asynchronously via virtual channels known as *queues*. A queue may have multiple receivers but only one can receive the message.

27.2 JMS API Basics

We certainly can't cover all of the ins and outs of using the JMS API in this chapter; that subject has filled entire books. Instead, we refer the interested reader to [Monson-Haefel] or [IBM-JMS] for the details of the API. Luckily, the API is based upon only a few simple concepts, which we can flesh out in the context of a very simple example. Once you understand this basic example you'll be in better stead to understand the more complete example presented later in the chapter.

As mentioned previously, the fundamental action of sending a message in JMS involves using a message producer to place a message on a destination. Let's first look at how these concepts are implemented in JMS and how you can use them in your programs.

The first concept we need to introduce is how to find a destination. Destinations are held in the JNDI namespace, just as EJBs are. The following syntax can be used (note that it is nearly identical to locating an EJB home interface).

```
InitialContext ctx = new InitialContext();

Object o = ctx.lookup("jms/QOrTopicName");

javax.jms.Queue aQueue = (javax.jms.Queue)

java.rmi.PortableRemoteObject.narrow(o,javax.jms.Queue.class);
```

However, unlike an EJB, you can't just start using a Queue to send messages. Remember that you must have a Message producer to send messages—to create a message producer, you must first obtain a connection. In that respect, JMS is much more like JDBC. The syntax for obtaining a Connection is shown next:

```
//Look up the QueueConnectionFactory in JNDI

Object o = ctx.lookup("jms/ivtQCF");

javax.jms.QueueConnectionFactory qcf =

(javax.jms.QueueConnectionFactory)


java.rmi.PortableRemoteObject.narrow(o,

    javax.jms.QueueConnectionFactory.class);

//Create a QueueConnection

javax.jms.QueueConnection conn = qcf.createQueueConnection();
```

Again, like in JDBC, you then need to obtain an object from a connection that you can
work with. The JMS Session object is the transactional object that you use to create message
producers. While the objects we've seen previously (Queues, Connection Factories, and Connections) are all thread-safe and can be shared across several threads of execution (and therefore
cached), the Session must be created for each individual thread, and should always be closed at
the end of its use.

```
//Create a QueueSession

javax.jms.QueueSession session  =

conn.createQueueSession(false,javax.jms.Session.AUTO_ACKNOWLEDGE);
```

Now that you've created a Session, you're finally ready to create a message producer on
the queue that we obtained in the first step:

```
javax.jms.QueueSender sender = session.createSender(aQueue);
```

Our example is nearly finished. We can now create a message and place it on a queue. In JMS,
messages come in several flavors. TextMessages are messages whose body (or payload) is a text
string. There are also ObjectMessages that carry serialized Java objects, MapMessages that carry
name/value pairs, ByteMessages, and StreamMessages. In our example, we'll use a TextMessage, which is probably the most commonly used message type:

```
// Create the Text Message

Message message = session.createTextMessage();

message.setJMSType("LogMessage");

message.setText("Hello World");

//Send the message

sender.send(message);
```

In this quick introduction to using JMS to send messages, we've omitted all of the exception processing that is necessary in a full example. We'll show that later in the chapter. We've also not covered receiving messages, which we'll cover later as well. However, this should serve as a good enough introduction to the concepts that you can understand the more complete examples presented later.

27.3 Message-Driven Beans

MDBs are a direct outgrowth of the JMS technology. MDBs are stateless, server-side, transaction-aware components for handling asynchronous JMS messages. MDBs are new to the EJB 2.0 specification.

An MDB is a very lightweight EJB which simply processes messages delivered by JMS. The container handles transactions, security, resources, concurrency, and message acknowledgement. A very nice feature is that an MDB can consume and process messages concurrently. Previously in JMS if you needed to process messages concurrently, you would have had to develop a custom framework to instantiate, manage, and synchronize resources across threads. MDBs allow the bean developer to focus on what has to happen when a message is delivered. But more importantly, MDBs allow JMS message consumption to be included in a transaction.

MDBs are indeed enterprise beans complete with XML deployment descriptor elements. However, an MDB does not have the familiar component interfaces (Home, LocalHome, etc.). MDBs have no need for component interfaces because the only way an MDB can process a message is for the subject destination (queue or topic) to have been given a message. MDBs only respond to asynchronous messages, not to client requests.

When creating an MDB, the only method which must be implemented is `onMessage(Message aMsg)` which is called when an asynchronous message is received. Inside the `onMessage()` method, the Message object can be examined to obtain the complete message delivered. The Message object may be a simple text message, a serializable object, or a MapMessage. A MapMessage is essentially a hash table containing keys and values.

While the primary purpose of an MDB is to consume messages, it is possible, and many times it will be necessary, to send messages from the MDB. Hence, MDBs can contact other EJBs using standard J2EE constructs or enqueue messages using JMS. For instance, imagine a simple workflow situation where a chain of asynchronous events needs to occur. Once the MDB has handled its message, it can send another asynchronous message to the next destination in the workflow.

27.3.1 Example MDB in WSAD

Now it's time to build a sample MDB and test client in WSAD. Since most clients of an MDB will be a servlet or session bean, we will use a test servlet to exercise the MDB. We could have used an application test client but using a servlet will allow us to show how to set up resource references in WSAD for the JMS resources.

We will perform the following steps in creating our example:

1. Create the enterprise project

2. Create the MDB

3. Create a test servlet

4. Configure the JNDI names

5. Test and debug

Now it is time to elaborate.

27.3.1.1 Create the Enterprise Project

Go to the J2EE Perspective and create and enterprise project by selecting the *File > New > Enterprise Application Project*. The dialog in Figure 27.2 will be displayed.

Select the radio button for a J2EE 1.3 enterprise application project and press the *Next* button to display Figure 27.3.

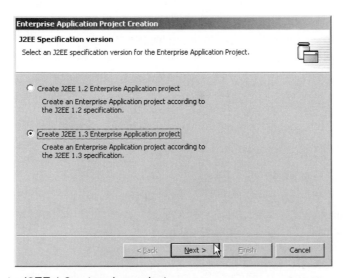

Figure 27.2 Create J2EE 1.3 enterprise project.

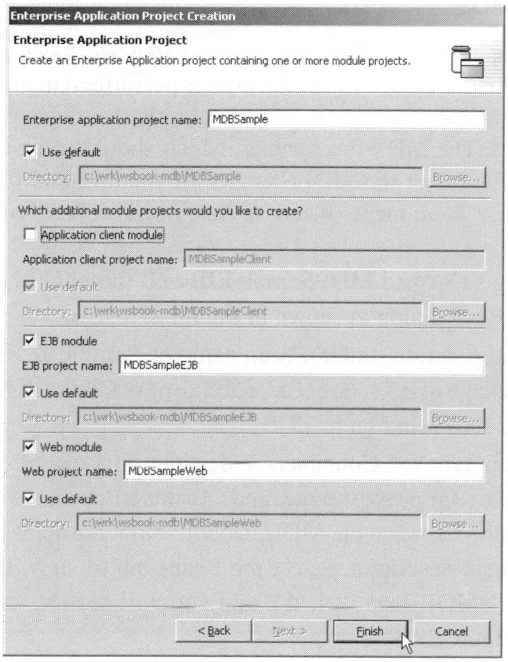

![Enterprise Application Project Creation dialog box showing project name MDBSample with EJB module MDBSampleEJB and Web module MDBSampleWeb]

Figure 27.3 Specify EAR modules.

Name the project MDBSample and specify that an EJB and Web project also be created for this EAR. Name the EJB module MDBSampleEJB and name the Web module MDBSampleWeb. Since we will be using a servlet for our JMS message sender, we do not need an application client project. Press the *Finish* button to create the three projects. The Navigator view in the J2EE perspective should now resemble Figure 27.4.

Notice that the MDBSample enterprise application contains two modules—MDBSampleEJB.jar and MDBSampleWeb.jar.

Figure 27.4 Navigation view in J2EE perspective.

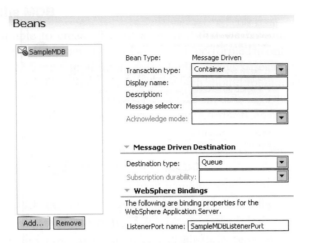

Figure 27.8 Bean details.

The next task is to write the code for the onMessage(Message aMsg) method. Double-click the SampleMDB to open the java editor on our MDB bean class. Replace the contents with the code in Listing 27.1.

Listing 27.1 The onMessage(MessageaMsg) method

```
package com.wsbook.mdbsample;

import javax.jms.TextMessage;

public class SampleMDBBean

    implements javax.ejb.MessageDrivenBean,javax.jms.MessageListener{

    private javax.ejb.MessageDrivenContext fMessageDrivenCtx;

    public javax.ejb.MessageDrivenContext getMessageDrivenContext() {

        return fMessageDrivenCtx;

    }

    public void setMessageDrivenContext(javax.ejb.MessageDrivenContext

      ctx) {

        fMessageDrivenCtx = ctx;

    }
```

```
public void ejbCreate() {

}

public void onMessage(javax.jms.Message msg) {

        try {

                System.out.println("Handling MDB onMessage() now.");

                System.out.println("Message Object is: " + msg);

                System.out.println("Text message is: " +

                        ((TextMessage) msg).getText());

        } catch (Exception e) {

                System.out.println("Exception occurred: " + e);

                e.printStackTrace();

        }

}

public void ejbRemove() {

}

}
```

The onMessage(Message msg) method is the only one of consequence in this class. In order to get the contents of the actual message, we need to cast the Message to a specific kind of Message called a TextMessage and then we can call getText() to obtain the String contents of the message. The TextMessage messages are just one of several different types of messages that can be sent. As we said earlier, there is no coupling between the producer and the consumer. However, we must now say that the message type does have to be in agreement in order for the consumer (the MDB) to be able to understand the message. Having said that, it is possible to use the java instanceof operator to determine which type of message has been sent and to then act accordingly. While this is possible, it is usually unnecessary. Most consumers and producers agree on the message type to be sent and code as such. This is very loose coupling.

27.3.1.3 Create a Test Servlet

For simplicity, we have decided to create a servlet as our message producer. In this servlet, we will find the queue connection factory from JNDI, find the queue from JNDI, create a message, and send it. The code, shown in Listing 27.2, needs to be placed in the JavaSource folder of the MDBSampleWeb project.

Listing 27.2 A test servlet as a message producer

```java
package com.wsbook.mdbsample.servlet;

import java.io.IOException;

import javax.jms.*;

import javax.naming.*;

import javax.servlet.*;

import javax.servlet.http.*;

public class MDBSampleServlet extends HttpServlet {

    public static final String CONN_FACTORY_NAME =

        "java:comp/env/Sample/jms/SampleQCF";

    public static String QUEUE_NAME =

        "java:comp/env/Sample/jms/SampleQ";


    public void doGet(HttpServletRequest req, HttpServletResponse resp)

        throws ServletException, IOException {

        try {

            ServletOutputStream out = resp.getOutputStream();

            out.println("<HTML><BODY>");

            out.println("<P>Getting Initial Context</P>");

            InitialContext context = new InitialContext();

            out.println("<P>Getting Connection Factory</P>");
```

```
QueueConnectionFactory qConnectionFactory =

    (QueueConnectionFactory)context.lookup(

        CONN_FACTORY_NAME);

out.println(qConnectionFactory.toString());

out.println("<P>Getting Queue</P>");

Queue queue = (Queue)context.lookup(QUEUE_NAME);

out.println("<P>Creating connection");

QueueConnection qConnection =

        qConnectionFactory.createQueueConnection();

out.println("<P>Creating Session</P>");

QueueSession qSession =

        qConnection.createQueueSession(false,

                Session.AUTO_ACKNOWLEDGE);

out.println("<P>Creating Sender</P>");

QueueSender sender = qSession.createSender(queue);

out.println("<P>Creating Text</P>");

TextMessage message = qSession.createTextMessage();

out.println("<P>Appending command Line</P>");

String messageToSend = req.getParameter("message");

if(messageToSend == null) {

        messageToSend = "Default Message";

}

out.println("<P>Setting Text</P>");
```

```
            message.setText(messageToSend);

            out.println("<P>Sending message</P>");

            sender.send(message);

            out.println("<P>Closing sender</P>");

            sender.close();

            out.println("<P>Closing session</P>");

            qSession.close();

            out.println("<P>Closing connection</P>");

            qConnection.close();

            out.println("<P>Connection closed</P>");

            out.println("</HTML></BODY>");

        }

    catch (NamingException ne) {

            ne.printStackTrace(out);

        }

    catch(JMSException e) {

            e.printStackTrace(out);

            Exception linked = e.getLinkedException();

            linked.printStackTrace(out);

        }

    }

}
```

The servlet is very straightforward. It honors one HTTP request parameter named `message` which will be placed into the message that is sent to the destination. Notice that Queue-ConnectionFactory and Queue are both obtained from JNDI.

27.3.1.4 Configure the JNDI names

In order for the servlet to be able to find QueueConnectionFactory and Queue from JNDI, we must add resource references to the deployment descriptor of the Web module. To do this, open the deployment descriptor of the Web module by selecting the Web module, MDBSampleWeb, right-click, and select *Open With > Deployment Descriptor Editor*. Select the References tab as shown in Figure 27.9.

Select the *Add* button to add a new reference to the list. Change the name to Sample/jms/SampleQCF for the QueueConnectionFactory. The type should be javax.jms.QueueConnection-Factory, the authentication should be set to Application, and the JNDI name should be set to jms/SampleQCF as shown in Figure 27.10.

Select the *Add* button again and add a reference named Sample/jms/SampleQ for the Queue. The type should be javax.jms.Queue, the Authentication should be set to Application, and the JNDI name should be set to jms/SampleQ as shown in Figure 27.11.

Notice that the servlet uses the JNDI references that we just set up in its final static variables:

```
public static final String CONN_FACTORY_NAME =

        "java:comp/env/Sample/jms/SampleQCF";

public static String QUEUE_NAME =

        "java:comp/env/Sample/jms/SampleQ";
```

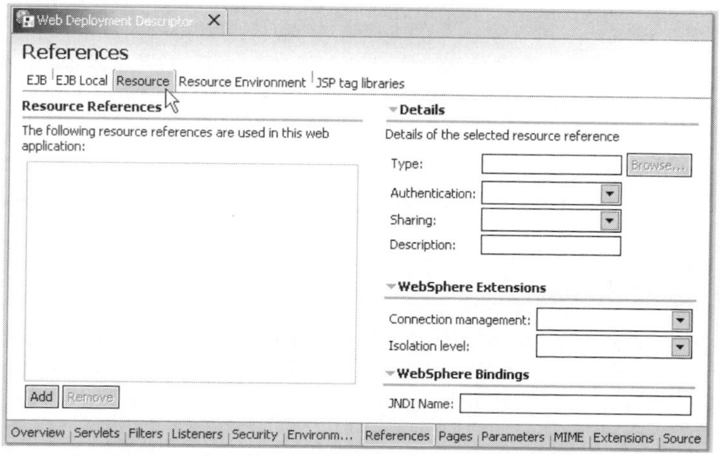

Figure 27.9 Select References, then Resources.

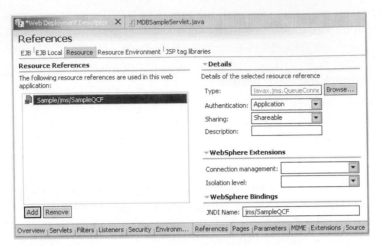

Figure 27.10 JNDI reference for QueueConnectionFactory.

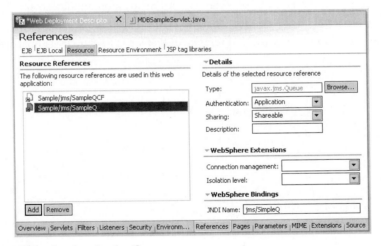

Figure 27.11 JNDI reference for the Queue.

Using references like this allows the name used in the java code to be different from the JNDI name defined for the Queue and QueueConnectionFactory which decouples the Java code from the JNDI name.

27.3.1.5 Set Up the Server

Before we can test and debug our MDB sample, we need to set up a WebSphere 5.0 test server with QueueConnectionFactory and Queue. From the J2EE perspective, select the Servers project from the tree and then use the right-click menu to select *New > Server and Server Configuration*. In the dialog that displays (Figure 27.12), name the server SampleServer and specify that this is the WebSphere version 5.0, Test Environment. Select the *Finish* button to create the server.

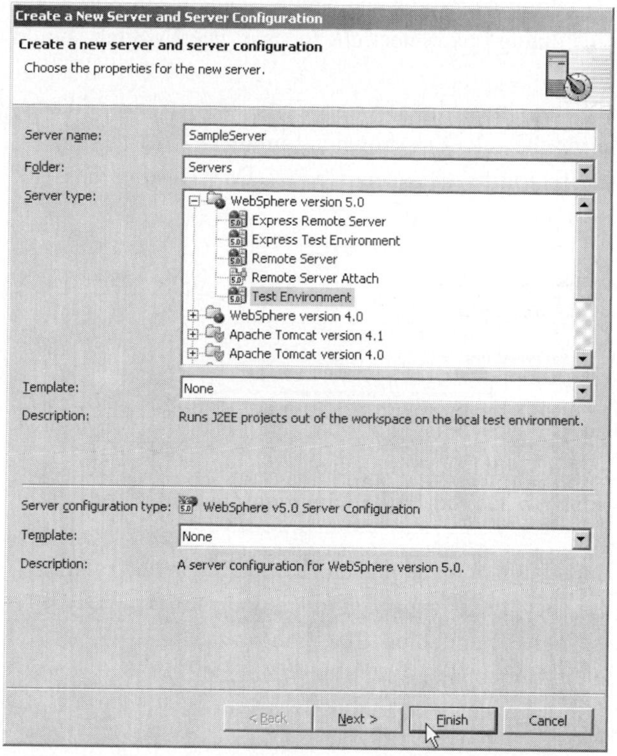

Figure 27.12 Server configurations.

Now, select the SampleServer from the J2EE perspective and double-click so that the WebSphere server editor displays. Select the JMS tab as shown in Figure 27.13 so that we can set up the Queue and QueueConnectionFactory. Notice that there are no queues named and that the initial state is STOP.

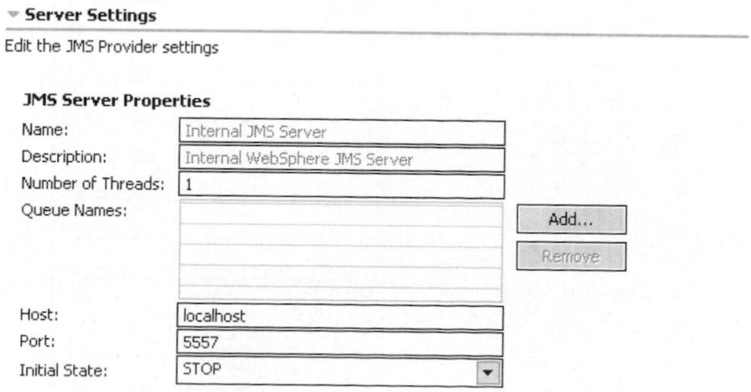

Figure 27.13 Server configuration JMS tab.

Select the *Add* button next to Queue Names: under JMS Server Properties, and enter the name SampleQ in the dialog box. Select *OK* to save. The JMS tab should now resemble Figure 27.14.

Click the *Add* button under JMS Connection Factories, and add a new WASQueueConnectionFactory by entering the values as shown in Figure 27.15.

Select the *Add* button by the queues under JMS Destinations, and create a WASQueue with the values shown in Figure 27.16.

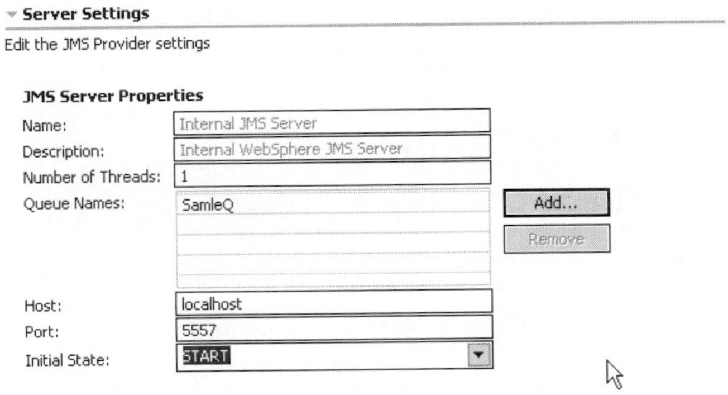

Figure 27.14 Server configuration—initially start with SampleQ.

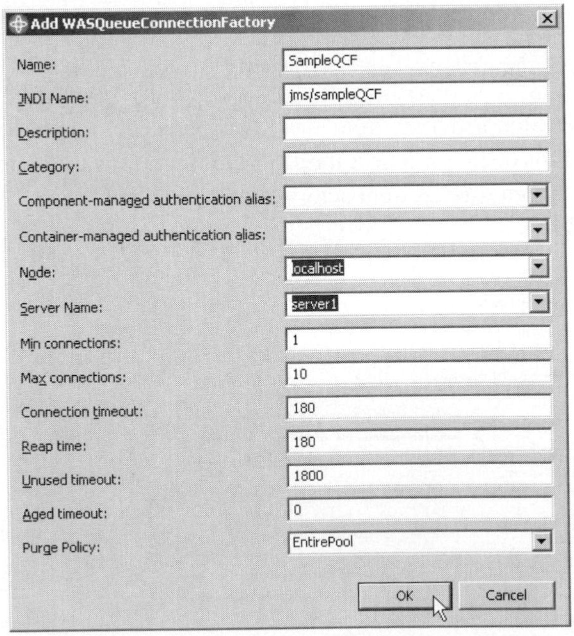

Figure 27.15 Create QueueConnectionFactory.

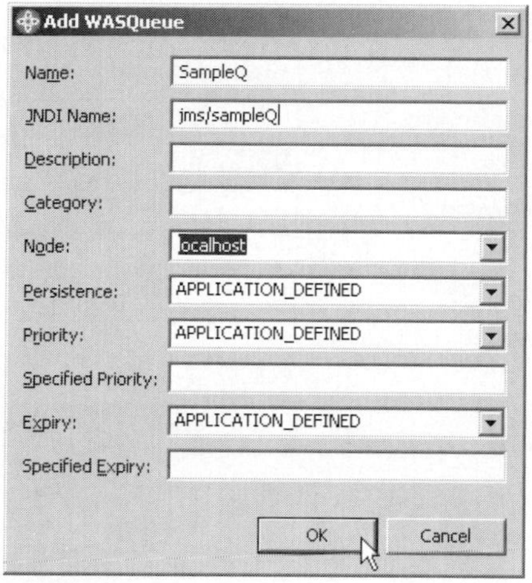

Figure 27.16 JMS configuration.

The JMS tab should now resemble Figure 27.17.

Now we need to add ListenerPort to the server configuration. It should have a JNDI name that matches the one set for the MDB in the EJB deployment descriptor editor. Select the EJB tab, then the *Add* button to enter the information as shown in Figure 27.18.

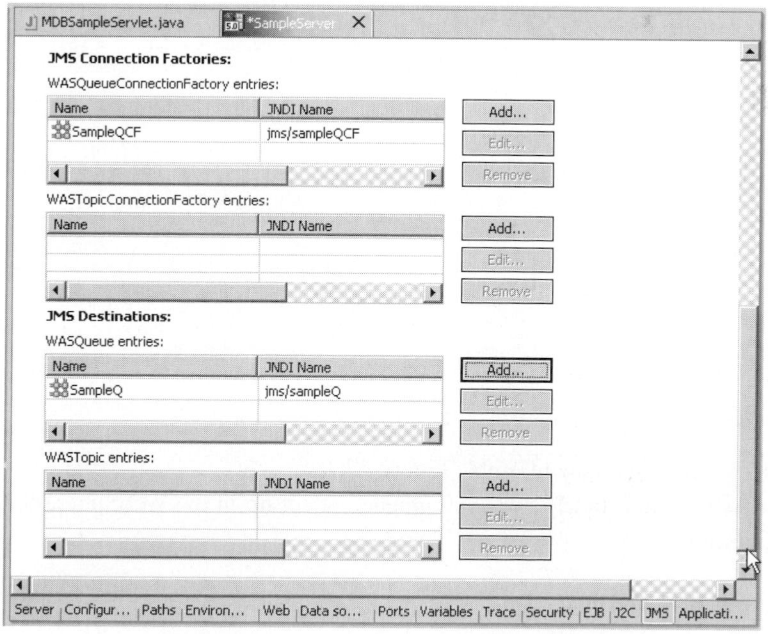

Figure 27.17 Adding a listener port.

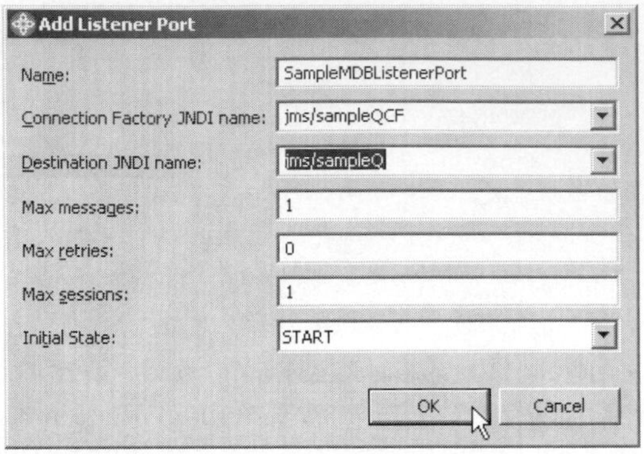

Figure 27.18 Listener port.

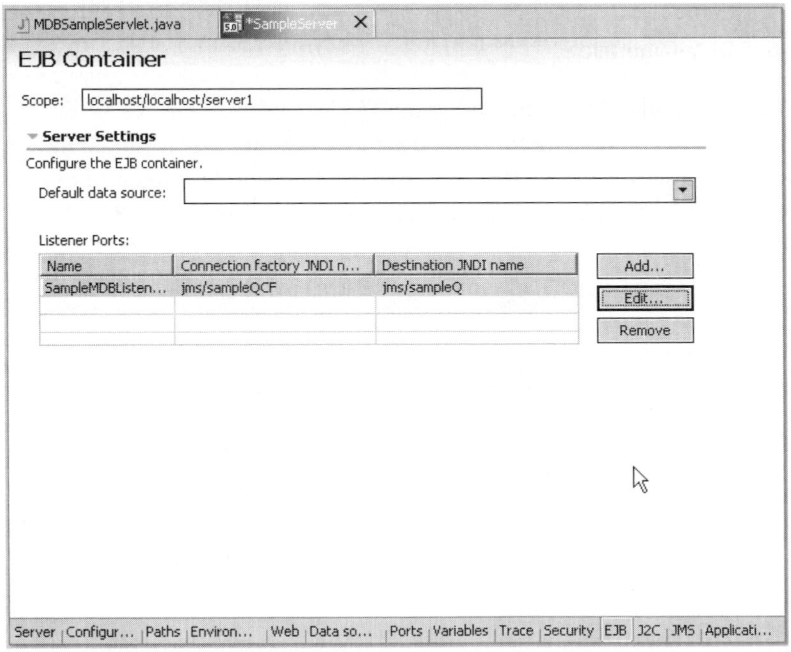

Figure 27.19 Listener port.

The EJB tab should now resemble Figure 27.19.

Now QueueConnectionFactory and Queue are set up in the WebSphere 5.0 TE. Save the server configuration.

27.3.1.6 Test and Debug

To test the MDBSample, simply start SampleServer. Once it has started, open a Web browser and enter *http://localhost:9080/MDBSampleWeb/MDBSampleServlet*. The browser will show the log messages that the servlet is generating and the console will show the log messages from the MDB, proving that the MDB is getting the message.

27.4 Summary

In this chapter we have covered the basics concepts of JMS and MDBs. Asynchronous messaging can add a new dimension to your enterprise solutions. We will examine more about asynchronous messaging in Chapter 28, when we'll see how transactions apply to JMS and EJBs.

Transactions in WebSphere 5.0

Transactions are one of those things that most Java programmers would rather ignore than try to understand. And, in fact, in most cases you can ignore them—the default settings of WAS and WSAD work well enough in most situations that many programmers can build large and complex applications without having to know the details about how transactions work. Unfortunately, at some point all of this blissful ignorance must end. Then you have to hunker down and learn how transactions operate in order to solve problems that have ramifications all the way up and down your architecture. We show all of the architectural layers that EJB transactions touch in Figure 28.1

In this chapter, we'll examine how transactions operate in WAS. We'll begin by looking at a type of transaction that most Java programmers are familiar with, those available through JDBC. After that review, we'll examine how EJB transactions are defined in the EJB specification, and how the specification is implemented in WAS and WSAD. Finally, we'll examine some of the more complex transactional issues that occur in real-world applications, and examine some of the WebSphere-specific mechanisms for handling concurrency and other gray areas of the EJB specification.

28.1 JDBC Transactions

In JDBC each `javax.sql.Connection` object has two ways of starting and ending a transaction. In the default mode (called autocommit), each individual JDBC statement is executed in its own transaction. So, if you created two separate `INSERT` statements, one for an employee and one for the employee's address within a method, it would be possible to create an address that refers to an employee that does not exist if the `INSERT` for the address succeeds while the `INSERT` for the employee fails.

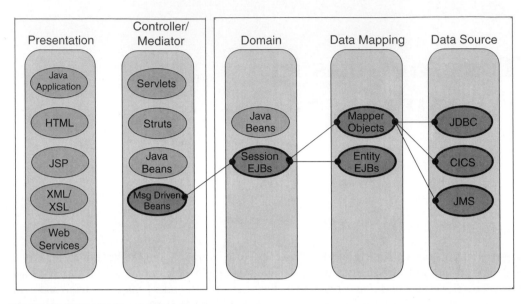

Figure 28.1 Architectural road map.

To get around this there is a second mode in JDBC whereby the transaction associated with a connection can encompass the execution of several `javax.sql.Statement` objects created from the connection. Therefore, you can have code like that in Listing 28.1.

Listing 28.1 Manually controlled JDBC transaction

```
// Begin the transaction by setting autocommit to false

connection.setAutocommit(false);

// First insert the new Employee's address

PreparedStatement insert = connection.createPreparedStatement("INSERT INTO

ADDRESS (id, street, city, state, zip) VALUES (? ? ? ? ?)");

insert.setString(1, "22333");

insert.setString(2, "101 Hummingbird Ln");

insert.setString(3, "Cary");

insert.setString(4, "NC");
```

```
insert.setString(5, "27502");

insert.executeUpdate();

// Now insert his information, including a foreign-key reference to

// the address inserted in the previous block

insert = connection.createPreparedStatement("INSERT INTO Employee (id, name,

salary, address) VALUES (? ? ?)");

insert.setString(1, "12345");

insert.setString(2, "Karl Johnson");

insert.setInteger(3, 23450);

insert.setString(4, "22333");

insert.executeUpdate();

// finally, commit the transaction

connection.commit();
```

As you see, it's possible to join multiple SQL statements in a single transaction using the features of the `javax.sql.Connection`, but there are problems with using this feature.

The first is that you must pass the physical connection object between all of the mappers (DAOs) that will operate on it. This can be tricky, and tends to mean that you have to expose the details of the persistence layer to the layers above it. Overall, it's not pretty.

Another issue is how concurrent transactions affect each other. If you run two transactions at the same time, how do you keep data updated in one transaction from being read in the other before it completes? JDBC solves this problem (as does the ANSI SQL-92 standard) using what are called isolation levels. You can set the isolation level of a JDBC connection by using the `setTransactionIsolation()` method. The isolation levels defined by the JDBC specification (as static fields in `java.sql.Connection`) are as follows:

- TRANSACTION_NONE—Transactions are not supported.
- TRANSACTION_READ_UNCOMMITTED—The transaction can read uncommitted data (data changed by a different transaction still in progress).
- TRANSACTION_READ_COMMITTED—The transaction is not able to read uncommitted data from other transactions. However, nonrepeatable reads (e.g., the first read within a transaction gets one result, while the second gets a different result due to

the data being updated by another transaction or program) can occur. Likewise, phantom records can occur—records can be inserted while the transaction (of which this transaction may be unaware) is in progress.

• TRANSACTION_REPEATABLE_READ—The transaction is guaranteed to always read back the same data on each successive read. Phantom records can still occur.

• TRANSACTION_SERIALIZABLE—All transactions are serialized (e.g., fully isolated from one another). All rows touched during the transaction are locked for the duration of the transaction.

So, why is this an issue? Why not just use `TRANSACTION_SERIALIZABLE` and always assume you are safe from phantom records and nonrepeatable reads? The answer lies in the performance of your transactions. In order to keep transactions fully isolated, even reads have to wait in line at the highest isolation level. We'll return to the subject of isolation levels and associated locking later in the chapter.

Finally, there's a yet more troublesome problem that JDBC transactions do not address. There is no easy way to join resources that are not part of JDBC together with JDBC statements within a single transaction. For instance, a common problem in many applications is the following: You have an application that takes orders for widgets over the Internet. The widget order-processing application is a legacy system that is accessed over WebSphere MQ—it's based on a batch system and it takes in orders from a queue and (eventually) process them so that widgets will be delivered to the customer.

This model doesn't fit well with the expectations of an Internet order-entry application. In that case, users will expect to check the status of their order at any time. However, that may not lend itself to a model where an order may sit in a queue for a long time while in between processing steps. It would be cumbersome to have to check several queues to determine where in the order-processing sequence the order resides.

What is often done is to have two different representations of the order—when the order is first received, a record is created in a relational database to represent the order, and the order information is then placed in the first queue for the order-processing system to be processed. As the orders move from one state to another, the information in the database is updated accordingly.

So, we have the following problem in our order entry application: We'd like to create the database record for the order and place it in the queue for processing at the same time and in the same transaction. It's not acceptable if the database record creation fails and the order processing enqueuing succeeds. That would result in a user having widgets delivered (and billed!) to him, but he would not be able to find out any information about the orders in the meantime.

What we need is to join the two resources—the WebSphere MQ Queue and the JDBC Connection that the statement executes on—in the same transaction. That is the domain of the two-phase commit (2-PC) transaction model, as you'll see in the next section.

28.2 Transactions and 2-Phase Commit

A key implementation feature of database systems and transaction processing systems like Web-Sphere is 2-PC. This feature allows multiple resources to be updated in a single transaction or to be returned to their pretransaction state if an error occurs. To understand how 2-PC works, we need to provide a few more definitions:

- Transactional object—An object whose behavior is affected by being invoked within the scope of a transaction. Transactional objects update resource managers through changing attributes managed by the resource managers.
- Resource manager—Manages the transaction for a single data source. An example of a resource manager in our case is a single relational database, or database driver.
- Transaction manager—Takes care of managing the details of transactions behind the scenes, determining when to instruct individual resource managers to commit a transaction to permanent storage, or to roll back to the previous state. WAS acts as a transaction Manager.

Some of the interactions between these object types are illustrated in Figure 28.2.

These objects are tied together through the 2-PC protocol. It involves two sets of messages from the transaction manager to the resource managers. Each resource manager initially and temporarily stores resource changes. The transaction manager then issues a prepare or "are you ready" message to each of the resource managers. If each resource manager responds with an acknowledgement saying that it can commit, the transaction manager sends the final commit message to the resource managers.

The Java API for managing 2-PC transactions is called JTA (the Java Transactions API). Understanding JTA is the subject of the next section.

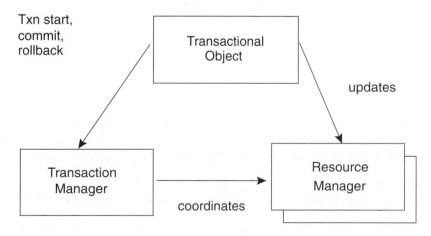

Figure 28.2 Transaction interactions.

28.3   JTA and Transaction Demarcation

JTA is a high-level API that provides for transactional management. Most of JTA is for internal use by transaction managers. However, a few APIs are intended for use by applications. These allow you to start, commit, and roll back transactions in an underlying Java transaction manager. The major benefit of JTA is that it controls a transaction manager that can span multiple data sources, so if you access both a JDBC DataSource and update a JMS Queue within a single JTA transaction they will both be either committed or rolled back together.

To understand how this works, look at the following methods defined in the interface javax.jts.UserTransaction:[1]

- begin()—Creates a transaction and associates it with the current thread.
- commit()—Completes the transaction associated with the current thread. When this method completes, the thread is no longer associated with a transaction.
- rollback()—Rolls back the transaction associated with the current thread. When this method completes, the thread is no longer associated with a transaction.
- setRollbackOnly()—Modifies the transaction associated with the current thread such that the only possible outcome is to roll back the transaction.

How does a client (meaning a servlet or JSP, or code inside an EJB declared to use bean-managed transactions [BMTs]) obtain an object that implements this interface? Clients should be able to obtain this by looking it up through JNDI.[2] The following code fragment illustrates this:

```
UserTransaction tranContext = (UserTransaction)

    initContext.lookup("java:comp/UserTransaction");

tranContext.begin();

// get and manipulate data sources or EJB's

tranContext.commit();
```

Where and how would you use JTA in this way? One of the little-known features of the WebSphere Web container is that it allows the use of JTA inside methods executing within the context of the Web container. This is important in that it allows you to gain some of the benefits of 2-PC transactions without having to use the EJB container. So, if you need to perform one of

---

1.   For a more complete listing of the messages in this interface, refer to the JTS specification [JTS]

2.   Session EJBs using BMTs should instead obtain the current transaction by using EJBContext.getCurrentTransaction(). Also, previous versions of WebSphere used a different name (jta/usertransaction) to look up the user transaction. WAS 5.0 requires java:comp/UserTransaction to be in compliance with the EJB 2.0 specification.

the more common tasks for which JTA is applicable (like placing a message to a JMS Queue and updating a database in the same transaction) you can do it entirely within the context of the Web container without even having to involve the EJB container. You simply need to enclose the appropriate JMS and JDBC code between the `begin()` and `commit()` statements and the 2-PC transaction will take place. (You should also provide for rolling back the transaction in case an error occurs between the two statements).

This same kind of transactional control is also available within the EJB container as BMT. In BMT, you can place the kind of code shown in the example within a session bean method that has been appropriately configured to use BMT.

As you can see, there are several advantages in using JTA over using the facilities of the JDBC connection for your transactions. In particular, moving the control external from the connection makes commitment independent of each particular connection. This makes it much easier to implement the mapper pattern. Each mapper can use the get Connection...use Connection...release Connection idiom; you are not required to pass the connection between mappers, making the control flow of your system simpler.

JTA isn't perfect. In fact, compared to the type of control we'll see next with container-managed transactions (CMTs) in EJBs, JTA is a blunt instrument:

- If you are using JTA there is no individual control over data sources and other resources. If you obtain a connection from a data source within a transaction, that connection will be enlisted within the transaction. You can't make it not enlisted or force it to commit otherwise.
- You can't suspend a JTA transaction; once the transaction is started it must be either committed or rolled back. If you try to start another JTA transaction on the same thread as an existing one, it will cause an error.

28.4   Enabling 2-PC in WebSphere 5.0

Now that you've seen how the 2-PC protocol works, and how the JTA API is structured, you may be asking yourself "How do I make this work within WAS?" To understand the answer to that question, we have to go back and look at some of the definitions of the actors in the 2-PC protocol. Do you remember how WAS acts as the transaction manager? The resource managers that it coordinates are implemented in J2EE by three different types of objects:

- JDBC Database Drivers may act as resource managers with either one-phase commit or 2-PC semantics. In order to support 2-PC transactions, a JDBC driver vendor must provide a database driver that provides implementations of the `javax.sql.XADataSource` and `javax.sql.XAConnection` interfaces.
- A JMS vendor may provide a JMS provider that implements the `javax.jms.XAConnectionFactory`, `javax.jms.XAConnection`, and `javax.jms.XASession` interfaces.

• A provider of a J2EE Connector Architecture (J2C) resource adapter may choose to implement the XAResource interface.

So, whether your resource (database driver, JMS provider, or J2C resource adapter) will participate in a 2-PC transaction depends entirely upon what your vendor provides, and the particular driver software you are using. Most vendors provide both an XA-compliant[3] and a non-XA compliant version of their driver or provider. If you see the need to use a 2-PC transaction, you must make sure that all of the resource managers involved in the transaction are XA compliant. If they are not (e.g., you enlist resources from one XA-compliant resource manager and another one that is not within the same transaction) the WebSphere transaction manager will throw a `java.lang.IllegalStateException` and you will find error messages like the following in the log:

```
[1/10/03 14:07:59:510 EST] 52d374a0 TransactionIm E WTRN0064E: An illegal

attempt to enlist a two phase capable resource with an existing one phase

capable resource has occurred.


[1/10/03 14:08:00:041 EST] 52d374a0 XATransaction E J2CA0030E: Method enlist

caught java.lang.IllegalStateException
```

After these exceptions are thrown your transaction will roll back. This doesn't mean that you always have to use an XA-compliant database driver or other resource manager in all instances. If a particular transaction only goes against a single resource manager, a standard resource manager will work fine, and, in fact, may be faster than using a corresponding XA resource manager. In fact, you should only use XA if you need it. The initial WebSphere 5.0 performance report [Willenborg] contains a study of the performance difference between XA and non-XA performance of basic operations on a database. The differences are relatively small; resource access is between 18-27 percent slower using an XA resource manager than a non-XA one. Note that this is for basic operations; in a real application the cost would be less since the database operations comprise a smaller percentage of the total. This difference is enough to be concerned about in performance-critical situations, but not large enough to prohibit the use of XA when it is necessary.

---

3.   XA is an X/Open standard specifying a protocol for communication between transaction monitors and resource managers.

28.5 EJBs and Container-Managed Transactions

So how do we get around the limitations of JTA with EJBs? First you need to review the three ways of controlling transactions defined in the EJB specification:

- Client demarcation—The programmer of a client uses the explicit programmatic transaction management of JTA. The methods of the interface `javax.jts.UserTransaction` are used to begin, commit, or roll back the transaction.
- Bean demarcation—A session EJB with the transaction attribute set to `TX_BEAN_MAN-AGED` can explicitly control a transaction through using the methods of `javax.jts.UserTransaction`.
- Container demarcation—The programmer does not write code to define when the transaction begins, commits, or rolls back. The EJB container instead defines this. The behavior of this object in a transaction is based on information in the transaction attribute fields of the deployment descriptor.

By far, the preferred way of managing a transaction (e.g., determining when it starts, and how it terminates) is through container demarcation. This is called declarative transaction management, since declarations in the deployment descriptor tell the container when to start and commit the transaction. To understand how this works, we should examine what values the transaction attribute can take on. Transaction attributes can be set on either the bean or the method level. (If it is set at the method level it overrides the setting, if any, on the bean level.) The values of this attribute are:

- Mandatory—The client of this EJB must create a transaction (either programmatically or declaratively through container demarcation) before invocation of a method. If a transaction context is not present, a `javax.transaction.TransactionRequired-Exception` is thrown if the client is a remote client, or a `javax.trans-action.TransactionRequiredLocalException` is thrown if the client is a local client. The execution of the EJB method will be associated with the client transaction (i.e., this object will participate in the transaction context associated with the calling thread).
- NotSupported—Transactions are not supported by this EJB or method. If a client provides a transaction, it is suspended. All methods marked with this value will execute within an unspecified transaction context. However, if an externally created transaction is so suspended, the transaction will be resumed and propagated to other objects called in this thread after the completion of the marked method(s).
- Required—The EJB requires that methods be executed within a transaction. If a client transaction is provided, it is used, and the execution of the method is associated with it. If no transaction context exists, a transaction context is created for this thread at the start of the method, and it commits when the method has completed. If other methods are called

within this method, the transaction context is passed along with the method invocation. This is the default transaction setting if one is not explicitly defined for the bean.

- RequiresNew—The EJB requires that a method be executed in a new transaction. If a client transaction is provided it is suspended for the method execution.[4] A new transaction is always created at the start of the method, and it commits when the method has completed.
- Supports—The EJB supports execution of the method in a transaction but does not require it. If this thread is associated with a transaction context the method execution will be associated with that transaction. If this thread is not associated with a transaction context, then the method executes in an unspecified transaction context.

To understand how transactions are propagated or passed by beans with different settings of this attribute, examine Table 28.1 derived from [Sun].

- Never—A mixture of NotSupported and Mandatory. If a client provides a transaction context, then the method will throw a `java.rmi.RemoteException` if the client is a remote client, or a `javax.ejb.EJBException` if the client is a local client. On the other hand, if the client does not provide a transaction context, the method acts the same as in the NotSupported case.

Table 28.1 Transaction attribute settings.

Transaction Attribute	Client Transaction	Transaction Associated with Bean Method
NotSupported	None	None
	T!	None
Required	None	T2
	T!	T1
Supports	None	None
	T!	T1
RequiresNew	None	T2
	T!	T2
Mandatory	None	ERROR
	T!	T1
Never	None	None
	T!	ERROR

---

4.   The EJB Specification [Sun] only describes support for flat transactions and does not include support for nested transactions. Only one transaction may execute within an object at a time.

Note that in Table 28.1 on the Required line, a transaction, T2, is created because the client does not have an existing transaction and the transaction attribute is Required. Also, note that in Mandatory, an error is produced because the client does not have an existing transaction when calling the method. Careful use of the transaction attributes can help to enforce application defined transactional integrity within a set of EJBs.

28.6   Participating in a Transaction

Now that you've seen how transactions are started and rolled back, what do you have to do to your EJB code to make this work? That depends on the type of EJB you are writing. For session EJBs the answer is usually nothing. Session EJBs are functional objects whose job it is to direct the action of entity EJBs or other data sources (like JDBC). In most cases, a session EJB will simply originate or propagate a transaction through declarative transaction management as described earlier.[5] You are not responsible for writing any code to support this behavior; it just happens because the transaction is propagated by the container by associating it along with the thread of control.

Likewise, for container-managed entity beans, you do not have to explicitly write anything to participate in a transaction. In this case, the generated persistence code handles persisting changed data to a database when a transaction commits. In BMP entity beans, (discussed in Chapter 26), you have to write code within the hook methods `ejbLoad()` and `ejbStore()` to load data from a database or store updated data to a database respectively in response to a transaction commit or rollback.[6]

But how does this work and where would you apply these settings? Let's says that you are developing an application to record stock trades. Brokers should be only able to record stock trades for customers that they are directly responsible for, so that a broker can't make any unauthorized trades for another broker's customers. Therefore, you can imagine a StockSales session bean that records the sale by writing to a database, and also checks to see that the broker entering the sale is the one responsible for this customer. If there is a mismatch, the transaction is rolled back (by using `SessionContext.setRollbackOnly()`.

Let's also say that if an unauthorized sale attempt occurs, a record needs to be written to an audit log table indicating when (and by whom) the attempt took place. However, here you're in a catch-22; if the transaction rolls back, the audit log will not be written. This is where the transaction settings can come to your rescue. If you wrap the audit log function in an AuditLog session bean, you can set the transaction setting of the AuditLog bean's `recordLogInforma-tion()` method to be RequiresNew, so that it always runs in a new transaction, regardless of

5.   An exception to this would be through the use of the SessionSynchronization interface for stateful session beans as described later.

6.   These methods are also defined in CMP beans, but you usually do not do anything in them. (The method implementations contain no code.)

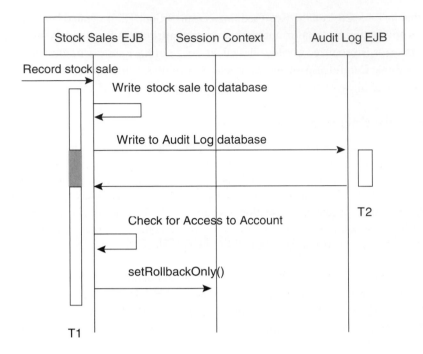

Figure 28.3 Stock sales example.

whether or not there was an existing transaction in the calling method's scope. Figure 28.3 illustrates the methods involved and the transaction scopes applied.

In this diagram, the stock sales EJB begins a new CMT (shown as T1) when the `record-StockSale()` message is received. It performs a database write within the context of that transaction. However, that transaction is paused (shown by the shaded area) when `recordLog-Information()` is called on the AuditLog EJB, which has its transaction attribute set to RequiresNew.

This creates a second transaction (T2) which will commit at the end of the `recordLog-Information()` method, ensuring that the log will be written to the database. When that method finishes, the original transaction is resumed, and, at some point, the business logic determines that this broker cannot actually perform this trade, and rolls back the transaction—preventing the sale from being recorded, but not preventing the audit log from being updated.

28.7 Using XA Resources with 2-PC in WebSphere

Now that you've seen where you might want to use transaction attributes, in what circumstances would you want to use 2-PC? There are many reasons to use 2-PC, ranging from needing to update two separate databases (requiring two different data source definitions, since a data source is uniquely bound to a single database), to needing to make a request of an EJB running

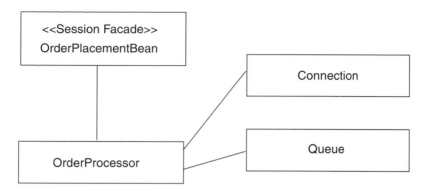

Figure 28.4 Order placement bean design.

in another EJB server (since there would be no way to manage this as a local transaction if it's running in another server).

However, one particular pattern occurs so often that it nearly defines the need for 2-PC: Many applications need to be able to write to both a database and place a message on a JMS queue within the same transaction.

An exceptionally common situation for this is when you need to update a local cache of information and notify another application of the update. For instance, let's say that you are building an application that takes product orders from the Internet. There is an existing mainframe application that can process the incoming orders. The application is naturally asynchronous. Since it was developed as a batch application, it does not process newly submitted orders immediately, but works continuously through the queue of submitted orders from the Web and from those received from other routes (such as retail store point of sale [POS] systems).

So how do you make this work in a Web environment, where fast response is everything, and where impatient shoppers will demand to know the status of their orders at any hour of the day? The answer is to combine writing to a local order cache (which can be later queried from a servlet to show our erstwhile shopper how the order is doing) with placing a request for processing on a queue shared with the mainframe application. A simple design for this is shown in Figure 28.4.

This is a standard design (explained in more detail in Chapter 30) that uses a stateless session bean (OrderPlacementBean) as a Session Façade onto a business object (OrderProcessor). The code to accomplish this can begin quite simply. First, let's examine the method in the Order-Processor that executes the database insert and the enqueuing of the message.

```
public void processOrder(Order anOrder) throws OrderException {

        storeOrderInOrderDatabase(anOrder);

        String xmlString = buildXML(anOrder);
```

```
                    writeOrderToOutputQueue(xmlString);

    }
```

Here we see the sequencing of the instructions. Next, look inside the storeOrderInOrderDatabase() message (Listing 28.2) to see how the insert into the database table is done.

Listing 28.2 Inserting into a database table

```
    void storeOrderInOrderDatabase(Order anOrder) throws OrderException

{

            Connection con = null;

            PreparedStatement stmt = null;

            try {

                    InitialContext ctx = new InitialContext();

                    DataSource ds =

                            (DataSource) ctx.lookup(

                            "java:comp/env/jdbc/Db2XADataSource");

                    con = ds.getConnection();

                    stmt = con.prepareStatement(insertStatement);

                    stmt.setString(1, anOrder.orderNumber);

                    stmt.setString(2, anOrder.customerNumber);

                    stmt.setDate(3, anOrder.placementDate);

                    stmt.setString(4, anOrder.status);

                    boolean updated = stmt.execute();
```

```
        } catch (Exception e) {

            System.out.println("Exception caught in

StoreOrderinDatabase");

            throw new OrderException(e.toString());

        } finally {

        try {

            if (stmt != null)

                stmt.close();

            if (con != null)

                con.close();

        } catch (Exception e2) {

            System.out.println("Exception in closing JDBC

resources");

            // log and ignore the exception

        }

        }


    }
```

There's no rocket science going on here. This is plain-vanilla JDBC code that simply obtains a connection, creates a prepared statement, executes the statement, and closes the connection. The only interesting thing is that if a problem is encountered that an OrderException (an application defined exception) is thrown, with the information on the originating exception enclosed within it. This idiom is called converting exceptions or wrapping exceptions—we'll look more deeply into this later. But first, we need to examine the message that puts the order creation message on the JMS queue (Listing 28.3):

Listing 28.3 The order creation message

```java
void writeOrderToOutputQueue(String text) throws OrderException

{

        QueueConnection connection = null;

        QueueSession session = null;


        try {

            InitialContext ctx = new InitialContext();


            QueueConnectionFactory qcf =

                (QueueConnectionFactory) ctx.lookup(

                    "java:comp/env/jms/

QueueConnectionFactory");

            Queue queue = (Queue) ctx.lookup(

                "java:comp/env/jms/OutputQueue");


            connection = qcf.createQueueConnection();

            session =

                connection.createQueueSession(true,

                    Session.AUTO_ACKNOWLEDGE);


            QueueSender sender = session.createSender(queue);
```

```
                         TextMessage message =

                             session.createTextMessage(text);

                         sender.send(message);



            } catch (Exception e) {

                  System.out.println("exception in put to queue " +

                      e);

                  throw new OrderException(e.toString());

            } finally {

                  try {

                        if (session != null)

                              session.close();

                        if (connection != null)

                              connection.close();

                  } catch (Exception e2) {

                        System.out.println("Exception in closing JMS

resources");

                        // log it and eat it

                  }

            }

      }
```

As you see, this method simply obtains a JMS connection from a QueueConnectionFactory, creates a session and a sender, sends the message, and then closes everything. Likewise, if it encounters any problems, it wraps the exception text in an OrderException and throws that.

The interesting bit comes in when we consider how the stateless session bean that wraps this code invokes this, and what kind of flexibility this design gives us. So, to understand that, look at the processOrder method in the OrderPlacementBean:

```
public void processOrder(Order anOrder) throws OrderException {

    try {

        OrderProcessor processor = new OrderProcessor();

        processor.processOrder(anOrder);

    } catch (OrderException e) {

        mySessionCtx.setRollbackOnly();

        throw e;

    }

}
```

This simple-looking code shows a general-purpose way to handle rolling back transactions when things go wrong. First, let's consider what happens when everything works correctly. In this code, we enter the `try` block, create an OrderProcessor, call the processOrder, and the method completes. That's the beauty of EJB declarative transaction management. There was no additional code needed to create a 2-PCconnection between the JDBC data source used in the `storeOrderInOrderDatabase()` method and the JMS session used in the `writeOrder-ToOutputQueue()` method. We didn't have to explicitly look the transaction up, tell it to start, or commit as you do when using the JTA API.

This simple example shows an easy way to handle things that go wrong too. In this simple application, we've used the Session Façade pattern from [Alur]. We wrap a session bean around a set of objects that implement the functional behavior of our application—the session bean acts as a façade around the other application objects. In this case, it is the OrderProcessor that does all of the real work in our application, but note that we've left handling the exceptional case out of scope of this object. Since the Session Façade implicitly knows about the transaction, it is the best place to handle the work of rolling back the transaction (using setRollbackOnly). There are many cases when applying this pattern that you will want to handle exceptional cases like this by explicitly rolling back the transaction, and then passing on the application exception to the client code.

Another way to force a transaction rollback explicitly is to throw a `javax.transaction.SystemException`. We have found that this mechanism is usually easier and cleaner than the other approach since it allows you to do cleanup that is not possible when you simply jump all the way out by throwing a SystemException.

We should point out one final thing about this example: The only reason that we can get a 2-PC in this example is because both the SQL DataSource and the JMS QueueConnection manager have been explicitly set up as XA resources. You do not get 2-PC if you don't use an XA connection manager; this opens you up to a particular class of error in the case where you try to mix one-phase commit and 2-PC resources within the same transaction.

What do you do in the case where you do not have an XA capable resource to work with? This situation may occur when using certain databases not directly supported by WebSphere, or when using certain JCA adapters (like the IBM JCA Adapter for CICS) that do not support XA from within WAS on distributed platforms. There are two ways of handling this: You can try to make this work yourself by using the SessionSynchronization interface or you can use the last participant support that is available in WAS EE.

First, you should examine how the SessionSychronization interface works. You can make a stateful session bean aware of transaction synchronization by implementing the interface `javax.ejb.SessionSynchronization`. This interface provides hook methods to a stateful session EJB that allows it to read or write its internal fields to or from external database storage. Likewise the session bean could also force a rollback using `sessionContext.setRollBack-Only()` if necessary. There are three methods in this interface that you should become familiar with. They are:

- afterBegin()—Receipt of this method notifies a session bean instance that a new transaction has started. Subsequent business methods on this instance are within the context of the transaction.
- beforeCompletion(boolean)—This method notifies the session bean instance that a transaction is about to be committed. The value of the boolean tells the instance whether the transaction has been committed or rolled back.
- afterCompletion(boolean)—This method notifies the session bean instance that a transaction commit protocol has completed. The value of the boolean tells the instance whether the transaction has been committed or rolled back.

So, if you needed to use a resource that is not XA compatible, one way to handle it is to perform your actions on the non-XA resource in the `beforeCompletion()` method, after first checking the value of the boolean argument to be assured that the rest of the data in this transaction will been committed.

In the `afterCompletion()` method, you would have to check the boolean value to see if everything else succeeded. If it did, you are finished. If not, you need to undo (or compensate for) the action you performed in `beforeCompletion()`. So, if you inserted a row in `before-Completion()` you would have to delete it in `afterCompletion()`. Likewise, if you updated a row in `beforeCompletion()` you would have to update it a second time with the old values in `afterCompletion()`. This is not guaranteed to work; if something fails in `afterComple-`

tion(), then data may be corrupted. Thus, while this technique may be your only option in some circumstances, it should not be confused with simulating a full 2-PC. Full transactional support requires support from both the application server and all the resources that participate in the transaction. This is why you should try to use XA-compliant resources whenever possible.

In addition, you should note that this would *only* work if WebSphere were not aware of the non-XA resource. If for instance you tried to use a 1-PC database driver from WebSphere together with other 2-PC transaction resources, you would receive an error that would inform you that you couldn't do that. Therefore, you would have to use the standard JDBC mechanism of using a JDBC DriverManager to obtain a database connection, which could potentially lead to a database connection leak if you don't remember to close the connection when you're finished with it.

As you can imagine, this isn't a desirable situation. To get around this limitation, WAS EE supports a special feature (called last participant support) that can correct for this in one special case. Last participant support orders the resource managers within the 2-PC protocol. Thus, a single 1-PC resource manager can be put off and be committed last, only after all of the 2-PCre-source managers have voted yes in the first (prepare) phase of the 2-PC process. If any 2-PC resources veto the transaction during the prepare phase, which occurs prior to this last participant being invoked, the 1-PC resource manager is not invoked, and the transaction rolls back. If the 1-PC resource manager successfully completes, the transaction is allowed to commit. If it fails, the entire transaction rolls back.

28.8 Transaction Settings for J2EE 1.3 in WAS 5.0

How do you set up WebSphere to use the transaction attributes? Since these settings are described in the EJB specification, remember that you will need to edit the EJB deployment descriptor to set them. The EJB Specification [EJB] describes the format of the <container-transaction> tag in detail, but we show the basic format in Listing 28.4. Let's see how you would set up transaction attributes for the order processing example described earlier. In this example, you will need to set the transaction attribute of the processOrder method to be required (since an EJB transaction is required in order for the 2-PC connection between the database insert and the enqueueing of the message to work). Likewise, you will set the transaction attribute of the retrieveOrder method to supports (since the EJB doesn't need to establish a transaction for this, single read, but will still work within one if it is provided). We show the <assembly-descriptor> section that describes this next:

Listing 28.4 The <assembly-descriptor> of the <container-transaction> tag

```
<assembly-descriptor>

    <container-transaction>

        <method>

            <ejb-name>OrderPlacement</ejb-name>
```

```
                    <method-intf>Remote</method-intf>

                    <method-name>processOrder</method-name>

                    <method-params>

                    <method-param>

                 com.ibm.ejb.tests.Order

                     </method-param>

                    </method-params>

            </method>

           <trans-attribute>Required</trans-attribute>

      </container-transaction>

     <container-transaction>

          <method>

                    <ejb-name>OrderPlacement</ejb-name>

                    <method-intf>Remote</method-intf>

                    <method-name>retrieveOrder</method-name>

                    <method-params>

                        <method-param>

                           java.lang.String

                      </method-param>

                    </method-params>

          </method>

           <trans-attribute>Supports</trans-attribute>

      </container-transaction>

 </assembly-descriptor>
```

This is a simple example that doesn't begin to cover all the different variations of setting up transaction attributes on home methods or using wild-card specifications. For more information on doing that, see [Monson-Haefel].

To begin your examination of setting transaction attributes in WSAD, you will need to open an EJB deployment descriptor editor on the deployment descriptor of the QueueAndDatabaseUpdateEJB project. Then, select the Assembly Descriptor tab and look for the Container Transactions section on the right-hand side of the page (Figure 28.5).

If you press the *Add* button in the Container Transactions section, you will see the following wizard page (Figure 28.6) for adding new Container Transaction settings.

Figure 28.5 Add container transactions.

Figure 28.6 Select beans for CMT.

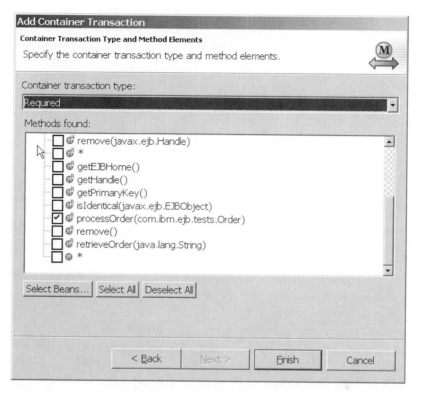

Figure 28.7 Add container transaction.

At this point, we're only interested in setting up transactions for the OrderPlacement EJB. OrderQueueClearingMDB is a simple way to verify that the order was placed on the queue (we'll examine it when we look at running the example). For now, select the OrderPlacement check box and press the *Next* button. That brings up the wizard page shown in Figure 28.7.

Begin by setting the container transaction type to Required in the top drop-down, and then scroll down the method list until you encounter the `processOrder()` method. Select it by checking the check box next to the method name and press *Finish* to create this container-transaction entry.

Repeat the process by again pressing *Add* to create a container-transaction entry, but this time set the container transaction type to Supports and then select the `retrieveOrder()` method before finishing the wizard. Once you are done, you will see two entries in the container-transaction section of the EJB deployment descriptor editor (Figure 28.8).

Figure 28.8 List of container transactions.

28.9 Advice on Using Transactions

The best set of advice about EJB transactions that I've come across is a set of simple rules that Keys Botzum (from the IBM Software Services for WebSphere group) came up with that give you the 90 percent case for dealing with transactions. Keys' rules of thumb are:

Always assume you're going to use container demarcated transactions when using EJBs. It's complicated and difficult to use the JTA API to do your own transaction demarcation, and not worth it in most circumstances.

If you need transactions with a servlet (e.g., outside the EJB container), use the JTA API for demarcating a transaction. The beauty of this rule and the previous one is that by doing this you will not have to write your database code one way (using `setAutoCommit()`) to work within the EJB container and another way to work outside the EJB container. In fact, you should try not to mess with `Connection.setAutoCommit()`—just assume that the container will handle transaction commit/rollback for you.

Assume that the container will handle the appropriate magic of managing local versus global transactions based on the number of participants. Also, assume that it will perform automatic 1-PC optimizations if appropriate. Thus, there is no penalty to global transactions.

Use XA enabled resources in the following situations:

If there may be more than one participant in a transaction (this could be two JDBC databases, or a database and a JMS connection or EIS connection, or any other combination). This allows the container to do any appropriate optimizations if there is only one participant, but to handle XA correctly if there are two or more.

If an EJB needs to access another EJB deployed in a different EJB container, then both containers should use XA resource managers. Sometimes one of your application's EJBs will need to use a utility EJB that provides some service to you. The only way to tie together the two EJBs into a single transaction is to use XA resources in both EJBs. This is an example of a distributed transaction; something relatively rare, but that also requires the use of XA resources.

These rules will work for most situations, but there are a few that you may find yourself in that will require you to go beyond the rules—in particular we need to look at some of the differences between the EJB 1.1 and EJB 2.0 specs with regard to local transactions. Let's look at the following sections from Section 6.5.7 of the EJB 1.1 spec:

"A session Bean's newInstance, setSessionContext, ejbCreate, ejbRemove, ejbPas-sivate, ejbActivate, and afterCompletion methods are called outside of the client's global transaction. For example, it would be wrong to perform database operations within a session Bean's ejbCreate or ejbRemove method and to assume that the operations are executed under the protection of a global transaction. The ejbCreate and ejbRemove methods are not controlled by a transaction attribute because handling rollbacks in these methods would greatly complicate the session instance's state diagram (see next section)."

This statement was modified a bit in the EJB 2.0 specification to make things less confusing. It said that the operations shouldn't be controlled by the transaction attribute of the bean, but it didn't specify what the behavior of these operations should be in relation to any ongoing global transaction. In particular, it didn't give the vendors much guidance as to how SQL statements in these methods should be handled. Should each statement be its own transaction (e.g., should it be as if the connection were in auto-commit mode) or should the method be a single transaction scope? So let's examine how this statement changed in EJB 2.0 (the following quote is from section 7.5.7 of the EJB 2.0 specification):

"A session bean's `newInstance`, `setSessionContext`, `ejbCreate`, `ejbRemove`, `ejbPas-sivate`, `ejbActivate`, and `afterCompletion` methods are called with an unspecified transaction context. Refer to Subsection 17.6.5 for how the Container executes methods with an unspecified transaction context."

What the section discusses is that it is up to the Container vendor to determine how methods in the unspecified transaction context operate. Now, in addition, you should turn your attention back to the table referenced previously. When an EJB's transaction attribute is Never or NotSupported (or Supported without an outer transaction context) the business methods also run within an unspecified transaction context. It is important to understand exactly what that means in WebSphere, and how to know what the behavior of methods running in the unspecified transaction context will be.

In WebSphere 5.0, there are extended transactional attributes that apply to the unspecified transactional context. The three settings we have to understand are:

- Boundary (Bean_Method or Activity_Session)
- Resolver (Application or Container_At_Boundary)
- Unresolved action (Commit or Rollback)

Let's leave aside the issue of activity sessions for the moment. So, for the moment, just go along with this and we'll discuss what happens when you set Boundary to Bean_Method. Basically this means that all resource manager local transactions [RMLTs]—we'll call them local transactions from now on) must be committed within the same enterprise bean method within which they are started.

What does Resolver mean? In short, Resolver specifies resolution control and determines who is responsible for handling the commitment of statements that are left hanging by being called within an unspecified transaction context. The two options for Resolver are Application, which means that your program is responsible for forcing commitment (either by using `setAutocommit(true)` or by using `LocalTransaction.begin()` and `LocalTransaction.commit()`) and `Container_At_Boundary`, which means the container is responsible for committing the local transaction.

If you set Resolver to `Container_At_Boundary` (and set the Unresolved Action to Commit) then the bean's method will act the same as it would if you had set the bean's transaction attribute to RequiresNew. That is, the container will begin a local transaction when a connection is first used, and the local transaction will commit automatically at the end of the method.

The difference is that this method will execute in a local transaction context, meaning it won't tie together two different data sources into a single 2-PC transaction within the same method. Likewise, you can't carry a connection over into a method that is being used in this way. You must obtain the connection, use it, and close it all within the same method. Any attempt to pass a connection carried over from another transaction context into a method set up in this way will throw an exception.

Things are a bit more complicated if you choose to set the Resolution Control to Application. Now the behavior of the local transaction depends upon what your code does. If your code specifies the behavior of each local resource (if you use `setAutoCommit(true)` in JDBC) then each statement will run in its own local transaction. Another option would be that you could delineate the transaction yourself by using `javax.resource.cci.LocalTransaction.begin()` and `javax.resource.cci.LocalTransaction.commit()` (or `rollback()`). The interesting bit occurs if you do neither of these things, and leave a transaction open or hanging. This could happen in one of two ways; either you could use `LocalTransaction.begin()` without a corresponding `LocalTransaction.commit()` at the end of the method, or you could use `setAutocommit(false)` after obtaining your JDBC connection and not add any code to control the transaction. As you can see, the state of the transaction at the end of the method is now ambiguous. To resolve that ambiguity, there is the Unresolved Action option. If Unresolved Action is set to Commit, then open local transactions will commit at the end of the bean method; if it is set to Rollback, they will roll back.

28.9.1 Activity Sessions in WAS EE

Why did we have to ignore the possibility of setting Boundary to Activity Session in the earlier discussion? Because Activity Sessions, the subject of this next discussion, are a feature of WAS EE only—they are not available in either other version of WebSphere 5.0. However, the feature is useful enough that it is worth a discussion for those who may be trying to determine whether to use the ND or EE versions of the product.

Activity Sessions provide an alternate unit of work model to standard EJB transactions. In particular, Activity Sessions can provide a way of solving the business transaction problem where a single business activity will have to cross more than one EJB transaction. Activity Sessions can be associated with an HttpSession so that the activity session can span several servlet invocations as well—spanning user think time, resolving the case where the application needs a human being to be involved in a process but does not want to give up the unit of work model. Using Activity Sessions require additional thought and planning be put into the design of your applications, since the transactional span is quite different from what most developers are used to. For more information, consult the WAS EE InfoCenter, and JSR-95, which is a proposal to standardize Activity Sessions through the JCP.

28.10 Extended Transaction Settings in WebSphere 5.0

Setting up the extended transaction settings in WebSphere Studio is quite simple. The extended settings apply for an entire bean; any method of that bean running in an unspecified transaction context will take on the same extended attributes. To set them in WSAD, open an EJB deployment descriptor editor, select the Beans tab, and select the bean from the list. Scroll down to the WebSphere Extensions section. You then select the Boundary, Resolver, and Unresolver Action settings from the drop-down menus as shown in Figure 28.9.

The big question that remains unresolved is where you would use this? In truth, this feature is not used that often. Probably the most common use would be in an `ejbCreate()` method of a stateful session bean; since those methods always run in an unspecified transaction contract, you would need to use the extended transaction settings if you wanted to perform an insert into a database during the `ejbCreate()` method. Stateful beans are not that useful, and are not a part of our best practices. We would recommend that instead of trying to make a stateful bean act like an entity bean, that instead you simply use an entity bean where it is applicable.

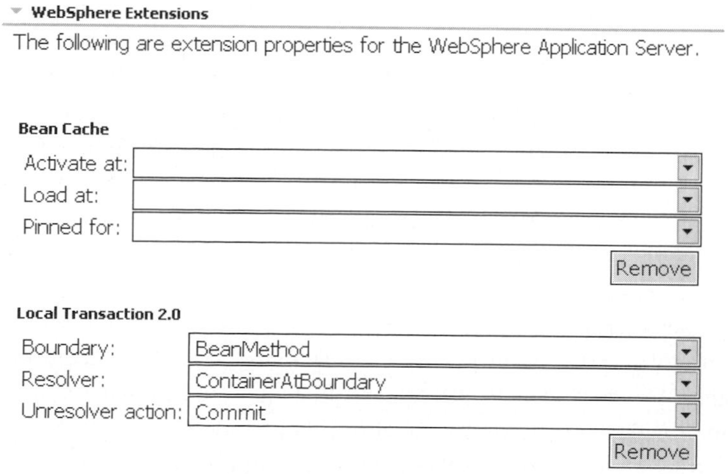

Figure 28.9 Extended transaction settings in WSAD.

28.11   Special Transaction Considerations for JMS

While EJB developers have been writing transactional systems using JDBC since the EJB 1.0 days (which, to us WebSphere developers means WebSphere 3.X), it's only more recently that we've been able to develop fully transactional EJB systems using JMS. WebSphere 4.0, for the first time, provided full transactional connection between JDBC and JMS when using WebSphere MQ. Because this capability has not been in the field as long, the patterns for using JMS within EJBs and WebSphere are not as well known as the patterns for using JDBC within EJBs.

For instance, in some situations, you can use JMS synchronously (i.e., a process can place a message on a queue, then turn around and wait for a response in the same thread). We call this the pseudosynchronous approach to using JMS. It is quite common in some older client/server systems that interfaced with legacy applications using MQ Series.

Unfortunately, this pattern will not work within the EJB container in WAS 5.0 because the EJB specification (section 17.3.5) specifically states, "The Bean Provider must not make use of the JMS request/reply paradigm (sending of a JMS message, followed by the synchronous receipt of a reply to that message) within a single transaction." The reason for this is that, within an EJB transaction, the request would not be sent until the end of the transaction—so the response would time out (after receiving nothing) and the entire operation would fail. This is not some arbitrary limitation of the J2EE specification, but rather an inherent property of a transactional system.

Another common approach that cannot be used in WAS 5.0 is to use the JMS message `Session.setMessageListener()` inside an EJB. The problem here is that if this were allowed, the messages received within the message listener would not be received within a specified transaction context. This makes sense in retrospect, as providing a way of involving both a message receipt and work done by the `onMessage()` method of an MDB is the raison d'etre of introducing MDBs into the EJB 2.0 specification. What will surprise some developers is that not only is the use of `Session.setMessageListener()` forbidden within the EJB container but within the Web container as well. There are some good reasons for this; foremost among them is that the J2EE 1.4 specification (which is not yet implemented in WebSphere 5.0) explicitly states in section J2EE.6.6 that `Session.setMessageListener()` may only be used by application clients running within an application client container. The J2EE 1.3 specification was not as strong in this regard as is the J2EE 1.4 specification. Therefore, many vendors allowed the use of `setMessageListener()` in the Web container in the absence of a strong J2EE 1.3 statement.

IBM, on the other hand, is anticipating the J2EE 1.4 requirement in WebSphere 5.0 by disallowing the use of `setMessageListener()`. This may cause a problem in porting applications from other Web containers to WebSphere. It should not be a huge issue; often the reason for this was to provide the same kind of functionality provided by MDBs. If you do run into this problem in porting an application to WebSphere 5.0, simply move the code from the Message Listener class into an MDB.

28.12   Dealing with Concurrency

Every application that uses a database in any form will at some point have to face an age-old question: How do I keep two different users from stepping on each other while they update their data? That is, if Tammy in the graphics department is updating our catalog to reflect the new look of our summer items, while Bob in accounting is also updating the catalog to reflect the new price list, how do we keep Bob's updates from overwriting Tammy's and vice versa? This comes down to the issue of managing concurrency and there are two general approaches: optimistic and pessimistic concurrency management.

Pessimistic concurrency management, probably the easiest to understand, is the idea of using a lock on a database record to keep more than one application from updating the database at the same time. So, at the beginning of Tammy's transaction, she obtains a lock on the catalog row. When Bob comes along, he may be restricted from reading the catalog row (if Tammy's lock was a lock on read) and forced to wait until Tammy is done. Another option would be a lock on write, meaning that Bob can read the original data, but he's restricted from writing new data to the row until Tammy's update completes (this would ensure that Bob's updates are additive to Tammy's).

The main problem with the pessimistic approach is the waiting. If several readers are kept from reading a row while another holds a lock that might result in an update, then this may lead to unacceptable runtime performance. In this case, the readers are needlessly waiting for a write that might never occur. To avoid this, another option is the idea of optimistic concurrency. This involves two things: (1) not obtaining locks, thus allowing for maximum concurrency in reading, and (2) performing a read immediately before a write to ensure that the data has not changed in the interim. If the data has changed, the writer will abort the writing process.

In our scenario, Bob would read his row at the beginning of his transaction, getting the original row without Tammy's updates. At the end of his transaction, under most circumstances, he would read the row again and discover it had not changed, and then complete the update. In some cases, he might read the row, discover Tammy's update, and abort his attempt to write the row since he would overwrite Tammy's intervening update in the process.

Detecting whether a row has changed requires one of two approaches. Bob could detect Tammy's update either by using a time stamp, which is applied at the end of each update, or by using an overqualified update which is where you use the originally read value of every column in the table as part of the WHERE clause of your update statement. In this case, if there are any mismatches (due, for instance, to Tammy's update), the WHERE clause of the SQL UPDATE statement will not locate that row and fail. The major advantage of optimistic concurrency control is that since it doesn't require locking, it allows for much better throughput—at the cost of some number of aborted updates when collisions occur.

28.12.1   Concurrency and EJBs

Historically, the specification has left questions of how to handle concurrency within entity EJBs to the vendor's discretion. In its releases, WebSphere has gone through several different options in trying to represent the best way to handle concurrency in entity beans. To begin with, in WebSphere 3.X (which implemented the EJB 1.0 specification) WebSphere maintained the following approaches:

- As per the EJB 1.0 specification, each entity bean specified an isolation level. This provided a hint to the database as to how transactions should be separated (the idea of an isolation level is still part of the JDBC specification [JDBC] as discussed earlier). The problem with this was that the effect the isolation levels had on EJB applications was determined by the locking mechanisms available in the database and how WebSphere's transaction manager uses those locking mechanisms. So, in fact, each database driver supported by WebSphere could have different locking semantics (we'll look more into this later). In addition, a more subtle issue with isolation levels is that every method of every EJB in a transaction had to have the same isolation level. Trying to change isolation levels in midstream led to a commit-time exception.
- WebSphere 3.X extended the EJB 1.0 specification by providing a special extension to handle deadlock in some databases in the case where the EJB isolation level was set to `TRANSACTION_SERIALIZABLE` (the safest level as described earlier). In this case, if two transactions both read the same row (entity), they both acquired a read lock on it. If one transaction then tried to write the entity, it would acquire a write lock, which must wait until all read locks are released to complete. If the other transaction also tried to write to the entity, deadlock would occur. For this purpose, WebSphere introduced the Find for update option. This option specified whether the container should get an exclusive lock on the enterprise bean when the find by primary key method is involved. If it is set to false, it will instead acquire exclusive locks on find by primary key methods, and the deadlock condition would not occur.

This changed a bit in WebSphere 4.0. First, the EJB 1.1 specification removed the isolation level from the deployment descriptor, and left it to the vendors to handle transaction isolation in a consistent way. IBM provided an IBM extension for isolation levels similar to what was provided in WebSphere 3.X. Now, to handle the find for update and the read-only problems, WebSphere 4.0 introduced an extension flag for all methods called access intent. The access intent flag could be set on all methods, but it had two different results. The valid values were read and update. If a business method (a getter method) were set to read, it would have the same effect as setting the read-only flag to true in WebSphere 3.X. Likewise, it were set to update then executing the method marked the bean as dirty. However, if the access intent flag were set to update on a home finder method, this had the effect of making this method use a find by update. WebSphere 3.X provided an option to reduce the number of write locks needed (while increasing overall performance) by providing a read-only flag. The issue here was that the EJB 1.0 specification did not describe any way for the container to find out if a bean's state has changed during a transaction. The specification implicitly assumed that all beans used during a transaction were dirty and must have their state written to the back-end store at the end of a transaction. To address this, WebSphere 3.X defined a read-only method flag in the deployment descriptor of entity beans. This allowed the EJB developer to tell the container which methods were read-only; i.e., which didn't change the state of the bean. WebSphere 3.X looked for the setting of this flag whenever a method is invoked. If only read-only methods (e.g., methods this flag set) were sent to a bean in a transaction, the container would not assume that the bean were dirty and would not execute an SQL `UPDATE` statement when the transaction is committed.

So far, you will notice that we have only discussed managing the effects of a pessimistic concurrency strategy. That is because until WebSphere 4.02, WebSphere did not support optimistic concurrency. In WebSphere 4.02, an IBM deployment descriptor extension was introduced, a setting for concurrency control, which had two values, pessimistic (the default, using the support described earlier) and optimistic.

If you chose optimistic concurrency control, WebSphere would use an overqualified update scheme to identify if any columns in the target row changed during the transaction. Web-Sphere would use all columns defined in the EJB deployment descriptor as CMP fields, with the exception of those columns having an ineligible column type (BLOB, CLOB, LONG VAR-CHAR, and VARCHAR having a length greater than 255).

This demonstrates everything that led up to the concurrency control support in Web-Sphere 5.0. How is all this managed in WebSphere and WSAD 5.0? WebSphere 5.0 simplified the process by combining all this into one setting now called access intent. You now define one or more access intent policies to apply to a set of entity EJB methods that will control both the concurrency scheme used (optimistic or pessimistic) and the locking strength used in a pessimistic scheme.

The cool thing about the new access intent approach in WebSphere 5.0 is that it also abstracts away the details of picking the right isolation level for each particular database; because different databases have different locking semantics, the access intent setting allows the container to pick the right isolation level based on a general hint.

There are seven different settings for Access Intent in WebSphere 5.0. To begin with, we have the two possible optimistic settings:

- wsOptimisticUpdate—Use this when you want to allow a method (or group of methods) to perform updates but use optimistic concurrency. This will not perform any locking on select statements, and will perform an overqualified update at the end of the transaction if any `set()` methods are used during the transaction.
- wsOptimisticRead—Use this when you want to allow one or more methods to only read from a database. If you attempt to perform any updates (e.g., if you send a `set()`) method during the execution of the transaction, a `PersistenceManagerException` will be thrown.

In addition, there are the five pessimistic settings: wsPessimisticRead, wsPessimisticUp-date-Exclusive, wsPessimisticUpdate-NoCollisions, wsPessimisticUpdate-WeakestLockAtoad and wsPessimisticUpdate. The setting wsPessimisticRead is nearly identical to wsOptimisti-cRead other than the fact that the underlying database isolation levels are set slightly differently (wsPessimisticRead sets the isolation level to RepeatableRead instead of ReadCommited as it is in wsOptimisticRead). As is the case with wsOptimisticRead, if an update is attempted, the container will throw a PersistenceManagerException. Note that the isolation level setting for this is different in Oracle

The four choices for pessimistic updates differ in both the isolation level used and in the approach taken to using the FOR UPDATE clause on select statements. Here are the different choices for pessimistic updates:

- wsPessimisticUpdate-Exclusive—Exclusive in this case means that your application needs exclusive access to the database rows it is using. This setting indicates that it will use the FOR UPDATE clause, and will set the isolation level to serializable. This setting will mean that you will not encounter either phantom reads or nonrepeatable reads, and that the deadlock that is possible with the TRANSACTION_SERIALIZABLE level alone (without the use of a FOR UPDATE clause) will not occur. This is terribly expensive—this will force every transaction to wait in line to acquire a write lock at the beginning of the transaction and will hold all other transactions until this transaction completes.
- wsPessimisticUpdate-NoCollision—No collision means that the application should be designed such that no concurrent transactions are expected to access the same database rows. This setting (as in the previous) uses the FOR UPDATE clause but sets the isolation level to ReadCommitted.
- wsPessimisticUpdate-WeakestLockAtLoad—The default setting for WebSphere. WeakestLockAtLoad is applicable only to those databases that support both read locks and write locks. If the database supports them both, a read lock is first acquired when a row is accessed and the lock is escalated (promoted) to a write lock if an update is performed on the bean. This setting uses an isolation level of RepeatableRead, but does not use a FOR UPDATE clause. It will work pretty well with nearly every database except Oracle. We will discuss more on that later.
- wsPessimisticUpdate—This setting uses a for-update clause on finder methods and sets the isolation level to RepeatableRead (as in WeakestLockAtLoad) except in Oracle.

Why is Oracle special? Because of the way that it implements its locking mechanism, Oracle does not support the TRANSACTION_REPEATABLE_READ isolation level in the same way as other databases (for example, DB2 or SQL Server). So, everywhere that in other databases the server would have used TX_REPEATABLE_READ the server instead has to use TX_READ_COMMITTED.

In addition, Oracle doesn't use locks in the same way as in other databases. In databases, there is usually a difference between read locks and write locks. A read lock is shared; multiple processes or threads can read an item simultaneously. A write lock is exclusive; only a single transaction holds the lock on the item. In Oracle the weakest lock is an update lock. This becomes interesting when you consider using wsPessimisticUpdate-WeakestLockAtLoad in Oracle, as mentioned earlier, for Oracle the server has to use the TX_READ_COMMITTED for this setting. What's more, in order, to maintain the semantics of the setting, the server must also use a SELECT...FOR UPDATE as well. This is only true of Oracle; no other database requires the server to use a FOR UPDATE clause for this setting. The problem is that in many cases using this access intent with Oracle will result in a runtime exception of the back-end datastore does not support the SQL Statement needed by this AccessIntent. This is because certain types of SQL statements (for instance multiple table joins) cannot use the FOR UPDATE clause.

28.12.2 Choosing the Right Access Intent

Given all of this, which access intent should you use for your applications? If the question were simple to answer then WebSphere wouldn't have included so many choices. The fact is this is a complicated question, often motivated by differences in the behavior of the databases themselves. So, let's work through some best practices, some decision points, and some recommendations to guide you.

First, what's the easiest route for access intent? In many cases you would have expected that to be wsOptimisticUpdate. In that case (as you remember), if an application writes to a database, and there are few expected collisions, then readers and writers entirely stay out of each others way, and writers will only cause each other problems once in a blue moon. What's more, it's even easy to write your domain logic so that if a transaction fails in this way that you can restart the entire process if you captured the original data the user was operating on (perhaps using the Command pattern).

However, optimistic locking is not appropriate in all cases, Sometimes you have to use one of wsPessimisticUpdate variants. wsPessimistic-WeakestLockAtLoad will work in most cases with nearly every database; that's why it's the default. However, if you are using Oracle, it will fail in joins, and wherever the DISTINCT keyword is used so you would have to move back to using wsPessimisticUpdate-NoCollision. However, this policy doesn't ensure data integrity. Since it doesn't hold locks, concurrent transactions can step on each other and overwrite each other's data. So, either you can live with that option (maybe by ensuring that you don't get simultaneous transactions against a row through some other approach) or choose to live with wsPessimisticUpdate-Exclusive, which would serialize access to each row for both readers and writers. In some applications, this would be a significant performance problem. In others, it wouldn't. Your mileage may vary.

Finally, there is a difference in how you set up the optimistic predicate in Websphere 5.0.0 and 5.0.1. In WebSphere 5.0, by default, all nonbinary columns were added to the predicate (as we saw was true in the 4.0.2 version as well). The problem here was that this is slow since not all the columns will be typically indexed. Also, this can lead to problems because now the predicate is too constrained. In Version 5.0.1, the default is instead not to add any columns to the predicate, meaning that for optimistic locking, no locking will take place. Instead, you need to manually set which columns are part of the predicate by selecting the mapping of a column in the overview of the WebSphere Studio map editor and then by setting the OptimisticPredicate property to true.

Setting up access intents for an EJB in WebSphere Studio is actually very simple. We covered this (in another context) in Chapter 25. The process is the same.

28.12.3 Application Profiles in WAS 5.0 EE

Now that you understand the benefits that you can gain from using WebSphere's access intent feature, you may be thinking that it can solve all of your locking problems. Not so fast. You should be aware of another issue that sometimes can bring EJB developers grief, and how it can be ameliorated in WAS EE. Let's say that we have a task that entails lots of simultaneous reads, and even the occasional update to a particular set of entity beans. For instance, consider an application for college registration. The college catalog is made up of courses, each with different sections taught by different instructors. Students register for a particular section in a course. Here, you will have many reads from the course catalog, and the occasional change to a student's individual class assignments as they drop or switch sections at the beginning of the semester. Therefore, optimistic locking will work most of the time. It would be a very rare situation in which a student's association to a course would need to be updated in two places at once. However, sometimes the situation arises where the college itself needs to make large-scale changes to the schedules of a number of students. If a course or section is dropped, or if a substitution is made for a section, then dozens of records may need to be changed at once.

If we're using optimistic locking, then during that lengthy change, a student might simultaneously make a change to his or her own schedule. The college's update could fail if the student's change "snuck in" during the transaction. So, we'd like to be able to lock the schedules of the students affected for the length of the transaction.

If we've set the access intent to be an optimistic intent, then we can't do that with our entity beans. Therefore, it seems we've come to a catch-22. In this situation, WAS EE provides an answer. There is a feature called Application Profiles that allows you to associate several different access intents with the same bean under the rubric of a Task. A Task is a way of specifying a particular point in an application to the WAS EE EJB container. You can associate Tasks with different methods. So, you could associate one Task (in turn associated with a pessimistic access intent policy for the course and schedule beans) to the method that dropped a course section altogether, while methods used in student registration could be associated with a different task that specified an optimistic access intent policy for the same entity beans. For more information, refer to the WAS EE InfoCenter or to [Francis].

28.13 Summary

You've seen a lot in this chapter. We've covered why you need EJB transactions, how they work, how you use the transactional features of the EJB specification in WebSphere, and what special features WebSphere provides above and beyond the EJB specification. While we've not covered all of the possible transactional problems that you can encounter in writing EJB applications, you should now have the necessary tools to do debugging and work out the issues on your own.

CHAPTER 29

J2EE Security in WebSphere

Let's face it, security is a painful subject. Far too often, developers take the attitude that security is "not my problem," leaving securing their applications up to the nameless, faceless security people in an organization. The results are tragic. It seems like almost daily you hear of major Web sites being hacked or defaced, sensitive information being stolen, or massive fraud being committed as a direct result of that attitude. Is this the fault of these security people? No, the reality is that building secure systems is the job of all developers, not just a privileged and knowledgeable few.

However, due to the way that WebSphere's J2EE security works, it's easy to get away with that attitude. By default, all security is turned off in WAS and WSAD. Unless you turn it on and think about what securing your application means, you'll never encounter it. Unfortunately, that's the way that it stays in far too many installations. Here are a couple of scenarios that might give you pause when you consider the results of leaving security turned off:

- Leaving J2EE security turned off leaves all administrative functionality exposed across the WebSphere cell. Severe damage can be done to production systems simply by a developer mistakenly connecting the WAS Admin Console to a production server and making changes there when they intended to modify a test server instead.
- If you use EJBs your application server will be listening for requests to those EJBs over RMI-IIOP. When WebSphere security is turned off, these requests do not require authentication nor perform any authorization checks before they are processed, and this communication is not encrypted. So, the entire application is open for intrusion from the inside. In the past, developers have argued that the obscurity of EJB requests (i.e., the obscurity of RMI-IIOP) makes this a moot point. The problem is that tools like WSAD UTC use introspection to determine available EJB method signatures and names, and from there provide a platform to execute these methods. Anyone with a

copy of WebSphere Studio can use the UTC to query an unsecured application server directly and possibly obtain confidential data by casually browsing the EJBs that are available.

Our recommendation is that in nearly every application, be it for an intranet or the Internet, at a minimum that you turn on WebSphere J2EE security and use the J2EE security model. This will begin to plug some of the holes in your security infrastructure. In the next sections we'll examine the basic parts of J2EE security, and see how WebSphere implements them. Finally, we'll take a look at the edges of dealing with security in WebSphere—handling some of the more interesting programmatic issues that using J2EE security can bring up. We won't cover most of the hard issues of developing a truly secure production environment; things like firewall placement, server hardening, and physical security are beyond the scope of this book. However, we will at least introduce you to basic things you can do for your own applications that will help you begin to create a more secure environment.

29.1 J2EE Security Overview

What does J2EE security, consist of? For the most part it boils down to answering basic questions about your system:

- Who is asking for this particular request? This is the problem of *authentication*. You don't necessarily want anyone off the street to access your application; instead you want to know exactly who makes each request, and you want to make sure that they are who they say they are.
- Should the person or program making this request be allowed to make this request? This is the problem of *authorization*.
- How do you know that a user's interactions with an application are private and not viewed by other persons? How do you know that requests and responses haven't been altered in mid-flight? These are issues of *privacy* (often dealt with through encryption) and *integrity* (the domain of checksums and digital signatures).

At its core, you have to determine how much risk you are willing to take for your application. As we've said earlier, implementing no security entails very little effort but comes with a very high risk. On the other hand, locking down everything can require a very high level of effort, but carries with it a relatively low risk. In the next section, we'll examine how these issues are addressed in WebSphere.

29.1.1 J2EE Security Architecture

Figure 29.1 shows some typical J2EE-defined paths into a WAS. Using this diagram as a guide, we'll quickly address where each of the areas identified in the previous section come into play in WebSphere.

The first path we'll examine is the most common—the one into the Web container from a Web browser (A in Figure 29.1). On this path, all three areas of concern may come into play.

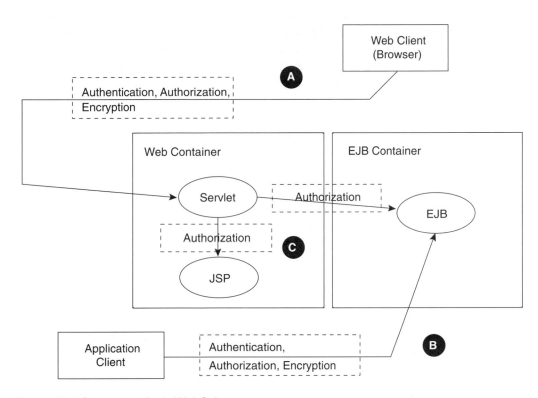

Figure 29.1 Secured paths in WebSphere.

First, you will want to make the conversation private; the way this is done is through the use of HTTPS (the version of HTTP that runs over the SSL). Configuring HTTPS for your Web server, application server, and the WebSphere Web Server plug-in is beyond the scope of this book, but is covered in the InfoCenter. Of more immediate concern to you here is how you identify your user to the Web container and how you determine whether or not that user can access that particular server.

29.1.2 J2EE Authentication in the Web Container

Secure interaction with a Web container initiates a challenge-response interaction where the Web server challenges the client to provide proper authentication before it will honor the request. Authentication consists of two processes: identification and validation. Identification means that a party making a request has to provide some proof of identity, called a credential. This is often in the form of a user ID and password pair (something that only that person would know) or a certificate (something only that person should possess). Validation consists of one partner presenting his credentials, with the other partner in the transaction validating them.

The servlet specification outlines four methods for providing credentials to a Web container:

- **HTTP Basic Authentication**—This method is the most straightforward. This uses a set of headers defined in the HTTP specification (the HTTP basic-authentication headers) and passes a user ID and password to the container in this header in response to the challenge. When a Web browser first attempts to access a page that is set up for basic authentication, the Web server and the browser coordinate with each other according to a flow set forth in the HTTP specification. The server issues a "challenge" to the browser, and the browser will then typically pop up a password dialog asking for a user ID and password. That information will then be sent to the container in the headers mentioned earlier. The user ID and password are not encrypted; they are instead merely base-64 encoded in the headers. This means that you should plan on securing your login page (if not the rest of your site) through HTTPS as we discussed earlier.
- **Form-based Authentication**—Form-based login is an alternative to basic authentication where you as a developer provide an HTML or JSP page that provides a login page with the custom look and feel of your application. Your login page must contain an HTML <FORM> tag that performs an HTTP POST to a special action called j_securitycheck with two specifically defined HTTP parameters, j_username and j_password.. When the request is POSTed to the j_securitycheck URL, the container will verify the user ID and password as in the basic auth case.
- **Certificate-based Authentication (HTTPS Client Authentication)**—Here, the client browser must possess a certificate and corresponding private key to identify the user. This is useful particularly where you want to physically restrict all access to your application to a specific set of users. However, you must plan on generating and disseminating the certificates to your users.
- **Digest authorization**—This is an optional authentication mechanism specified in the servlet specification that WebSphere does not support. Digest authentication is similar to basic authentication, but uses an encrypted password. Few browsers support this option.

The particular mechanism you want to support in your application is specified on a web-app basis through the Web deployment descriptor (web.xml). So, let's say you wanted to support form-based authentication in your application. First, you would need to implement an HTML page or JSP page as your login page, following the rules described earlier. You'd also want to specify a login error page. You would then add the following lines to your web.xml file:

```
<login-config id="LoginConfig_1">

<auth-method>FORM</auth-method>

<realm-name>My Form-based Authentication</realm-name>

<form-login-config id="FormLoginConfig_1">

<form-login-page>/login.html</form-login-page>
```

```
<form-error-page>/error.jsp</form-error-page>

</form-login-config>

</login-config>
```

How does the second part of authentication work? How does WebSphere know what people correspond to particular user IDs and passwords and if a particular combination is valid? Luckily for you, in most cases, you don't have to do anything programmatically to perform this lookup. WebSphere does this for you through the use of user registries. There are three options for user registries in WebSphere:

- WebSphere can use the local operating system (UNIX, Linux, or Windows) to obtain user IDs and passwords.
- WebSphere can use an LDAP 3.0 compliant directory server to provide user IDs and passwords. WebSphere directly supports the IBM Directory Server, Lotus Domino Enterprise Server, the Sun ONE Directory Server, and Windows 2000 Active Directory. However, WebSphere can be made to work with almost any LDAP 3.0 directory server if you provide the proper configuration information.
- You can build your own custom user registry to look up user IDs and passwords from a file, a database, or any other place you choose.

Once a user has been authenticated into WebSphere, WebSphere generates a special client credential to keep the user from having to log in again. This credential uniquely identifies the user and is kept in a cookie that is stored in memory on the user's browser. It has an expiration time associated with it to keep someone else from finding the cookie and using it to surreptitiously log in as the original user (called a replay attack) after which it is regenerated and retransmitted.

There is a ramification associated with this when you consider the different authentication mechanisms. If a user does not allow cookies from your site in his browser, then *every* Web request must be reauthenticated. This works with basic-authentication since the user ID and password are still in the HTTP header and it can still reauthenticate every request. This will be very expensive but workable. In forms-based authentication, it will force your application into a loop where every action goes back to the login page. So, the moral of the story is either inform your users that they must leave cookies turned on if they are using a secured application or plan on using basic or certificate-based authentication and having a slow application.

29.1.3 EJB Client Mechanisms (JAAS)

Now that you've seen how encryption and authentication are done along the A path from the Web browser into the Web container, you may be wondering what happens on the B path from an application client to the EJB container (Figure 29.1). Unlike in the servlet case, this case is not specified by the J2EE specification. The mechanism for providing credentials to an EJB container is left up to the vendor's discretion.

In WebSphere 5.0, IBM has chosen to use the JAAS (Java Authentication and Authorization Service) APIs for programmatic login for EJBs. JAAS is a very broad API that allows the definition of custom authentication, authorization, and access control mechanisms. WebSphere does not fully support all of the JAAS API in this way. It instead supports a limited subset of the JAAS API. In this context, the support that is valuable is the programmatic login API.

In many cases, developers have used JAAS in other servers without a predefined security model (like Tomcat) to define their own lookup mechanisms for user IDs and passwords. In WebSphere, as we have described earlier, you would want to use a user registry instead in that situation. In effect, JAAS is a more standards-compliant replacement for the old CORBA programmatic login APIs that were supported in WebSphere 3.5 and WebSphere 4.0.

How would you actually use JAAS in practice? First there are a number of steps that you need to perform such as setting up a sas.client.props file, which will be used by WebSphere security infrastructure to determine the type of authentication.   All of these steps are described in detail in the WebSphere InfoCenter. Once you have performed these setup steps, then you can begin using the JAAS LoginContext API (Listing 29.1).

Listing 29.1 The JAAS LoginContext API

```
LoginContext lc = null;

String username = "myUserName";

String password = "myPassword"

String realm = "myRealm"

 try {

     lc = new LoginContext("WSLogin",

          new WSCallbackHandlerImpl(myUserName ,myRealm, myPassword));

 } catch (LoginException e) {

    System.out.println("Cannot create LoginContext. " + e.getMessage());

       // do any error processing here

 } catch(SecurityException se) {
```

```
        System.out.printlin("Cannot create LoginContext." + se.getMessage();

            // do any error processing here

    }

    try {

            lc.login();

    } catch(LoginException le) {

        System.out.printlin("Cannot create Subject. " + le.getMessage());

            // do your error processing here

    }
```

This example assumes that you'll provide your own username and password to the WSCallbackHandlerImpl. This means that you would have your own Swing-based dialog to obtain the user ID and password from the user prior to calling this API. That's not your only option. There are also two other CallbackHandler implementations: WSStdinCallbackHandler-Impl and WSGUICallbackHandlerImpl. The former reads a user ID and password from standard input, while the latter pops up a dialog box to prompt the user for the user ID and password. You can use whichever of these is most appropriate for your particular situation.

Just as there are security credentials that are passed back and forth from the browser to the Web container to provide the authentication status of a principal[1], there are similar credentials that are passed between an EJB client and an EJB. In WebSphere, there are two different credential mechanisms to choose from: the CORBA Common Secure Interoperability, 2.0 (CSIv2) protocol, which is new to WebSphere 5.0, and the WebSphere Secure Association Service (SAS) protocol. Your clients can be configured to use either or both. In practice, this choice has hardly any impact on you; it's only if you need to interoperate with earlier versions of WebSphere or another application server vendor that you'll ever care. The only result you care about is that credentials are passed along transparently with every EJB call. This is also how the path marked C in Figure 29.1 is handled. If you are authenticated into a Web container, WebSphere will automatically flow your credentials into the EJB container without your having to provide any special credentials to the EJB or the InitialContext (as is the case with some other application servers).

---

1.   A java.security.Principal is the J2EE representation of an entity that can be authenticated. Think of it as being a
     named user.

29.2 J2EE Authorization

Authorization is the process of controlling access to resources. The basic process of authorization involves an idea called an access control list, which is a way of specifying a mapping between users and resources, and showing which users have access to which resources.

J2EE bases its authorization model on the notion of a role. You can think of a role as a job that a user might perform; for example, clerk, manager, or supervisor. Each user may participate in more than one role.

Each J2EE component (a servlet, or an EJB, for instance) is associated with a set of abstract, developer-defined roles that are granted access to run the methods of a particular EJB, or to use a particular servlet or JSP. At deployment time, these abstract roles are mapped to actual users that are stored in the user registry. To facilitate this, WebSphere keeps a mapping of groups and users in the user registry to J2EE roles, so you must configure this as part of the deployment process of your application.

Here's how it works. Roles may have different access rights to the same resource. Let's say we were working in a bank where we have two roles: tellers and loan officers. If you're a loan officer you need to be able to view a person's bank account balance to determine if she is a good credit risk. So, if we had an account EJB, LoanOfficers should be allowed to call `getAccountBalance()` on that EJB. On the other hand, Tellers can call not only `getAccountBalance()` in order to tell a depositor how much money she in that account, but also the `deposit()` and `withdraw()` methods to update the account balance.

Likewise, if we had a servlet called AdminServlet that allowed someone to perform administration functions in your application, you would want to restrict access to that servlet to users who were in the admin role. It is important to understand the roles are specific to each application. Thus, the admin role we are describing is unrelated to the administrator role used in the administration of WAS.

SECURITY IN THE WEBSPHERE ADMINISTRATIVE CONSOLE

Remember from our earlier discussions that the WebSphere administration console is really just another WebSphere application that runs on an application server (in the core product) or on a deployment manager server (in the ND product). Just as with your own applications, the WebSphere administrative subsystem is protected through WebSphere's J2EE role-based security mechanism. WebSphere defines a number of administrative roles to provide levels of authority needed to perform WebSphere administrative functions from the Web-based admin console. The authorization policy is only enforced when global security is enabled. Administrative roles provide authorization for groups and users:

•Monitor—Least privileged, allows a principal to view the WebSphere configuration and current state
•Configurator—Monitor privileges plus the ability to configure WebSphere

•Operator—Monitor privileges plus the ability to change the WebSphere runtime state

•Administrator—Operator privileges plus configurator authority.

You can add or remove principals such as users and groups to the administrative roles from the WebSphere admin console at anytime. A best practice is to map groups rather than individual users to admin roles because it is easier to administer. By mapping a group to an admin role, adding or removing users occurs outside of WebSphere and doesn't require a server restart for the change to take effect.

29.2.1   Specifying Authorization in the Web Container

As you can imagine from the way in which authentication was specified in the Web deployment descriptor, authorization is similarly specified there as well. The basic mechanism in specifying Web container authorization is to create a set of tuples of role, resource, and action through the security constraint tag in the web.xml.

This XML element will usually contain two subelements, Web-resource-collection and auth-constraint. (A third possible subelement, user-data-constraint, can be used to ensure that a particular collection should be accessed through either HTTP or HTTPS, but it will not enter into this discussion.) The Web-resource-collection element is used to specify a named collection of URL patterns and HTTP methods that can be used to access those elements.

So, if we wanted to limit deposits and withdrawals in our imaginary bank to only Tellers, we would first create a Web-resource collection containing the URLs to the servlets and JSPs that implement those functions.

The second part of the security-constraint element is the auth-constraint subelement. This XML element is used to define a collection of J2EE role names. These role names are references to role names declared elsewhere in the web.xml file in a security-role tag. So, putting it all together, the security portions of the web.xml in our bank example might look like Listing 29.2.

Listing 29.2 A security portion of a web.xml file

```
<security-constraint>

    <web-resource-collection>

        <web-resource-name>Protected Area</web-resource-name>

      <!-- Define the context-relative URL(s) to be protected -->

          <url-pattern>/finance/account/*.jsp</url-pattern>

        <url-pattern>/finance/account/MakeDepositServlet</url-pattern>

      <url-pattern>/finance/account/MakeWithdrawalServlet</url-pattern>
```

```
        <!-- If you list http methods, only those methods are protected -->

            <http-method>GET</http-method>

            </web-resource-collection>

        <auth-constraint>

        <!-- Anyone with one of the listed roles may access this area -->

            <role-name>Teller</role-name>

        </auth-constraint>

    </security-constraint>

<security-role>

<role-name>Teller</role-name>

</security-role>
```

One of the interesting things about the way that Web-resource collections are specified is that what you are specifying here are particular URLs and not individual servlets and JSPs declared elsewhere in the Web deployment descriptor. This makes it possible, for instance, to easily declare different security constraints on different parts of a struts application. Since in the struts deployment descriptor you declare the full URL of each action, you can simply add that complete URL to a Web-resource-collection in a security-constraint element.

29.2.2 Specifying Authorization in the EJB Container

While there are some parallels between the way security elements are specified in the EJB deployment descriptor and the Web deployment descriptor, there's not a one-to-one correspondence. However, the basic idea is the same: You want to specify a set of tuples of role, EJB, and method on that EJB just as you earlier specified tuples of role, URL, and HTTP method to be used to access that URL.

Unlike in the Web deployment descriptor, there's no top level security element per se. This often confuses people when they're learning how to read an EJB deployment descriptor. Instead, security elements are contained inside the assembly-descriptor element along with other items general to either all the EJBs in the EJB JAR file or a subset of those EJBs. This is, by the way, the same place where elements like container-managed transactions are declared, as described in Chapter 28.

The first subelement we'll need to deal with is the security-role element. This element has the same meaning as it has in the Web deployment-descriptor; it allows you to declare a particular security role to be used elsewhere. The second subelement we will examine is more interesting. The method-permission element is roughly analogous to the security-constraint element we saw earlier. In a method-permission element, you specify a set of roles, and then a set of method elements. Each method element corresponds to one or more methods on a particular EJB. This can include methods defined on the local or remote interface, or even in the home or local home interfaces. Wildcards (*) are also allowed if you want to specify all methods for an EJB.

So, our bank example, which would allow Tellers to access the account balance, deposit, and withdraw from an account, while LoanOfficers can only check an account balance, would have the elements shown in Listing 29.3 in its deployment descriptor.

Listing 29.3 Specifying the web.xml assembly descriptor

```
<assembly-descriptor>

        <security-role>

                <role-name>Tellers</role-name>

        </security-role>

        <security-role>

                <role-name>LoanOfficers</role-name>

        </security-role>

        <method-permission>

                <role-name>Tellers</role-name>

                <method>

                        <ejb-name>Account</ejb-name>

                        <method-name>deposit</method-name>

                </method>

                <method>

                        <ejb-name>Account</ejb-name>

                        <method-name>withdraw</method-name>

                </method>
```

```
            <method>

                <ejb-name>Account</ejb-name>

                <method-name>getAccountBalance</method-name>

            </method>

        </method-permission>

        <method-permission>

            <role-name>LoanOfficers</role-name>

            <method>

                <ejb-name>Account</ejb-name>

            <method>

                <ejb-name>Account</ejb-name>

                <method-name>getAccountBalance</method-name>

            </method>

        </method-permission>

</assembly-descriptor>
```

There is another option for the role-name in method permissions. Within the method-per-missions element, the role-name element can contain one or more roles or the special element Unchecked. Unchecked means that method permissions will not be checked for the methods specified within this permissions element. This can be potentially useful, for instance, in reducing the security overhead of local interfaces by turning off all authorization checking for local interface methods.

There is another section of the method-permissions element that we haven't examined, called the excludes list. Methods added to the exclude-list element cannot be called at all. While this sounds like insanity of the first order (why have a method that can't be called) you can imagine situations where test methods can be allowed to be called in development, but restricted in production. There are many other options for specifying the details of security in the deployment descriptor. For more information on those options beyond this basic survey, see [EJB20] or [Monson-Haefel].

29.3   Securing Resources with WebSphere Studio

Now that you understand the theory of how role-based security works in WebSphere and J2EE, you're ready to try an example of securing some resources. We will secure the example you completed in Chapter 21 in order to show you how to secure Web and EJB resources, and how to configure a test server for security. After that, we'll talk about basic issues in deploying secured applications to WAS.

29.3.1   Defining an Authentication Mechanism in WSAD

Earlier we discussed how each Web deployment descriptor that contains secured resources must describe its authentication mechanism in its web.xml deployment descriptor. The first task we will take on in securing our EmployeeManagementWeb Web application is to set the authentication mechanism for that Web app to be HTTP basic authentication. To begin, turn to the J2EE perspective in WSAD and open the J2EE Hierarchy view. You'll start by securing the Web resources in the application, so open the Web modules tree and double-click EmployeeManagementWeb to open the Web deployment descriptor editor. Once you are in the Web deployment descriptor editor, turn to the Pages tab (Figure 29.2).

In this page, in the Login section, set the authentication method drop-down to Basic. Set the realm name to myRealm. Realm is an artifact of the HTTP basic authentication mechanism—in HTTP basic authentication; a realm is a set of related Web pages that share the same user ID and password. The realm name is passed along with the server challenge that requests authentication. It does not matter what you place here. Adding these settings adds the following lines to the web.xml:

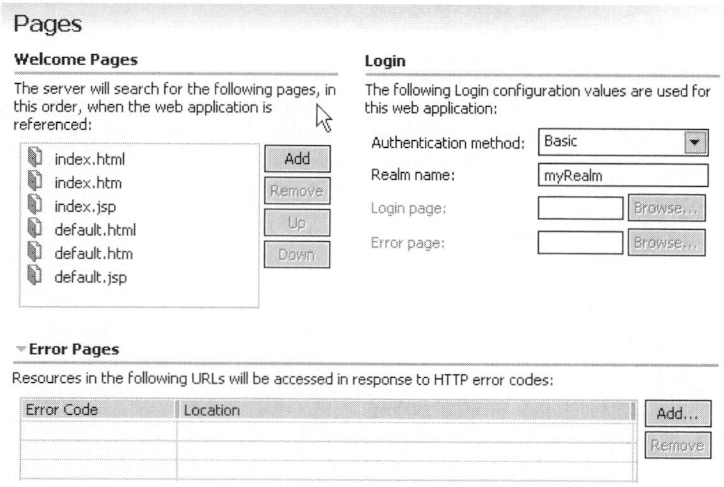

Figure 29.2 Setting the authentication method.

```
<login-config>

    <auth-method>BASIC</auth-method>

    <realm-name>myRealm</realm-name>

</login-config>
```

29.3.1.1   Securing Web Resources in WSAD

Now that we have set up the authentication mechanism, we are ready to specify which Web resources are secured. Make sure you have the Web deployment descriptor editor open on the EmployeeManagementWeb Web app. Turn to the Security tab at the bottom of the Web deployment descriptor editor (Figure 29.3). You'll see two tabs at the top: Security Roles and Security Constraints. The first job you have is to add a new Security Role to the Web deployment descriptor.

Adding and removing Employees from our company is the job of an administrator, so we are going to create an Administrators J2EE role. Make sure you are looking at the Security Roles page and then press the *Add* button beneath the Security Roles list box. This will create a Security Role and highlight it. Type the name Administrators while it is selected (it is editable) and then click outside the text box. At this point, if you switch to the Source tab in the Web deployment descriptor editor, you'll find that you've added a Security Role to the web.xml file like so:

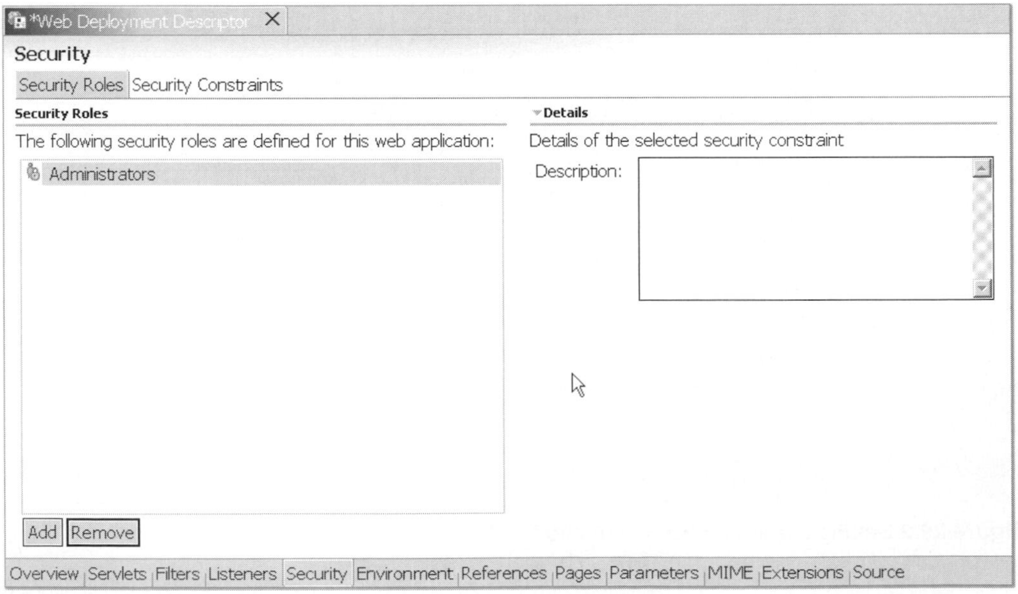

Figure 29.3 Web Security tab.

Figure 29.4 Security Constraints tab.

```
<security-role>

    <description></description>

    <role-name>Administrators</role-name>

</security-role>
```

Now, switch back to the Security tab in the Web deployment descriptor editor and click the *Security Constraints* tab at the top of the page (Figure 29.4).

Press the *Add* button at the bottom of the page to add a new Security Constraint (note that its name of the security constraint). Make sure the Security Constraint is selected and you will notice a Web resource collection (named [New Web Resource Collection]) in the Web resource collections list box. Select the Web resource collection and press the *Edit...* button. This will bring up the Web resource collections dialog (Figure 29.5).

You'll want to do several things in this dialog. First, change the name to be EmployeeManagement. Next, select both the GET and POST HTTP methods so authorized users can read resources in the resource collection.[2] Next, use the *Add* button and type into the editable fields in the list box to add the URL patterns *.jsp, *.html, /CreateEmployee, and /UpdateEmployee.

---

2.   If you leave all the HTTP methods unchecked, it will (by default) apply to all methods.

Figure 29.5 Web resource collection dialog.

Finally, press *OK* to dismiss the dialog. This will create the following section in the web.xml that specifies the Web resources that are secured in this Web application.

```
<security-constraint>

    <web-resource-collection>

        <web-resource-name>EmployeeManagement</web-resource-name>

        <description></description>

        <url-pattern>*.jsp</url-pattern>

        <url-pattern>*.html</url-pattern>

        <url-pattern>/CreateEmployee</url-pattern>

        <url-pattern>/UpdateEmployee</url-pattern>

        <http-method>GET</http-method>

        <http-method>POST</http-method>

    </web-resource-collection>

</security-constraint>
```

The final action you'll take in the Web deployment descriptor editor is to associate the Web resource collection you just created with the administrators role you previously created. To do that, make sure the EmployeeManagement Web resource collection is selected, and then press the *Edit* button next to the Authorized Roles list box. In the dialog that appears, select the administrators role in the list and then press *OK* to dismiss the dialog. That will tie all of the pieces together within the web.xml file by adding an auth-constraint tag linking the resource collection to the administrators role as is shown in Listing 29.4.

Listing 29.4 Tying the pieces together

```
<security-constraint>

    <web-resource-collection>

        <web-resource-name>EmployeeManagement</web-resource-name>

        <description></description>

        <url-pattern>*.jsp</url-pattern>

        <url-pattern>*.html</url-pattern>

        <url-pattern>/CreateEmployee</url-pattern>

        <url-pattern>/UpdateEmployee</url-pattern>

        <http-method>GET</http-method>

        <http-method>POST</http-method>

    </web-resource-collection>

    <auth-constraint>

        <description></description>

        <role-name>Administrators</role-name>

    </auth-constraint>

</security-constraint>

<security-role>
```

```
<description></description>

<role-name>Administrators</role-name>
```

```
</security-role>
```

29.3.1.2   Securing EJB Resources in WSAD

Now that you've secured your Web resources, it's time to move on to securing the EJB resource in this application. This time, open the EJB modules tree in the J2EE Hierarchy view and double-click the EmployeeManagementEJB module to open the EJB deployment descriptor editor. Note that there's no Security tab here—it's not quite as obvious what you need to do to secure your EJBs. Instead, you need to remember the structure of the EJB deployment descriptor that we discussed at the beginning of the chapter. To add security constraints, you must first select the Assembly Descriptor tab (Figure 29.6). In the Assembly Descriptor page, press the *Add* button under the Security Roles list box to add a new Role. In the dialog that pops up, name the Role Administrators as we did in the first step.

Now it is time to add method permissions to go along with the Security Role we just defined. Press the *Add* button beneath the Method Permissions list box. This will bring up a dialog box with several pages.

• In the first page (Method Permission), select the Administrators security role. This will tie this role into the selected EJBs and their methods. Press *Next* to move to the second page.

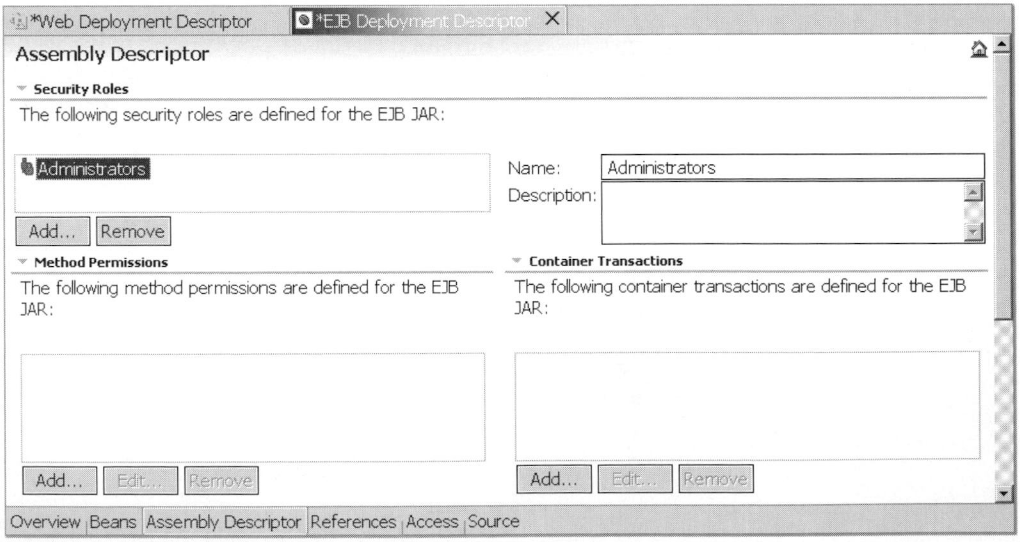

Figure 29.6 Assembly Descriptor tab.

- In the second page (enterprise bean selection), select the EmployeeManagement EJB and press *Next*.
- In the third page (Method Elements), check the box next to the EmployeeManagement bean This selects the wildcard method element which means select all methods in all interfaces (home, remote, local, and LocalHome). Press *Finish*.

Adding method permissions and the security role in the Assembly Descriptor page will create the following Assembly-Descriptor section in the ejb-jar.xml deployment descriptor file:

```
<assembly-descriptor>

    <security-role>

        <description></description>

        <role-name>Administrators</role-name>

    </security-role>

    <method-permission>

        <role-name>Administrators</role-name>

        <method>

            <ejb-name>EmployeeManagement</ejb-name>

            <method-name>*</method-name>

        </method>

    </method-permission>

</assembly-descriptor>
```

Finally, press CONTROL+S to save your work in the EJB deployment descriptor editor.

29.3.1.3 Reconciling Roles in the Enterprise Application Deployment Descriptor

Now that your work in the EJB deployment descriptor editor is finished, you have one more thing to do to effect the way your EAR file is configured. You have to reconcile the roles between the WAR and EJB JAR files. This step is necessary because the J2EE spec requires that the roles be specified at the EAR level in order to support deployment of EARs. To do this, in the J2EE Hierarchy view, open the Enterprise Applications folder and double-click the EmployeeManagement deployment descriptor to bring up the its editor.

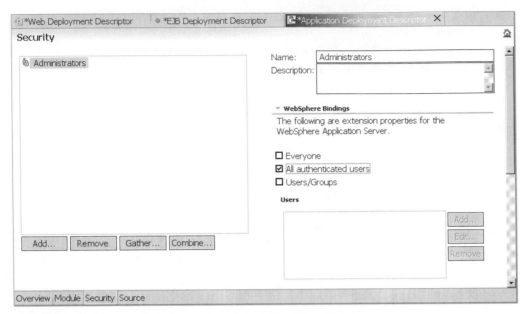

Figure 29.7 Application deployment descriptor editor Security tab.

Next, switch to the Security tab of the application deployment descriptor editor (Figure 29.7). Underneath the Security list box, press *Gather...* This will add the Administrators role to the security list. Select the Administrators role. For simplicity, check the check box marked All Authenticated Users. Ordinarily, you would map such a powerful role to a more restricted set of users, but for now, this is sufficient. This binding can be overridden during deployment by the Application Deployer.

To understand what you have done, recall how we discussed that WebSphere allows for several different user registries, and that one of the features of WebSphere was that it was capable of mapping from users and groups defined in a user registry to J2EE roles defined inside a J2EE application. That is exactly what this page allows you to do. If you were to select the Users/Groups check box, you could add user or group names into the Users list box and that would define the mapping between the group and the list of users or names.

But where does this mapping go? This mapping isn't part of the J2EE specification, so it can't go inside the application.xml file. Instead, as we've seen earlier, this kind of information goes into a special extension file for WebSphere, in this case one called ibm-application-bnd.xmi. The contents of the file you just created are shown here:

```
<?xml version="1.0" encoding="UTF-8"?>

<applicationbnd:ApplicationBinding xmi:version="2.0" xmlns:xmi="http://

www.omg.org/XMI" xmlns:applicationbnd="applicationbnd.xmi"
```

```
xmlns:common="common.xmi" xmlns:application="application.xmi"

xmi:id="ApplicationBinding_1050688790267">

  <authorizationTable xmi:id="AuthorizationTable_1050688790267">

    <authorizations xmi:id="RoleAssignment_1050688790267">

      <specialSubjects xmi:type="applicationbnd:AllAuthenticatedUsers"

xmi:id="AllAuthenticatedUsers_105068879026&ame="AllAuthenticatedUsers"/>

      <role href="META-INF/application.xml#SecurityRole_1050688790267"/>

    </authorizations>

  </authorizationTable>

  <application href="META-INF/application.xml#Application_ID"/>

</applicationbnd:ApplicationBinding>
```

This file is used by WebSphere to determine which users it finds in a registries (based on user ID and password or other credentials) correspond to what J2EE roles in a particular application. In this particular application, it shows the link between the role defined in the applica-

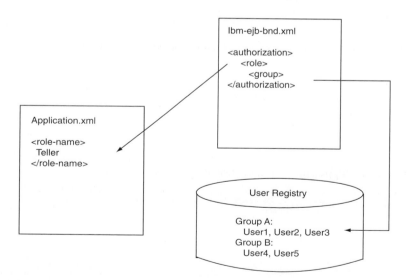

Figure 29.8 Binding file mapping for user registries and application DD.

tion.xml file and the special subject allAuthenticatedUsers. In a more common case, it would link particular group names in a user registry to corresponding roles in the application.xml file as Figure 29.8 indicates.

29.3.1.4 Creating a Secured Server and Running the Example

You're almost done now. If you haven't done so, make sure you've saved all of your work by using *File>Save All* or CONTROL+SHIFT+S to save all of the configuration files you've worked on. Now you've done everything that needs to be done for the EAR file. In fact, you could now export your EAR file to WebSphere and make it work there. However, we want to test our newly secure application in a WAS TE first.

To do so, create a server and server configuration that is set up with security enabled. You've created servers and server configurations before, so this process should seem familiar. In the J2EE Hierarchy view in the J2EE perspective, select the Servers group and select *New>Server>Server configuration* from the context menu. Name the server Secured Test Server. Make sure that the server type is set to WebSphere 5.0 TE and press *Finish* to create the Server.

Open the new secured test server in the server configuration editor by double-clicking the new server within the Servers group. Turn to the Security tab (Figure 29.9) and check the check box that says Enable Security. Type your Windows login ID and password in the appropriate fields. Type your password a second time into the confirm password field.

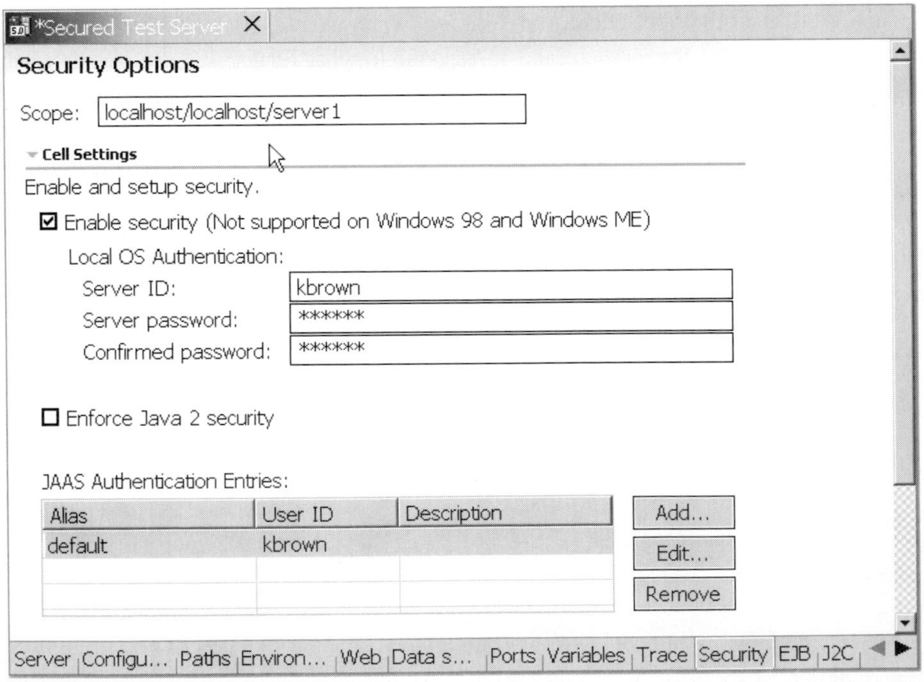

Figure 29.9 Server Security tab.

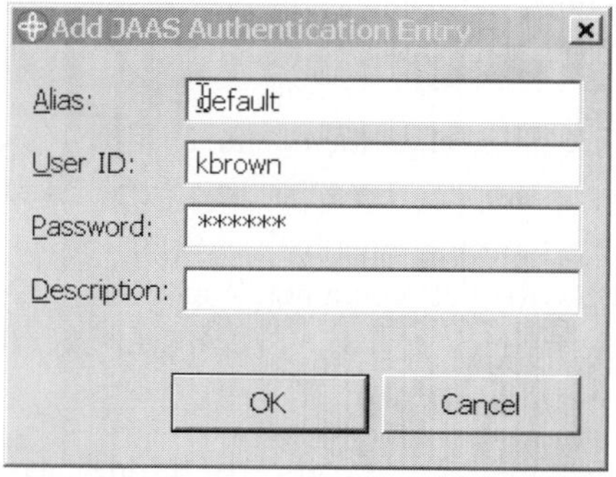

Figure 29.10 Basic authentication dialog.

Now let's test the newly secure application. Switch back to a Web perspective and open the EmployeeManagementWeb project. Select the index.html file and select *Run on Server...* from the context menu. When the Web container comes up and the Web browser goes to the index.html page, you should see a browser basic authentication dialog (Figure 29.10) asking you for your user ID and password.

You are being challenged here because WebSphere has found a security constraint on the index.html (the *.html value) and that constraint specifies All Authenticated Users. Thus, WebSphere will need to challenge you to determine that you can be authenticated. After you enter the user ID and password, you have been authenticated into the Web application and you can use it as you did in Chapter 21.

29.4 EJB Security Recommendations

At a minimum, all session and entity EJBs should be secured to all authenticated users, so that only users that have authenticated into the application can access the EJBs. This simplest level of authentication should discourage the casual browser with a tool like the UTC. However, this will not prevent attack by a user who has the ability to authenticate. Since WebSphere is generally designed to work with an enterprise registry, this level of protection limits access to the EJBs to everyone listed in the registry. While a good start, this is often not sufficient for most applications, so you will want to limit access by group.

Finally, there's one more security entry you should be aware of. The security-identity element is an optional entry in the definition of any EJB. It can look like the following:

```
<security-identity>

    <run-as>

        <role-name>admin</role-name>

    </run-as>
```

```
</security-identity>
```

The security-identity element informs the container how it is supposed to propagate identity from caller to callee. What is happening here is this: We've assumed that when you log in as a particular user, your identity is passed along on all of the calls that are made in the servlet container, and then passed again into the EJB container. What's more, this is the identity that is used to compare against the roles defined in the method-permissions for this EJB.

At this point, a bean deployer has a choice:

- They can specify that the same identity be propagated further down to all other methods called. This is done with the `<use-caller-identity/>` element.
- They can use the `<run-as>` element to specify that any EJB methods called by this EJB will instead run using another role.

You might not think this second option (`<run-as>`) would be very useful until you consider the ramifications of MDBs. In a MDB there is no identity associated with the receipt of a message and the invocation of an `onMessage()` method. So, in that case, you would need to use `<run-as>` to specify what role under which you would run any other beans that are called from the `onMessage()` method.

29.5 Handling Instance-Based Security

So far, everything we've seen with EJB and servlet security has dealt with what is termed declarative security. That is, we've not had to write any code to perform any security actions; everything has been done in the deployment descriptor. There are a few methods that you can use to access information about the user under whose auspices a method in a servlet or EJB is being called. You can get to these methods either from the HttpServletRequest or from the EJB context. In the EJB context, the two methods you can use are:

```
java.security.Principal getCallerPrincipal();
```

```
boolean isCallerInRole(String roleName);
```

The first method allows you to obtain the principal that represents the user. Principal implements the `getName()` method that will obtain for you the user ID with which the user signed in. The second method allows you to determine if any particular user has been associated with a particular role whose name you supply.

There are similar methods in HttpServletRequest with the following signatures:

```
public java.security.Principal getUserPrincipal();
```

```
public boolean isUserInRole(String role);
```

Up to now, our discussion has focused on how the EJB specification allows you to define access rights at a method or EJB level, but only to an entire class of EJBs. Sometimes this is not appropriate for all applications.

Consider the following problem: A team is building a customer relationship management (CRM) application for their company's sales force. One requirement of this application is that each salesperson be only able to view their own clients, not the clients belonging to other sales-people. This is, obviously, to prevent the unscrupulous salesperson from stealing the accounts of others. It is also to protect the company by prohibiting the transfer of sensitive data to our cus-tomer's competitors. If a salesperson can't find out what a competitor of a customer has ordered, he can't relay that information to the customer. This is called the problem of instance-based security, since you need to restrict access to a particular EJB instance, rather than to the entire class of EJBs.

How would we implement this as a set of EJBs? A simple solution would be to create a single entity EJB class called Customer. This EJB would have a set of appropriate finder meth-ods in the home interface that allows us to retrieve the customers for a particular salesperson. This solution is shown in the following home interface:

```
/**

 * This is a Home interface for the Entity Bean

 */

public interface CustomerHome extends javax.ejb.EJBHome {

com.ibm.ejb.examples.utilities.Customer create(int argKey) throws

javax.ejb.CreateException, java.rmi.RemoteException;


com.ibm.ejb.examples.utilities.Customer

findByPrimaryKey(com.ibm.ejb.examples.utilities.CustomerKey key) throws

java.rmi.RemoteException, javax.ejb.FinderException;


java.util.Enumeration findBySalesperson(String salespersonId)   throws

java.rmi.RemoteException, javax.ejb.FinderException;

}
```

Now here lies the problem with this implementation. According to the EJB security model we can grant rights to different identities for each method, but there is no way to restrict access to a particular EJB. You can only restrict access to the EJB type as a whole, or a set of methods in the type.

So in our example, we can restrict access to the finder methods in the EJB home to only those users whose identities we verified and who should be granted access rights to those methods (for example the set of all salespeople). However, we can not restrict access to any individual EJB returned by those finder methods. So, for instance, we couldn't prevent one salesperson (John with logon ID johnm) from looking at the customers of another salesperson (Mary, with logon ID maryq) as long as John knew Mary's logon.

What we need in this particular situation is a way of restricting access to a particular EJB. Some way of keeping a user from gaining access to an EJB for which they have no rights. To that end, let's examine a session wrapper approach to solving our example problem, which applies the EJB security APIs we've examined earlier to make access by unauthorized users more difficult.

29.5.1   A Session Wrapper Approach for Instance-Based Security

The heart of our solution revolves around the following assumption: John may know Mary's SalesPerson logon ID, but does not know her private password. In that case, the identity reported to the system will always be John (since he can only log in as himself) even though he may make queries (e.g., call finder methods) with Mary's ID as a parameter. So we can assume that access should be granted to a particular EJB only if the identity of the caller is on a list that is allowed to access that particular ID.

To implement this solution, we are going to place a session EJB (a wrapper) around the queries in the EJB home to validate the user's identity when we make a query. Consider the following remote interface:

```
package com.ibm.examples.security.ejbs;

public interface IdentityCheckWrapper extends javax.ejb.EJBObject {

java.util.Collection getCustomersForSalesperson(String salespersonID) throws

ImproperAccessException;

}
```

In this remote interface, we have defined a method named `getCustomersForSalesperson()` that takes as its parameter a SalesPerson's unique ID. Listing 29.5 shows the implementation of this method.

Listing 29.5 The implementation of getCustomersForSalesperson()

```
public class IdentityCheckingBean implements SessionBean {

/**

 * This method is a simple security hack to allow a verification of an

 * identity

 * before it sends a query on to an EJB Home.

 * @return java.util.Collection

 * @param salespersonId String

 */

publicjava.util.CollectiongetCustomersForSalesperson(StringsalespersonId)

throws ImproperAccessException {

      java.util.Collection value = null;

      try {

      java.security.Principal principal =

            mySessionCtx.getCallerPrincipal();

      if (checkAccessForSalesperson(principal, salespersonId)) {

            value = getCustomerHome().findBySalesperson(salespersonId);

      } else {

            throw new ImproperAccessException("Access not allowed to +

                salesperson + " by " + principal.getName());

      }

      return value;
```

```
}


public boolean checkAccessForSalesperson(principal, salespersonId) {

        String name = principal.getName();

        // now would do a database lookup to see if this person can

        // access this salesperson's sales.

}

}
```

What we show here is a mechanism by which you can check to see if any person (identified by the name returned from the principal) can access the information for a particular Sales-Person. We've not shown the implementation of `checkAccessForSalesperson()` but you can readily imagine how it would work. For instance, it could be implemented as a database table lookup where you `SELECT`ed against a table that mapped individual names against the IDs of the salesperson they corresponded to. This would allow for almost arbitrarily complex business rules in the implementation of this wrapper bean. For instance, perhaps a salesperson's manager can access their customers, in addition to the salespersons themselves. By adding the proper rows into this lookup table, you can specify exactly the access that needs to be granted.

29.6 GUI-Based Security

In the previous discussion of instance-based security we outlined ways of dealing with a finer granularity of control than is possible with the role-based controls that the J2EE specification provides. Both actions occur a bit too late to help those who shouldn't have access to particular data, but who access that data inadvertently, or through programmer error. For instance, let's say that in our time card application we've used for the case study that we have the case where any Employee can see the pending time sheets that are available, but that only Managers can approve them. So, in the first version of the display_pending.jsp we might see the following code:

```
The current time sheet has NOT been approved, click to

<A href="/TimeAppStruts/ApproveTimeSheet.do">approve</A>
```

How would we change this to set it so that only Managers see this message? One way would be to wrap the code in two scriptlets that use the HttpRequest methods we saw earlier like so:

```
<% if (request.isUserInRole("Manager")) { %>

The current time sheet has NOT been approved, click to

<A href="/TimeAppStruts/ApproveTimeSheet.do">approve</A>

<% } %>
```

As you can imagine, this is error prone, and not in the spirit of the way JSPs are normally written. Another option is to write a simple custom tag library that wraps this common scriptlet like so:

```
<sec:rolespecific role="Manager">

 The current time sheet has NOT been approved, click to

<A href="/TimeAppStruts/ApproveTimeSheet.do">approve</A>

</sec:rolespecific>
```

There are other options that you can manage in the same way. For instance, in many cases you have the situation where you want some users to see a field, and others to be able to edit it. With the scripting approach you can have:

```
<% if (request.isUserInRole("Manager")) { %>

<html:text property="customer.name"/>

<% } else if (request.isUserInRole("Employee")) { %>

<%=customer.getName() %>

<% } %>
```

As the number of unique cases for each role grows, the scripting becomes more repetitive and error prone and the need for a custom tag library grows. While we will not present such a custom tag library here, you certainly have the tools necessary to build one on your own to solve this (and other similar) problems.

Finally, a significant advantage of the XML/XSLT approach to page generation is that it makes data restriction of this type extremely easy. In particular, [Fowler] describes a two-stage approach to generating user interfaces with XSLT in which an initial XML document is generated from domain objects to a domain-like schema, and that document is then transformed into a user interface-like schema that is then transformed into any of a number of different user interface styles. It is at this intermediate transformation that you can apply rules based on the identity of the user, or user preferences. So, in the example case you might choose to render an entry field tag into the intermediate, user interface-like document if a person were a Manager, or a text field tag if he were not. To very cleanly separate model from view, you might even provide a kind of hint in the domain-like XML where each tag could include a read-only or read-write attribute that can be generated at the model level.

29.7 Summary

In this survey of J2EE security in WebSphere, you've seen how the J2EE specifications define role-based security, and how authentication and authorization are described. You've seen a simple example of role-based security in WebSphere Studio, and also learned about some mechanisms for implementing more finely-grained security solutions in your J2EE code.

Building Layered Architectures for EJB Systems

In a previous chapter, we laid out the requirements and design of our case study and, in the last few chapters, you've learned a great deal about how to develop EJBs. Now it's time to put everything you've seen together into a single perspective. In this chapter, we'll examine how to build a complete domain and mapper layer using EJB technology. In the next chapter, after we've seen how the groundwork has been laid by building the domain and mapper layers of our application, we'll examine the design of the user interface of our case study.

Figure 30.1 shows where we fit in our architectural road map as we examine session beans, CMP entity beans, and POJOs.

In this section of the case study, we'll walk through the following patterns and how they are applied, and show the benefits that they convey. Some of the patterns we'll use in this chapter are new, but many of them you've seen before.

- **Business Delegates**—The Business Delegate pattern ([Alur]) allows you to isolate your controller logic from the details of how domain logic is distributed. The basic approach is to give the appearance of local-remote transparency where it doesn't exist.
- **Session Façades**—Session Façades allow you to present a single point of contact to a logical subsystem and they provide distributed access to that subsystem. This allows you to use large-grained distributed objects and to avoid the problems that fine-grained distribution causes.
- **Mappers**—Mappers allow you to hide persistence details from your application and allow you to develop to a logical interface that does not depend on the particular details of a persistence solution such as CMP EJBs or JDBC. In addition, you can take advantage of the Simulated Mapper pattern to test the layers above your persistence layer in the absence of a functioning persistence layer.

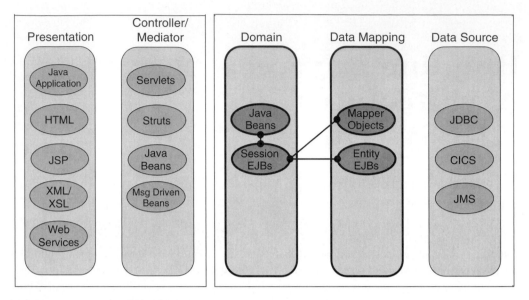

Figure 30.1 Architectural road map.

30.1 Problems with an All-Entity EJB Solution

To understand why the patterns discussed in this chapter are important, let's first talk about the different types of EJBs that we've seen so far, discuss what architectures can be developed using them, then weigh the pros and cons of each architectural choice.

In Chapter 19 we discussed the idea of the session façade, whose purpose is to simplify the API of your system by limiting the number of business methods that EJB clients must deal with. In Chapter 21, we implemented a simple session façade that sat on top of a set of data mapper objects that hid the fact that our Employee domain objects were being persisted in a relational database. However, that design still entailed a lot of complexity. When we covered data mappers in detail in Chapter 16 you saw that there are many considerations that must go into building data mappers that persist objects into JDBC.

In Chapters 23 through 26 we investigated a part of the EJB specification that helps alleviate some of the complexity of building Data Mappers on top of JDBC—CMP entity beans. Are we done now? Can we simply declare that all of our domain objects should only be implemented as CMP beans and go home early? Unfortunately, it's not that simple. Let's consider what would happen if we took that approach.

Remember the TimeSheet domain model we introduced in Chapter 2, and implemented as a set of CMP entity beans in Chapters 23-25. What we've not done is consider how to obtain and manipulate our TimeSheet objects from an EJB client like a servlet or a struts action. So, let's examine a simple example, and work through the ramifications of some different design choices. Let's say we want to retrieve and display the TimeSheets for a particular Employee. No problem, you say! You would simply implement a `findByEmployee()` method on the TimeSheetLocal-Home, code the appropriate EJB QL in the deployment descriptor, and then you may obtain a collection of TimeSheet entity beans.

So now our hypothetical GetTimeSheetsForEmployee servlet can receive back from the TimeSheetLocalHome a collection that would contain EJB client references to the corresponding local TimeSheet entity EJBs. The servlet could then iterate through the collection and ask each bean reference for the week ending Date, current approval state, and TimeSheetEntries for its EJB. However, therein lays the crux of our problem. You see, each call to the methods of our TimeSheet or TimeSheetEntry CMP entity beans from our servlet would be a *different* EJB transaction.

Recall from Chapter 28 how we described the transaction attribute settings for EJBs, and how if a call is made to an EJB where there is not an existing transaction context that the EJB may (depending on the setting) start a new EJB transaction, throw an exception, or start a local resource transaction. Let's say that the transaction setting for our TimeSheet CMP was set to required, which is the default. In this case, the call to `TimeSheet.getWeekEndingDate()` would start a new transaction, since none exists so far. The ramification of this would be that the TimeSheet entity bean would have to reload all its data from the database based on the primary key value (e.g., it would perform a `SELECT` statement on the database) and then return the week ending date.

The problem then is that when the servlet would send the `getState()` method to display the approval state, the same thing would occur again. The container would perform another `SELECT` statement, refetch all of the data for the EJB, and then (in effect) throw it away again at the end of the transaction. As the servlet would proceed to retrieve each TimeSheetEntry, the number of `SELECT` statements would grow as every EJB call results in yet another `SELECT` statement.

One potential way around this would be to use the facilities of JTA (described in Chapter 28) to obtain a UserTransaction within the servlet, and thus provide a shared transactional context for all of the entity bean calls within the servlet method. The downside of this is that you are now placing a requirement on all of your EJB client methods. Missing this and allowing bare entity bean access in just a single method could have an enormous performance impact on your system. What's more, this complication is simply at the wrong level. You've forced what is a business-layer or persistence-layer decision into the Controller layer, where it does not belong. One of the points of EJBs was to avoid this sort of complication in the first place.

As if that weren't bad enough, let's say that our client wasn't a servlet or struts action, but instead an application client. In that case, we couldn't use a local EJB; we would have to expose our entity beans through remote interfaces. Then, in addition to the overhead caused by all of the `SELECT` statements, we would additionally have serialization and network call overhead added on.

So, it seems we're at an impasse. We want the benefits that CMP entity beans give us in isolating us from the complexity of database coding, but we can't stand the performance impact that an all-entity solution would create. Luckily, our old friend, the Session Façade pattern, can help us out of this situation.

30.2 The Session Façade and DTO Solution

The way to avoid the problems of an all-entity bean solution is to gather a set of related data for the client within the context of a single transaction (and remote call, if necessary) instead of accessing it a piece at a time from the server.

What you must do is to use a pass-by-value approach to obtain information from your CMP entity beans rather than a pass-by-reference approach. Instead of making requests to an entity bean from a client for each individual piece of business data, ask a session EJB (a session façade) for a serializable Java object, called a data transfer object (DTO), that contains all the information necessary to display an entire business result or perform a business operation. Remember that any serializable object can be passed as a method argument to an EJB remote method call, or returned as a method result from an EJB remote method call.

When we need to update information contained in an EJB, we can send that information as a DTO to the session façade, which will determine which EJBs to update so that all updates can happen within the context of a single EJB transaction.[1] The DTO can be used to perform validations before they are passed on to the EJB. If a DTO can determine if it is complete or not before the EJB call is made, you can avoid unnecessary transaction and remote overhead.

Figure 30.2 illustrates the process just described.. In Figure 30.2 you see a servlet asking a session EJB for a DTO. The session EJB is responsible for obtaining the information that will make up the data bean from one or more entity EJBs. It is then responsible for creating a serializable object (i.e., a DTO) and copying the information into the data bean. Finally, the DTO is returned as the result of the message sent to the session EJB.

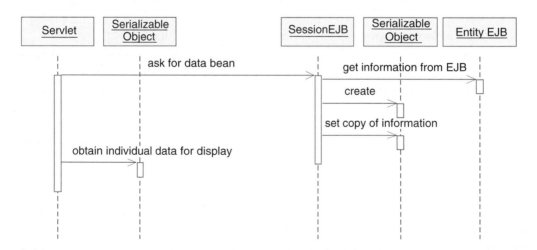

Figure 30.2 Interaction diagram using session façade.

---

1.   Although sending a DTO can work for most update messages, there are some situations where it is best to send a Command object, as we will discuss later.

On the client side, the servlet will obtain the individual data items from the data bean and display them to the user by either embedding the bean directly in a JSP or by some other mechanism. All of the calls made from the servlet to the data bean are all calls to a local Java object, not network calls. More importantly, since we encapsulate all of the calls to the entity bean(s) within a single EJB transaction, there will only be one SELECT statement issued for each entity bean, not the several per bean we encountered earlier. This avoids the additional overhead of the all-entity EJB solution, and will result in a faster system overall.

We should note here you want to avoid doing business logic on the client using data objects. They should only be used to display results or get new values. We must be careful not to pull business logic into the controller and presentation layers where it has to be repeated for each new view resulting in code redundancy and poor reuse.

30.3   Design Points for Session Façades

Since the publication of the first edition of this book, the Session Façade pattern has become almost ubiquitous. It has been well described in both [Alur] and [Fowler]. If we take a look at the original definition of the Façade pattern in [Gamma] we can discover a few details about the implementation of Session Façades that are often missed. [Gamma] describes the Façade pattern as: "...provide a unified interface to a set of interfaces in a subsystem. Façade defines a higher-level interface that makes the subsystem easier to use."[2] The application of this idea to EJBs has been generally construed to mean that you should create a session EJB that acts as a façade and then wraps a set of entity beans that make up a subsystem. In this way, the clients are isolated from the details of the entity bean implementation, and do not have to manage the details of transaction management themselves.

This overly simple approach is often not sufficient. In the following sections, we'll take a closer look at the Façade pattern in order to understand its ramifications in EJB design and to see a number of other beneficial design possibilities inherent in the pattern.

30.3.1   Key Points of the Façade Pattern

There are a number of key points made about the Façade pattern in [Gamma] that we need to understand. The first two are found in the applicability section, which describes when you will want to apply the Façade pattern. They are: "Use the Façade pattern when...you want to provide a simple interface to a complex subsystem" and "Use the Façade pattern when... you want to layer your subsystems. Use a Façade to define an entry point to each subsystem level."[3]

There are a couple of ideas we can extract from that discussion of the Façade pattern. The first is that a façade should provide an abstract view of the subsystem, rather than simply directly wrapping the API of the whole subsystem itself. Taken to an extreme, a session façade could be created for every entity bean and provide direct access to each of its properties. However this

2.   [Gamma] p. 185.

3.   [Gamma] p. 186.

would introduce additional interfaces in the application without providing any additional abstraction. The idea of the pattern is to reduce complexity, not simply to shift it to another part of the application.

The second, subtler point involves layering. The idea here is that you may employ multiple façades to hide the details of successive subsystems. So here you can imagine that a session façade might be layered on top of other façades that further abstract away the details of the underlying business logic. This crucial point becomes clearer when you look at the following two statements from the Collaborations Section and the Related Patterns section of the Façade pattern in [Gamma] respectively:

- "Clients communicate with the subsystem by sending requests to the façade, which forwards them to the appropriate subsystem object(s)."[4]
- "A façade merely abstracts the interface to subsystem objects to make them easier to use; it doesn't define new functionality."[5]

To summarize: Façades don't do the real work of a system—they instead delegate to other objects that in turn do the work. The ramification of that is that you must have these objects in place in order to make the pattern work as intended.

This point is very important. One thing you don't want is for your designs to be unnecessarily EJB-centric. You should certainly not assume that the only objects in your system are EJBs. We have seen that this can result in bloated session objects that are not reusable at all across projects, and can pose problems when there are slightly different requirements within the same project. The approach we will describe next will avoid this problem.

A final point is that you can apply the same pattern several times to different areas of your application. Different session façades can provide different abstractions to clients for different purposes or use cases. Viewed this way, you're not so much abstracting underlying business logic, as providing business logic applicable to the needs of the particular client. The façades act as a filter on the parts of the underlying system, only allowing what each client needs to show through.

30.4 Rules for Session Façades

So how do you apply these rules about façades to sessions and what does this mean for your EJB designs? There are three basic principles that you should apply when designing session façades:

4.   [Gamma] p. 187.

5.   [Gamma] p. 193.

1. Session façades should delegate to other objects to do the real work of the system. This means that each method in a session façade should be small (five lines of code or less, not counting exception handling logic).

2. Session façades should provide a simple interface. This means that the number of façade methods should be relatively small (no more than two dozen or so in each session bean).

3. Session façades act as the client interface to the underlying system. They should encapsulate the subsystem-specific knowledge and not unnecessarily expose it.

So how does this work? What other types of objects can you delegate work to, and what advantage does that confer in your designs? In general, there are four kinds of objects that you find in most EJB designs:

- **DTOs**—As described earlier DTOs are serializable Java beans that contain data requested by a client. They contain a subset of the data contained the entity beans and other data sources. They are the return types for session EJB methods. (Note: DTOs are called value objects in [Sun 2001] and [EJB 2.0] but [Fowler] uses the more descriptive term that we have chosen to follow).

- **Mappers** [Fowler]—Mappers are responsible for building DTOs. In that sense, they act as factories, and are often called factories in recognition of this. Mappers know about the different data sources an object's data is drawn from, create instances of the value objects, fill in the instances of the value objects, and so on. There should be a mapper for every root object in your object model. (Root objects are those that contain other objects.) In a way, a mapper is also acting as a façade onto the JDBC or entity bean persistence subsystem, implementing the layering principle from [Gamma].

- **Entity EJBs**—These should be standard data sources that can be globally useful across the enterprise. Entity beans should not contain application-specific domain logic, nor should they be constrained to only work within a single application. Entity beans are optional and are not a required part of this architecture. A mapper could just as simply obtain data directly from a data source like a JMS queue or a JDBC connection as we will demonstrate later.

- **Action objects**—An action object represents a unique business process that a session bean may invoke. Action objects are required to handle business processes that are not related to simply creating, reading, updating, or deleting data. Like mappers, action objects also act as inner-layer façades.

Figure 30.3 illustrates how the participants in our template architecture are applied. In this figure we show how some of the classes in our case study take on the roles we have just described (we show the roles as UML stereotypes). You will see more about how these classes interact in a later section.

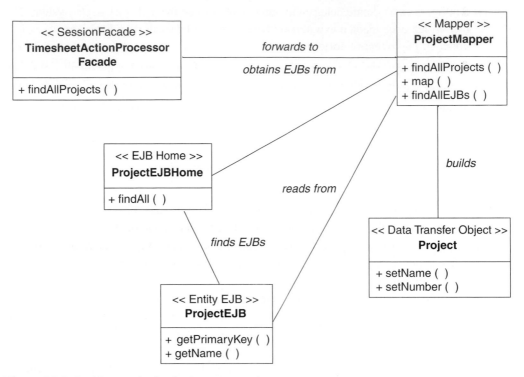

Figure 30.3 Architectural roles in the case study.

30.5 Reasons for EJB Objects

Why do we need this second layer of objects? Didn't we move to EJBs from CORBA and RMI to make things simpler? Why not just put all of the logic in your EJBs? There are several reasons for this. First and foremost, this is simply an application of layering. It is never a good idea to place too much behavior in a single object. If you layer the objects called by your EJBs in this way, you can gain the following benefits:

- Placing the behavior in a set of objects one level in from the session makes it easier to test them in isolation, perhaps even outside of the context of a J2EE application server.
- Multiple session façade objects can use the same inner-layer objects without fear of inappropriate transaction semantics and without the potential network and marshalling/unmarshalling overhead of cross-session bean calls.
- A second layer of objects allows you to vary the implementation of those objects (by using the Strategy pattern from [Gamma]) in order to take advantage of particular features of an application server, while still allowing the entire design to remain portable across application servers. For instance, [Brown 2000a] describes some particular caching strategies for speeding up EJB performance that work under the WAS AE, but that would not work under the IBM CICS EJB support. By providing two

implementations of the same Mapper or Action class, you can keep the overall design portable, while taking maximum advantage of the peculiarities of each server.

- In cases where you do not need a JTA transaction context (e.g., you are working against a single data source) this pattern allows you to choose to deploy and build your applications either with or without EJBs. For instance, in some simple query cases it may be significantly more efficient to call a factory directly from a servlet in order to avoid the overhead of the EJB calls.

Also, we have found through review of several projects that reuse only rarely occurs at the session level. Each session will have a specific combination of transactional settings and method signatures for a specific application. Having a second layer of objects can instead result in reuse at the inner-layer level, where we have seen reuse in many projects, both within projects (across different session beans) and across projects in the enterprise.

We have seen that if you employ this design strategy then your designs can often use stateless session beans as your façade objects. Since each stateless session bean is not unique to a single user, this allows you to gain the additional scalability that stateless beans provide.

Now we can start to look at what kind of methods the façade will present to the outside world. We have seen that façade methods will usually fall into the following types:

- **Collectors**—Collector methods often begin with get and return a single object or a collection of objects (represented as an enumeration in EJB 1.0 or a Java collection in EJB 1.1 and 2.0). The collector method will defer its implementation to a mapper object (possibly through the intermediary of a helper object).
- **Updaters**—This method will locate and update an entity bean or a set of entity beans based on information held in value objects passed in as the arguments. The method name will often begins with update or set. An updater method's implementation can be either deferred to a mapper or enclosed a separate class.
- **Actions**—An Action method (e.g., `AccountBean.transfer(String fromAcctNum, String toAcctNum, BigDecimal amount)`) will defer its implementation to an action object.

A last point to make about this template architecture involves why we have chosen to use mappers (or factories) to create our DTOs from our entity beans. A potential competing solution to the use of mappers is what [Monson-Haefel] describes as bulk accessors—methods on an entity bean that create and return value objects to represent the data in the entity bean. This is, in fact the solution employed by the CopyHelper access beans in WebSphere Studio. However, this has the unfortunate downside that it assumes that all requests will need all of the data in the EJB—resulting in returning unnecessary data to the user, and (in remote calls) incurring additional overhead for marshalling and unmarshalling the larger DTOs.

30.6   A Simple Example from the Case Study

Now that you have seen the basic outline of the session façade/DTO solution, you are ready to start stepping through the code of one of the simplest examples of how this solution is put to use in our case study. In this example, you will see how to obtain a set of data beans that correspond to the list of projects available for selection. This will be used a few times in our case study code. For example, EmployeeTimeSheetAction asks for a list of projects to display in a drop-down so that someone entering a new TimeSheetEntry can assign that entry to a project. This is an example of the collector method type that we discussed earlier.

Figure 30.4 presents a high-level object interaction diagram of how the list of project is accessed. After exploring the diagram, we'll take an in-depth look at the example code to see how each class plays its role.

The interaction begins with an instance of TimeSheetActionProcessorImpl, which acts as a Business Delegate ([Alur]) and wraps our Session Façade. Since we haven't discussed this pattern yet, now is an appropriate time to mention why this is needed. If you recall from Chapter 22 on EJB clients, obtaining an EJB instance takes several steps: you have to create a JNDI Initial-Context, look up the EJB home in the InitialContext, then obtain the EJB reference from the EJB home. The Business Delegate pattern simply provides a way to roll all of these steps into the methods of a single, reusable class that clients can use whenever they need to obtain an instance

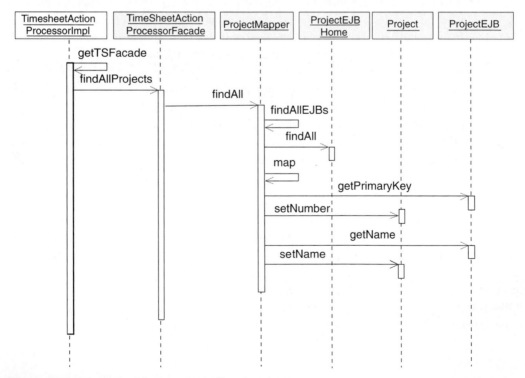

Figure 30.4 Interaction diagram to get list of projects.

of a particular EJB type. The business delegate resides on the client, and is not part of the server-side implementation of the EJB, but instead wraps the EJB to simplify access to its methods.

All of the interactions that we will examine take place on a single session bean, the TimeSheetActionProcessorFacade. Each DTO class has a corresponding Mapper class that is responsible for retrieving instances of the class from the data in one or more entity beans. To illustrate, let's take a look at the `findAllProjects()` method in the TimeSheetActionProcessorImpl (business delegate) class (Listing 30.1).

Listing 30.1 The findAllProjects()method

```
public ArrayList findAllProjects() throws ModelException {

    TimeSheetActionProcessorFacade modelFacade = null;

    try {

        modelFacade = getTSFacade();

        if (modelFacade != null)

            return modelFacade.findAllProjects();

        else

            throw new ModelException("Could not create Facade");

    } catch (RemoteException re) {

        throw new ModelException(re, "Remote Exception caught");

    } finally {

        try {

            modelFacade.remove();

        } catch (Exception e) {


            AppService.log(TraceCapable.ERROR_LEVEL,

                "Exception caught trying to remove facade" + e);

        }

    }
```

```
}
```

As you can see, there's not much to this method. All of the real work is done on the server side. To see this, look inside the implementation of `findAllProjects()` in the TimesheetActionProcessorFacadeBean class:

```java
public ArrayList findAllProjects() throws ModelException {

    ArrayList list = null;

    try {

        Mapper mapper =



MapperFactory.getSystemMapperFactory().getMapper(Project.class);

        list = mapper.findAll();

    } catch (MappingException e) {

        throw new ModelException(e,

                "Mapping Exception caught in findAllProjects() ");

    }

    return list;

}
```

The TimesheetActionProcessorFacade EJB is a session façade. Since it's a façade, that means that it shouldn't do much on its own, but instead should provide an interesting and useful abstraction of an underlying subsystem. In this case, the entity beans and the mappers that we will examine next make up the subsystem hidden by this façade.

Figure 30.5 illustrates some of the features of the mapper hierarchy. ProjectMapper inherits a number of template methods from its superclass, DomainEJBMapper. One of these methods is `findAll()`:

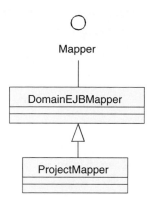

Figure 30.5 ProjectMapper hierarchy.

```
/**

 * Return a ArrayList of all Domain objects of the type created by this

factory.

* @return java.util.ArrayList

 */

public ArrayList findAll() throws MappingException {

        Iterator allEJBs = findAllEJBs().iterator();

        ArrayList list = new ArrayList();

        while (allEJBs.hasNext()) {

                Object next = allEJBs.next();

                Object mapped = map((EJBLocalObject) next);

                list.add(mapped);

        }

        return list;

}
```

This method relies on three abstract hook methods that are redefined in each of the sub-classes of DomainEJBMapper. The first, findAllEJBs(), returns an ArrayList of all of the entity EJBs that correspond to the domain object type. To see what is meant, look at the implementation of findAllEJBs() in ProjectMapper:

```
/**

 * This method retrieves all ProjectEJBs from the store

 */

protected Collection findAllEJBs() throws MappingException {

        try {

                return projectHome.findAll();

        } catch (Exception e) {

                throw new MappingException(e,

                        ("Wrapped exception caught in findAllEJBs : " + e));

        }

}
```

At this point we've almost unwound all the way to the bottom. The findAll() method in ProjectHome is a custom finder method. As with all custom finders in WebSphere, this is implemented with EJB QL that is found in the EJB deployment descriptor. In our case, the following section of the EJB deployment descriptor defines this EJB QL:

```
<query>

<query-method>

<method-name>findAll</method-name>

<method-params></method-params>

</query-method>

<ejb-ql>select object(o) from ProjectEJB o</ejb-ql>

</query>
```

Note that as is common with `findAll` methods, that there is no `WHERE` clause in this EJB QL.

There is one more hook method that `findAll()` uses that you should examine. That method, `map(EJBLocalObject obj)`, returns a domain object that contains the information contained in the `EJBObject` passed into it as an argument. The implementation of `map()` in ProjectMapper (Listing 30.2) shows a simple example of this.

Listing 30.2 Implementing map() in ProjectMapper

```
/**

 * Return an instance of Project created from the

 * ProjectEJB passed in as an argument

*/

public TsObject map(EJBLocalObject input) throws MappingException {

        ProjectEJB ejb;

        try {

                ejb = (ProjectEJB) input;

        } catch (ClassCastException e) {

                throw new MappingException(e, "Attempt to map a non ProjectEJB

in ProjectFactory");

        }

        Project proj = null;

        try {

                proj = new Project();

                proj.setNumber((String) ejb.getPrimaryKey());

                proj.setName(ejb.getName());

        } catch (Exception e) {
```

```
        AppService.log(TraceCapable.ERROR_LEVEL,"Exceptioncaughtin

ProjectFactory.map(): " + e);

        throw new MappingException(e, "Wrapped Exception caught in

ProjectFactory.map()");

    }

    return proj;

}
```

The first `try...catch` block in the method is meant to catch runtime problems that would result from trying to map something that is not a ProjectEJB. The second `try...catch` block does the bulk of the work of this method. As you can see, the method first creates an instance of Project then sets its number and name variables to the values obtained from the ProjectEJB passed in as an argument. Presuming that this all works correctly, the result returned from this method is an instance of Project. This instance works its way back to the previous method and is finally added to the `ArrayList` that is returned by TimesheetProcessorActionFacade.

30.7   A More Complex Example

Now that you understand the basic way in which facades, mappers, DTOs, and entity beans interact, you are ready to move on to understanding a more complex interaction—the way in which TimeSheets, including all of their component objects, are fetched for display.

In order to understand how this works, you will need to revisit the hierarchy of mappers that we have employed in our solution (Figure 30.6).

As you can see from the diagram, most of the complexity in this solution is in the TimesheetMapper and TimeSheetEntryMapper classes. A TimesheetMapper contains references to both an EmployeeMapper and a TimeSheetEntryMapper. In fact, a TimeSheetEntryMapper will only exist in the context of a TimesheetMapper. You never map TimeSheetEntries to their corresponding EJBs outside of the context of a TimeSheet. Likewise, a TimeSheetEntryMapper contains a reference to a ProjectMapper. These relationships parallel those of the JavaBeans these factories create and the entity EJBs from which they store and retrieve their data.

The TimeSheet creation process matches that of the project creation process because they share most of the same classes and methods. Since the business delegate methods upstream of the TimesheetProcessorActionProcessorFaçade are very nearly the same, you can start learning about the differences by examining the creation of Timesheets in the `findPendingForEmployee()` method of TimeSheetActionProcessorFaçade:

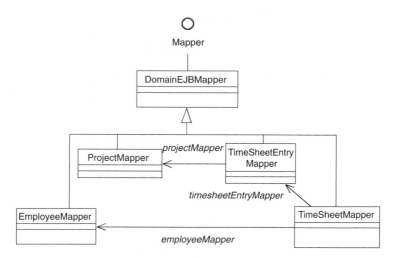

Figure 30.6 Factory relationships for underlying object relationships.

```
public ArrayList findPendingForEmployee(String empId)

    throws NoSuchEmployeeException, MappingException {

    TimeSheetMapper mapper =

    (TimeSheetMapper)MapperFactory.getSystemMapperFactory().getMapper(

                TimeSheet.class);

    return mapper.findPendingForEmployee(empId);

}
```

Remember that in the previous example, the implementation of findAll() in Domain-EJBMapper relies on the findAllEJBs() and map() hook methods. The implementation of findPendingForEmployee() in the TimeSheetMapper class is similar, but different enough to point out some unique aspects in building mappers for entity EJBs. Look at the implementation of this method:

```
    public ArrayList findPendingForEmployee(String empId) throws

MappingException {

        Collection selectedTS = null;

        try {
```

```
        selectedTS =

            timesheetHome.findPendingByEmployee(empId);

    } catch (FinderException fe) {

        throw new MappingException(fe,

        "Wrapped Exception caught in

        findPendingForEmployee()");

    }

    ArrayList list = new ArrayList();

    Iterator it = selectedTS.iterator();

    EJBLocalObject local;

    while (it.hasNext()) {

        local = (EJBLocalObject) it.next();

        Object mapped = map(local);

        list.add(mapped);

    }

    return list;

}
```

This method doesn't use findAllEJBs(), but instead goes directly to the entity bean home to execute a custom finder method (findPendingByEmployee()) that returns all of the pending time sheets for this employee. It does so through the following EJB QL:

```
select object(o) from TimeSheetEJB o where (o.state = 'PENDING') AND

(o.submitter.empId = ?1)
```

What this EJB QL does is to request only those TimeSheets for which the state is "PENDING" (which is the constant string that a PendingState returns for its state name) and whose submitter's employee ID matches the argument passed in. Note that EJB QL is an object query language—it may resemble SQL, but it is defined in terms of the EJB model, and not a database model. Therefore the domain model is not compromised by putting domain behavior in the EJB QL.

The major benefit of performing queries to populate data used in façades using EJB QL is speed. Since EJB QL will be translated (at deployment time) into an SQL query, the filtering of the pending from the approved time sheets will occur at the database, rather than within the application server.[6] By way of comparison, let's look at the corresponding implementation of find-ApprovedByEmployee(), in which we chose to implement the filtering in the mapper method:

```
public ArrayList findApprovedForEmployee(String empId) throws

MappingException {

    ArrayList allSheets = findForEmployee(empId);

    // remove Pending timesheets

    ListIterator iterator = allSheets.listIterator();

    while (iterator.hasNext()) {

        TimeSheet currentTS = (TimeSheet) iterator.next();

        if (currentTS.isPending())

            iterator.remove();

    }

    return allSheets;

}
```

In this implementation, the data must be transferred from the database to instantiated EJBs, and then filtered using the test in the Iterator. Doing the selection directly in the database eliminates all this unnecessary data transfer and object creation. Now, while query implementation is an interesting and useful diversion, you will find that the real differences between this collector method implementation and that of the previous example is in the implementation of

6. If you want to see the exact SQL query that this translates to, open the package com.wsbook.case-study.ejb.websphere_deploy.DB2UDBNT_V72_1 and locate the class whose name begins with TimeSheetEJBBeanFunctionSet. You will find methods that execute SQL statements corresponding to the EJB QL defined in the DD.

`map()`. Examine the code in Listing 30.3 from TimeSheetMapper and then take a look at the explanation that follows.

Listing 30.3 TimeSheetMapper

```
/**

* Return the domain object this EJB object maps to.

* @return com.wsbook.casestudy.domain.TimeSheet

* @param ejb com.wsbook.casestudy.ejb.TimeSheetEJB

*/

public TsObject map(EJBLocalObject input) throws MappingException {

    TimeSheetEJB ejb;

    TimeSheet timeSheet;

    try {

        ejb = (TimeSheetEJB) input;

    } catch (ClassCastException e) {

        throw new MappingException(e,

            "Attempt to map a non TimeSheetEJB in

        TimeSheetMapper");

    }

    try {

        timeSheet = new TimeSheet();

        shallowMap(timeSheet, ejb);

        Iterator entries = ejb.getEntries().iterator();

        TimeSheetEntryEJB entryEJB;

        ArrayList newEntries = new ArrayList();
```

```
        while (entries.hasNext()) {

                entryEJB = (TimeSheetEntryEJB) entries.next();

                TimeSheetEntry entry =

(TimeSheetEntry)getEntryFactory().map(entryEJB);

                entry.setTimeSheet(timeSheet);

                newEntries.add(entry);

            }

            timeSheet.setEntries(newEntries);

    } catch (Exception e) {

            AppService.log(TraceCapable.ERROR_LEVEL,"Exception " + e + "

caught in TimeSheetMapper.map()");

            throw new MappingException(e,

                "Wrapped Exception caught in TimeSheetMapper.map()");

    }

    return timeSheet;

}


private void shallowMap(TimeSheet timeSheet, TimeSheetEJB ejb) throws

java.rmi.RemoteException, javax.ejb.FinderException, MappingException {

    timeSheet.setTimesheetID(((TimeSheetEJBKey)

ejb.getPrimaryKey()).timeSheetId);

    EmployeeEJB employee = ejb.getApprover();

    if (employee != null) {
```

```
        Employee approver = (Employee)

          getEmployeeFactory().map(employee);

        timeSheet.setApprovedBy(approver);

    }

    employee = ejb.getSubmitter();

    if (employee != null) {

        Employee submitter = (Employee)

          getEmployeeFactory().map(ejb.getSubmitter());

        timeSheet.setEmployee(submitter);

    }

    timeSheet.setWeekendFromFormattedString(ejb.getWeekend());

    String stateName = ejb.getState();

    TimeSheetState state = null;

    if (stateName.equals("APPROVED"))

        state = TimeSheetState.getApprovedState();

    else

        state = TimeSheetState.getPendingState();

    timeSheet.setState(state);

}
```

If you dissect these methods you will learn how the different pieces work and understand the concept as a whole. First, note that split this into two methods; map() represents the mapping of the entire TimeSheet object, including its dependent parts. However, the details of mapping the submitter, approver, week end, and state are taken care of in the method shallow-Map(). So, shallowMap() is roughly equivalent to the entire map() method we examined previously for Projects.

The first real difference occurs when the method begins to handle the relationships between the Timesheet and the Employees that submit and approve the Timesheet. Look at the following code snippet taken from the beginning of the `shallowMap()` method:

```
EmployeeEJB employee = ejb.getApprover();

if (employee != null) {

        Employee approver = (Employee) getEmployeeMapper().map(employee);

        timeSheet.setApprovedBy(approver);

}
```

What this snippet of code does is turn over the problem of creating an instance of Employee from an EmployeeEJB to the EmployeeMapper class. It uses the EJB relationship getter method `getApprover()` to obtain an EJB object (an EmployeeEJB) and then asks the EmployeeMapper to return an Employee that is created from that information. Finally, it sets the time sheet domain object's approving employee to be that Employee. The same solution is repeated for the submitting employee a few lines later.

Next, the `shallowMap()` method performs some Date manipulation to take the String that is returned from the EJB and convert it into a Calendar so that it can be set into the TimeSheet. Only the last part of this method, which creates the TimeSheetState, deserves more inspection:

```
String stateName = ejb.getState();

TimeSheetState state = null;

if (stateName.equals("APPROVED"))

        state = new ApprovedState(timeSheet);

else

        state = new PendingState(timeSheet);

timeSheet.setState(state);
```

This method creates a brand new state object whose type is based upon the information stored in the state attribute of the EJB. This kind of object creation based on static information is common in cases where the object that is created has no internal state, or whose internal state can be entirely recreated (as it can here). When storing objects like this (which are often flyweights, as in [Gamma]), you are often better off storing a simple String that can be interpreted at runtime than storing a more complex representation of the object.

Going back to the `map()` method, the last problem addressed is creating the TimeSheetEntry instances that a TimeSheet holds. The following code snippet taken from the `map()` method illustrates how this is done:

```
Iterator entries = ejb.getEntries().iterator();

TimeSheetEntryEJB entryEJB;

ArrayList newEntries = new ArrayList();

while (entries.hasNext()) {

    entryEJB = (TimeSheetEntryEJB) entries.next();

    TimeSheetEntry entry =

      (TimeSheetEntry)getEntryMapper().map(entryEJB);

    entry.setTimeSheet(timeSheet);

    newEntries.add(entry);

}

timeSheet.setEntries(newEntries);
```

First, the method obtains the list of entries (which, remember, are TimeSheetEntryEJBs) from the TimesheetEJB. It then iterates over this list of entries. Once the method has obtained the EJB reference returned from the Iterator, it calls the `map()` method in TimeSheetEntryMapper to map this EJB to a TimeSheetEntry DTO. Having done this, it adds the new TimeSheetEntry to the ArrayList and loops around again. Finally, the method sets the list of entries in the TimeSheet to the ArrayList of TimeSheetEntries that is has just created.

30.8 Mappers Revisited

Now, let's review a couple of fine design points. Remember that the intent of the Mapper pattern is to provide a single, common point of contact to a particular data source. The Mapper pattern provides a separation of concerns in your designs. In our case, it keeps business logic independent from database persistence code.

However, the mappers you've seen in the two previous examples are different than those discussed in Chapter 14 because they don't have to deal with a lot of the things that come with dealing with JDBC on your own—units of work, lazy load, etc.—since this is done by the entity EJBs themselves. As a result, these mappers are significantly simpler than then ones we saw in the previous chapters.

However, the basic responsibility of the mappers (acting as an insulating layer between two subsystems) remains the same, as we have seen. Just like the data mappers we saw in previous chapters, our EJB mappers contain methods that are collectively known as CRUD that operate on DTOs. What you may not have noticed in our design is that all of our mapper classes have implemented interfaces that define these methods. For instance, our ProjectMapper class implements the following interface (in the package com.wsbook.casestudy.mapping).

```java
public interface ProjectMapper extends Mapper {

    public Project findByName(String projectName) throws MappingException;

    public Project findById(String projectId) throws MappingException;

}
```

As you can see, in our example, `ProjectMapper` extends the Mapper interface, which we show in Listing 30.4.

Listing 30.4 Extending the mapper interface

```java
/**

 * Mapping API implemented by data source access mechanisms that access

 * specific

 * data sources, such as JDBC or EJB, and "maps" results to objects.

 * This interface specifies a set of persistent operations in order to

 * retrieve and store Objects to and from specific data sources.

 * */

public interface Mapper {

    /**

     * Delete a TsObject from its store

     */

    public void remove(TsObject anObject) throws NoSuchObjectException,
MappingException;
```

```
    /**

     * Insert a new TsObject into the store

     */

    public void insert(TsObject anObject) throws DuplicateKeyException,
MappingException;

    /**

     * Return a ArrayList of all TsObjects (use carefully in practice!)

     * We use this in our example, but in fact more "wise" enumerators

     * That would directly query the datasource (e.g. through EJB finders)

     * @return ArrayList

     */

    public ArrayList findAll() throws MappingException;

    /**

     * Retrieve a single object matching this object.

     * @return TsObject

     */

    public TsObject findByPrimaryKey(TsObject anObject) throws
NoSuchObjectException, MappingException;

    /**

     * Update this object (e.g. change its state in the store)

     */

    public void update(TsObject anObject) throws NoSuchObjectException,
MappingException;

}
```

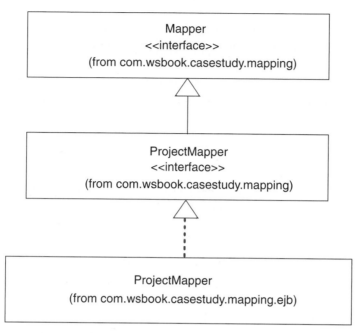

Figure 30.7 ProjectMapper hierarchy.

Declaring this interface is a standard part of implementing the Mapper pattern. For example, [Alur] shows the use of such an interface in nearly all of the design diagrams that illustrate the implementation of the DAO pattern (which, you'll remember, is the same as Fowler's Mapper pattern). So, each of our concrete Mapper implementations implement a specific mapper interface (Figure 30.7).

30.9 Simulated Mappers

Now we can show why the declaration of this (seemingly redundant) interface is important. In [Alur], the DAO interface is declared in order to allow for the creation of additional DAOs that sit on top of other data sources. For instance, [Alur] refers to the possibility of having DAOs for both an XML file format and a relational database in the case where your application has two different data feeds.

There is another possibility. What we can also do is to create a mapper that in fact sits on *no* external data source. This may seem like insanity of the first order, but there are a number of benefits that you can derive from the implementation of this idea (which is similar in form to the idea of mock objects, described in [Mackinnon]). In particular:

- Building a simulated mapper allows you to test your code without having to have a database in place with the application server. This means (for instance) that you don't have to have an instance of DB2 on every developer's desktop if you don't want it.

- When building an application using servlets, JSPs, and EJBs you have enough to worry about without having to deal with database errors too. This idea of layered testing allows you to work out the problems with your presentation and business logic without simultaneously dealing with database issues.
- Being able to separate a layer allows you to more easily isolate problems that occur in testing. For instance, let's assume that you have an error that's difficult to locate. You see a generic exception (like `TransactionRollbackException`) but you can't pinpoint the source of the error. The ability to remove the database layer from the equation entirely allows you to more closely identify where the problem is occurring in your code.
- This approach can come in handy for performance profiling and testing as well. By replacing the database layer you can isolate many performance and multithreading problems. While some classes of performance problems (database deadlock, etc.) still require the database to resolve, you can obtain useful measurements of domain and GUI performance, and more easily resolve problems in those layers, by using this technique.

To show you what these simulated mappers look like, let's examine part of the in-memory version of ProjectMapper (Listing 30.5). Some methods have been left out for brevity.

Listing 30.5 The in-memory mapper of ProjectMapper

```
/**

 * This class is the "in-memory" Mapper for Projects.

 * It creates the default collection of Projects.

 */

public class ProjectMapper extends ObjectMapper implements

  com.wsbook.casestudy.mapping.ProjectMapper {

      protected static ArrayList cache = null;

      /**

       * ProjectMapper constructor.

       */

      public ProjectMapper() {

            super();

      }
```

```
/**

 * Return the singleton cache of Project objects.

 */

protected ArrayList getCache() {

        if (cache == null) {

                cache = initialLoad();

        }


        return cache;

}
/**

 * Create and return a ArrayList of Project Objects.

 */

ArrayList initialLoad() {

        ArrayList v = new ArrayList();

        Project p = new Project();

        p.setNumber("P1");

        p.setName("Development at ABC Corp.");

        v.add(p);

        p = new Project();

        p.setNumber("P2");

        p.setName("Project work at XYZ Corp.");

        v.add(p);

        return v;
```

```
    }

    /**

     * Return a specific Project object matching the input id

     */

    public Project findById(String id) throws NoSuchProjectException{

            ArrayList projects = getCache();

            ListIterator iter = projects.listIterator();

            Project currentProj = null;

            while (iter.hasNext()) {

                    currentProj = (Project)iter.next();

                    if (currentProj.getNumber().equals(id))

                            return currentProj;

            }

            throw new NoSuchProjectException("No project matching " + id +
" found");

    }

    /**

     * Implement the findByPrimaryKey method defined in the Mapper

     * interface

    * by returning the Project matching the id of the Project passed in.

     */

    public TsObject findByPrimaryKey(TsObject input) throws

      NoSuchProjectException {

            Project proj = (Project) input;
```

```
        return findById(proj.getNumber());

    }

    /**

     * Clear the cache.   This is only used in testing.

     */

    public void clearCache() {

            cache = new ArrayList();

    }

}
```

All this class does is store an instance of `ArrayList` in the static variable `cache`, and allow access to that cache. When the first instance is initialized, it will load the cache with a set of starter Projects. Users of this class can then locate Projects by using the `findById()` and `findByPrimaryKey()` methods that search the collection for the appropriate elements. To understand how elements are added and removed from this cache, look at the implementation of the Object-Mapper class (Listing 30.6):

Listing 30.6 Implementing ObjectMapper

```
/**

 * This class represents a simple, "in-memory" mapper for TsObjects.

 * It stores the objects in a ArrayList.

*/

public abstract class ObjectMapper implements Mapper, Serializable {

    /**

     * ObjectMapper constructor.

     */

    public ObjectMapper() {

            super();
```

```java
    }

    protected abstract ArrayList getCache();

    /**

     * Remove all entries from the cache.

     * Required for the JUnit Test Cases.

     */

    public abstract void clearCache();

    /**

     * Remove this TsObject from the cache.

     */

    public void remove(TsObject anObject) {

            ArrayList cache = getCache();

            synchronized(this.getClass()) {

                    cache.remove(anObject);

            }

    }

    /**

     * Return a ArrayList of TsObjects for a Mapper.

     * This should be overridden for each Mapper that requires

     * an initial population of objects

     * @return java.util.ArrayList

     */

    abstract ArrayList initialLoad();

    /**
```

```
      * Insert TsObject into cache.

     */

    public void insert(TsObject anObject) {

          synchronized(this.getClass()) {

                ArrayList cache = getCache();

                cache.add(anObject);

          }

    }

    /**

      * Retrieve all objects in this mapper.

     */

    public java.util.ArrayList findAll() {

          ArrayList cache = getCache();

          return (ArrayList) cache.clone();

    }



    /**

      * Retrieve a single object matching the input object.

     */

    public abstract TsObject findByPrimaryKey(TsObject anObject) throws

       NoSuchObjectException;

    /**

      * The default update() method does a remove and an insert

     */
```

```
public void update(TsObject anObject) {

        remove(anObject);

        insert(anObject);

    }

}
```

Now, to make this work in our case study, we must have an easy way to replace the real Mapper class with our new simulated Mapper class that polymorphically substitutes for the original class. The answer we need is even provided for us by [Alur] in the discussion of the use of object factories in the implementation of the Mapper pattern.

What we wanted to do was to make our client code avoid references to either the concrete `com.wsbook.casestudy.mapping.ejb.ProjectMapper` class or the new `com.ws-book.casestudy.mapping.memory.ProjectMapper` class; using an object factory allows us to provide the client code with instances of the concrete class when one is necessary.

A key concept here is that our object factory uses a software switch that allows it to return an instance of either the real Mapper class or the simulated Mapper class as necessary. In our case, the switch itself is held in a properties file named wasBookConfig.properties, stored in the TimeApp-AppLogic project and dependent JAR file. You've saw the invocation of the object factory back in the `ProjectModelHelper.findAllProjects()` method. In that method, the mapper was obtained by using the code:

```
Mapper mapper =

MapperFactory.getSystemMapperFactory().getMapper(Project.class);
```

The MapperFactory class implements this switch. It returns an appropriate instance of a MapperFactory subtype from `getSystemMapperFactory()` as shown in Figure 30.8.

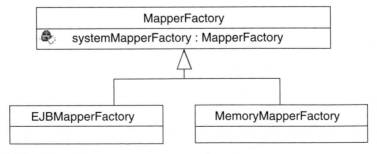

Figure 30.8 Mapper factories.

As you run your tests you will often begin by setting this switch to return the simulated class so that you can test the remainder of the system in isolation from the database. Only in later tests will you ever set the switch to return the real EJB-based Mapper.

There are several ways in which we could have implemented our simulated Mapper class. What we've done in the case study is the simplest implementation where results are simply fetched from an in-memory collection that must be populated during the test. Another common extension of this idea is to prefill the collection with default values in the constructor of the class. The major disadvantage of using a singleton as we have done in the example is that you must clear the singleton between each test. If you miss it in one test, it can cause a failure in a later test. Luckily most unit test frameworks (like JUnit [Beck]) provides facilities to make this easy. For instance, in JUnit, you can put code to clear the singleton in the `teardown()` method of your test class, and put any prefill code in the `setUp()` method of the test class. We will show that in the JUnit tests for the case study.

A second approach, which is slightly more complicated, but also provides for more realistic tests, is to use Java serialization to read a set of objects from a file or to use XML for the same purpose. The advantage of this is that it is possible to use several files to represent different initial conditions for the test.

In general, we would often recommend that the first mapper that you should build is the default Mapper going to an in-memory collection of DTOs. You can then pass this version off to the team building the upper layers of your application (servlets and JSPs, for instance) while then working with another team to build the mappers that will actually work with the database. This allows you to keep both teams working simultaneously, with the interaction between the teams being defined by a shared contract (the Mapper interface).

30.10 An Updating Example

Now that you've mastered the complexity of creating a Timesheet from the corresponding EJB, you should be ready for the inverse operation—updating the state of a TimeSheetEJB from information held in a TimeSheet DTO. Before we dive into the implementation of how updating is done in the case study, we need to talk about the theory of updating with session beans.

Recall that in Chapter 21 in our simple example of using a session bean that we included an update method that took as its argument a map that contained the constituent elements of our Employee class. That approach could be extended to include sending an entire domain object as the argument to an updater method. So, if we wanted to update a simple domain object, like a Project, we would simply have a method called `update()` on the business delegate, façade, and mapper that takes the information in the domain object and replaces the information in the database by updating the corresponding EJB. We use that approach for Employees and Projects in our case study. Let's look at the Mapper implementation of `update()` in ProjectMapper to see how this works:

```
public void update(TsObject obj) throws MappingException{
```

```
    try {

            Project proj = (Project) obj;

            ProjectEJB projectEJB =

                    projectHome.findByPrimaryKey(proj.getNumber());

            projectEJB.setName(proj.getName());

    } catch (Exception e) {

            AppService.log(TraceCapable.ERROR_LEVEL,"Exception " + e +

                    "caught in ProjectFactory.update()");

            throw new MappingException(e,

                    "WrappedExceptioncaughtinProjectFactory.update()");

    }

}
```

There's nothing unexpected here. The Mapper simply locates the right ProjectEJB using `findByPrimaryKey()` and then sends the `setName()` method to that EJB to update the name of the project if it has changed. You can't change a project number in this method because project number is the primary key. Changing it would mean that you aren't updating a project, you're creating one.

While this works approach fine for simple objects like Projects, what would happen if we tried this with more complex objects like Timesheets? Since a TimeSheet contains several other objects inside it (TimeSheetEntries, Employees, and even Projects) this could present a problem. For instance, if the change was to remove a TimeSheetEntry, how would you detect that? If you sent in the entire Timesheet, then the only mechanism for doing that would be to laboriously compare all of the TimeSheetEntries in the TimeSheet to the list of TimeSheetEntryEJBs returned for the corresponding TimeSheetEJB and then determine if one had been added, removed, or changed.

In that case, it might be easier to simply delete all of the existing TimeSheetEntryEJBs and insert all new ones, which could work for our simple TimeSheet example, but, as you could imagine, would cause problems if the number of contained objects were much larger than the few TimeSheetEntries that we're dealing with.

So, we need a different approach. The preferred mechanism for dealing with changes to deeply contained objects like the TimeSheetEntries is to instead capture the changes as they occur. Instead of saying figure out what changed in this object we need to somehow tell our Session Façade, "This is *exactly* what changed in this object." The way out of our quandary is to use the Command pattern from [Gamma] to represent each change as an object in itself that is communicated with the façade. So, we in effect would send delete this particular time sheet entry to the façade instead of sending the time sheet and making it the job of the façade and the mappers to determine how to accomplish that task.

Is it considered cheating that you're moving the complexity to the GUI instead of putting the burden on the back-end? In fact, we're making the GUI simpler as a result. When you're building a GUI element like a struts action, you are already representing a particular user interface action like adding or deleting a TimeSheetEntry. So, it's often easier to simply build a Command object from the information you have in the GUI than it would be to find and update the corresponding domain object.

To show you how this is done, let's again start at the TimesheetActionProcessorImpl class, this time in the `updateTimesheet()` method.

```
public TimeSheet updateTimesheet(UpdateTimesheetFormCommand command)

    throws NoSuchTimeSheetException {

    TimeSheetActionProcessorFacade modelFacade = null;

    try {

        modelFacade = getTSFacade();

        if (modelFacade != null)

            return modelFacade.updateTimesheet(command);

        else

            throw new NoSuchTimeSheetException("No Facade Found");

    } catch (RemoteException re) {

        throw new NoSuchTimeSheetException(re,

            "Remote Exception caught in updateTimesheet");

    } finally {

        try {

            modelFacade.remove();
```

```
        } catch (Exception e) {

        }

    }

}
```

Moving into the TimesheetActionProcessorFacadeBean class, you see the following code, which is a major change from what we've seen previously:

```
public TimeSheet updateTimesheet(UpdateTimesheetFormCommand command)

    throws NoSuchTimeSheetException {

    return command.updateTimesheet();

}
```

Note that all this does is turn the problem around and tell the command object to render the update to the TimeSheet. That is basically the essence of the Command pattern; to treat an action as an object that can be passed around. So, to see how the job is accomplished, we need to look inside UpdateTimesheetFormCommand. We'll start by examining its class definition and instance variables:

```
public class UpdateTimesheetFormCommand implements Serializable {

    // ------------------ Instance Variables

    private String employeeId;

    private String weekending;

    private int[] removeEntryId;

    private String addDate;

    private String addProjectId;

    private String addHours;

    ...

}
```

First, note that the class implements `java.io.Serializable`. It has to be since it will be passed in its entirety as an argument to the session façade. The instance variables that the command class contains are tailored to the needs of the user interface that will generate this class. The user interface (which we will examine in the next chapter) allows a user to select one or more TimeSheetEntries within a TimeSheet for deletion or to add a new TimeSheetEntry. It doesn't allow changing an existing entry, but that can be accomplished in two steps by deleting the old entry and replacing it with a new one.

However, the real work of the class happens in `updateTimeSheet()`, shown in Listing 30.7.

Listing 30.7 The updateTimesheet() method

```
/**

* Command execution

* Given the encoded add and remove TimeSheetEntry commands, update the

* corresponding TimeSheet.

*/

public TimeSheet updateTimesheet() throws ModelException {

    TimeSheet tsheet = null;

    TimeSheetMapper tsMapper =

    (TimeSheetMapper)MapperFactory.getSystemMapperFactory().getMapper(

            TimeSheet.class);

    TimeSheetEntryMapper entryMapper =

        (TimeSheetEntryMapper)

MapperFactory.getSystemMapperFactory().getMapper(TimeSheetEntry.class);

    try {

        // get the owning TimeSheet

        tsheet=tsMapper.findByKey(getEmployeeId(),getWeekending());

        // process command

        // first check if there are any Entries to be removed
```

```
        int[] removeIds = getRemoveEntryId();

        if (removeIds != null) {

                for (int i = 0; i < removeIds.length; i++) {

                        tsheet =
entryMapper.removeByKey(tsheet.getTimesheetID(), removeIds[i]);

                }

        }

        TimeSheetEntry entry = getEntry();

        // check if there is an Entry to be added

        if (entry != null) {

                // Persist

                tsheet = tsMapper.addEntry(tsheet.getTimesheetID(),

                        entry);

        }

        return tsheet;

    } catch (Exception e) {

        throw new ModelException(e,

        "Wrapped Exception caught in updateTimeSheet");

    }

}
```

Again, take a look at the method as a whole, then dissect it into its component parts. The first few lines are quite simple. The method locates a TimeSheetMapper and a TimeSheetEntry-Mapper which it will need to handle the rest of the steps. Next, it locates the owning TimeSheet using the `TimeSheetMapper.findByKey()` method. From then on it uses the information in the command to decide what to do about the TimeSheetEntries for this TimeSheet. First, it iterates through its list of `removeId`'s (which are the second part of the primary key of the TimeSheetEntries) and deletes all of the TimeSheetEntries that were supposed to be removed using the `TimeSheetEntryMapper.removeByKey()` method. Finally, if there is an entry to be added, it determines that by calling the `getEntry()` method:

```
public TimeSheetEntry getEntry() {

  if (validateAddEntryData())

    return new TimeSheetEntry(getAddDate(), getAddProjectId(),

                              getAddHours());

  else

    return null;

}
```

This method runs validation checks (which make sure that all the required fields are filled in) and, if the validation passes, creates a TimeSheetEntry and returns it. Otherwise, it returns null. If a TimeSheetEntry is returned from this method, the `updateTimeSheet()` method will then insert that TimeSheetEntry using the `TimeSheetMapper.addEntry()` method. We'll wrap up our examination of updates by looking at this method and its follow-on methods. We'll begin at `TimeSheetMapper.addEntry()`:

```
public TimeSheet addEntry(int tsId, TimeSheetEntry entry) throws

MappingException {

    TimeSheetEJB ejb = (TimeSheetEJB) findEJBObjectMatching(

        new TimeSheet(tsId));

  if (ejb == null) {

    throw new MappingException("No TimeSheet with id = " + tsId);

  }

  // create new Entry
```

```
        entryMapper.addEntry(entry, ejb);

        return (TimeSheet) map(ejb);

}
```

The method begins by locating the TimeSheetEJB matching the ID for the TimeSheet that is passed in. If there is no corresponding TimeSheetEJB, it throws a `MappingException`, else it then calls `addEntry()` in TimeSheetEntryMapper:

```
public void addEntry(TimeSheetEntry entry, TimeSheetEJB parent)

        throws MappingException {

        ProjectEJB projEJB = (ProjectEJB)

                projectFactory.findEJBObjectMatching(entry.getProject());

        try {

                timesheetEntryHome.create(entry.getHours(),

                        entry.getFormattedDate(), projEJB, parent);

        } catch (Exception e) {

                throw new MappingException(e, "Exception caught in addEntry");

        }

}
```

This method locates a ProjectEJB matching the project ID, and then invokes a `create()` method on TimeSheetEntryEJBHome passing in the hours, a string representation of the date, and the references to ProjectEJB and TimeSheetEJB required.

You've now made it all the way to the end. The `createEjb()` method called by this `create()` method is implemented in TimeSheetEntryEJB, which you have seen in an earlier chapter. There's nothing much else to note in this method, other than the ever-present date to string format conversion already covered by the converters discussed in the earlier chapter.

30.11   Testing the Session Façade Example with JUnit

So now that you understand how the case study EJBs function, you're ready to see them in action. Before we start looking into using the Web front-end to our case study, you should first become familiar with the operation of the JUnit test cases that we've set up to demonstrate the operation of the case study. As we described earlier in the book, you should always plan on writing unit tests for your applications; the test cases make it possible for you to perform regression tests when you add any functions to your application or when you refactor your application.

It's also usually easier to understand the functioning of a system by reading the JUnit test cases than it is to puzzle out the implementation of a complex GUI front-end consisting of several servlets and JSPs.

In our situation, we're going to demonstrate a common way of testing EJB applications, which is to build JUnit test cases in an application client JAR file and then use the JUnit test runner as the application client itself. You want to build your test cases into an application client because it allows the test cases to run against the EJBs. There's no way to run the JUnit TestRunner in the EJB container itself, so running it in an application client allows you to test your EJBs externally. You can use either the Java Swing GUI as your application client, or the JUnit text user interface. In our example, we'll use the text user interface.

Open WSAD, switch to the J2EE perspective, then open the TimeAppTestClient project. Begin by double-clicking the Client deployment descriptor for the project (from either the J2EE Hierarchy or Navigator views), and click the Edit button next to the Main-Class field on the Overview page to open the JAR dependency editor. You can also open the JAR dependency editor by opening the Manifest.MF file in the META-INF directory. Remember that the manifest file includes a reference to the Main-Class of an application client. If you look at the Source page for this file you'll see that the Main-Class of our application client is junit.textui.TestRunner.

```
Manifest-Version: 1.0

Main-Class: junit.textui.TestRunner

Class-Path: TimeSheet-AppLogic.jar

 TimeSheetGroup.jar

 junit.jar
```

The application client manifest also declares that this J2EE module depends on two other modules: the TimeSheet-Applogic dependent JAR (which contains the domain logic of our case study) and the TimeSheetGroup.jar, which is the EJB JAR file that contains our EJBs. It also depends on the junit.jar dependent JAR, which contains the JUnit classes (Figure 30.9).

Next, go back to the client deployment descriptor (or open the application-client.xml file), and switch to the source pane of the application client deployment descriptor editor. Listing 30.8 shows the EJB references called by the file.

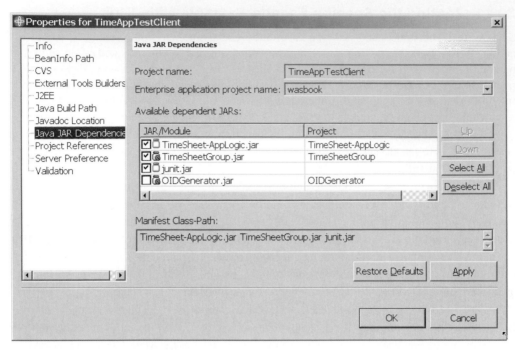

Figure 30.9 JAR dependencies for JUnit.

Listing 30.8 Calling EJB references

```
<?xml version="1.0" encoding="UTF-8"?>

<!DOCTYPE application-client PUBLIC "-//Sun Microsystems, Inc.//DTD J2EE

Application Client 1.3//EN" "http://java.sun.com/dtd/application-

client_1_3.dtd">

<application-client id="Application-client_ID">

        <display-name>TimeAppTestClient</display-name>

        <ejb-ref id="EjbRef_1051066552052">

                <description></description>

                <ejb-ref-name>ejb/TimeSheetActionProcessor</ejb-ref-name>
```

```
            <ejb-ref-type>Session</ejb-ref-type>

       <home>com.wsbook.casestudy.ejb.TimeSheetActionProcessorFacadeHome</
home>



<remote>com.wsbook.casestudy.ejb.TimeSheetActionProcessorFacade</remote>

            <ejb-link>TimeSheetGroup.jar#TimeSheetActionProcessorFacade</
ejb-link>

       </ejb-ref>

       <ejb-ref id="EjbRef_1051666731161">

            <description></description>

            <ejb-ref-name>ejb/ReportActionProcessorFacade</ejb-ref-name>

            <ejb-ref-type>Session</ejb-ref-type>

       <home>com.wsbook.casestudy.ejb.ReportActionProcessorFacadeHome</home>

       <remote>com.wsbook.casestudy.ejb.ReportActionProcessorFacade</remote>

            <ejb-link>TimeSheetGroup.jar#ReportActionProcessorFacade</ejb-
link>

       </ejb-ref>

</application-client>
```

In our test cases, we'll be able to refer to the TimeSheetActionProcessor Façade through its reference of java:comp/env/ejb/TimeSheetActionProcessor Façade instead of having to use the full JNDI name, which is shown in the deployment descriptor editor and is (as described earlier) defined in the bindings file.

Now let's look at the actual test cases you'll run. We'll begin by examining the AllEJBTests class in `com.wsbook.casestudy.tests.junit.ejb`.

```
/**

 * This is an AllTests class that runs all of the tests in the

 * com.wsbook.casestudy.tests.junit.ejb package.  The use of an AllTests

 * class in each package is a common practice for regression testing.

 */

public class AllEJBTests extends TestCase {

    /**

     * Constructor for AllEJBTests.

     * @param arg0

     */

    public AllEJBTests(String arg0) {

        super(arg0);

    }

    public static Test suite() {

        TestSuite suite =  new TestSuite();

        suite.addTest(new

            TestSuite(TimesheetActionProcessorTests.class));

        suite.addTest(new

            TestSuite(ReportActionProcessorTests.class));

        return suite;

    }

}
```

This AllEJBTests class will be the class that we run the JUnit Test runner against. But we still haven't gotten to the actual tests. To see those, begin by opening the TimesheetActionProcessorTests class. You can read the entire set of code on your own, but let's look at an example of the type of JUnit tests we've written, the testAddFindDeleteProject() method:

```java
public void testAddFindDeleteProject() {


    // test adding, finding and removing a Project from the model

    TimeSheetActionProcessor processor =

        (TimeSheetActionProcessor) ActionProcessorFactory

                        .getActionProcessor("TimeSheet");
    try {

        Project purple = new Project();

        purple.setNumber("99");

        purple.setName("Project Purple");

        processor.addProject(purple);

        Project clone = processor.findProjectByKey("99");

        assertEquals("Names don't Match for Project",

                    purple.getName(),

                    clone.getName());

        processor.removeProject("99");

        try {

            processor.findProjectByKey("99");

            fail("Should have raised NoSuchProjectException");

        } catch (Exception e) {

            // Eat it -- it should fail

        }
```

```
        } catch (MappingException e) {

            fail("MappingException caught " + e);

        }

    }
}
```

We won't go through this code line by line but you can see that it does exactly what its method name describes: it adds, finds, and removes a Project. Since there's not much to a Project, there aren't many assertions to verify—only the name need be compared when the project is retrieved. Likewise, the only negative test we need to make is to ensure that a NoSuch-ProjectException is raised when you try to retrieve a Project by a key that is not present. Instead, you may want to investigate some of the more complex Test cases that are in this class for testing TimeSheets. In particular, you will want to investigate the different checkForDeep-Equality() methods that compare TimeSheets, TimeSheetEntries, Employees, and Addresses.

The only other aspect of this TestCase class that we need to point out involves the way in which test cases are run by a JUnit test runner. In a JUnit TestCase, the individual test methods run in a random order. There's no assurance as to which method will run before any other method, so you can't rely on the results of one method in the next. (This is a good thing, since if there were order dependencies it would become difficult to make changes to your test cases; with the existing JUnit design each test method is a world unto itself.) What JUnit provides also is a couple of optional methods (setUp() and tearDown()) that will run before and after each test method respectively. You can use these methods in your test cases to ensure that all of the preconditions are met prior to each test method running, and to ensure that you fully clean up after the end of each test method.

In particular, you need to be very careful as to the state of the database when testing against a database. When you are using a local database, it is often best to clear out the test data you are using between each test method so that the test methods can themselves add all of the necessary test information into the system and then be assured that they are running from a known configuration.

We do this in our TestCase subclass through the use of the deleteAllRows() method, which uses JDBC to remove all of the rows from the tables used in our example. However, this creates another issue, which is how to obtain the JDBC connections needed to delete the rows from the tables in a J2EE application client.

The problem, as described in the InfoCenter, is that WebSphere J2EE application clients cannot access DataSources defined inside WebSphere "because the J2EE application client does not support Java 2 Connection Factories." The upshot of this is that you have to define your own WAS4 DataSources within the application client itself. There is a tool (the application client resource configuration tool) that allows you to do this for WebSphere, but there is no way to do the same thing within WSAD.

This tool creates an XML file (called client-resource.xmi) that defines the data sources and other J2EE resources within the client container. So, the easiest thing to do in WSAD is to take the following file and edit it yourself and then place it in the META-INF directory of your application client. You will simply need to edit the file in Listing 30.9 (which is in the META-INF directory of your application client project).

Listing 30.9 Defining data sources

```
<?xml version="1.0" encoding="UTF-8"?>

<xmi:XMI xmi:version="2.0" xmlns:xmi="http://www.omg.org/XMI"

xmlns:resources.mail="http://www.ibm.com/websphere/appserver/schemas/5.0/

resources.mail.xmi" xmlns:resources.jms="http://www.ibm.com/websphere/

appserver/schemas/5.0/resources.jms.xmi" xmlns:resources.jdbc="http://

www.ibm.com/websphere/appserver/schemas/5.0/resources.jdbc.xmi"

xmlns:resources="http://www.ibm.com/websphere/appserver/schemas/5.0/

resources.xmi">

 <resources.mail:MailProvider xmi:id="MailProvider_1" name="Default Mail

Provider" description="IBM JavaMail Implementation">

    <protocolProviders xmi:id="ProtocolProvider_1" protocol="smtp"

type="TRANSPORT"/>

    <protocolProviders xmi:id="ProtocolProvider_2" protocol="pop3"

type="STORE"/>

    <protocolProviders xmi:id="ProtocolProvider_3" protocol="imap"

type="STORE"/>

  </resources.mail:MailProvider>

 <resources.jms:JMSProvider xmi:id="JMSProvider_1" name="MQ JMS Provider"

description="Default - cannot be changed"/>
```

```
<resources.jms:JMSProvider xmi:id="JMSProvider_2" name="WebSphere JMS
Provider" description="Default - cannot be changed"/>
<resources.jdbc:JDBCProviderxmi:id="JDBCProvider_1"name="DefaultDB2JDBC
Provider" description=""
implementationClassName="COM.ibm.db2.jdbc.DB2ConnectionPoolDataSource">
    <classpath>C:\EJBTwoExperiments\db2java.zip</classpath>
    <factories xmi:type="resources.jdbc:WAS40DataSource"
xmi:id="WAS40DataSource_1" name="jdbc/WSBOOK" jndiName="jdbc/WSBOOK"
description="" databaseName="SAMPLE">
      <propertySet xmi:id="J2EEResourcePropertySet_1">
       <resourceProperties xmi:id="J2EEResourceProperty_1" name="user"
value="my_userid"/>
      <resourceProperties xmi:id="J2EEResourceProperty_2" name="password"
value="my_password"/>
      </propertySet>
    </factories>
    <propertySet xmi:id="J2EEResourcePropertySet_2"/>
  </resources.jdbc:JDBCProvider>
</xmi:XMI>
```

First, you'll need to edit the `<classpath>` element of the file to point to a copy of db2java.zip, which is the DB2 JDBC driver jar file. Also, you'll need to edit the value attributes for `userid` and `password` to be a valid user ID and password on your machine. Note that you are using an unencrypted password in this case; only the Application Client Resource Configuration tool can encrypt passwords. While you can use the unencrypted ones in WSAD you should plan on running the ACRCT after you deploy your EAR if you need to run them at the command line.

30.12   Running the Test Client

Once you've edited the client-resource file, you're almost ready to run the example. First, you'll need to create an application client configuration. In WSAD, select *Run > Run...* from the menu bar to open the Launch Configurations editor. Select WebSphere V5 Application Client in the Launch Configurations Tree view. Press the New button at the bottom of the page to create a configuration.

Change the name (at the top of the page) to TimeApp Test Client. Set the enterprise application to be wasbook by selecting wasbook from the pull-down. Then switch to the Arguments tag and provide a parameter to the JUnit TestRunner. After -CCverbose=true add the line com.wsbook.casestudy.tests.junit.ejb.AllEJBTests. This will ensure that the `AllEJBTests` subclass of `TestCase` will run when you run the application client.

There's one more problem to resolve. The issue here is that no matter what you put in the classpath section of the client-resource file for DB2, WSAD still won't find your driver. (If you want to run your application client at the command line against WebSphere or WSAD, this classpath does matter!)   Instead, to make this work for WSAD you will need to add the db2java.zip JAR file with the DataSource implementation to the runtime classpath of your application client in the Launch Configurations Editor. To do this, open the Launch Configurations Editor (with either *Run > Run* or *Debug > Debug*) and select the TimeApp Test Client. Turn to the Classpath tab and use the Add External Jars button to add db2java.zip (wherever it is stored on your machine, usually <db2install>/SQLLIB/java/db2java.zip) where <db2Install> is often C:\Program Files in Windows.

Now that you've edited your client-resource file, you're finally ready to run the test case against our case study. First, switch to a server perspective and make sure that the WAS 5.0 server you created in an earlier chapter is running. If not, start it. Then, switch to the J2EE perspective and use `Run-->Run...` to bring up the launch configurations editor. Select the TimeApp TestClient and press the Run button. If everything goes as expected, you should see the following output at the end of the WebSphere console (your time will vary, of course):

```
WSCL0900I: Initializing and starting components.

WSCL0910I: Initializing component:

com.ibm.ws.activity.ActivityServiceComponentImpl

WSCL0911I: Component initialized successfully.

WSCL0901I: Component initialization completed successfully.

WSCL0035I: Initialization of the J2EE Application Client Environment has

completed.
```

```
WSCL0014I: Invoking the Application Client class junit.textui.TestRunner

........

Time: 9.363



OK (8 tests)
```

If you see anything at the end other than OK (8 tests) you need to go back over your configuration steps and determine what went wrong.

30.13 Rules for Creating Session Façades

Now that you've learned what session façade interfaces look like, and what objects sit behind the session façades, the question you may have is "How many of these things will I have?" You don't want to have too many session façades, otherwise you lose the benefits of the Façade pattern. However, a single session façade for an entire application might become a "God Object"[7] and cause problems of it own. Here are some rules for designing session façades to achieve the right level of granularity.

- Look for functional subsystems in your application. Subsystems named Order Management, Billing, and Shipping might be the source of three potential Façade objects in an application.
- Go back to your use cases and look for related groups of use cases. A group of related use cases (like buy a stock, sell a stock, get a price quote) might suggest a cohesive subsystem like Stock Trading. This single cohesive subsystem will probably share many inner-layer objects and be a good candidate for a session façade. [Sun 2001] discusses this approach in more depth.
- Do *not* make each individual use case into a session façade. This results in a system with far too large of a distribution cross section. The clients will have to manage too many EJB references and homes in this case.
- After an initial pass, look at the relationships between the second-layer objects in your design. If you see that there are disjoint groups of value objects, factories, and actions, separate the façade into two or more façades based around the actual groupings.

30.14 Should Session Façades Return XML?

One of the bigger questions people struggle with in regard to the previous architecture is the question of what the parameters and return types of the façade methods should be. In particular,

---

7.   [Brown 98] p. 73.

there's a common antipattern that has found its way into several projects that should be squashed before it infects more projects and causes more grief.

What we have been assuming in our preceding discussion is that Session Façade methods could take as arguments and return simple, serializable Java objects (DTOs or value objects). However, others have recommended that instead Façade methods could take as arguments and return an XML (string) representation of the data requested.

In fact, a common question that we find ourselves addressing quite often on mailing lists and bulletin boards like JavaRanch is "How do you pass a DOM into an EJB?" The short answer is you can't. DOM objects are not serializable, and, as you've learned, all EJB arguments must be declared as being serializable. But the more insidious question is why do you want to do that? What advantage would sending a DOM (or a string representation of XML, which is all you could really send) to an EJB possibly convey?

First, let's begin with a consideration of DTOs. DTOs have the advantage that they can be very efficiently serialized. In most cases, the size of a binary value object representation of a data set would be smaller than the corresponding XML representation of the same data. Also, since the Java serialization mechanism is a highly optimized part of the Java base classes and JVM, the serialization process is usually significantly (an order of magnitude or more) faster than generating and parsing corresponding XML. What's more, DTOs are particularly attractive since the JSP specification has been explicitly designed to make displaying the parts of a Java-Bean easy and efficient. This is true even if the desired output of the JSP is XML.

To be fair, DTOs have some drawbacks. The biggest is that it forces you to closely tie the releases of your business tier and presentation tier together. Since the return values form a contract between the two tiers, any change in the business tier (say to add or rename a field in a value object) will necessitate a change in the presentation tier. Often the presentation tier code must change, but in any case, the new data transfer classes must always be redeployed on the presentation tier to avoid serialization problems. It is often out of a desire to avoid this tie between tiers that designers seek to use XML for intertier communication.

However, this is a false distinction. While you may not need to recompile anything or redistribute classes if an XML schema changes, the fact is that the code that parses and uses the resulting XML (especially if it is a SAX parser) would still have to change to deal with the update. It is only the rare (and insignificant) change to an XML schema that would not necessitate code changes on both ends of a conversation.

One case where you might be able to make a valid argument about using XML directly would be if the data you are manipulating is already in XML form, perhaps if it comes directly from an external system in that form. However, in this case, what you are writing is probably better represented as a Web service—something we'll cover in a later chapter.

30.15 Summary

In this chapter, you've learned how to build an architecture that reduces the total number of network-crossing EJB remote method calls, while still allowing for the display and manipulation of complex data. You've also seen how to make entity EJBs generic data sources for multiple projects, enterprise-wide, while maintaining the ability to have application-specific business logic. The key to achieving this is to have the following types of objects in your architecture:

- DTOs are serializable Java objects that contain a subset of the information held in an entity EJB. They should contain some of the business logic in a system like validation, dynamic calculations (e.g., things not stored in the database), etc. They can manage their own relationships to other data beans (so for instance, an Employee can contain an Address). These JavaBeans are suitable to being displayed by a JSP.
- Session façades are session EJBs that provide distributed access to common ways of creating, updating, and managing data beans for client programs (like servlets). Making the façades session EJBs allows for flexibility in distributing the database lookup logic to other machines beyond the second-tier application servers running presentation logic and provides an excellent place to handle things like transactions and security.
- Mappers are responsible for building DTO and updating data sources from the information passed to them as data beans that have changed. They know about the different data sources, manage connections to the data sources, create instances of the data beans, fill in the instances of the data beans, etc. They are standard Java classes. There should be a mapper for every root object in your object model. (Root objects are those that contain other objects.)
- Entity EJBs are standard data sources that can be globally useful across the enterprise. Entity beans should not contain application-specific domain logic, nor should they be constrained to work within a single application.

You've learned about building these objects, and how these interact with each other to form a layered architecture that takes the best advantage of EJBs.

Implementing the Case Study User Interface

In Chapter 2 we described the basic requirements of our complete case study and outlined some of the objects found in its design. In Chapter 30 we examined the detailed design of the EJB portion of the case study. In this chapter, we will study the user interface design of our case study and its implementation using the Struts framework. We'll use the EJBs defined in Chapter 30 and examine how the case study implements the design principles we've discussed so far. Figure 31.1 illustrates where this fits into our architectural road map.

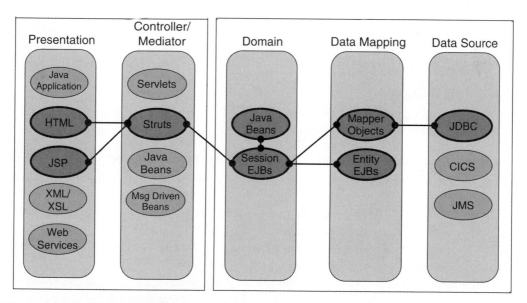

Figure 31.1 Architectural road map of the case study.

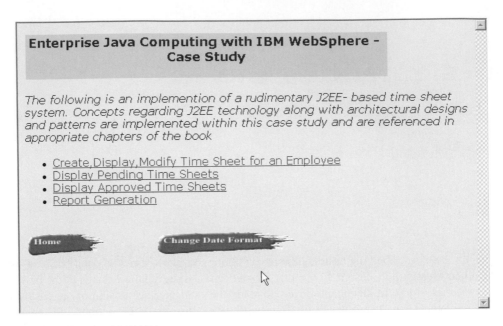

Figure 31.2 Case study initial screen.

31.1   User's Guide

Our time sheet application allows the user to create, modify, and report on time sheet entries. From the primary entry point into the Web-based application the user can take any of three navigation paths. We will explain each path by showing the generated HTML as it is rendered in a browser.

31.1.1   Initial Screen

This screen presents a description of the time sheet application with links to time sheet creation, modification, display, and reporting functions (Figure 31.2).

31.1.2   Create, Display, Modify Time Sheet for an Employee

This action searches for and displays a time sheet based upon an employee name and week-ending date (Figure 31.3).

If a time sheet for a week-ending date exists for the named employee, the time sheet is displayed; if not, the employee can choose to create a time sheet (Figure 31.4).

Only pending, not approved, time sheets can be edited. Time sheet entries can be marked for deletion and entries can be added. (Figure 31.5).

Once an employee is finished entering time for his time sheet, his manager can approve it by using the approve link. That brings up the page (Figure 31.6) that allows the manager to select the name from the list, perform a final review of the time sheet, and approve the time sheet.

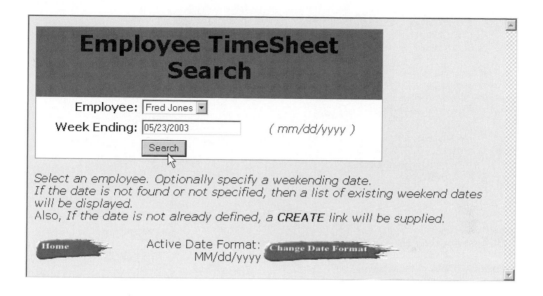

Figure 31.3 Time sheet search.

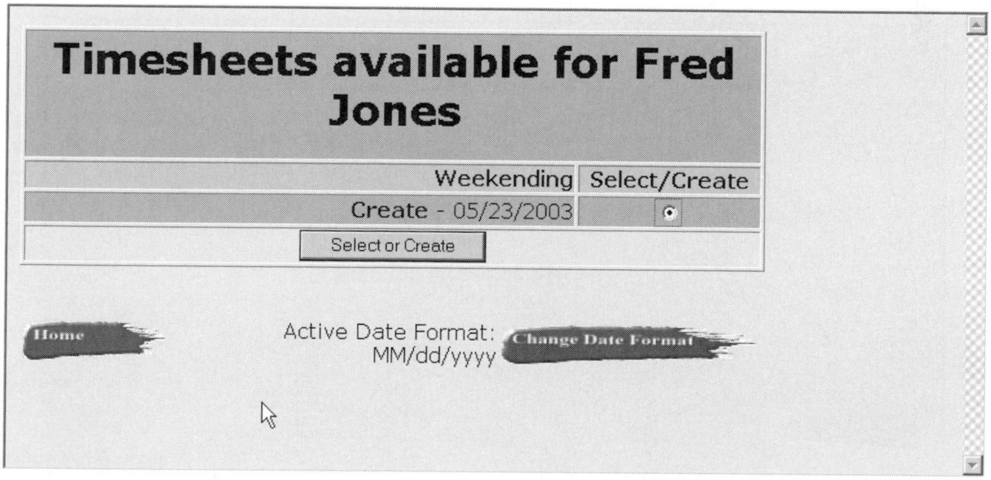

Figure 31.4 Create or select time sheets.

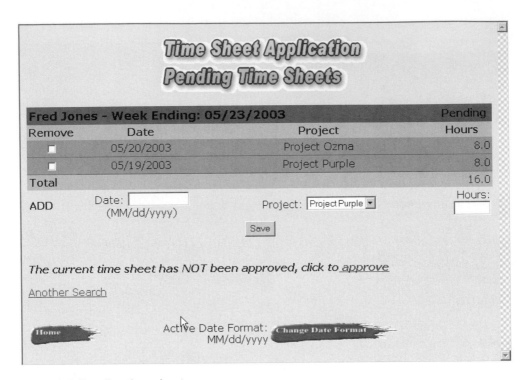

Figure 31.5 Pending time sheet.

Figure 31.6 Approve time sheets.

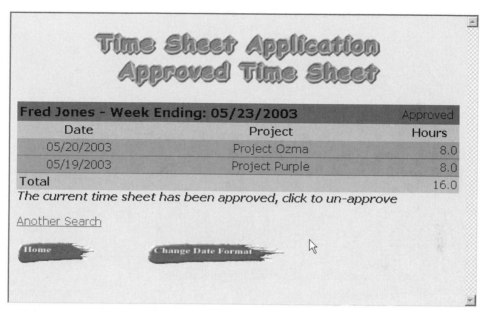

Figure 31.7 Approved time sheets.

31.1.3 Display Pending and Approved Time Sheets

In Figure 31.7, the details of an approved time sheet is displayed.

We discussed how you can start out in understanding the flow of a Web application by first drawing a diagram that indicates how the pages are connected through the different go buttons on the pages. The diagrams for the time sheet portion of our case study are more complicated than any of the diagrams we have seen in previous chapters, with more pages and more links. In fact, the case study flow is large enough and complicated enough that it doesn't fit on a single diagram; we will show it to you in pieces. In addition, the case study is not fully implemented even in the code that comes on the CD; we've left some parts (for instance, some parts of report generation) that are similar to existing parts incomplete. This can provide you with an opportunity to exercise your own design and implementation skills by building on what you've learned in the case study. Figure 31.8 illustrates the first part of the implemented portions of our case study.

This first section shows the flow from the Index page to the linked pages. The link that results in the week_search page is grayed out since we will examine it in another diagram. The remainder of the pages that make up the case study are shown. First, there are the two links that display the pages listing all pending and approved time sheets. In the former case, the pages are shown with the Display_pending.jsp. However, since this is a strict MVC implementation using struts, the link on the index.html page first refers to the ListAllPending action. Listing 31.1 shows the code for this action.

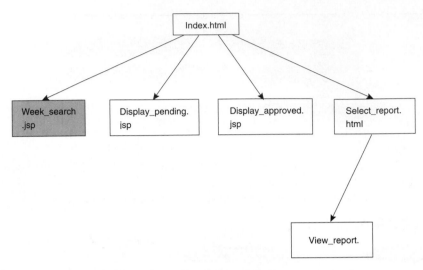

Figure 31.8   Flow diagram for time sheet reporting and display.

Listing 31.1 The ListAllPending action

```
public class ListPendingTimeSheetsAction extends Action {


    public ListPendingTimeSheetsAction() {

        super();

    }


    public ActionForward perform(

        ActionMapping mapping,

        ActionForm form,

        HttpServletRequest request,

        HttpServletResponse response)

        throws IOException, ServletException {
```

```
// Get actionprocess (model) and delegate
ActionForward forward = null;
try {

    TimeSheetActionProcessor processor =

        (TimeSheetActionProcessor)

        ActionProcessorFactory.getActionProcessor(

            "TimeSheet");

    TimeSheets sheets = processor.getPendingTimeSheets();

    if (sheets != null) {

        // Add ValueBean to request context

        // and forward response

        request.setAttribute(BeanKeys.PENDING, sheets);

        forward = mapping.findForward("success");

        if (forward == null) {

            forward = mapping.findForward("error");

        }

    } else

        forward = mapping.findForward("error");

} catch (MappingException e) {

    forward = mapping.findForward("error");

}

return forward;

    }

}
```

This sets the stage for a number of common struts mechanisms that are repeated throughout the code of our case study. First, Action obtains a reference to a TimeSheetActionProcessor. Then, it asks ActionProcessor to invoke a business method and obtains the result. If no exceptions were thrown and if the result is good, the result is placed on the Request and Action looks up the forward for the success page. If any errors resulted, it looks up the forward for the error page. Finally, it returns ActionForward.

If you examine the code for the ListApprovedTimeSheetsAction, you will find that the flow in it is virtually identical to the flow in this action—the only difference being the business method that is invoked on the Action processor.

The other portion of the diagram illustrates report generation. If you look at the code of the select_report HTML page, you'll see that the only report that has been implemented is the Employee by Month report. In that case, the URI used to invoke Action is /TimeApp/GenerateReport.do?primary=employee&secondary=month. The code for generating the report is shown in Listing 31.2.

Listing 31.2 Generating a report

```
public class GenerateReportAction extends Action {



    public GenerateReportAction() {

        super();

    }



    public ActionForward perform(

        ActionMapping mapping,

        ActionForm form,

        HttpServletRequest request,

        HttpServletResponse response)

        throws IOException, ServletException {



        // Obtain the ActionForm object
```

```
ReportForm dForm = (ReportForm) form;

Report report = null;

// Get action processor (model) and delegate

ReportActionProcessor processor =

        (ReportActionProcessor)

         ActionProcessorFactory.getActionProcessor(

                "Report");

try {

        if (dForm.isByEmployeeFirst() &&

                dForm.isByMonthSecond())

                report =

                    processor.generateEmployeeByMonthReport();

} catch (ModelException e) {

        ActionForward forward = mapping.findForward("error");

        return forward;

}

request.setAttribute(BeanKeys.REPORT, report);

ActionForward forward = mapping.findForward("success");

if (forward == null) {

        forward = mapping.findForward("error");

}

return forward;

    }

}
```

Again, notice the similarities to the previous example in that Action obtains a reference to a processor, invokes a business method, and sets the result on the request prior to obtaining a forward to return. The only difference in this example is that Action uses the information in the ReportForm to determine which business method to invoke (currently only generateEmployee-ByMonthReport is implemented, but it would be easy to add the other reports as needed).

31.1.4 Time Sheet Processing

This section of the case study is the most interactive and complicated of the entire case study. We will cover how to create, update, and approve time sheets by reviewing the implementations of the actions and JSPs. The flow diagram in Figure 31.9 is connected to the previous diagram through the week_search.jsp page. The darker lines on the flow diagram represent the path through the case study classes that we will examine. We'll begin with week_search.jsp and discuss design decisions that went into developing this part of the case study.

The first thing to consider is the design of the week_search JSP. If you refer to the picture of the week_search JSP (Figure 31.2) you'll see that it contains a form with two fields: a drop-down containing a list of employees and a text field for entering a week. Using a text field is a user interface decision that we need to examine. There are several ways to enter a date into an HTML form—but most are more complex than we want to consider for our case study. For instance, you could include a drop down of available dates, but the number of elements in the drop down would have to be quite large. If we wanted to enable entering time for any time within a year, it would contain 52 different week-ending dates.

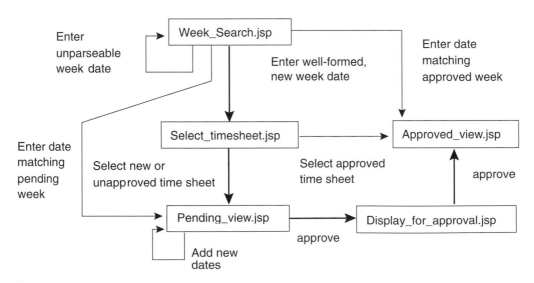

Figure 31.9 Time sheet entry and approval flow.

Another possibility would be to display a calendar, but since HTML does not have a calendar control, this could be a complicated feature requiring significant JavaScript development.[1] Instead, we'll stick with a simple text field, and then rely on Strut's validation logic to ensure that the date entered is a valid date in the right format. The form is submitted through the section from week_search.jsp shown in Listing 31.3.

Listing 31.3 Entering a date

```
<html:form action="EmployeeTimeSheet.do">

<TABLE WIDTH="75%" BORDER="0" BGCOLOR="#777999" CELLSPACING="0"

    CELLPADDING="1">

    <TBODY>

      <TR>

        <TD>

          <TABLE width="100%" border="0" bgcolor="#FFFFFF"

                   cellspacing="0"

                   cellpadding="3">

          <TBODY>

              <TR>

                <TD colspan="3" bgcolor="#009900" align="center">

                  <H1><B>Employee TimeSheet Search</B></H1>

                </TD>

              </TR>

              <TR>

                  <TD ALIGN="right"><B>Employee:</B></TD>

                  <TD><html:select property="submitterId">
```

---

1. Alternatively, you could buy a commercial JavaScript calendar.

```
                         <html:options collection="employees"

                                property="id"

                                labelProperty="name"></html:options>

                    </html:select></TD>

                    <TD> </TD>

          </TR>

          <TR>

               <TD ALIGN="right"><B>Week Ending:</B></TD>

               <TD><html:text property="weekending"/></TD>

               <TD ALIGN="left"><I>( mm/dd/yyyy )</I></TD>

          </TR>

          <TR>

             <TD> </TD>

             <TD><html:submit>Search</html:submit></TD>

             <TD> </TD>

          </TR>

                    </TBODY>

          </TABLE>

          </TD>

        </TR>

      </TBODY>

   </TABLE>

   </html:form>
```

In this JSP we use the Struts `html:options` tag to display the drop down of employees. The options tag iterates over the collection that has been placed in the session scope under the name employees. The Struts `html:select` tag places the selected option in the `submitterId` property of TimeSheetForm ActionForm. The list of Employees was earlier placed in the session by TimeSheetSearchAction, which retrieved the list from the TimeSheetProcessor. Likewise, the `html:text` tag places the date typed into the text field into the week-ending field of TimeSheet-Form. Struts will then handle the validation of that form when it is submitted by creating and populating an instance of TimeSheetForm, then running the form's `validate()`:

```
publicActionErrorsvalidate(ActionMappingmapping,HttpServletRequestreq){

    ActionErrors errors = new ActionErrors();



            if ((submitterId == null) || (submitterId.length() < 1))

                errors.add("submitter",new

                    ActionError("errors.missing.submitter"));

            if ((weekending == null) || (weekending.length() < 1))

                errors.add("weekending", new

                    ActionError("errors.missing.weekending"));

            Formatter fmt = Formatter.getDefaultFormatter();

            Calendar dt = fmt.convertToDate(weekending);

            if (dt == null)

                errors.add("weekendingformat", new

                    ActionError("errors.weekending.format"));

        return errors;

    }
```

If any errors are returned, the form will redisplay automatically, otherwise, the flow will proceed to the following method in EmployeeTimeSheetAction (Listing 31.4):

Listing 31.4 EmployeeTimeSheetAction

```
public ActionForward perform( ActionMapping mapping,

        ActionForm form,

        HttpServletRequest request,

        HttpServletResponse response)

        throws IOException, ServletException {



    // Look at the ActionForm object

    TimesheetForm tsForm = (TimesheetForm) form;

    ActionForward forward = null;

    String msg = null;

    if (tsForm != null) {

        // See if corresponding Timesheet exists

        TimeSheet timeSheet = null;

        try {

            TimeSheetActionProcessor processor =

                (TimeSheetActionProcessor)

                    ActionProcessorFactory.getActionProcessor(

                        "TimeSheet");

            timeSheet =

                processor.findTimeSheetByKey(

                    tsForm.getSubmitterId(),

                    tsForm.getWeekending());

            if (timeSheet != null) {
```

```
                        request.setAttribute("timesheet", timeSheet);

                        addProjectsBean(request);

                        if (timeSheet.isPending())

                                forward mapping.findForward("pending");

                        else

                                forward =

                                    mapping.findForward("approved");

                } else { // setup to list weekend dates for employee

                        WeekEndings weekendings =


                processor.getWeekEndings(tsForm.getSubmitterId());

                if (weekendings.getWeekEnding().length == 0 ) {

                        ArrayList calendars = new ArrayList();

                        Calendar weekend =

                            Formatter.convertToDate(

                             tsForm.getWeekending());

                        calendars.add(weekend);

                        weekendings=newWeekEndings(calendars);

                        }

                        request.setAttribute("weekendings",

                                weekendings);

                        Employee employee =

                                processor.findEmployeeByKey(

                                tsForm.getSubmitterId());
```

```
                        request.setAttribute("employee",

                            employee);

                        request.setAttribute("create",

                            tsForm.getWeekending());

                        forward=mapping.findForward("select");

                    }

            } catch (NoSuchEmployeeException e) {

                    // Handle this as a recoverable error (even


                    // (though the display shouldn't allow this)

                    ActionErrors errors = new ActionErrors();

                    ActionError err= new

                        ActionError("errors.no.such.employee");

                    errors.add("no such employee", err);

                    saveErrors(request,errors);

                    forward = mapping.findForward("tryagain");

            } catch (MappingException e) {

                    // Handle this as an unrecoverable error

                    AppService.log(TraceCapable.ERROR_LEVEL,

                        "Exception caught in" +

                        "EmployeeTimeSheetAction.perform:" + e);

                    forward = mapping.findForward("error");

            }

    }
```

```
        return forward;

}
```

This is by far the most complex controller we've examined. However, it also has the most to do. Aside from the error path back to the week_search JSP we just considered, the user can reach three possible destinations after submitting a week date in the form:

- If the date matches an existing time sheet in the pending state, the user is sent to the pending_view.jsp, which allows him to add or remove hours from the time sheet, or request approval.
- If the date matches an existing time sheet in the approved state, the user is sent to the approved_view.jsp.
- If the date does not match an existing time sheet, the user is sent to select_time-sheet.jsp, which allows him to either select an existing time sheet with a different date or create a time sheet.

The logic in this Action class has to handle all three cases, which, you will notice, rely not just on the input data, but on information retrieved from the domain model (the state of the time sheet) as well. That is the reason that this method has not just one, but three separate ActionForwards that it can return, not even counting the two error cases. It is worth studying this method well, since this is the kind of complexity that is typical of many Struts Action classes. Luckily, for our example, this is the high-water mark. None of the remaining paths is as complex as this.

In the most common case, what would happen next is that the date entered into week_search.jsp would be a week that doesn't correspond to an existing time sheet, and that the user would select the create link on the select_timesheet.jsp to create a time sheet. This leads the user to pending_view.jsp (Figure 31.3) where he can enter new hours against a project. Pressing the Add button on this form leads to the following perform method being executed in the UpdateTimesheet action.

```
public ActionForward perform(

        ActionMapping mapping,

        ActionForm form,

        HttpServletRequest request,

        HttpServletResponse response)

        throws IOException, ServletException {
```

```
// Look at the ActionForm object

UpdateTimesheetForm tsForm = (UpdateTimesheetForm) form;

// Build the command object

UpdateTimesheetFormCommand updateCommand = buildCommand(tsForm);

TimeSheet timeSheet = null;

try {

    TimeSheetActionProcessor processor =

    (TimeSheetActionProcessor)

            ActionProcessorFactory.getActionProcessor(

                "TimeSheet");

    timeSheet =

            processor.updateTimesheet(updateCommand);

} catch (Exception e) {

    AppService.log(TraceCapable.ERROR_LEVEL,"Exception caught in"


                + "TimeSheetSelectAction.perform:" + e);

    ActionForward forward = mapping.findForward("error");

    return forward;

}

addProjectsBean(request);

request.setAttribute("timesheet", timeSheet);

ActionForward forward = mapping.findForward("pending");

return forward;

}
```

This action is similar to the ones we've seen before in that it processes a form by reading information from the input data, but the slight difference here is in how the data is passed to TimesheetProcessor. As we covered in Chapter 30, the updateTimesheet() method uses the Command pattern to avoid the expense of constructing and passing an entire time sheet to TimesheetProcessor. The buildCommand method, shown next, constructs this object.

```
protected UpdateTimesheetFormCommand buildCommand(

    UpdateTimesheetForm tsForm) {

UpdateTimesheetFormCommandupdateCommand=newUpdateTimesheetFormCommand();

    updateCommand.setAddDate(tsForm.getAddDate());

    updateCommand.setAddHours(tsForm.getAddHours());

    updateCommand.setAddProjectId(tsForm.getAddProjectId());

    updateCommand.setEmployeeId(tsForm.getSubmitterId());

    updateCommand.setWeekending(tsForm.getWeekending());

    updateCommand.setRemoveEntryId(tsForm.getRemoveEntryId());

    return updateCommand;

}
```

Since it uses a command, the action does not need any special logic to handle adding and removing a time sheet differently. In both cases, if the processing was successful, it simply returns the user to pending_view.jsp. Finally, if the user clicks the approve link, the display_for_approval.jsp (Figure 31.4) page is shown. If the user selects the approving employee (presumably not the same person as the employee submitting the time sheet) from the list, then presses the approve button, the following code is executed in the ApproveTimeSheet action:

```
public ActionForward perform(

    ActionMapping mapping,

    ActionForm form,

    HttpServletRequest request,

    HttpServletResponse response)

    throws IOException, ServletException {
```

```
ApprovingTimesheetForm tsForm = (ApprovingTimesheetForm) form;

TimeSheet timeSheet = null;

// invoke approve behavior on Model

TimeSheetActionProcessor processor =

(TimeSheetActionProcessor)ActionProcessorFactory.getActionProcessor(

          "TimeSheet");


try {

   timeSheet =

       processor.approveTimeSheetByKey(tsForm.getSubmitterId(),

              tsForm.getWeekending(), tsForm.getApproverId());

} catch (Exception e) {

      AppService.log(TraceCapable.ERROR_LEVEL,"Exception caught in"


                         + "ApproveTimeSheetAction.perform:" + e);

      ActionForward forward = mapping.findForward("error");

      return forward;

}

request.setAttribute("timesheet", timeSheet);

ActionForward forward = mapping.findForward("approved");

return forward;


}
```

As you can see, there's nothing new here. This action simply invokes the `approveTimeSheet-ByKey` method in TimesheetProcessor and then forwards the user to approved_view.jsp if the method execution is successful. At this point, we've completed our set of use cases and finished our look at the case study Struts implementation.

31.2 Summary

In this chapter, you've examined the Struts implementation of the time sheet case study application and examined how it uses the mechanisms provided by Struts (the html tag library, Action-Forms, and Actions) and also how it uses the methods provided by the TimesheetProcessor business delegate we discussed in Chapter 30. We are now finished with our examination of the different parts of J2EE 1.3 and how J2EE applications are developed in WebSphere.

In the next two chapters, we'll begin looking forward past the current implementation of the J2EE standard and examine how WAS provides support for Web services, which will be a key part of the J2EE 1.4 specification.

An Introduction to J2EE Web Services for WebSphere

Web services promise to revolutionize the Internet by enabling integration of requests for services across a number of vendors. However, achieving this promise will not be without challenge. Web services are defined by a number of different specifications. This implementation of these specifications varies depending on the vendor and version of the application server, including WAS. There is also significant variability across the tools supporting the development, deployment, and use of Web services including WSAD tools. The result is a conglomeration of technology that can often confuse and overwhelm the software developer.

Amid all the confusion, we may forget to ask ourselves the more fundamental question: When is it appropriate to use Web services? Applying technology for technology's sake, because it's the latest buzz word, is a recipe for disaster.

The following chapters will help the developer and technical manager through this maze of specifications and technology and provide an overview of Web services relative to the J2EE environment, and specifically, how it is implemented within the WAS runtime. Chapter 33 will provide a hands-on example that uses the tools included with WAS and WSAD that aid the developer in creating and deploying Web services. Chapter 34 will extend the example and conclude with a discussion of the best practices to employ when implementing a solution that utilizes Web services.

32.1 If Web Services Is the Solution, What's the Problem?

We know from reading all trade journals, conference agendas, and marketing material that Web services *is* the solution to all our problems. Of course, by now we've got a loaded six-gun filled with silver bullets—OOP, CORBA, EJBs, etc.—and our problems are still around. IT professionals realize that technology in and of itself does not solve problems. It is the application of technology, used in its proper context, which facilitates the construction of robust systems that solve real business problems. In other words: Use the right tool for the right job. When talking about Web services, that job is application integration.

32.1.1 The Integration Problem

Application integration is a problem that has been around for a long time. Today's companies are looking for solutions that help effectively manage the changing business environment. Companies looking for ways to preserve the value of existing software assets because the cost and time involved in recreating them in the latest and greatest programming language is prohibitive. IT executives must manage budget decreases, forcing an even more careful evaluation of build-versus-buy decisions, with the trend being to find ready-made parts to snap into the development process.

As companies merge and form alliances with strategic partners, disparate information systems must be integrated to form a synergistic business process to provide a comprehensive solution. And throughout all of this turbulence, executives are demanding that IT managers reduce the cost of creating, maintaining, and deploying applications!

To help companies find a solution to these problems, an industry has evolved around IT. In the last decade, there has been tremendous growth in this industry and the success of companies such as Crossworlds (now part of IBM) that specialize in integration, and products like IBM's MQSeries Integrator, are evidence of the vibrancy of this industry. It is business, not technology, that is driving the application integration market. And it is business, not technology, that has driven the creation of Web services.

32.1.2 The Rise of Web Services

Despite its meteoric rise, Web services did not appear overnight. It is the result of the convergence of trends in both application architecture and business needs. As people began to assemble large-scale solutions, they realized that many of the same lessons learned from creating robust software could be applied when integrating these applications. Many of these lessons became embodied in patterns, like those described by the Gang of Four,[1] while others became established as best practices. However expressed, there were two patterns that kept recurring.

- Most fundamental is that distinct behavior should be isolated. In OO languages, when each class has a well-defined set of responsibilities, the result is an object model that has a cleanly factored set of interfaces. Adaptation to new business requirements results in minimal impact to existing classes, reducing the cost of development and testing.
- There should be a layer of indirection in place when establishing a reference to an object. There are several techniques used to accomplish this, many of them covered in the Creational Patterns section in the Design Patterns book [Gamma].

These patterns are reflected in the EJB component model. For example, a typical J2EE implementation is for business models to be expressed as a collection of stateless session EJBs,

---

1.   Design Patterns, Elements of Reusable Software, [Gamma]

with their state persisted using an associated set of container managed EJBs. By using the implementation JNDI provided with the WAS, along with EJB homes, application developers can properly isolate business logic as a separate tier within an application.

However, the underlying themes that these patterns address are how applications should be coupled. Previous chapters presented in detail how to build a properly layered enterprise application. The goal with Web services is to present a well-described unified logical view into the business layer of the application.

32.1.3 A Shared Understanding: Why XML?

One step in solving the integration problem is to establish a universal way to represent structured data. The industry agreed upon XML primarily for two reasons: (1) XML is a simple, text-based mechanism that allows data to be exchanged between systems in a string format; (2) XML embraces the notion of metainformation. XML documents often conform to a XML Schema definition (XSD). This XML Schema provides a means to define the structure, content, and semantics of an XML document. In this regard it plays a role very similar to a Java class in that it governs the structure of its instances. In fact, XML documents that conform to a schema are said to be instance documents.

The use of XML Schema in this manner allows the validation of data to be represented external of any programming language and platform. For example, a schema can declare that its instance documents will have a tag called `id`, that it is a `positiveInteger`, and that it must be present in the document. When this instance document is received, the XML parser uses the schema as a means to validate it without the need to invoke application logic. However, this does not eliminate the need for application validation logic. For example, a schema cannot do dependence validation; that is, if the value of Element A is 100, then Element B must be either X or Y.

A second advantage to using XML is namespaces. A common problem is that names are frequently repeated; e.g., `id`. However, there could be many different uses of `id`. In some systems, this could be an integer, in others, it is a string. Namespaces provide an elegant solution to this problem. Using Java again as a reference, an XML namespace is like a Java package in that it fully qualifies elements. Therefore, within one instance document two elements may have an identical name only if they are uniquely qualified by different namespaces.

32.1.4 What Is a Web Service?

To this point, we've described the business rationale for Web services: application integration. We've also described technical issues with existing integration techniques and distributed computing solutions. But what exactly is a Web service and how does it address these problems? Here is the formal definition provided in IBM's paper defining the conceptual architecture of Web services.

DEFINING WEB SERVICES

"A Web service is an interface that describes a collection of operations that are network accessible through standardized XML messaging. Web services fulfill a specific task of a set of tasks. A Web service is described using a standard, formal XML notion, called its service description, that provides all of the details necessary to interact with the service, including message formats (that detail the operation), transport protocols, and location."[2]

It is these basic properties that give Web services the flexibility to be an effective enterprise integration solution. Businesses experience a direct benefit in adopting Web services because it formalizes the separation of interface, implementation, *and* transport protocol. Thus, rates of change can be effectively managed by allowing the service API to remain constant while the underlying network location and implementation change.

32.2 Web Services Architecture

In order to achieve integration across heterogeneous environments, vendors must agree upon how to invoke, describe, and locate services. Traditionally, these have been some of the most difficult problems that architects of distributed systems have had to solve. This section explains how the Web services community has defined a collection of specifications that address each of these concerns, and then brings them together to form a Services-Oriented Architecture (SOA).

32.2.1 The Role of SOAP (Simple Object Access Protocol)

SOAP provides an industry standard mechanism for XML-based messaging. Because SOAP is XML-based, it is by nature programming language and platform neutral. SOAP was designed to be lightweight and flexible. The specification defines an enveloping structure that contains the business information which is conveyed as an XML string. Initial implementations of SOAP favored encoding business data in a format that was suitable to an RPC style of computing. SOAP also supports a document-centric style of message exchange. Often referred to as the document-literal, this is now the preferred style for business data transferred within a SOAP message.

SOAP also has provisions for message headers and faults. Headers represent information that is orthogonal to the business content of the message; for example, security or transaction information. The fault mechanism described by the specification allows for the identification of the source of the error and provides the ability to return meaningful structured diagnostic information. Because of these features, SOAP has emerged as the de facto standard for XML messaging and Web services.

---

2.   *http://www.ibm.com/software/solutions/webservices/pdf/WSCA.pdf*; pg.6.

32.2.2 The Role of the Web Services Description Language (WSDL)

WSDL is the standard, formal XML notion that is referred to in IBM's definition of Web services. In many aspects, WSDL can be compared to other IDLs, in that its primary responsibility is to describe an interface.

However, WSDL has unique qualities and capabilities that make it an extremely flexible and powerful tool. Because WSDL is based upon XML, instance documents can be validated against a schema as well as leverage the flexibility of namespaces. Also, description documents are easily readable by a wide variety of nonspecialized tools. WSDL documents can also be separated into distinct sections that isolate the argument types, the operational interface, the message encoding and transport format, and the service location. In fact, the complete service description need not be contained in a single physical document. Rather, each section can exist independently as a unique file. At runtime, multiple physical documents can be combined into one single logical interface definition.

A key aspect of constructing well-factored, robust, scalable applications is properly isolating the responsibilities of each application layer, then exposing it through a well-defined façade. When these interfaces are exposed as services, WSDL is the mechanism in which they are described.

32.2.3 UDDI and the Problem of Service Location

From the aspect of building distributed applications, two of the fundamental concerns—message protocol and description—have been addressed with SOAP and WSDL. Distributed systems also have a registry that provides a standard mechanism of locating remote object references. For example, Java provides JNDI, which we used earlier to get a reference to our EJBs. To locate services in a heterogeneous environment, there needs to be a mechanism that facilitates the browsing and querying of service descriptions.

As Web services began to gain popularity, vendors such as IBM and Microsoft began working together to develop an industry—standard way to locate a service. The result was a global registry, based upon the standard Universal Description Discovery and Integration[3] specification. UDDI, as this registry is typically called, is collection of replicated nodes that are operated by Web services providers such as IBM, Microsoft, and SAP. The goal of UDDI is to benefit "businesses of all sizes by creating a global, platform-independent, open architecture for describing businesses and services, discovering those businesses and services, and integrating businesses using the Internet."[4] UDDI allows businesses to classify themselves and the services they offer based upon well-established categorization schemes; e.g., the North American Industry Classification System (NAICS) or the Universal Standard Products and Services Classification (UNPSC). Currently, the operators of the major UDDI nodes do not charge for business to use the registry.

---

3.   For detailed information regarding UDDI, please see *http://www.uddi.org.*

4.   *http://www.uddi.org/faqs.html#who.*

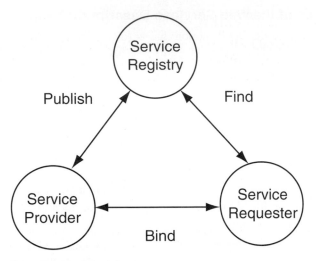

Figure 32.1 The Services-Oriented Architecture.

32.2.4 Putting It All Together: The Service-Oriented Architecture

SOAP, WSDL, and UDDI are the building blocks for the Web services architecture by providing industry-standard mechanisms that address the issues of message protocol, description, and discovery. Together, these technologies form the basis of SOA. Figure 32.1 is the most widely used picture of a SOA as it illustrates the basic interactions of the primary actors.

The interaction works as follows: Service providers describe their business function using WSDL and publish it to the service registry; e.g., UDDI. A service requestor can query the registry in order to find a service that meets its requirements. Once found, the service requestor can examine the description and bind to the service in order to invoke the methods expressed in the WSDL. By incorporating the service registry, service requestors are able to gain access to the services of the service provider from anywhere in the network, using whatever protocol is appropriate.

IBM considers anything to be a Web service whose interface can be fully described in WSDL. This encompasses the more limited definitions (requiring SOAP and even HTTP) that Microsoft and Sun hew to, but it also encompasses the ability to use JMS over MQSeries as a transport layer, or even to choose JCA (the J2EE Connector Architecture) as a Web services implementation as we have done in WSAD-IE.

The conclusion to draw from this definition is that an SOA is a superset of other distributed computing approaches; thus, Web services can fully encompass the J2EE distributed computing approaches as well as the emerging ones that focus more tightly on SOAP and HTTP. This means that we can not only base our Web services technology on existing J2EE infrastructures, but we can also draw from our existing J2EE best practices and apply them within an SOA context. So, while in effect, every distributed service in J2EE is a service in the broadest definition, architectural prudence has taught us that there are still places under which you would not want to use specific Web services technologies and design principles.

32.3   Web Services in J2EE

Given the road map outlined by the SOA, it is possible to map how this architecture should be supported relative to the J2EE platform. To describe this mapping, the JCP introduced two standards—JAX-RPC (JSR-101) and JSR-109—that represent the core infrastructure of J2EE based-Web services.

The JAX-RPC specification identifies the client and server programming model for J2EE based-Web services. In addition, is also defines the Java-to-WSDL type mappings. The *JAX-RPC* specification defines the core APIs, as well as mappings from XML/WSDL to Java and Java to XML/WSDL. It is this specification that defines how tools take a Java interface and produce a WSDL document. Likewise, a WSDL document can be converted into a set of Java classes that can, in turn, be used to invoke a service specified by the WSDL document.

The Web Services for J2EE (JSR-109) specification complements JAX-RPC by extending the programming model into the J2EE environment. JSR 109 defines how J2EE services are to be deployed into the runtime environment. This includes refinement of the client and server programming models, the deployment model, handler support, and WSDL publication rules.

Figure 33.2 illustrates the relationships between the specifications that comprise the J2EE Web services environment.[5]

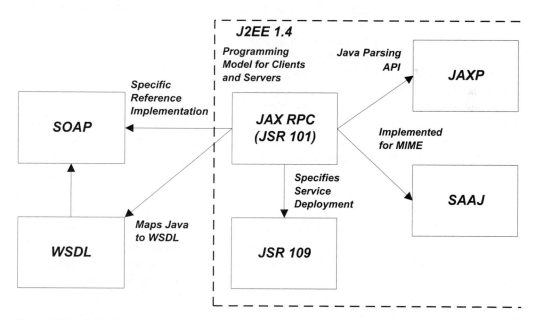

Figure 32.2 Relationship between Java and Web services specifications.

---

5.   Note that although JAX-RPC and JSR 109 are supported by WAS 5.0.2, they are not officially part of J2EE until release 1.4. Likewise, JAXP and SAAJ are presented here for completeness.

32.4   Web Services in WAS

WAS 5.0.2 supports an optimized Web services runtime based architecturally on Apache AXIS. This allows for the definition of handlers for the orthogonal extension of the engine's runtime behavior. Also provided with WAS 5.0.2 is an open source version of the Web Services Invocation Framework (WSIF). WSIF provides for the calling of Web services based upon the WSDL document.

In addition to the runtime engine, WebSphere 5.0.2 provides the Web Services Gateway and an implementation of UDDI. As its name implies, the Web Services Gateway acts as a proxy between external services that should be made available to internal business applications, as well as your services that must be exposed outside the firewall. In addition, the Gateway can use WSDL to map from one transport to another and provide a single point of control for access and validation of service requests. The UDDI component of WebSphere is a fully functional Web services registry. Companies may use this to host their own private UDDI as a mechanism to classify their own internally developed services.

32.5   The Standardization Nightmare

The rapid success of Web services resulted in the creation of a collection of specifications each tailored to a particular problem. For example, SOAP addressed the need for a standard XML messaging, while WSDL addressed service description. UDDI was defined to help solve the location and discovery process. JAX-RPC and JSR-109 were developed so Web services could become first class constructs in the J2EE platform. In addition, there is a host of other nonstandard specifications—commonly referred to as the WS-* specifications—such as WS-Security, WS-Transaction, and WS-Secure Conversation.

The problem with all of these specifications is not in their number, but rather that they are managed by different organizations, and sometimes, as in the case of the WS-* specifications, no organization at all. For example, of the five non-WS-* specifications listed earlier, there are multiple governing bodies: W3C (SOAP, WSDL), OASIS (UDDI), JCP (JAX-RPC, JSR 109).

The amount of functionality that is becoming available for Web services shows no sign of slowing. For the architect and developer, this results in even more specifications to understand and manage. Fortunately, the industry has responded with the formation of the Web Services Interoperability Organization, or WS-I. The goal of this organization is to promote the adoption of Web services by working "across the industry and standards organizations to respond to customer needs by providing guidance, best practices, and resources for developing Web services solutions." [6]

---

6.   The WS-I home page—*http://ws-i.org*.

32.6 Summary

Application integration remains a difficult and expensive problem. Although maturing at a rapid pace, Web services is to date, industry's best attempt at providing a comprehensive solution based upon open standards. However, in order to fully understand how Web services work, it is necessary to build several examples. The next chapter continues the discussion by walking you through the steps to construct a J2EE Web service.

Constructing J2EE Web Services for WebSphere

In this chapter, we will build an example Web service from the RandomIDGenerator EJB. In addition to providing a running solution, this example will be the basis for explaining WSDL as well as SOAP. The goal of this first example is to break down implementing Web services into the most basic steps. We'll then use this example to illustrate how the tools provided by WebSphere generate artifacts compliant with the various specifications. This first example exposes the simple session bean introduced in Chapter 20 as a Web service. In Chapter 34, we will enable the reporting feature of the time sheet application, as well as discuss some best practices for Web services.

In a J2EE environment, the programming model is often session EJBs. Web services, as an extension to this model, are an alternate way of providing access to these EJBs. This subtle, but important, point is reflected in how the J2EE specifications and common best practices help guide vendors in the construction of productivity tools that aid developers in the creation of Web services.

Since this is the first time we've examined Web services within our architectural road map (Figure 33.1), you may be wondering why we chose to place them in the presentation layer. In identifying the design patterns and design approaches that should be taken for Web services, it has become apparent that many of the decisions that you must make when designing a Web service are the same that you must make when designing an MVC architecture for a user interface. In particular:

- Web services should be large-grained. Each business service should return a functionally complete set of semantically related information. This is similar to a user interface, where each page of an interface to the user should present as much information as the particular interface technology is capable of conveying. In other words, just as good interfaces are information-rich (but not overwhelming) good business services should also be information-rich so as to convey to the Web services

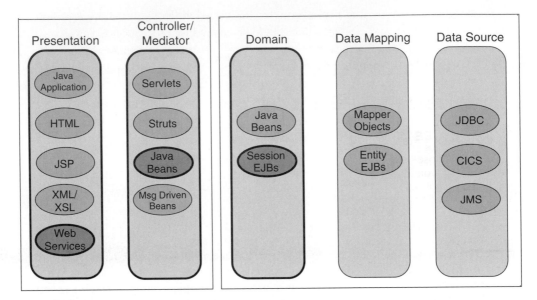

Figure 33.1 Architectural road map.

requestor enough information to make a valid and informed business decision. The reason here is not that a person can only comprehend so much information at a time, but that a Web service is limited most fundamentally by the overhead of the protocol over which the information is conveyed. Usually the speed of XML parsing and the transmission speed of a large XML document over an HTTP connection are the limiting factors.

• Web services implement the same patterns used in building controller and mediator layers (the Adapter pattern and the Façade pattern). The Adapter pattern [Gamma] describes how to transform one API into another. In user interfaces, this occurs when the business objects are rendered as HTML, or where string parameters are converted into business object representations so that they can be operated upon in the domain object layer. This problem also occurs in building Web services. In Web services we must be able to convert from the schema of the XML that it presents to the outside world to the internal data models used by the internal components that it wraps. Part of this conversion may include aggregating the results of several different functional calls into lower level components into a single composite object, or hiding the dependencies between two lower level objects, which, as we have seen, is the reason for the Façade pattern.

There is one major difference: Presentations are inherently synchronous; Web services are not. Many Web services may be synchronous, but that this is not true all of the time. In any case, designing for asynchronicity is something that most developers are not comfortable with. Asynchronous design has its own unique set of patterns (described in [Hohpe]) that must be applied, regardless of the kind of design patterns that should be applied for other service aspects.

As a result of these similarities in construction and intent, we've decided the best place to show where Web services apply to be the presentation layer of an application. In any case, the domain layer (and other layers below it) should be unaffected by the presence or absence of a Web service, since it presents only an alternate interface to your business logic.

WHY USE EJBS FOR WEB SERVICES

Those of you familiar with the JAX-RPC and JSR-109 specifications may be wondering why we are insisting on using EJBs as the implementation vehicles of our Web services rather than JavaBeans (which, according to these specifications, may be implemented as Web services). The reason is simple— Security. In Chapter 29 we examined how EJBs can have each method separately secured to a different set of J2EE roles. This is not possible with JavaBeans. Since Web services are by their nature Remote services, the inability to adequately secure JavaBean methods makes them unattractive for many services. Also (as we will see in Chapter 34), there are very good reasons for choosing to use EJBs rather than JavaBeans when you are considering making your service available over multiple protocols.

33.1 Getting Started with Web Services

This first example will be the functional equivalent of the famous *Hello World!* and the now infamous *Stock Quote!* There are two parts of this example: the creation of the service that will run inside of WebSphere and two clients that will be used to invoke its behavior.

We'll start by creating a specialized Java interface for our session bean. This is the *service endpoint interface (SEI),* which conforms to the rules outlined in JAX-RPC. Once completed, a command line tool (Java2WSDL) will be used to create a WSDL document that another command line tool (WSDL2Java) needs to generate the corresponding JSR-109 deployment artifacts. These tools are provided with WebSphere 5.0.2 and are located in the bin directory; e.g., C:\WebSphere\AppServer\bin.

Once generated, these files will be packaged as part of an enterprise application. The final step prior to deployment is to add the code to handle HTTP requests. This is done through the endptEnabler command line tool. Finally, we'll walk through the deployment steps for the WAS. The result will be our session bean exposed as a Web service running inside of the WAS.

33.1.1 Creating the Service Endpoint Interface

An SEI is the Java description of what methods will be exposed when the WSDL is created. Since Web services are simply a technique of exposing domain objects, one way to create an SEI is to copy an existing interface. This chapter's example uses an existing EJB stateless session bean interface, with some minor changes required to ensure compliance with JAX-RPC (Section 5.2), as the SEI. However, this does not imply that there is a one-to-one mapping between every stateless session bean and a Web service. Care must be taken to determine the right interface to your application.

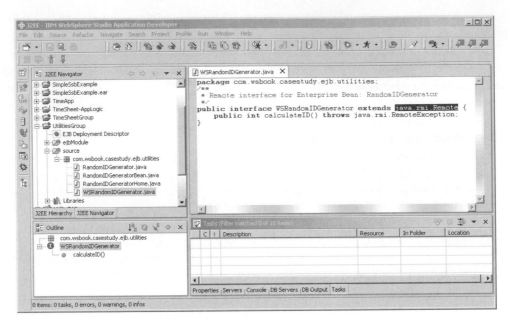

Figure 33.2 The service endpoint interface.

For our simple example, we will work with the random ID generator from the utilities group created in Chapter 20. In the J2EE Navigator, copy the interface *com.wsbook.case-study.ejb.utilities.RandomIDGenerator.java* to *com.wsbook.casestudy.ejb.utilities.WSRandom-IDGenerator.java*. When finished, there will be two interfaces in the package. Open up the newly copied interface in a Java editor (Figure 33.2).

One change needs to be made because the interface can no longer extend *javax.ejb.EJB-Object*; JAX-RPC does not allow methods that have a parameter of *java.lang.Object*. After changing the parent interface, the declaration should be as follows:

```
public interface WSRandomIDGenerator extends java.rmi.Remote
```

33.1.2 Using WSDL to Express the Service Description

An important aspect of IDLs (Interface Definition Language) is that they separate the concerns of distributed computing. In distributed computing solutions where there are heterogeneous consumers of objects, IDLs are critical because they provide a description of the interface as the programming model, and thus make it possible to keep separate the actual implementation. For distributed systems to work, three pieces of information are necessary:

1. The interface of the remote object to be invoked
2. A wire format for the data, or the encoding scheme of the data
3. The location of the object

Web services is about distributed computing, these three responsibilities are facilitated by the WSDL.

The next step in our example is to create a WSDL file based upon the SEI. To build the necessary constructs for our Web service, we will be using a combination of WSAD 5.0 and the command line. This is because as of this writing, the JAX-RPC rules have not been completely integrated into WSAD 5.0. Since we will be moving between two tools, it is recommended that you change to the ejbModule directory underneath the project in your WSAD workspace. This allows the code to be generated by the command line tools in the proper place relative to WSAD. The tool to use for creating the WSDL file is Java2WSDL, which will generate a Web services description compliant with the rules outlined in Section 5 of the JAX-RPC specification. Because this is a command line tool, the Java classpath must contain references to the j2ee.jar file. Once the classpath has been set, from the command line invoke Java2WSDL.

```
Java2WSDL -verbose -implClass

com.wsbook.casestudy.ejb.utilities.RandomIDGeneratorBean

com.wsbook.casestudy.ejb.utilities.WSRandomIDGenerator

-output .\META-INF\wsdl\WSRandomIDGenerator.wsdl
```

The output of Java2WSDL is shown here—

```
WSWS3004W: Warning: The -location was not set, the value

"file:undefined_location" is used instead.

WSWS3010I: Info: Generating portType {http://

utilities.ejb.casestudy.wsbook.com}WSRandomIDGenerator

WSWS3010I: Info: Generating message {http://

utilities.ejb.casestudy.wsbook.com}calculateIDRequest

WSWS3010I: Info: Generating message {http://

utilities.ejb.casestudy.wsbook.com}calculateIDResponse

WSWS3010I: Info: Generating binding {http://

utilities.ejb.casestudy.wsbook.com}WSRandomIDGeneratorSoapBinding
```

```
WSWS3010I: Info: Generating service {http://

utilities.ejb.casestudy.wsbook.com}WSRandomIDGeneratorService

WSWS3010I: Info: Generating port WSRandomIDGenerator
```

Before examining the WSDL output, let's look at the information the Java2WSDL command used to generate the file. Java2WSDL was invoked with three arguments: the implementation class, which was specified by –implClass; the SEI; and an output location, specified by the output option.

The implementation class is an optional argument that allows the tool to generate a more customer-friendly WSDL. There is one caveat. The class must be compiled with debug information (javac –g) because classes, unlike interfaces, carry the complete message signature when compiled for debug. Without the implementation class, the Java2WSDL tool would not have sufficient information to generate WSDL parts that match the method signatures. Instead, default part names would be used, resulting in a less readable, although technically accurate, WSDL document. Thus, the only requirement placed on this class is that the message signatures match those of the SEI. It is not necessary for the class to implement the interface. Fortunately, classes are compiled with the debug information by default when using WSAD.

The second parameter is the SEI (`com.wsbook.casestudy.ejb.utilities.WSRandomIDGenerator`) that we created in the first step.

The last parameter is an output location and file name. Because we are using an EJB and will ultimately be deploying an EAR file, the WSDL file will need to be inside the META-INF directory. We entered it directly from the command line.

The Java2WSDL tool analyzes the SEI and generates a corresponding WSDL document. The WSDL in Listing 33.1 was generated based on the public method inside WSRandomIDGenerator, `calculateID()`.

Listing 33.1 WSDL generated based on calculateID()

```
<?xml version="1.0" encoding="UTF-8"?>

<wsdl:definitions targetNamespace="http://

utilities.ejb.casestudy.wsbook.com" xmlns="http://schemas.xmlsoap.org/wsdl/"

xmlns:apachesoap="http://xml.apache.org/xml-soap" xmlns:impl="http://

utilities.ejb.casestudy.wsbook.com" xmlns:intf="http://

utilities.ejb.casestudy.wsbook.com" xmlns:soapenc="http://

schemas.xmlsoap.org/soap/encoding" xmlns:wsdl="http://schemas.xmlsoap.org/
```

```
wsdl/" xmlns:wsdlsoap="http://schemas.xmlsoap.org/wsdl/soap/"

xmlns:xsd="http://www.w3.org/2001/XMLSchema">

 <wsdl:types/>

   <wsdl:message name="calculateIDResponse">

     <wsdl:part name="calculateIDReturn" type="xsd:int"/>

   </wsdl:message>

   <wsdl:message name="calculateIDRequest">

   </wsdl:message>

   <wsdl:portType name="WSRandomIDGenerator">

     <wsdl:operation name="calculateID">

       <wsdl:input message="intf:calculateIDRequest"

    name="calculateIDRequest"/>

       <wsdl:output message="intf:calculateIDResponse"

    name="calculateIDResponse"/>

     </wsdl:operation>

   </wsdl:portType>

   <wsdl:binding name="WSRandomIDGeneratorSoapBinding"

      type="intf:WSRandomIDGenerator">

     <wsdlsoap:binding style="rpc"

      transport="http://schemas.xmlsoap.org/soap/http"/>

     <wsdl:operation name="calculateID">

       <wsdlsoap:operation soapAction=""/>

       <wsdl:input name="calculateIDRequest">
```

```
        <wsdlsoap:body

    encodingStyle="http://schemas.xmlsoap.org/soap/encoding/"

    namespace="http://utilities.ejb.casestudy.wsbook.com" use="encoded"/>

        </wsdl:input>

        <wsdl:output name="calculateIDResponse">

            <wsdlsoap:body

    encodingStyle="http://schemas.xmlsoap.org/soap/encoding/"

    namespace="http://utilities.ejb.casestudy.wsbook.com" use="encoded"/>

        </wsdl:output>

    </wsdl:operation>

  </wsdl:binding>

  <wsdl:service name="WSRandomIDGeneratorService">

    <wsdl:port binding="intf:WSRandomIDGeneratorSoapBinding"

     name="WSRandomIDGenerator">

        <wsdlsoap:address location="file:undefined_location"/>

    </wsdl:port>

  </wsdl:service>

</wsdl:definitions>
```

33.1.3 Understanding WSDL

WSDL is an XML document that can easily be broken down into these three main sections: (1) the interface is represented by the portType WSDL element, (2) the wire format by the binding element, and (3) the location by the port element.

In fact, the complete description of a service need not reside in a single file. WSDL provides a mechanism to import other documents. This allows a single logical WSDL document to be comprised of multiple physical files. This layering of WSDL into distinct sections—from the interface, to the binding, and, ultimately, the location, as expressed in the port element—is a key feature of WSDL and Web services in general as it facilitates multiple implementations sharing a common interface. Specifically, it is possible for two services to reference the same WSDL interface and binding, but provide their own port, which specifies a different location. Also, it is possible to further abstract the `portType` by separating the type element into a separate document.

Because the description is simply an XML document, it is important that each element be properly qualified. Java2WSDL will automatically generate the target namespace based upon the package name of the SEI, `http://utilities.ejb.casestudy.wsbook.com`. When designing and understanding software systems, it is often helpful to start by thinking about the function they need to support.

Understanding WSDL is no different, so let's start with the interface, or the `portType`, which represents the interface of the Web service. Like almost all WSDL elements, a `portType` is a composite of smaller pieces. In this case, operations (the logical equivalent of method signatures) are the smaller pieces that are combined to form the complete interface. Although a WSDL document may contain any number of `portTypes`, the typical practice is for them to contain only one.

```
<wsdl:portType name="WSRandomIDGenerator">

    <wsdl:operation name="calculateID">

      <wsdl:input name="calculateIDRequest"

        message="intf:calculateIDRequest"/>

      <wsdl:output name="calculateIDResponse"

        message="intf:calculateIDResponse"/>

    </wsdl:operation>

</wsdl:portType>
```

Every element inside of a WSDL document is named, and this `portType` is called WSRandomIDGenerator, which was derived from the name of the SEI. The easiest way to conceptualize an operation element is to think of it as a Java method. The input element represents the parameters, and the output element the return value. More complex WSDL documents would also define one or more fault elements used for handling exceptional conditions. Each public method in the SEI is translated into a WSDL operation. Since WSRandomIDGenerator contains only one method, there is only one corresponding operation element. The element name is generated using the name of the method, `"calculateID"`.

The method signature is then broken down into WSDL messages. The messages contain optional part elements that represent the actual parameter. The `calculateID()` method takes no arguments and returns an integer. Therefore, the message used as the input for the operation, "calculateIDRequest" does not contain a part. Likewise, the message used as the response "calculateIDResponse" contains a single part that is typed to an integer.

```
<wsdl:message name="calculateIDRequest">

    </wsdl:message>

<wsdl:message name="calculateIDResponse">

    <wsdl:part name="calculateIDReturn" type="xsd:int"/>

</wsdl:message>
```

The final section of the WSDL that relates to the `portType` is the type element. This is where complex types, if any, would be mapped to XML according to the JAX-RPC rules. There is a fairly straightforward mapping between types defined by XML schema and Java primitives. Since `calculateID()` returns a simple type, no additional mapping is necessary and the type section is empty. Chapter 34 contains an example of a WSDL that maps a complex type for the reporting Web service.

What has been covered in the WSDL document thus far has been the protocol and location-independent interface. In order to deploy a Web service so it can be accessed by clients, it is necessary to specify the particular protocols the Web service implementation supports, and where the service can be located. The WSDL binding element brings together the interface and the implementation. It is the binding element (Listing 33.2) that tells us how a particular interface is to be encoded onto the wire and what protocol is to be used.

Listing 33.2 The WSDL binding element

```
<wsdl:binding name="WSRandomIDGeneratorSoapBinding"

            type="intf:WSRandomIDGenerator">

  <wsdlsoap:binding style="rpc"

      transport="http://schemas.xmlsoap.org/soap/http"/>

    <wsdl:operation name="calculateID">

      <wsdlsoap:operation soapAction=""/>

      <wsdl:input name="calculateIDRequest">

        <wsdlsoap:body use="encoded"

      encodingStyle=http://schemas.xmlsoap.org/soap/encoding/
```

```
namespace="http://utilities.ejb.casestudy.wsbook.com"/>

      </wsdl:input>

      <wsdl:output name="calculateIDResponse">

       <wsdlsoap:body use="encoded"

encodingStyle=http://schemas.xmlsoap.org/soap/encoding/

namespace="http://utilities.ejb.casestudy.wsbook.com"/>

      </wsdl:output>

    </wsdl:operation>

</wsdl:binding>
```

The first part of the binding element provides its name, `"WSRandomIDGeneratorSoap-Binding"`, as well as a type, `"intf:WSRandomIDGenerator"`. Therefore, the binding declares the encoding and transport information for the service that conforms to the WSRandomIDGenerator interface, or `portType`.

In order to facilitate multiple encoding schemes and styles of invoking behavior, WSDL supports extensibility elements. Rather than embed information about the SOAP encoding and HTTP transport directly into WSDL, extensibility elements are leveraged. Therefore, SOAP is said to extend WSDL. This is an incredibly flexible and powerful approach, as the number of extensions is independent of WSDL itself.

In the binding in Listing 33.2, the `"wsdlsoap"` namespace prefix indicates that this is a SOAP extension. The style attribute is set to `"rpc"`, which indicates that parameters will map to XML elements in the SOAP body. An alternate style, document, is also supported. Document style assembles method parameters into *one or more* XML elements. To generate WSDL that uses the document style, rerun JAVA2wsdl with the `style` option. The transport value of *http://schemas.xmlsoap.org/soap/http* indicates that the transport is HTTP.

Each operation in the port type must be *bound* with a specific encoding and any other protocol specific information. This example indicates through the `use="encoded"` and the `encoding-Style=http://schemas.xmlsoap.org/soap/encoding/`optionsthattheinformationwillflow across the wire following the encoding rules specified by the SOAP specification. In addition to the encoding information, SOAP requires the special `soapAction` extension. The value of this element must be placed into the HTTP header when the `post` request is made to the server.

At this point, the WSDL document has indicated what the service interface is and how its information will be transmitted over the wire. All that is left is to determine where the service can be invoked. For this, we turn to the port element (Listing 33.3).

Listing 33.3 The port element

```
<wsdl:port name="WSRandomIDGenerator"

      binding="intf:WSRandomIDGeneratorSoapBinding">

  <wsdlsoap:address

     location="http://localhost:9080/TSS/services/WSRandomIDGenerator"/>

</wsdl:port>
```

Notice:

- The port element is associated with a specific binding, in this case, `"intf:WSRan-domIDGeneratorSoapBinding"`.
- The location is specified by `wsdlsoap:address`. This is the address used by clients where the HTTP `post` should be directed.
- The address is specified within the `wsdlsoap` namespace, indicating that the address is an extension element specific to SOAP. The address is typically specified during the deployment stage, not at the time of WSDL generation.

The final element of interest is the service element. The service element is nothing more than a named collection of ports. WSDL is a well-layered, extensible mechanism for describing services. Even this simple document is illustrative of how the various constructs such as types, `portTypes`, bindings, and ports can be assembled to form a clear and cohesive service definition. By leveraging these constructs, complex services interfaces can be developed independently of how and where they are exposed on the network.

33.1.4 Creating the Deployment Descriptors

At this point, we have a WSDL document that conforms to the JAX-RPC specification, as well as a stateless session bean that will implement the behavior of the exposed methods. The next step is to create the necessary deployment artifacts for the J2EE environment that are required by JSR-109. To generate these files, use the command WSDL2Java.

```
wsdl2java -verbose -r server -c ejb -j No .\META-

INF\wsdl\WSRandomIDGenerator.wsdl
```

The results of the WSDL2Java are shown here—

```
WSWS3185I: Info: Parsing XML file: .\META-INF\wsdl\WSRandomIDGenerator.wsdl

WSWS3282I: Info: Generating META-INF\webservices.xml.
```

```
WSWS3282I: Info: Generating META-INF\ibm-webservices-bnd.xmi.

WSWS3282I: Info: Generating META-INF\ibm-webservices-ext.xmi.

WSWS3282I: Info: Generating META-INF\WSRandomIDGenerator_mapping.xml.
```

This usage of WSDL2Java is fairly straightforward. The `-verbose` parameter simply causes detailed output to appear on the command line. The second parameter, `-r server`, indicates that role for which files should be generated. Since we are creating the deployment descriptors for the server, role should be server. The `-c ejb` parameter is used because the implementation of our service is a stateless session bean. Because we already have a stateless session bean implementation, we don't need WSDL2Java to generate any additional Java classes or interfaces. To prevent WSDL2Java from creating any Java files, we use the `-j No` parameter. Later, when creating a client, we will use WSDL2Java to generate additional files that will be used as starting points for invoking the service.

Now, if we refresh the J2EE navigator view in WSAD, we should see four new files underneath the META-INF folder of the EJB module (Figure 33.3). Here is a summary of each of the four files:

- ibm-webservices-bnd.xmi: This is a WebSphere-specific file, hence the ibm prefix. Typically, this file contains binding information for security.
- ibm-webservices-ext.xmi: This is an extension file for Web services deployment, also used for securing the Web service.

Figure 33.3 Files created by WSDL2Java.

- webservices.xml: This is the deployment file, specified by Section 7.1.2 of JSR-109, used to indicate the deployment characteristics of the Web service. This file contains several interesting sections and is worth a closer look.
- WSRandomIDGenerator_mapping.xml: This file is generated in response to Section 7.3 of the JSR-109 specification and is used to associate entries in the WSDL to the Java constructs specified in the service interface.

33.1.4.1 Understanding the webservices.xml Deployment Descriptor

The webservices.xml file in Listing 33.4 was generated from the WSDL2Java command. This deployment descriptor ties together the implementation and the service description, as well as the mapping file to use.

Listing 33.4 The webservices.xml file

```xml
<?xml version="1.0" encoding="UTF-8"?>

<!DOCTYPE webservices PUBLIC "-//IBM Corporation, Inc.//DTD J2EE Web services

1.0//EN" "http://www.ibm.com/webservices/dtd/j2ee_web_services_1_0.dtd">

<webservices>

  <webservice-description>

    <webservice-description-name>WSRandomIDGeneratorService

    </webservice-description-name>


    <wsdl-file>META-INF/wsdl/WSRandomIDGenerator.wsdl</wsdl-file>


    <jaxrpc-mapping-file>META-INF/WSRandomIDGenerator_mapping.xml

    </jaxrpc-mapping-file>


    <port-component>

      <port-component-name>WSRandomIDGenerator</port-component-name>

      <wsdl-port>
```

```
            <namespaceURI>http://utilities.ejb.casestudy.wsbook.com</

            <namespaceURI>

            <localpart>WSRandomIDGenerator</localpart>

        </wsdl-port>

          <service-endpoint-interface>

              com.wsbook.casestudy.ejb.utilities.WSRandomIDGenerator

          </service-endpoint-interface>

        <service-impl-bean>

      <ejb-link>??SET THIS TO ejb-name ELEMENT OF ejb-jar.xml??</ejb-link>

        </service-impl-bean>

      </port-component>

    </webservice-description>

</webservices>
```

The values of the subelements `namespaceURI` and `localpart` are used to uniquely identify the correct port that is contained inside the WSDL document. The deployment descriptor also specifies the fully qualified SEI.

33.1.5 Updating the Deployment Descriptor

The last element, `<service-impl-bean>`, describes how the particular Web service is implemented. In this case, our Web services implementation is the RandomIDGenerator stateless session EJB. Therefore, an `<ejb-link>` subelement is present. However, since WSDL2Java does not infer the name of the EJB implementation automatically, it must be supplied by the developer. The name of the provided EJB *must* match the value of the `ejb-name` element in the ejb-jar.xml. According to JSR-109, "The ejb-link element may not refer to a session element defined in another module."[1] In the example, WSAD was used to manually set the value of this to `RandomIDGenerator`.

---

1.   JSR-109 7.1.2.

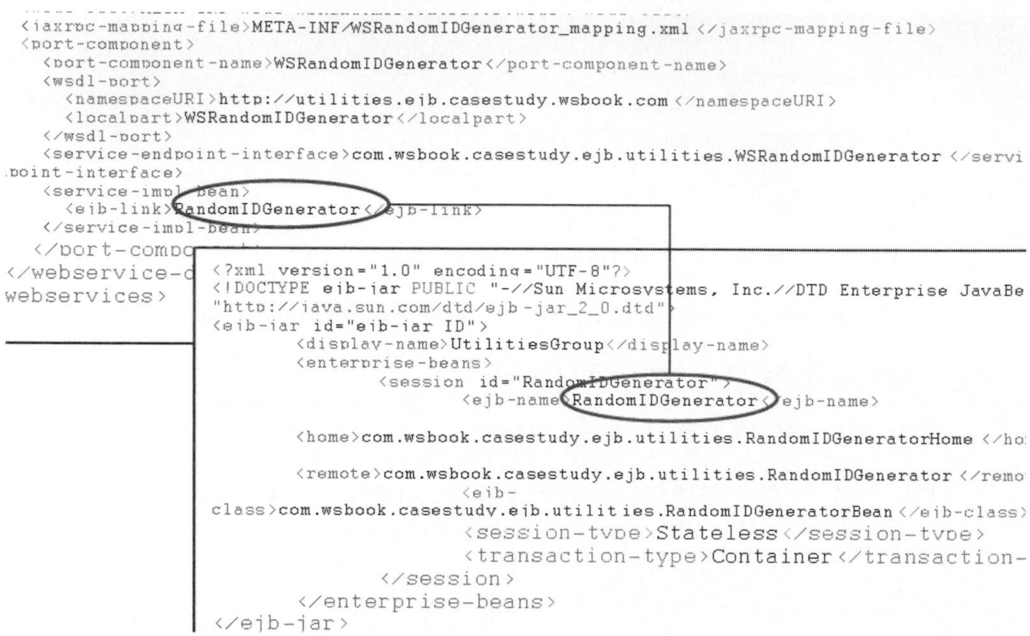

```
<jaxrpc-mapping-file>META-INF/WSRandomIDGenerator_mapping.xml</jaxrpc-mapping-file>
<port-component>
  <port-component-name>WSRandomIDGenerator</port-component-name>
  <wsdl-port>
    <namespaceURI>http://utilities.ejb.casestudy.wsbook.com</namespaceURI>
    <localpart>WSRandomIDGenerator</localpart>
  </wsdl-port>
  <service-endpoint-interface>com.wsbook.casestudy.ejb.utilities.WSRandomIDGenerator</servi
.point-interface>
  <service-impl-bean>
    <ejb-link>RandomIDGenerator</ejb-link>
  </service-impl-bean>
</port-comp
</webservice-d   <?xml version="1.0" encoding="UTF-8"?>
webservices>     <!DOCTYPE ejb-jar PUBLIC "-//Sun Microsystems, Inc.//DTD Enterprise JavaBe
                 "http://java.sun.com/dtd/ejb-jar_2_0.dtd">
                 <ejb-jar id="ejb-jar ID">
                         <display-name>UtilitiesGroup</display-name>
                         <enterprise-beans>
                                 <session id="RandomIDGenerator">
                                         <ejb-name>RandomIDGenerator</ejb-name>

                         <home>com.wsbook.casestudy.ejb.utilities.RandomIDGeneratorHome</ho:

                         <remote>com.wsbook.casestudy.ejb.utilities.RandomIDGenerator</remo
                                         <ejb-
                 class>com.wsbook.casestudy.ejb.utilities.RandomIDGeneratorBean</ejb-class>
                                         <session-type>Stateless</session-type>
                                         <transaction-type>Container</transaction-
                                 </session>
                         </enterprise-beans>
                 </ejb-jar>
```

Figure 33.4 Connecting the deployment descriptors.

33.1.6   Preparing the Web Service for Deployment

There are two steps necessary to prepare the Web service for deployment. The first is to export the EAR file. This is done using WSAD. The second is to enable the HTTP endpoint. This is done through a command line tool, endptEnabler, which adds a Web application to the service EAR that handles incoming SOAP requests.

To export the EAR from WSAD, right-click the UtilityEAR application under the Enterprise Applications folder in the J2EE hierarchy and select Export EAR File. The dialog box shown in Figure 33.5 should appear for you to fill in the location of the .ear file.

Once the EAR has been exported, the endptEnabler command may be run. This tool will gather from the developer information necessary to add the SOAP HTTP Web application. From the command line type the following: endptEnabler. Then type the following into the endptEnabler prompts—

```
IBM WebSphere Application Server Release 5

Web Services Enterprise Archive Enabler Tool.

Copyright IBM Corp., 1997-2002



Please enter the name of your ear file: Utility.ear
```

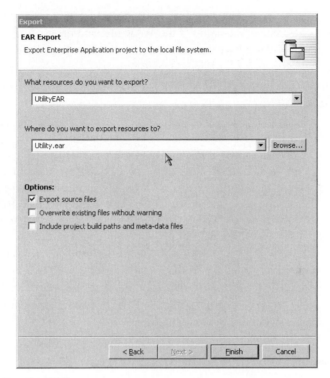

Figure 33.5 Exporting the EAR.

```
*** Backing up EAR file to: Utility.ear~


JSR 109 enabled EJB Jar file at name UtilitiesGroup.jar.


Please enter a file name for your endpoint [UtilitiesGroup.war]:

WSUtilitiesGroup.war


Please enter a context root for your endpoint [/UtilitiesGroup]: TSS
```

When invoking this tool, the developer is prompted for three pieces of information: the name of the enterprise archive, the name of the WAR file, and the context root of the endpoint. Effectively, this step provides a URL for your service. Examination of the web.xml deployment descriptor that was added to the EAR file would reveal the `<url-pattern>/services/*</url-pattern>` element. The complete URL for the service would be *http://localhost:9080/TSS/services/RandomIDGenerator.*

33.1.7 Deploying the Web Service into WebSphere

Currently WSAD 5.0 does not provide an integrated test environment for the WAS Web services implementation. Therefore, the deployment of the service must occur in a stand-alone instance of the application server. Deployment of this EAR begins at the WebSphere admin console and follows the same steps outlined in the previous chapters. However, JSR-109 permits the additional declaration of publishing the WSDL files that are generated with the proper service location at the time of deployment (Figure 33.6).

During the deployment process, one of the options you will be asked is to map the modules to the application server instances. In the .ear file, there will be two modules, one that contains our application EJBs, the UtilitiesGroup, and another, that was added by the `endptenabler` command. This group is necessary because EJBs need a lightweight mechanism to listen on HTTP. Deployment options are shown in Figure 33.7.

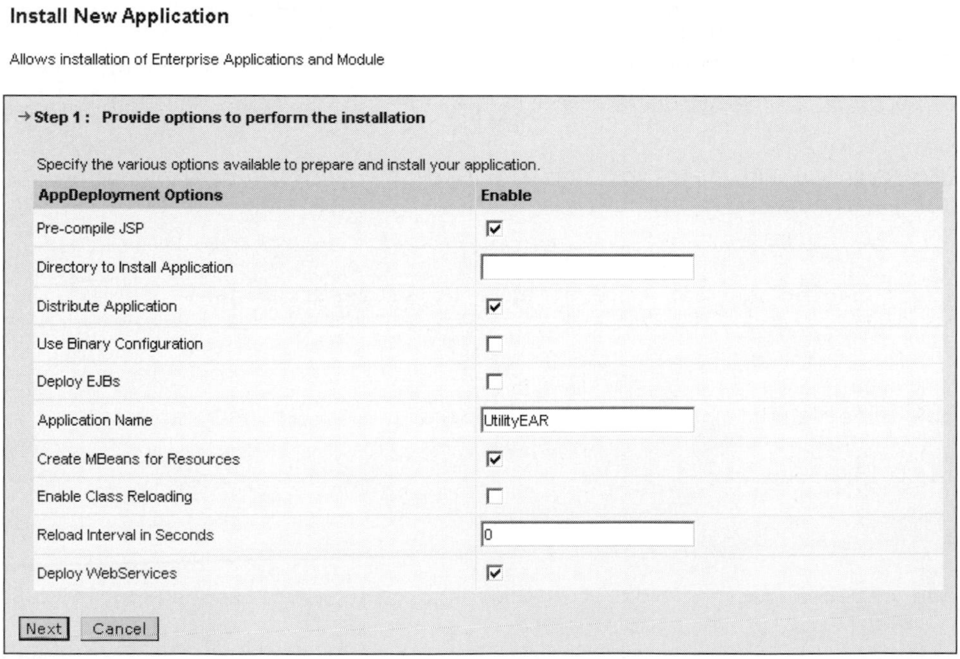

Install New Application

Allows installation of Enterprise Applications and Module

→ **Step 1 : Provide options to perform the installation**

Specify the various options available to prepare and install your application.

AppDeployment Options	Enable
Pre-compile JSP	☑
Directory to Install Application	
Distribute Application	☑
Use Binary Configuration	☐
Deploy EJBs	☐
Application Name	UtilityEAR
Create MBeans for Resources	☑
Enable Class Reloading	☐
Reload Interval in Seconds	0
Deploy WebServices	☑

Next   Cancel

Figure 33.6 WebSphere Web services deployment option.

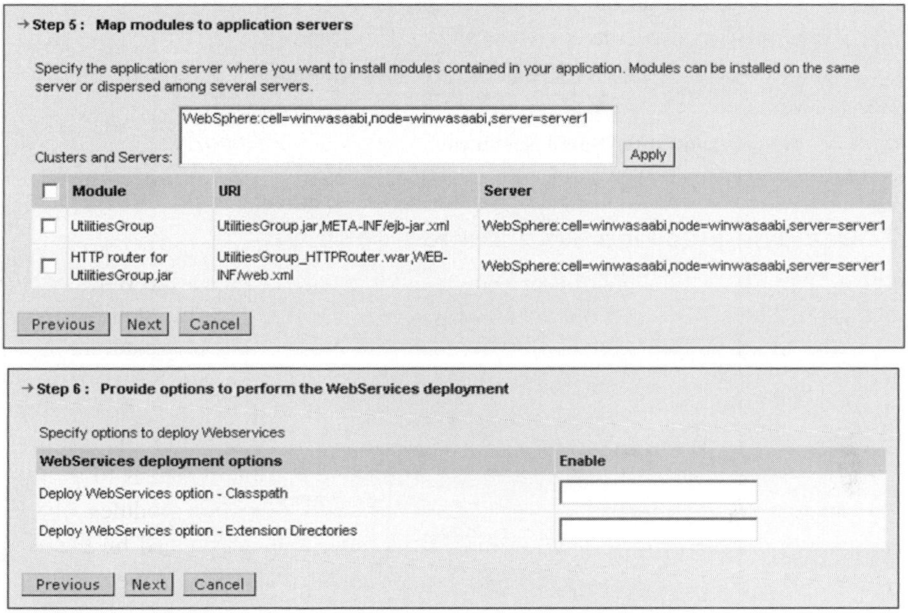

Figure 33.7 Web Services deployment options.

The default values for the server name and the host are applicable for our example. Select *Next to* move to the summary page, then Finish. WebSphere will now install the application. When the installation completes successfully, be sure to save the master configuration and start the application.

After saving the master configuration, start the application from the Enterprise Applications admin page. To validate the service is available, enter the following URL from a browser, *http://localhost:9080/TSS/services/WSRandomIDGenerator*. Figure 33.8 shows the result from the WebSphere Web services engine. This engine has been implemented in such a way that when the URL for a service is invoked with an HTTP `get`, it will respond with an acknowledgement that the service is available.

In addition to the standard acknowledgement page that the WebSphere runtime provides, it is also possible to retrieve the WSDL for the service. For our example, the WSDL is located at the following URL: *http://localhost:9080/TSS/services/WSRandomIDGenerator/wsdl/WSRandomIDGenerator.wsdl*. When the client for the service is built, this URL will be used as the location of the description (Figure 33.9).

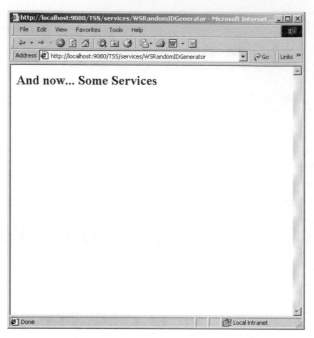

Figure 33.8 Invoking the service from a browser.

Figure 33.9 Viewing the WSDL from a browser.

33.1.8   Publishing the WSDL

In order to create the Web services client, we will need the generated WSDL. We can get this information by resolving the URL, as in Figure 30.9, or by publishing the WSDL from WebSphere into a zip file. To export a zip file, you must use the WebSphere Admin console. Select the UtilityEAR from the enterprise applications list. An option to publish WSDL is in the Additional Properties section (Figure 33.10).

Once the Publish WSDL link is selected, a page is presented that allows you to select which .jars contain the information to export. In this example, the UtilitiesGroup.jar is the file we are interested in and should be checked. Pressing *OK* will present a named link that, when selected, will ask you for the name of the .zip file through the standard save file mechanism supported by your browser (Figure 33.11).

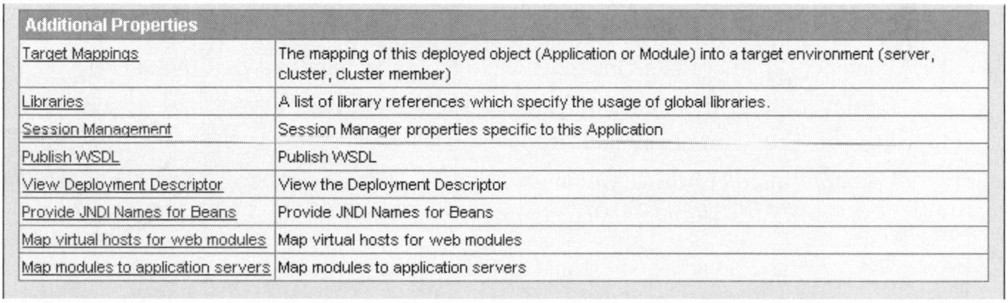

Additional Properties	
Target Mappings	The mapping of this deployed object (Application or Module) into a target environment (server, cluster, cluster member)
Libraries	A list of library references which specify the usage of global libraries.
Session Management	Session Manager properties specific to this Application
Publish WSDL	Publish WSDL
View Deployment Descriptor	View the Deployment Descriptor
Provide JNDI Names for Beans	Provide JNDI Names for Beans
Map virtual hosts for web modules	Map virtual hosts for web modules
Map modules to application servers	Map modules to application servers

Figure 33.10 Publish WSDL option in WAS admin console.

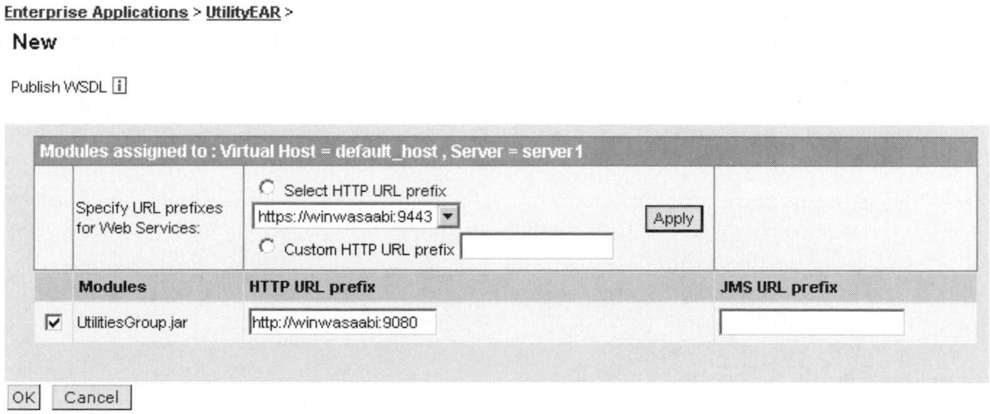

Enterprise Applications > UtilityEAR >

New

Publish WSDL [i]

Modules assigned to : Virtual Host = default_host , Server = server1			
Specify URL prefixes for Web Services:	○ Select HTTP URL prefix https://winwasaabi:9443 ▼ ○ Custom HTTP URL prefix	Apply	
Modules	**HTTP URL prefix**		**JMS URL prefix**
☑ UtilitiesGroup.jar	http://winwasaabi:9080		

OK   Cancel

Figure 33.11 Publishing WSDL for the Utilities Group.

33.1.9   Creating a Web Service in Summary

This list summarizes the steps we took to create and deploy the RandomIDGenerator EJB as a Web service.

1) Created the service description
    a. Copied the EBJ remote interface to create the JAX-RPC-compliant SEI
    b. Used Java2WSDL to create a Web services description language document
2) Created the deployment information
    a. Used WSDL2Java to create JSR109-compliant deployment information, including the deployment descriptor and the mapping files
    b. Edited the webservices.xml deployment descriptor `<ejb-link>` to insert the corresponding name of the ReportIDGenerator EJB found in module's ejb-jar.xml.
3) Packaged and deployed the application
    a. Used WSAD to export the EAR file
    b. Ran endptEnabler to add the SOAP HTTP request handler WAR to the EAR
    c. Deployed the EAR into a stand-alone installation WAS
4) Tested for successful deployment
    a. Using an internet browser, requested the URL of our service, *http://localhost:9080/ TSS/services/WSRandomIDGenerator* to verify our service endpoint is available

Now that we have exposed the RandomIDGenerator as a service, what remains is to develop the necessary clients that will be used to invoke the behavior. In the next section, two different styles of clients will be used to call the Web service.

33.2   Building Web Service Clients

The client programming model for Web services is similar to other distributed computing models. Essentially, the client needs to have a proxy representation of the service to invoke. JAX-RPC and JSR-109 refer to this as a service reference. Once obtained, this reference behaves just like any other Java object and methods can be invoked in a standard fashion. JAX-RPC defines a ServiceFactory that is used by J2SE clients to obtain a service proxy. However, in J2EE, JNDI is the preferred lookup mechanism. Section 4.2 of the JSR-109 specification outlines how JNDI is to be used by J2EE application clients to look up the service proxy. In this section, we will build two examples: a J2SE client, then a J2EE client. The examples will be written and run inside of WSAD.

33.2.1   The J2SE Client

Building the J2SE client is simple and straightforward (Figure 33.12). Unfortunately, even though the end product can be executed by WSAD, it is currently not possible to build the entire example using the development environment. The command line tool necessary to generate the necessary JAX-RPC and JSR-109 constructs is the same one used when the service implementation was built—WSDL2Java.

Export WSDL Zip file

Click on the application to download a zip file that contains the application's published WSDL files

Export WSDL Zip file
UtilityEAR.ear_WSDLFiles.zip
Back

Figure 33.12 Creating a Java project.

The first step in creating a J2SE client is to create a project for the classes. In WSAD, create a Java project named WSUtilityClientJ2SE (Figure 33.13).

After entering the project name, the wizard collects information about the structure of the project. Since this is a simple Java project, it is okay to use the project as the source folder. However, the JAX-RPC client will require several additional jar files, so the next step is to edit the properties of the WSUtilityClientJ2SE project. From the Libraries tab, select *Add External Jars* and add the necessary libraries (Figure 33.14). The jar files can be found in the \AppServer\lib directory underneath the stand-alone WebSphere installation that you used in the earlier service deployment example.

Table 33.1 shows the necessary JAR files for reference. Since this is a J2SE client, it is necessary only to have these libraries on the classpath. No additional assembly or deployment steps are necessary.

Figure 33.13 Setting the project source.

Figure 33.14 Setting up the classpath.

Table 33.1 JAR files.

commons-discovery.jar
commons-logging-api.jar
j2ee.jar
qname.jar
xerces.jar
webservices.jar
ws-commons-logging.jar
wsdl4j.jar

After adding the required jars, press *Finish*. Because we will be creating metainformation about the classes inside this project (i.e., deployment descriptors), it is necessary to create a META-INF folder in the WSUtilityClientJ2SE project.

Now that the project is properly set up, we can generate the Java constructs from WSDL2Java and then build the main client class. From the command line, switch to the directory underneath the workspace location for WSUtilityClientJ2SE project. Enter the following WSDL2Java command from an MS-DOS prompt.

```
<WSAD Workspace Directory>\WSUtilityClientJ2SE>wsdl2java -verbose

-rclient-cclienthttp://localhost:9080/TSS/services/WSRandomIDGenerator/

wsdl/WSRandomIDGenerator.wsdl
```

The output of WSDL2Java is shown here—

```
WSWS3185I: Info: Parsing XML file:  http://localhost:9080/TSS/services/

WSRandomIDGenerator/wsdl/WSRandomIDGenerator.wsdl

WSWS3282I: Info: Generating

com\wsbook\casestudy\ejb\utilities\WSRandomIDGeneratorService.java.

WSWS3282I: Info: Generating

com\wsbook\casestudy\ejb\utilities\WSRandomIDGeneratorServiceLocator.java.

WSWS3282I: Info: Generating

com\wsbook\casestudy\ejb\utilities\WSRandomIDGenerator.java.

WSWS3282I: Info: Generating

com\wsbook\casestudy\ejb\utilities\WSRandomIDGeneratorSoapBindingStub.java.

WSWS3282I: Info: Generating META-INF\webservicesclient.xml.

WSWS3282I: Info: Generating META-INF\ibm-webservicesclient-bnd.xmi.

WSWS3282I: Info: Generating META-INF\ibm-webservicesclient-ext.xmi.

WSWS3282I: Info: Generating META-INF\WSRandomIDGenerator_mapping.xml.
```

In this example, the WSDL2Java tool takes the URL of the WSDL for the service we deployed into WebSphere. In addition, -r and -c options indicate we are building a client. The result is the eight files necessary to invoke the Web service (Table 33.2).

Table 33.2 Files to invoke the Web service.

WSRandomIDGeneratorService.java	This is the JAX-RPC service used to access the port through the WSDL model.
WSRandomIDGeneratorServiceLocator.java	This is the class that does much of the heavy lifting. It is used to get the proxy to the service and is an implementation of the service interface. It should not be invoked directly from client code.
WSRandomIDGenerator.java	This is the service interface that the client uses when invoking methods on the service proxy.
WSRandomIDGeneratorSoapBindingStub.java	This is an implementation of the SEI. It is part of the plumbing and should not be used directly by a client.
webservicesclient.xml	This is the JSR-109 deployment descriptor for a client.
WSRandomIDGenerator_mapping.xml	The mapping information as specified by JSR-109.
ibm-webservicesclient-bnd.xmi	A WebSphere-specific binding file.
Ibm-webservicesclient-ext.xmi	An extension file used by WebSphere.

Back in WSAD, select the WSUtilityClientJ2SE project and click *Refresh*. You should see the generated files appear in the folder structure (Figure 33.15). Specifically, a package was created, `com.wsbook.casestudy.ejb.utilities`, that contains the generated Java files. Underneath the META-INF directory we created earlier, are the generated xml and xmi files.

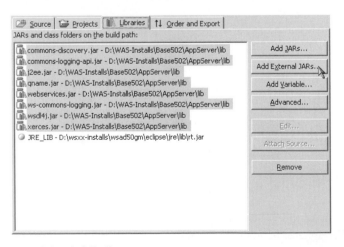

Figure 33.15 Contents of the J2SE client.

We are now ready to create the client that will invoke our service. Create a Java class called WSRandomIDGeneratorClient in the `com.wsbook.casestudy.utilities.wsclient` package. In this simple class we will invoke the Web service directly from the main method. The complete method is shown in Listing 33.5.

Listing 33.5 Invoking the Web service from the main method

```java
public class WSRandomIDGeneratorClient {

    public static void main (String[] args) throws Exception {

        try{

            Service aService =

                ServiceFactory.newInstance().createService(

                new URL("http://localhost:9080/TSS/services/
WSRandomIDGenerator/wsdl/WSRandomIDGenerator.wsdl "),


                new QName("http://
utilities.ejb.casestudy.wsbook.com","WSRandomIDGeneratorService") );


            WSRandomIDGenerator idGenService =

                (WSRandomIDGenerator)

                aService.getPort(

                new QName(

        "http://utilities.ejb.casestudy.wsbook.com","WSRandomIDGenerator"),

                WSRandomIDGenerator.class);


            int result = (int)idGenService.calculateID();

            System.out.println("And now for a random number...");
```

```
                    System.out.println(result);

          } catch (Exception e)

                    {e.printStackTrace();}

     }

}
```

The method is broken down into three steps. The first step is to acquire a reference to the service.

```
     Service aService = ServiceFactory.newInstance()

          createService(

     new URL("http://localhost:9080/TSS/services/

     WSRandomIDGenerator?wsdl"),

     new QName("http://utilities.ejb.casestudy.wsbook.com",

      "WSRandomIDGeneratorService") );
```

A service reference is instantiated by creating a Java model of the WSDL service description using the framework provided in the `javax.xml.rpc.*` package. Because the service reference represents the description of the service, it is helpful to think of it as service metainformation that is available at runtime. ServiceFactory is used as the lookup mechanism for J2SE clients.

ServiceFactory takes two arguments, the location of the WSDL file and the qualified name of the service description inside it. Notice that the URL will be resolved when this method is invoked. Also note that it is the same one we used to retrieve the WSDL when we deployed the service. The QName must match a port definition inside the resolved WSDL document. If this method fails, a `javax.xml.rpc.ServiceException` will be thrown.

The second step in service invocation uses the service reference to get a stub, cast to the service interface, which can be used to invoke the behavior.

```
WSRandomIDGenerator idGenService = (WSRandomIDGenerator)

aService.getPort(

  new QName("http://utilities.ejb.casestudy.wsbook.com",

    "WSRandomIDGenerator"),
```

Figure 33.16 Setting the main class.

```
WSRandomIDGenerator.class);
```

The last step in the code is to invoke the service.

```
int result = (int)idGenService.calculateID();

System.out.println("And now for a random number...");

System.out.println(result);
```

We can run this example in WSAD by creating a Launch Configuration from the Run…
menu (Figure 33.16). When selected the Launch Configuration dialog box will open. Enter
WSRandomIDGeneratorClient as the name, WSUtilityClientJ2SE as the project, and `com.ws-book.casestudy.utilities.wsclient.WSRandomIDGeneratorClient` as the main class.

Press *Apply* to update the dialog, then *Run*. The result should be out text and a random
integer printed in the console.

33.2.2   Building the J2EE Client

The J2SE and J2EE client programming models are the same in that the developer gets a reference to service and invokes behavior on remote service. Where they differ is in how the service
reference is resolved. J2EE clients perform a JNDI lookup, rather than using a service factory.

To create the J2EE client that will invoke the RandomIDGenerator service, the first step is
to create an application client project. In the J2EE perspective of WSAD, create a J2EE applica-

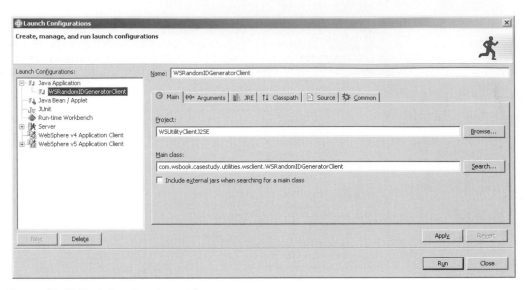

Figure 33.17 Updating the classpath.

tion client project. When the wizard opens, choose to create a J2EE 1.3 application client project and press *Next*. The project name should be WSUtilityClientJ2EE and the enterprise application project name should be WSUtilityClientJ2EE-EAR. Press *Finish* and the application client modules and the EAR are created.

The next step is to add the WSUtilityClientJ2SE project to the EAR deployment descriptor as a utility .jar file. To do this, follow the same steps outlined in Chapter 18. It is also necessary to modify the properties of the WSUtilityClientJ2EE application client module to contain the proper JAR file dependencies, which is also explained in Chapter 18.

Next, select the Java Build Path properties on the lefthand side of the dialog. In this step, we will be adding the libraries for our client (Figure 33.17).

Select *OK* to close the properties wizard. We are now ready to add a class to the application client module that will invoke the Web service. From the J2EE navigator, create a class called WSRandomIDGeneratorClientJ2EE in the appclientModule folder of the WSUtilityClientJ2EE project, and in package com.wsbook.casestudy.utilities.wsclient.j2ee. Listing 33.6 shows the implementation of the WSRandomIDGeneratorClientJ2EE class.

Listing 33.6 Implementing the WSRandomIDGeneratorClientJ2EE class

```
public class WSRandomIDGeneratorClientJ2EE {

    public static void main (String[] args) throws Exception {

        try{
```

```
                    InitialContext aContext = new InitialContext();

                    Service aService = (Service)

                            aContext.lookup(

                    "java:comp/env/service/WSRandomIDGeneratorService");

                    WSRandomIDGenerator idGenService =

                    (WSRandomIDGenerator)

                            aService.getPort(WSRandomIDGenerator.class);

                    int result = (int)idGenService.calculateID();

                    System.out.println("And now for a random number...");

                    System.out.println(result);

            } catch (Exception e)

                    {e.printStackTrace();}

        }

}
```

There are two minor changes in the main method of the J2EE client. The first and most important is the use of JNDI to get the service reference.

```
        InitialContext aContext = new InitialContext();

        Service aService = (Service)

            aContext.lookup("java:comp/env/service/

WSRandomIDGeneratorService");
```

Second, an alternate form of the getPort() method has been used. Instead of passing in the service class and the qualified name as in the J2SE example, the runtime is allowed to determine a port that matches the provided SEI.

```
WSRandomIDGenerator idGenService = (WSRandomIDGenerator)

        aService.getPort(WSRandomIDGenerator.class);
```

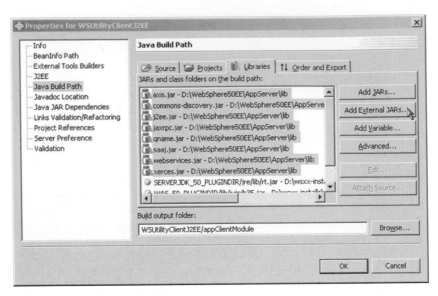

Figure 33.18 Setting Jar Dependencies.

Now that we have created the J2EE client that will invoke our service, we are ready to package the EAR for deployment. The WebSphere 5.0 application client launcher requires that the client module have a main class specified. To specify this for WSUtilityClientJ2EE, open it with the Jar Dependency Editor, which is an option under the *Open With* context menu. The class that will be invoked will be the one just created, `com.wsbook.casestudy.utili-ties.wsclient.j2ee.WSRandomIDGeneratorClientJ2EE` (Figure 33.18).

Next, move the webservicesclient.xml file from the J2SE application to the J2EE application. This file is a JSR-109 deployment descriptor and is needed only by J2EE clients. The file should be placed into the META-INF folder of the WSUtilityClientJ2EE application. In addition, the mapping file, WSRandomIDGenerator_mapping, will also need to be made available in the META-INF folder. Because the webservicesclient.xml file expects the WSDL for the service to be available, a folder should be created and the service description placed inside it. The default location for the WSDL file is META-INF/wsdl. The file can be extracted from the published .zip file created earlier in this example. The result of these file operation is reflected in Figure 33.19.

At this point, the enterprise application is ready to be run. The EAR can be exported and the launch client invoked from the command line. Alternately, the WSAD launch client can be configured and the client application can be run from within the development environment.

33.2.3 Running the WSAD Application Client

The WSAD application client runner is available from the *Run* menu. From the Launch Configurations wizard, choose a new WebSphere 5.0 application client (Figure 33.20).

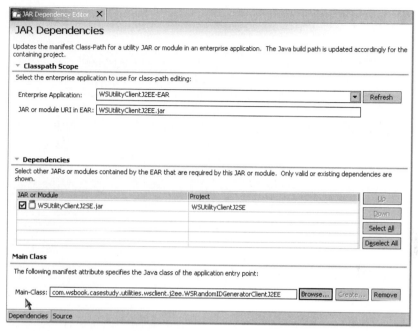

Figure 33.19 J2EE and J2SE folder structures.

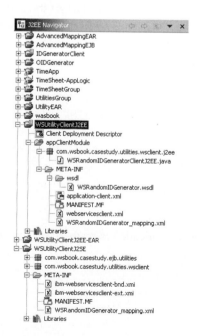

Figure 33.20 Application client configuration.

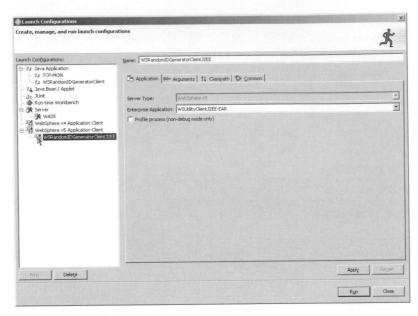

Figure 33.21 Adding all JAR files.

Since we are using the 5.0.2 version of the application server, which is different from the version provided inside of WSAD 5.0, we will need to set the classpath of the application client to point to the runtime files of the 5.0.2 application server. Because this type of client requires the J2EE container, it is recommended that the entire collection of 5.0.2 jar files be selected (Figure 33.21). These can be found in the lib folder underneath the WAS install; e.g., D:\Web-Sphere\AppServer\lib.

Once the JARs have been added, select *Apply*, then *Run*. The output of the command should appear in the console (Figure 33.22).

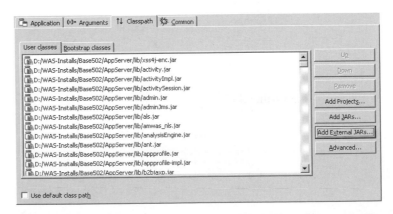

Figure 33.22 Output in the command console.

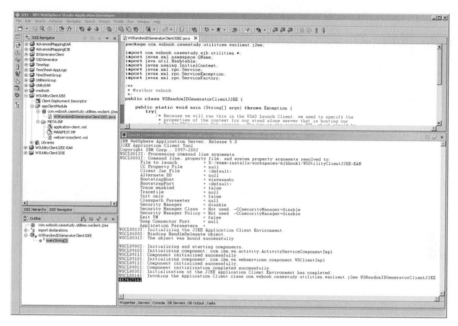

Figure 33.23 Exporting the EAR file.

33.2.4   Running the Client from a Command Line

From the *File* menu, select *Export* and choose EAR File in the first page of the wizard. The next page of the export wizard allows you to select the enterprise resource, along with its location (Figure 33.23).

Select WSUtilityClientJ2EE-EAR from the drop-down list, then enter the directory and name to be used for exporting the EAR. When this is complete, the WebSphere launchClient can be invoked from the command line to test the service. From the command line, execute the launch client:

```
%WSRoot%\AppServer\bin\launchClient WSUtilityClientJ2EE-EAR.ear

  -CCverbose=true
```

The output will look like Listing 33.7:

Listing 33.7 Invoking the WebSphere launchClient

```
IBM WebSphere Application Server, Release 5.0

J2EE Application Client Tool

Copyright IBM Corp., 1997-2002
```

```
WSCL0012I: Processing command line arguments.

WSCL0001I: Command line, property file, and system property arguments

resolved to:

            File to launch          = WSUtilityClientJ2EE-EAR.ear

            CC Property File        = null

            Client Jar File         = <default>

            Alternate DD            = null

            BootstrapHost           =

            BootstrapPort           = <default>

            Trace enabled           = false

            Tracefile               = null

            Init only               = false

            Classpath Parameter     = null

            Security Manager        = disable

            Security Manager Class  = Not used.  -CCsecurityManager=disable

            Security Manager Policy = Not used.  -CCsecurityManager=disable

            Exit VM                 = false

            Soap Connector Port     = null

            Application Parameters  =

WSCL0013I: Initializing the J2EE Application Client Environment.

WSCL0600I: Binding HandleDelegate object.

WSCL0031I: The object was bound successfully.


WSCL0900I: Initializing and starting components.
```

```
WSCL0901I: Component initialization completed successfully.

WSCL0035I: Initialization of the J2EE Application Client Environment has

completed.

WSCL0014I: Invoking the Application Client class

com.wsbook.casestudy.utilities.wsclient.j2ee.WSRandomIDGeneratorClientJ

2EE

And now for a random number...

1385193498
```

Success! The J2EE client invoked the WSRandomIDGenerator, which returned an integer.

33.2.5 Inspecting the SOAP messages

Earlier in the chapter we provided a very high level overview of SOAP. Now that we have SOAP messages traveling across the wire from client to server, we can inspect them to see how they were formed using the information specified by WSDL and the code generated by the tools.

In order to see the SOAP messages, a TCP monitor needs to be set up. In WSAD, a TCP monitor is just another type of server. From the File menu, select *New > Other*, select Server on the left-hand side, and then Server and Server Configuration on the right. Pressing *Next* will bring up the configuration for the type of server to create (Figure 33.24).

Enter the server name and select an appropriate project from the drop-down list. If you do not have your own server project, then you can select wasbookServers. Click *Finish* to create the server and configuration using the information supplied. Switch to the Servers perspective and open the server configuration by double-clicking UtilityTCPMonitor (Figure 33.25).

In the configuration from Figure 33.26, the UtilityTCPMonitor will listen on Port 9081 and forward the requests to localhost 9080. By default, the TCP monitor will act as a proxy server. Because this does unnecessary translations of the HTTP requests it needs to be disabled. Uncheck the HTTP Proxy enabled box, save the configuration, and start the TCP monitor.

Before we can run our service, we need to make a slight change. Recall that the J2SE client will resolve the WSDL document for the Web service using *http://localhost:9080/TSS/services/WSRandomIDGenerator/wsdl/WSRandomIDGenerator.wsdl*. However, this will return a port that has a `<wsdlsoap:address>` element with the value of 9080 as the port. Thus, the TCP monitor will never hear the incoming SOAP request. In order to monitor our Web service, two things need to happen.

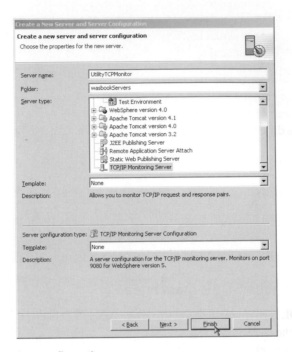

Figure 33.24 TCP monitor configuration.

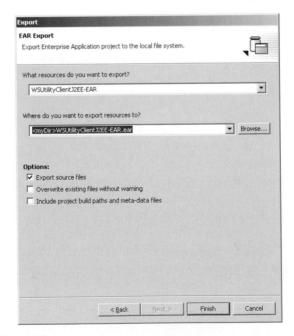

Figure 33.25 The TCP monitor.

- We will need a WSDL document that has a service location that points to the TCP monitor, and not the actual application server (the monitor will forward the request).
- The client will be updated to use the modified WSDL document.

To fix the WSDL, start with the one that we published from the application server during deployment. Here, we can update the port to be 9081. Using a file editor, change the location of the `wsdlsoap:address` element to be 9081. In order to avoid confusion, the WSDL document can be saved under a different name; e.g., WSRandomIDGenerator-monitored.wsdl.

```
<wsdl:port name="WSRandomIDGenerator"

    binding="intf:WSRandomIDGeneratorSoapBinding">

 <wsdlsoap:address

    location="http://localhost:9081/TSS/services/WSRandomIDGenerator"/>

</wsdl:port>
```

Save the WSDL file and rerun the J2SE client.

Next, update the WSRandomIDGeneratorClient.java file to resolve the updated WSDL document. Specifically, change the location of the WSDL URL. In the code, replace `<my directory>` with the location of the file.

```
Service aService = ServiceFactory.newInstance().createService(

    new URL("file:///<my directory>/WSRandomIDGenerator-monitored.wsdl"),

new QName("http://

utilities.ejb.casestudy.wsbook.com","WSRandomIDGeneratorService") );
```

By default, when the TCP monitor detects activity on the port, the reporting view will open. Selecting this view presents the HTTP request and response as a pair. The outgoing SOAP request is on the left, and the corresponding response is on the right (Figure 30.26).

However, the TCP monitor will not format the information that it intercepts. In order to see this information presented in an easily readable format, create a scratch project and add a new XML file. The XML portion of the request or response can then be copied into this document so that the WSAD XML editor can be used to format and view the content.

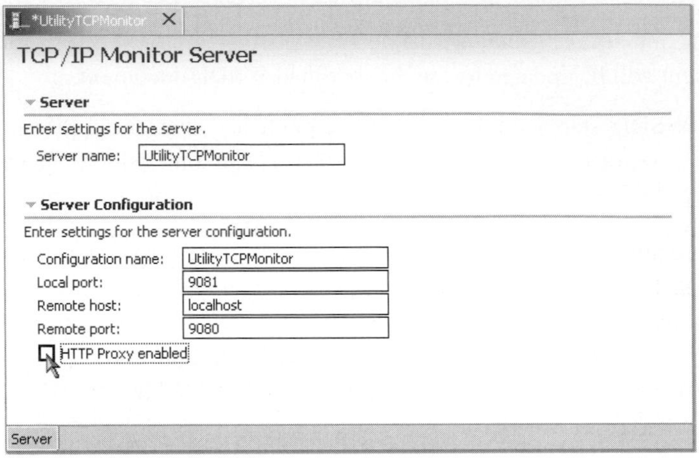

Figure 33.26 Monitoring SOAP messages.

33.2.5.1 Adding a WSDL Port

In the previous example, it was easy to monitor the SOAP requests by changing the endpoint of the service in the WSDL document. However, an alternate approach is to leverage the well-layered structure of WSDL. In WSDL documents, it is possible for a service to have multiple port elements. Therefore, instead of changing the existing location to listen on 9081, it is possible to define an entirely new port element to the WSDL that defines a new service location.

To add a new port element, simply make a copy of the WSDL port named WSRandomID-Generator, calling it WSRandomIDGeneratorMonitored. It is required that each port be uniquely named within the scope of a service. The service element with the two ports is listed below.

```
<wsdl:service name="WSRandomIDGeneratorService">

    <wsdl:port binding="intf:WSRandomIDGeneratorSoapBinding"

            name="WSRandomIDGenerator">

    <wsdlsoap:address location="http://localhost:9080/TSS/services/

WSRandomIDGenerator"/>

    </wsdl:port>


    <wsdl:port binding="intf:WSRandomIDGeneratorSoapBinding"

            name="WSRandomIDGeneratorMonitored">
```

```
    <wsdlsoap:address location="http://localhost:9081/TSS/services/

WSRandomIDGenerator"/>

    </wsdl:port>

  </wsdl:service>
```

All that is required is a simple modification to the client to resolve the new port in the `get-Port`(...) method. Try changing the name between WSRandomIDGenerator and WSRandomID-GeneratorMonitored. Notice the behavior of the TCP monitor confirms the port usage.

```
WSRandomIDGenerator idGenService = (WSRandomIDGenerator)

    aService.getPort(

    new QName("http://utilities.ejb.casestudy.wsbook.com",

    "WSRandomIDGeneratorMonitored"),

    WSRandomIDGenerator.class);
```

Although this is a simple example, it illustrates one of the powerful features of WSDL—the ability to expose the same service over multiple ports. Keep in mind that WSDL ports are not limited to the same type. In the example, WSRandomIDGeneratorMonitored could have flowed over a JMS transport (assuming there is a JMS binding as well), rather than TCP. Imagine having WSRandomIDGeneratorSecured that flows over HTTPs or incorporates other aspects of security; for example, basic authorization.

There is a larger aspect to this. Because WSDL documents can be composed, it is possible to have a common port type (the interface), along with a common set of bindings, that are associated with a wide range of WSDL ports. Therefore, there can be multiple providers of the same service. These services can be discovered and bound to dynamically over the Web, which enables large-scale integration of applications across the Internet.

33.2.5.2 Understanding the SOAP Message

It is important to realize that SOAP, like all Web services, is not a programming model. SOAP is not a system architecture either and nowhere in the SOAP specification will you find how to build a robust, scalable, distributed system. That is what EJBs are for. SOAP is one of many tools in an architect's distributed computing toolbox that should be used when the goal of information exchange is interoperability across heterogeneous systems.

Fundamentally, SOAP is an XML-based protocol for exchanging messages in a distributed computing environment. The protocol is simple: It specifies only an envelop structure that can be used to carry the body of the message. Figure 33.27 shows the basic structure of a SOAP message.

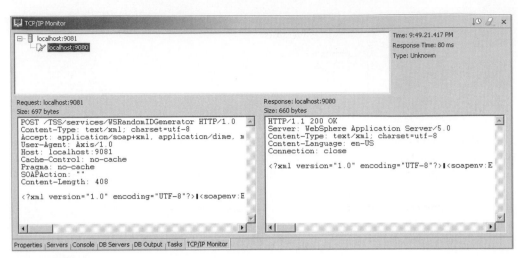

Figure 33.27 Structure of a SOAP message.

The message is composed of two primary parts—headers and the body. SOAP is extremely flexible because it allows for the use of message headers, which provide orthogonal layers of expandability (e.g., transactions and security). Because it is based on XML, and in particular XML Schema, SOAP is well-positioned to be both simple and flexible. The use of XML facilitates versioning through namespaces, as well as the ability to express complex data types. SOAP, because of XML, is agnostic of programming language and runtime platform. Although it is possible to utilize SOAP without a description language, the combination of SOAP and WSDL allows the software engineer to build, design, and implement robust and flexible distributed computing solutions. The body of a SOAP message is where the RPC call or document is carried.

When exchanging information between systems using Web services, the basic communication unit is called a message. A message is, typically, an XML document with the SOAP envelope as the root element. Figure 33.28 shows the SOAP envelope structure.

The envelope is defined within the namespace *http://schemas.xmlsoap.org/soap/envelope/*, which resolves to its schema. Contained inside the envelope is the SOAP body, which contains the information to invoke the behavior remotely. For WSRandomIDGenerator, the method to invoke, `calculateID`, is represented as an element tag within the SOAP body. It is empty because it accepts no parameters. Notice the namespace on the tag is the same as the targetNamespace in the service's WSDL document. You may recall that this was generated by the Java2WSDL tool and was based upon the package name of the Java class.

Messages returned from a SOAP call are very similar to requests. Information is returned inside a body contained within a SOAP envelope. Figure 33.29 is the output from the calculateID request.

The return value is contained within the calculateIDResponse element tag and is within the same namespace, *http://utilities.ejb.casestudy.wsbook.com*. The encoding is indicated by the

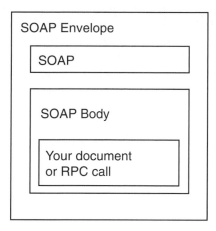

Figure 33.28 SOAP envelope.

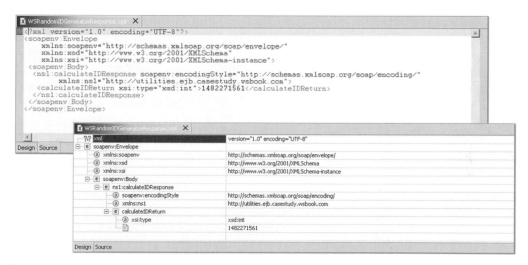

Figure 33.29 CalculateIDResponse SOAP envelope.

`encodingStyle` attribute of the calculateIDResponse tag, *http://schemas.xmlsoap.org/soap/encoding/'*. This URL will resolve to the XML schema that governs the encoding rules outlined by the SOAP specification. In addition, the SOAP encoding rules cause the `xsi:type` attribute to be specified with the return value, indicating that the information contained in the element is conformant with the schema type `int`, which is an integer.

33.3 Summary

This chapter introduced the basic concepts of Web services and demonstrated how to use them to provide more opportunities for integrating enterprise applications. An overview of the WSDL and SOAP was presented, along with the JAX-RPC and JSR-109 specifications that drive the implementation inside of WAS. In addition, we covered the tools necessary to create the J2EE constructs to support Web services, including Java2WSDL, WSDL2Java, endptEnabler, and WSAD. The next chapter continues our exploration of Web services by presenting best practices guidelines as well as examples of other aspects such as document-literal Web services.

Web Services Architectures and Best Practices

In the previous chapters you've seen a little about the promise of using Web Services in Web-Sphere. In this chapter we'll cover some of the architectural challenges posed by Web services, examine how to use (and not to use) Web services, and see some best practices in applying Web services for solving tough architectural problems.

Web services are the final piece of our architectural road map. You will see in this chapter (as you have seen as the previous chapters on Web services) how Web services in WebSphere usually use stateless session beans as their component implementation. The position of Web services in our road map is shown in Figure 34.1.

34.1   Some Web Services Dos and Don'ts

There is a common set of emotions that go along with adopting any new technology. First, when you begin to hear the buzz about a technology, you start to think that it might be useful in solving your particular problems, and feel positively inclined toward it. As you learn more, your excitement grows—perhaps a short proof-of-concept is successful and leads you to jump in with both feet and adopt the new technology for a big new project. Then, the reality of the state of the technology begins to set in, and you start to find the limitations of the new technology. At this point, you might be able to muddle through and make the project successful despite the technology's limitations, or the project may crash around you amid a shattering of lost hopes and dreams. The old adage "all panaceas become poison" applies to most new technologies, and it applies no less to Web services.

In the past two or three years since Web services have started to be used in practical applications, a number of basic dos and don'ts have emerged about when Web services are practical, and when they are not. Next, we'll examine some of these basic principles, and discuss some situations where disregarding them have made projects go awry.

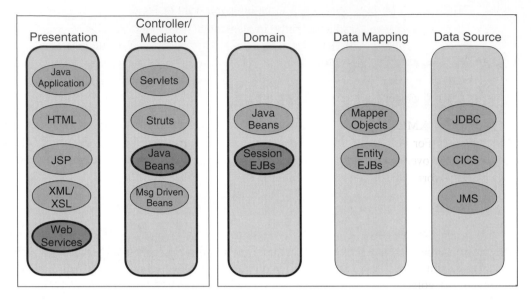

Figure 34.1 Architectural road map.

Principle: *Try not to use XML-based Web services between the layers of a logical application.*

Web services function best where they complement other J2EE technologies, not replace them. For instance, a wonderful way to use Web services is when connecting from an application client running on the global Internet to business logic written in EJBs inside WAS. Here you get a nice, clean separation of communication between the controller and domain layers of your application. This is the same place in which you would use EJBs (see Chapter 22) and so, if you consider Web services as another object distribution mechanism, then you can see why this would be appropriate. SOAP over HTTP can work in places where RMI over IIOP can't (as we saw in Chapter 22), allowing the XML-based Web services to complement the existing EJBs.

However, where people often go wrong with this is to assume that if this works between one pair of layers, it would work well between another. For instance, a common antipattern that we've seen far too often is a design where a persistence layer is wrapped inside an XML API and then placed in a process separate from the business logic that needs to invoke the persistence layer. In versions of this design, we've seen people actually serialize Java objects into XML, send them over the network, deserialize them, perform a database query with the objects thus sent in as an argument, convert the database result set to XML, then send the result set back across the network, only to be converted into Java objects, and, finally, operated on. There are two major problems with this approach:

  • As we discussed in the chapters on CMP and BMP design, persistent objects should *always* remain local to the business object that operates on them. The overhead of serialization and deserialization is something you want to avoid whenever possible.

- There is not yet a workable, fully implemented transaction specification for Web services. In EJBs with RMI-IIOP you have the option of including persistence operations in an outer transaction scope if you use entity beans or session beans with mapper objects if you so choose. If you introduce a layer of Web services between the persistent objects and the business objects operating on them, you lose that ability.

In general, XML Web services aren't appropriate for fine-grained interactions, even less so than RMI-IIOP. For instance, don't put it between the view layer and the controller layer of an application. The overhead of the parsing/XML generation and the garbage generation overhead will kill the performance of your overall application.

Principle: *Be very careful when using Web services between application servers*

In many ways, interoperability between systems is the raison d'etre of Web services. So, if you're connecting to a system written using Microsoft .NET, the use of Web services is almost a given. While you could use other mechanisms like WAS's COM support, the best solution for interoperability going forward for both the Microsoft and IBM platforms is Web services.

Sometimes using Web Services makes sense as when connecting disparate Java application servers from different vendors, but this is a less common occurrence. It is possible to connect to EJBs written in WebSphere from a JBoss or Weblogic server by using the WebSphere thin application client described in Chapter 22. This would be a much better performing solution than one using HTTP and SOAP-based Web services.

On the other hand, a more common occurrence is when you want asynchronous invocation of business logic written either in another application server or in some sort of legacy server. In this case, sending XML over JMS makes a lot of sense, and if you wrap your document-oriented XML in a SOAP envelope it makes even more sense; you can take advantage of the header structure of SOAP and even possibly gain some out-of-the box features like WS-security support.

34.2   Addressing the Limitations of Web Services

Web services have proven to be a useful approach for addressing some of the interesting problems of distributed objects. Since its introduction, SOAP over HTTP has become nearly the de facto standard for application-to-application communication over the Internet. With major Web sites like UPS, Amazon, and Google supporting the Web services standards, this technology has become quite entrenched in the corporate IT world.

However, when we look at using Web services in an intranet environment, the issues are not quite as clearly defined as they are when discussing systems made available over the Internet. Web services provide a number of advantages when using them over the Internet. For instance:

- Since the most common transport protocol for Web services is HTTP (which is also the protocol that most of the Internet infrastructure is built around), handling, managing, load-balancing, and allowing access to applications through HTTP is often much less troublesome than allowing access through other protocols. For instance, most corporations already employ a DMZ firewall policy that allows a set of protected servers to receive incoming traffic on HTTP or HTTPs but over no other protocols. This is rather an ironic situation; most businesses allow HTTP because it is believed to be a safe protocol for accessing Web content. Now with Web services, all sorts of business traffic can flow through the corporate firewall. Simply assuming that because your Web services traffic flows over HTTP that it is safe is inappropriate. You need to instead open a dialogue with your security organization on what business functions should be exposed over the Internet, and what precautions should be taken to protect them.

- Web services are quickly becoming ubiquitous. This is due to the curious historical occurrence that for the first time, both Microsoft and the Java industry have backed a single distributed technology. Since SOAP engines and tools that understand the basic protocols are now common, there is no requirement that a Web services client be written using the same tool as a Web services server. This enables communication between companies over the Internet since business partners need not assume anything about the way in which either side of the conversation is implemented.

However, when we're considering a system in which the majority of users will be working within a corporate intranet, some of the following hurdles to overcome with Web services and SOAP become more crucial. They are:

- We have found that, with the current SOAP engines, there is literally an order-of-magnitude performance difference between Web services calls and equivalent calls using the remote EJB protocol (RMI-IIOP). While a very large-grained approach with Web services may be applicable to infrequent communication between business partners, using them in tightly coupled, high-volume internal applications is likely to be inappropriate. For instance, a call-center application where there are dozens or hundreds of requests per minute from each user is probably not a good candidate for Web services because the overhead of generating and parsing XML is problematic.

- Even though the industry is making progress with standardized authentication and authorization for Web services, unfortunately most of the current set of J2EE products do not yet provide full support for this to the extent that they do for the J2EE protocols (like RMI-IIOP).

Looking forward, many of these problems could be addressed in a very elegant way by an expansion of the promised multiprotocol support for Web services. For instance, if a standard RMI-IIOP binding for WSDL were available through JAX-RPC, then you could simply choose the right port for the job in your WSDL. However, pending standardization of this approach, these problems are still real issues.

So, since no one distribution approach solves all problems, what many organizations have concluded is that they need to support multiple distributed-object protocols and access mechanisms within their enterprise. A single application API may need to be available as an external

Web service using SOAP over HTTP, over RMI-IIOP for internal remote clients, using local EJB references within an application server, and potentially even using SOAP over MQ for asynchronous interaction.

There are two pieces to solving this puzzle: how do we provide access to business logic over multiple distribution protocols, and what client programming model do we use to provide access to the remote business logic.

The second problem is the more interesting one, although we will need to discuss some approaches for the first one as well. In short, the solution to providing a common, unified client programming model (that is independent of which of several different remote technologies are used) can be found by applying an extension to the Business Delegate pattern from [Alur].

34.2.1 Multiple Business Delegates

Business Delegate is a pattern that allows a client to remain ignorant of the implementation details of a particular remote business service. The participants of the pattern are shown in Figure 34.2 (adapted from [Alur]).

The key here is that you have a client that needs to use a remote business service. The Business Delegate pattern hides the implementation details of how to obtain the business service and invoke its methods by providing an external API that is nearly the same as that of the business service, minus the details of things like remote exception handling. It does so by delegating the details of object lookup to a lookup service (usually implemented as a Service Locator pattern from [Alur]) and by handling remote exceptions (as well as other issues like retry) inside the methods of the Business Delegate itself.

In Figure 34.2, note the uses relationship between the delegate and the business service represents a set of remote calls. That is the key to this pattern. As [Alur] states on page 249, "The main benefit is hiding the details of the underlying service." An explicit consequence of this pattern (discussed on page 255 of [Alur]) is to hide remoteness of the business service. In fact, the pattern contains the seeds of more than just hiding remoteness. By providing a purely local mechanism for accessing a remote object, it hides the underlying remote protocol used so that (with only a slight modification to the pattern) you can allow the client to choose from several different remote protocols.

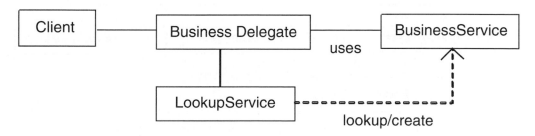

Figure 34.2 Business delegate participants.

The problem is that when most J2EE developers think of the Business Delegate pattern, they only think of it in terms of remote EJB access. The code examples in [Alur] only show this application of the pattern, and the vast majority of the text in the pattern itself also only refers to using it with EJBs. However, the pattern is not limited to EJBs alone.

Consider using a Web service through the JAX-RPC API. The same issues that led to the use of this pattern for EJBs (e.g., the need to know how to obtain the remote object reference, and the need to know how to handle remote exceptions and retry logic) apply for Web services as well. What's more, the pattern also provides a useful way to abstract the details of the differences between local and remote interfaces in EJB 2.0. Rather than having to make your application programmers explicitly pick which home interface (remote or local) and which of the local or remote interface to use, you can abstract that detail away by hiding the decision behind a set of two Business Delegates.

What we are arriving at is a slight modification of the pattern where we explicitly recognize that there are several different Business Delegate implementations that might apply to a single business service, each depending upon the particular access mechanism that is needed for a specific circumstance.

We can make this explicit by introducing another couple of elements into the pattern. First, we have to decide that there needs to be a specific interface that defines the methods of the Business Delegate itself. Each of the implementations (for Web services, remote EJB access, local EJB access, etc.) must implement the delegate interface. Second, we need to provide a mechanism for allowing clients to create the particular Business Delegate implementation that is needed. The most common solution is to create a Factory that can (based on a set of input parameters, or a set of configuration parameters preset in the class) create one of many different implementations of the business delegate interface. The result of applying these two changes can be seen in Figure 34.3.

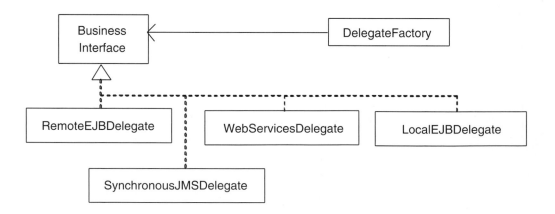

Figure 34.3 Business delegates with factory and interface.

Astute observers may note that this does remove one of benefits of the Business Delegate pattern—the original pattern kept the client from having to use a factory (in this case, the EJB-Home) to create an object (the EJB reference), while we have reintroduced a factory into the mix. This slight complication to the programming model is well worth the benefits that it conveys. What we have done is to replace multiple factories (such as the EJBHome and the JAX-RPC service) with a single factory that returns a local business delegate adapted for a specific distribution protocol.

This design allows you to take advantage of each of the available protocols without having to have your client depend on the specifics of which protocol is being used. Consider the case where you have an application client that can run both inside and outside your corporate firewall. By setting a configuration parameter for the factory, the same code could be used in both situations; inside the firewall you could choose RMI/IIOP while outside you could choose SOAP over HTTP.

If the code that communicated with the remote object was part of a larger business component, that component could also be incorporated into a servlet or JSP by configuring the parameter to instruct the factory to use a local EJB reference instead. Our final configuration might look like Figure 34.4.

In fact, this pattern could be extended to any number of additional protocols, so long as they maintain the same basic RPC semantics. Of course, the qualities of service may differ for each protocol. For instance, transactions (at least today) will not flow over a SOAP/HTTP invocation, while they will over an RMI-IIOP invocation. There are also subtleties of security to consider. However, for many situations, these differences are irrelevant and the pattern provides great value.

A final note about this pattern is that it provides value to you specifically on the client side only for the particular language in which you implement your business delegates. If you, for

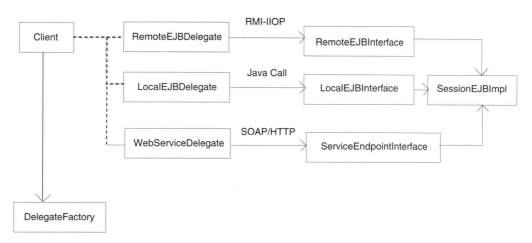

Figure 34.4 Multiple delegates and servers.

instance, implemented a business delegate framework in Java that allowed you to connect transparently over either RMI-IIOP or SOAP/HTTP, it would not help you at all if your Web services clients could be written in C#.

34.2.2 WSDL and WSIF

You would think that a pattern that (in retrospect) is as obvious as this one would have managed to find its way into one or more open-source projects or commercial products. That has happened, although it has appeared to have sneaked by most developers. In 2002 IBM donated a technology called WSIF to the Apache consortium. The WSIF home page at *http://apache.org* describes WSIF as "…a simple Java API for invoking Web services, no matter how or where the services are provided." The key difference here is that WSIF is designed around using WSDL as a normalized description of a piece of software using a protocol. If you have a WSDL document with different bindings for a set of technologies (such as SOAP over HTTP or EJBs), then you could use WSIF providers to connect to remote objects implemented using different distribution technologies.

WSIF is primarily used through an API whose constructs closely match those of WSDL. However, it is possible for tools to develop proxy classes that use the WSIF API in such a way that the external API of the proxy matches the equivalent Java definition of a WSDL-described Web service using the JAX-RPC mappings. Some IBM tools (like WSAD-IE) can generate proxy classes like this to provide a simple Java interface to the WSIF API in some cases. So, in the case of a JCA interface built using WSAD-IE, a proxy class (in effect, a Business Delegate) can be generated on top of the WSIF API, which would then call into a JCA WSIF provider. So, WSIF provides one way to handle what is needed on the left-hand side of the diagram, but only if the entire system is described with WSDL and you have (or can write) all of the appropriate providers.

One final word on WSIF: While it is an intriguing technology, and can be a useful approach for many users, remember that it is an open-source technology, and not one that has been standardized as part of the JAX-RPC specification. In the future, we expect JAX-RPC to evolve to take on the same multiprotocol capabilities that WSIF has. At this point the WSIF APIs will prove to be more of a liability than a help. So, while WSIF may be used as a point solution, you should be cognizant of the future of the approach. While IBM uses WSIF internally in its own products extensively, it should probably not be viewed as an accepted standard Web services API. For your own implementations you should stick with JAX-RPC and other fully standardized APIs.

34.3 Choosing the Right Level of Granularity in SOA

In Chapter 32 you learned the basic outlines of the approach which IBM has christened SOA. The most difficult portion in developing a SOA lies in determining what the right level of granularity of a Web service should be. To a large extent, this consists of determining what constitutes a good Web service, and what does not. Earlier in the chapter we've seen appropriate uses of Web Services technology as a mechanism for communicating between disparate system types (such as servers written in .NET and servers written for WebSphere) and as a way to facilitate client/server communication over the Internet. But Web services is a much broader approach than just these two canonical examples. In the following sections we'll talk about some appropriate uses of Web services that might help you better understand where in your designs to apply the technology.

34.3.1 Unified Logical View

In Chapter 30 we discussed best practices around the use of session EJBs and tips in applying the Session Façade pattern. One of the things we discussed was that a good level of granularity for a Session Façade is at the service level, meaning that you identify a logical service provided to a common group of clients and then create a Session Façade at that level.

What you are doing is, in effect, creating a unified logical view on a subsystem. This large-grained Session Façade is especially appropriate when you consider how to use Web services. First, for efficiency's sake you would not want to have a fine-grained, chatty interface to a Web service. As we discussed earlier, the overhead involved in XML parsing and generation would take a flaw that would be noticeable in an EJB design and magnify it. So, you would look for as few methods as possible to represent the whole scope of your subsystem's function, and then work on making the methods large-grained, so that each method does one complete logical function.

As an example, consider if you were building a system to run an E-commerce site on the Internet. You can readily imagine the different subsystems that would be needed based on the parts of the domain: order processing, shipping and shipment tracking, returns, and inventory management quickly come to mind. This would be exactly the level of component that would be appropriate as a Web service. By presenting a single logical view of the entire subsystem, clients would be protected from knowing the details of how the subsystem is implemented and isolated from changes in the implementation of the subsystem over time.

34.3.2 Replaceable Component

Another common theme we have seen in many Web services designs is the need to represent several implementations of a particular component, where you need to be able to isolate requestors from change in the implementation and provide access to many different flavors of that component, either at once or over time.

Let's say you're building a Web site that will provide customers with insurance quotes. To do so, you have an agreement with several insurance companies to provide you with quotes. But you have a problem: Each of the insurance companies has a different mechanism for accepting quote requests and providing quotes to you. How do you design you Web site to deal with this? In a nutshell, this is the place where the Adapter pattern from [Gamma] can come to your rescue (Figure 34.5).

What you could write is a broker component that would look in a local UDDI repository for the references to different adapters that implemented a particular WSDL interface, then use that common WSDL interface to get quotes from all of the insurers by sending the same get-Quote request to all of the adapters. Each insurer-specific adapter (which you would be responsi-

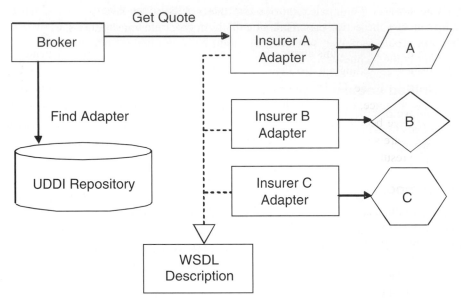

Figure 34.5 Insurance broker design.

ble for writing) would translate the Web services request into a request that the insurer's own
quote system could understand. There could be several ways of doing this:

- The easiest way (a no-op) is to have the insurer implement the WSDL document
  describing the getQuote interface themselves. In this case you don't need an adapter,
  and you simply pass through the request. However, it may be useful to have a simple
  adapter—you might want to log outgoing requests, or translate from one protocol
  (HTTP) to another (HTTPs). This sort of intermediation is the function of a component
  of WAS ND called the Web Services Gateway. It allows you to set up filters that can
  perform logging, protocol translation, or a number of other useful features. You can
  even write your own filters for deployment in the gateway as well.
- If your business partners won't implement your WSDL, but provide you with a
  document type that is similar, you might be able to write an adapter that could
  transform from their existing format into your format. For instance, your partners may
  provide you with an existing system that you can access through HTTP to a quote
  presented as an XML document in their own unique, proprietary format. In this case,
  you could write a Web service that uses an XSLT document to transform from their
  XML format into the format your WSDL document specifies.
- If you have access to existing business logic through a standard J2EE protocol (like JMS
  over WebSphere MQ, or JCA with IBM CICS), you can write a Web service as an EJB
  or JavaBean that uses that protocol and the appropriate JCA, JDBC, or JMS connectors
  to send the request on to the target system, get back the quote, and then translate the

response into the format you need. Here you could use the WSDL2Java tool to generate a simple skeleton for you to fill out with the appropriate translation logic

The great thing about this approach is that your broker system is now independent of the individual insurers—adding another insurer could be as simple as implementing a new adapter and registering it to the UDDI repository. Likewise, changes to the implementation of the adapter (if, for instance, one of your insurers decides to implement its own compliant Web service after you have been using an adapter written for CICS) do not affect the broker at all. The Web client software would simply ask the broker for quotes for a particular set of circumstances and present the results to the user.

34.3.3 Composable Component

Finally, you need to ask yourself if you have a need to take parts of your system and compose it into a larger system in a configurable way. In other words, do you need to implement one or more workflows that use the different parts of your system? A workflow is a way of describing a set of steps (often called activities) that are combined to execute a particular business process. For instance, in the insurance industry, there are a number of steps that make up paying a claim. If you imagine that each of these steps is implemented as individual Web services, then the process of paying the claim will consist of invoking the different services in a particular order, perhaps with some services being skipped or bypassed, depending upon the results of previous service invocations.

In 2002 a specification was released by IBM, BEA, and Microsoft called BPEL4WS (Business Process Execution Language for Web Services) that describes how to compose Web services into workflows, and, thus, form larger, composite Web services. Note that this does not necessarily mean Web services using SOAP over http; this means all WSDL-defined services, which could include EJBs using RMI-IIOP. BPEL4WS features the following capabilities:

- A mechanism for specifying tasks (Web services) and transitions between tasks
- The ability to support either microflows (flows that occur within an atomic transaction, such as within a single EJB invocation) or macroflows (flows that span several transactions, and may span large periods of time)
- A simple mechanism for specifying conditional execution and task selection
- A sophisticated error-handling mechanism that includes handling of compensating transactions in cases where a workflow must be rolled back to a specific point

A workflow system consists of two parts: a workflow specification tool and a workflow execution engine. The advantage of using a standard specification language like BPEL4WS between the two is that it allows both to become pluggable over time.

IBM has a very sophisticated workflow specification and optimization tool called the WebSphere Business Integration Modeler (formerly known as HoloSofx). By mid-late 2003 this tool will fully support BPEL4WS. Currently, IBM WAS EE supports a predecessor of BPEL-4WS called WSFL (the Web Services Flow Language) but it will be updated with BPEL4WS capabilities by late 2003 as well.

There are also workflow specification tools that are part of IBM WSAD-IE that will be updated to work with the BPEL4WS-compliant version of the WebSphere Business Process Choreographer.

34.4 Interoperability Lessons Learned

Interoperability between Web services providers and Web services requestors written in different languages, or using different tool sets, has been the prime example of the benefits that Web services can convey. In fact, it's probably the only reason why they are so popular. The IT industry is divided into two warring camps, Microsoft and Java, and anything that can be done to call a truce must be considered to be a good thing.

In real-world situations, having some way to call code written using one technology from the other is extremely useful. It can allow systems from different organizations within the same company to communicate for the first time (not an uncommon event given the rapid rate of corporate mergers) and can allow companies to work with business partners that use a different set of technologies. Although the promise of interoperability is the major reason why we're looking at Web services, the reality is that interoperability isn't free. You have to work at it and design it into your systems from the beginning, just like you have to design in scalability, performance, reliability, and security.

Luckily for developers, some order has begun to emerge out of the chaos of spec interpretation through the action of WS-I, an industry consortium with a charter to promote interoperability among Web services vendors. One of the first, and most crucial, specifications produced by the WS-I is its basic profile, which describes a subset of the ways in which the four main Web services specifications (WSDL, SOAP, HTTP, and UDDI) can be used to ensure interoperability.

While most of the recommendations in the WS-I basic profile deal with issues that are of interest only to the vendors of Web services toolkits, there are some steps that you must take to ensure that your Web services are interoperable and in compliance with the WS-I basic profile. In particular, two issues in the WSDL (and the SOAP) spec come into play here: encoding style and binding style.

34.4.1 Encoding Style and Interoperability

The SOAP specification specifies a mode called encodingStyle that can take on two values, encoded and literal.[1] This refers to how the XML representing parameters is defined on the wire. Encoded refers to Section 5 of the SOAP specification, which defines a primitive mechanism for mapping programming language types to XML. Literal means don't do that. Instead, the type information is provided by an external mechanism, more likely than not a WSDL document that uses XML Schema to define exactly what types are used in the SOAP message.

This came about because the SOAP specification was written prior to the adoption of the XML Schema specification. Thus, the original SOAP specification had to provide a way of

---

1.   If no encodingStyle is specified, the value is assumed to be literal.

encoding type information along with the parameters being sent for method calls because there was no accepted way of specifying it. Where this really differs from XML Schema is with arrays. Section 5.4.2 of the SOAP specification lists a particular mechanism for representing programming language arrays in XML that uses a special SOAPEnc:Array schema type. Also, encoding information (such as `<item xsi:type="xsd:string">`) was usually associated with SOAP message body elements encoded using the SOAP encoding standard.

However, since the adoption of XML Schema (which, you'll remember, WSDL uses to represent its types), most languages have rendered the need for SOAP encoding obsolete by specifying their own mappings (or serialization rules) from XML Schema to the programming language types.

For instance, the JAX-RPC specification covers how Java types are mapped to XML Schema elements and vice versa. This obviates the need for extra encoding information in the XML. As a result, SOAP encoding has been superceded by literal encoding with the mapping being specified externally by an XML Schema document, usually in the form of a WSDL document.

You should not plan on making your Web services use SOAP encoding if interoperability is ever likely to be required. Instead you should plan on using literal encoding, whenever possible. Most of the interoperability problems that have been encountered by developers using Web services stem from differing interpretations of SOAP encoding, so avoiding the issue is a useful tactic. In fact, the WS-I has gone so far as to specifically exclude the use of SOAP encoding from its basic interoperability profile.[2]

34.4.2 Binding Style and Interoperability

WSDL specifies two different binding styles in its SOAP binding. The values of the binding style attribute are RPC and document. This means that if a WSDL document specifies an operation that has a binding style attribute set to RPC the receiver must interpret that message using the rules in Section 7 of the SOAP specification.

This means, for instance, that the XML element inside the SOAP body (called a wrapper element) must have a name identical to the name of the corresponding programming-language operation that is to be invoked. Each message part within that element must correspond exactly (in name and order) to a parameter of that programming-language operation. There must be only a single element returned (which must be named XXXResponse, where XXX is the name of the corresponding operation in the language) that contains inside it exactly one element, the return value of the operation.

The document binding style is looser. A message in the document binding style must be made up of well-formed, namespace-qualified XML. It is up to the SOAP engine that receives it to determine how to interpret it. Having said that, it is common (i.e., among Microsoft tools) to use document binding style and literal encoding to represent RPCs. In that case, the sender will still follow many or all of the rules of Section 7 of the SOAP spec in formulating the message,

---

2.   See section 4.1.7 of the WS-I basic profile.

but it is up to the receiver to determine how to handle the message, either as an RPC call or as a document to be processed. In particular, there is still an outer element that represents (and names) the operation, while that element contains elements that represent message parameters.

Perhaps the most curious dichotomy to emerge in the Web services design community has been the conflict arising from those who approach Web services from a messaging background, and those who approach it from an OOP background. [Sun] typifies this dichotomy when it makes a mistaken distinction between document-oriented Web services and RPC-style Web services. [Sun] states that document-oriented Web services apply only to asynchronous messaging processing while RPC-style Web services apply to synchronous services.

[Sun] missing a valuable point: how the choice of a usage scenario applies to the binding style. To understand, let's examine the three usage scenarios defined in the WS-I usage scenarios). They are:

- **One-way**—A message that does not require a response from a Web services provider. The Web services consumer issues a request to a provider, but does not wait for a response. This was defined in [WSDL] and has been clarified in [WS-I].
- **Synchronous Request/Response**—The most commonly used scenario. In it, a Web services consumer issues a request to a provider and synchronously waits (blocks) while the provider processes the request and provides a response. This is the operating semantic that all RPC mechanisms implement since this is the standard function-call semantic in procedural and OOP languages.
- **Basic Callback**—Combines two synchronous request/response scenarios to enable asynchronous processing. An initial request is issued to a provider containing information that identifies the receiver. The request immediately results in an acknowledgement of receipt from the provider (without returning a value to the receiver). At some point, the receiver would then issue a request to the initial receiver (the callback) providing it with the full set of information requested by the initial request; the response to this request will be another acknowledgement. The two interactions are tied together by a correlation identifier ([Hohpe]).

A key point to derive from this is that RPC-style Web services are simply a subset of document-style services in general. While a document-style service can be used in any of the three usage scenarios defined in WS-I, an RPC-style Web service is limited to only the synchronous request/response scenario. The more important point is that if you choose to use document-style messages across the board, they will work regardless of the usage scenario you choose. There are some distinct advantages to taking this approach, namely that a single set of design principles can guide you regardless of the usage. This results in systems that are more consistent and more easily maintained

34.4.3   Choosing When to Use Document vs. RPC Binding Style

Despite the architectural arguments for or against using document style across the board, the fact is that the WS-I has declared that both RPC-literal and document-literal style Web services are allowable for interoperability. In particular, you need to evaluate whether to use document-style or RPC-style messaging in your Web services based on the details of the particular scenario you are implementing. While you want to be consistent in your processing model, you can achieve this by using either document or RPC style in a consistent way. You do not have to choose just one style throughout your business.

Some guidelines that can help you identify which mode to use in a particular scenario are:

- Some XML is intended to be treated as documents (for instance, a news feed). Document style should be used when the message payload is going to be processed as XML; for example, when it is to be transformed into another format and stored directly into a database or if the payload is going to be merged with other XML and then sent on to another destination.
- If your application already has XML interfaces, you will probably want to use document style. Likewise, if you are sending data conforming to an industry XML vocabulary.
- When executing functions or sending data which will be analyzed, you need to carefully evaluate the choice between document and RPC style. RPC offers simplicity and sometimes better tooling support. Document offers greater flexibility and decoupling, and, under some circumstances (large messages with many elements), vast reduction in message size, but may require more XML expertise and hand-coding.

Despite the fact that both models have been accepted, there have been fewer problems found when using document-literal style communications than RPC style. Thus, if you anticipate any interoperability with your services, we strongly advocate that you plan on using the document-literal style for your Web services. When doing so, be very cognizant of the limitations placed on what XML Schema elements can be understood by JAX-RPC[3] and other vendor tool sets.

34.4.4   An Example of Document-Literal Processing in WebSphere

In Chapter 33 you saw a simple example of building an RPC Web service from our simple random ID generator EJB. In this example we will return to our case study and examine a more realistic example: building a document-literal Web service from the report generator EJB. You will find that most of the steps are the same as the ones you followed in the previous chapter; only a few parameters to Java2WSDL are different, and the structure of the generated WSDL is only slightly different from the WSDL you have seen earlier.

---

3.   Chapter 4 of the JAX-RPC specification lists the allowable WSDL to Java mappings

As in the previous example, we will begin by creating an SEI in accordance with the JAX-RPC specification. In our case, this interface will be named `com.wsbook.case-study.ejb.WSReportActionProcessorFacade.java`:

```
package com.wsbook.casestudy.ejb;

import java.rmi.RemoteException;

import com.wsbook.casestudy.exception.ModelException;

import com.wsbook.casestudy.value.Report;


public interface WSReportActionProcessorFacade extends java.rmi.Remote {

        public Report generateEmployeeByMonthReport()

                throws ModelException, java.rmi.RemoteException;

}
```

Create this class in the appropriate package using the create class wizard within WSAD. Once you have added the SEI to the EJB module, you are ready to generate the WSDL file from the SEI. As in the previous example, several directories must be on your classpath in order for the command line tools to locate the necessary classes, and other directories must be added to the PATH variable to allow you to run the tools. To help you with that, we have provided a bat file (setupWSEnv.bat) on the accompanying CD that will help you set up these paths. Copy this file (whose template is shown next) to your local hard drive and edit it to match the path where your WSAD workspace is installed.

```
REM SetupWSEnv Batch file

REM Edit the following line to match the directory

REM Where you have installed WebSphere 5.02

set WS_ROOT=C:\WebSphere\AppServer

REM Edit the following line to match the directory

REM Where your WSAD Workspaces are installed

set WSAD_ROOT=C:\Documents and Settings\kbrown\My Documents\IBM\wsad
```

```
call %WS_ROOT%\bin\setupcmdline

set WSADWorkspacePath=%WSAD_ROOT%\newbookworkspace

set UtilityJarPath=\TimeSheet-AppLogic\classes

set EJBModulePath=\TimeSheetGroup\ejbModule

set CLASSPATH=

%WAS_HOME%\AppServer\lib\j2ee.jar;.;%WSADWorkspacePath%%UtilityJarPath%;%WSA

DWorkspacePath%%EJBModulePath%;%CLASSPATH%

set PATH=%WAS_HOME%\bin;%PATH%
```

Open a command prompt and run the setupWSEnv batch file to set up your directories. Then, as in the previous chapter, `cd` to the TimeSheetGroup/ejbModule directory underneath your WSAD workspace. As in the previous examples, we must then create a wsdl directory to hold the generated wsdl, so `cd` to the META-INF directory and use mkdir to create a wsdl directory under META-INF. Then, `cd` back to the TimeSheetGroup/ejbModule directory to run `java2WSDL` (which, you will remember, is part of the WAS 5.0 Fixpack 2 installation underneath the bin directory of the WebSphere/AppServer installation root). Run `java2WSDL` with the following parameters:

```
java2WSDL -verbose

-style document

-use literal

-implClass com.wsbook.casestudy.ejb.ReportActionProcessorFacade

-output META-INF\wsdl\WSReportActionProcessorFacade.wsdl

com.wsbook.casestudy.ejb.WSReportActionProcessorFacade
```

Two of these parameters need more explanation. We are using two parameters that you have not seen in the previous use of the Java2WSDL tool in Chapter 33—the `-style` parameter with the argument `document` and the `-use` parameter with the argument `literal`. As you can guess, this is what allows us to generate document-literal WSDL from the SEI. In the previous examples, we've taken the default, which is RPC style (and since RPC style is used, encoded is the default for the use parameter).

The generated WSDL is similar to the WSDL generated for an RPC Web service, with one noticeable exception. Take a look at the wsdl:binding section from the generated WSDL file:

```
<wsdl:binding name="WSReportActionProcessorFacadeSoapBinding"

        type="impl:WSReportActionProcessorFacade">

    <wsdlsoap:binding style="document" transport="http://

            schemas.xmlsoap.org/soap/http"/>

    <wsdl:operation name="generateEmployeeByMonthReport">

        <wsdlsoap:operation soapAction=""/>

        <wsdl:input name="generateEmployeeByMonthReportRequest">

            <wsdlsoap:body use="literal"/>

        </wsdl:input>

        <wsdl:output name="generateEmployeeByMonthReportResponse">

            <wsdlsoap:body use="literal"/>

        </wsdl:output>

        <wsdl:fault name="ModelException">

            <wsdlsoap:fault name="ModelException" use="literal"/>

        </wsdl:fault>

    </wsdl:operation>

</wsdl:binding>
```

First, notice that in the wsdlsoap:binding element, the style attribute is set to document. Likewise, all of the wsdlsoap:body elements have their use attribute set to literal. This means that all of the operations within the binding element will use documents mode. Similarly, all of the operations are set to use literal XML encoding. It is possible to mix encoding modes (for instance, if there were several operations in a port type you could set one operation to use literal XML encoding, and another to use SOAP encoding) but that should be discouraged for clarity's sake.

In the previous chapter we discussed why you want to provide an implementation class, how to provide the SEI class, and why you want to set the output directory as we've shown here, so we will not cover that again. Instead, we are ready to move on to the next part of the example, which is using `WSDL2Java` to create the JSR-109 deployment descriptors so that we can export the EAR file to WAS 5.02.

While executing the next step, you need to be very careful to get the parameters right. It is worth double-checking the parameters you provide to WSDL2Java because one of the parameters, the `-j` option, stands for Java generation. In our case, we are only using WSDL2Java to generate JSR-109 deployment descriptors, but you will remember that it is also capable of generating Java skeleton classes from a WSDL file. If you do not set the `-j` option to `No` (as shown next), your implementation classes will be overwritten.

While you are still in the same directory as you were while you executed WSDL2Java, execute the following command:

```
wsdl2Java

-verbosc

-r server

-c ejb

-j No

META-INF\wsdl\WSReportActionProcessorFacade.wsdl
```

Here we are setting the `-r` parameter (role) to server, so that only the JSR-109 server-side deployment descriptors are generated. We are informing WSDL2Java to generate code for an EJB (with `-c` [container] being set to `ejb`), and, most importantly, we are telling it not to generate any Java code from this WSDL. At this point, we are nearly done at the command line. However, first we need to move back into WSAD for just a moment. Go back into WebSphere Studio, refresh the TimeSheetGroup project and open the webservices.xml deployment descriptor file. In that file, update the ejb-link element to point back to the ReportActionProcessorFacade as shown here:

```
<service-impl-bean>

  <ejb-link>ReportActionProcessorFacade</ejb-link>

</service-impl-bean>
```

After saving this file, select the wsbook EAR project, and export the EAR file (using the *File > Export...* option or the corresponding context menu option) to a directory on your local hard drive so that we can then run the endpoint enabler tool. You may want to name the file ws-wsbook.ear to remind yourself that this is a version of the wsbook application enabled for Web services.

As in Chapter 33, go back to the command line, cd to the directory where you exported the EAR file and run the endpoint enabler by typing endptenabler. In this instance, though, the first thing you want to do is to give it the name of the EAR file (ws-wsbook.ear), then accept all of the defaults for the name of the endpoint and context root.

After that, you can then deploy the EAR file into WAS 5.02 using the same set of deployment steps you used in the previous chapter. Chief among those steps is that you need to check the deploy Web services box, start the enterprise application after it has been deployed, and publish the WSDL after the application is started so that you can use the published WSDL to build a Web services client.

You will follow the same set of steps from the last chapter to create a Web services client to test your new document-literal service. Begin by creating a Java project named WSTimeSheetReportClientJ2SE. Add the same set of JAR files from WebSphere 5.02 onto the Java project build path as you added in the previous chapter to the J2SE client. Then, create the following class in the package `com.wsbook.casestudy.wsreport.client` (Listing 34.1):

Listing 34.1 Testing a document-literal service

```
package com.wsbook.casestudy.wsreport.client;



import com.wsbook.casestudy.value.*;

import com.wsbook.casestudy.ejb.*;

import java.net.MalformedURLException;

import java.net.URL;

import javax.xml.namespace.QName;

import javax.xml.rpc.Service;

import javax.xml.rpc.ServiceException;

import javax.xml.rpc.ServiceFactory;



public class WSReportByMonthClient {
```

```
public static void main (String[] args) throws Exception {

    try{

Service aService = ServiceFactory.newInstance().createService(

    new URL("http://localhost:9080/TimeSheetGroup/services/

WSReportActionProcessorFacade/wsdl/WSReportActionProcessorFacade.wsdl"),

    new QName("http://

ejb.casestudy.wsbook.com","WSReportActionProcessorFacadeService") );

WSReportActionProcessorFacade reportService =

(WSReportActionProcessorFacade)

                aService.getPort(

                new QName("http://ejb.casestudy.wsbook.com",

                "WSReportActionProcessorFacade"),

                WSReportActionProcessorFacade.class);

        Report result =

        (Report)reportService.generateEmployeeByMonthReport();

        System.out.println(result);

    } catch (Exception e)

        {e.printStackTrace();}

    }

}
```

The only thing new here is that we are obtaining a complex object (a report) back from our Web service. However, we're not ready to test our new service yet, even after adding this class. We have yet to generate the client-side Java classes and JSR-109 deployment descriptors necessary to make this client run. You do that with the WSDL2Java tool, this time pointing at the published WSDL from the previous step.

At a command prompt, change to the directory structure underneath your new WSTimeSheetReportClientJ2SE project. Create a META-INF subdirectory of WSTimeSheetReportClientJ2SE, just as you did in Chapter 33. Then invoke WSDL2Java with the following parameters:

```
wsdl2java

-r client

-c client

-verbose http://localhost:9080/TimeSheetGroup/services/

WSReportActionProcessorFacade/wsdl/WSReportActionProcessorFacade.wsdl
```

Note that you are creating Java and JSR-109 files for the client role, for the client container, and that you are pointing to the previously published WSDL for the input to the wsdl2Java tool. Once you have finished running this command, you should be able to refresh the project, and then use the launch configuration editor in WSAD to set up the runtime classpath of the J2SE client (use the same JAR files as in Chapter 33) and test your new client.

34.4.5 A Final Note about Interoperability

Interoperability between systems is one of the primary reasons for using Web services. However, you can't just assume that your Web services will be interoperable, even if you do follow the procedures we've discussed; you need to test your services to ensure interoperability.

Our recommendation is to plan to simultaneously test your services with as many different clients as you anticipate will use your services. We recommend that nearly all services be tested against both Java and .NET clients. This is critical to avoid being unpleasantly surprised later. Also, make sure that you keep abreast of the latest interoperability issues that have been found. Use *http://ws-i.org* and *http://soapbuilders.org* as resources for discovering these issues.

34.5 Summary

While Web services are not the solution to all problems, they can certainly make some problems, notably those of cross-language or cross-system integration, easier. In this chapter, you've seen a bit more about how a SOA can help you obtain these benefits, and how to design your systems to make interoperability easier and to make it possible to take advantage of the best communication mechanism available for each service. In particular, you've learned the following major points:

- Web services are not appropriate for all situations. They are quite effective in solving different types of interoperability questions (interoperability with Microsoft tools, connecting with existing Web services-enabled systems, or when dealing with firewall issues) but are not as effective in many designs where both sides of a conversation can be mandated.

- Use the Business Delegate pattern to allow for situations where clients may choose different transports based on differing quality of service needs.
- When planning to use Web services, be cognizant of the differences between Microsoft and Java tools with regard to processing style. We recommend the use of document-literal Web services wherever interoperability is a possibility.

A Final Look

Throughout this book, we have demonstrated how J2EE and WebSphere combine to form an architecture and runtime suitable for large, mission-critical applications. Through hands-on examples, we have illustrated how IBM's WebSphere Studio family of tools helps you master enterprise application development. Along the way, we used these examples to show many J2EE best practices intended to make your development tasks easier, your code more maintainable, and your enterprise projects successful. We've also provided rationale for our approaches to building enterprise applications.

So what have we hoped you've learned through this journey? First, if we had to identify the single architectural principle that is the cornerstone of everything we have discussed, and the key to understanding how to navigate through the WebSphere product forest, we would have to declare layering to be that principle.

35.1 Application Layering

Application layering is applying the idea of separation of concerns to your software. Understanding how each of the J2EE technologies fits within an overall architectural road map is the key to writing flexible, maintainable applications whose components do not step on each other's toes. In explaining our approach, we have described these five layers in detail:

- **Presentation**—The presentation layer consists of objects defined to accept user input and display application outputs.
- **Controller/Mediator**—The controller isolates the user interaction from the business model while the mediators capture and decouple application-specific functionality from presentation technology by performing domain model requests for presentation or controller objects that drive a specific application use case. Mediator classes are defined

to satisfy a specific application user interface function or use case; they are less granular than controllers.

- **Domain**—The domain objects are the primary assets of a J2EE application. The domain contains business rules and logic. Domain objects know nothing of how data is presented or persisted.
- **Data Mapping**—The data mapping layer moves data from domain objects to back-end data sources and vice versa.
- **Data Source**—The data source layer physically stores and retrieves data from back-end data sources.

We've demonstrated how this five-layer architecture can map to the different parts of the J2EE standard, and how you can use the WebSphere tool set and runtime to build and deploy applications that use those technologies. We hope that our architectural road map and the comparisons of different approaches to similar ends (like JSP and XML/XSLT) have helped you understand how to choose which approach to take.

Also, we have discussed application responsibilities that developers must apply to all application development efforts. Implementing these activities consistently using a design that is extendible facilitates reuse and minimizes side effects when requirements change. Moreover, standardizing these services across all applications can yield efficiencies in determining and communicating new development and maintenance activities.

35.2 Case Study and J2EE Technologies

It's not enough to simply discuss a complex architectural topic like application layering in an abstract way, especially when this is a book to be used by practitioners. In this book we have also presented examples of how you use each technology in the context of a case study about a company developing a simple J2EE application for tracking time worked on projects. The example was sufficiently complicated, both from a user interface and a domain object perspective to provide an appropriate backdrop to show how to apply J2EE technologies in a real-world environment.

In order to illustrate to you how the different J2EE technologies work together, we have provided an overview of the J2EE architecture, a brief discussion of the specifications and described a component design with the solutions they provided. We described which J2EE technologies are available for enterprise application components and where they fall in the layered application architecture. We've provided examples (both small, stand-alone examples, and larger examples in the context of our case study) to show you how these technologies fit together, and how alternative technology choices (like using Struts or servlets as controllers) play out in the context of an application design.

The J2EE only defines the interfaces, life cycles, and interactions of components they must carry out and the roles that can be held by developers involved in the development and deployment of server-based applications. It does not provide you with detailed guidance on how to combine those components in the best way. That is what we hope to have provided you in our book.

35.3 Tooling

Throughout we have also provided a guide to how to use IBM's best-of-breed application development platform—WebSphere Studio—to build, test, debug, and maintain your application assets. WebSphere Studio provides a highly productive platform in which to develop extensive J2EE applications. One of the common themes throughout is to take advantage of the vast array of wizards available to accelerate your development and free you to concentrate on your design.

One of the great challenges is ensuring the quality of your code assets. A combination of the robust test environments and tools within WebSphere Studio and a conscientious use of test frameworks can reap tremendous benefits.

35.4 A Parting Thought

In this book we have attempted to describe the most common J2EE technologies and best practices that can help you deliver enterprise solutions and presented these technologies in the context of IBM's WebSphere family of products. We recognize the complexity of the task of building large-scale enterprise applications. While one book cannot answer all questions about a subject, we hope that we've set you firmly on the path toward architecting, designing, and implementing your WebSphere solutions in the best way possible. Good luck in all your development efforts.

Installing Products and Examples from the CDs

The case study and all other examples referenced in this book are delivered on CD #3 within the examples.zip file. The examples are packaged as WSAD projects within this zip file. Each project will need to be imported into WSAD. We do not provide the source code in another format; since the purpose of this book is to teach you to use WSAD and the other WebSphere tools, we encourage you to try these projects out in that environment.

We expect that most of you install WSAD, DB2 and WAS from the included CDs that come with this book. If you already have copies of WSAD 5.01, WAS 5.02 and DB2 Universal Database 8.1.2 on your machine, you can skip the next section and move on to the section on installing the case study examples.

A.1 Installing the Products from the CDs

Before you begin installing the products from the CDs, you should make sure that your machine meets the minimum requirements. The set of products you will install will require a minimum of a 500 Mhz (or greater) machine with 512Mb of RAM and 4 GB of free disk space running Windows 2000 or Windows XP. The installation also requires a live internet connection to download a WSAD fix pack from the IBM Web site. Follow these steps to install the product set:

Step 1: Install WSAD. Insert Disc 1 into your CD drive. The WSAD installation process should automatically start. If it does not, run setup.exe from the root of the CD. From the WSAD Install screen, select "Install IBM WebSphere Studio Application Developer" and follow the prompts to install WSAD. At some point, the installation process will prompt you to insert Disc 2.

Step 2: Install DB2 Universal Database Personal Edition, version 8.1. Re-insert Disc 1 into your CD drive. Press Exit to cancel the WSAD installation dialog. Use the Windows Explorer or *Start > Run* to run the file setup.exe in the directory DB2PE821. Follow the prompts to complete the installation of DB2.

Step 3: Upgrade to WSAD 5.01. Start WSAD by choosing *Start > IBM WebSphere Studio > Application Developer 5.0* from the Windows Start Menu. Once WSAD has loaded, select *Help > Software Updates > New Updates* from the WSAD Help Menu. WSAD will automatically locate the WSAD 5.01 updates. Install both of the selected updates.

Step 4: Fix APAR #jr18488. Unfortunately, the versions of DB2 and WSAD that we ship with the book have a compatibility problem that makes it impossible to execute some of our examples unless it is addressed. The details of this fix (including its symptoms) are found at: http://www.ibm.com/support/docview.wss?uid=swg21111633 . To fix the problem, exit WSAD. Replace the db2locale.dll file in your WebSphere Studio tools installation with the db2locale.dll file from DB2 V8.1.2. To do this, copy the file:

db2_home\bin\db2locale.dll

to *ws_home*\wstools\eclipse\plugins\com.ibm.etools.subuilder.win32_5.x.x

Where

- *db2_home* is the directory where DB2 is installed.
- *ws_home* is the directory where WSAD is installed.
- _5.x.x is the WebSphere tools plugin version, based on your current install configuration.

Step 5: Install WAS 5.0. Insert Disc 3 into your CD drive. Using the Windows Explorer, or *Start > Run* from the Windows Start Menu, run the file Install.exe in the directory WAS50. Follow the prompts to install WAS 5.0.

Step 6: Install the WAS 5.02 Fix pack. Before starting the upgrade, make sure that all WebSphere processes (including the IBM HTTP Server) have been stopped. Use the Windows Explorer or *Start > Run* from the Windows Start Menu to run the file updateWizard.bat inside the WAS5Fixpack2 directory on Disc 3. Follow the prompts to upgrade WAS to fix pack 5.02.

A.2   Installing the Case Study Examples

A new feature called Project Interchange has been developed for WSAD to make it easier to import projects from a zip file. This feature is also delivered on Disc 3 in the com.ibm.etools.project.interchange.feature.zip file. Before you begin importing and using the case study or any other example, you must first install this feature using the steps which follow.

> ### MORE INFORMATION FOR THE PROJECT INTERCHANGE FEATURE
>
> More information regarding the Project Interchange feature can be found in "Share and Share Alike: Project Interchange in Eclipse and WebSphere Studio Made Simple" located on IBM's Developer Domain. You can use the following link for this article: *http://www.ibm.com/websphere/developer/library/techarticles/0309_bergschacher/bergschacher.html.*

A.2.1 Installing the Project Interchange Feature

1. Unzip the com.ibm.etools.project.interchange.feature.zip file to your WSAD install directory.

2. Start WSAD. You should be prompted that you have pending changes. Click *Yes*. If a prompt does not appear, select *Help > Software Updates > Pending Changes*.

3. Expand the tree in the Pending Configuration Changes window that appears. Select the top level date which includes the Project Interchange feature (this should be the first and only entry).

4. Click *Finish*.

5. Select *Yes* when prompted to restart so the changes will take effect.

Now that the Project Interchange feature is successfully installed, you may proceed to import the necessary projects for an example referenced within the book. The next steps describe how to install the case study.

A.2.2 Installing the Case Study

6. Select *File > Import > Project Interchange* to launch the new Project Interchange wizard.

7. Browse to the **examples.zip** file on the CD for the **From zip file**.

8. Select the **wasbook** and **wasbookServers** projects from the list.

9. Click the *Select Referenced* button to automatically select all required projects.

10. Click *Finish* to have the selected projects imported into your current workspace.

Now the wasbook case study projects are installed in your workspace and you are ready to proceed. Whenever you need to install another example, follow these steps except you will select the required project(s) for the example you wish to use in Step 3.

A.2.3 Running the Case Study

To run the case study, perform the following steps:

1. Select the wasbook application from the J2EE Hierarchy view and select the *Generate Deploy Code* context menu action by right-clicking. This will generate deploy code for all EJB modules contained in the application.

2. Use the procedure from the Export Database Tables section in Chapter 24 to export the tables for both the OIDGenerator and TimeSheetGroup EJB module projects. Since the TimeSheetGroup was generated with the NULLID schema name, you do not want to export the tables using fully qualified names and you want to use a valid database login ID.

3. Open the WAS5 server configuration editor by double-clicking on the WAS5 server in the J2EE Hierarchy view under the Servers group. Flip to the Security tab and edit the

wsbook JAAS authentication alias entry so that the user ID and password match those used in Step 2. Be sure to press Control-S to save the server configuration.

4. Add sample data into the tables created in Step 2. Locate the file fillTables.clp located on the CD. The contents of this file are shown here:

```
CONNECT TO SAMPLE;

INSERT INTO ADDRESSEJB (CITY, STATE1, STREETADDRESS, ZIPCODE, ADDRESSKEY)

VALUES ('Apex', 'NC', '214 Maple Leaf Way', '27555', 199);

INSERT INTO ADDRESSEJB (CITY, STATE1, STREETADDRESS, ZIPCODE, ADDRESSKEY)

VALUES ('Cary', 'NC', '277 Broadcloth Street', '27545', 299);

INSERT INTO EMPLOYEEEJB (EMPID, HOMEADDRESS_ADDRESSKEY, NAME, STATE, CITY,

BUILDING, OFFICE) VALUES ('99', 199, 'Fred

Jones','NC','Durham','501','D318');

INSERT INTO EMPLOYEEEJB (EMPID, HOMEADDRESS_ADDRESSKEY, NAME,STATE, CITY,

BUILDING,OFFICE)VALUES('49',299,'JamieWoo','NC','Durham','501','D320');

INSERT INTO PROJECTEJB(NAME, PROJNUMBER) VALUES ('Project Purple', '22');

INSERT INTO PROJECTEJB(NAME, PROJNUMBER) VALUES ('Project Ozma', '48');
```

5. Execute this file by opening a DB2 command window and typing

```
db2 -t -f filltables.clp
```

at the command prompt.

6. Select the TimeApp project in the J2EE Navigator pane, and invoke *Run on Server* from the context menu. When the select server dialog appears, select the existing WAS5 server. You should see the index.html file pictured in Chapter 31. You can then use the user guide in Chapter 31 as a guide to using the application.

A.2.4 Installing the Web Services Example

The steps for installing the Web services example are similar to those of the case study except you will use the WSUtilityClientJ2EE-EAR application project and its required projects. The Web services example also requires that you have WebSphere Application Server 5.0.2 installed. Following the next set of steps will correct the compile errors that are found with this example.

1. Select the *Window > Preferences* workbench menu option.

2. Expand Java from the list and select Classpath Variables.

3. Click the *New* button.

4. Enter WAS_V502 for the name of the new classpath variable and browse to the Web-Sphere 5.0.2 install directory for the Path.

5. Click the *OK* button to create the Classpath Variable.

6. Select *OK* on the properties page to accept the changes.

7. Select *Yes* at the prompt to perform a full build and recompile the projects.

Constructing J2EE Web Services Using WSAD 5.1

At the time of this writing, WSAD 5.0.1 was the latest commercially available product set offered by IBM and is therefore the base tooling for this book. Chapter 33 walked you through an example of creating a Web service from the RandomIDGenerator utility class using a combination of command line tools and WSAD. The reason for using command line tools, rather than the Web services wizards provided with WSAD 5.0.1, is the wizards in WSAD 5.0.1 are tooled for Apache SOAP and do not generate artifacts that are compliant with the JAX-RPC and JSR-109 runtime provided with WAS 5.0.2. In other words, the tool and the runtime were out of sync.

Fortunately, the Web services support included with WSAD 5.1 is tooled to generate artifacts for WAS 5.0.2—the tool and the runtime are back in sync. This section will present the same example from Chapter 33 using the next release of WSAD, version 5.1. We will also use this opportunity to explore some of the new features presented to the Web services developer.

B.1 What's New?

The support for Web services in WSAD 5.1 is greatly enhanced from prior versions. WSAD's UTC has been upgraded to 5.0.2, the latest version of WebSphere, which includes a JSR-101 (JAX-RPC)- and JSR-109-compliant Web services engine. The command line tools used in Chapter 33 in conjunction with Version 5.0 are now integrated directly into the tool and exposed through context aware menu options and wizards. Here is a high-level overview of additional features included in WSAD 5.1.

- WSDL editor that presents a graphical layout and source views of a WSDL document
- First-class deployment descriptor editors
- Integrated JAX-RPC handler support
- Automatic inclusion of Web project to enable HTTP transport for EJBs (same function as the `endptenabler` command)

- Integrated support for security
- Rules to validate the creation of Web services compliant with the WS-I profiles
- Better support for UDDI, including an explorer and publishing options
- Cheat sheets for top-down and bottom-up Web service creation
- Full complement of help documents

There are a few notes before we get started. Relative to the Web services tooling, Version 5.1 represents a significant increase in function and integration. Because the WebSphere tooling must be compliant with industry specifications, this affects how code can be generated. The way development organizations choose to structure their projects for separating the EJB projects into source and module folders may sometimes result in minor inaccuracy in artifact generation. Because this appendix is based on a prerelease version of WSAD 5.1, some of the screen shots you see may differ slightly from what you may see in the released product.

B.2   Creating the RandomIDGenerator Service

In Chapter 33, we started with the RandomIDGenerator stateless session bean and created an SEI, then used the command-line tools to generate the remaining Web service artifacts such as the deployment descriptors. Because the code provided with this book is configured for this environment, it will be necessary to make some modifications to the UtilityGroup. In particular, you will remove the Web service artifacts that are needed to complete the example in Chapter 33. Why not provide a new project? As we wrote this book, it became evident that developers building Web services-based solutions with WSAD 5.0 will want to move these projects into Version 5.1. Using the existing example will serve to illustrate the basic steps to begin using your existing EJB projects in the latest version of the IBM tooling.

B.2.1   Project Setup

The first step to using WSAD 5.1 is to delete the files from the UtilitiesGroup that we created in Chapter 33. From the J2EE Project Navigator view (Figure B.1), expand the ejbModule META-INF folder. Also expand the WSDL folder. Select and delete the following files:

- WSRandomIDGenerator.wsdl
- ibm-webservice-*.xmi
- webservices.xml
- WSRandomIDGenerator_mapping.xml.

In the source folder, expand the `com.wsbook.casestudy.ejb.utilities` package and delete the WSRandomIDGenerator.java file.

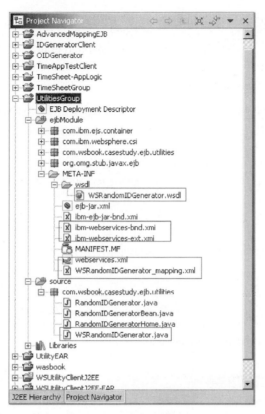

Figure B.1 Existing Web service artifacts to be removed.

B.2.2 Create the RandomIDGenerator Service

The next step is to create a Web project that will contain the Web services servlet. In Chapter 33, this was added for you by the endptenabler command line tool. WSAD 5.1 incorporates this function into the Web services wizard and will automatically add the necessary constructs to a Web project.

From the J2EE Hierarchy view, expand the Enterprise Applications folder and select the UtilityEAR. Right-click and choose *New > Dynamic Web Project*. When the wizard opens, enter WSUtilityGroupRouter as the project name and mark the Configure Advanced Options check box, as shown in Figure B.2. Click *Next*.

The second page of the wizard (Figure B.3) will present options to specify the EAR, the project's context root, and the J2EE level. Accept the defaults and press *Next*.

The Features page allows you to specify a default style sheet. Since we will use this project only for the Web services router, it is not necessary to have a style sheet. Deselect the check boxes and click *Finish*. Since we are modifying an EAR that is associated with an existing

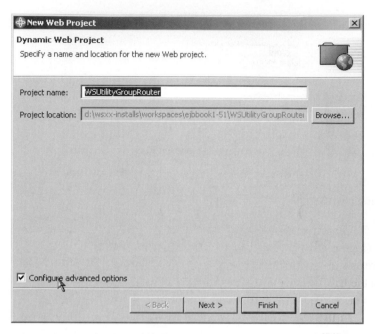

Figure B.2   Creating a dynamic Web project.

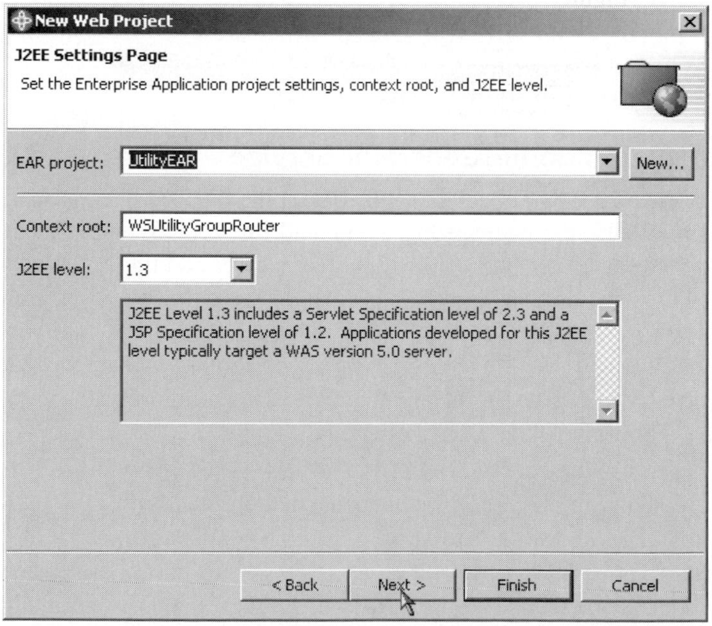

Figure B.3   Web project J2EE settings.

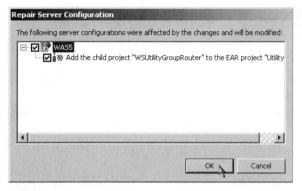

Figure B.4 Repair WAS5 server configuration.

server, during the project generation you will be asked to repair the server configuration for the WAS 5 server (Figure B.4). When prompted, select *OK*.

If you are asked to switch to the Web perspective, choose No. The result will be a new Web module within the UtilityEAR called WSUtilityGroupRouter.war.

At this point, we can use WSAD to generate the Web service from the RandomIDGenerator session bean. In the J2EE hierarchy browser expand the UtilitiesGroup that is under EJB Modules. Expand Session Beans and right-click RandomIDGenerator. In WSAD 5.1 there is a Web Services menu option with three choices: *Generate WSDL Files*, *Deploy as Web Service*, and *Endpoint Enabler* (Figure B.5).

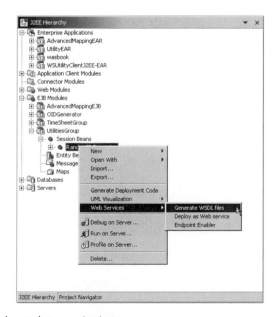

Figure B.5 WSAD Web services context menu.

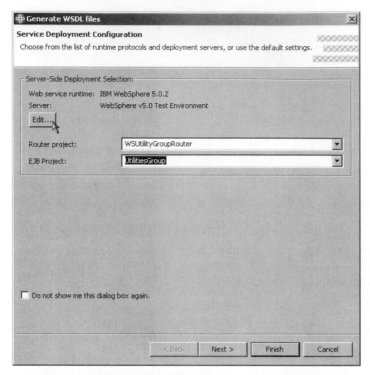

Figure B.6 Generate RandomIDGenerator WSDL files.

Because we are using an existing session bean, we will choose to generate the WSDL files (Figure B.6). This will generate the WSDL, the deployment descriptors, and the mapping files. To begin, select *Generate WSDL files* from the *Web Services* menu of the RandomIDGenerator.

Update the Router project option to be the Web project added in the previous step. Change the EJB Project to be the UtilitiesGroup. Since we already have a server, select the *Edit* button at the top of the page.

When the dialog box shown in Figure B.7 opens, scroll to the top of the Server selection box. Expand the Existing Server and highlight WAS5. Click *OK* to close the dialog box, then *Next* to advance to the Web Service EJB Selection page. Accept the defaults and click *Next*.

Figure B.8 shows the Web Service Java Bean Identity page of the Web services wizard. Information on this page translates directly into the description of the service, as expressed in WSDL. The Web service URI is the endpoint that will be entered into the port element as the location of the service. The Methods section is the publicly available behavior that, when checked, will become WSDL operations.

The Style and Use section contains the options that will build the binding section of the service description. The WS-I recommends that Document/Literal be the preferred message style and, therefore, it is enabled by default. However, our existing J2SE client was created using

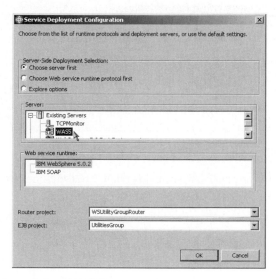

Figure B.7 Selecting the existing WAS 5 server.

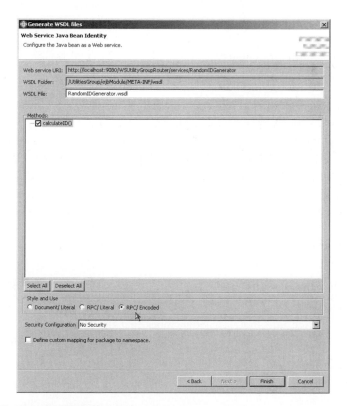

Figure B.8 Configuring the Web service.

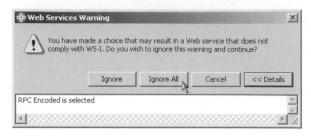

Figure B.9 WS-I compliance warning.

SOAP encoded RPC. Because we will reuse this client after making two minor changes, select RPC/Encoded. Click *Finish* to close the wizard and generate the WSDL files.

A nice feature about WSAD 5.1 is the built-in validation rules for WS-I compliance. Whenever a user choice violates a rule, a warning box is displayed (Figure B.9).

You may recall that the services created in Chapter 33 were defined to use SOAP-encoded RPC. While technically correct, the SOAP encoded/RPC style is out of favor with the WS-I recommended best practice of using the document/literal style. This is because document/literal is a more flexible way of encoding information. However, because this is a simple example, and for illustrative purposes we would like to reuse the J2SE client created in Chapter 33, we will ignore this warning. Click *Ignore All* to continue the Web services generation.

When the generation is complete, select the Project Navigator view of the J2EE perspective. You will notice that the ejbbModule and the source folders of the UtilitiesGroup contain errors (Figure B.10).

The UtilitiesGroup project is structured according to the best practice of partitioning source code and generated code into separate folders. However, the current driver of WSAD 5.1 does not recognize this distinction and, because it cannot locate the home or the remote interface, it generates new files within the ejbModule folder. The result is that the same class is created twice. The task list in Figure B.11 shows the root cause of the problems.

Fortunately, correcting the problem is very straightforward. In the ejbModule folder, delete the RandomIDGenerator.java and RandomIDGeneratorHome.java files, right-click the UtilitiesGroup, and rebuild the project. The errors should be cleared up and the project is now ready to be tested *within* WSAD.

B.3 Running and Testing the RandomIDGenerator Service

Because WSAD 5.1 includes WebSphere 5.0.2 as a test server, it is possible to deploy the RandomIDGenerator service into the UTC. Remember that the UtilityEAR is already associated with the WAS 5 server created in earlier chapters. Therefore, the only thing necessary to deploy the service is to run the UtilityEAR on the server. From the J2EE Hierarchy view, right-click the UtilityEAR and select *Run on Server* (Figure B.12).

Figure B.10 Errors caused by WSDL file generation.

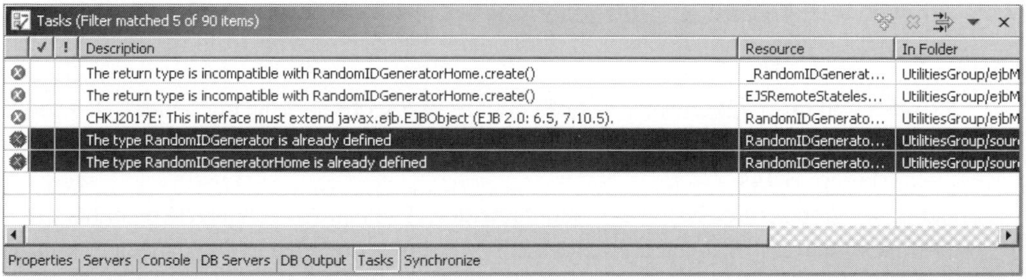

Figure B.11 Task list.

To verify that our service was deployed, we can enter its URL, *http://localhost:9080/WSUtilityGroupRouter/services/RandomIDGenerator*, into a Web browser. The result is the standard Web services welcome page with the text And now… Some Services.

Figure B.12 Deploying the RandomIDGenerator service.

B.3.1   Using the Web Services Explorer

An exciting new feature of WSAD 5.1 is the Web Services Explorer (WSE). This feature works in a similar fashion to the EJB test client. Given any WSDL file, the WSE will automatically generate the necessary classes to generate a full-featured client. We will use the WSE to verify that the RandomIDGenerator service was properly deployed. From the J2EE Project Navigator, select the RandomIDGenerator.wsdl file located in the wsdl folder within the META-INF folder. Right-click this file and select *Test with Web Services Explorer* option from the Web Services menu (Figure B.13).

The WSE will open a Web browser that contains two sections: one, on the left, that shows a tree view of the WSDL file; and one, on the right, that shows actions corresponding with the selected item (Figure B.14).

Testing the Web service becomes a simple matter of selecting calculateID by either clicking on the link in the Actions panel, or expanding the RandomIDGeneratorSoapBinding in the Navigator panel (Figure B.15).

The Go button will invoke the service and the result will be displayed within the Status panel on the bottom. Also contained in the Status panel is a link for Source. Selecting this link will display the contents of the SOAP request and response (Figure B.16). This provides an easy way to examine the contents of the messages and is an alternative to using the TCP monitor.

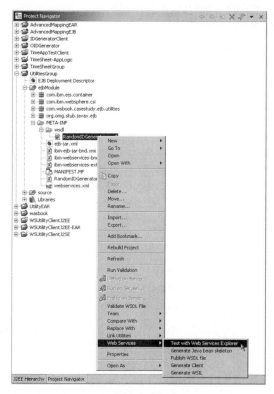

Figure B.13 Testing with the Web Services Explorer.

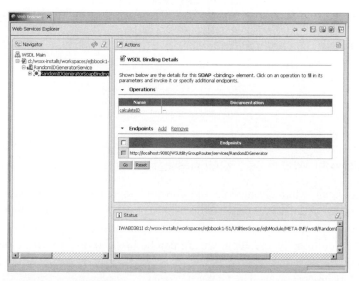

Figure B.14 The Web Services Explorer.

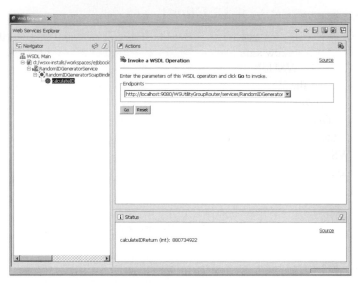

Figure B.15 Invoking the calculateID operation.

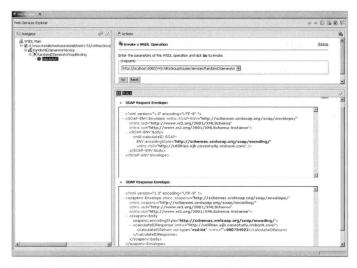

Figure B.16 Using the WSE to view SOAP message contents.

The WSE is an extremely flexible and powerful tool. This example has only touched on several of its base functions. You can use the WSE to examine *any* WSDL document, including those that reside outside of the workbench. WSDLs can then be imported to the file system or the workbench. Additionally, the client wizard can be invoked directly from the WSE. In addition to manipulating WSDL files, the WSE is able to work with Web Service Inspection Language (WSIL) documents, as well as UDDI registries.

B.4 Using the Existing J2SE Client

Now that we have a working service within WSAD, we would like to use our exiting J2SE client to invoke it. This requires a few simple changes to the main method of the WSRandomIDGeneratorClient.java file in the WSUtilityClientJ2SE project.

First, the URL of the WSDL file should be provided in the create service method. The service's URL is *http://localhost:9080/WSUtilityGroupRouter/wsdl/com/wsbook/casestudy/ejb/utilities/RandomIDGenerator.wsdl.*

Next, since the service endpoint was generated by WSAD, the service name and port do not contain the WS prefix that was used earlier, making it necessary to update the service name and the port name in the code. The following is the updated createService and getPort methods:

```
public static void main (String[] args) throws Exception {

    try{Service aService = ServiceFactory.newInstance().createService(

    new URL"http://localhost:9080/WSUtilityGroupRouter/wsdl/com/wsbook/

casestudy/ejb/utilities/RandomIDGenerator.wsdl"),

    new QName

("http://utilities.ejb.casestudy.wsbook.com","RandomIDGeneratorService"));

    WSRandomIDGenerator idGenService = (WSRandomIDGenerator)

        aService.getPort(

            new QName("http://utilities.ejb.casestudy.wsbook.com",

                "RandomIDGenerator"),

                WSRandomIDGenerator.class);

...
```

Note that in the last line of the code, the class file still contains the WS prefix. The WSRandomIDGenerator.class is the client side interface that resides in the com.wsbook.casestudy.ejb.utilities package within the WSUtilityClientJ2SE project. The client can be executed from the Run menu option just as in Chapter 33. The results will be a random number conveniently displayed in the console.

B.5 Summary

WSAD 5.1 includes a robust, feature-rich tool set the helps the developer create and use industry standard, WS-I compliant Web services for the J2EE platform.

Bibliography

[Alur] Deepak Alur, John Crupi, and Dan Malks, *Core J2EE Patterns: Best Practices and Design Strategies*, (Reading, MA: Addison-Wesley, 2001).

[Beck] Kent Beck, *Extreme Programming Explained: Embrace Change* (Reading, MA: Addison-Wesley, 2000).

[Blueprints] Sun Microsystems, Java Blueprints, available from: *http://java.sun.com/blueprints/*.

[Booch] Grady Booch, *Object-Oriented Analysis and Design with Applications*, 2nd Ed. (Reading, MA: Addison-Wesley, 1993).

[Brooks] Frederick Brooks, *The Mythical Man Month: Essays on Software Engineering*, Ann. Ed. (Reading, MA: Addison-Wesley, 1995).

[Brown00] Kyle Brown, "Choosing the Right EJB Type," VisualAge Developer's Domain, October 2000, available at: *http://www7.software.ibm.com/vad.nsf/data/document2361?OpenDocument&p=1&BCT=1&Footer=1*.

[Buschmann] Frank Buschmann, Regine Meunier, Hans Rohnert, Peter Sommerlad, and Michael Stal, *Pattern Oriented Software Engineering: A System of Patterns* (West Sussex, England: John Wiley & Sons, 1996).

[EJB] Sun Microsystems, EJB 2.0 Specification, available from: *http://java.sun.com/products/ejb/docs.html*.

[Evans] Eric Evans, *Domain Driven Design: Tackling Complexity at the Heart of Software* (Reading, MA: Addison-Wesley, 2003).

[Fowler99] Martin Fowler and Kendall Scott, *UML Distilled: A Brief Guide to the Standard Object Modeling Language*, 2nd Ed. (Reading, MA: Addison-Wesley, 1999).

[Fowler] Martin Fowler with David Rice, Matthew Foemmel, Edward Hieatt, Robert Mee, and Randy Stafford, *Patterns of Enterprise Application Architecture*, (Reading, MA: Addison-Wesley, 2002).

[Francis] Tim Francis, Eric Herness, Rob High, Jim Knutson, Kim Rochet, and Chris Vignola, *Professional IBM WebSphere 5.0 Application Server* (Birmingham, United Kingdom: Wrox Books, 2003).

[Gamma] Erich Gamma, Richard Helm, Ralph Johnson, and John Vlissides, *Design Patterns: Elements of Reusable Object-Oriented Design* (Reading, MA: Addison-Wesley, 1996).

[Hohpe] Gregor Hohpe and Bobby Woolf with Conrad D'Cruz, Sean Neville, Jonathan Simon, Martin Fowler, and Kyle Brown, *Patterns and Best Practices for Enterprise Integration* (Reading, MA: Addison-Wesley, 2003).

[IBM-JMS] MQ Series Using Java, available from: *http://www.ibm.com/software/integration/mqfamily/library/manualsa/csqzaw04/csqzaw.htm*.

[Jacobson] Ivar Jacobson, Grady Booch, and James Rumbaugh, *The Unified Software Development Process*, (Reading, MA: Addison-Wesley, 1999).

[JDBC] Sun Microsystems, JDBC 2.0 Specification, available at: *http://java.sun.com/products/jdbc/download.html*.

[MacKinnon] Tim MacKinnon, "Endotesting: Unit Testing with Mock Objects," available at *http://www.mockobjects.com/endotesting.html*.

[Marinescu] Floyd Marinescu, *EJB Design Patterns: Advanced Patterns, Processes and Idioms* (New York, NY: John Wiley & Sons, 2001).

[Monson-Haefel] Richard Monson-Haefel, *Enterprise JavaBeans*, 3rd Ed. (Sebastapol, CA: O'Reilly & Associates, 2001).

[Orfali] Robert Orfali and Dan Harkey, *Client Server Programming with Java and CORBA*, 2nd Ed. (New York, NY: John Wiley & Sons, 1998).

[RFC 2396] W3C RFC 2396, Uniform Resource Identifiers Generic Syntax, available at: *http://www.ietf.org/rfc/rfc2396.txt*.

[Shavor] Sherry Shavor, Jim D'Anjou, Dan Kehn, Scott Fairbrother, Dan Kellerman, and Pat McCarthy, *The Java Developer's Guide to Eclipse* (Reading, MA: Addison-Wesley, 2003).

[Sun] Sun Microsystems, Web Services blueprints, available from: *http://java.sun.com/blueprints/webservices*.

[Willenborg] Ruth Willenborg, "WebSphere version 5.0 Performance Report," available from: *http://www.ibm.com*.

[WSDL] W3C, Web Services Definition Language Specification, available from: *http://www.w3.org/TR/wsdl*.

[WS-I] Web Services Interoperability Organization, WS-I Basic Profile, available from: *http://www.ws-i.org/Documents.aspx*.

Index

Register Your Book

at www.awprofessional.com/register

You may be eligible to receive:

- Advance notice of forthcoming editions of the book
- Related book recommendations
- Chapter excerpts and supplements of forthcoming titles
- Information about special contests and promotions throughout the year
- Notices and reminders about author appearances, tradeshows, and online chats with special guests

Contact us

If you are interested in writing a book or reviewing manuscripts prior to publication, please write to us at:

Editorial Department
Addison-Wesley Professional
75 Arlington Street, Suite 300
Boston, MA 02116 USA
Email: AWPro@aw.com

Addison-Wesley

Visit us on the Web: http://www.awprofessional.com

Company's only obligation under these limited warranties is, at the Company's option, return of the warranted item for a refund of any amounts paid by you or replacement of the item. Any replacement of SOFTWARE or media under the warranties shall not extend the original warranty period. The limited warranty set forth above shall not apply to any SOFTWARE which the Company determines in good faith has been subject to misuse, neglect, improper installation, repair, alteration, or damage by you. EXCEPT FOR THE EXPRESSED WARRANTIES SET FORTH ABOVE, THE COMPANY DISCLAIMS ALL WARRANTIES, EXPRESS OR IMPLIED, INCLUDING WITHOUT LIMITATION, THE IMPLIED WARRANTIES OF MERCHANTABILITY AND FITNESS FOR A PARTICULAR PURPOSE. EXCEPT FOR THE EXPRESS WARRANTY SET FORTH ABOVE, THE COMPANY DOES NOT WARRANT, GUARANTEE, OR MAKE ANY REPRESENTATION REGARDING THE USE OR THE RESULTS OF THE USE OF THE SOFTWARE IN TERMS OF ITS CORRECTNESS, ACCURACY, RELIABILITY, CURRENTNESS, OR OTHERWISE.

IN NO EVENT, SHALL THE COMPANY OR ITS EMPLOYEES, AGENTS, SUPPLIERS, OR CONTRACTORS BE LIABLE FOR ANY INCIDENTAL, INDIRECT, SPECIAL, OR CONSEQUENTIAL DAMAGES ARISING OUT OF OR IN CONNECTION WITH THE LICENSE GRANTED UNDER THIS AGREEMENT, OR FOR LOSS OF USE, LOSS OF DATA, LOSS OF INCOME OR PROFIT, OR OTHER LOSSES, SUSTAINED AS A RESULT OF INJURY TO ANY PERSON, OR LOSS OF OR DAMAGE TO PROPERTY, OR CLAIMS OF THIRD PARTIES, EVEN IF THE COMPANY OR AN AUTHORIZED REPRESENTATIVE OF THE COMPANY HAS BEEN ADVISED OF THE POSSIBILITY OF SUCH DAMAGES. IN NO EVENT SHALL LIABILITY OF THE COMPANY FOR DAMAGES WITH RESPECT TO THE SOFTWARE EXCEED THE AMOUNTS ACTUALLY PAID BY YOU, IF ANY, FOR THE SOFTWARE.

SOME JURISDICTIONS DO NOT ALLOW THE LIMITATION OF IMPLIED WARRANTIES OR LIABILITY FOR INCIDENTAL, INDIRECT, SPECIAL, OR CONSEQUENTIAL DAMAGES, SO THE ABOVE LIMITATIONS MAY NOT ALWAYS APPLY. THE WARRANTIES IN THIS AGREEMENT GIVE YOU SPECIFIC LEGAL RIGHTS AND YOU MAY ALSO HAVE OTHER RIGHTS WHICH VARY IN ACCORDANCE WITH LOCAL LAW.

ACKNOWLEDGMENT

YOU ACKNOWLEDGE THAT YOU HAVE READ THIS AGREEMENT, UNDERSTAND IT, AND AGREE TO BE BOUND BY ITS TERMS AND CONDITIONS. YOU ALSO AGREE THAT THIS AGREEMENT IS THE COMPLETE AND EXCLUSIVE STATEMENT OF THE AGREEMENT BETWEEN YOU AND THE COMPANY AND SUPERSEDES ALL PROPOSALS OR PRIOR AGREEMENTS, ORAL, OR WRITTEN, AND ANY OTHER COMMUNICATIONS BETWEEN YOU AND THE COMPANY OR ANY REPRESENTATIVE OF THE COMPANY RELATING TO THE SUBJECT MATTER OF THIS AGREEMENT.

Should you have any questions concerning this Agreement or if you wish to contact the Company for any reason, please contact in writing at the address below.

Robin Short
Prentice Hall PTR
One Lake Street
Upper Saddle River, New Jersey 07458

About the CD-ROMs

Contents

Disc 1—

- IBM® WebSphere® Studio Application Developer, Version 5.0.2, for Windows® (Trial Edition)
- IBM® DB2® Universal Database™ Personal Edition, Version 8.1.2, for Windows® Operating Environments (Evaluation Copy)

Disc 2—

- IBM® WebSphere® Studio Application Developer, Version 5.0.2, for Windows® (Trial Edition)

Disc 3—

- IBM® WebSphere® Application Server Version 5.0, for Windows® (Trial Edition)
- IBM® WebSphere® Application Server, 5.0.2 Update
- Examples and source code from the book

The CD-ROMs can be used on Microsoft Windows® 2000 and XP.

License Agreement

Use of the material on these CDs is subject to the terms of the License Agreement and Limited Warranty, found on the previous two pages.

Warranty

Addison-Wesley warrants the enclosed CD-ROM to be free of defects in materials and faulty workmanship under normal use for a period of ninety days after purchase. If a defect is discovered in the CD-ROM during this warranty period, a replacement CD-ROM can be obtained at no charge by sending the defective CD-ROM , postage prepaid, with proof of purchase to:

Editorial Department
Addison-Wesley Professional/Pearson Technology Group
75 Arlington Street, Suite 300
Boston, MA 02116
Email: AWPro@aw.com

Addison-Wesley makes no warranty or representation, either expressed or implied, with respect to this software, its quality, performance, merchantability, or fitness for a particular purpose. In no event will Addison-Wesley, its distributors, or dealers be liable for direct, indirect, special, incidental, or consequential damages arising out of the use or inability to use the software. The exclusion of implied warranties is not permitted in some states. Therefore, the above exclusion may not apply to you. This warranty provides you with specific legal rights. There may be other rights that you may have that vary from state to state. The contents of this CD-ROM are intended for personal use only.

More information and updates are available at:
http://www.awprofessional.com/